S0-BEA-815

THE DIR GUIDE TO JAPANESE ECONOMIC STATISTICS

THE DIR GUIDE TO JAPANESE ECONOMIC STATISTICS

Mikihiro Matsuoka and Brian Rose

OXFORD UNIVERSITY PRESS
1994

Oxford University Press, Walton Street, Oxford OX2 6DP

Oxford New York Toronto
Delhi Bombay Calcutta Madras Karachi
Kuala Lumpur Singapore Hong Kong Tokyo
Nairobi Dar es Salaam Cape Town
Melbourne Auckland Madrid

and associated companies in
Berlin Ibadan

Published in the United States
by Oxford University Press Inc., New York

British Library Cataloguing in Publication Data
Data available.

Library of Congress Cataloging in Publication Data
Data available

ISBN 0-19-828861-1

Typeset by Pentacor PLC, High Wycombe
Printed in Great Britain
on acid-free paper by
Biddles Ltd., Guildford and King's Lynn

To Yoko, Chigako and Keigo

Preface

This book is intended to be a 'hands-on' guide for those who are interested in the macro-economy of Japan: economists at universities, governments and private research institutions, journalists, businessmen, investors, and students. It contains basic descriptions of the major economic statistics of Japan, including full treatment of the monetary economy. Without this information it is impossible to fully understand the Japanese economy, yet until now this information has been largely inaccessible to non-Japanese. The book examines the inter-relationships between the statistics as well as the relationship between each statistic and the Japanese economy as a whole. Problems with the statistics are revealed, so that readers will be able to use and interpret them correctly. Information on how to obtain the statistics covered in this book is provided in the appendices.

Part I presents statistics on the *real* economy, beginning with statistics covering the entire economy: national income statistics (Chapter 1), System of National Accounts (Chapter 2), and Diffusion and Composite Indexes (Chapter 3). These are followed by more detailed statistics on the household sector (Chapters 4–8), the corporate sector (Chapters 9–17), the construction and housing sector (Chapters 18–20), prices (Chapters 21–4), labor markets and population (Chapters 25–9), international trade and investment (Chapters 30–3) and the government sector (Chapter 34).

Part II presents statistics on the *monetary* economy, beginning with a brief explanation of financial institutions and money markets in Japan (Chapters 35–7). Measures of money stock are discussed in Chapters 38 and 39, followed by an explanation of the monetary policies of the Bank of Japan and their effects on money markets (Chapters 40–5). Two related government organizations, the Trust Fund Bureau of the Ministry of Finance and Postal Savings, are discussed in Chapters 46 and 47. Interest rates are discussed in Chapters 48 and 49, followed by banks' balance sheets (Chapter 50). Bond and stock markets are described in Chapters 51 and 52. Household savings are covered in Chapters 53 and 54.

Each chapter consists of three sections. The first section provides summary information, such as the organization preparing the statistics, frequency, timing of release, and availability. The second section describes coverage, method of calculation, and other details. The third section provides any special features or problems which are important for correctly interpreting the statistics, and comparisons with related statistics. The chapters are designed so that they can be read individually, with related chapters referred to where appropriate.

Appendixes 1 and 2 contain a basic description of index numbers and seasonal adjustment procedures used in Japan. Appendix 3 includes a list of source statistics available from various governmental and non-governmental organizations. Appendix 4 provides information on capital investment surveys which are not covered in this book. Appendix 5 contains charts showing the date of release for each statistic. A Select Bibliography provides a list of references on the Japanese economy to assist those who want to study Japan's economy further.

The data presented throughout this book were the latest available in June 1993.

Acknowledgments

We have benefited greatly from discussions with our colleagues at DIR: Seiji Adachi, Guy Canessa, Hideki Hayashi, Takunori Kobayashi, Takeshi Minami, Yasushi Okada and Susumu Okano. Takashi Kodama contributed greatly to Part II, and developed the method for estimating the average outstanding of monetary base in Chapter 40. Takeji Yamashita kindly provided the chapter on stock markets. We are grateful to the outside reviewers who contributed comments on the manuscript: Aaron M. Cohen (Daiwa Securities Co. Ltd. and Reitaku University), Jun Kurihara (Mitsubishi Research Institute, Inc.), Hiroyuki Odagiri (University of Tsukuba), Masanori Okura (Senshu University), Allen Shiau (WEFA Group), numerous government officials, and anonymous referees. Of course, remaining errors are our own.

We would like to thank Sakiyo Yamashiro (Booklink International Co. Ltd.) for assisting in arranging publication of the book. We should also thank Makoto Honjo and Yasushi Okada for providing us the time to complete this book and for their continuous encouragement. June Anderson, Enid Barker, Tracy Mawson, Andrew Schuller, and other staff at Oxford University Press were encouraging and helpful in guiding us to finish the manuscript.

We welcome comments and criticisms from readers. Please write to us in care of:

Economic Research Department
Daiwa Institute of Research Ltd.
15-6, Fuyuki, Koto-ku
Tokyo 135
Japan

Mikihiro Matsuoka
Brian Rose

Tokyo,
July 1993.

Contents

Prices

Labor Markets and Population

International Trade and Investment

Government Sector

Part II Monetary Economy

Financial Institutions and Money Markets

Money

Operations of the Bank of Japan

Part I

The Real Economy

General Business Conditions

1 National Income Statistics

Source: Economic Research Institute, Economic Planning Agency.

Frequency: Quarterly.

Release: Preliminary estimates or 'QE' (Quick Estimates) for the previous quarter are released near the end of each quarter (around the middle of March, June, September, and December). Preliminary estimates are revised several times, but are usually close to the 'final figures'. All figures for the preceding fiscal year are consolidated and released as 'final figures' during the period from October to December. For example, the real growth rate for the January to March 1991 quarter was released in June 1991 as a 'preliminary estimate' of 11.2%, which was revised in September to 11.0% and again in December, then released as the 'final figure' of 8.3%. Disaggregated figures (e.g. the components of private consumption) are not released in preliminary estimates. They are provided in the *Annual Report on National Accounts*, which is published every March.

Availability: Figures based on the SNA (see Chapter 2) are available from 1955 onward.

Real economic growth rates from national income statistics (rates of annual increase in real GNP or real GDP -- 'Gross National Product' or 'Gross Domestic Product' adjusted for inflation) are the most typical indicators of economic trends. This chapter provides only an outline of national income statistics. Chapter 2 presents the System of National Accounts and includes more detailed data.

Details

Demand Items

1. Private final consumption expenditure: consumption of the household sector and private non-profit institutions serving households.
2. Private residential investment: expenditure on construction and repair of housing, and miscellaneous expenditures related to housing.
3. Private non-residential investment: investment for construction, plants, machinery, and equipment.
4. Private inventory investment.
5. General government final consumption expenditure: the expression 'general government' refers to the central government and local governments, as well as social security funds.

6. Public fixed capital formation: the 'public' sector includes general government and public enterprises.
7. Public inventory investment.
8. Exports: exports of goods and services, and factor income receipts.
9. Imports: imports of goods and services, and factor income payments.

Items 1–4 above are collectively called private demand and items 5–7 are collectively called public demand. These are consolidated as domestic demand. The figure for exports less imports is called net external demand. Table 1.1 shows the growth rates and relative sizes of the major demand components.

Table 1.1. Demand Components of Gross National Product
Calendar Years 1987–1992

	% of GNP (1992)		Real Growth Rate (%) -- Calendar Year					
	Nominal	Real	1987	1988	1989	1990	1991	1992
GNP	100.0	100.0	4.3	6.2	4.8	4.8	4.1	1.5
Private consumption	56.5	56.8	4.2	5.2	4.3	3.9	2.2	1.7
Private residential investment	4.9	4.6	22.6	11.9	0.5	4.7	−8.6	−5.4
Private non-residential investment	18.1	20.5	6.7	14.8	16.6	11.4	5.7	−4.1
Increase in private inventories	0.5	0.7						
Government consumption	9.4	8.4	0.4	2.2	2.0	1.9	1.7	2.5
Public fixed capital formation	7.3	7.2	7.3	5.2	−2.2	4.5	4.4	12.2
Increase in public inventories	−0.0	−0.0						
Net exports	3.3	1.8						
Exports	14.2	18.4	4.6	10.7	14.9	10.7	4.8	2.4
Imports	10.9	16.6	10.5	21.3	22.1	12.0	−2.8	−2.6

Source: Economic Planning Agency, *Annual Report on National Accounts* (1993), 125, 129.

Percentage Contribution

The expression 'percentage contribution' is frequently used in discussions of economic growth factors. For example, the percentage contribution of domestic demand is defined as: ('domestic demand for current period' – 'domestic demand for the preceding period') divided by 'GNP for the preceding period'. This tells us how much of GNP growth is accounted for by growth in domestic demand. Percentage contribution of other demand components are calculated in a similar manner (see Fig. 1.1).

The GNP growth rate is sometimes stated as the sum of 'percentage contribution of domestic demand' and 'percentage contribution of external demand'. For example, in FY 1992 real GNP grew by 0.84%; the percentage contribution of domestic demand was 0.96% and that of external demand was –0.12%.

Fiscal Year

The fiscal year (FY) in Japan runs from 1 April to 31 March of the following year.

Features and Problems

Declining Rate of Real Growth

The annual average real GNP growth rate of the Japanese economy in the 1960s was 10.0%. After the first oil crisis in 1973–4, the rate fell to 4.4% in 1974–80, 3.8% in 1980–5, and 4.6% in 1985–91, respectively. In 1991 Japan entered into the first classical recession (due to autonomous stock adjustment caused by excess capacity) since World War II. This contrasts sharply with past recessions where external factors such as balance of payment constraints, the oil crises, and the yen's sharp appreciation led to economic downturns. Japan's medium-term potential growth rate is usually estimated to be around 4%.

Changes in the Leading Sector

The sector leading economic growth has changed several times (see Fig. 1.1). During the 1977–9 boom, public sector investment led private consumption and investment. In the first half of the 1980s, exports grew rapidly while domestic demand was stagnant due to tight fiscal policy and cautious private consumption and investment. After the 1985–6 recession caused by sharp appreciation of the Japanese Yen against other major currencies, accommodative monetary and fiscal policies led to economic expansion in 1987–90. This boom was led by strong domestic demand. Private capital investment showed three-year double-digit growth. The contribution of net exports to GNP growth was negative during this period.

Ratio of Private Capital Investment to GNP: Useful Indicator

A useful rule of thumb in analyzing Japan's economic activity is the ratio of nominal private non-residential investment to nominal GNP. Past experience suggests that if it approaches 20 percent, economic activity is likely to peak out the following year due to excess capacity in plant and equipment.

Privatization and National Income Statistics

The effects of the privatization of government corporations on national income statistics appeared in 1985 and 1987. Nippon Telegraph and Telephone (NTT) and Japan Tobacco (JT) were privatized in 1985 and Japan Railway (JR) was privatized in 1987. Private non-residential investment was higher and public non-residential investment was lower for these two years than they would have been otherwise.

Seasonal Adjustment

Original and seasonally adjusted figures are available. The Census X-11 method is employed for seasonal adjustment. No adjustment is made for the extra day in leap years.

Seasonal Fluctuation

There are several factors which have affected GNP in such a way that their irregular movements could not be smoothed out by seasonal adjustment:

1. Voluntary restraints on auto exports to the United States.
2. Front-loading of public-works expenditures into the first half of the fiscal year.
3. Factor income receipts and payments.

The first two factors contributed to a lower GNP growth rate in the January–March quarter and to a higher rate in the April–June quarter during the first half of the 1980s. Receipts and payments of factor income grew rapidly in the second half of the 1980s (see Table 2.1), and fluctuate widely even after adjustment for seasonal factors. This has led to greater emphasis on GDP, which is GNP excluding net factor income.

Base Year and Its Revision

The base year, which is used when calculating real (inflation adjusted) figures, is revised every five years. The currently applied base year is calendar year 1985. When the base year is revised, substantial changes may be made in the statistics, both in real and nominal terms. For example, the base year was revised from 1980 to 1985 in November 1990, and at that time the real GNP growth rate for FY 1988 was revised upward from 5.3% to 5.7%, while the nominal rate was revised upward from 6.0% to 6.3%.

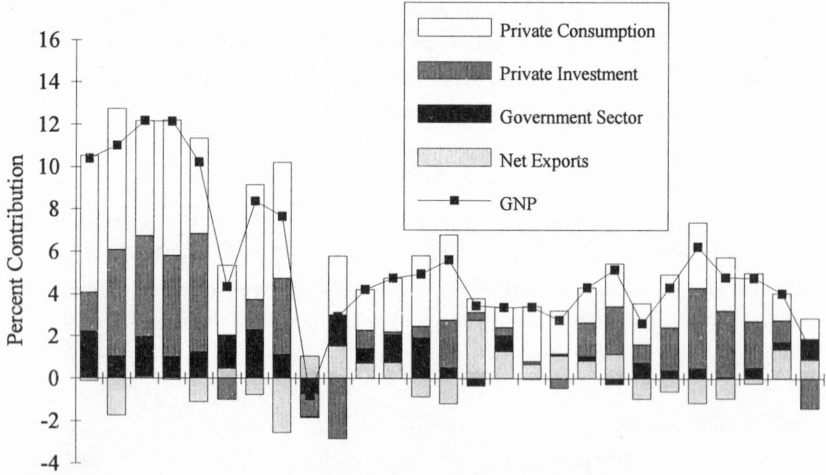

Fig. 1.1. GNP Growth and Contribution of Demand Components

2 System of National Accounts (SNA)

In 1978, Japan adopted the System of National Accounts (SNA) proposed by the United Nations. Historical data (for major categories) from 1955 onward is now available on the SNA basis. The SNA integrates five types of economic accounts: (1) national income accounts; (2) input-output tables of inter-industry relations; (3) flow-of-funds accounts; (4) balance sheet of the economy; and (5) balance of payments statistics. The SNA is designed to analyze the relationship of various types of economic activity as income (flows), assets (stocks), goods and services (real transactions), and money (financial transactions). This chapter consists mainly of tables from the National Accounts; very brief explanations accompany each table.

Table 2.1 shows the main table of Gross National Expenditure (which is equal in value to Gross National Product, but with economic activity classified by the source of final demand rather than production).

Classification of Economic Activities

There are two types of classifications adopted in the SNA: by type of economic activity; and by institutional sector.

Tables 2.2 and 2.3 show Gross Domestic Product and Factor Income disaggregated by type of economic activity.

Tables 2.4–2.11 are based on classification by institutional sector, the basis for analysis of the process of distribution (disposition) of income brought about as a result of economic activity. In the SNA there are five institutional sectors:

1. Non-financial incorporated enterprises.
2. Financial institutions.
3. General government.
4. Private non-profit institutions serving households.
5. Households.

In this classification, *companies* (rather than business establishments as in Table 2.2) are the basic units. They are classified based on their major line of business. *Non-financial incorporated enterprises* include not only private companies (excluding those engaging in finance and insurance) but also large unions and a part of special accounts of the government which operate in a similar manner to private companies and whose financial statements (balance sheets and profit/loss statements) are made available. 'General government' consists of three sub-sectors: central government, local government, and social security funds. 'Households' include not only consumers but also non-financial personal businesses.

Public financial institutions such as the Bank of Japan, the Japan Development Bank, and the Export Import Bank of Japan, are classified as financial institutions rather than general government.

The consolidated accounts give the sum of these five institutional sectors plus the foreign sector. It includes four accounts: (1) Gross Domestic Product and Expenditure; (2) National Disposable Income and its Appropriation; (3) Capital Finance Account; and (4) External Transactions (see Tables 2.4 and 2.5). Detailed figures for external transactions are given in Tables 2.15 and 2.16.

Activity in each of the five institutional sectors is revealed in four accounts: (1) income-outlay account (see Tables 2.6 and 2.7); (2) capital finance account (see Tables 2.8 and 2.9); (3) closing balance-sheet account (see Tables 2.10 and 2.11); and (4) reconciliation account (included in Tables 2.10 and 2.11). These accounts are connected through balancing items. It should be noted that in these accounts, private non-profit institutions serving households are unified into the household sector.

Tables 2.13 (capital formation by type of capital goods) and 2.14 (household consumption by type and object) are examples of the supporting tables published in the *Annual Report on National Accounts* which provide various types of disaggregated figures.

Inventory (Stock) Valuation Adjustment

The *Statistical Survey of Incorporated Enterprises* (hereafter, *Quarterly Financial Report of Non-Financial Businesses* or QFR) released by the Ministry of Finance (see Chapter 15) is one of the major sources of data for the preparation of national account statistics. In the QFR, an increase in inventories in period t is calculated as the difference of stock values of inventories at the end-of-period t and t–1. This is a standard concept in corporate accounting and includes changes in the price of inventories (i.e. capital gains/losses). The increase in inventories in the SNA, however, does *not* include the changes in price of inventories. The difference in the two concepts (QFR vs. SNA) of increase in inventories is accounted for by the item 'inventory value adjustment'. The following relationship holds:

Increase in Inventories in SNA = Increase in Inventories in QFR
– Inventory Value Adjustment

Table 2.1. Main Table of Gross National Expenditure at Constant Prices
Calendar Years 1987–1992, Trillions of 1985 Yen

	1987	1988	1989	1990	1991	1992
1. Private final consumption expenditure	203.3	214.0	223.2	231.9	237.1	241.1
(1) Household final consumption expenditure	200.8	211.3	220.4	229.3	234.1	***
a. Domestic final consumption expenditure	198.7	207.6	216.2	225.0	230.2	***
b. Purchases of resident households abroad	2.5	4.1	4.7	4.8	4.3	***
c. (Less) domestic purchases of non-resident households	0.3	0.4	0.4	0.5	0.4	***
(2) Private non-profit institutions serving households	2.5	2.7	2.8	2.7	3.0	***
2. Government final consumption expenditure	32.1	32.8	33.5	34.1	34.7	5.5
3. Gross domestic capital formation	102.0	116.1	127.3	137.2	142.3	139.8
(1) Gross domestic fixed capital formation	101.1	113.1	123.6	134.6	138.6	137.1
a. Private sector	77.0	87.8	98.9	108.7	111.6	106.7
(a) Residential	19.3	21.6	21.7	22.8	20.8	19.7
(b) Machinery and equipment	57.7	66.2	77.1	85.9	90.8	87.1
b. Public sector	24.1	25.3	24.8	25.9	27.0	30.3
(a) Residential	0.8	0.8	0.8	0.8	0.9	***
(b) Machinery and equipment	5.5	5.4	5.1	5.3	5.6	***
(c) General government	17.8	19.1	18.9	19.7	20.5	***
(2) Increase in inventories	0.9	3.0	3.7	2.6	3.6	2.7
a. Private enterprises	0.8	3.2	3.8	2.5	3.8	2.8
b. Public enterprises	0.1	−0.2	−0.1	0.1	−0.2	−0.1
4. Net exports	6.9	2.9	−0.5	−1.5	4.1	7.8
(1) Exports of goods and services and receipts of factor income	51.7	57.2	65.8	72.8	76.3	78.2
a. Exports of goods and services	44.2	47.3	51.6	55.3	58.0	60.9
b. Receipts of factor income	7.5	9.9	14.2	17.4	18.2	17.3
(2) (Less) imports of goods and services and payments of factor income	44.8	54.3	66.3	74.2	72.2	70.3
a. Imports of goods and services	39.3	46.7	54.9	59.6	56.9	56.9
b. Payments of factor income	5.5	7.7	11.4	14.7	15.3	13.4
5. Gross national expenditure (GNE)	344.3	365.8	383.4	401.8	418.1	424.3
Gross domestic expenditure	342.3	363.6	380.7	399.0	415.2	420.5
Gross domestic demand	337.4	362.9	384.0	403.3	414.1	416.5
Private demand	281.2	305.0	325.8	343.2	352.5	350.7
Public demand	56.3	57.9	58.2	60.1	61.5	65.8

Notes: Gross National Expenditure (GNE) = Gross National Product (GNP).

Gross National Expenditure = Private Final Consumption Expenditure + Government Final Consumption Expenditure + Gross Domestic Capital Formation + Net Exports.

Gross Domestic Expenditure = GNE – Receipts of Factor Income + Payments of Factor Income.

Private Demand = Private Final Consumption Expenditure + Private Fixed Capital Formation + Increase in Private Inventories.

Public Demand = Government Final Consumption Expenditure + Public Fixed Capital Formation + Increase in Public Inventories.

*** not available until March 1994.

Source: Economic Planning Agency, *Annual Report on National Accounts* (1993), 120–1.

Table 2.2. Gross Domestic Product and Factor Income by Kind of Economic Activity [1]
Calendar Year 1991, Trillion Yen at Current Prices

	Gross Output at Producers' Prices	Inter-mediate Inputs	Gross Domestic Output at Producers' Prices	Cons-umption of Fixed Capital	Net Domestic Output at Producers' Prices
	(1)	(2)	(3) = (1)–(2)	(4)	(5) = (3)–(4)
1. Industry	860.5	429.4	431.1	64.8	366.3
(1) Primary	18.0	7.6	10.4	1.9	8.5
(2) Mining	2.3	1.0	1.3	0.3	1.0
(3) Manufacturing	365.6	234.9	130.7	17.8	112.9
1) Food	37.7	23.6	14.1	1.0	13.1
2) Textile and apparel	7.6	5.2	2.4	0.2	2.2
3) Pulp and paper	10.1	6.7	3.4	0.8	2.6
4) Chemical	27.5	17.1	10.3	1.8	8.5
5) Petroleum and coal	13.1	7.9	5.2	0.4	4.8
6) Stone and ceramic	10.6	5.9	4.7	0.6	4.1
7) Primary metals	38.5	28.6	10.0	1.6	8.3
8) Metal products	17.5	9.4	8.1	0.9	7.1
9) General machinery	45.2	27.9	17.3	2.7	14.6
10) Electrical machinery	56.1	36.0	20.1	3.6	16.5
11) Transportation machinery	46.2	33.5	12.7	1.7	11.0
12) Precision machinery	5.3	3.2	2.1	0.3	1.8
13) Other manufacturing	50.2	29.8	20.4	2.2	18.3
(4) Construction	94.1	49.7	44.4	3.7	40.7
(5) Electricity, gas, and water supply	20.4	8.0	12.4	5.1	7.3
(6) Wholesale and retail trade	90.0	32.1	57.9	5.1	52.9
(7) Finance and insurance	36.3	13.4	22.9	1.5	21.4
(8) Real estate	55.5	6.4	49.1	13.6	35.5
(9) Transportation and communications	46.0	17.0	29.1	5.5	23.6
(10) Services	132.1	59.4	72.7	10.3	62.4
2. Producers of government services	49.2	15.0	34.2	2.5	31.7
(1) Electricity, gas, and water supply	2.6	1.2	1.5	0.6	0.9
(2) Services	18.0	4.0	14.0	1.2	12.8
(3) Public operations	28.6	9.9	18.7	0.7	18.0
3. Producers of private non-profit services to households	14.0	5.1	8.8	1.0	7.8
Sub-Total (1 + 2 + 3)	923.6	449.6	474.1	68.3	405.7
Import taxes	2.9	0.0	2.9	0.0	2.9
Others	−2.3	0.0	−2.3	0.0	−2.3
Imputed interest	0.0	22.7	−22.7	0.0	−22.7
Grand total	924.2	472.2	452.0	68.3	383.7

Source: Economic Planning Agency, *Annual Report on National Accounts* (1993), 188–9.

Tables 2.2 and 2.3 show economic activity classified into three types: (1) industry; (2) producers of government services; and (3) producers of private non-profit services to households. *Business establishments* are the basic unit in classifying production. 'Producers of government services' include both government institutions and non-profit institutions which are strictly supervised and supported by the government.

Table 2.3. Gross Domestic Product and Factor Income by Kind of Economic Activity [2]
Calendar Year 1991, Trillion Yen at Current Prices, unless otherwise noted

	Indirect Taxes less Subsidies	Domestic Factor Income	Compen-sation of Employees	Operating Surplus	Gross Domestic Output at Constant Prices
	(6)	(7)=(5)−(6)	(8)	(9)=(7)−(8)	(10)
1. Industry	30.4	335.9	212.5	123.4	402.3
(1) Primary	0.1	8.5	2.4	6.1	9.5
(2) Mining	0.1	1.0	0.5	0.5	1.1
(3) Manufacturing	13.1	99.8	66.4	33.5	132.8
1) Food	3.8	9.3	5.9	3.4	11.6
2) Textile and apparel	0.2	2.0	1.9	0.1	2.0
3) Pulp and Paper	0.2	2.4	1.7	0.7	3.1
4) Chemical	0.7	7.9	3.9	4.0	11.7
5) Petroleum and coal	2.5	2.3	0.4	1.8	1.1
6) Stone and ceramic	0.3	3.7	2.6	1.1	4.1
7) Primary metals	0.8	7.6	3.8	3.8	9.2
8) Metal products	0.4	6.7	4.4	2.3	6.6
9) General machinery	0.9	13.6	9.0	4.7	17.4
10) Electrical machinery	1.1	15.4	10.9	4.5	31.1
11) Transportation machinery	0.9	10.1	8.3	1.8	14.6
12) Precision machinery	0.1	1.7	1.4	0.3	2.2
13) Other manufacturing	1.1	17.2	12.3	4.9	18.1
(4) Construction	1.9	38.8	24.8	14.0	36.0
(5) Electricity, gas, and water supply	1.1	6.3	3.2	3.1	14.0
(6) Wholesale and retail trade	3.8	49.0	39.6	9.5	57.4
(7) Finance and insurance	0.1	21.2	15.0	6.3	24.7
(8) Real estate	3.1	32.4	2.3	30.2	40.7
(9) Transportation and communications	1.9	21.7	19.6	2.1	26.6
(10) Services	5.3	57.1	38.9	18.3	59.5
2. Producers of government services	0.0	31.7	31.7	−0.0	26.9
(1) Electricity, gas, and water supply	0.0	0.9	0.9	0.0	1.2
(2) Services	0.0	12.8	12.8	0.0	11.1
(3) Public operations	0.0	18.0	18.0	0.0	14.6
3. Producers of private non-profit services to households	0.1	7.7	7.7	0.0	7.4
Sub-total (1 + 2 + 3)	30.5	375.3	251.9	123.4	436.6
Import taxes	2.9	0.0	0.0	0.0	3.2
Others	−2.3	0.0	0.0	0.0	0.0
Imputed interest	0.0	−22.7	0.0	−22.7	−23.8
Grand total	31.1	352.6	251.9	100.7	416.0

Note: All figures are at current prices except those in column (10), given at 1985 prices.

Source: Economic Planning Agency, *Annual Report on National Accounts* (1993), 188–9, 192.

'Producers of private non-profit services to households' are defined as those who supply to households social and regional services that cannot be supplied by private enterprises by other means. Labor unions, political parties, religious organizations, some hospitals, and all private schools are included in this category.

Table 2.4. Consolidated Accounts for the Nation [Flow], [1]
Calendar Years 1987–1991, Trillion Yen

	1987	1988	1989	1990	1991
1. Gross domestic product and expenditure					
1.1 Compensation of employees	189.1	200.1	214.8	233.4	251.9
1.2 Operating surplus	86.6	93.3	96.4	99.8	100.7
1.3 Consumption of fixed capital	48.9	52.3	57.9	62.8	68.3
1.4 Indirect taxes	28.4	30.9	32.2	35.2	34.9
1.5 (Less) subsidies	3.4	3.4	3.1	4.6	3.9
1.6 Statistical discrepancy	−1.1	−1.7	−2.0	−2.0	−1.2
Gross domestic product	348.4	371.4	396.2	424.5	450.8
1.7 Private final consumption expenditure	204.6	215.1	228.5	243.6	255.3
1.8 Government final consumption expenditure	33.0	34.2	36.3	38.8	41.2
1.9 Gross domestic fixed capital formation	99.2	111.1	122.8	136.7	142.8
1.10 Increase in inventories	0.7	2.6	3.1	2.3	3.2
1.11 Exports of goods and services	36.2	37.5	42.4	45.9	46.8
1.12 (Less) imports of goods and services	25.2	29.1	36.8	42.9	38.5
Gross domestic expenditure	348.4	371.4	396.2	424.5	450.8
2. National disposable income and its appropriation					
2.1 Private final consumption expenditure	204.6	215.1	228.5	243.6	255.3
2.2 Government final consumption expenditure	33.0	34.2	36.3	38.8	41.2
2.3 Saving	64.8	73.5	78.1	83.9	90.0
Appropriation of national disposable income	302.3	322.8	342.8	366.3	367.6
2.4 Compensation of employees	189.1	200.1	214.8	233.4	251.9
2.5 Net compensation of expatriate employees	0.1	0.1	0.1	0.1	0.1
2.6 Operating surplus	86.6	93.3	96.4	99.8	100.7
2.7 Net receipts of property income from abroad	2.0	2.2	2.7	2.8	3.1
2.8 Indirect taxes	28.4	30.9	32.2	35.2	34.9
2.9 (Less) subsidies	3.4	3.4	3.1	4.6	3.9
2.10 Other net transfers from abroad	−0.4	−0.4	−0.3	−0.3	−0.3
National disposable income	302.3	322.8	342.8	366.3	386.6
National disposable income at market prices	302.7	323.1	343.1	366.7	386.9
National disposable income at factor cost	277.7	295.7	314.1	336.1	355.8

Source: Economic Planning Agency, *Annual Report on National Accounts* (1993), 80–1.

Gross Domestic Product vs. Gross National Product

Gross Domestic Product (GDP) is the sum of value added produced in the country analyzed from the production side. By definition, GDP is equal to Gross Domestic Expenditure (GDE) which is the value added analyzed from the expenditure side.

The term ‘domestic’ refers to the geographical territory of Japan. GDP includes the value added produced by non-Japanese people and companies in Japan. On the other hand, the concept ‘national’ means nationality of people and companies. Gross *National* Product (GNP) includes the value added produced not only by the Japanese living in Japan but also by the Japanese living in foreign countries. Factor income is the sum of compensation of employees, corporate income, and property income received from abroad. For Japan, it consists largely of dividends and interest

Table 2.5. Consolidated Accounts for the Nation [Flow], [2]
Calendar Years 1987–1991, Trillion Yen

	1987	1988	1989	1990	1991
3. Capital finance (1): non-financial transactions					
3.1 Gross domestic fixed capital formation	99.2	111.1	122.8	136.7	142.8
3.2 Increase in inventories	0.7	2.6	3.1	2.3	3.2
3.3 Net increase in claims on foreign assets	12.5	10.2	7.9	5.2	9.8
Uses of investment	112.4	123.9	133.7	144.3	155.7
3.4 Saving	64.8	73.5	78.1	83.9	90.0
3.5 Consumption of fixed capital	48.9	52.3	57.9	62.8	68.3
3.6 Net capital transfer from abroad	−0.2	−0.2	−0.2	−0.4	−1.4
3.7 Statistical discrepancy	−1.1	−1.7	−2.0	−2.0	−1.2
Sources of investment	112.4	123.9	133.7	144.3	155.7
4. Capital finance (2): financial transactions					
4.1 Net increase in foreign assets	25.1	21.3	24.9	16.4	15.2
Net increase in foreign assets	25.1	21.3	24.9	16.4	15.2
4.2 Net increase in claims on foreign assets	12.5	10.2	7.9	5.2	9.8
4.3 Net increase in foreigners' liabilities	12.6	11.1	17.0	11.2	5.5
Net increase in foreign assets	25.1	21.3	24.9	16.4	15.2
5. External transactions (1): current transactions					
5.1 Exports of goods and services	36.2	37.5	42.4	45.9	46.8
5.2 Compensation of Japanese employees abroad	0.3	0.3	0.4	0.4	0.4
5.3 Receipts of property income from abroad	7.3	9.8	14.4	18.1	19.3
5.4 Receipts of other transfers from abroad	0.1	0.1	0.1	0.1	0.2
Receipts	43.9	47.7	57.3	64.6	66.7
5.5 Imports of goods and services	25.2	29.1	36.8	42.9	38.5
5.6 Compensation of non-Japanese employees in Japan	0.3	0.2	0.3	0.3	0.4
5.7 Payments of property income to abroad	5.3	7.6	11.6	15.3	16.2
5.8 Payments of other transfers to abroad	0.5	0.5	0.5	0.5	0.5
5.9 Surplus on nation's current account	12.4	10.4	8.1	5.6	11.2
Payments	43.9	47.7	57.3	64.6	66.7
6. External transactions (2): capital transactions					
6.1 Surplus on nation's current account	12.7	10.4	8.1	5.6	11.2
6.2 Net capital transfers from abroad	−0.2	−0.2	−0.2	−0.4	−1.4
6.3 Net increase in foreigners' liabilities	12.6	11.1	17.0	11.2	5.5
Receipts	25.1	21.3	24.9	16.4	15.2
6.4 Net increase in foreign assets	25.1	21.3	24.9	16.4	15.2
Payments	25.1	21.3	24.9	16.4	15.2

Source: Economic Planning Agency, *Annual Report on National Accounts* (1993), 82–3.

on stocks and securities. GNP includes factor income (net of payments) while GDP does not.

In the past, the distinction between GNP and GDP was not important in Japan because of the relatively small size of factor income. However, as Japan became a major creditor country, factor income grew to include more than a quarter of all external transactions, and more emphasis has been placed on GDP than GNP.

Table 2.6. Income and Outlay Account for the Non-Financial Corporate Sector
Calendar Years 1987–1991, Trillion Yen

	1987	1988	1989	1990	1991
1. Income and outlay account					
1.1 Payments of property income	33.2	34.7	39.6	50.0	55.8
(1) Interest	26.8	27.8	30.3	41.3	46.6
(2) Dividends	4.2	4.4	6.5	5.6	5.8
(3) Rents	2.2	2.5	2.8	3.1	3.3
1.2 Casualty insurance premiums	0.9	0.9	1.0	1.2	1.6
1.3 Direct taxes	15.2	17.7	21.0	20.6	19.9
(1) Corporate income tax	15.0	17.4	20.7	20.3	19.6
(2) Other taxes	0.2	0.3	0.3	0.3	0.3
1.4 Penalty charges	0.1	0.1	0.2	0.2	0.1
1.5 UEWBCI	0.1	0.1	0.1	0.1	0.1
1.6 Other net current transfer	0.9	1.0	1.1	1.3	1.4
1.7 Savings	13.7	15.7	13.5	11.4	8.6
Total payments	64.1	70.2	76.4	84.8	87.5
1.8 Operating surplus	53.5	59.0	63.7	68.6	69.6
1.9 Receipts of property income	9.7	10.2	11.6	14.9	16.2
(1) Interest	6.2	5.9	5.5	8.7	9.4
(2) Dividends	3.0	3.6	5.3	5.3	5.8
(3) Rents	0.6	0.6	0.8	0.9	1.0
1.10 Receipts of casualty insurance	0.9	0.9	1.0	1.2	1.7
1.11 UEWBCI	0.1	0.1	0.1	0.1	0.1
Total receipts	64.1	70.2	76.4	84.8	87.5

Note: *UEWBCI* Unfunded Employee Welfare Benefits and Contributions Imputed.
Source: Economic Planning Agency, *Annual Report on National Accounts* (1993), 86–9.

The income-outlay account reveals receipts and dispositions of income in each sector. Tables 2.6 and 2.7 show the income-outlay accounts for the non-financial corporate sector and the household sector. The categories and definitions in each table vary by sector. For example, disposable income is equal to the sum of final consumption expenditure and saving for the household and government sectors, while it is equal to saving for non-financial incorporated enterprises and financial institutions.

For the household sector, receipts of income such as compensation of employees, operating surplus, and transfers are disposed in the form of consumption, non-consumption expenditures, and saving. Saving is defined as disposable income less consumption expenditure. Disposable income is defined as total receipts less non-consumption expenditure.

The income-outlay account is connected to the capital finance account via saving. Capital gains (and losses) are not income (value added) resulting from production activity and are thus not included in the income-outlay account.

Table 2.7. Income and Outlay Account for the Household Sector
Calendar Years 1987–1991, Trillion Yen

	1987	1988	1989	1990	1991
1. Income and outlay account					
1.1 Final consumption expenditure	202.0	212.2	225.4	240.5	251.8
1.2 Payments of property income	13.0	13.6	14.5	18.5	20.7
(1) Interest on consumers' liabilities	1.4	1.6	1.9	2.5	3.2
(2) Other interest	11.2	11.6	12.2	15.6	17.0
a. Payments to primary industries	0.9	0.8	0.8	0.9	1.0
b. Payments to other industries	5.4	5.3	5.1	6.4	6.9
c. Owner-occupied housing	4.9	5.4	6.2	8.2	9.1
(3) Rents	0.4	0.4	0.4	0.5	0.5
1.3 Casualty insurance premiums	1.8	1.9	2.0	2.2	2.7
1.4 Direct taxes	25.1	26.3	27.9	33.4	37.7
(1) Corporate income taxes	23.8	24.9	26.5	31.8	36.1
(2) Other taxes	1.2	1.3	1.4	1.5	1.6
1.5 Penalty charges	0.3	0.2	0.2	0.3	0.3
1.6 Social security contributions	29.7	31.4	33.4	39.0	41.3
1.7 Current transfers to private non-profit institutions serving households	2.8	3.1	3.4	3.7	3.8
1.8 UEWBCI	0.1	0.1	0.1	0.1	0.1
1.9 Other current transfers	15.9	17.0	16.8	18.0	19.6
1.10 Savings	34.8	35.5	38.5	39.5	44.3
Total payments	325.4	341.3	362.3	395.0	422.3
1.11 Compensation of employees	189.1	200.2	215.0	233.5	252.0
1.12 Operating surplus	43.9	45.3	45.7	46.6	47.5
Owner-occupied housing	14.6	15.4	16.4	17.4	18.3
1.13 Receipts of property income	32.1	32.3	36.6	43.4	48.3
(1) Interest	23.9	23.4	23.9	30.9	35.6
(2) Dividends	6.4	6.8	10.4	10.0	10.0
(3) Rents	1.9	2.1	2.3	2.5	2.7
1.14 Receipts of casualty insurance	1.9	1.9	2.0	2.2	2.6
1.15 Social security benefits	34.2	35.9	37.4	42.4	42.8
1.16 Social assistance grants	8.2	8.5	8.7	8.8	9.1
1.17 UEWBCI	0.1	0.1	0.1	0.1	0.1
1.18 Other current transfers	15.9	17.1	16.9	18.0	19.8
Total receipts	325.4	341.3	362.3	395.0	422.3
Disposable income of households	236.7	247.7	263.9	280.0	296.1
Household saving rate (%)	14.7	14.3	14.6	14.1	15.0

Notes: UEWBCI Unfunded Employee Welfare Benefits and Contributions Imputed.
Disposable income = Total receipts less items 1.2 through 1.9.
= Final consumption expenditure (1.1) + Saving (1.10).
Household saving rate = Saving / Disposable income (%).
The household sector includes private unincorporated non-financial enterprises.

Source: Economic Planning Agency, *Annual Report on National Accounts* (1993), 90–1.

Table 2.8. Capital Finance Account for the Non-Financial Corporate Sector
Calendar Years 1987–1991, Trillion Yen

	1987	1988	1989	1990	1991
2. Capital finance account (1): non-financial transactions					
2.1 Gross fixed capital formation	52.8	59.9	68.6	78.7	83.9
2.2 Increase in inventories	0.6	2.6	3.0	2.3	3.1
2.3 Net purchases of land	5.1	8.1	9.8	12.4	8.2
2.4 Saving-investment balance	−12.9	−20.7	−29.6	−40.2	−40.1
Uses of investment	45.5	49.8	50.8	53.2	55.1
2.5 Saving	13.7	15.7	13.5	11.4	8.6
2.6 Consumption of fixed capital	30.3	32.7	36.8	40.1	44.4
2.7 Net capital transfer	1.4	1.4	1.5	1.7	2.1
Sources of investment	45.5	49.8	50.8	53.2	55.1
3. Capital finance account (2): financial transactions					
3.1 Cash	0.2	0.3	0.5	0.0	0.0
3.2 Demand deposits	−1.8	3.3	−6.5	3.3	9.1
3.3 Other deposits	29.5	19.8	27.5	−4.3	−17.0
3.4 Short-term securities	−1.0	−0.1	−0.2	0.4	−0.4
3.5 Long-term securities	0.9	0.9	−1.5	3.6	1.2
3.6 Stocks	3.5	2.9	3.3	3.1	−1.2
3.7 Commercial Paper	0.1	1.7	1.0	2.3	−0.9
3.8 Loans from government	−0.0	−0.0	0.0	−0.0	0.0
3.9 Accounts receivable	28.3	17.9	31.4	15.2	12.8
3.10 Others	−0.7	6.7	9.2	15.3	1.7
Increase in financial assets	59.0	53.4	64.8	39.0	5.4
3.11 Financial surplus or deficit	−22.4	−23.1	−30.0	−48.8	−41.1
3.12 Short-term securities	−0.2	−0.6	−0.2	−0.1	−0.2
3.13 Long-term securities	7.0	7.2	12.6	8.6	13.8
3.14 Stocks	4.1	5.3	10.1	4.4	1.3
3.15 Commercial Paper	1.7	7.6	3.8	2.7	−3.4
3.16 Borrowings from private financial institutions	25.9	30.0	38.0	39.5	24.2
3.17 Borrowings from government	0.8	2.2	3.9	2.1	5.7
3.18 Transfer from government	0.0	0.0	0.0	0.0	0.0
3.19 Accounts payable	27.6	15.6	23.2	9.6	7.7
3.20 Others	14.6	9.2	3.6	21.0	−2.7
Increase in liabilities and net financial assets	59.0	53.4	64.8	39.0	5.4

Source: Economic Planning Agency, *Annual Report on National Accounts* (1993), 94–5.

The capital finance account consists of two tables: non-financial (or, real) transactions and financial transactions (see Tables 2.8 and 2.9). The former reveals the sources and uses of investment while the latter reveals increases in assets and debts. The sources of investment consist of saving, consumption of fixed capital, and net capital transfers. The consumption of fixed capital is calculated on a book-value basis. The uses of investment consist of gross fixed capital formation, increase in inventories, net land purchases, and saving-investment balance. The saving-investment balance is a balancing item between the non-financial and financial transactions tables.

Table 2.9. Capital Finance Account for the Household Sector
Calendar Years 1987–1991, Trillion Yen

	1987	1988	1989	1990	1991
2. Capital finance account (1): non-financial transactions					
2.1 Gross fixed capital formation	26.2	29.0	30.4	31.9	31.2
2.2 Increase in inventories	0.1	0.1	0.1	0.0	0.1
2.3 Net purchases of land	−8.8	−12.5	−14.5	−17.5	−14.2
2.4 Saving-investment balance	29.1	31.4	36.3	39.6	43.2
Uses of investment	46.7	48.0	52.2	54.0	60.3
2.5 Saving	34.8	35.5	38.5	39.5	44.3
2.6 Consumption of fixed capital	14.4	15.3	16.4	17.6	18.8
2.7 Net capital transfer	−2.5	−2.8	−2.7	−3.1	−2.9
Sources of investment	46.7	48.0	52.2	54.0	60.3
3. Capital finance account (2): financial transactions					
3.1 Cash	2.1	2.6	4.5	0.3	0.7
3.2 Demand deposits	4.3	3.4	5.7	0.7	2.3
3.3 Other deposits	21.8	24.9	35.3	40.9	39.2
3.4 Long-term securities	6.3	−0.7	5.5	3.0	−3.1
3.5 Stocks	4.6	−1.6	−1.3	2.1	−2.9
3.6 Life insurance	17.2	20.9	22.3	18.1	15.8
3.7 Others	1.7	0.4	1.8	2.2	0.4
Increase in financial assets	58.0	50.0	73.8	67.4	52.4
3.8 Financial surplus or deficit	31.7	28.0	34.7	38.6	35.3
3.9 Borrowings from private financial institutions	22.5	17.3	26.7	20.1	8.0
3.10 Borrowings from government	3.2	2.6	4.4	3.2	4.1
3.11 Accounts payable	0.6	2.1	8.1	5.4	5.0
3.12 Others	0.0	0.0	0.0	0.0	0.0
Increase in liabilities and net financial assets	58.0	50.0	73.8	67.4	52.4

Note: The household sector includes private unincorporated non-financial enterprises.
Source: Economic Planning Agency, *Annual Report on National Accounts* (1993), 102–3.

The financial asset table is obtained by arranging 'Flow of Funds' statistics released by the Bank of Japan (see Chapter 36).

Land transactions which have no production activity (i.e. do not produce value added) are not shown in income-outlay accounts in the SNA (transactions which do produce value added, such as land development and preparation of land, are included in gross capital formation). However, all financial transactions must be recorded in the capital finance account, as the exclusion of land transactions would result in a missing linkage between real (non-financial) and financial transactions. Net purchases of land by each institutional sector appears under non-financial transactions. It should be noted that the net purchase of land in the whole country is by definition *zero*. Therefore, no value for this item appears in the capital finance account in the consolidated accounts. The household sector has been a net seller (supplier) of land while private non-financial businesses and government have been net purchasers.

Table 2.10. Balance-Sheet Accounts for the Non-Financial Corporate Sector
Calendar Years 1987–1991, Trillion Yen

	1987	1988	1989	1990	1991
4. End-of-year balance-sheet account					
4.1 Inventories	56.2	58.2	63.4	67.3	69.3
4.2 Net reproducible tangible assets	330.9	355.2	394.7	437.0	475.4
4.3 Irreproducible tangible assets	442.6	497.3	592.4	674.2	611.6
(1) Land	433.0	487.6	582.1	663.7	601.4
(2) Forest	8.7	8.8	9.4	9.7	9.4
(3) Underground resources	0.9	0.8	0.9	0.8	0.8
4.4 Financial assets	640.3	756.0	861.8	804.8	803.9
(1) Cash	2.8	3.1	3.5	3.6	3.7
(2) Demand deposits	43.1	46.4	35.7	39.0	48.1
(3) Other deposits	138.6	159.2	183.7	179.3	162.3
(4) Short-term securities	0.3	0.2	0.0	0.4	0.0
(5) Long-term securities	13.0	12.1	11.6	12.5	13.3
(6) Stocks	181.3	250.7	339.7	236.0	230.9
(7) Commercial Paper	0.1	1.8	2.8	5.1	4.2
(8) Loans from government	0.0	0.0	0.0	0.0	0.0
(9) Accounts receivable	222.4	239.7	231.6	253.4	268.4
(10) Others	38.8	42.8	53.1	75.4	73.1
Total assets	1,470.0	1,666.7	1,912.3	1,983.3	1,960.3
4.5 Liabilities, excluding stocks					
(1) Short-term securities	1.5	0.9	0.7	0.5	0.4
(2) Long-term securities	68.6	74.3	85.8	98.5	111.2
(3) Commercial Paper	1.7	9.3	13.1	15.8	12.4
(4) Borrowings from private financial institutions	327.2	357.2	395.2	434.7	458.8
(5) Borrowings from government	65.1	67.2	71.1	73.2	78.9
(6) Transfers from government	0.1	0.1	0.1	0.1	0.2
(7) Accounts payable	175.4	185.6	179.7	193.9	204.9
(8) Others	16.1	20.3	25.2	38.4	41.3
4.6 Stocks and net worth	814.3	951.8	1,141.4	1,128.1	1,052.3
(1) Stocks	367.0	519.7	726.4	495.7	487.3
(2) Net worth	447.3	432.1	415.1	632.5	565.0
Total liabilities and net worth	1,470.0	1,666.7	1,912.3	1,983.3	1,960.3
5. Reconciliation account					
5.1 Inventories	–0.2	–0.5	2.2	1.6	–1.1
5.2 Net reproducible tangible assets	–4.1	–2.9	7.6	3.7	–1.0
5.3 Irreproducible tangible assets	109.8	46.6	85.3	69.4	–70.8
(1) Land	109.3	46.5	84.7	69.2	–70.5
(2) Forest	0.5	0.1	0.6	0.2	–0.2
(3) Underground resources	–0.0	0.0	0.0	–0.1	–0.0
5.4 Financial assets	38.7	62.3	41.0	–96.1	–6.2
Stocks	36.7	66.5	85.7	–106.9	–3.9
Total	144.1	105.4	136.2	–21.4	–79.1
5.5 Liabilities excluding stocks	–11.2	–12.1	–28.7	0.9	7.7
5.6 Stocks and net worth	155.3	117.5	164.9	–22.3	–86.8
(1) Stocks	61.3	147.5	196.5	–235.1	–9.6
(2) Net worth	94.0	–30.0	–31.6	212.9	–77.2
Total	144.1	105.4	136.2	–21.4	–79.1

Source: Economic Planning Agency, *Annual Report on National Accounts* (1993), 334–5.

Table 2.11. Balance-Sheet Accounts for the Household Sector
Calendar Years 1987–1991, Trillion Yen

	1987	1988	1989	1990	1991
4. End-of-year balance-sheet account					
4.1 Inventories	8.8	8.8	9.2	9.6	9.8
4.2 Net reproducible tangible assets	184.0	194.0	212.3	227.4	236.8
4.3 Irreproducible tangible assets	1,116.7	1,216.6	1,411.3	1,531.5	1,412.6
(1) Land	1,085.9	1,183.2	1,376.7	1,495.0	1,375.7
(2) Forest	30.1	32.6	33.9	35.8	36.2
(3) Underground resources	0.7	0.7	0.7	0.8	0.7
4.4 Financial assets	715.2	816.3	958.7	949.6	1,003.7
(1) Cash	24.8	27.4	31.9	32.2	33.0
(2) Demand deposits	41.3	44.8	52.9	53.6	56.0
(3) Other deposits	337.4	362.3	397.6	438.7	477.9
(4) Long-term securities	60.4	59.7	66.2	69.1	65.9
(5) Stocks	123.7	173.4	237.3	162.7	161.8
(6) Life insurance	112.3	133.2	155.5	173.6	189.4
(7) Others	15.2	15.5	17.3	19.7	19.8
Total assets	2,024.6	2,235.8	2,591.7	2,718.1	2,662.9
4.5 Liabilities excluding stocks	238.7	265.5	294.1	325.1	340.9
(1) Borrowings from private financial institutions	150.5	167.8	194.5	214.6	222.6
(2) Borrowings from government	43.3	45.9	50.3	53.5	57.6
(3) Accounts payable	44.9	51.8	49.4	56.9	60.7
(4) Others	0.0	0.0	0.0	0.0	0.0
4.6 Net worth	1,785.9	1,970.3	2,297.5	2,393.0	2,321.9
Total liabilities and net worth	2,024.6	2,235.8	2,591.7	2,718.1	2,662.9
5. Reconciliation account					
5.1 Inventories	0.0	−0.0	0.3	0.3	0.1
5.2 Net reproducible tangible assets	−1.0	−3.7	4.4	0.8	−2.9
5.3 Irreproducible tangible assets	268.1	112.5	209.3	137.7	−104.7
(1) Land	267.5	109.9	208.0	135.8	−105.0
(2) Forest	0.6	2.5	1.3	1.9	0.4
(3) Underground resources	−0.0	0.0	−0.0	0.0	−0.1
5.4 Financial assets	24.7	51.1	68.6	−76.5	1.7
Long-term securities	0.7	−0.0	1.0	−0.1	−0.1
Stocks	23.0	51.3	65.2	−76.8	2.0
Total	291.8	159.9	282.6	62.2	−105.8
5.5 Liabilities	1.3	4.8	−10.5	2.1	−1.2
5.6 Net worth	290.6	155.1	293.1	60.1	−104.6
Total	291.8	159.9	282.6	62.2	−105.8

Notes: The household sector includes private unincorporated non-financial enterprises.

Source: Economic Planning Agency, *Annual Report on National Accounts* (1993), 350–1.

Tables 2.10, 2.11, and 2.12 show the closing balance-sheet account for the non-financial corporate sector, the household sector, and the consolidated account, respectively. The closing balance-sheet account reveals end-of-calendar-year outstanding of physical assets, as well as financial assets and liabilities. Most items in the closing balance-sheet account adopt market valuation or replacement cost valuation, while most items in

Table 2.12. The Consolidated Accounts of National Income Statistics [Stock], Japan
Calendar Years 1987–1991, Trillion Yen

	1987	1988	1989	1990	1991
1. End-of-year balance-sheet account					
1.1 Inventories	65.0	67.1	72.7	76.9	79.1
1.2 Net reproducible tangible assets	755.4	805.9	888.6	972.3	1,043.4
1.3 Irreproducible tangible assets	1,720.6	1,888.6	2,204.5	2,442.6	2,244.9
1.4 Financial assets, excluding stocks	2,326.9	2,560.0	2,815.5	3,067.1	3,217.8
1.5 Stocks	472.9	669.0	889.9	594.3	586.5
Total assets	5,340.8	5,990.6	6,871.2	7,153.2	7,171.7
1.6 Liabilities, excluding stocks	2,279.6	2,513.2	2,756.9	3,005.6	3,149.3
1.7 Stocks and net worth	3,061.2	3,477.4	4,114.2	4,147.6	4,022.4
(1) Stocks	483.9	678.7	910.3	606.6	603.3
(2) Net worth (national wealth)	2,577.3	2,798.7	3,203.9	3,541.0	3,419.1
Total liabilities and net worth	5,340.8	5,990.6	6,871.2	7,153.2	7,171.7
2. Capital finance account					
2.1 Increase in inventories	0.7	2.6	3.1	2.3	3.2
2.2 Net fixed capital formation	50.3	58.8	64.8	73.9	74.4
2.3 Increase in financial assets excluding stocks	269.4	253.4	282.7	228.3	163.4
2.4 Stocks	22.1	18.6	27.3	11.2	–3.0
Uses of investment	342.5	333.4	377.9	315.8	238.0
2.5 Increase in liabilities excluding stocks	272.9	253.3	287.2	228.1	149.2
2.6 Stocks	6.1	8.4	15.0	6.2	1.4
2.7 Savings	64.8	73.5	78.1	83.9	90.0
2.8 Net capital transfer from abroad	–0.2	–0.2	–0.2	–0.4	–1.4
2.9 Statistical discrepancy	–1.1	–1.7	–2.0	–2.0	–1.2
Sources of investment	342.5	333.4	377.9	315.8	238.0
3. Reconciliation account					
3.1 Inventories	–0.2	–0.5	2.5	1.9	–1.0
3.2 Net reproducible tangible assets	–6.8	–8.2	17.9	9.7	–3.3
3.3 Irreproducible tangible assets	416.5	168.0	315.8	238.1	–197.7
3.4 Financial assets excluding stocks	–23.3	–20.3	–27.2	23.3	–12.7
3.5 Stocks	76.0	177.5	193.6	–306.7	–4.8
Total	462.2	316.5	502.6	–33.8	–219.6
3.6 Liabilities excluding stocks	–26.1	–19.7	–43.5	20.6	–5.5
3.7 Stocks and net worth	488.3	336.1	546.1	–54.3	–214.1
(1) Stocks	88.4	186.4	216.6	–309.9	–4.8
(2) Net worth (national wealth)	399.9	149.8	329.4	255.6	–209.3
Total	462.2	316.5	502.6	–33.8	–219.6

Note: Valuation of stocks is at market value basis for liabilities, as well as assets of the household, private corporate, and financial sectors; valuation is at book value basis for assets of other sectors.

Source: Economic Planning Agency, *Annual Report on National Accounts* (1993), 328–9.

the capital finance account adopt book value estimation. The difference between the market and book values (and statistical discrepancies) can be regarded as realized and unrealized capital gains/losses which are available in the reconciliation account.

The asset inflation which occurred in the second half of the 1980s resulted in huge capital gains on stocks and land (irreproducible tangible assets).

Table 2.13. Gross Domestic Capital Formation by Type of Capital Goods
Calendar Years 1987–1991, Trillions of 1985 Yen, unless otherwise noted

	1987	1988	1989	1990	1991	% of Total in 1991
1. Gross domestic fixed capital formation	101.1	113.1	123.6	134.6	138.6	100.0
(1) Residential	20.1	22.4	22.5	23.6	21.7	15.6
(2) Buildings other than residential	15.2	16.2	18.6	20.1	22.1	15.9
(3) Other structures	19.7	21.3	22.2	23.5	24.4	17.6
(4) Improvement and development of land	4.8	5.1	5.4	5.7	5.9	4.2
(5) Transportation machinery	9.0	10.1	12.2	14.6	15.2	11.0
(6) Other machinery and equipment	32.2	38.1	42.7	47.1	49.4	35.6
2. Increase in inventories	0.9	3.0	3.7	2.6	3.6	--
(1) Manufactured goods	0.0	0.3	0.8	0.6	1.1	--
(2) Goods in process	0.2	0.9	0.7	1.2	1.2	--
(3) Raw materials	0.1	0.1	0.5	0.3	0.1	--
(4) Wholesale and retail inventories	0.6	1.7	1.7	0.6	1.3	--
Gross domestic capital formation	102.0	116.1	127.3	137.2	142.3	--

Note: Gross domestic fixed capital formation includes both private and public sectors.
Source: Economic Planning Agency, *Annual Report on National Accounts* (1993), 251.

Table 2.14. Households' Final Consumption Expenditure by Type and Object
Calendar Years 1987–1991, Trillion 1985 Yen, unless otherwise noted

	1987	1988	1989	1990	1991	% of Total in 1991
By Type						
1. Durable goods	14.5	17.0	18.4	19.5	20.7	9.0
2. Semi-durable goods	23.4	23.8	24.8	26.2	26.7	11.6
3. Non-durable goods	60.0	61.5	63.5	65.9	66.3	28.8
4. Services	100.8	105.3	109.5	113.3	116.5	50.6
Domestic final consumption expenditure of households	198.7	207.6	216.2	225.0	230.2	100.0
By Object						
1. Food, beverage, and tobacco	43.0	43.9	45.4	46.6	46.7	20.3
2. Clothes and footwear	13.0	13.0	13.2	13.5	13.7	5.9
3. Rent, light, and water charges	37.0	38.5	40.2	42.0	43.7	19.0
4. Furniture, utensils, and miscellaneous	12.4	13.1	13.6	14.8	15.6	6.8
5. Medical care	21.0	22.0	22.6	23.6	24.6	10.7
6. Transportation and communications	19.6	21.3	23.0	24.7	25.1	10.9
7. Recreation and education	20.2	21.6	22.5	23.3	24.7	10.7
8. Others	32.4	34.0	35.5	36.4	36.2	15.7
Domestic final consumption expenditure of households	198.7	207.6	216.2	225.0	230.2	100.0
Imputed rent on owner-occupied housing (nominal)	25.9	27.6	29.6	31.7	33.9	

Source: Economic Planning Agency, *Annual Report on National Accounts* (1993), 243, 245.

'Imputed Rent on Owner-Occupied Housing' is the value of the service provided by housing occupied by owners. It is calculated as the market price of equivalent rental housing less maintenance costs, and is added to operating surplus (hence disposable income), even though no transactions actually take place. Similarly, imputed medical expenditure (which benefits households but is actually borne by the government) is included in households' medical expenditure.

Table 2.15. External Transactions [1]: Current Transactions
Calendar Years 1987–1992, Trillion Yen

	1987	1988	1989	1990	1991	1992
1. Exports of goods and services	36.2	37.5	42.4	45.9	46.8	47.4
(1) Merchandise (FOB)	32.5	33.4	37.4	40.7	41.4	***
(2) Transportation and communications	1.7	1.9	2.3	2.4	2.4	***
a. Freight charges	1.1	1.1	1.2	1.3	1.3	***
b. Others	0.7	0.8	1.1	1.1	1.1	***
(3) Insurance	0.0	0.0	0.0	0.0	–0.0	***
a. Freight insurance	0.0	0.1	0.1	0.1	0.0	***
b. Others	–0.0	–0.3	–0.0	–0.1	–0.0	***
(4) Others	1.3	1.5	1.9	2.1	2.3	***
(5) Domestic purchases by non-resident households	0.3	0.4	0.4	0.5	0.5	***
(6) Purchases by foreign government organizations	0.3	0.3	0.3	0.3	0.2	***
2. Receipts of factor income from abroad	7.6	10.1	14.8	18.5	19.8	19.1
(1) Compensation of employees	0.3	0.3	0.4	0.4	0.4	***
(2) Property income	7.3	9.8	14.4	18.1	19.3	***
3. Other current transfers from abroad	0.1	0.1	0.1	0.1	0.2	***
(1) General government	0.0	0.0	0.0	0.0	0.0	***
(2) Other sectors	0.1	0.1	0.1	0.1	0.2	***
4. Current receipts	43.9	47.7	57.3	64.6	66.7	***
5. Imports of goods and services	25.2	29.1	36.8	42.9	38.5	36.2
(1) Merchandise (FOB)	18.7	21.3	26.9	31.6	27.7	***
(2) Transportation and communications	2.4	2.6	3.2	3.6	3.6	***
a. Freight charges	1.0	0.9	1.0	1.0	1.0	***
b. Others	1.4	1.7	2.2	2.5	2.6	***
(3) Insurance	0.2	0.2	0.2	0.2	0.1	***
a. Freight insurance	0.1	0.1	0.1	0.1	0.2	***
b. Others	0.1	0.1	0.0	0.0	–0.1	***
(4) Others	2.3	2.5	3.3	3.8	3.8	***
(5) Purchases by resident households abroad	1.6	2.4	3.2	3.7	3.3	***
(6) Overseas purchases by the government	0.0	0.0	0.0	0.0	0.0	***
6. Payments of factor income to abroad	5.6	7.8	11.9	15.6	16.6	14.8
(1) Compensation of employees	0.3	0.2	0.3	0.3	0.4	***
(2) Property income	5.3	7.6	11.6	15.3	16.2	***
7. Other current transfers to abroad	0.5	0.5	0.5	0.5	0.5	***
(1) General government	0.1	0.1	0.1	0.1	0.1	***
(2) Other sectors	0.4	0.4	0.3	0.3	0.3	***
8. Current payments	31.2	37.4	49.2	59.0	55.6	***
9. Surplus on nation's current account	12.7	10.4	8.1	5.6	11.2	***
10. Net capital transfers from overseas	–0.2	–0.2	–0.2	–0.4	–1.4	***
(1) General government	–0.2	–0.2	–0.2	–0.4	–1.4	***
(2) Other sectors	0.0	0.0	0.0	0.0	0.0	***
11. Net increase in claims on foreign assets	12.5	10.2	7.9	5.2	9.8	***

Note: *** not available until March 1994.

Source: Economic Planning Agency, *Annual Report on National Accounts* (1993), 256–7.

Table 2.16. External Transactions [2]: Capital Transactions
Calendar Years 1987–1991, Trillion Yen

	1987	1988	1989	1990	1991
1. Increase in foreign reserves	5.7	2.1	−1.8	−1.2	−1.1
(1) Gold and SDR	0.1	0.1	−0.1	0.1	−0.1
(2) Other foreign reserves	5.6	2.0	−1.8	−1.3	−1.1
2. Outward foreign direct investment	2.8	4.4	6.1	7.0	4.2
3. Export credits	0.1	0.9	0.6	−0.1	−0.5
4. Loans	2.4	2.0	3.1	3.2	1.8
5. Outward foreign securities investment	12.9	11.2	15.8	5.8	10.0
6. Increase in other foreign assets	1.3	0.8	1.2	1.7	1.0
7. Net increase in foreign assets	25.1	21.3	24.9	16.4	15.2
8. Inward foreign direct investment	0.2	−0.1	−0.1	0.3	0.2
9. Import credits	−0.0	−0.0	−0.0	−0.0	−0.0
10. Borrowings	−15.5	−10.2	2.6	5.6	5.1
11. Inward foreign securities investment	−4.7	−0.2	0.8	−0.9	8.6
12. Net issue of foreign bonds	4.4	4.6	10.5	4.4	6.4
13. Other increase in foreign liabilities	12.7	6.8	3.4	1.9	−14.8
(1) Long- and short-term capital and statistical discrepancy	2.7	1.0	0.5	1.7	-3.5
(2) Balance on monetary movements excl. foreign reserves	10.0	5.8	2.8	0.2	−11.3
14. Net increase in foreign liabilities	12.6	11.1	17.0	11.2	5.5
15. Net increase in claims on foreign assets	12.5	10.2	7.9	5.2	9.8

Note: SDR is not included in 'net increase in foreign assets' (item 7) because SDR is not used for ordinary economic transactions.

Source: Economic Planning Agency, *Annual Report on National Accounts* (1993), 256–7.

Tables 2.15 and 2.16 show external transactions in the SNA. These are derived from balance of payments statistics (BOP statistics, see Chapter 31), with Table 2.15 showing transactions on the current account and Table 2.16 showing transactions on the capital account. Note that the item 'Errors and Omissions' in BOP statistics is included in capital transactions.

The bottom line in Table 2.15, 'Net Increase in Claims on Foreign Assets', is equivalent to the current balance (current account surplus) in BOP statistics. The difference between merchandise trade exports and imports is equal to the trade balance in BOP statistics.

In Table 2.16, all figures have the opposite sign when compared with BOP figures. In BOP statistics, negative figures in the capital account are equivalent to increases in claims on foreigners. Thus 'Net Increase in Claims on Foreign Assets' is equivalent to the capital account *deficit* (minus Errors and Omissions) in BOP statistics.

Note that in SNA statistics, all figures must be in yen, while in BOP statistics most detailed figures are shown in terms of US dollars.

3 Indexes of Business Conditions

Source:	Research Bureau, Economic Planning Agency.
Frequency:	Monthly.
Release:	Figures are released at the end of each month with a two-month lag. Indexes are revised as each component is revised, but revision in the value of Diffusion Indexes (DI) is rare because of the method of calculation (see below). Unless a revision results in a change in the direction (e.g. from an increase to a decrease) of a component, there will be no revision in the value of the DI.
Availability:	DI are available from 1956 onward. Composite Indexes (CI) are available from 1971 onward.

The Economic Planning Agency releases a leading index, a coincident index and a lagging index as 'Diffusion Indexes' (DI) and 'Composite Indexes' (CI) collectively. The indexes are used to determine the official dates of peaks and troughs in the business cycle (see Table 3.1). DI and CI are calculated using the sets of statistics given in Tables 3.2, 3.3, and 3.4. The DI receive much more attention than the CI; following their release, typically the values of the DI only are published in newspapers.

Details

DI and CI each consist of three indexes: (1) Leading Index -- used to look at future business movements; (2) Coincident Index -- used to gauge the current situation of business activity; and (3) Lagging Index -- used to trace and confirm past business movements.

Calculation of DI

DI are stated in percentage terms. The most recent value of each component is compared with its three months' prior value (some components are published monthly, others quarterly). Components showing an increase are called 'expansive components'. The DI is the ratio of the total number of expansive components to the total number of components. For each component with no change in its value, 0.5 is added to the number of expansive components.

Table 3.1. Duration of Business Cycle (Months)

Cycle No.	Trough	Peak	Trough	Expansion	Contraction	Total
1st		June 51	Oct. 51		4	
2nd	Oct. 51	Jan. 54	Nov. 54	27	10	37
3rd	Nov. 54	June 57	Jun. 58	31	12	43
4th	June 58	Dec. 61	Oct. 62	42	10	52
5th	Oct. 62	Oct. 64	Oct. 65	24	12	36
6th	Oct. 65	July 70	Dec. 71	57	17	74
7th	Dec. 71	Nov. 73	Mar. 75	23	16	39
8th	Mar. 75	Jan. 77	Oct. 77	22	9	31
9th	Oct. 77	Feb. 80	Feb. 83	28	36	64
10th	Feb. 83	June 85	Nov. 86	28	17	45
11th	Nov. 86					

Source: Economic Planning Agency.

Table 3.2. Components of DI and CI -- Leading Index (13 indicators)

	Name of Indicator	Source	Chapter No.	Seasonal Adjustment	Frequency
L1.	Index of producers' inventory-to-shipment ratio, final demand goods (reversed scale)	MITI	10	MITI-III-R	Monthly
L2.	Index of inventory-to-consumption ratio, raw materials, manufacturing sector (reversed scale)	MITI	--	MITI-III-R	Monthly
L3.	New job offers, excluding new school graduates	ML	27	X-11	Monthly
L4.	New orders for machinery industries, private sector, excluding shipbuilding and electric power, deflated by the wholesale price index for domestic capital goods	EPA	9	X-11	Monthly
L5.	Construction starts, floor area for mining, construction, manufacturing, and commercial and services	MC	--	X-11	Monthly
L6.	New housing construction started, floor area	MC	20	X-11	Monthly
L7.	Months of construction works order backlog (ratio of unfilled orders to completed works)	MC	18	X-11	Monthly
L8.	Index of producers' shipments, durable consumer goods	MITI	10	Y-Y (%)	Monthly
L9.	Nikkei's commodity index, 42 kinds, end-of-month	Nikkei	--	Y-Y (%)	Monthly
L10.	Money supply, average balance of M2+CDs	BJ	38	Y-Y (%)	Monthly
L11.	Index of operating rate adjusted by input and output prices (index of operating rate for manufacturing sector multiplied by output price index divided by input price index)	MITI/BJ	11	MITI-III-R	Monthly
L12.	Operating profit divided by total assets (manufacturing sector) minus yield on telecommunication bonds	MF/TSE	15	MITI-III-R	Quarterly
L13.	Outlook in the business conditions survey of small- and medium-sized companies for the next quarter	SBFCJ	--	X-11	Quarterly

Notes: *BJ* Bank of Japan, *EPA* Economic Planning Agency, *MC* Ministry of Construction, *MF* Ministry of Finance, *MITI* Ministry of International Trade and Industry, *ML* Ministry of Labour, *Nikkei* Nihon Keizai Shimbun Sha, *SBFCJ* Small Business Finance Corporation of Japan, *TSE* Tokyo Stock Exchange. *Y-Y (%)* Year-on-year increase (%).

Source: Economic Planning Agency.

Table 3.3. Components of DI and CI -- Coincident Index (11 indicators)

	Name of Indicator	Source	Chapter No.	Seasonal Adjustment	Frequency
C1.	Index of industrial production, mining and manufacturing sectors	MITI	10	MITI-III-R	Monthly
C2.	Index of raw material consumption, manufacturing sector	MITI	--	MITI-III-R	Monthly
C3.	Total electric power consumption	FPC	--	X-11	Monthly
C4.	Index of operating rate, manufacturing sector	MITI	11	MITI-III-R	Monthly
C5.	Total hours worked of all workers, manufacturing sector (index of total hours worked multiplied by index of employed persons)	ML/MCA	10	X-11	Monthly
C6.	Index of producers' shipments of investment goods, mining and manufacturing sectors excluding transportation equipment	MITI	10	MITI-III-R	Monthly
C7.	Sales of large-scale retail stores, department stores	MITI	5	Y-Y (%)	Monthly
C8.	Index of wholesale and retail sales, wholesale sector	MITI	--	Y-Y (%)	Monthly
C9.	Current profit, non-financial business	MF	15	X-11	Quarterly
C10.	Index of shipments, medium- and small-sized companies, multiplied by the wholesale price index for these companies	SBFCJ	--	MITI-III-R	Monthly
C11.	Ratio of effective job offers to applicants, excluding new school graduates	ML	27	X-11	Monthly

Notes: *BJ* Bank of Japan, *FPC* Federation of Power Companies, *MCA* Management and Coordination Agency, *MF* Ministry of Finance, *MITI* Ministry of International Trade and Industry, *ML* Ministry of Labour, *SBFCJ* Small Business Finance Corporation of Japan. *Y-Y (%)* Year-on-year increase (%).
Source: Economic Planning Agency.

Table 3.4. Components of DI and CI -- Lagging Index (8 indicators)

	Name of Indicator	Source	Chapter No.	Seasonal Adjustment	Frequency
Lg1.	Index of producers' inventory of finished goods, mining and manufacturing sectors, final demand goods	MITI	10	MITI-III-R	Monthly
Lg2.	Index of raw materials inventory, manufacturing sector	MITI	--	MITI-III-R	Monthly
Lg3.	Employment index of regular workers, establishments with 30 or more regular workers	ML	26	X-11	Monthly
Lg4.	Plant and equipment investment by non-financial corporate sector divided by the implicit price deflator for private plant and equipment investment	MF/EPA	15	X-11	Quarterly
Lg5.	Living expenditure, workers' households	MCA	4	Y-Y (%)	Monthly
Lg6.	Corporation tax revenue	MF	--	X-11	Monthly
Lg7.	Unemployment rate (reversed scale)	MCA	25	X-11	Monthly
Lg8.	Average contracted interest rates on loans and discounts of All Banks	BJ	49	--	Monthly

Notes: *BJ* Bank of Japan, *EPA* Economic Planning Agency, *MCA* Management and Coordination Agency, *MF* Ministry of Finance, *MITI* Ministry of International Trade and Industry, *ML* Ministry of Labour. *Y-Y (%)* Year-on-year increase (%).

Source: Economic Planning Agency.

Calculation of CI

Step 1

Calculate the growth rate of the ith indicator (Y_{it}) in period t (χ_{it}):

$$\chi_{it} = 200 * \frac{(Y_{it} - Y_{it-1})}{(Y_{it} + Y_{it-1})}$$

This gives the change in the indicator as a percentage of the average value of the current and previous periods. If the indicator has a negative or zero value, or it is already in percentage or ratio form, χ_{it} is calculated as:

$$\chi_{it} = Y_{it} - Y_{it-1}$$

Step 2

For each indicator, calculate the average (μ_{it}) and standard deviation (σ_{it}) of the growth rate (χ_{it}) over the previous five years. Then calculate the normalized growth rate (Z_{it}) as:

$$Z_{it} = \frac{\chi_{it} - \mu_{it}}{\sigma_{it}}$$

Step 3

Calculate the average values (over the indicators at time t) of μ, σ, and Z to obtain the growth rate (V_t):

$$V_t = \text{avg}_t\,(\mu_{it}) + \text{avg}_t\,(\sigma_{it}) * \text{avg}_t\,(Z_{it})$$

When calculating the growth rate (V_t) for the leading and lagging indicators, the average of μ for the coincident indicator is used.

Step 4

Calculate the index as:

$$I_t = I_{t-1} * \frac{(200 + V_t)}{(200 - V_t)}$$

Finally, calculate the value of the index relative to the base year (currently calendar year 1985):

$$I_{new} = \frac{I_t}{I_{base}} * 100$$

where I_{new} is the rebased index, and I_{base} is the value of the index in the base year.

Features and Problems

Interpretation of DI and CI

For each DI (leading, coincident and lagging), a level of 50% is used to determine the trend in the economy. In the past, when the coincident index showed less than 50% for some period of time, an economic slowdown was announced. The numerical values of DI do not necessarily indicate a specific degree of business strength. They are always used to grasp the turning points of business cycles by comparing the indexes with the 50% level.

By contrast, the CI are designed such that the growth rate of the CI reflect the magnitude of the business cycle, with higher values indicating stronger business conditions.

DI Adjusted Ex-post When Inaccurate

Diffusion Indexes are constructed in such a way that they follow the past peaks and troughs of the business cycle. Their construction is based on the judgement of the Business Cycle Dating Committee, a group expert on business cycles. The Economic Planning Agency then gathers and compares a large number of indicators to choose those which most appropriately follow peaks and troughs of the cycle. DI therefore do not necessarily reflect current economic conditions as accurately as they reflect past conditions. For example, the leading and coincident DI dropped to less than 50% in several months of 1988 and 1989 despite Japan's economy expanding at a rate exceeding potential growth. When the leading sector of the economy is not the same as in the previous expansion, the DI's ability to reflect business conditions weakens. The EPA reselected the components of the DIs in 1988 so that they can correctly reflect the business conditions of the non-manufacturing industries, whose weight in Japan's economy has grown.

Delayed Announcement of Peaks and Troughs of Business Cycle

The official determination of peaks and troughs requires a long period of time, because of the complex process and the reluctance of the government to admit any downturns. For example, the peak of the past business cycle (starting from the trough of November 1986) has not yet been determined (as of July 1993), although unofficial statements from the EPA suggest the peak was the first quarter of 1991.

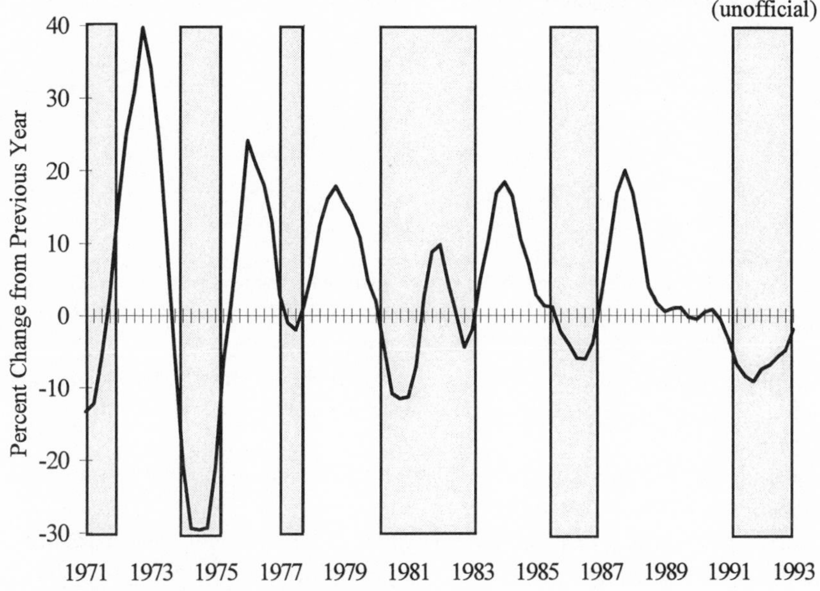

Note: Shaded areas indicate economic downturns.

Fig. 3.1. Composite Indexes: Leading Index

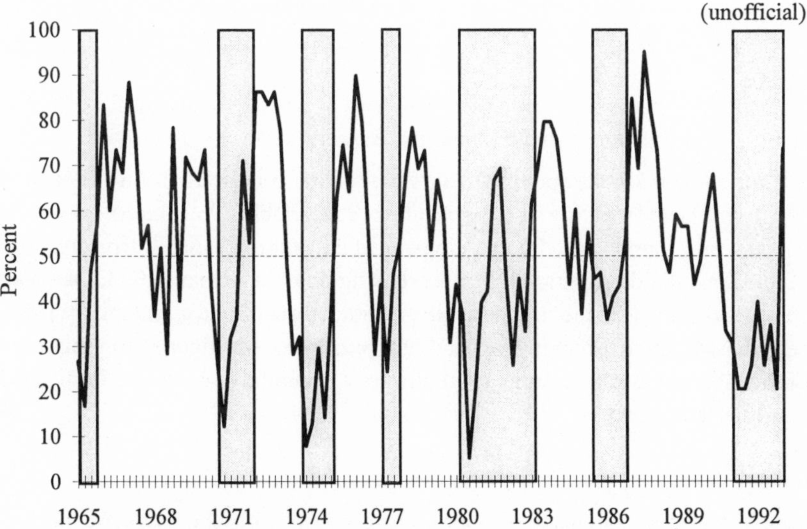

Note: Shaded areas indicate economic downturns.

Fig. 3.2. Diffusion Indexes: Leading Index

Household Sector

4 Family Income and Expenditure Survey

Source: Statistics Bureau, Management and Coordination Agency.

Frequency: Monthly and annual.

Release: Figures are released at the end of each month with a two-month lag. The *Annual Report on the Family Income and Expenditure Survey*, which contains historical as well as monthly data, is published each June.

Availability: Annual series are available from 1947 onward. Monthly expenditure and income series are available from August 1946 and September 1950, respectively.

The Family Income and Expenditure Survey (FIES) is an important resource for analyzing the behavior of the household sector and it is one of the sources for estimating private final consumption expenditures in GNP. Highly detailed data on household expenditure is made available on a timely basis (national income statistics provide disaggregated expenditure data only in the 'final figures' reports -- see Chapter 1). A related survey, the *National Survey of Family Income and Expenditure*, is conducted once every five years and provides broader coverage than the FIES.

Details

History of Family Income and Expenditure Survey

The Family Income and Expenditure Survey was first conducted in July 1946, and has been conducted monthly since September 1950. In July 1962, the coverage was expanded, and figures based on this expanded coverage (available from January 1963 onward) are discontinuous with earlier figures. In January 1973, Okinawa prefecture was added to the survey, again creating a discontinuity. In January 1981, a new classification of living expenditure was adopted; figures for this new classification are available from 1970 onward for monthly series and from 1963 onward for annual series.

Coverage

A sample survey is conducted on approximately 8,000 households in 168 municipalities. The households are divided into two categories: workers' households and other households. Households engaged in farming, fisheries, and forestry, as well as one-person households and foreigners, are excluded from the sample. Workers' households include employees in the public or private sector, except that households whose heads are executives of companies or corporations are classified as 'other households'. The types of households included in the survey comprise about 71% of total households in Japan, and 84% of the total population.

A survey is conducted for six consecutive months on each household. One-sixth of the households surveyed are replaced each month.

Explanation of Terms

The survey reveals total living expenditures for both workers' and other households. Living expenditures are broken into ten major categories as shown in Table 4.1. Income, disposable income, and average propensity to consume are available only for workers' households. Disposable income is obtained by subtracting non-living expenditures such as income tax and social security payments from income. Surplus is defined as disposable income less living expenditures, and the surplus rate is defined as the ratio of surplus to disposable income.

The following relationships hold in the survey (see Table 4.1):

Total receipts (A)
= Income (B) + Receipts other than income (E)
+ Carry-over from previous month (F)

Income (B)
= Current income (C) + Non-current income (D)
= Living expenditure (I) + Non-living expenditure (J) + Surplus (N)

Total disbursements (G)
= Expenditure (H) + Disbursements other than expenditure (K)
+ Carry-over to next month (L)

Disposable income (M)
= Income (B) – Non-living expenditure (J)

Surplus (N)
= Income (B) – Expenditure (H)
= Disposable income (M) – Living expenditure (I)
= Net increase in financial assets (O)
+ Net decrease in debts, installment/credit purchases
+ Net increase in property, others, and carry-over
= Disbursements other than expenditure (K) + Carry-over to next month (L)
– [Receipts other than income (E) + Carry-over from previous month (F)]

Table 4.1. Monthly Receipts and Disbursements per Household: Workers' Households
Calendar Year 1992, Yen, unless otherwise noted

Total receipts (A)		Total disbursements (G)	1,001,938
Income (B)	563,855	Expenditure (H)	442,937
Current income (C)	551,411	Living expenditure (I)	352,820
Wage and salaries	529,490	Food	83,445
Business and homework	5,583	Housing	20,191
Other current income	16,337	Fuel, light, and water charges	18,094
Property income	2,534	Furniture and household utensils	13,560
Social security benefits	13,479	Clothes and footwear	24,033
Remittances	324	Medical care	9,125
Non-current income (D)	12,444	Transportation and communication	35,304
Gifts	7,113	Education	18,625
Others	5,331	Reading and recreation	34,279
Receipts other than income (E)	338,749	Other living expenditures	96,164
Deposit withdrawals	311,090	Non-living expenditures (J)	90,117
Insurance proceeds	3,371	Taxes	51,152
Debts	5,550	Social security contributions	38,558
Installment/credit purchases	16,750	Others	407
Securities/property sold	1,502	Disbursements other than expend. (K)	460,169
Others	486	Deposits	361,149
Carry-over from previous month (F)	99,334	Insurance premium payments	39,733
		Payments of debts	28,010
Disposable income (M)	473,738	Payments of installments/credit	20,533
Surplus (N)	120,918	Purchase of securities/property	9,953
Net increase in financial assets (O)	88,368	Others	790
Net increase in saving (P)	86,422	Carry-over to next month (L)	98,832
Net increase in deposits	50,059		
Net increase in insurance	36,363		
Net increase in securities	1,946	Average propensity to consume (Q)	74.5%
Net decrease in debts	22,460	Ratio of surplus to disposable income (R)	25.5%
Net decrease in installment/credit purchases	3,783	Ratio of net increase in financial assets to disposable income (S)	18.7%
Net increase in property, others	6,809	Ratio of saving to disposable income (T)	18.2%
Net increase in carry-over	−501		

Note: Some sub-category items are omitted.

Source: The Management and Coordination Agency, *Annual Report on the Family Income and Expenditure Survey*, 1992, 114-23.

Average propensity to consume (Q)
= Living expenditure (I) / Disposable income (M) ∗ 100 (%)

Surplus rate
= Surplus (N) / Disposable income (M) ∗ 100 (%)

Savings rate
= Net increase in saving (P) / Disposable income (M) ∗ 100 (%)

The surplus rate is closer to the concept of saving in the SNA than the FIES 'savings rate', and should be used when comparing figures to the savings rate in the SNA.

Seasonal Adjustment and Real Figures

Although seasonally adjusted figures are available, it is recommended that the year-on-year increase of non-adjusted figures be used. The Census X-11 method is used for seasonal adjustment of monthly figures. A forecast of seasonal coefficients for the current year is used in calculating seasonally adjusted figures. Seasonally adjusted figures for the previous year are revised when January figures for the new year are released. Figures in real terms are obtained by dividing the nominal values by the consumer price index (specifically, the CPI for all Japan excluding imputed rent on owner-occupied housing).

Features and Problems

Bias in FIES Statistics -- Disparities with SNA Statistics

Households Surveyed

As mentioned above, the FIES excludes certain types of households, so the sample survey does not accurately reflect the true distribution of households. The FIES shows far fewer young household heads than the population census, since most are single householders and thus excluded from the survey (see Table 4.2). Even excluding one-person households, census data still indicates more young household heads. Overall, low-income households (and to a lesser extent high-income households) tend to be under-represented in the FIES.

Table 4.2. Distribution of Household Head by Age
Calendar Year 1990, Percent of Total, unless otherwise noted

	FIES	Population Census		
Age of Household Head		All Private Households	One-Person Households	Excluding One-Person Households
–24	0.5	7.2	27.4	1.1
25–29	3.7	6.2	13.7	4.0
30–34	8.7	7.1	7.1	7.1
35–39	12.4	9.3	6.0	10.3
40–44	14.8	12.4	6.4	14.3
45–49	13.2	11.5	5.5	13.3
50–54	11.4	10.7	5.3	12.3
55–59	11.1	10.4	5.6	11.8
60–64	10.1	9.0	5.8	9.9
65–	14.0	16.2	17.3	15.8
Number of Households	7,976	40,670,475	9,389,660	31,280,815

Sources: Management and Coordination Agency, *Annual Report on the Family Income and Expenditure Survey* (1990), 230–1. *Population Census of Japan* (1990), 286–7.

Another manifestation of this bias appears in the figures for inter-household transfers, such as receipts and payments of 'remittances' (typically money sent to children attending university and living in a separate household) and money gifts. In theory, receipts and payments would be equal if we aggregated all households together. In practice, the figures are completely different, as shown in Table 4.3.

The substantial difference between receipts and payments reflects the fact that the FIES sample does not include single householders, who are likely to be the beneficiaries of these remittances and money gifts. Another factor may be that respondents simply tend to under-report receipts of these items relative to payments.

Table 4.3. Remittances and Money Gifts
Workers' Households (Monthly)
Calendar Year 1992, Yen

	Receipts	Payments
Remittances	324	9,290
Money gifts	7,113	15,893

Source: Management and Coordination Agency, *Annual Report on the Family Income and Expenditure Survey* (1992), 146, 160.

Interest Payments

In SNA statistics, repayment of principal of debt is included in saving, while interest payments are not. In FIES however, interest payments are not distinguished from repayment of principal, since respondents would have difficulty separating debt payments (such as mortgage payments) into principal and interest. Thus, interest payments are included in FIES surplus.

Housing Expenditure

In SNA statistics, housing expenditure is adjusted to include the service flow from owner-occupied housing (imputed rent, see Chapter 2 for details), but since no actual transfer of money takes place, no expenditure appears in FIES. As shown in Table 4.4, the weight of housing rent, water supply, and light charges in FIES (11.1%) is substantially smaller than in SNA statistics (19.7%).

Medical Expenditure

FIES covers only direct medical expenditure incurred by households, excluding indirect expenditures (Japan has a nationalized health-care system) which are included in households' medical expenditure in SNA. As shown in Table 4.4, the weight of medical expenditure in total living expenditure is only 2.8%, a fraction of the 10.7% in SNA statistics.

Table 4.4. Comparison of Household Consumption
Calendar Year 1991, Percent of Total

	SNA	FIES: All Households	
Domestic household consumption	100.0	100.0	Living expenditure
Food, beverage, and tobacco	20.6	25.1	Food
Clothes and footwear	6.5	7.3	Clothes and footwear
Housing rent, water supply,		5.5	Housing
and light charges	19.7	5.6	Fuel, light and water charges
Furniture, household utensils,			
and miscellaneous	6.2	4.1	Furniture and household utensils
Medical care	10.7	2.8	Medical care
Transportation and communications	10.1	9.3	Transportation and communications
Recreation, education,		4.3	Education
and cultural services	10.2	9.6	Reading and recreation
Others	16.0	26.9	Other living expenditure
Durable goods	7.0	6.8	Durable goods
Non-durable goods	12.0	13.5	Non-durable goods
Semi-durable goods	28.2	42.4	Semi-durable goods
Services	52.8	37.3	Services

Sources: Economic Planning Agency, *Annual Report on National Accounts* (1993), 243, 245. Management and Coordination Agency, *Annual Report on the Family Income and Expenditure Survey* (1992), 120–1, 416.

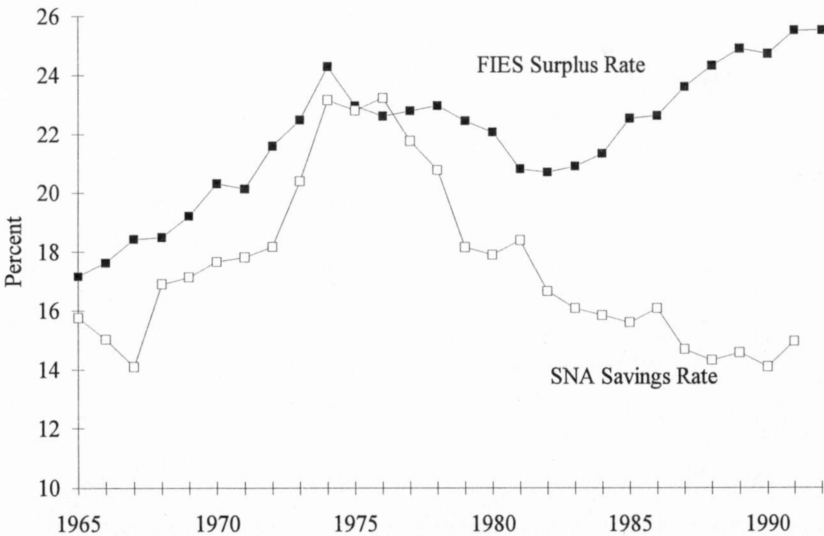

Fig. 4.1. Household Savings Rate -- FIES Surplus Rate vs. SNA Savings Rate

Payment of Insurance Premiums

FIES and SNA both include net payment of insurance premiums in saving (surplus). SNA also includes policyholders' implicit return on investment in insurance as disposable income.

Divergence in Savings Rate

As shown in Fig. 4.1, there is a considerable gap between the surplus rate for the household sector in FIES and the SNA savings rate. Of the differences mentioned above, exclusion of one-person households, inclusion of interest payments as surplus, and exclusion of imputed rent (which lowers consumption and disposable income by equal amounts) increase the FIES surplus rate relative to the SNA savings rate; differences relating to medical expenditure and insurance policies should work in the opposite direction.

Another factor may be underestimation of savings in the SNA due to its treatment of land purchases (see Chapter 2). Land sales by the household sector are calculated as a residual from the figures for land sales by the other sectors (net land sales must be zero by definition). If the value of land purchases by the other sectors is overestimated (which seems likely when land prices are rising), then land sales by the household sector will be overestimated and household savings underestimated.

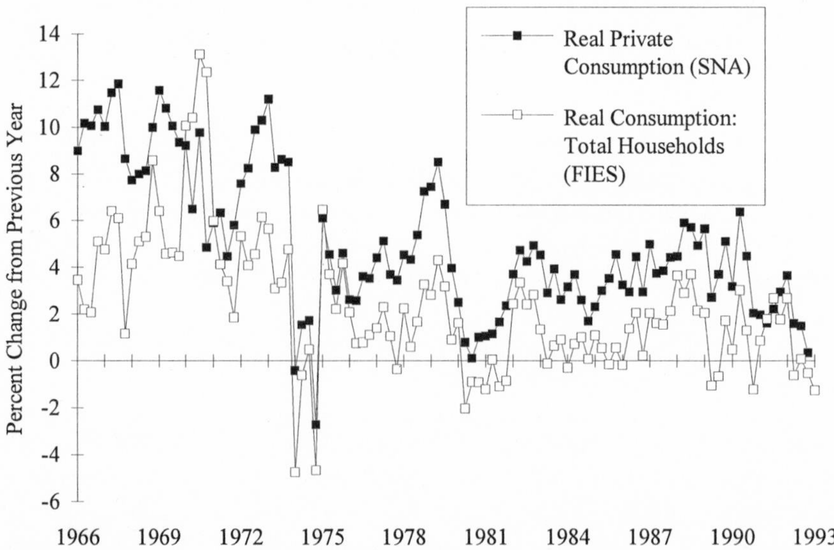

Note: Real figures for FIES were obtained by dividing nominal values by CPI-excluding rent for owner-occupied housing.

Fig. 4.2. Growth in Private Consumption

Growth Rate of Consumption Expenditure

The real growth rate of consumption expenditure in FIES is typically 2 or 3% lower than in SNA (see Fig. 4.2). One reason for this is that FIES measures expenditure per household, while SNA measures total expenditure. The number of members per household is decreasing, whereas the total population of Japan is increasing, so the FIES figures are downward biased. Further, the use of the Consumer Price Index (Laspeyres Index) lowers the growth rate in real terms when compared with SNA figures, which use a Paasche Index (see Appendix 1).

Consumption Expenditure on Durable Goods

It is often argued that the expenditure on durable goods, especially that on automobiles, is underestimated in FIES. In calendar 1992, the average annual expenditure on automobile purchases was only 63,288 yen for all households and 77,748 yen for workers' households. Given that annual passenger car sales were more than 4 million units (even if we take into account that corporate purchases are a substantial portion of total sales), these figures imply underestimation.

Related Statistics

Historical Data for FIES

Historical annual series are available in *Comprehensive Time Series Report on the Family Income and Expenditure Survey: 1947-1986* published by the Management and Coordination Agency.

National Survey of Family Income and Expenditure

The *National Survey of Family Income and Expenditure* (NSFIE) has been conducted by the Management and Coordination Agency every five years since 1959. This survey covers not only income and consumption, but also the stock of durable consumer goods, savings, and liabilities of households. It also covers one-person households, giving a basis for adjusting FIES figures to more closely match an unbiased sample of households (using the census data in Table 4.2 to give the proper weight to one-person households).

The 1989 survey consists of 12 volumes covering 55,008 households with two or more members and 4,084 one-person households in 1,191 municipalities. The wider coverage of NSFIE data allows for more detailed cross-section analysis than the FIES. In addition to total households, figures by type of household are available, such as: households with dual income earners; households without jobs; households receiving pension benefits; households with person aged 65 years old or over; households of mother and child(ren); and households with/without liabilities for housing.

5 Sales of Large-Scale Retail Stores

Source: Ministry of International Trade and Industry.

Frequency: Monthly.

Release: Preliminary figures are released at the end of each month with a one-month lag. Revised figures are released one month later.

Availability: Figures for the aggregate series are available from July 1971 onward. Those for department stores only are available from January 1966 onward.

Statistics for sales of large-scale retail stores cover department stores and supermarkets. They are frequently used to gauge private consumption activities because of their quick release. Department store sales are included in the coincident index of Diffusion Indexes (DI) compiled by the EPA.

Details

A monthly survey of retail sales, number of staff, total floor area, and number of business days is conducted by MITI on designated large-scale retail stores. Large-scale retail stores consist of department stores and supermarkets. A supermarket is defined as a store with a staff of 50 or more, total floor area of 1,500 square meters or more, and which employs a self-service system for 50 percent or more of its total floor area. A department store is defined as a store other than a supermarket, with a staff of 50 or more and total floor area of 3,000 square meters or more (for stores in 12 large cities; 1,500 square meters or more otherwise). Department stores account for 55 percent of total large-scale retail store sales, supermarkets for 45 percent.

The survey reveals retail store sales by type of store and merchandise, and by area. As the data in Table 5.1 shows, the distinction between supermarkets and department stores is not great in Japan. Most supermarkets are multi-level, with one floor selling food and beverages, and other floors selling clothing, appliances, etc. Department stores also often contain one floor which sells food, with a relatively large portion being processed (pre-cooked) food.

Number-of-Stores Adjusted Index

There are two types of figures shown in the statistics: original figures and the

Table 5.1 Composition of Sales of Large-Scale Retail Stores
Calendar Year 1992, % of Total, unless otherwise noted

	Total	Department Stores	Supermarkets
Total	100.0	100.0	100.0
Clothes	40.9	50.3	30.0
For men	8.5	10.2	6.5
For women and children	20.7	25.7	14.9
Other clothes	4.9	5.5	4.2
Accessories	6.9	8.9	4.5
Food and beverages	32.2	21.8	44.3
Others	26.9	27.9	25.7
Furniture	3.3	4.3	2.1
Electric appliances	2.7	1.3	4.4
Household goods	4.9	4.0	5.9
Others	14.4	15.9	12.6
Restaurants and coffee shops	1.6	2.4	0.7
Total value in billion yen	22,204	11,930	10,274
Percent (%)	100.0	53.7	46.3

Source: Ministry of International Trade and Industry.

number-of-stores adjusted index, which is calculated to exclude sales increases caused by an increase in the number of stores surveyed; the latter has been available only since 1988.

Seasonal Adjustment

Seasonally adjusted figures (using the MITI-III-R method) for both original and the number-of-store adjusted index are available from January 1977 onward for department store and supermarket sales, and from July 1980 onward for total sales. When the revised numbers for March are released, seasonal coefficients for January of the previous year onward are revised. It is recommended that the year-on-year rate of increase of the *original* figures be used because seasonally adjusted figures tend to fluctuate widely.

Features and Problems

Department store sales tend to be stronger than that of supermarkets in boom periods (and vice versa in recessions) due to consumers' increasing orientation toward higher quality merchandise (see Fig. 5.1). Supermarket sales tend to move more steadily due to the larger share of food and beverages.

Large-scale retail store sales cover only a small part of the total private consumption expenditures. In 1992, total sales of large-scale retail stores was 22.2 trillion yen, while nominal private consumption expenditures in the SNA was 265 trillion yen.

Further, a significant portion of sales (more for department stores than supermarkets, probably more than 20% overall) are to businesses. Thus large-scale retail store sales do not always accurately reflect household consumption (see Fig. 5.2).

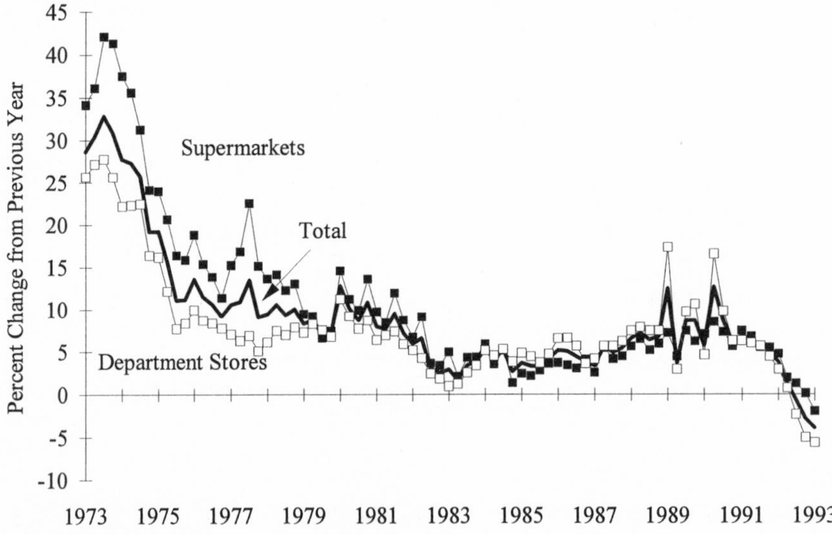

Fig. 5.1. Sales of Large-Scale Retail Stores

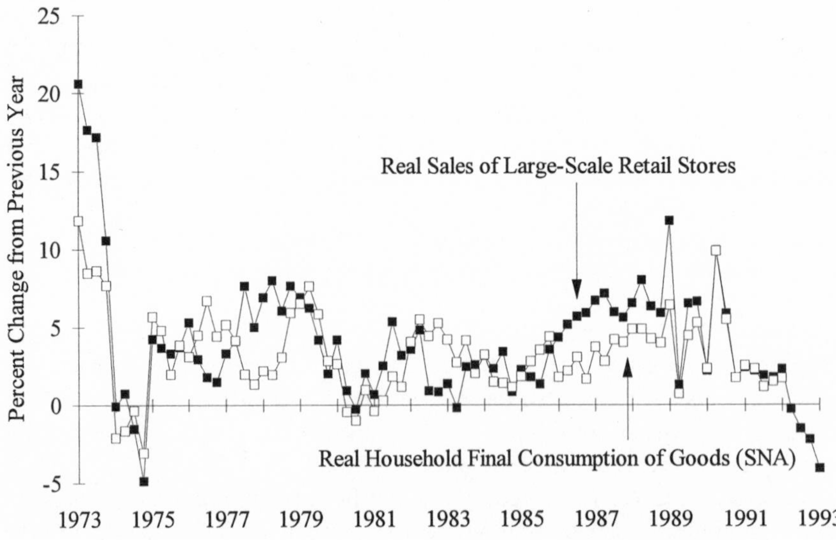

Fig. 5.2. Sales of Large-Scale Retail Stores vs. Household Consumption (SNA)

6 Department Store Sales

Source:	Japan Department Stores Association.
Frequency:	Monthly.
Release:	Preliminary figures are released at the end of each month with a one-month lag. Revised figures are released one month later.
Availability:	Figures are available from January 1980 onward.

Department store sales statistics are frequently used to gauge private consumption activities because of their quick release. These statistics are similar to 'Sales of Large-Scale Retail Stores' published by MITI (see Chapter 5).

Details

The Japan Department Stores Association conducts a monthly survey on retail sales by merchandise, floor area, number of staff, and business days. As of December

Table 6.1. Department Store Sales By Type of Merchandise
Calendar Year 1992

	Sales (billion yen)	Percent of Total
Total	9,519.6	100.0
Clothes	3,861.8	40.6
Men	951.2	10.0
Women	2,077.2	21.8
Children	305.1	3.2
Other	528.3	5.5
Accessories	840.4	8.8
Miscellaneous	1,243.8	13.1
Household goods	1,055.1	11.1
Furniture	554.2	5.8
Electrical appliances	106.8	1.1
Others	394.1	4.1
Food and beverages	1,973.0	20.7
Restaurants and coffee shops	220.8	2.3
Services	88.8	0.9
Others	235.9	2.5

Source: Japan Department Stores Association.

1992, there are 116 participating companies with 271 stores. Only stores with floor area of 1,500 square meters or more are included in the survey. Sales by type of merchandise are classified as shown in Table 6.1. Sales by region is divided into two major groups: six large metropolitan areas and eight other separate regions.

There are no seasonally adjusted figures. It is recommended that the year-on-year rate of increase be used to avoid the wide fluctuation of monthly sales. The year-on-year growth rate adjusted for the number of stores is available. This growth rate is adjusted so that the effect of a sales increase due to an increase in the number of stores surveyed can be excluded. The JDSA also publishes a deflator for sales.

Features and Problems

Department store sales published by the JDSA were 9.5 trillion yen in 1992, while department store sales published by MITI (see Chapter 5) were 11.9 trillion yen. Growth rates of these two statistics show very close movement (see Fig. 6.1).

Department store sales are considered to be sensitive to changes in general business conditions because the proportion of high quality (luxury) merchandise is large. They include purchases by business firms as well as by households.

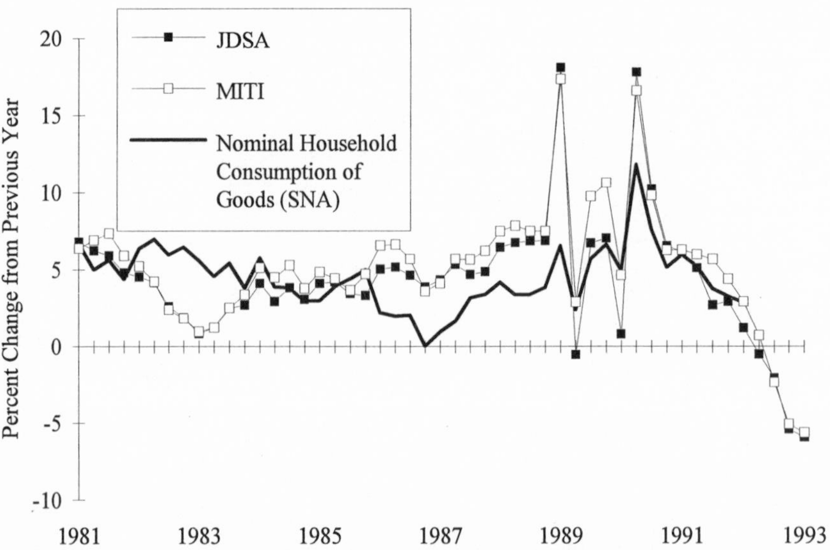

Fig. 6.1. Comparison of Department Store Sales Statistics

7 New Vehicle Registrations

Source: Japan Automobile Dealers Association.

Frequency: Monthly.

Release: Figures for the previous month are released at the beginning of each month.

Availability: Figures are available from January 1968 onward.

New vehicle registrations are considered to reflect the strength of consumption expenditures on durable goods. These statistics are particularly useful due to their quick release.

Details

The Japan Automobile Dealers Association compiles the number of vehicles sold each month. The number of vehicles sold is also called the number of new vehicle registrations. It includes cars, trucks, and buses. Cars and trucks with engine displacements of 660 cc or less are excluded from the statistics.

Vehicles are classified by size of engine (for cars) or carrying capacity (for trucks) and by company. Table 7.1 shows the number and type of new vehicle registrations for calendar year 1992.

Table 7.1. New Vehicle Registrations
Calendar Year 1992

	Units	Percent of Total
Total vehicles	5,333,784	100.0
Total cars (excluding engine 660 cc or less)	3,679,831	69.0
Engine 2,000 cc or less	2,966,003	55.6
Engine over 2,000 cc	713,828	13.4
Total trucks (excluding engine 660 cc or less)	1,632,376	30.6
Carrying capacity of 2 metric tons or less	1,485,009	27.8
Carrying capacity of over 2 metric tons	147,367	2.8
Buses	21,577	0.4

Source: Japan Automobile Dealers Association.

Only the number of new vehicle registrations is released. Neither the value of vehicles sold nor seasonally adjusted figures are available.

Features and Problems

The number of new vehicle registrations excluding trucks and buses is frequently used. The recent trend shows a higher growth rate of cars with engines over 2,000 cc than those with engines of less than 2,000 cc. This reflects consumers' increasing preference for luxury cars.

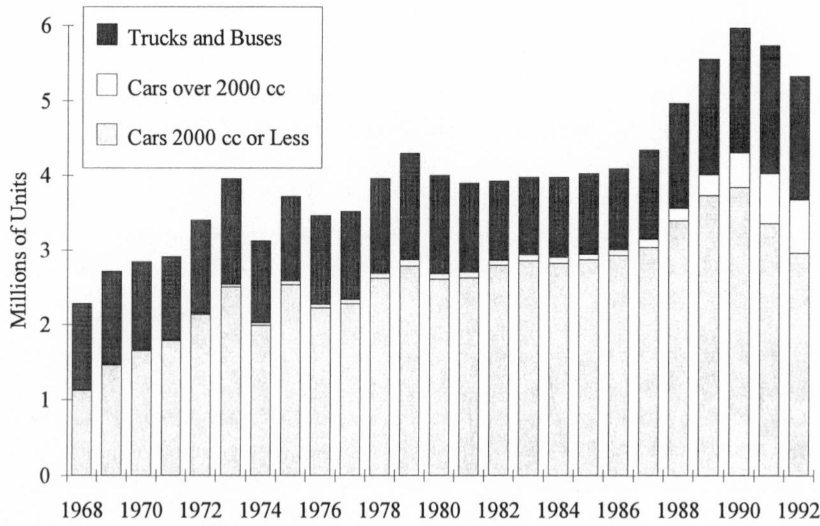

Fig. 7.1. New Vehicle Registrations

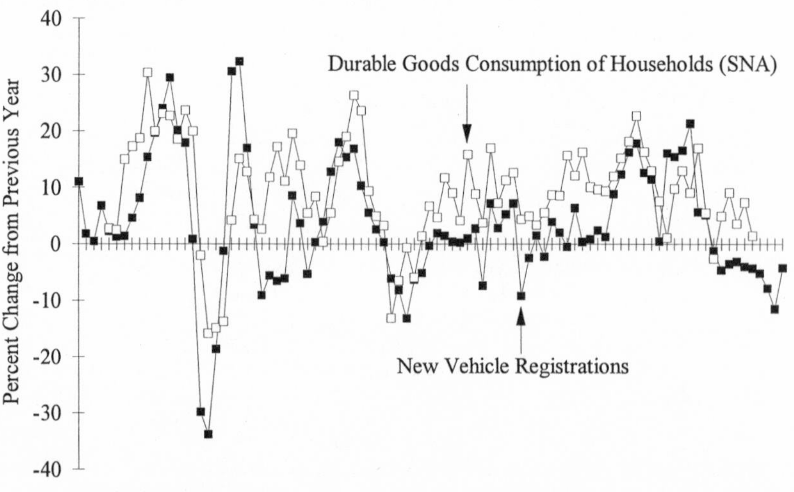

Fig. 7.2. Growth in New Vehicle Registrations vs. Durable Goods Consumption

8 Consumer Behavioral Survey

Source: Research Bureau, Economic Planning Agency.

Frequency: Quarterly.

Release: Figures for the previous quarter are released in the latter half of the first month of each quarter.

Availability: The Consumer Attitude Index is available from fiscal year 1972 onward. Consumer durable ownership statistics begin in 1957 (annual data).

The Consumer Behavioral Survey reveals consumers' attitude toward current and future consumption, income, and business conditions. Planned and realized expenditure on travel and durable goods, and planned expenditure on services, are also available. The March survey contains the ownership rates of various consumer durables.

Details

The Consumer Behavioral Survey is conducted every March, June, September, and December on a sample of 5,040 households in 231 municipalities nationwide. One-person households and foreigners are excluded from the survey.

Consumers' Attitude

The surveyed households are asked seven questions about their general sentiment on: (1) standard of living; (2) income; (3) price developments; (4) job security; (5) expenditure on consumer durables; (6) expenditure on leisure; and (7) value of their assets. The respondents are asked how the situation six months later will compare with the current situation, using one of five choices: (a) will improve; (b) will somewhat improve; (c) will not change; (d) will somewhat worsen; or (e) will worsen.

Five consumer sentiment indexes are constructed based on questions 1–5 above (questions 1–3 only prior to fiscal year 1982). Answers are assigned a score: 1 point for (a); 0.75 for (b); 0.5 for (c); 0.25 for (d); and 0 for (e). The consumer sentiment index is the average score for the question (in percent). If all the households expect improvement in the future, the value will be 100, while if all expect the situation to worsen, the value will be 0. The 'Consumer Attitude Index' is the simple average of these five consumer sentiment indexes.

Planned and Realized Expenditure

The households are asked about their planned and realized expenditure on travel and consumer durables, and planned expenditure on various services.

Ownership Rate and Service Lives of Consumer Durables

The service lives of 10 types of consumer durables are available each quarter. The March survey includes the ownership rates of 46 types of consumer durables.

Seasonal Adjustment

The Census X-11 method is applied to all time series except for the ownership rates, which are published only once a year.

Features and Problems

The Consumer Behavioral Survey is the only official survey on consumer sentiment and has useful micro-level data, but is not widely followed by financial analysts. As Fig. 8.1 shows, the Consumer Attitude Index is not a reliable predictor of household consumption expenditure.

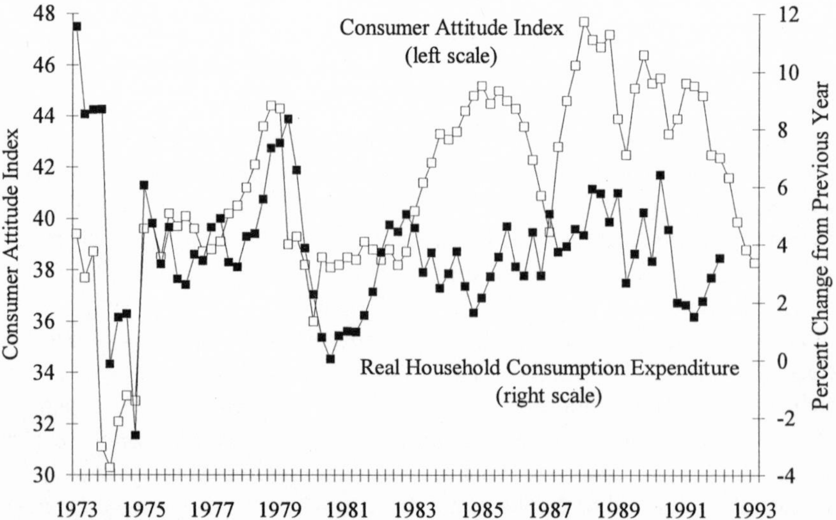

Fig. 8.1. Consumer Attitude Index (Seasonally Adjusted)

Corporate Business Sector

Introduction to the Corporate Business Sector: The Capital Investment Process

Capital investment is the most volatile of the major GNP components, and an important factor in determining both current and future economic growth. Capital investment appears in statistics in two ways: it adds to demand when expenditures are made on equipment and structures; and later, it adds to capacity (supply) following the completion of the equipment and structures. This chapter outlines the process of capital investment and how it may be followed using the various statistical series introduced in this book.

Business Surveys -- Capital Investment Plan

In the first stage, each company makes an annual capital investment plan. These are compiled in business surveys conducted by various institutions, although most are available only in Japanese. One of the most important of these is the Short-Term Economic Survey of Enterprises (TANKAN) conducted by the Bank of Japan, which is available in English (see Chapter 14). Appendix 5 provides a list of business surveys.

Ordering

After each company determines its annual capital investment plan, it begins to place orders for capital goods and construction. Statistics for these orders are available in New Orders, Sales, and Unfilled Orders of Machinery Industries (Chapter 9) and Orders Received for Construction (Chapter 18).

Production

Upon receipt of orders, machinery and construction companies start producing various types of goods. Of course, there are many interactions between industries in the production process. Production activities are covered by the following statistics: Industrial Production (Chapter 10); Public Construction Started (Chapter 19); and Construction Starts (available in the *Monthly of Construction Statistics*).

Shipment, Sales

Produced goods are delivered from the warehouses of manufacturing companies. Shipments are covered by the following statistics: 'shipment index' in Industrial

Production (Chapter 10); 'machinery sales' in New Orders, Sales, and Unfilled Orders of Machinery Industries (Chapter 9); and 'imports of capital goods' in the Summary Report on Trade (Chapter 30).

Delivery

Finally, machinery equipment and structures are delivered to the ordering companies. They are included in fixed capital formation in national income statistics (Chapters 1 and 2), Quarterly Financial Report of Non-Financial Businesses (Chapter 15), and the Business and Investment Survey of Incorporated Businesses (published by the Economic Planning Agency).

Operation

Once machinery equipment starts its operation, the capital investment leads to an increase in capacity, which is covered by Operating Rate and Production Capacity statistics (Chapter 11) and Gross Fixed Capital Stock of Private Enterprises (Chapter 13).

9 New Orders, Sales, and Unfilled Orders of Machinery Industries

Source: Research Bureau, Economic Planning Agency.

Frequency: Monthly.

Release: Machinery orders statistics are released around the middle of each month with a two-month lag. The *Annual Report on Machinery Orders*, published every November (no English translation provided), includes detailed figures. In the first half of the second month of each quarter, the *Outlook of New Machinery Orders* is published. It contains the outlook for the next two quarters.

Availability: Figures for machinery orders for 178 companies are available from April 1969 onward. Figures for an expanded sample of 280 companies are available from April 1987 onward. To avoid discontinuity, some statistics for the 178-company sample are still released. Figures prior to 1969 are available on a different basis of sample companies (127 machinery manufacturers).

Machinery orders statistics are considered to be a leading indicator of firms' capital investment and business activities. Machinery orders (private sector, excluding shipbuilding and electric power) deflated by the wholesale price index of domestic capital goods is included in the leading index of Diffusion Indexes compiled by the EPA.

Details

The EPA conducts a survey of 308 designated manufacturers of machinery and related products, with 280 being manufacturers of machinery (industries 1–9 in Table 9.1). Contents of the survey include new orders, sales, and unfilled orders for machinery equipment. The recent change in Japan's economic structure (declining share of manufacturing industries and increasing share of tertiary industries) forced the EPA to increase the number of firms from 202 (of which 178 firms are machinery manufacturers) to 308 and to enlarge the coverage of the survey, so that orders from tertiary industries can be properly measured. Figures based on the wider coverage have been published only since April 1992, but figures from April 1987 onward were made available retroactively.

Machinery orders are classified by the source of demand (see Table 9.2). Statistics for domestic private demand by industry (of demanders) are also available. In these statistics, orders from a company which produces a variety of goods are

Table 9.1. Types of Companies Surveyed in Machinery Orders
As of March 1991

	Current Sample [280]	Previous Sample [178]
1. Engine and motor manufacturing	31	28
2. Electric power machinery	20	14
3. Electronic and communication machines	53	15
4. Industrial machinery	190	126
5. Machine tools	56	42
6. Railway vehicles	17	17
7. Road vehicles	5	0
8. Aircraft	12	12
9. Shipbuilding	20	10
Sub-Total	280	178
10. Steel structures	32	27
11. Bearings	6	6
12. Cable and wire	21	21
Total	308	202

Note: Figures do not sum to total because firms may be counted more than once.

Source: Economic Planning Agency, *Annual Report on Machinery Orders*, November 1992.

Table 9.2. Machinery Orders by Source of Final Demand
Calendar Year 1992, 280 Company Sample

	Billion Yen	Percent of Total
Total	25,771	100.0
External demand	5,283	20.5
Domestic public demand	3,852	14.9
Domestic private demand	14,760	57.3
Manufacturing	5,526	21.4
Non-manufacturing	9,234	35.8
Demand through agencies	1,876	7.3
Total excluding shipbuilding	24,822	96.3
Domestic private demand excl. shipbuilding	14,514	56.3
Domestic private demand excl. shipbuilding and electric power	12,165	47.2

Note: Demand through agencies include those via intermediaries such as trading and construction companies and via unidentifiable final demanders. This is considered to represent a part of small business demand.

Source: Economic Planning Agency.

classified by the industry of the company's major line of business.

Figures with and without seasonal adjustment are available. Figures are seasonally adjusted retroactive to 1969 by Census X-11 in May each year (when March figures become available). Figures are always subject to revision as new and corrected survey data become available.

Features and Problems

Leading Indicator of Capital Investment

Domestic private demand excluding shipbuilding and electric power usually leads non-residential investment in national income statistics by about two quarters (see Figure 9.1). Orders *received* by shipbuilders and orders *placed* by electric power companies are usually excluded because they show wide fluctuations. Single contracts are large, and orders for shipbuilding are mainly determined by foreign demand while orders by electric power companies are often politically influenced.

Privatized Companies

Orders received by the privatized Japan Railway (JR) and Nippon Telegraph and Telephone (NTT) have been included in private domestic demand since September 1988 for the series 'Transportation and Other Non-Manufacturing'; for other related series, they have been included since April 1987.

Possible Double Counting

There is the possibility of double counting of orders when the manufacturers surveyed do not subtract from their total amount of orders received those which are subcontracted out to their subsidiaries and/or outside subcontractors. If the subcontractor is also one of the manufacturers included in the survey, the same order may be counted twice.

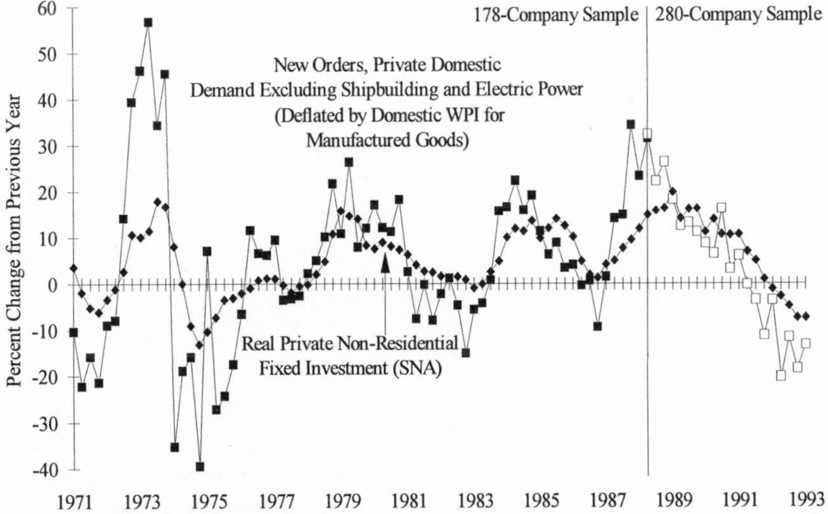

Fig. 9.1. Growth Rate of New Orders

10 Industrial Production, Shipments and Inventory Statistics

Source:	Research and Statistics Department, Ministry of International Trade and Industry.
Frequency:	Monthly and Annual.
Release :	Preliminary figures for the previous month are released at the end of each month. Revised figures are released around the middle of the following month. Seasonally adjusted figures are also available. Annual revision for seasonal adjustment is made for the previous calendar year figures in May, by the MITI-III-R method. Detailed figures are available in the *Year Book of Indexes of Industrial Production*, published in July or August.
Availability:	Figures are available from 1950 onward. It should be noted that there are some discontinuities every five years because of the change in the benchmark year and corresponding change in the coverage of commodities.

The industrial production, shipments, and inventory statistics cover mining and manufacturing industries, which account for about 30 percent of GNP. They include four indexes:

1. Industrial production index.
2. Producers' shipments index.
3. Producers' inventory index.
4. Inventory-shipment ratio index.

These indexes are valuable in analyzing business conditions due to their prompt availability, sensitive nature in response to changes in business conditions, and detailed components by industry and market groups.

Details

Method of Calculation

522 commodities are included in the production and shipment indexes, 395 for the inventory index, and 378 for the inventory-shipment ratio index. First, a Laspeyres quantity index (see Appendix 1) for each commodity is calculated (in the inventory-shipment ratio index, the inventory/shipment ratio is used as the quantity). The overall index is then calculated as a weighted average of the commodity indexes,

with weights determined by value added for the production index, and total value for the other indexes. Table 10.1 shows the weights for the current benchmark year (1990), classified by industry and by market group. Values of the indexes for these classifications are also available.

Table 10.1. Weights Used in Production, Shipment, and Inventory Indexes Classification by Industry and by Market Group
Benchmark Year 1990

	Production Index	Producers' Shipment Index	Producers' Inventory Index	Inventory-Shipment Ratio Index
Classification by industry				
Total	100.0	100.0	100.0	95.0
Manufacturing	99.7	99.8	99.8	94.9
Iron and steel	5.7	6.3	9.8	9.4
Non-ferrous metals	2.0	2.7	1.9	1.9
Fabricated metals	6.5	4.8	5.2	4.0
Machinery and equipment	45.0	47.9	34.0	31.3
Industrial machinery	13.5	11.4	9.1	8.5
Electrical machinery	18.7	18.8	15.7	13.6
Transportation equipment	11.5	16.5	8.1	8.1
Precision instruments	1.3	1.2	1.1	1.1
Ceramics, stone and clay products	5.0	3.8	5.8	5.8
Chemicals	10.1	8.0	11.3	11.3
Petroleum and coal products	0.8	3.0	4.8	4.8
Plastic products	3.9	3.7	3.5	3.5
Pulp, paper and paper products	3.0	3.1	3.0	2.8
Textiles	5.9	3.9	7.1	7.1
Foods and tobacco	6.0	7.5	7.6	7.6
Other manufacturing	6.0	5.1	5.7	5.4
Mining	0.3	0.2	0.2	0.1
(Public utilities)	[5.2]	[5.0]	--	--
Classification by market group				
Total	100.0	100.0	100.0	95.0
Final demand goods	55.6	56.4	54.2	50.0
Investment goods	30.8	28.7	20.5	19.9
Capital goods	21.2	20.7	10.6	10.0
Construction goods	9.6	8.0	9.9	9.9
Consumer goods	24.7	27.8	33.7	30.0
Durable consumer goods	11.0	14.3	18.1	14.9
Non-durable consumer goods	13.7	13.5	15.5	15.2
Producer goods	44.4	43.6	45.8	45.1
Producer goods for mining and manufacturing	43.2	41.6	43.2	42.5
Producer goods for other uses	1.2	2.0	2.7	2.6

Note: Weights for the inventory-shipment ratio index are the value of inventory as a percentage of total inventory included in the producers' inventory index. Some commodities included in the producers' inventory index are not included in the inventory-shipment ratio index, so the sum of weights is less than 100. This does not affect the actual value of the index.

Source: Ministry of International Trade and Industry.

Classification by industry basically follows the Japan Standard Industry Classification. Although public utilities are normally not included in mining and manufacturing, an additional index which includes public utilities is provided.

For classification by market group, 'final demand goods' are those not used as an input for other industries. 'Producer goods' are those used as an input for other industries. 'Investment goods' are those used for final demand of capital investment. 'Consumer goods' are those purchased by households. They consist of 'durable consumer goods' (service life of over one year or relatively expensive) and 'non-durable consumer goods' (service life less than one year, or relatively inexpensive).

Features and Problems

Production, Shipment, and Forecast Indexes

The Production Index shows current business conditions in the manufacturing sector and is included in the coincident index of Diffusion Indexes (DI) compiled by the EPA. Inventory levels tend to lag the business cycle, and the Producers' Inventory Index is included in the lagging index of DI. The producers' inventory-shipment ratio index is included in the leading index of DI. The shipment index for durable consumer goods is also included in the leading index of the DI, while the shipment index for investment goods (excluding transportation) is included in the coincident index of DI.

In connection with the production index, a forecast index (based on the firms' forecast of production in the next two months) is released. When production is rising, the forecast index will be nearly the same as the actual value, while it tends to be above the actual value when production is slackening.

The shipment indexes for domestic and foreign demand are released on a quarterly basis, concurrent with the release of final figures for the final month of the corresponding quarter.

Changes in the Benchmark Year

When the benchmark year is changed, data for the two years prior to the benchmark year are recalculated to reflect the benchmark year weights, while earlier data are rescaled so that there is no jump in the historical series (the weights used are not revised). For example, in April 1993 the benchmark year was changed from 1985 to 1990. The figures for 1988 (two years prior to the benchmark year) onward were revised to reflect the 1990 weights, while figures for 1987 and earlier were simply rescaled. Thus, figures for 1983–7 will always be weighted in the old benchmark year of 1985. When the benchmark year is changed to 1995, only data for 1993 onward will be reweighted, so the data for 1988–92 will always use the 1990 weights.

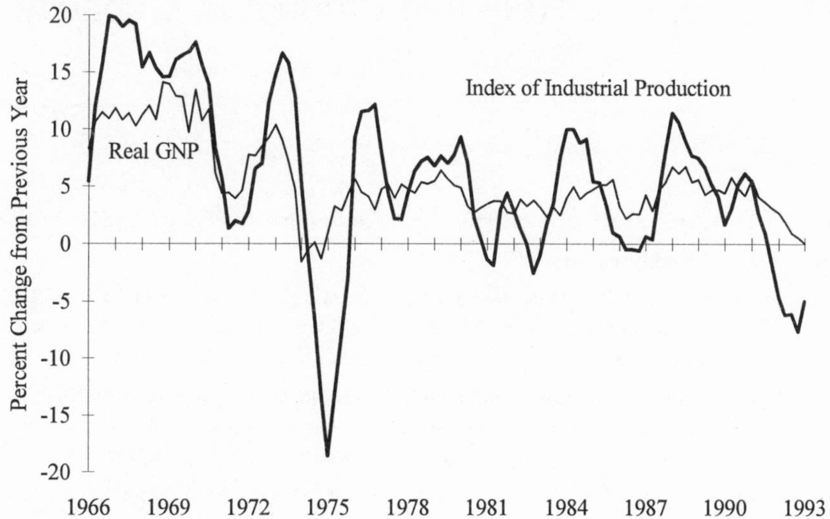

Fig. 10.1. Index of Industrial Production

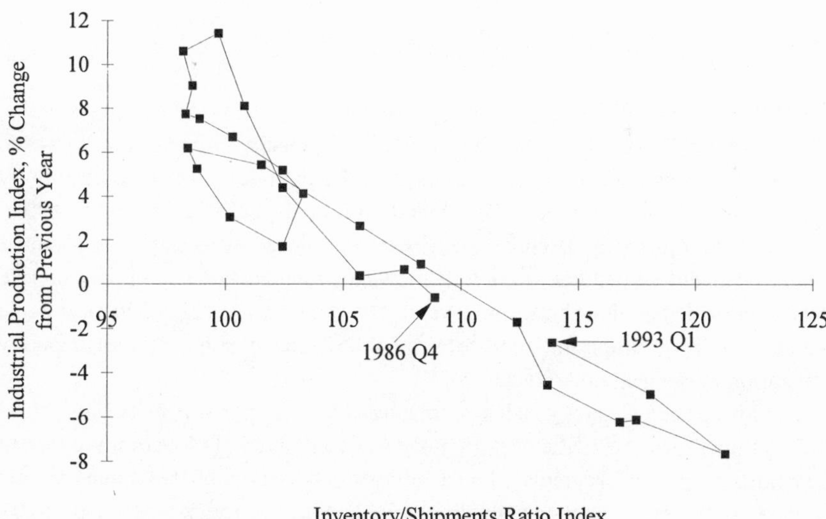

Fig. 10.2. Inventory Cycle

11 Operating Rate and Production Capacity

Source: Research and Statistics Department, Ministry of International Trade and Industry.

Frequency: Monthly and Annual.

Release: Indexes of operating rate and production capacity are released around the middle of each month with a two-month lag, concurrently with the revised production, shipments, and inventory statistics (see Chapter 10).

Availability: Monthly indexes of operating rate and production capacity are available from January 1965 onward. Monthly figures are available only for major categories. Figures for disaggregate classifications are available in the *Year Book of Indexes of Industrial Production*, published every July or August.

Indexes of operating rate and production capacity cover the manufacturing sector of the economy. The Operating Rate Index is used in the coincident index of Diffusion Indexes compiled by the EPA.

Details

Method of Calculation

The Operating Rate Index (sometimes called the capacity utilization index -- see Figure 11.1) is calculated by dividing the Production Index for manufacturing by the Production Capacity Index. The Operating Rate Index, by definition, is 100 in the base year (currently calendar year 1990), and does not measure the absolute level of capacity utilization. Rather, it shows the relative capacity utilization rate compared with that of the benchmark year. The absolute level of the operating rate is obtained by multiplying the index by 0.857, the average rate of capacity utilization in the benchmark year.

The Production Capacity Index is calculated in a similar way as the Industrial Production Index, with the weight for each commodity (146 commodities in benchmark year 1990) calculated on a value-added basis. The benchmark year is changed in the same manner as the Industrial Production Index (see Chapter 10).

Seasonal Adjustment

Seasonally adjusted figures for the Operating Rate Index are available, but not for the Production Capacity Index. Annual revision for seasonal adjustment is made for the previous calendar year figures in May by the MITI-III-R method.

Features and Problems

Production Capacity: Net or Gross Concept?

It is unclear whether the Production Capacity Index is a *net* (of depreciation) or *gross* concept (the precise method of calculation used has never been published). It is derived from MITI's own survey on actual production capacity of factories in each industry, not from the balance sheets of companies. It should reflect the changes in production capacity resulting from wear and obsolescence, i.e. a net concept. As shown in Figure 11.2, the growth rate of MITI's Production Capacity Index is lower than that of EPA's Real Gross Fixed Capital Stock for the manufacturing sector. It therefore seems likely that the index includes some adjustment for depreciation.

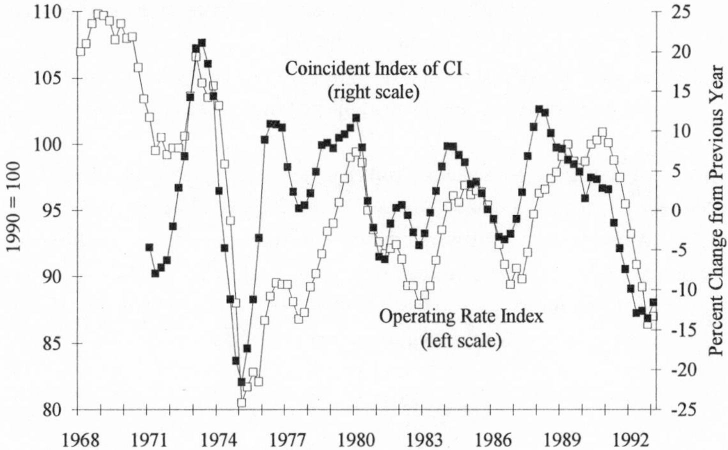

Fig. 11.1. Operating Rate Index (Capacity Utilization Index)

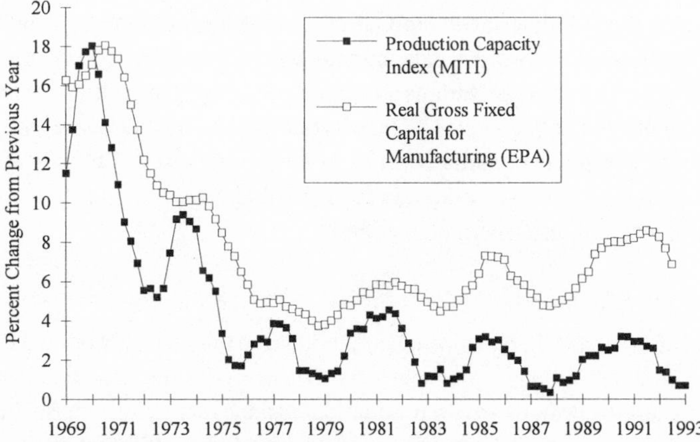

Fig. 11.2. Growth Rate of Production Capacity

12 Index of Tertiary Industries Activity

Source: Ministry of International Trade and Industry.

Frequency: Monthly, Quarterly, and Annual.

Release: Monthly and quarterly series are released four times a year in March, June, September, and December with a three- to five-month lag (figures for the January–March period are released in the first half of June). Some series are revised with the next period's release. All figures are revised when those for the January–March period are released.

Availability: Figures are available from January 1973 onward, although some series begin in 1979 or 1983. Seasonally adjusted figures are also available.

The Index of Tertiary Industries Activity is the only comprehensive statistic available which covers tertiary industries in Japan. The percentage of GDP accounted for by tertiary industries has increased dramatically, reaching 63.7% of GDP in calendar 1991 (48.0% of total gross output). This index can be used with the Index of Industrial Production (see Chapter 10) to (at least roughly) examine the relative strength of the manufacturing and non-manufacturing sectors.

Details

Concept of the Index

Activity of tertiary industries is defined as market transactions by producers of services (including non-profit organizations), and therefore includes market transactions by government organizations and private non-profit institutions even if their services are offered at below cost. The various types of production of the tertiary industries are compiled from many different source statistics. Roughly speaking, the index measures gross real output in the sense that it incorporates not only value added produced but also intermediate inputs.

Compilation of the Index

For each sub-industry, indexes which are thought to most closely approximate the activity of the sub-industry are selected. Where available, production quantity indexes are used. If there are no production statistics in quantity terms, nominal production value is deflated by an appropriate price index. If there are no statistics

Table 12.1. Weights Used for Index of Tertiary Industries Activity
Benchmark Year 1985

Total tertiary industry	100.0
Electricity, gas, heat, and water supply	5.1
Transportation and communications	11.1
Transportation	8.2
Communications	2.9
Wholesale and retail trade and restaurants	26.7
Wholesale trade	11.7
Retail trade	10.8
Restaurants	4.3
Finance and insurance	10.0
Banking and finance	7.4
Insurance	2.7
Real estate	6.7
Services	33.3
Services for individuals	8.5
Services for business establishments	8.3
Public services	16.9
Government services	6.6

Source: Ministry of International Trade and Industry.

Table 12.2. Weights Used in Special Classification of Activity Index
Benchmark Year 1985

Tertiary industries excluding electricity, gas, heat, and water supply	94.9
Tertiary industries excluding government services	93.5
Wholesale and retail trade	22.5
Production and trade-related industries	31.0
Information and communications related industries	6.0
Leisure related industries	4.9
Industries mainly for business establishments	27.0
Industries mainly for individuals	25.1
Industries both for business establishments and individuals	24.5
Public-related industries	23.4

Source: Ministry of International Trade and Industry.

on production at all, other types of data, such as earnings, inputs, or expenditures are employed.

Coverage

Indexes are scaled to 100 in calendar 1985. The overall index for tertiary industries is a weighted average of the sub-industry indexes. The value added for each industry in the input-output tables in 1985 is used to determine the weights (see Tables 12.1 and 12.2). When the value added in each industry cannot be obtained from the input-output tables, it is estimated from other source statistics.

Seasonal Adjustment

Seasonally adjusted and non-adjusted monthly and quarterly figures are released. The MITI-III-R method is employed for seasonal adjustment. All figures are revised when the January–March figures are released.

Features and Problems

Varying Definition of Production Activity

As discussed in the previous section, there are difficulties in standardizing the definition of production activity in each sub-industry. For some industries, there are no suitable statistics representing gross production activity.

Volatile Monthly Movement

As shown in Fig. 12.1, the year-on-year growth rate sometimes suddenly jumps up or down for just one period, even with seasonally adjusted quarterly figures; monthly figures are much more volatile. One reason for this is that each sub-index is deflated by price indexes which may be strongly affected by monthly fluctuation in commodity prices and the foreign exchange rate. The volatility in monthly figures increased considerably during 1986 and 1987 when the yen appreciated substantially and domestic wholesale prices declined at a double-digit rate. It is therefore recommended that the index be interpreted with caution, especially when using monthly figures.

Comparison with Manufacturing Sector

It is also worth comparing the movement of this index with that of the manufacturing sector (Index of Industrial Production: see Chapter 10). As shown in Fig. 12.1, the growth rates of these two indexes roughly move together, with the manufacturing sector showing larger cyclical movements. Note how in 1986–7 the yen's sharp appreciation hit the export-oriented manufacturing industries hard while the tertiary industries continued to grow. In 1992, both indexes showed negative growth, demonstrating the breadth of the recession at that time.

Combining Two Indexes to Reflect the Level of Economic Activity

One way to get a more accurate picture of overall economic activity is to combine (using a weighted average) the index of tertiary industries activity and the index of industrial production. Although these two indexes differ in many aspects, their basic concept of measuring fixed-weight gross real output is a common property. The weights for gross output of manufacturing and tertiary industries in the benchmark year (1985) are 0.484 and 0.516, respectively. Fig. 12.2 shows year-on-year increases in the combined series (called the Integrated Index) and the Coincident Index of Composite Indexes (CI). Note how the Integrated Index indicates the same turning points in the business cycle as the Coincident Index of CI.

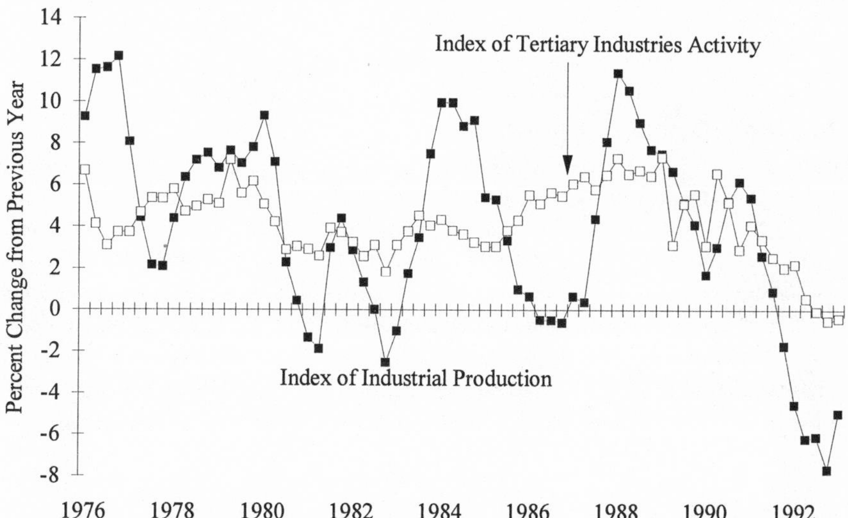

Fig. 12.1. Index of Tertiary Industries Activity

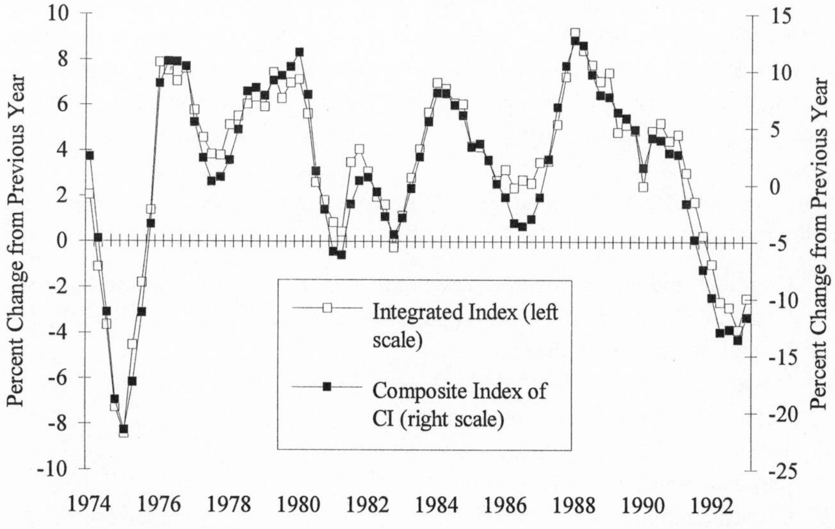

Fig. 12.2. Integrated Index

13 Gross Fixed Capital Stock of Private Enterprises

Source: Economic Research Institute, Economic Planning Agency.

Frequency: Quarterly and Annual.

Release: Figures for the previous quarter are released in the last month of each quarter (along with the QE release of GNP figures). This preliminary release includes only the total figures for all industries. Detailed figures are available one quarter later. Annual revision is incorporated into the December issue.

Availability: Figures are available from the first quarter of 1955 onward. Figures for some minor classifications are available only from the first quarter of 1975 onward.

These statistics reveal gross fixed capital stock and new capital investment of private enterprises. Only capital which contributes to production capacity is included.

Details

Coverage

These statistics are intended to measure capital stock from the viewpoint of total *production capacity* of the corporate sector of Japan. Some types of capital stock such as company-owned housing, inventories, and bric-a-brac are excluded from the statistics because they are not considered to contribute to production capacity. Land is also excluded. Figures for gross fixed capital stock and gross new capital investment of private enterprises are available. Private enterprises include financial institutions but exclude private non-profit institutions serving households. The following types of reproducible tangible fixed capital stock are included:

1. Buildings and related facilities excluding company-owned housing.
2. Structures (transportation, power generation, telecommunication facilities).
3. Machinery and equipment.
4. Vessels.
5. Vehicles and transportation equipment.
6. Tools, utensils, and fixtures.
7. Large animals and trees.
8. Construction in progress accounts.
9. Land development and improvement excluding acquisition of land.

Measurement

There are two measures of capital stock: *installation-in-progress* basis and *end-of-installation* basis. The latter includes only equipment for which installation or construction is completed, while the former also includes equipment for which installation or construction is in progress. More precisely, the former includes all types of capital stock in items 1–9, while the latter excludes the construction in progress accounts (item 8).

Valuation of Capital Stock

Capital stock and new capital investment are currently valued at calendar 1985 prices. There is no valuation at current prices. Both fixed capital and new capital investment are valued in *gross* terms, including depreciation (capital consumption). The EPA assumes that the gross value is a better proxy for production capacity than the net value (gross value less depreciation). The use of gross value implies that the production capacity of capital stock is constant until it suddenly vanishes at the end of its service life. This contrasts with the production capacity index for manufacturing sector compiled by Ministry of International Trade and Industry (see Chapter 11). MITI's production capacity index is closer to a net concept, although the methodology used is quite different.

Valuation of Assets

The value of gross assets is first estimated by type of asset and by year of acquisition. *Acquisition cost*, or *historical cost* estimates are employed. *Inflators* by type of asset and by year of acquisition are calculated, then multiplied by the nominal value of each asset in each year to obtain the constant price value of assets, or the *gross asset value*. The *net asset value* is obtained by subtracting capital consumption based on the fixed percentage method of depreciation.

Estimation of Capital Stock

The value of the capital stock is estimated based on the following formula:

$$K_t = K_{t-1} * (1 - r_t) + I_t * (1 + s_t)$$

where K_t denotes the capital stock at the end of the period t, r_t the rate of capital retirement, I_t new capital investment during period t, and s_t the acquisition rate of used equipment.

Treatment of Privatized Enterprises

The following four privatized companies have been included in the statistics:

Company	Industry	Included Since
NTT	Transportation and Communications	Apr.–June 1985
JT	Manufacturing	Apr.–June 1985
EPDC	Electricity, Gas, and Water Supply	Oct.–Dec. 1986
7 JRs	Transportation and Communications	Apr.–June 1987

Note: *NTT* Nippon Telegraph and Telephone, *JT* Japan Tobacco, *EPDC* Electric Power Development Company, *JR* Japan Railways.

Seasonal Adjustment

Both original and seasonally adjusted figures are available. The Census X-11 method is employed for seasonal adjustment.

Relationship between New Capital Investment and National Income Statistics

The value of total new capital investment in these statistics is equal to 'gross private domestic fixed capital formation excluding private non-profit institutions serving households and corporations' in national income statistics.

Classification by Industry

Table 13.1 shows the classifications available in quarterly preliminary estimates. In the annual revision, more detailed classifications are available, especially for the manufacturing industries. Figures for new capital investment are available with the same classifications. This classification is in accordance with that employed in national income statistics. There are identical figures for the capital stock of proprietorships on both an installation-in-progress basis and end-of-installation basis.

Table 13.1. Gross Fixed Capital Stock by Industry, Installation-in-Progress Basis
Calendar Year 1992, Trillions of 1985 Yen (constant prices)

	Capital Stock	New Investment
Total industries	810.3	83.5
Agriculture, forestry, and fishery	97.9	5.6
Mining	2.7	0.2
Construction	29.7	4.3
Manufacturing	295.7	28.8
Wholesale and retail trade	81.7	7.7
Finance and insurance	18.0	2.5
Real estate	24.4	2.8
Transportation and communications	80.4	8.6
Electricity, gas, and water supply	70.8	6.5
Services	109.0	16.5
Incorporated enterprises	658.8	72.6
Proprietorships	151.4	10.9

Note: Figures for capital stock are end-of-calendar year values.

Features and Problems

Comparison with Capacity Index of MITI

While the capacity index developed by MITI (Chapter 11) covers only manufacturing sectors, gross fixed capital in these statistics covers the whole corporate sector. When comparing MITI's capacity index to the EPA's gross capital stock measure, the capacity index consistently shows lower growth than gross capital (see Figs. 11.2 and 13.1), which seems to indicate some adjustment for depreciation in the capacity index.

Estimation Bias Resulting from the Historical Cost Method

EPA adopts the historical cost method to obtain gross asset values. The accuracy of this method critically depends on how precisely inflators are constructed. If the inflators are overestimated, then gross asset value in constant prices would also be overestimated.

Quality Improvement and Technological Change

In theory, the value of gross fixed capital stock should reflect improvements in quality and technological progress. These statistics make no adjustment for these factors due to the difficulties involved with incorporating them.

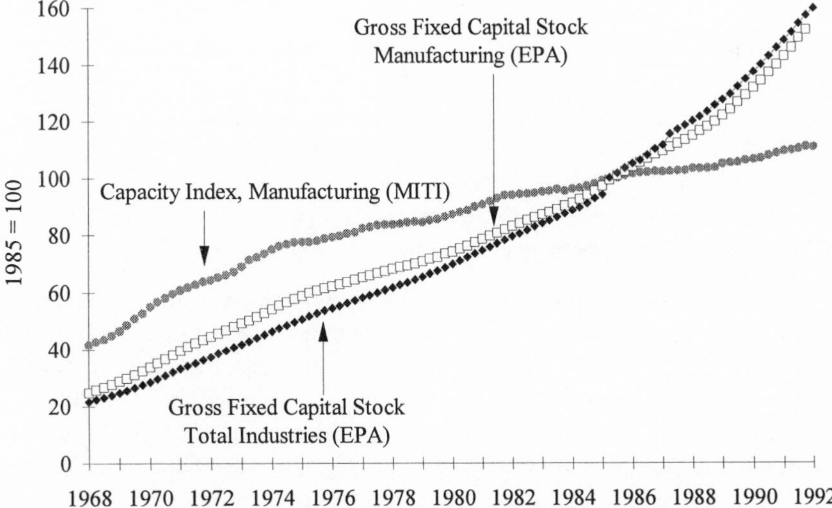

Fig. 13.1. Production Capacity in MITI and EPA Statistics

14 Short-Term Economic Survey of Enterprises (TANKAN)

Source: Research and Statistics Department, Bank of Japan.

Frequency: Quarterly.

Release: The survey is conducted in February, May, August, and November. Figures are released in the first weeks of the following month, in March, June, September, and December respectively.

Availability: Figures for several series are available from the July–September quarter in 1957 onward. Additional series and more companies were included in later years.

Enterprises are surveyed on various indicators of business conditions during the previous quarter. The outlook for the current quarter and next quarter (or year) is also surveyed. The survey is widely used in the analysis of business conditions because of its early release and vast coverage. It is one of the most important of the surveys on capital investment plans (see Appendix 5 for a list of such surveys).

Details

Coverage

The survey is conducted on three major groups of enterprises:

1. Principal non-financial enterprises (716 companies).
2. Non-financial enterprises throughout Japan (7,394 companies).
3. Financial institutions (202 companies).

(The number of enterprises given is for the May 1993 survey.)

The first group covers principal non-financial corporations with annual sales of over 1 billion yen. The sample corporations are basically fixed, consisting of 393 manufacturing and 323 non-manufacturing firms. The second group covers large, medium-sized and small non-financial enterprises, with manufacturing and non-manufacturing firms equally represented. The third group covers major banks, securities, and insurance companies. The third group was added to the survey because of their increasing role in capital investment. In the English language version of the report, statistics are provided for the first group only.

Content and Methodology

The survey contains 38 questions, which are consolidated into seven main groups:

1. Judgement of business conditions.
2. Production and sales.
3. Judgement of demand-supply conditions and of price developments.
4. Corporate profit.
5. Capital investment.
6. Judgement on employment.
7. Judgement on financial conditions.

Quarterly data are available for items 1, 3, 6, and 7. Semi-annual and annual data are available for items 2, 4, and 5 on a fiscal year basis. Financial institutions are surveyed only on their capital investment (item 5). Table 14.1 shows the schedule for the release of quarterly and semi-annual data.

Table 14.1 Schedule for the Release of Quarterly and Semi-Annual Data

Quarterly data							
	Survey period:	Nov. 93	Feb. 94	May 94	Aug. 94	Nov. 94	Feb. 95
	Release date:	Dec. 93	Mar. 94	June 94	Sept. 94	Dec. 94	Mar. 95
Data for:	Oct.–Dec. 93	R	A	--	--	--	--
Data for:	Jan.–Mar. 94	I	R	A	--	--	--
Data for:	Apr.–June 94	--	I	R	A	--	--
Data for:	July–Sept. 94	--	--	I	R	A	--
Data for:	Oct.–Dec. 94	--	--	--	I	R	A
Semi-annual data							
	Survey period:	Nov. 93	Feb. 94	May 94	Aug. 94	Nov. 94	Feb. 95
	Release date:	Dec. 93	Mar. 94	June 94	Sept. 94	Dec. 94	Mar. 95
Data for:	Apr. 93–Sept. 93	A	A	A	A	A	--
Data for:	Oct. 93–Mar. 94	R	R	A	A	A	--
Data for:	Apr. 94–Sept. 94	--	I	R	A	A	A
Data for:	Oct. 94–Mar. 95	--	I	R	R	R	R
Data for:	Apr. 95–Sept. 95	--	--	--	--	--	I
Data for:	Oct. 95–Mar. 96	--	--	--	--	--	I

Note: *I* Initial forecast, *R* Revised forecast, *A* Actual result.

The survey includes both quantitative and qualitative data. The latter is called the 'Judgement Survey'. Items 2, 4, and 5 are mainly quantitative, while items 1, 3, 6, and 7 are mainly qualitative. In the quantitative analysis, corporations are asked to show the actual and expected levels of various indicators such as production, sales, inventories, profit, investment, and liquidity. The Bank of Japan compiles these raw data so that growth rates from the previous period and various ratio indexes are calculated without discontinuity of the series. In the qualitative analysis, Diffusion

Indexes (DI) are used. The reporting enterprises choose between three alternatives, roughly corresponding to 'good/neutral/bad'. The Diffusion Indexes are constructed by subtracting the portion responding with negative tone from the portion responding with positive tone. The following are examples of Diffusion Indexes for various indicators:

Item	Diffusion Index
Business conditions	favorable less unfavorable
Demand-supply condition	excess demand less excess supply
Inventory	excessive less short
Price of input and product	increase less decrease
Production capacity	excessive less short
Employment	excessive less short
Financing	easy less difficult
Banks' lending standard	easy less tight
Liquidity	enough less short
Interest rate on borrowing	rising less declining

Features and Problems

Business Conditions DI as an Indicator of the Business Cycle

The survey is widely used in the analysis of current and future business conditions because of its early release and vast coverage. The Business Conditions DI is acknowledged as reflecting current business sentiment as much as business conditions.

Comparison of DI in TANKAN with DI Published by the EPA

It is important to distinguish between the DI in TANKAN and the DI published by the EPA. Fig. 14.1 shows how the Business Conditions DI of TANKAN (DI-BOJ) and the Coincident Index of DI published by the EPA (DI-EPA) relate to the business cycle and each other. The economy is said to be in an expansionary (recessionary) phase when it is growing faster (slower) than its long-run trend (approximately 4% for Japan). The economy is said to hit a peak (trough) when it stops growing (starts growing) faster than its long-term trend. The DI-EPA should be high (more than 50%) when the economy is in an upturn (between points A and C) and low (less than 50%) in downturns (between points C and E), while the Business Conditions DI should be increasing during upturns and decreasing during downturns. The DI-EPA tends to peak at around the same time the Business Conditions DI turns positive (point B). At this point, the economy is growing at its fastest, so all of the components of DI-EPA are increasing, while the Business

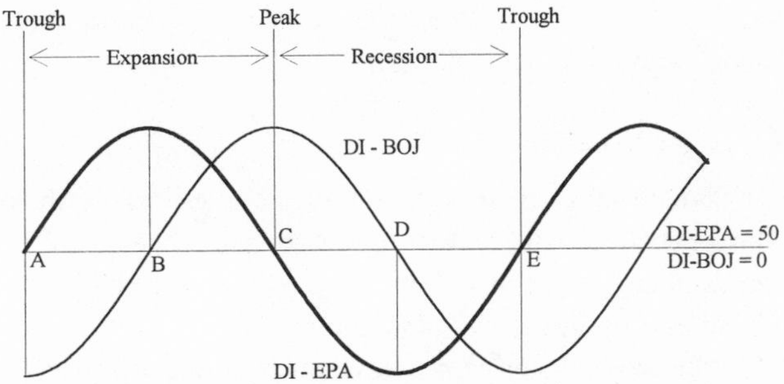

Fig. 14.1. Comparison of Business Conditions DI (DI-BOJ) and DI Published by the EPA

Conditions DI is increasing rapidly (business sentiment is improving). The Business Conditions DI should peak at around the same time the DI-EPA falls to 50% (point C). At this point, the economy is growing just at its long-term trend and business sentiment peaks, while some of the components of DI-EPA turn negative. The DI-EPA tends to reach a trough at around the same time the Business Conditions DI turns negative (point D), while the Business Conditions DI should reach its trough at around the same time the DI-EPA recovers to 50% (point E).

Comparison of DI in TANKAN with CI Published by the EPA

Fig. 14.2 compares the Business Conditions DI with the Coincident Index of Composite Indexes (CI) released by the EPA. Since both are supposed to measure current business conditions, in theory the two variables should move concurrently, but in reality peaks in the Business Conditions DI tend to come a few quarters after the peaks in the Coincident Index of CI. The *change* in the Business Conditions DI

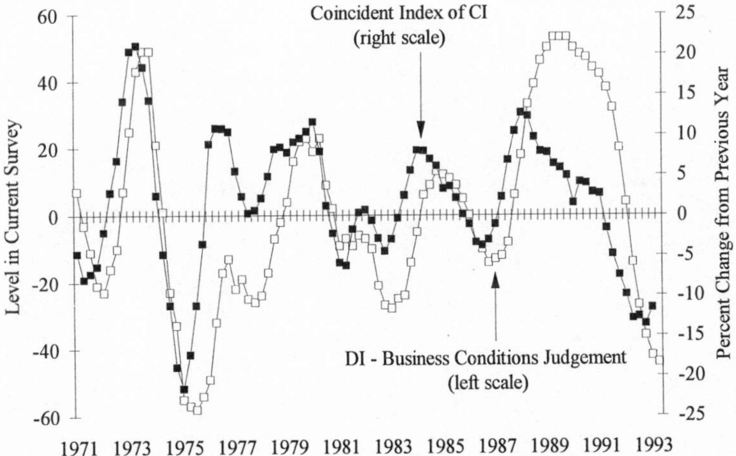

Fig. 14.2. Business Conditions DI

(value in current survey minus value in previous year's survey) actually shows closer movement with the Coincident Index of CI (see Fig. 14.3).

Some Indicators are Biased

The survey contains some bias in several indicators, especially those involving forecasts, which usually do not predict the future accurately. The judgement of enterprises tends to lag behind actual developments because they usually assume that current business conditions will continue.

For example, the outlook for capital investment in the February survey (first outlook for the next fiscal year) tends to underestimate actual investment when the economy is expanding, while it tends to be an overestimate when the economy is in recession (such as in FY 1986). During a business expansion, the November survey tends to show the highest figures (see Table 14.2).

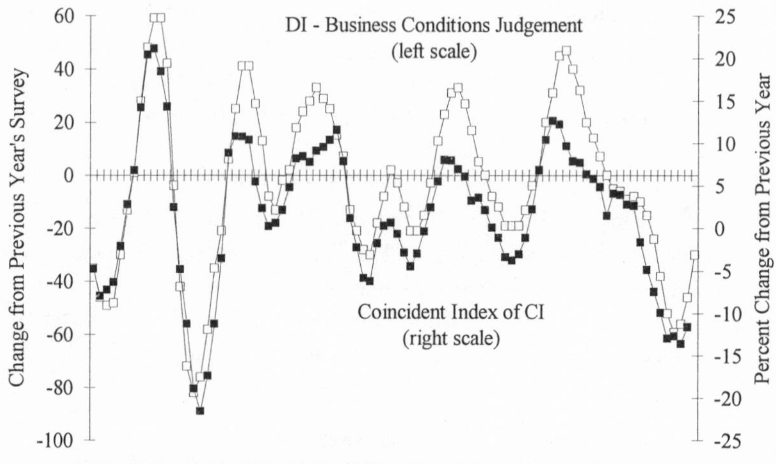

Fig. 14.3. Business Conditions DI (Change from Previous Year)

Table 14.2 Capital Investment Plan and Actual Investment (Manufacturing Sector)
Fiscal Year, Percent change from previous fiscal year

	83	84	85	86	87	88	89	90	91	92	93
Feb.	−6.8	0.3	6.8	1.6	−4.8	7.0	9.1	7.5	−1.1	−8.2	−9.9
May	−2.5	11.0	15.0	−4.5	−2.6	18.6	17.6	16.5	6.2	−8.9	−10.5
Aug.	−1.2	13.3	15.2	−6.1	−1.2	23.8	20.4	17.3	6.7	−10.4	n.a.
Nov.	−1.5	16.8	14.5	−8.1	1.7	28.8	25.7	20.7	5.6	−13.6	n.a.
Feb.	−2.7	16.9	12.1	−9.2	1.3	28.6	24.9	21.2	4.6	−14.5	n.a.
Actual (TANKAN)	−8.2	13.4	13.2	−11.9	−2.2	28.0	22.1	19.6	3.0	−17.2	n.a.
Actual (SNA)	3.8	12.2	12.2	1.3	7.1	16.1	14.0	13.0	2.9	−5.8	n.a.

Note: The first line shows the plan before the beginning of the fiscal year (February 1983 for FY 1983), while the fifth line shows the plan near the end of the fiscal year (February 1984 for FY 1983).

15 Quarterly Financial Report of Non-Financial Businesses

Source:	Institute of Fiscal and Monetary Policy, Ministry of Finance.
Frequency:	Quarterly and Annual.
Release:	Figures for the previous quarter are released in the first half of the final month of each quarter. Annual figures for the previous fiscal year are released in October each year in the *Monthly Statistics on Government Finance and Banking* (no English translation is provided).
Availability:	Quarterly figures are available from 1950 onward. There have been changes either in estimation methods or survey items for the annual figures in 1968, 1975, and 1983.

The official name of this report is the *Statistical Survey of Incorporated Enterprises*. It is the most comprehensive sample survey available for the non-financial corporate sector. Major items in balance sheet and income statements, such as sales and profits, are available. Capital and inventory investment figures are used for the compilation of the corresponding SNA series. The operating profit/assets ratio for the manufacturing sector is included in the leading index of Diffusion Indexes (DI) compiled by the EPA. Current profit of all industries is included in the coincident index of DI, while plant and equipment investment is included in the lagging index of DI.

Details

The Quarterly Financial Report uses data compiled in a survey conducted by the Ministry of Finance via its regional offices. It covers more than 20,000 non-financial private companies with paid-in capital of 10 million yen or more. It covers all those with paid-in capital of 1 billion yen or more. The annual survey includes corporations with paid-in capital of 2 million yen or more. The sample is fixed for one year, beginning with the April–June quarter. The following items are available classified by amount of paid-in capital and by type of industry (also see Table 15.1):

Assets

Liquid assets (cash and deposits, accounts receivable, inventories, securities).
Fixed assets (land, tangible assets, investment securities).

Liabilities

Liquid liabilities (accounts payable, short-term borrowing).

Fixed liabilities (long-term bonds, long-term borrowing).

Net Worth

Paid-in capital.

Sales and Profits

Sales, cost of sales, general administrative cost, operating profits, net interest, ordinary profits, capital consumption, personnel cost.

Rate of Return

Operating profit to sales ratio, ordinary profit to sales ratio, liquidity to sales ratio, capital asset ratio.

Table 15.1. Sales and Capital Investment of Non-Financial Businesses
Calendar Year 1992

	Sales		Capital Investment	
	Trillion Yen	% of Total	Billion Yen	% of Total
Classification by industry				
Total	1,238.1	100.0	57,795	100.0
Manufacturing	372.1	30.1	20,466	35.4
Food	38.7	3.1	1,860	3.2
Chemical	34.2	2.8	2,525	4.4
Petroleum and coal	12.3	1.0	619	1.1
Steel	15.9	1.3	1,630	2.8
General machinery	25.9	2.1	1,190	2.1
Electric machinery	65.7	5.3	3,247	5.6
Transportation machinery	49.8	4.0	2,800	4.8
Other manufacturing	129.7	10.5	6,595	11.4
Non-manufacturing	866.0	69.9	37,329	64.6
Construction	131.0	10.6	2,701	4.7
Wholesale and retail trade	542.0	43.8	6,403	11.1
Real estate	26.6	2.1	3,347	5.8
Transportation and communications	55.7	4.5	7,334	12.7
Electricity	14.6	1.2	4,804	8.3
Business and household services	87.9	7.1	11,888	20.6
Classification by amount of paid-in capital				
1 billion yen and over	524.6	42.4	33,878	58.6
100 million to less than 1 billion yen	201.1	16.2	8,648	15.0
10 million to less than 100 million yen	512.4	41.4	15,269	26.4

Note: All figures shown are estimated figures for all non-financial companies in Japan, not only for the companies surveyed. The raw data is modified to reflect the sampling ratio.

Source: Ministry of Finance.

Capital Investment

Capital investment is the sum of new purchases of land and other fixed tangible assets (such as machinery, equipment, and structure), and the construction-in-progress account. It does not include transfers from the construction-in-progress account and purchase of existing fixed tangible assets from other companies to avoid double counting. It does not exclude capital consumption. Thus, the definition of capital investment in QFR is a *gross* concept and is very similar to that in the *Census of Manufactures* compiled by MITI (see Chapter 17 and Fig. 15.1).

Features and Problems

Annual Figures Considered More Accurate

Most companies have to rely on their preliminary financial results when reporting for the quarters ending in June and December because their financial year ends at the end of March or September. This may result in over- or underestimation in some items in the income statements. The figures in the annual survey are considered more accurate because they reflect actual financial results.

Seasonal Factors

There is a tendency toward overestimation in sales figures for the April–June quarter, when the sample changes and the number of companies with paid-in capital with more than 10 million yen increases. There are also seasonal fluctuations in the sales and profits of several industries, such as retail trade. To avoid these fluctuations, it is recommended that the year-on-year growth rate be used.

During the sampling period, marginal companies tend to drop from the survey. All figures are adjusted for this to maintain the continuity of the series.

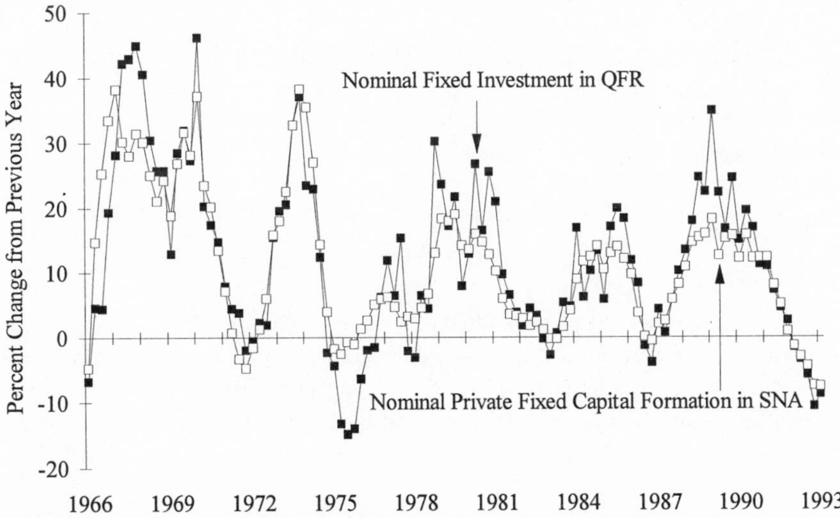

Fig. 15.1. Comparison of Investment Statistics

16 Establishment Census of Japan

Source:	Statistics Bureau, Management and Coordination Agency.
Frequency:	Once every five years.
Release:	Figures are released approximately 12 to 18 months after the survey date.
Availability:	The census was first conducted in 1947, then in 1948 and every three years afterward until 1981, then again in 1986 and 1991.

The *Establishment Census of Japan* provides basic information on the business activities of every establishment in Japan, including kind of business activities, location, number of employees, and year established. Although designed primarily for government use, others may find it useful for its universal coverage.

Details

The Census covers all establishments in Japan where production of goods or provision of services was carried out as of the date of the census (the latest Census was taken as of 1 July 1991). Individual proprietorship establishments in agriculture, forestry, and fisheries are excluded.

The Census consists of two surveys: 'A' (privately-owned establishments) and 'B' (establishments under the management of national or local government). Items surveyed include: location, kind of legal organization, year established, number of persons engaged, kind of business activities and type of operation, and type of establishment.

Explanation of Terms

Persons Engaged

Persons engaged consist of: individual proprietors; family workers, salaried managers or directors; regular employees; and temporary employees. Regular employees include workers contracted with an employment period of more than one month, or employed for 18 days or more in each of the two months prior to the survey. Regular employees make up around 75% of persons engaged (see Table 16.1).

Type of Establishment

Type of establishment consists of: shop or eating place; office; business outlet; factory, workshop or mining station; private warehouse or oil depository; establishment resembling ordinary dwelling houses; and others (hotels, hospitals, shrines, schools, etc.).

Publications for the 1991 Establishment Census of Japan

Volume 1, Part 1:Number of Establishments and Persons Engaged

Gives results cross-tabulated by industry, kind of legal organization, size of establishment (persons engaged), type of establishment, head- or branch-office, opening year, etc. (see Tables 16.1 and 16.2).

Volume 1, Part 2:Results for Regular Employees

A continuation of Part 1, with size defined according to the number of regular employees instead of persons engaged.

Volume 1, Part 3:Results for Municipalities

Contains data for individual municipalities. Parts 1 and 2 contain data only for Japan, prefectures, and major cities and metropolitan areas.

Volume 2: Results for Prefectures (47 parts)

The data for each prefecture was published in separate books and then used to compile Volume 1 (Volume 2 was published prior to Volume 1).

Volume 3: Results for Incorporated Enterprises

Presents the number of incorporated enterprises by industry, type of enterprise, size (regular employees), etc. Based on survey A only.

Features and Problems

Industry classifications are given in Japanese only, along with their industry code (based on the Standard Industrial Classification for Japan, available from the Government Publication Service Center). The English translation of the classifications appears in Volume 1, Part 1.

Possible Double Counting

Since the Census is a survey of establishments and not individuals, it is possible for an individual working at more than one establishment to be counted more than once.

Table 16.1. Establishment Census of Japan
As of 1 July, Millions, unless otherwise noted

	1986	1991	% Change
Establishments	6.71	6.75	0.67
Privately owned	6.51	6.56	0.73
Individual proprietorships	4.11	3.75	–8.69
Persons engaged	54.37	60.02	10.39
Male	33.12	35.76	7.96
Female	21.25	24.26	14.18
Privately owned	49.22	55.01	11.76
Male	29.57	32.48	9.85
Female	19.65	22.53	14.63
Individual proprietorships	12.01	11.02	–8.26
Male	5.73	5.12	–10.72
Female	6.28	5.90	–6.03
Regular employees	40.49	45.50	12.39
Male	25.56	27.70	8.38
Female	14.93	17.81	19.27
Privately owned	35.48	40.68	14.64
Male	22.04	24.47	11.04
Female	13.45	16.21	20.54
Individual proprietorships	4.21	4.53	7.79
Male	1.81	1.72	–4.79
Female	2.40	2.82	17.25

Source: Management and Coordination Agency

Table 16.2. Establishments and Persons Engaged, by Industry
As of 1 July, Thousands, unless otherwise noted

	1986		1991		% Change	
	Establ.	Persons	Establ.	Persons	Establ.	Persons
Total	6,708.8	54,370.5	6,753.9	60,018.8	0.67	10.39
Agriculture, forestry, and fisheries	21.5	281.5	21.0	259.1	–2.31	–7.96
Non-agricultural	6,687.3	54,089.0	6,732.9	59,759.7	0.68	10.48
Mining	6.0	102.6	5.3	77.6	–12.07	–24.34
Construction	576.4	4,796.7	602.6	5,281.9	4.54	10.12
Manufacturing	874.6	13,351.2	857.0	14,095.8	–2.01	5.58
Electricity, gas, heat, and water supply	10.1	317.7	9.8	312.5	–3.08	–1.62
Transportation and communications	168.7	3,383.1	182.3	3,679.7	8.05	8.77
Wholesale, retail trade, eating and drinking establishments	3,048.2	15,709.0	2,923.2	16,913.2	–4.10	7.67
Finance and insurance	95.1	1,807.6	104.6	2,083.6	10.05	15.27
Real estate	257.9	712.6	287.3	924.2	11.40	29.69
Services	1,604.4	12,162.5	1,715.1	14,613.9	6.90	20.16
Government (including those not elsewhere classified)	45.8	1,745.9	45.7	1,777.2	–0.23	1.79

Source: Management and Coordination Agency

17 Census of Manufactures

Source: Research and Statistics Department, Ministry of International Trade and Industry.

Frequency: Annual.

Release: A prompt report for the previous year is released in December of each year. Detailed reports consisting of six or more volumes are released around six months after the prompt report.

Availability: Figures are available from 1948 onward.

The Census of Manufactures is the most comprehensive survey of its type, covering every manufacturer in Japan. Data on the number of factories and employees, total compensation of employees, total shipment value and value added, and increase in fixed tangible assets (capital investment) are available by industry, prefecture, and number of employees. The weights of shipment values are used as the benchmark-year weights of the wholesale price index compiled by the Bank of Japan (see Chapter 21).

Details

Coverage and Methodology of the Survey

The title 'Census' indicates that this is not a sample survey but rather a survey covering every manufacturing factory (whose primary business is to make and/or assemble manufactured goods) in Japan. Head offices and other business establishments which do not make and/or assemble goods are excluded from the survey, even if they are part of manufacturing companies. The 'Census' survey is conducted as of the end of December each year. Flow figures such as sales and capital investment are expressed in calendar year terms, while stock figures such as the number of employees and fixed tangible assets are given as of the end of the calendar year.

Two types of questionnaires are prepared: one for factories with 30 or more employees and the other for those with less than 30 employees. Factories with less than 4 employees are not surveyed in some years (for example 1987 and 1989). As shown in Table 17.1, most factories have only a small number of employees, but exclusion of factories with less than 4 employees does not affect statistics such as shipments and value added substantially. Table 17.2 shows statistics disaggregated by industry.

Table 17.1. Major Statistics in the Census of Manufactures by Number of Employees
Calendar Year 1990, Billion Yen, unless otherwise noted

	Total	4 or More Employees		30 or More Employees	
			% of Total		% of Total
Number of factories	728,853	435,997	59.8	60,386	8.3
Number of employees (000's)	11,788	11,173	94.8	7,442	63.1
Compensation of employees	43,292	42,655	98.5	31,596	73.0
Value of raw material used	190,540	189,046	99.2	160,562	84.3
Value of shipments	327,093	323,374	98.9	269,058	82.3
Value added	121,243	119,028	98.2	94,464	77.9

Source: Ministry of International Trade and Industry, *Census of Manufactures*, 1990.

Table 17.2. Census of Manufactures
Calendar Year 1991, Billion Yen, unless otherwise noted

	Shipments		Value Added		Employees		Capital Investment	
		(%)		(%)	(000's)	(%)		(%)
Total manufacturing	340,610	100.0	125,607	100.0	11,354	100.0	18,922	100.0
Material industry	119,747	35.2	46,410	36.9	3,434	30.2	7,444	39.3
Lumber and wood	4,625	1.4	1,690	1.3	245	2.2	98	0.5
Pulp and paper	8,969	2.6	3,117	2.5	283	2.5	698	3.7
Chemical	24,253	7.1	11,595	9.2	406	3.6	1,766	9.3
Petroleum and coal	8,885	2.6	1,138	0.9	34	0.3	394	2.1
Plastics	11,568	3.4	4,374	3.5	456	4.0	683	3.6
Rubber	3,801	1.1	1,689	1.3	173	1.5	286	1.5
Ceramics and stone	11,080	3.3	5,267	4.2	459	4.0	660	3.5
Steel	18,629	5.5	6,501	5.2	340	3.0	1,398	7.4
Non-ferrous metals	7,697	2.3	2,159	1.7	174	1.5	577	3.1
Metal products	20,240	5.9	8,878	7.1	866	7.6	885	4.7
Assembly industry	149,187	43.8	50,851	40.5	4,457	39.3	8,727	46.1
General machinery	36,174	10.6	14,740	11.7	1,233	10.9	1,777	9.4
Electrical machinery	58,608	17.2	21,378	17.0	1,987	17.5	3,569	18.9
Transportation machinery	48,902	14.4	12,628	10.1	983	8.7	3,085	16.3
Precision machinery	5,504	1.6	2,104	1.7	254	2.2	296	1.6
Life-related industry	71,676	21.0	28,346	22.6	3,462	30.5	2,752	14.5
Food	24,089	7.1	8,672	6.9	1,105	9.7	893	4.7
Beverage, feed, and tobacco	10,523	3.1	2,734	2.2	129	1.1	445	2.4
Textile	7,975	2.3	3,202	2.5	520	4.6	362	1.9
Apparel	4,900	1.4	2,379	1.9	583	5.1	120	0.6
Furniture	4,235	1.2	1,844	1.5	230	2.0	138	0.7
Publication and printing	13,286	3.9	6,692	5.3	567	5.0	611	3.2
Leather	1,306	0.4	504	0.4	79	0.7	21	0.1
Other	5,361	1.6	2,321	1.8	249	2.2	162	0.9

Note: Value added for factories with less than 10 employees is gross value added where capital consumption is included. Value of capital investment covers only factories with 30 employees or more. It is the sum of the acquired value of fixed tangible assets and net increase in the construction-in-progress account. All figures are for factories with 4 or more employees.

Source: Ministry of International Trade and Industry, *Census of Manufactures*, Prompt Report (1991), 38–9.

Prompt Report and Detailed Reports

Prompt reports with data for the previous year are released each December. They cover only factories with 4 or more employees. Detailed reports are released around 15 or 18 months after the survey date, and consist of the six regular volumes listed below as well as others which are released only occasionally. The statistics included in each volume vary somewhat from year to year.

1. Report by Industries (all factories).
2. Report by Commodities (all factories).
3. Report on Industrial Land and Water (factories with 30 or more employees).
4. Report by Cities, Towns, and Villages (factories with 4 or more employees).
5. Report by Industrial Districts (factories with 4 or more employees).
6. Report by Enterprises (all factories).

Explanation of Terms

Employees

The number of employees is the sum of regular employees, self-employed, and their family workers as of 31 December each year. Regular employees include day and temporary employees who are employed for 18 days or more in November and December, as well as regular unpaid family workers of the self-employed.

Total Compensation of Employees

The total compensation of employees is the sum of regular salary, allowance, and special salary (such as bonuses) paid to regular employees during the calendar year. It includes retirement allowances and allowances for day and temporary employees.

Value of Raw Material Used

The value of raw material used is the sum of the following:

a. cost of raw material, parts, packages, material for factory maintenance, and office supplies
b. cost of electricity consumption
c. cost of production commissioned to other companies' factories.

Value of Shipments of Manufactured Goods

The value of shipments of manufactured goods includes shipments to other factories within the same company, in-house consumption, shipments for commissioned sales, and other revenue from storage and advertisement. It also includes various consumption taxes (indirect taxes) such as consumption tax, alcohol tax, tobacco tax, oil tax, and local road tax. The value of any discounts are subtracted from the value of shipments.

Fixed Tangible Assets

The acquired value of fixed tangible assets is the increase of fixed tangible assets from the previous end-of-calendar-year figure, including capital consumption. It is expressed on a book value basis. It consists of the following four types:

a. land
b. buildings and structures
c. machinery and equipment
d. others (vessels, motor vehicles and rolling stock, and other assets with service life of one year or longer).

Investment in fixed tangible assets is the acquired value of fixed tangible assets plus the net increase in the construction suspense account (temporary account). Retirement of fixed tangible assets consists of sales to other companies, removal, write-offs, and transfers to other factories within the same company.

The stock of fixed tangible assets is expressed in the following formula:

Fixed tangible assets as of the end of the current year
= Fixed tangible assets as of the end of the previous year
+ Acquired value on fixed tangible assets
+ Net increase in construction suspense account
– Retirement of fixed tangible assets
– Capital consumption of fixed tangible assets (on a book value basis)

Features and Problems

Comparison of Output and Value Added Statistics

Figs. 17.1 and 17.2 compare growth rates of output and value added of the manufacturing sector in national income statistics (SNA) and the Census of Manufactures. The growth rates of Gross Output and Shipments are similar, but the growth rate of Gross Domestic Product at Producer's Cost shows less volatility than Value Added.

The value added in the SNA, or gross domestic product at producer's cost, is the sum of compensation of employees, operating surplus, net indirect tax (indirect taxes less subsidies), and capital consumption. Value added in the Census excludes consumption taxes and capital consumption (see Table 17.3).

Comparison of Capital Investment Statistics

Table 17.4 compares the definition of 'gross capital investment' in three statistics: the Census of Manufactures; the Quarterly Financial Report (QFR) compiled by the Ministry of Finance (Chapter 15); and national income statistics (SNA).

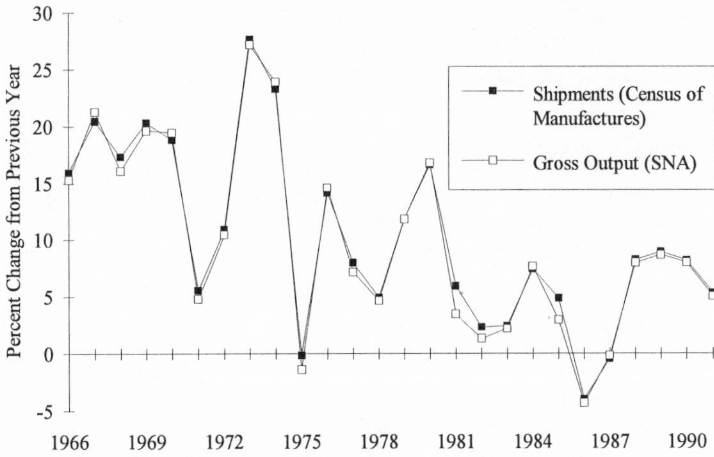

Fig. 17.1. Comparison of Gross Output Statistics

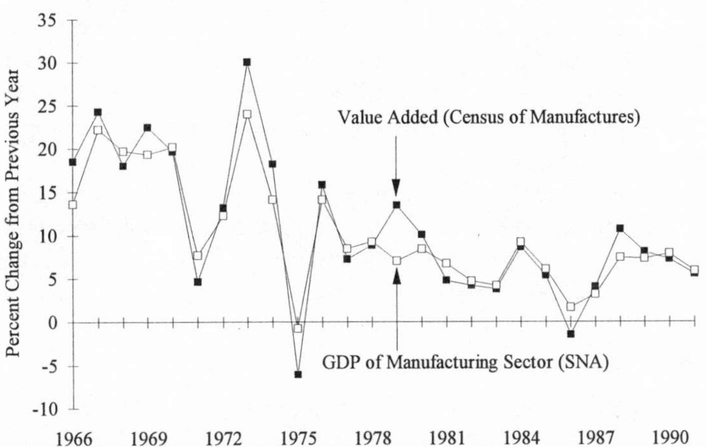

Fig. 17.2. Comparison of Value Added Statistics

Table 17.3. Comparison of Value Added Statistics

Census of Manufactures[1]			System of National Accounts
Value of Shipments (A)	323,373.6		
Increase in Inventory (B)	1,888.8		
Value of Production (C)=(A)+(B)	325,262.4	348,072.0	Gross Output (F)
Value of Raw Material Used (D)	189,046.0	224,628.8	Intermediate Inputs (G)
Capital Consumption + Consumption Taxes[2] (E)	17,188.2	30,428.8	Capital Consumption + Indirect Taxes (H)
Value Added (C)-(D)-(E)	119,028.3	123,443.2	Gross Domestic Product (F)-(G)

Notes: 1. Includes factories with less than 4 employees. 2. Includes consumption tax, alcohol tax, tobacco tax, oil tax, and local road tax; subsidies are not subtracted out.

Sources: Ministry of International Trade and Industry, Economic Planning Agency.

Table 17.4. Comparison of Definition of Gross Capital Investment

	Census	QFR	SNA
Acquisition of Land	x	x	
Construction Suspense Account	x		
Capital Consumption	x (book value)	x (book value)	x (book value)

Sources: Ministry of International Trade and Industry, Ministry of Finance, and Economic Planning Agency.

Comparison of Statistics on Number of Employees

The number of employees in the manufacturing sector based on the Labor Force Survey conducted by the Management and Coordination Agency (Chapter 25) is considerably higher than the Census of Manufactures figure (in calendar 1990, 15.05 million in the Labor Force Survey and 11.17 million in the Census of Manufactures). Since the Census is a survey of establishments, employees can be double-counted if the same person is working at two different factories. It seems, however, that this over-estimation is more than offset by differences in the definition of employee. The Census of Manufactures adopts a narrower definition of employees than the Labor Force Survey, particularly for non-regular employees such as temporary employees and day laborers. For example, in the Labor Force Survey a person is counted as employed when he or she worked for pay or profit for at least one hour during the reference week. In the Census of Manufactures, only people who worked for at least 18 days each in November and December are counted as employees.

Double-Counting in Shipments

Since the Census of Manufactures covers transactions of factories, it counts shipment/production from one factory to another factory within the same company as shipment/production, resulting in double-counting (in value added there is no such double-counting).

Variation in Coverage

When making time-series comparisons, it should be noted that coverage differs from year to year.

Construction and Housing Sector

18 Orders Received for Construction

Source: Economic Affairs Bureau, Ministry of Construction.

Frequency: Monthly.

Release: Figures for (new) orders for the previous month are released at the end of each month. Figures for completed works and unfilled orders are released at the end of each month with a two-month lag.

Availability: Figures for Series-A are available from April 1959 onward. Figures for Series-B are available from April 1974 onward. In April 1984 coverage expanded to 50 companies from 43, causing a discontinuity in Series-A.

These statistics reveal the amount of new construction orders, completed works, and unfilled orders. Construction orders are said to lead construction activity by about six months. The ratio of unfilled orders to completed works is included in the leading index of Diffusion Indexes compiled by the EPA.

Details

Construction orders statistics are collected in a monthly survey conducted by the Ministry of Construction. It includes a number of series in two survey categories: Series-A, which covers 50 large construction companies, and Series-B, which covers medium-sized and small construction companies. Series-A data is more frequently used than Series-B. It includes the amount of new construction orders, completed works, unfilled orders, and ratio of unfilled orders to completed works, for the categories shown in Table 18.1.

Completed works and unfilled orders are available only by type of construction works. Unfilled orders for the current month are calculated as unfilled orders for the previous month plus new orders for the current month less completed works for the current month.

Seasonally Adjusted Figures

Seasonally adjusted figures are available for the following statistics: total orders; private domestic orders (manufacturing and non-manufacturing); public orders; residential and non-residential construction; engineering works; completed works; and unfilled orders. Figures are seasonally adjusted by Census X-11 each year when December figures become available.

Table 18.1. Orders Received for Construction: Series-A
Calendar Year 1992

	Billion Yen	Percent of Total
Total orders	24,123	100.0
Classification by type of construction works		
Residential and non-residential construction (offices, factories, housing, schools, etc.)	15,903	65.9
Engineering works (roads, railways, water systems, etc.)	8,221	34.1
Classification by source of orders		
Total domestic	23,344	96.8
Private domestic	15,958	66.2
Manufacturing	2,848	11.8
Non-manufacturing	13,110	54.3
Public domestic	6,861	28.4
Central government	2,842	11.8
Local government	4,019	16.7
Foreign	779	3.2

Source: Ministry of Construction.

Features and Problems

Series-A excludes orders that a construction company receives from another construction company as a subcontract, while Series-B includes such orders. Orders from companies with various lines of business are classified by the industry in which the company principally engages.

Construction orders show wide fluctuations because of the basic characteristics of the construction industry. Construction activity is affected by weather conditions and other seasonal factors. It is also strongly affected by public demand, which tends to be counter-cyclical.

Unusual Movement of Ratio of Unfilled Orders to Completed Works

Although the ratio of unfilled orders to completed works is included in the leading index of DI published by the EPA, it has recently been an unreliable predictor of economic activity. It has remained in a upward trend since 1988 even though the economy fell into recession in the January–March quarter of 1991 (see Fig. 18.2).

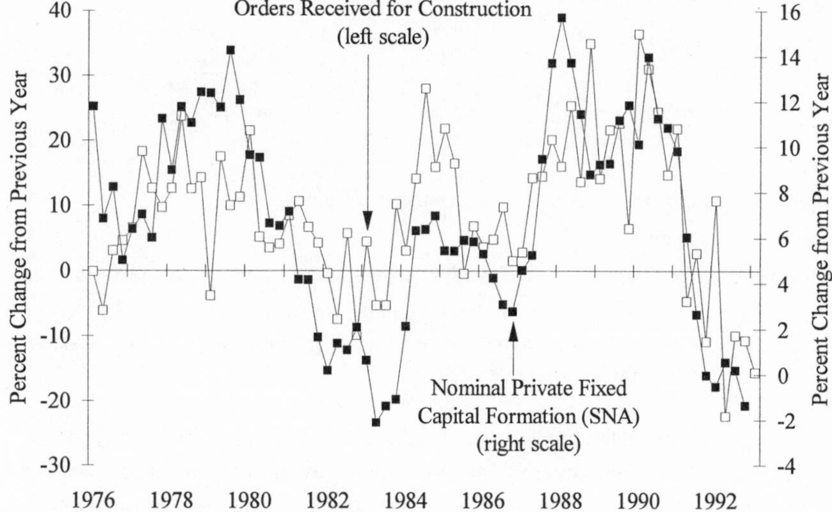

Fig. 18.1. Total New Orders Received for Construction

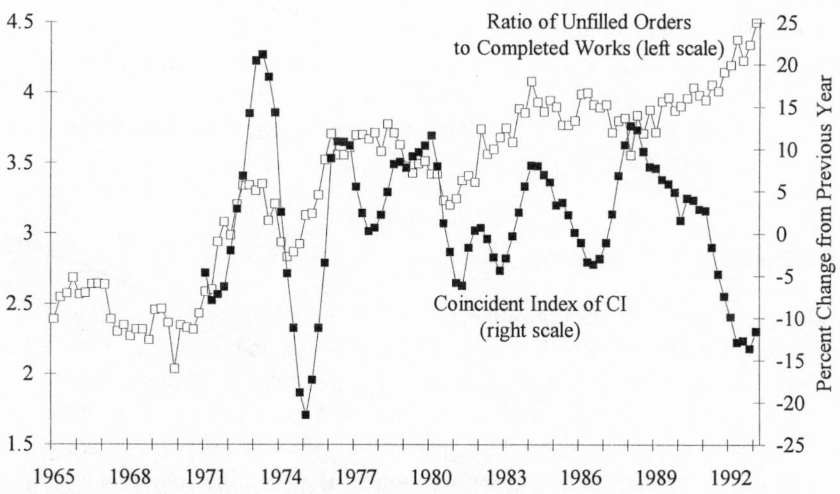

Fig. 18.2. Ratio of Unfilled Orders to Completed Works

19 Public Construction Starts

Source: Economic Affairs Bureau, Ministry of Construction.

Frequency: Monthly.

Release: Figures are released in the first 10 days of each month with a two-month lag.

Availability: Quarterly figures are available from the April–June quarter of 1960 onward. Monthly figures are available from April 1969 onward. No seasonally adjusted figures are released.

These statistics reveal the number of public construction works started on orders by the central and regional governments, as well as government corporations. They provide tangible signs of the nation's fiscal policy stance as well as regional developments in public construction works.

Details

Statistics on public construction started are collected in a monthly survey conducted by the Ministry of Construction via regional governments. The survey covers all construction companies nationwide with annual public construction contracts of over 300 million yen, and a quarter of the companies with annual public construction contracts of between 30 and 300 million yen. The surveyed companies provide data regarding public contracts received with an appraised value above 500,000 yen each. Figures for appraised value, number of works, and estimated number of workers to be employed are available by type of ordering unit, by type of construction (see Table 19.1), and by prefecture.

Features and Problems

Public construction figures show considerable seasonal fluctuation, especially for regional governments. Public construction works tend to be executed during the period from June through December and at the end of the fiscal year (March).

The most frequently used statistics are those by type of ordering unit. The role of the regional governments in public construction activity should be stressed. Their share of the total value of public construction is far greater than that of the central government and government corporations.

Table 19.1. Appraised Value of Public Construction Started
Calendar Year 1992

	Billion Yen	Percent of Total
Total	18,148	100.0
Classification by type of ordering unit		
Central government and govt. corporations	4,357	24.0
Central government	1,977	10.9
Central government corporations	2,380	13.1
Regional governments and govt. corporations	13,791	76.0
Prefectural (state) governments	5,566	30.7
Municipal governments	6,180	34.1
Regional government corporations	1,179	6.5
Others	866	4.8
Classification by type of construction works		
Flood prevention and irrigation	1,498	8.3
Agriculture, forestry, and fisheries	1,233	6.8
Roads	4,534	25.0
Ports and airports	720	4.0
Sewerage and parks	2,382	13.1
Education and hospitals	2,251	12.4
Housing	986	5.4
Offices	2,528	13.9
Restoration from disasters	515	2.8
Land development	367	2.0
Railroads	188	1.0
Postal services	58	0.3
Electric power and gas	49	0.3
Water supply	361	2.0
Maintenance	477	2.6

Source: Ministry of Construction.

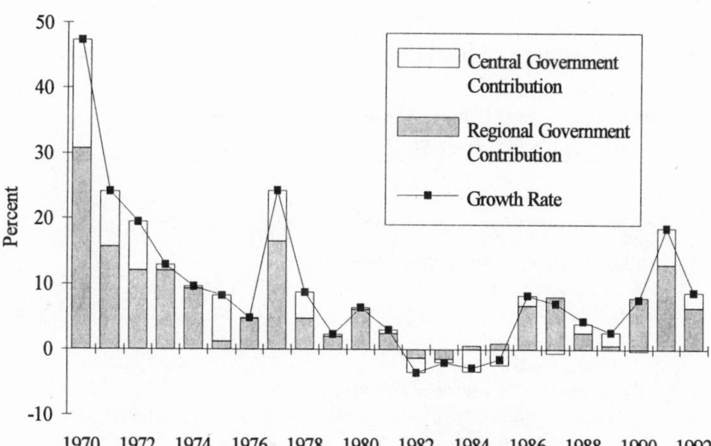

Fig. 19.1. Appraised Value of Public Construction (Growth Rate and Contributions)

20 New Housing Construction Started

Source: Economic Affairs Bureau, Ministry of Construction.

Frequency: Monthly.

Release: Figures for the previous month are released at the end of each month. Revised figures are released one month later.

Availability: Monthly figures are available from January 1951 onward.

Statistics on new housing construction starts are a part of statistics on 'Building Construction Starts' which covers not only housing construction, but also other types of construction such as factories, buildings, and structures. These statistics are used to judge current developments in the demand for housing. They are considered to move sensitively to changes in business conditions, especially interest rates, and are watched carefully because of their tendency to lead general economic activities. The total floor area of new housing starts is included in the leading index of Diffusion Indexes compiled by the EPA.

Details

The statistics on new housing construction starts are collected in a survey conducted by the Ministry of Construction via regional governments (builders are required to notify their regional governors whenever the construction area exceeds 10 square meters). Both the number and total floor area of new housing starts are available.

Table 20.1. New Housing Construction Starts
Calendar Year 1992

	Units	Sq. meters (000's)
Total	1,402,590	120,318
Classification by ownership of housing		
Owner-occupied	477,611	65,620
Rental	671,989	32,582
Company-owned	35,863	2,496
Built-for-sale	217,127	1,962
Classification by source of financing		
Private sources	853,510	61,355
Public sources	549,080	58,964

Source: Ministry of Construction.

Disaggregated series are available as shown in Table 20.1 and Fig. 20.1.

Seasonally adjusted annualized figures are available in *Monthly of Construction Statistics* published by the Ministry of Construction.

Features and Problems

Definition of 'New'

The term 'new' refers to construction which produces an additional housing unit via the construction of a new dwelling, increase in floor area, or partial rebuilding. Construction which does not produce an additional housing unit is referred to as 'others' in the statistics. The 'new' housing construction starts series is the most frequently used in analyzing demand for housing and general business conditions.

Comparison with Other Housing Data

The statistics on new housing construction starts are reported on an initiation basis, while residential investment in national income statistics (SNA) are estimated on a construction-in-progress basis. The former, therefore, leads the latter by one or two quarters (see Fig. 20.2).

The *number* of new housing starts can not take account of the distinction between constructions of dwellings with large floor area and those with small floor area, while *total floor area* of new housing starts can. Quality improvement in terms of increases in floor area per housing unit are reflected in the total floor area series.

Another measure of the quality of housing is the housing price per unit of floor area, which has been incorporated into the residential investment data in the SNA. The change in real residential investment in the SNA thus can be decomposed into three components: change in the number of new housing units, change in floor area per housing unit, and change in price per unit of floor area (quality improvement).

Housing Starts and the Tax System

The surge in the number of rental housing starts (especially in metropolitan areas) from 1987 to 1990 is considered to be in part the result of generous tax incentives which favor heavy borrowing in calculating the inheritance tax base. As land prices increased, the prospective inheritance tax to be paid also increased; by borrowing money to build rental housing, the inheritance tax liability could be reduced. Another surge in rental housing starts in 1992 is partly attributed to a tax law change which raised the tax rates on some farm land in metropolitan areas and encouraged the construction of housing on the land.

Stock Data

The Management and Coordination Agency conducts a comprehensive survey on the stock of residential properties once every five years. Results are published in the *Housing Survey of Japan.*

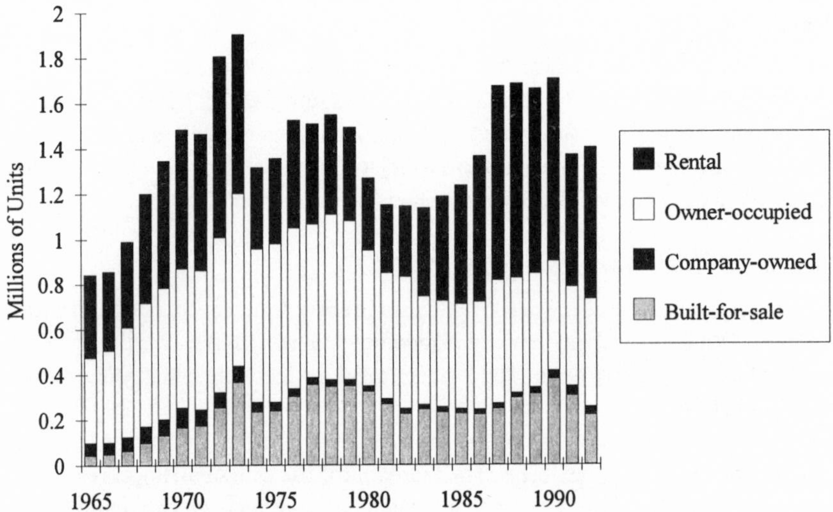

Fig. 20.1. New Housing Construction Starts

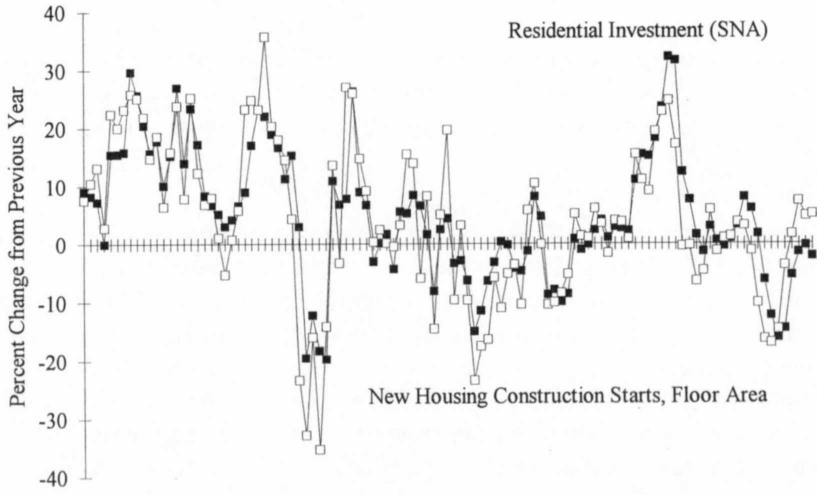

Fig. 20.2. Comparison of Housing Statistics

Prices

21 Wholesale Price Index

Source: Research and Statistics Department, Bank of Japan.

Frequency: Three times a month, monthly, and annual.

Release: Figures for the previous month are released in the middle of each month. Detailed and historical series are available in *Price Indexes Annual* published every February or March.

Availability: Monthly figures are available from January 1960 onward. Pre-war based monthly (overall index) and annual (by basic group) series are available from October 1900 and 1931 onward, respectively.

The wholesale price index measures the price of commodities traded in the business sector. It is calculated as the weighted average of three price indexes: Domestic Wholesale Price Index; Export Price Index; and Import Price Index. Prices for services, labor income, and financial services are not included in the index.

Details

Method of Calculation

The Bank of Japan surveys the price of each commodity from at least two different sources. For a commodity used domestically, the price offered by the initial wholesaler is used. If there is no intermediary between the manufacturer and the final demander, the price offered for shipment from the factory is used. For export commodities, the FOB price is used. For import commodities, the CIF price is used. (See Chapter 30 for definitions of FOB and CIF.)

The Domestic Wholesale Price Index covers 945 commodities, the Export Price Index 184 and the Import Price Index 184. The weighted average of these three indexes is called the Overall Wholesale Price Index, or simply the Wholesale Price Index (WPI). The current weights are 79.7% for the domestic wholesale price index, 11.7% for the export price index and 8.6% for the import price index.

The Wholesale Price Index is constructed by Laspeyres formula (see Appendix 1). The current benchmark year is calendar year 1990, and is changed every five years. Seasonally adjusted figures are not available for any of the components in the WPI.

Figures for components of the WPI are available by basic group (see Table 21.1) and by stage of demand and use (see Table 21.2).

Table 21.1. Weights in Overall Wholesale Price Index
Benchmark Year Calendar 1990, Percent

	Weight	Change in Weight
All commodities	100.0	
Classification by basic group		
Manufacturing industry products	90.3	4.3
Processed foodstuffs	8.1	−0.0
Textile products	3.7	−0.4
Lumber and wood products	1.6	0.1
Pulp, paper, and related products	2.6	−0.1
Chemicals	7.3	−0.1
Plastic products	3.2	0.3
Petroleum and coal products	3.0	−2.4
Ceramics, stone, and clay products	3.1	0.1
Iron and steel	5.1	−0.8
Nonferrous metals	2.8	0.1
Metal products	3.9	0.6
General machinery	11.6	1.6
Electrical machinery	16.2	3.4
Transportation equipment	9.3	1.3
Precision instruments	1.6	0.1
Others	7.3	0.6
Agricultural, forestry, and fishery products	3.4	−1.0
Mining products	3.0	−2.2
Electric power, gas, and water	3.0	−1.0
Scrap and waste	0.3	−0.1
Classification by destination of commodities		
Domestic wholesale price	79.7	3.0
Export price	11.7	−1.8
Import price	8.6	−1.2

Note: 'Change in weight' indicates the change in percentage-points from the previous benchmark-year (1985) weights.

Source: Bank of Japan.

Features and Problems

Wholesale prices are considered to move more sensitively than consumer prices in response to business conditions because they include only commodities traded in the business sector. Consumer prices include the price of services, which is largely dependent on wages and thus slow to change. Wholesale prices tend to lead consumer prices by three to six months. Wholesale prices are also affected by external factors such as changes in the price of oil and foreign exchange rates. It is therefore useful to examine the components of the WPI (domestic, export, and import prices) individually to understand the underlying cause of its movements.

Introduction of Consumption Tax in April 1989

The Japanese government introduced a 3% Consumption Tax on 1 April 1989,

Table 21.2. Weights in Overall Wholesale Price Index -- Classification by Stage of Demand and Use
Benchmark Year Calendar 1990, Percent

	Weight	Change in Weight
All commodities	100.0	
Domestic demand products	88.3	1.8
Domestic products	79.7	3.0
Imports	8.6	−1.2
Raw materials	5.2	−3.0
Raw materials for processing	4.0	−2.5
Construction materials	0.4	0.1
Fuel	0.5	−0.5
Others	0.3	−0.1
Intermediate materials	43.5	−2.1
Semi-finished goods	27.0	−1.4
Construction materials	7.5	1.2
Fuel and energy	4.3	−2.4
Others	4.7	0.5
Final goods	39.6	6.9
Capital goods	15.4	5.4
Consumer goods	24.3	1.5
Durables	7.6	1.5
Non-durables	16.6	0.0
Exports	11.7	−1.8
Semi-finished goods	3.5	−0.6
Construction materials	0.3	−0.4
Capital goods	4.5	1.0
Consumer goods	3.4	−1.8
Durables	2.9	−1.6
Non-durables	0.5	−0.2

Note: 'Change in weight' indicates the change in percentage-points from the previous benchmark-year (1985) weights.

Source: Bank of Japan.

which is estimated to have raised the WPI by 1.0 to 1.5%. The year-on-year increase in the WPI (and other price indexes) shows a small but sudden jump during the period from April 1989 to March 1990.

Benchmark Year Change and Price Movement

When the benchmark year was changed from 1985 to 1990, the weight of some commodity groups changed substantially. This reflects changes in the industrial structure of Japan, such as the increasing importance of high technology products. For example, the weights of general machinery and electrical machinery in the overall index increased from 10.0% and 12.8% to 11.6% and 16.2%, respectively (see Table 21.1). The weights of energy related commodities fell substantially, particularly for the Import Price Index (see Tables 21.2 and 21.3), due mainly to the decline in oil prices and the yen's appreciation.

Table 21.3. Export and Import Price Indexes
Classification by Basic Group
Benchmark Year Calendar 1990, Percent

	Weight	Change in Weight
Export Price Index		
All commodities	100.0	
Textiles	2.7	−1.2
Chemicals	6.4	1.0
Metals and related products	7.4	−4.3
General machinery	18.1	1.6
Electrical machinery	31.3	6.6
Transportation equipment	24.2	−2.6
Precision instruments	3.9	0.0
Miscellaneous goods	6.2	−1.1
Import Price Index		
All commodities	100.0	
Foodstuffs and animal feed	11.3	0.6
Textiles	7.1	2.1
Metals	14.2	2.0
Wood, lumber, and related products	5.2	1.3
Petroleum, coal, and natural gas	27.9	−20.4
Chemicals	7.2	1.0
Machinery and equipment	20.3	10.9
Miscellaneous goods	6.8	2.6

Note: 'Change in weight' indicates the change in percentage-points from the previous benchmark-year (1985) weights.
Source: Bank of Japan.

Revision for Changes in Benchmark Year

When the benchmark year changes, data for the period before the new benchmark year are simply rescaled so that the figure for 1990 equals 100. There is no change in the weights used to calculate the historical data.

Price Indexes and Quality Change

Price increases in certain goods are often accompanied by quality improvements, such as when new models of computers are introduced. If no adjustment were made for the improved quality, a price index would erroneously indicate that computers had become more expensive. The Bank of Japan attempts to measure only pure price increases in the wholesale price index, and has recently adopted the *hedonic indexes* (see Appendix 1) to adjust for the quality improvement in high-technology products.

Related Statistics

Another useful source of information on wholesale prices is *Input-Output Price Indexes of Manufacturing Industry by Sector* published in the BOJ's *Economic Statistics Monthly*. In these statistics, input indexes cover only material inputs used in current production (raw and manufactured materials and fuels and energy) and do not include the cost of labor, interest, advertisement, etc.. Output indexes cover manufactured goods produced by each sector. The indexes are given on two different bases: *gross*-weighted base, which include intra-sector transactions, and *net*-weighted base, which exclude them. The Indexes are calculated using Laspeyres formula with 1985 as the benchmark year. Monthly figures are available from January 1975 onward.

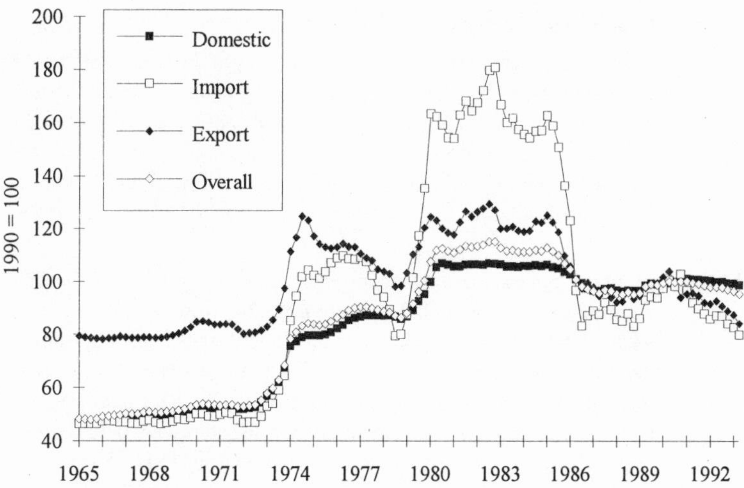

Fig. 21.1. Wholesale Price Index and its Components

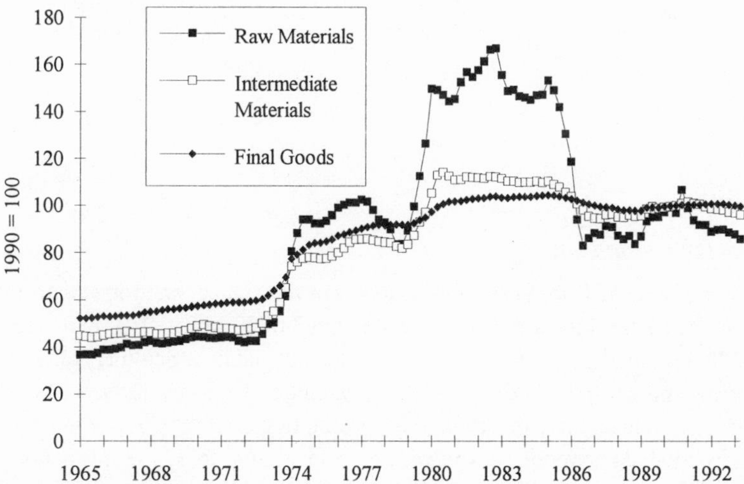

Fig. 21.2. Wholesale Price Index by Stage of Demand and Use

22 Consumer Price Index

Source: Statistics Bureau, Management and Coordination Agency.

Frequency: Monthly and Annual.

Release: Figures for all Japan are released on the Friday of the week including the 26th of the month, for the preceding month. Preliminary figures for the second ten days of the current month for the Tokyo metropolitan area (Tokyo's 23 wards or ku-area) are released on the same day. Revised figures for all Japan are released around the middle of the following month. Detailed and historical series are available in the *Annual Report on the Consumer Price Index* published every March.

Availability: Monthly general (overall) consumer price indexes for both the Tokyo metropolitan area and all Japan are available from January 1970 onward. General indices excluding imputed rent for owner-occupied housing for both the Tokyo metropolitan area and all Japan are available from August 1946 onward. They are shown in Tables 9 and 10-1 in the *Annual Report on the Consumer Price Index*. Annual figures for the general index excluding imputed rent for the Tokyo area are available from 1947 onward.

The Consumer Price Index is designed to capture the average price of goods and services that consumers purchase. While the Wholesale Price Index published by the Bank of Japan (Chapter 21) covers only commodities traded in the business sector, the Consumer Price Index covers both commodities and services purchased by final consumers.

Details

Method of Calculation

The monthly Retail Price Survey is conducted by the Management and Coordination Agency in 167 municipalities nationwide with 34,000 stores, 24,000 households, and 540 inns and lodges. Households mainly engaged in agriculture, forestry, and fisheries, and one-person households are excluded from the survey. The survey covers 561 items which are selected according to the relative importance of each item in total consumption expenditures, the ability to represent major price movements, and continuity of price data collection, so that the selected index items may represent the price movements of all the goods and services purchased by consumers.

The prices used in the index are normal (one-time discounts are excluded) retail prices of goods and services actually sold on the survey date. The survey is usually conducted once a month, except for fresh food, which is conducted three times a month. Items such as non-consumption expenditures (taxes and social security contributions), savings, purchases of securities and land, and housing construction are not included in the index. The Consumer Price Index is calculated as a Laspeyres Index. The benchmark year (currently 1990) is revised every five years.

Figures are available for all of the classifications shown in Table 22.1.

Seasonal Adjustment

Seasonally adjusted figures are available only for the following indexes (for both Japan and Tokyo metropolitan area): (1) General; (2) General excluding fresh food; (3) General excluding imputed rent; and (4) General excluding fresh food and imputed rent. The Census X-11 method is used for seasonal adjustment. Annual revision for seasonally adjusted figures for the previous year is made when the December figures are released.

Features and Problems

The Consumer Price Index tends to lag behind the movement in the Wholesale Price Index because the CPI captures the prices of goods and services sold downstream to final consumers, while the WPI covers only goods traded by the business sector. The prices for services mainly reflect labor costs, which tend to increase steadily. For example, in 1986 and 1987, when the yen's appreciation and the collapse of oil prices caused wholesale prices to fall significantly, the CPI still showed a small increase (see Figs. 22.1 and 22.2). This feature of the CPI is called 'downward rigidity'.

Figures for the Tokyo metropolitan area are worth using for their rapid release. Figures for 'general excluding imputed rent' (for Japan) are used for deflating nominal expenditures in the Family Income and Expenditure Survey (see Chapter 4).

Introduction of Consumption Tax

As is the case for the Wholesale Price Index (Chapter 21), the introduction of a 3% consumption tax in April 1989 is estimated to have raised the Consumer Price Index by 1.0 to 1.5%. The year-on-year increase in price indexes shows a small but sudden jump in the growth rate during the period from April 1989 to March 1990.

Revision for Changes in Benchmark Year

When the benchmark year changes, data for the period before the new benchmark year are simply rescaled so that the figure for 1990 equals 100. There is no change in the weights used to calculate the historical data. Figures from July 1990 onward use the 1990 benchmark year weights.

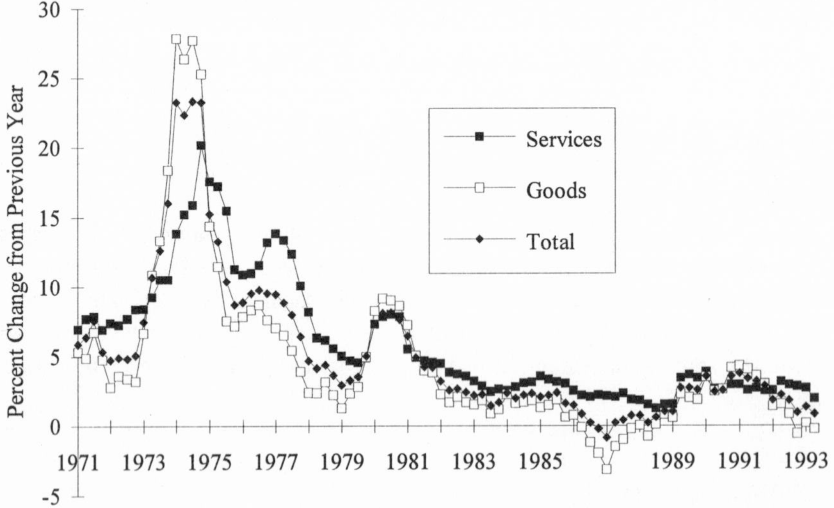

Fig. 22.1. CPI - All Japan

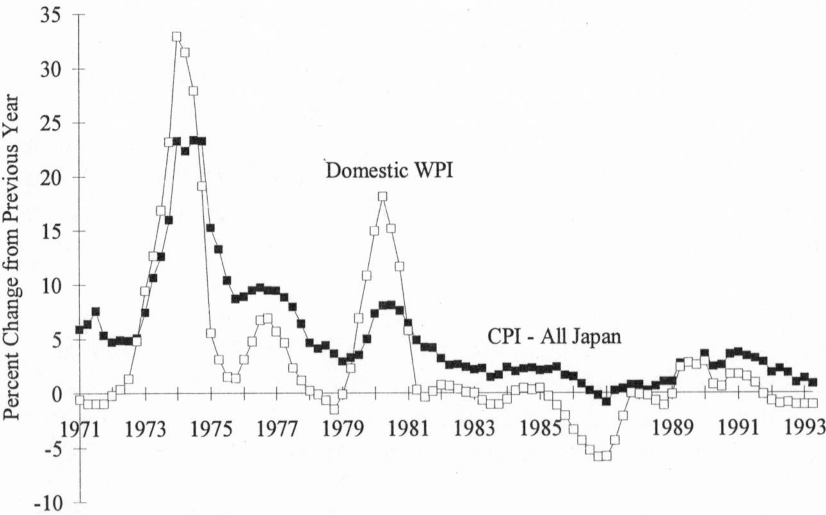

Fig. 22.2. Comparison of CPI and Domestic WPI

Table 22.1. Weights in Consumer Price Index
Benchmark Year Calendar 1990

	All Japan	Tokyo Ku-Area
Classification by major group		
General	100.0	100.0
Food	31.4	29.3
Housing	14.8	18.3
Fuel, light, and water charges	5.5	5.1
Furniture and household utensils	4.4	3.9
Clothes and footwear	8.6	8.9
Medical care	3.1	3.3
Transportation and communications	11.9	9.9
Education	4.7	5.6
Reading and recreation	11.2	11.3
Miscellaneous	4.5	4.6
General excluding imputed rent	90.1	87.8
General excluding fresh food	94.4	94.5
General excluding imputed rent and fresh food	84.5	82.3
Classification by commodity and service group		
General	100.0	100.0
Commodities	55.8	50.5
Agricultural and fishery products	10.1	9.3
Industrial products	39.8	35.3
Food products	14.1	12.6
Textiles	8.4	8.3
Durable goods	5.7	5.1
Other industrial products	11.6	9.3
Electricity, gas, and water charges	4.2	4.3
Publications	1.8	1.6
Services	44.2	49.6
Private house rent	2.3	4.0
Imputed rent	9.9	12.2
Public services	10.9	10.7
Personal services	13.4	14.9
Eating out	7.6	7.8
Classification by type of city and prefecture		
All cities		
Major cities (population more than 1,000,000)		
Middle cities (population ranging from 150,000 to 999,999)		
Small cities-A (population ranging from 50,000 to 149,999)		
Small cities-B (population less than 50,000)		
Towns and villages		
47 cities with prefectural government		

Source: Management and Coordination Agency.

23 Corporate Service Price Index

Source: Research and Statistics Department, Bank of Japan.

Frequency: Quarterly (monthly from July 1993 onward).

Release: Figures for the previous quarter are released in the latter half of the first month of each quarter (monthly release from July 1993 onward).

Availability: Figures are available for 1985 onward.

The Corporate Service Price Index was developed by the Bank of Japan in 1991 to measure the prices for corporate services which play an important role in the economy, where the weight of tertiary industries has been increasing. The Corporate Service Price Index is considered to supplement the traditional Wholesale Price Index which covers only commodities traded in the corporate sector.

Details

The Corporate Service Price Index covers 54 percent of the total transaction value in tertiary industries. It consists of the seven basic groups of services shown in Table 23.1. Some common services, such as public administration, education and research, and medical service and health care, are not included.

The Corporate Service Price Index is calculated as a Laspeyres index. The current benchmark year is 1985. Seasonally adjusted figures are not available.

Features and Problems

Because of its unique composition, movement of the Corporate Service Price Index is affected not only by general business conditions, but also by other macroeconomic variables such as nominal wages, labor productivity, and foreign exchange rates. The introduction of the Corporate Service Price Index in 1991 might have been related to efforts by the Bank of Japan to justify its tight monetary policy.

Introduction of Consumption Tax in April 1989

As is the case for the Wholesale and Consumer Price Indexes (Chapters 21 and 22), the introduction of a 3% consumption tax in April 1989 raised the Corporate Service Price Index. There is a sudden jump in the series in the April–June quarter of 1989.

Table 23.1. Weights in Corporate Service Price Index by Basic Group
Benchmark Year 1985

	Weight
All services	100.0
Finance and insurance	6.3
Financial services	3.0
Insurance services	3.2
Real estate	13.7
Transportation	29.8
Land freight	10.1
Sea freight	6.6
Air freight	0.5
Passenger transportation	7.8
Storage and other transportation services	4.9
Information services	7.3
Communications	7.2
Advertising services	6.4
Other services	29.4
Leasing and renting	10.1
Building maintenance, civil engineering and construction services	13.3
Judicial and accounting services	3.6
Industrial waste disposal and sewerage systems	2.4

Source: Bank of Japan.

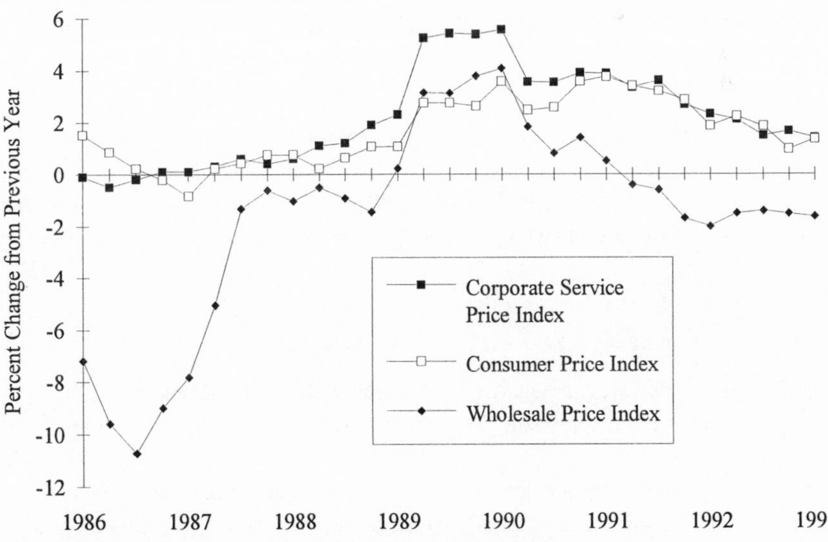

Fig 23.1. Corporate Service Price Index

24 Official Land Price Survey

Source: National Land Agency.

Frequency: Annual (Survey Date: January 1).

Release: Figures are released at the end of March each year.

Availability: Land prices in each observation block are available from 1970 onward.

The Official Land Price Survey conducted by the National Land Agency is the most important source of statistics on land prices in Japan. It provides a benchmark for land appraisers, land purchases by the public sector, etc. It is also used as the basis for evaluating inheritance, donation, and land price taxes (national taxes), and fixed property taxes (municipal tax). Several related surveys are available.

Details

History of Land Price Survey

In 1970, the first land price survey was conducted in eight prefectures; the survey was enlarged to cover the entire country in 1974. Observation blocks were substantially re-examined in 1983. New appraisal methods were adopted in 1991.

Land Appraisal Committee

Official land prices are surveyed as of 1 January each year by the Land Appraisal Committee. At least two real estate appraisers or assistant appraisers are required to conduct the appraisal of each observation block. The Land Appraisal Committee then examines and adjusts (when necessary) the results.

Determination of Observation Blocks

Each observation block is selected based on four criteria:

1. The block should represent the land prices of the neighboring area.
2. The block should represent the typical use, environment, and shape of the neighboring area.
3. The block should be located in an area where the type of land use is stable.
4. The block should be distinguishable from those of the neighboring blocks by land registration, address, building, land shape, etc.

Types of Observation Blocks

In the January 1993 survey, 20,555 observation blocks were selected (see Table 24.1). They cover 70,312 square kilometers of 1,124 municipalities. They were chosen to be evenly distributed nationwide. Observation blocks are classified into three types of areas, each of which is further divided based on the use of the land. Observation blocks may be subject to change in each survey.

Table 24.1. Official Land Price Survey
As of 1 January 1993

	Total Blocks	Area per Block (Square Km.)
Total	20,555	-
1. Urbanized areas	18,057	-
a. Residential areas	13,099	0.7
b. Prospective residential areas	113	0.7
c. Commercial areas	3,397	0.3
d. Quasi-industrial areas	1,147	0.3
e. Industrial areas	414	1.2
2. Urbanization-controlled areas	1,698	-
f. Residential areas	1,629	20
g. Woodlands	69	60
3. Other areas	800	23
h. Residential areas	533	-
i. Commercial areas	267	-

Source: National Land Agency, *Official Land Price Survey*, January 1993.

Available Figures

The price per square meter is available in each observation block. In addition, the distribution of land prices by type of use is available for three metropolitan areas and nine geographical regions. The average, highest, and lowest priced observation blocks for each municipality in the three metropolitan areas are listed. The growth rate of prices from the previous year are available by type of use. When calculating growth rates, only observation blocks continuously surveyed are included.

Methods of Land Appraisal

1. Previous Comparable Transactions

If there were land transactions in a neighboring area which is similar in type of use and other properties to the observation block, the prices in these transactions can be used as a proxy for the land price of the observation block after adjusting for the type of use, time elapsed, and other factors.

2. Discounted Expected Future Return on Land Acquisition

The net return on a land acquisition is the difference between the expected flow of revenues and expenses resulting from the acquisition. The land price is calculated from the net return adjusted (discounted) for the relevant rate of interest.

3. Replacement Cost Estimate

The land price of the observation block may be determined as the replacement cost of the block.

Features and Problems

General Trend of Land Prices

In the early 1970s, land prices surged at double digit rates for four years; the average price of land increased 127% from January 1970 to January 1974. At the beginning of the 1980s, land prices again increased at a double digit rate following the second oil crisis, when land was bought to hedge inflation risks. After the Bank of Japan lowered and maintained historically low interest rates in 1986, the average land price soared by 84% in Japan overall, 140% in the Tokyo metropolitan area, and 170% in the Osaka metropolitan area by the beginning of 1991 (see Figures 24.1 and 24.2). Prices first rose in Tokyo, then spread over to other metropolitan and suburban areas. In the past two years (1991–3), the average land price has declined by 13% overall, 22% in the Tokyo area, and 35% in the Osaka area.

Higher Land Prices for Commercial Use

Land prices in commercial areas are, in general, five to ten times higher than those in residential areas.

Measurement Bias in Land Prices

It is said that the prevailing market price of land is approximately 20–30 percent higher than the official land price. This is especially the case when land prices are surging. On the other hand, in 1991–3 when land prices collapsed, especially in the metropolitan areas, the prevailing market price has been below the official land price.

Related Land Price Surveys

1. Prefectural Land Price Survey

The Prefectural Land Price Survey has been conducted annually by each prefecture since 1975 (survey date is 1 July, results are released at the end of September). These surveys supplement the Official Land Price Survey. Land prices in this survey are called 'standard land prices'.

The types of data collected are almost the same as those in the Official Land Price Survey. The following statistics are available: land prices in the three major metropolitan areas and nine geographical regions; growth rates of land prices by type of use in each geographical region; average, highest, and lowest land prices in each municipality in the three metropolitan areas; and a land price index for the three metropolitan areas, with land prices for July 1983 = 100.

The Prefectural Land Price Survey includes more observation blocks located in woodland and non-metropolitan areas than the Official Land Price Survey, which may reduce the apparent size of land price hikes in recent years (see Tables 24.2 and 24.3). For example, land prices increased by 84% from January 1986 to January 1991 in the Official Land Price Survey while they increased by only 48% from July 1986 to July 1991 in the Prefectural Land Price Survey. There are about 1,400 identical observation blocks surveyed in the Official and Prefectural Land Price Surveys.

Table 24.2. Observation Blocks in the Prefectural Land Price Survey
As of 1 July 1992

	Blocks
Total	25,786
1. Urbanized and urbanization-controlled areas	19,954
a. Residential areas	12,491
b. Prospective residential areas	327
c. Commercial areas	4,058
d. Quasi-industrial areas	1,125
e. Industrial areas	579
f. Urbanization-controlled residential areas	1,374
2. Other areas	4,679
g. Residential areas	3,583
h. Commercial areas	956
i. Industrial areas	140
3. Woodlands	1,155

Source: National Land Agency, *Prefectural Land Price Survey*, 1 July 1992.

Table 24.3. Comparison of Distribution of Observation Blocks

	Official Land Price Survey (Jan. 1993)		Prefectural Land Price Survey (July 1992)	
	Blocks	(%)	Blocks	(%)
Total observation blocks excluding woodland	20,486	100.0	24,633	100.0
Sub-Total of the three metropolitan areas	7,754	37.9	6,371	25.9
Tokyo metropolitan area	4,354	21.3	3,592	14.6
Osaka metropolitan area	2,211	10.8	1,792	7.3
Nagoya metropolitan area	1,189	5.8	987	4.0

Source: National Land Agency.

2. Quarterly Land Price Survey

The Quarterly Land Price Survey has been conducted since January 1991 by the National Land Agency to monitor land prices. It surveys 804 observation blocks where land prices are thought to respond sensitively to market conditions. It does not show actual land prices in these blocks, and instead gives the change in land prices from the previous quarter, classified into five categories: (i) increase (3% and over), (ii) small increase (1 to 3%), (iii) stable (–1 to 1%), (iv) small decline (–1 to –3%), and (v) decline (–3% and over).

3. Appraisal Value for Inheritance Tax

The appraisal value for inheritance tax is calculated each year by the National Tax Administration Agency and its local offices. It is used for the evaluation of inheritance, donation, and land price taxes (all national taxes). The survey is conducted as of 1 January. Land prices on 'major routes' (called 'rosenka' in Japanese), with about 390,000 observation blocks that are released in August the previous year, are used for the basis of the appraisal. In general, land prices on major routes are lower than land prices in the Official Land Price Survey, which gives a substantial advantage to landholding as a legal tax avoidance measure. To eliminate this advantage, since 1992 land prices on major routes have been guided to equal to 80% of the price in the Official Land Price Survey.

4. Appraisal Value for Fixed Property Tax

The appraisal value for fixed property tax (local tax) is evaluated once every three years by municipalities. The price for the highest valued land in each prefectural capital is first determined as a certain percentage of the land price in the Official Land Price Survey two years earlier. Then, each municipality sets its own appraisal values, totalling 40,000 observation blocks nationwide. In general, the appraisal value for fixed property tax is substantially lower than those in either the Official Land Price Survey or the appraisal value for inheritance tax. The government intends to raise the appraisal value for fixed property tax to 70% of land prices in the Official Land Price Survey, effective 1994.

5. Land Price Index of City Areas

The Land Price Index of City Areas is released by the Japan Real Estate Institute twice a year. It covers only city areas and classifies land prices by three types of use: residential, commercial, and industrial. There are 2,230 observation blocks in 223 major cities nationwide (in 1991, the number of cities surveyed was enlarged to 223 from 140). The survey is conducted at the end of March and September. The results are released in the latter half of May and November, respectively. Figures are available for 1936 onward. The frequency of the survey was changed from once to twice a year in 1947. March 1980 is the current benchmark period for the index.

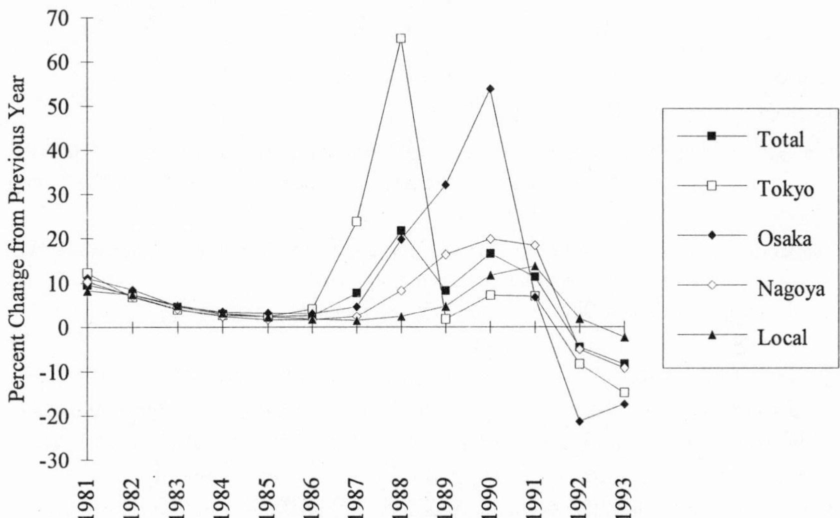

Fig. 24.1. Growth Rate of Land Prices (As of 1 January of Year Indicated)

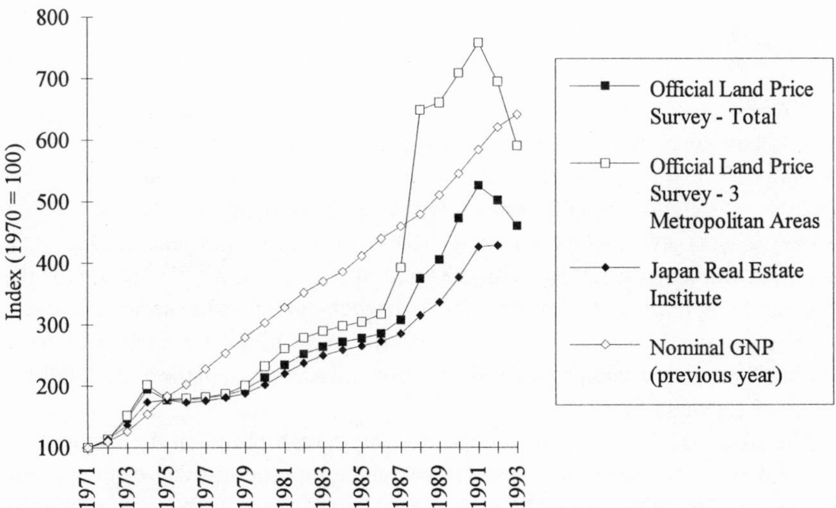

Fig. 24.2. Historical Trend of Land Prices (As of 1 January of Year Indicated)

Labor Markets and Population

25 Monthly Report on the Labor Force Survey

Source: Statistics Bureau, Management and Coordination Agency.

Frequency: Monthly and Annual.

Release: Figures for the previous month are released at the end of each month. Detailed data series are available in the *Annual Report on the Labor Force Survey* published every April.

Availability: The Labor Force Survey was first conducted in September 1946. Survey methodology was altered in September 1967. There is a discontinuity in July 1972 when Okinawa prefecture was included in the survey.

The Labor Force Survey is one of the two major sources of labor market statistics (the Monthly Labour Survey, Chapter 26, is the other), providing data on the size of the labor force, employed, unemployed, persons not in the labor force, rate of unemployment, labor force participation rate, and hours worked. The rate of unemployment is included in the lagging index of Diffusion Indexes compiled by the EPA. An annual report is published in the spring of each year, and a special survey is conducted once a year to gather more detailed information about workers' employment status.

Details

Coverage

The Labor Force Survey is conducted by the Management and Coordination Agency. The survey covers about 40,000 households nationwide with about 100,000 household members of age 15 and over (by contrast, the Monthly Labour Survey is a survey of establishments). Sample households are selected based on stratified two-stage sampling, with selection of population census districts as the first sampling unit and that of households in each district as the second. Sample districts are fixed for four months and a quarter of the districts are replaced every month. Sample households are fixed for two months, and half of the households are replaced each month.

The survey is conducted at the end of every month based on the situation of respondents in the reference period (week ending on the last day of the month, except for December, when it is the 20th to the 26th). The survey reveals employment status, characteristics, and desire for work of the respondents.

Table 25.1. Employment Status
Calendar Year 1992, Million Persons, unless otherwise noted

	Total	Male	Female
Population of age 15 and over	102.83	50.02	52.81
Labor force	65.78	38.99	26.79
Employed	64.36	38.17	26.19
By current status			
At work	63.38	37.60	25.79
Engaged mainly at work	53.78	36.66	17.12
Engaged partly in work besides school attendance	1.04	0.60	0.44
Engaged partly in work besides housekeeping	8.56	0.33	8.23
Not at work	0.98	0.58	0.40
By type of job			
Self-employed	8.43	5.80	2.63
Family workers of self-employed	4.56	0.81	3.75
Employees	51.19	31.45	19.74
Totally unemployed	1.42	0.82	0.60
Unemployment rate (percent)	2.16	2.10	2.24
Not in the labor force	36.79	10.90	25.90

Note: Unemployment Rate = ratio of totally unemployed to labor force.

Source: Management and Coordination Agency, *Annual Report on the Labor Force Survey*, 1992.

Explanation of Terms

'Employed at work' is defined as persons who worked for pay or profit for at least one hour during the reference period. Family workers are also included even if they were not paid.

'Employed not at work' include self-employed workers who did not work during the reference period and whose absence from work has not exceeded 30 days. Employees who did not work during the reference period but who received or expected to receive wages or salary are also included in this category.

'Totally unemployed' are persons who were ready to work, wishing to work, or actively seeking or prepared for work, but not employed. 'Persons not in the labor force' are those not classified as either employed or totally unemployed. They primarily consist of housewives, students, and aged persons.

The 'ratio of totally unemployed in labor force' (totally unemployed divided by labor force) is usually called the unemployment rate.

The 'labor force participation rate' is defined as the labor force divided by the population of age 15 and over.

'Self-employed workers' are persons who own and operate an unincorporated enterprise. 'Family workers' are those who work in an unincorporated enterprise operated by a member of the family. 'Employees' are those employed for wages or salary.

Table 25.2. Employment by Industry
Calendar Year 1992, Million Persons

	Employed Persons	Employees
Total	64.36	n.a.
Agriculture and forestry	3.75	n.a.
Non-agricultural	60.61	50.86
Fishery	0.36	0.13
Mining	0.06	0.06
Construction	6.19	4.97
Manufacturing	15.69	13.82
Textile mill products	1.99	1.33
Chemical and related products	2.15	1.96
Metal and machinery	7.59	7.08
Other	3.95	3.44
Electricity, gas, heat, and water supply	0.33	0.33
Transport and communications	3.85	3.63
Wholesale trade	4.32	4.00
Retail trade and eating and drinking establishments	10.03	7.02
Finance, insurance, and real estate	2.62	2.44
Services	14.81	12.31
Government including those not elsewhere classified	2.04	n.a.

Source: Management and Coordination Agency.

Figures in the Labor Force Survey are estimated results for the entire population (see Tables 25.1 and 25.2), based on the survey results and the *Monthly Report on Current Population Estimates* (see Chapter 29). When benchmark figures in the Population Census (see Chapter 28) are revised, the historical data in the Labor Force Survey are also revised.

Seasonal Adjustment

Figures in major categories are seasonally adjusted by the Census X-11 method. The seasonal coefficients are revised when the January figures are released. Seasonally adjusted figures are available for the following categories:

Number of employed by sex.
Number of employed by major industry.
Number of employees by sex.
Number of employees in non-agricultural industry by size of company.
Number of totally unemployed by sex.
Ratio of totally unemployed in labor force.
Total number of hours worked, non-agricultural industry.

Features and Problems

Japan's Low Unemployment Rate

The level and movement of the unemployment rate in Japan deserves special attention. Prior to the first oil crisis in 1973–4, it hovered between 1 and 2 percent (see Fig. 25.1). After the oil crisis, its level has moved upward to 2 or 3 percent, but this is still extremely low and stable compared with other industrial countries. Two important factors contribute to the low unemployment rate in Japan: the narrow definition of unemployed and the nature of the labor market.

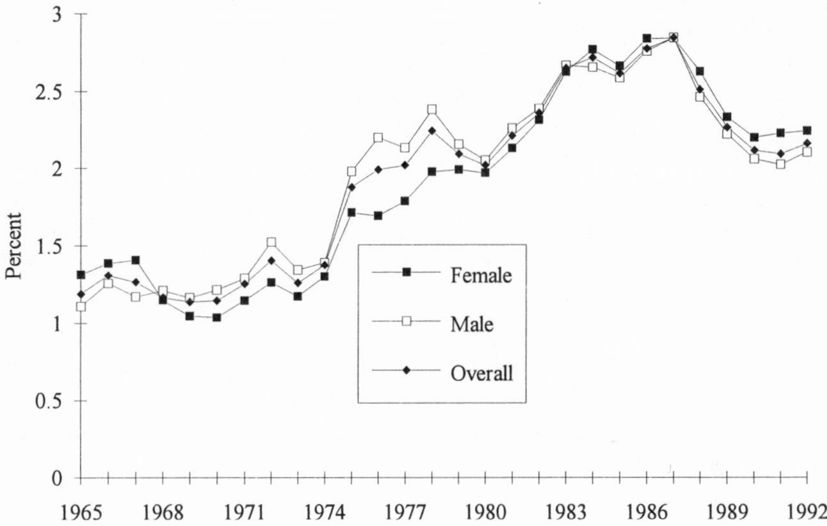

Fig. 25.1. Unemployment Rate

Comparison of Japan and USA Definitions of Unemployment

One of the reasons for the low unemployment rate in Japan is due to the narrow definition of unemployed. The major differences between the Japanese and USA definitions are: (1) People who worked less than 15 hours for a family business or family farm are classified as not in the labor force in the USA . (2) People who are laid off but still received salary or wages are classified as employed in Japan. In the USA, people who have been laid off from their former jobs and are awaiting recall are classified as unemployed. (3) The reference period is limited to one week in Japan while it is four weeks in the USA . People awaiting the results of job search in the five or more weeks prior to the survey date and not working in the last one week (for Japan, four weeks for the USA) are classified as unemployed in Japan while classified as not in the labor force in the USA. (4) People who have already committed themselves informally to begin work within 30 days are classified as not in the labor force in Japan, but classified as unemployed in the USA .

The *Special Labor Force Survey* conducted by the Management and Coordination Agency is usually used in Japan when comparing the labor statistics of Japan with those of the USA . This special survey is conducted every March when new graduates are waiting to start jobs in April. If the USA definition of item (4) were used, the number of people classified as unemployed in Japan would be higher.

Japan's Labor Market

Another reason for Japan's low unemployment rate is the characteristics of the labor market. Prevalent practices such as lifetime employment (mainly for male employees of large companies), large bonuses, seniority-based wages, and labor unions organized by company (rather than by industry) contribute to low frictional unemployment and infrequent strikes. In addition, Japanese companies first reduce working hours and use intra-company personnel transfers (or even transfers between companies within the same group) before reducing the number of workers in a recession. During a recession, 'hidden unemployment' tends to rise as much as the unemployment rate: lifetime workers are retained by their companies even if there is no work for them to do, while many part-time workers (especially women) who lose their jobs are classified as not in the labor force.

In this respect, attention should be paid to other variables in the Labor Force Survey such as the labor force participation rate, and other labor market indicators such as overtime worked (see Chapter 26) and the ratio of job offers to applicants (see Chapter 27) which are thought to move more sensitively than the unemployment rate in response to changes in general economic conditions.

Shorter Working Hours

As shown in Fig. 25.2, there has been a noticeable decline in the weekly average working hours for men since 1988, and a long-term decline for women. There are many possible explanations for this, including: revision of the Labor Standards Law which now restricts weekly scheduled working hours to 44, down from 48 hours previously; the trend toward 5-day work weeks; the recession which began around the first quarter of 1991; increasing participation of part-time workers (especially among women); and the shift toward some industries with lower than average working hours (such as services). It is a stated goal of the government to further reduce working hours, and the Labor Standards Law is to be revised again in April 1994, restricting scheduled hours to 40 (smaller companies, unable to easily reduce working hours, will be given a two-year exemption until April 1996).

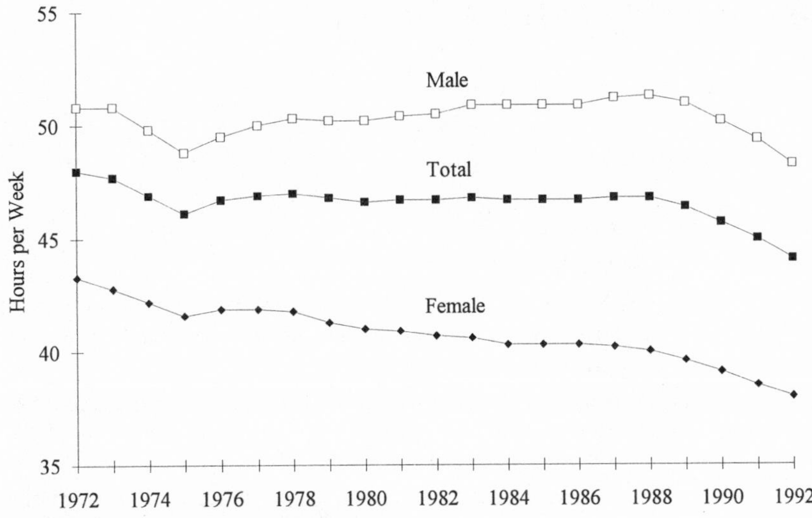

Fig. 25.2. Average Weekly Working Hours

Labor Force Participation Rates

The male labor participation rate among elderly workers is unusually high in Japan (see Fig. 25.3). Although the female participation rate has risen since the mid-1970s, it has retained an 'M'-shape. It is still typical for Japanese women to exit the labor force upon marriage or first childbirth.

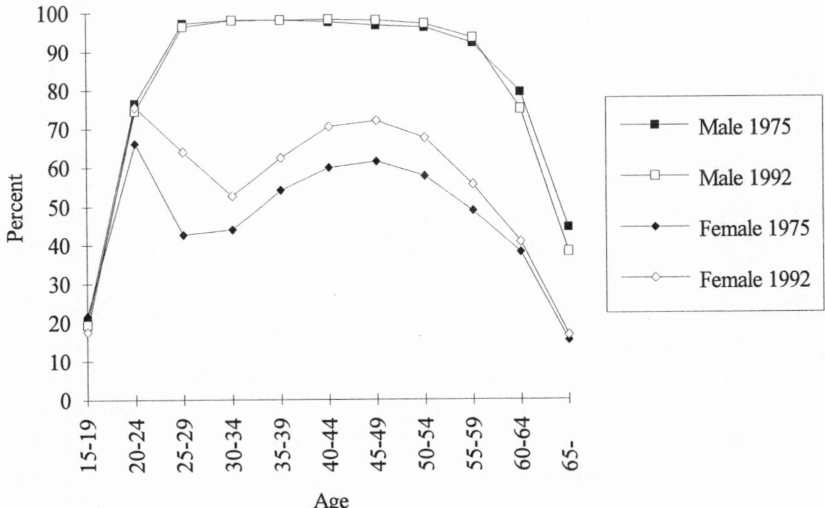

Fig. 25.3. Labor Force Participation Rate

26 Monthly Labour Survey

Source:	Policy Planning and Research Department, Ministry of Labour.
Frequency:	Monthly and Annual.
Release:	Preliminary estimates for the survey of establishments with 30 or more employees are released at the end of each month with a one-month lag. Revised estimates are released one month later.
Availability:	Monthly figures are available from January 1950 onward, with inclusion of the construction industry in January 1952 and service industries in January 1971.

The Monthly Labour Survey is one of the two major sources of labor market statistics (the Labor Force Survey, Chapter 25, is the other), providing data on total cash earnings, total hours worked, overtime hours worked, regular employment (index), and labor turnover. The survey covers nine major industries, excluding primary industries and government services. The index of total hours worked in manufacturing multiplied by the total employment index is included in the coincident index of Diffusion Indexes (DI) compiled by the EPA. The regular employment index in manufacturing is included in the lagging index of DI. The *Year Book of Labour Statistics* contains data from a variety of sources, including both the Monthly Labour Survey and Labor Force Survey.

Details

Coverage

The Monthly Labour Survey actually consists of two monthly surveys (National and Prefectural), and a Special Survey which is conducted annually, covering establishments in the nine major industries shown in Table 26.1 (by contrast, the Labor Force Survey is conducted on households).

The National Survey is conducted monthly on two different samples, one containing establishments with 5–29 regular employees, and the other containing establishments with 30 or more regular employees. The survey on establishments with 5–29 employees is conducted on a sample of about 16,500 establishments. Each establishment is surveyed for 18 months, and one-third of the sample is replaced every six months. The survey on establishments with 30 or more employees is conducted on a sample of about 16,700 establishments which is fixed for three years.

Table 26.1. Employment in Nine Major Industries (by Size of Establishment, National Survey)
Calendar Year 1992, Million Persons

	Establ. with 5 Employees or More	Establ. with 30 Employees or More
Total	40.89	24.07
Mining	0.08	0.03
Construction	3.71	1.55
Manufacturing	11.71	8.43
Electricity, gas, heat, and water supply	0.31	0.25
Transportation and communications	3.30	2.42
Wholesale and retail trade, eating and drinking establishments	9.40	3.99
Financing and insurance	1.80	1.10
Real estate	0.29	0.13
Services	10.29	6.16
Total excluding services	30.60	17.91

Source: Ministry of Labour.

The Prefectural Survey is conducted monthly on approximately 43,500 establishments with 5 or more regular employees. It has been conducted in addition to the National Survey since 1952 to provide accurate data for each prefecture.

The Special Survey has been conducted annually (as of the end of July) since 1957. Survey districts are first selected, then within those districts every establishment with less than 5 employees is surveyed. It should be noted that the surveys for 1980–9 covered establishments with 1–29 employees.

Figures for all Japan are based on the National Survey only, while figures by prefecture are based on the Prefectural Survey only. Figures for establishments with 5 or more employees, 30 or more employees, and 1–4 employees are given separately.

Explanation of Terms

The following major categories are available (per-capita basis):

- Total cash earnings
  - Contractual cash earnings
    - Scheduled cash earnings
    - Non-scheduled cash earnings (overtime pay)
  - Special cash earnings (bonus pay)
- Total hours worked
  - Scheduled hours worked
  - Non-scheduled hours worked (overtime)
- Regular employment
  - Part-time workers

'Total cash earnings' is the sum of 'contractual cash earnings' and 'special cash earnings' (before deductions of income tax, social security contributions, labor union dues, etc.). 'Contractual cash earnings' are earnings paid according to labor contracts, collective agreements, or wage regulations of establishments. 'Special cash earnings' is the amount paid for temporary or unforeseen reasons not based on any previous agreement, contract, or rule. Summer and year-end bonuses are included in this category.

'Regular employees' consist of: persons hired for an indefinite period or for longer than one month; persons hired for 18 days or more in each of the two preceding months; board directors of corporations who work regularly and are paid a monthly salary; and family workers who work regularly and are paid a monthly salary. 'Part-time workers' are those who are among regular employees and whose scheduled daily working hours or weekly working days are less than that of normal regular employees. Published figures for employees are estimated total values for all establishments (not only those surveyed), calculated using results from the survey in conjunction with the Establishment Census of Japan (see Chapter 16).

Indexes

Indexes for the major categories are available. The benchmark year is currently 1990 and is revised every five years. Real wage indexes are calculated by dividing nominal wage indexes by the overall consumer price index for Japan. Indexes for total cash earnings and contractual cash earnings for total industries, total industries excluding services, and manufacturing are available. Hourly earnings are calculated by dividing the index of total cash earnings by that of total hours worked. Indexes are more frequently used than absolute values for reasons described below.

Seasonal Adjustment

Seasonally adjusted indexes are available for the following series (establishments with 30 or more employees): total cash earnings; contractual cash earnings; total hours worked; non-scheduled hours worked; and regular employment. The Census X-11 method is used for the calculation of seasonal factors, which are applied to the entire period when the February figures are released.

Features and Problems

Non-scheduled hours worked, or overtime, is considered to be a leading indicator of business conditions, especially industrial production (see Fig. 26.1). In Japan, where long-term employment is prevalent, firms first tend to adjust their operations by changing the amount of overtime work rather than the number of employees.

Scheduled hours worked has been declining in recent years, corroborating the trend shown in the Labor Force Survey (see Fig. 25.2).

Large bonus payments in summer and winter are prevalent in Japan. These result in unusually high special cash payments (and total cash earnings) in June, July, and December.

Problems with Absolute Level Figures

As described above, the National Survey for establishments with 30 or more employees fixes its sample for three years. The sudden change in the sample establishments which occurs every three years is likely to result in discontinuities in the data series. For the index figures, an adjustment is made to account for the sample change, while there is no such adjustment for absolute level figures.

Another problem (even with index figures) is that as time passes the fixed sample tends to become more and more biased, because new establishments are not added to the sample (i.e. after three years the sample will contain only firms established more than three years ago). Since new establishments tend to pay less and grow faster than older ones, figures for cash earnings tend to become upward biased and figures for number of employees (total for Japan) downward biased. The only statistic adjusted for this effect is the Index of Regular Employment, which is adjusted annually using statistics on employment insurance (Employment Security Bureau, Ministry of Labour, *Report on Employment Insurance Activities*).

It is worth noting that the movement of total cash earnings (per-capita basis) reflects not only general business conditions, but also the change in composition of workers. For example, if the percentage of female workers among total workers increases, this will lower both total cash earnings and hourly earnings because average hourly earnings of female workers is lower than that of male workers.

Year Book of Labour Statistics

The *Year Book of Labour Statistics* is published around February each year. It contains various statistics on labor markets in addition to those described in this book, including:

1. Employment Referral Statistics.
2. Basic Survey on Schools.
3. Surveys on Employment Management.
4. Industry Labour Situation Survey.
5. Basic Survey on Wage Structure.
6. General Survey on Wages and Working Hours System.
7. Surveys on Wage Increases.
8. Conditions Relating to Spring Wage Increase (Shunto).
9. Survey on Labour Dispute Statistics.

Among these, the Basic Survey on Wage Structure contains particularly valuable information on wages and working hours by age, education, corporation size, industry, and tenure. Population Census data can be used to adjust for the bias in the sample survey (only companies with 10 or more employees are included).

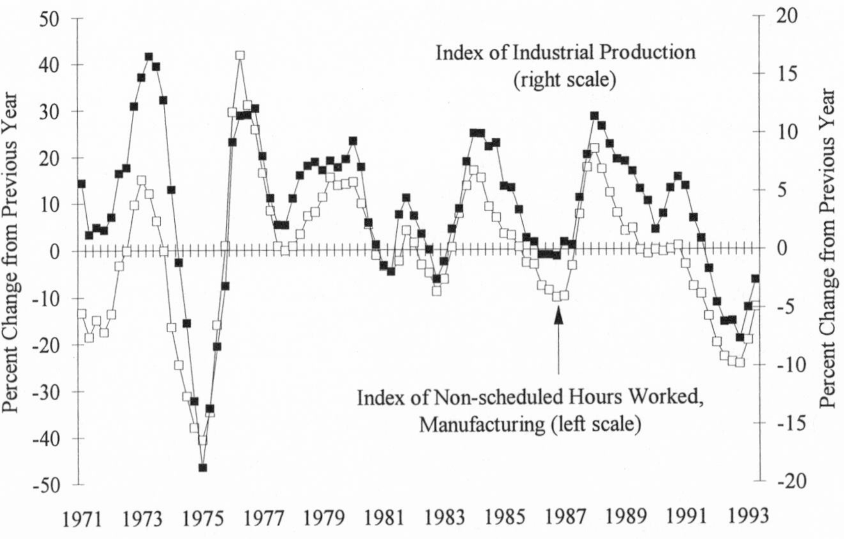

Fig. 26.1. Non-scheduled Hours Worked (Overtime)

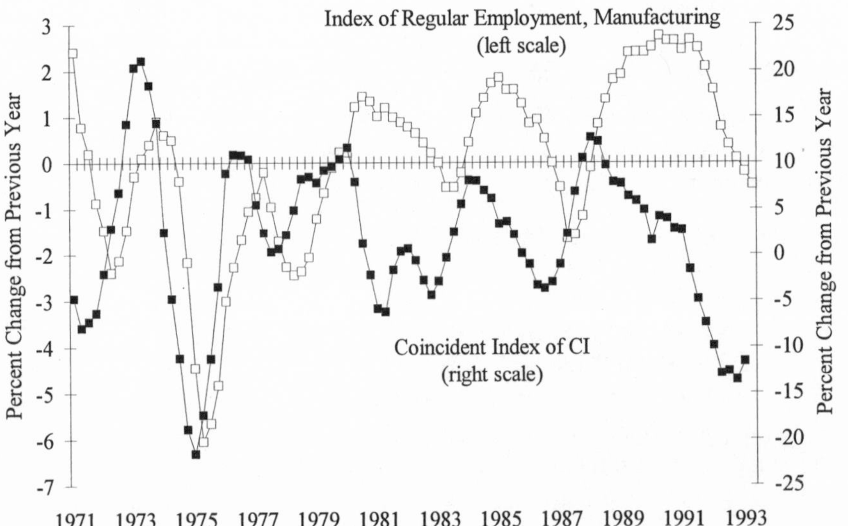

Fig. 26.2. Index of Regular Employment, Manufacturing Industries

27 Job Offers and Applicants

Source:	Employment Security Bureau, Ministry of Labour.
Frequency:	Monthly.
Release:	Figures for the previous month are released around the end of each month.
Availability:	Monthly figures for the job offers-to-applicants ratio are available from January 1961 onward.

Statistics on job offers and applicants reflect labor market conditions. The ratio of effective job offers to applicants for regular employment (excluding new graduates) is most commonly used, and is included in the coincident index of Diffusion Indexes (DI) compiled by the EPA. The number of new job offers for regular employment excluding new graduates is included in the leading index of the DI. These statistics are published in the *Monthly Report of Employment Security Business*.

Details

Statistics on job offers and applicants are collected via 599 public employment agency offices nationwide. 'New job offers' is the number of jobs newly offered by employers via the employment agencies during the month. 'New job applicants' is the number of job seekers applying at the employment agencies during the month. Job offers and applicants are kept registered for three months. The number of job offers and applicants registered are called 'effective job offers' and 'effective job applicants' respectively.

Jobs are classified by the length of contract: 'regular jobs' are those for four months or longer (or no specified period); 'temporary jobs' are for periods between one month and four months; and 'daily jobs' are those for less than one month. Part-time jobs are those which have shorter monthly working hours than regular jobs.

Seasonal Adjustment

Seasonally adjusted figures (using the Census X-11 method) are available for major variables such as effective job offers and applicants, new job offers and applicants, ratio of effective job offers to applicants, and ratio of new job offers to applicants. Seasonally adjusted figures for the previous five years are revised retroactively upon the release of January figures.

Features and Problems

At least in theory, the number of new job offers has a straightforward relationship with business conditions: the stronger the economy, the more jobs are offered. The relationship between business conditions and the number of job applicants, on the other hand, is ambiguous (see Fig. 27.1). Job applicants include both the unemployed and those who have jobs but are seeking an additional job or wish to change jobs. Thus the increase in applications by the unemployed in a recessionary period may be offset by a decrease in applications by the employed seeking better jobs.

Statistics on job offers and applicants cover only a portion of the labor market. They do not cover job searching activities outside the employment agencies. It is estimated that the statistics cover only 20 percent of job searches.

Table 27.1. Job Offers and Applicants
Calendar Year 1992

	General	Regular Employees
Effective job applicants (A)	1,433,026	1,307,775
New job applications (B)	344,639	297,077
Effective job offers (C)	1,553,333	1,438,175
New job offers (D)	554,035	506,361
Effective job offers-to-applicants ratio (C)/(A)	1.08	1.10
New job offers-to-applicants ratio (D)/(B)	1.61	1.70

Note: Figures exclude new graduates and include part-time workers.
Source: Ministry of Labour.

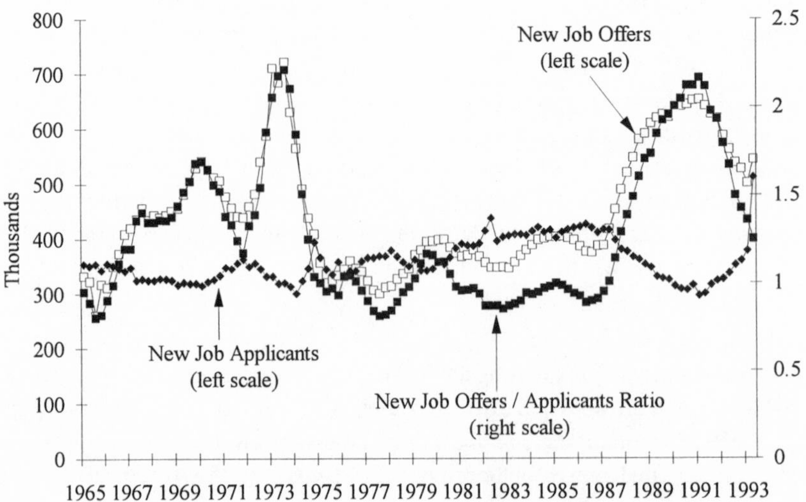

Fig. 27.1. New Job Offers and Applicants (General, Excluding New Graduates)

28 Population Census

Source: Statistics Bureau, Management and Coordination Agency.

Frequency: Once every five years.

Release: Figures are released over a period of years following the census. Details on the release of 1990 census figures are given below.

Availability: Data is available for 1920 onward, except for 1945.

A census is conducted every five years to obtain the basic demographic and economic statistics of the Japanese population. There are two types of census: a 'large-scale' census, conducted in years ending with '0', and a 'simplified' census, with fewer questions asked, conducted in years ending with '5'. Since census data is one of the few data sources which does not suffer from serious biases, it is useful as a benchmark for preparing (and a benchmark against which to compare) other statistics. (Note that actual data on the population of Japan is given in Chapter 29.)

Details

Topics Covered in the 1990 Census

For household members:

1. Name.
2. Sex.
3. Year and month of birth.
4. Relationship to the head of the household.
5. Marital status.
6. Nationality.
7. Place of five years previous residence.
8. Education.
9. Type of activity.
10. Name of establishment and kind of business (Industry).
11. Kind of work (Occupation).
12. Employment status.
13. Place of work or location of school.
14. Transportation to the place of work or school.
15. Commuting time to the place of work or school.

For households:

16. Type of household.
17. Number of household members.
18. Source of household income.
19. Type and tenure of dwelling.
20. Number of dwelling rooms.
21. Area of floor space of dwelling.
22. Type of building and number of stories.

All of the information reported in the census is as of 1 October 1990.

Publications for the 1990 Census

All of the publications listed below are available as of the date of writing, unless otherwise noted. Preliminary releases, which have now been superseded by final counts, are not listed. The official title of the following volumes takes the form: '1990 Population Census of Japan, Volume xx: . . ., Part yy . . .'. It should be noted that the contents and volume numbers change from census to census.

Complete Tabulation

The complete tabulation is conducted in three stages, summarized in volumes 2, 3 and 4 respectively. Each of these volumes consists of two parts: (1) Japan, containing statistics on the whole country and summary statistics for each prefecture; (2) Prefecture and Municipalities, one book for each prefecture (47 books in all), containing detailed statistics on the prefecture and its municipalities. Results for part 2 are released first, prefecture by prefecture; after the results for all 47 prefectures are released, results for the whole country (part 1) are published.

Volume 1: Total Population

Contains the population and area of each municipality, as well as of each prefecture, the whole country and each densely inhabited district. Based on the first basic complete tabulation.

Volume 2: Results of the First Basic Complete Tabulation

Includes statistics on the basic characteristics of population, households and dwellings, and statistics on aged persons' households, mother–child(ren) and father–child(ren) households, for the whole country, prefectures and municipalities.

Volume 3: Results of the Second Basic Complete Tabulation

Includes basic statistics on labor force status, industry and education of population.

Volume 4: Results of the Third Basic Complete Tabulation

Contains statistics on the occupation structure of the population. Part 1 is to be released in September 1993.

Volume 5: Results of Detailed Sample Tabulation

Provides more detailed tables for the whole country and prefectures. Included are detailed cross-classified results, with statistics based on detailed classifications of industry and occupation. Part 2 is to be released successively, prefecture by prefecture, by October 1994. Part 1 is to be released in October 1994.

Volume 6: Commutation

Part 1 Place of Work or Schooling of Population by Sex, Age, and Industry (Major Groups).
Part 2 Place of Work or Schooling of Population by Occupation (Major Groups).
Part 3 Place of Work or Schooling of Population by Industry and Occupation (Medium Groups).

Designed to track the daily movement of workers and students commuting between their homes and places of work or schooling in terms of the number, direction, and economic characteristics of commuters. The results are also used to calculate the daytime population in each locality, to be compared with the respective night-time (i.e. census) population. Part 1 contains statistics on the basic characteristics of the population, except for occupation by the place of work or schooling. Part 2 will include the results on the occupational structure of population by place of work, and is to be released in November 1993. Part 3 will be prepared after the completion of the detailed sample tabulation (Volume 5), and will provide detailed data concerning the industry and occupation of the commuters. It is to be released in December 1994.

Volume 7: Results of Tabulation on Internal Migration

Part 1 Basic Characteristics.
Part 2 Occupation.

Provides statistics concerning the number, direction, and characteristics of those who changed their usual place of residence. Part 1 provides basic statistics, while Part 2 contains data classified by occupation. Part 2 is to be released in December 1993.

Population Maps of Japan Series

These volumes contain highly detailed maps showing population density, change in population, age of population, etc. Some volumes are already available, but the final volume is not scheduled to be released until December 1994.

29 Monthly Report on Current Population Estimates (and Related Population Statistics)

Source: Statistics Bureau, Management and Coordination Agency.

Frequency: Monthly and Annual.

Release: Figures for the previous month are released as provisional estimates around the 10th of each month. They are revised as final estimates four months later. Figures for the Japanese population are available in the final estimates only. Detailed population estimates are released each June. Figures for the previous five years are revised following the release of census data.

Availability: Population by gender and age group (and by prefecture) in the post-World War II period is available.

The *Monthly Report on Population Estimates* provides up-to-date population statistics in the periods between censuses. The current population is calculated as the population in the latest census plus changes in population, which is divided into two parts: natural increase (births less deaths) and net migration (entries less exits). Statistics on natural increase and net migration are taken from *Monthly (Annual) Vital Statistics* (Ministry of Health and Welfare) and *Monthly (Annual) Report of Statistics on Legal Migrants* (Ministry of Justice), respectively.

Details

Total Population and Japanese Population

Population is calculated as of the 1st of each month. Two series are available:

Total population in Japan as of 1st of the current month [A]
= population in Japan as of 1st of the previous month
+ (births – deaths) in the previous month
+ (legal entries – legal exits) in the previous month

Japanese population as of 1st of the current month [B]
= Japanese population as of 1st of the previous month
+ (births – deaths) in the previous month
+ (legal entries – legal exits) in the previous month
+ net increase by change of citizenship in the previous month
(people obtaining Japanese citizenship – people losing Japanese citizenship)

Total population in Japan [A] includes both Japanese and non-Japanese living in Japan while the Japanese population [B] includes only the Japanese.

As shown in the above equations, the change in population can be expressed as the sum of two factors: natural increase and net migration. Natural increase is the number of births less deaths. Net migration is the number of legal entries less legal exits. Legal entrants are foreigners staying in Japan for more than 90 days as of the survey date. They do not include illegal migrants or stationed armed force members and their families. In Japan, net migration is small in comparison with natural increase (see Table 29.1).

Table 29.1. Current Population Estimates
As of 1 October 1992, Thousand Persons

	Total Population	Japanese Population
Population	124,399	123,476
Male	6,110	6,060
Female	6,336	6,288
Net increase	409	374
Natural increase	374	371
Live births	1,228	1,219
Deaths	854	848
Net migration	34	−7
Entries	12,720	11,912
Exits	12,685	11,918

Note: Net increase is for the one-year period ending 1 October 1992.
Source: Management and Coordination Agency.

The total population is calculated as the total population from the most recent census (currently the 1990 census) plus the change in population since the census. Since a census is conducted only once every five years, the monthly estimates become more uncertain in the years following the census. When a new census is conducted, monthly figures for the previous five years are revised. In addition, population by five-year age groups and gender is also available (see Table 29.2).

Features and Problems

Japan experienced a rather large but brief baby boom in the aftermath of World War II (see Fig. 29.1). The total fertility rate (expected number of children born to each woman over her lifetime) has declined to well below the rate necessary to maintain the size of the population in the long run (also see Figs. 29.2 and 29.3).

There was a sudden drop in the number of live births in 1966. This was caused by a Japanese superstition about girls born in certain years (once every 60 years), which led some people to avoid having children in 1966.

Table 29.2. Total Population by Age and Gender
As of 1 January 1993, Ten Thousand Persons

	Total	Male	Female
Total Population	12,440	6,108	6,332
0–4 years old	617	317	301
5–9	711	364	346
10–14	793	407	387
15–19	955	490	465
20–24	965	493	472
25–29	829	420	409
30–34	780	395	386
35–39	814	411	404
40–44	1,071	538	533
45–49	909	454	455
50–54	847	420	428
55–59	797	391	407
60–64	714	345	369
65–69	578	262	315
70–74	408	163	245
75 and over	651	239	411
0–14 years old	2,121	1,088	1,034
15–64	8,682	4,355	4,326
65 and over	1,637	665	972

Source: Management and Coordination Agency.

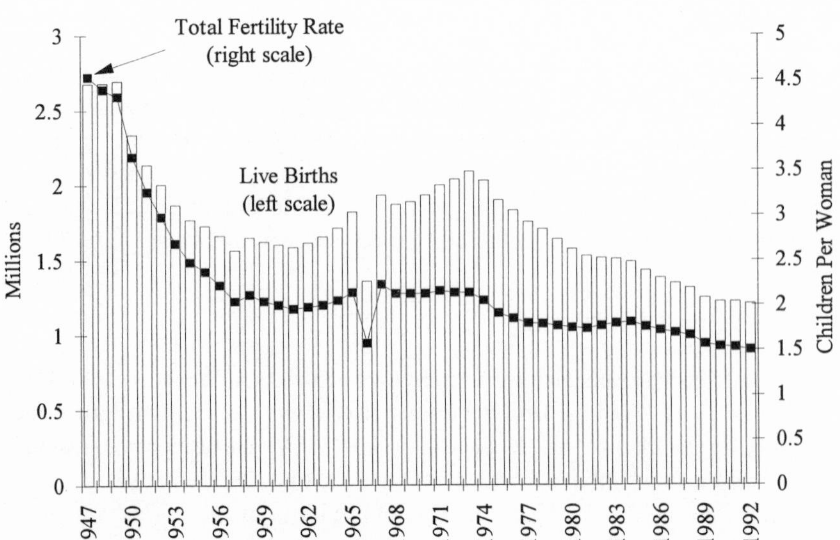

Fig. 29.1. Live Births and Total Fertility Rate

Related Statistics on Population

1. Population Estimates as of October 1

To supplement monthly population estimates, *Population Estimates as of October 1* is released each June. It is compiled from the same source statistics as Current Population Estimates. Population by age (with one- and five-year intervals), gender, and prefecture are available. It is not published in years when a census is conducted.

2. Vital Statistics

Statistics used to calculate natural increase (live births less deaths) are compiled in *Vital Statistics* by the Ministry of Health and Welfare. *Monthly Vital Statistics* is released with a two-month lag, and is called a prompt report. It is revised as a preliminary report three months later. More detailed statistics are available in the three volumes of *Annual Vital Statistics* released in September (annual statistics are available from 1899 onward). *Live Births: Special Report of Vital Statistics* released in March 1992 provides detailed statistics on live births by mother's age, mother's type of job, prefecture, etc. *Latest Trends of Vital Statistics in Japan* published every March contains a brief summary of the information in *Vital Statistics*. All of these reports are compiled by the Statistics and Information Department of the Ministry of Health and Welfare and published by the Health and Welfare Statistics Association.

Table 29.3 shows the main variables included in *Vital Statistics*. These data are also available by prefecture. The causes of deaths are analyzed in detail by type, age, and prefecture.

Table 29.3. Vital Statistics
Calendar Year 1992

	Number	Rate (Per 1,000)	Average Frequency (Min. Sec.)
Live births	1,208,977	9.8	0′26″
Deaths	855,436	6.9	0′37″
Natural increase	353,541	2.9	
Baby deaths	5,470	4.5	96′21″
Newborn baby deaths	2,902	2.4	181′37″
Stillbirths	48,884	38.9	10′24″
Marriages	754,442	6.1	0′42″
Divorces	179,198	1.5	3′07″

Note: Baby: age of less than one year old; newborn baby: age of less than four weeks old; baby deaths rate = baby deaths/live births * 1,000; newborn baby deaths rate = newborn baby deaths/live births * 1,000. Denominator for rates of other items is Japanese population as of 1 October 1992.

Source: Ministry of Health and Welfare.

3. Population Projection for Japan 1991–2090

Population Projection is released by the Institute of Population Problems, Ministry of Health and Welfare. It is published about once every five years. The latest edition was published in September 1992, with the data from the 1990 census used as a base for the projection. Most long-run forecasts involving population use the figures from *Population Projection.*

Three projection paths are described, based on varying assumptions: (1) high population growth; (2) medium population growth; and (3) low population growth. Total population and population in two sets of age groupings (ages 0–15, 16–64, and 65 and over; ages 0–19, 20–69, and 70 and over) are forecast until 2090. Population within one-year age groups are available only for the medium growth population projection, up until 2025. As shown in Table 29.4, the population of Japan is expected to peak around 2010, and the elderly population is expected to increase dramatically between 1990 and 2020.

Table 29.4. Assumptions and Results in the Population Projection
September 1992

Assumptions	Medium	High	Low
Average year of first marriage for females			
1950 cohort	24.4	24.4	24.4
1973 cohort and later	27.2	26.9	27.5
Females never marrying (percent of total)			
1936–40 cohort	4.2%	4.2%	4.2%
1965 cohort and later	11.0%	4.2%	16.4%
Summary of Projection			
Peak population (millions)	130.44	134.46	127.14
Peak year	[2011]	[2015]	[2006]
Total Population (millions)			
1990	123.61	123.61	123.61
2000	127.39	128.46	126.38
2010	130.40	133.74	126.76
2020	128.35	133.82	122.15
2030	122.97	131.26	113.86
2040	117.29	129.46	104.24
2050	111.51	127.60	94.42
Population of age 65 and over (% of total)			
1990	12.1	12.1	12.1
2000	17.0	16.9	17.2
2010	21.3	20.7	21.9
2020	25.5	24.5	26.8
2030	26.0	24.4	28.1
2040	28.0	25.3	31.5
2050	28.2	24.6	33.3

Source: Institute of Population Problems, Ministry of Health and Welfare, *Population Projection for Japan 1991–2090*, September 1992.

4. Life Tables

Life Tables are released by the Statistics and Information Department of the Ministry of Health and Welfare every five years, after the latest census data becomes available. At present, the life tables for 1990 released in March 1992 are the latest available. Abridged Life Tables are released in September every year.

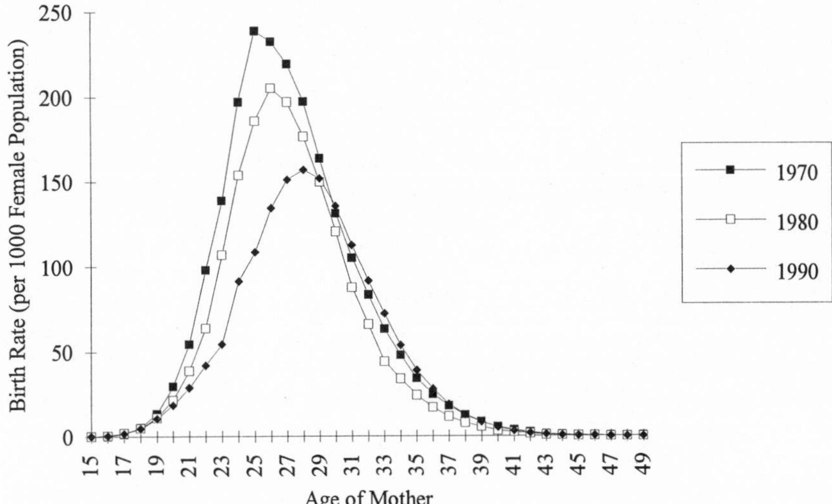

Fig. 29.2. Birth Rate by Age of Mother

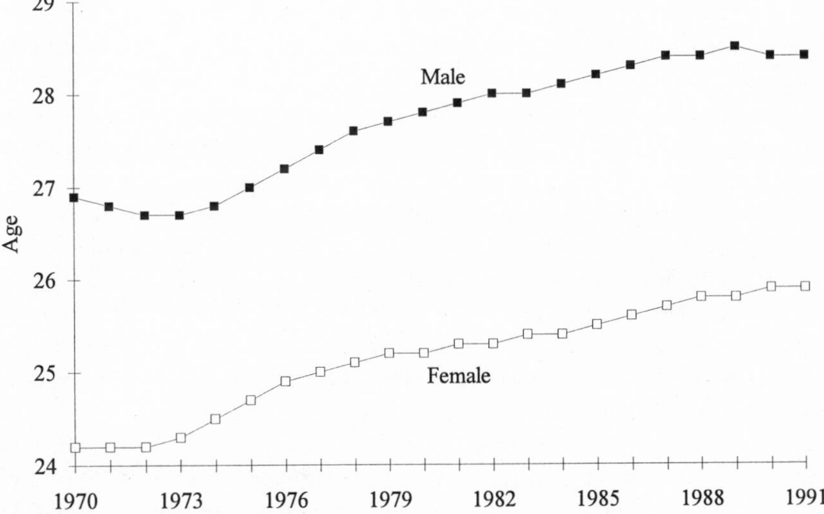

Fig. 29.3. Average Age at First Marriage

International Trade and Investment

30 Summary Report on Trade

Source: Customs and Tariff Bureau, Ministry of Finance.

Frequency: Three times per month.

Release: Figures are released for each 10-day period, with a 10-day lag. Preliminary figures for the previous month are released around the middle of each month, and revised figures are released around the end of the month. Annual revisions are incorporated after the release of figures for December.

Availability: Monthly figures are available for the entire post-World War II period.

This report is often called 'customs clearance statistics'. The report reveals values of merchandise exports and imports by commodity and country. Quantity and price (unit value) indexes and the terms of trade index (in yen terms) are also available. Because of its quick release and wide coverage, it is frequently used for the analysis of the external sector of Japan.

Details

The *Summary Report on Trade of Japan* is based on information gathered from export and import declaration reports submitted to the customs office. The report covers most commodities, excluding freight valued less than 200,000 yen, sample commodities, gifts, and freight for the stationed US military in Japan.

The value of each export commodity is recorded at the time of departure of the craft. The value of each import commodity is recorded at the time of import approval of the commodity.

The value of exports is expressed on a free-on-board (FOB) basis. FOB includes the cost of transportation and insurance until the goods are loaded on to the ship/airplane. The value of imports is expressed on a cost-insurance-freight (CIF) basis. CIF includes the cost of transportation and insurance until the goods arrive at the port of destination. Using the CIF value for imports allows the data to be released quickly, but has the effect of making the trade surplus seem smaller than if goods and exports were both valued on a FOB basis.

The values of exports and imports are expressed both in terms of Japanese yen and US dollars. Customs declaration reports require that trade values be expressed in terms of yen. Foreign currency contracts are converted into yen using the exchange rate quoted by the customs office. This quoted rate is the weekly average of the exchange rate two weeks ago. About 40 percent of exports and 10 percent of imports are yen contracts. The rest are mostly $US contracts, and the trade balance is usually expressed in terms of $US.

Values of exports and imports by commodity and country are available in terms of both the yen and $US. In the preliminary release, a limited number of disaggregated figures are available; the particular figures given are subject to change. Seasonally adjusted figures are available only for the total value of exports, imports, and trade-balance.

Table 30.1. Merchandise Trade by Country
Calendar Year 1987–1992, Billion $US, unless otherwise noted

	Balance (Billion $US)						Percent of Total in 1992	
	1987	1988	1989	1990	1991	1992	Exports	Imports
Developed countries	71.3	67.1	60.0	50.6	60.1	70.9	54.4	48.9
USA	52.1	47.6	44.9	38.0	38.2	43.6	28.2	22.4
Canada	−0.5	−1.9	−1.8	−1.7	−0.4	−0.6	2.1	3.3
Western Europe	22.8	25.4	21.4	20.7	29.7	34.1	21.2	16.3
EC	20.0	22.8	19.8	18.5	27.4	31.2	18.4	13.4
UK	5.3	6.4	6.3	5.5	6.0	7.4	3.6	2.1
France	1.1	0.7	−0.2	−1.5	0.3	0.9	1.9	2.3
Germany	6.7	7.7	6.9	6.3	9.9	9.6	6.0	4.6
Italy	−0.0	−0.1	−1.0	−1.6	−0.7	−0.3	1.1	1.8
Others	−3.2	−4.1	−4.4	−6.4	−7.4	−6.2	2.9	6.9
Developing countries	7.1	10.5	7.2	8.6	24.9	42.4	41.3	42.0
Asia	14.4	19.3	20.6	28.1	37.4	46.9	30.7	24.7
Asian NIEs	20.6	24.8	25.6	30.7	39.5	46.5	21.4	11.2
ASEAN	−8.0	−7.0	−6.1	−3.4	−2.9	−0.7	8.2	12.2
Middle East	−11.0	−10.2	−14.5	−21.5	−17.0	−14.0	4.5	12.6
Latin America	2.4	1.0	0.5	0.4	3.0	7.1	4.7	3.7
Africa	1.5	0.7	0.8	1.5	1.7	2.6	1.2	0.7
Others	−0.1	−0.3	−0.2	0.0	−0.1	−0.2	0.2	0.4
Former Communist countries	1.3	−0.0	−2.9	−7.1	−7.2	−6.6	4.3	9.1
Eastern Europe	0.2	0.1	--	--	--	--	0.0	0.0
Total	79.7	77.6	64.3	52.1	77.8	106.6	100.0	100.0

Note: Figures for Eastern Europe are included in Western Europe since 1989.
Source: Ministry of Finance.

Merchandise trade by country (see Table 30.1) reveals that the US is the largest single trading partner of Japan, followed by Asian countries, especially Asian NIEs (Korea, Taiwan, Hong Kong, and Singapore). Japan currently records trade surpluses for most regions except for resource-exporting countries such as ASEAN and the Middle East.

Merchandise trade by commodity (see Table 30.2) reveals that machinery and equipment accounts for three-quarters of total exports, but less than one-fifth of imports. Foodstuffs, raw material, and mineral fuels still account for half of all imports.

Table 30.2. Merchandise Trade by Commodity
Calendar Year 1987–1992, Billion $US, unless otherwise noted

	1987	1988	1989	1990	1991	1992	% of Total in 1992
Total exports	229.2	264.9	275.2	286.9	314.5	339.6	100.0
Foodstuffs	1.5	1.7	1.7	1.6	1.8	1.9	0.6
Textiles	6.9	6.9	6.9	7.2	7.9	8.6	2.5
Chemicals	11.7	14.0	14.8	15.9	17.5	19.1	5.6
Non-metallic mineral manufactures	2.5	2.9	3.1	3.2	3.5	3.9	1.1
Metals	18.0	21.8	21.6	19.5	21.1	21.3	6.3
Machinery and equipment	171.1	197.0	205.5	215.1	236.6	256.8	75.6
General machinery	44.8	56.0	61.1	63.5	69.5	76.3	22.5
Electrical machinery	40.9	62.0	64.5	65.9	73.7	77.4	22.8
Transportation machinery	63.9	65.7	66.6	71.8	77.9	87.1	25.7
Precision machinery	13.7	13.2	13.3	13.8	15.5	16.0	4.7
Others	17.5	20.7	21.7	24.4	26.0	28.0	8.2
Total imports	149.5	187.4	210.8	234.8	236.7	233.0	100.0
Foodstuffs	22.4	29.1	31.0	31.6	34.5	37.3	16.0
Raw materials	22.0	28.0	30.7	28.5	27.2	26.0	11.2
Mineral fuels	39.1	38.4	43.1	56.7	54.8	52.7	22.6
Petroleum and coal products	27.4	25.8	29.8	41.3	37.8	36.4	15.6
Chemicals	11.8	14.8	15.9	16.0	17.4	17.4	7.4
Machinery and equipment	19.1	26.7	32.4	40.9	42.9	42.9	18.4
Others	35.0	50.3	57.8	61.1	60.1	56.8	24.4
Iron and steel products	2.5	4.6	5.1	4.6	5.5	3.8	1.6
Textile products	7.6	10.6	13.3	12.8	13.7	15.3	6.6
Nonferrous metals	5.6	9.3	9.9	9.9	9.6	7.0	3.0
Overall trade balance	79.7	77.6	64.3	52.1	77.8	106.6	--

Source: Ministry of Finance.

Trade Indexes

Trade volume, price, and value indexes are available for total exports and total imports. They are available only in terms of yen. The base year was revised from calendar 1985 to calendar 1990 in the July 1993 release. The Trade Value Index is calculated by dividing the total value of exports and imports during the month by the monthly average of the total value for the base year. The Trade Price Index, or Unit Value Index, is expressed as a Fisher index (see Appendix 1). The Trade Volume Index is obtained by dividing the Trade Value Index by the Trade Price Index.

The Terms of Trade Index is obtained by dividing the export price index by the import price index. This index is considered to represent the amount of import goods obtainable in exchange for a unit of exports. An increase due to either an increase in export prices or a decrease in import prices implies improvement of national welfare. For example, the appreciation of the yen or a decline in oil prices would be reflected as an increase in the Terms of Trade Index.

Features and Problems

It is often useful to watch the movement of the volume indexes rather than the value indexes because value indexes are affected by the movement of both quantity and price. This is especially the case when prices fluctuate sharply due to a rapid change in the value of the yen or the price of oil.

J-curve Effect

When the value of the yen changes (relative to other currencies), movements in the volume of exports and imports tend to lag changes in prices. Thus, in the short run, when exchange rates change Japan's trade surplus tends to move in the 'wrong' direction: appreciation of the yen lowers the price of imports relative to exports, trade volumes show little change, and the trade surplus goes up instead of down. This is called the J-curve effect (in the long run, trade volumes respond to the price changes, and Japan's trade surplus moves in the 'right' direction).

Further, Japanese firms have placed an emphasis on maintaining market shares, so they try to limit price increases (in terms of foreign currencies) in foreign markets when the yen appreciates (the decrease in raw material and fuel costs associated with the yen's rise help make this possible). This behavior reinforced the J-curve effect during the yen's rapid appreciation following the Plaza Agreement in 1985, prolonging the period in which the trade surplus remained at high levels.

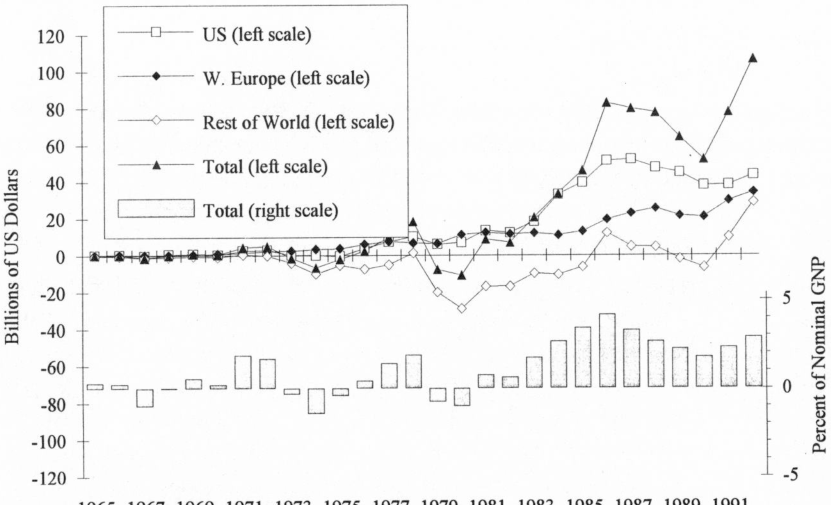

Fig. 30.1. Trade Balance (Customs Clearance Basis)

31 Balance of Payments Statistics

Source: International Department, Bank of Japan.

Frequency: Monthly and semi-annually.

Release: Figures are released at the beginning of each month with a two-month lag in *Balance of Payments Monthly*. Regional balance of payments for the first and second half of the calendar year are released in the November and April issues. More detailed figures are available in the August issue of *Monthly Statistics on Government Finance and Banking* published by the Ministry of Finance.

Availability: Quarterly figures are available from 1950 onward, and monthly figures from April 1966 onward.

Balance of payments statistics provide data on Japan's international economic transactions, including goods, services, investment income, and capital movements. This is one of the source statistics for compiling the System of National Accounts. The current account balance is the most frequently used measure of Japan's international trade.

Details

Source of Statistics

The Bank of Japan collects original figures from 'Customs Clearance Statistics' published by the Ministry of Finance (see Chapter 30), reports on receipts and payments of services submitted by authorized foreign exchange banks, and transportation income statements submitted by transportation companies.

Basic Concept of Balance of Payment Statistics

The statistics released in *Balance of Payments Monthly* (hereafter 'BOP statistics') is based on the fourth edition of the *Balance of Payments Manual* issued by the International Monetary Fund (IMF). BOP statistics employ a double-entry system, with every transaction represented by two entries that have exactly equal values. One entry is designated as a credit and is given a positive arithmetic sign, while the other entry is called a debit and given a negative sign. Under the conventions of the system, Japan records credit entries for real resources denoting exports and for financial items reflecting either a reduction in foreign assets or an increase in foreign liabilities. In other words, for assets, both real and financial, a positive figure (credit) represents a decrease in holdings, while a negative figure (debit) represents an increase in holdings. For liabilities, a positive figure shows an increase and a negative one a decrease. In principle, the sum of all the positive entries is identical to the sum of all negative entries, and the net balance (credits less debits) is zero, as in equation 3 below.

Balance of payment statistics cover: (a) transactions in goods, services, and income between Japan (residents) and the rest of the world (non-residents); (b) change of ownership and other changes in Japan's monetary gold, special drawing rights (SDRs), and claims on and liabilities to the rest of the world; and (c) unrequited transfers. The relationship between these items is summarized in the following identities (see Table 31.1):

$$\text{TB} + \text{SB} + \text{UT} = \text{Current Balance} \quad [1]$$

$$\text{TB} + \text{SB} + \text{UT} + \text{LTCB} = \text{Basic Balance} \quad [2]$$

$$\text{TB} + \text{SB} + \text{UT} + \text{LTCB} + \text{STCB} + \text{BMM} = 0 \quad \text{(theory only)} \quad [3]$$

$$\text{TB} + \text{SB} + \text{UT} + \text{LTCB} + \text{STCB} + \text{E\&O} = \text{BMM} = \text{Overall Balance} \quad [4]$$

TB: (Merchandise) Trade Balance
SB: Services Balance
UT: Unrequited Transfers
LTCB: Long-Term Capital Balance
STCB: Short-Term Capital Balance
E&O: Errors and Omissions
BMM: Balance on Monetary Movements

Table 31.1. Balance of Payments Statistics
Calendar Years 1987–1992, Billion $US

	1987	1988	1989	1990	1991	1992
Current account balance (A) = (B) + (C) + (D)	87.0	79.6	57.2	35.8	72.9	117.6
Trade balance (B)	96.4	95.0	76.9	63.5	103.0	132.3
Exports	224.6	259.8	269.6	280.4	306.6	330.9
Imports	128.2	164.8	192.7	216.8	203.5	198.5
Services balance (C)	–5.7	–11.3	–15.5	–22.3	–17.7	–10.1
Unrequited transfers (D)	–3.7	–4.1	–4.2	–5.5	–12.5	–4.7
Long-term capital balance (E)	–136.5	–130.9	–89.2	–43.6	37.1	–28.5
Basic balance (F) = (A) + (E)	–49.5	–51.3	–32.1	–7.8	110.0	89.1
Short-term capital balance (G)	23.9	19.5	20.8	21.5	–25.8	–7.0
Errors and omissions (H)	–3.9	2.8	–22.0	–20.9	–7.8	–10.5
Overall balance (I) = (F) + (G) + (H)	–29.5	–29.0	–33.3	–7.2	76.4	71.6
Above the line						
Below the line						
Balance of monetary movements (J) = (I)	–29.5	–29.0	–33.3	–7.2	76.4	71.6

Source: Bank of Japan.

The trade balance is the difference between the value of exports and imports of merchandise. Services consist of transportation, travel, investment income, and others. Unrequited transfers are unilateral, uncompensated transfers such as economic assistance to foreign countries. Long-term capital includes foreign financial assets and liabilities with maturities of more than one year, while short-term capital covers those with maturities of one year or less (except those covered under Monetary Movements).

Monetary Movements covers the short-term capital of the official sector (the government and BOJ) and authorized foreign exchange banks. In an exception to the usual rule, Balance of Monetary Movements is given with *reversed* sign (i.e. an increase in assets is represented by a positive sign). This is done purely for convenience, so that equation 4 can be written without a '–' sign in front of BMM (in equation 3, BMM is given with the usual sign). Overall Balance is equivalent to BMM, interpreted as a sum of balances.

Further details on each of the components in equation 4 are given below.

Trade Balance

The source of exports and imports of merchandise trade is the customs clearance statistics published by the Ministry of Finance. In BOP statistics, both exports and imports are recorded on a FOB basis, so the customs clearance values for imports (CIF basis) are adjusted by deducting estimated freight and insurance costs (from the time the goods were loaded until the time they arrive in Japan). Both export and imports are adjusted to account for the differences in coverage between the statistics. See the 'Features and Problems' section for further details.

Services Balance

Services consist of transportation, travel, investment income and others (see Table 31.2). Transportation covers international transportation of goods and passengers (including insurance), port disbursement, charterage, and other transportation. Travel covers expenditures by non-resident travellers in Japan (credits) and those by resident travellers overseas (debits). Investment income covers interest and dividends on direct investment, portfolio investment, deposits, money loans, trade credits, and external bond issuance. Others includes labor income and patent royalties.

Unrequited Transfers

Unrequited transfers includes gifts, donations, grants for economic assistance, government contributions to international organizations, remittance of annuities, income tax, legacies, sustenance, and migrants' funds. A surge in unrequited transfers in 1991 was the result of payments to the US in support of the Gulf War (see Fig. 31.1).

Table 31.2. Services Trade in Balance of Payments Statistics
Calendar Years 1987–1992, Billion $US

	1987	1988	1989	1990	1991	1992
Total						
Credits	79.6	111.8	143.9	165.8	188.5	193.9
Debits	85.3	123.0	159.4	188.1	206.2	204.0
Balance	–5.7	–11.3	–15.5	–22.3	–17.7	–10.1
Transportation						
Credits	13.0	15.5	18.1	18.1	19.6	20.3
Debits	19.1	23.0	25.8	27.6	29.9	30.3
Balance	–6.1	–7.4	–7.8	–9.5	–10.3	–10.0
Travel						
Credits	2.1	2.9	3.1	3.6	3.4	3.6
Debits	10.8	18.7	22.5	24.9	24.0	26.8
Balance	–8.7	–15.8	–19.3	–21.4	–20.5	–23.2
Investment income						
Credits	49.2	74.8	101.8	122.2	140.6	142.1
Debits	32.6	53.8	78.3	99.0	113.8	105.9
Balance	16.7	21.0	23.4	23.2	26.7	36.2
Others						
Credits	15.3	18.5	20.8	22.0	24.9	28.0
Debits	22.9	27.6	32.7	36.6	38.5	41.0
Balance	–7.6	–9.1	–11.9	–14.6	–13.6	–13.1

Source: Bank of Japan.

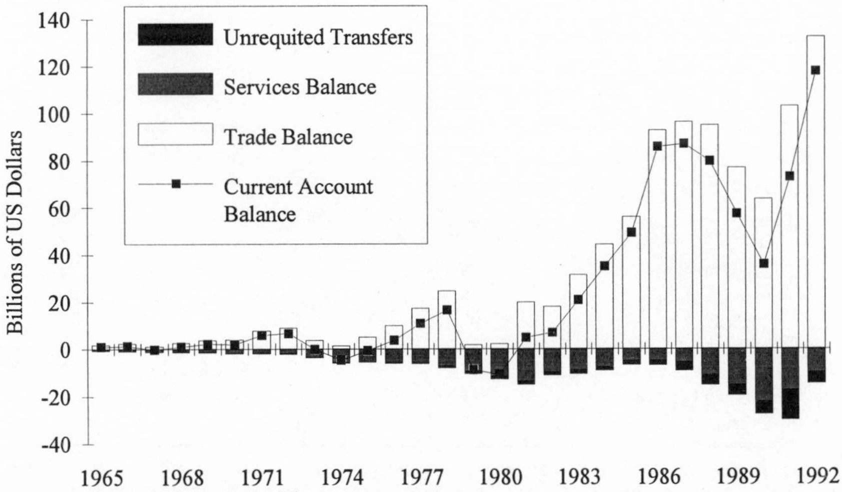

Fig. 31.1. Current Account Balance

Capital Account (Financial Items)

The capital account comprises all transactions which involve changes of legal ownership in Japan's foreign financial assets and liabilities (as well as some special cases such as SDRs and gold).

Long-term capital consists of direct investment, (long-term, i.e. more than one year) trade credits, loans, securities (excluding Gensaki transactions) and others (see Table 31.3). The short-term capital account includes (short-term) trade credits, loans, securities (including Gensaki transactions) and others.

Balance of Monetary Movements

Monetary movements covers the short-term external assets and liabilities of the government and BOJ (gold and foreign exchange reserves) and the authorized

Table 31.3. Long-Term Capital Balance in Balance of Payments Statistics
Calendar Years 1987–1992, Billion $US

	1987	1988	1989	1990	1991	1992
Assets	132.8	149.9	192.1	120.8	121.4	58.0
Direct investment	19.5	34.2	44.1	48.0	30.7	17.2
Trade credits extended	0.5	6.9	4.0	−0.7	−3.9	−5.3
Loans extended	16.2	15.2	22.5	22.2	13.1	7.6
Securities	87.8	86.9	113.2	39.7	74.3	34.4
Stocks	16.9	3.0	17.9	6.3	3.6	−3.0
Bonds	72.9	85.8	94.1	29.0	68.2	35.6
Yen-denominated bonds etc.	−2.0	−1.9	1.2	4.5	2.5	1.7
Others	8.8	6.6	8.3	11.6	7.2	4.0
Liabilities	−3.7	19.0	102.9	77.2	158.5	29.5
Direct investment	1.2	−0.5	−1.1	1.8	1.4	2.7
Trade credits received	−0.0	−0.0	−0.0	−0.0	−0.0	−0.0
Loans received	−0.1	−0.1	17.8	39.1	38.1	15.9
Securities	−6.1	20.3	85.1	34.7	115.3	8.2
Stocks	−42.8	6.8	7.0	−13.3	46.8	8.7
Bonds	6.7	−21.6	2.4	17.0	21.2	−8.2
External bonds	30.1	35.1	75.7	30.9	47.3	7.6
Others	1.3	−0.8	1.0	1.7	3.7	2.7
Balance	−136.5	−130.9	−89.2	−43.6	37.1	−28.5
Direct investment	−18.4	−34.7	−45.2	−46.3	−29.4	−14.5
Trade credits	−0.5	−7.0	−4.0	0.7	3.9	5.3
Loans	−16.3	−15.3	−4.7	16.9	25.0	8.3
Securities	−93.8	−66.7	−28.0	−5.0	41.0	−26.2
Stocks	−59.7	3.8	−10.9	−19.5	43.1	11.7
Bonds	−66.2	−107.4	−91.7	−12.0	−47.0	−43.8
Other bonds etc.	32.1	37.0	74.5	26.5	44.8	5.9
Others	−7.5	−7.3	−7.3	−9.9	−3.5	−1.3

Note: For items in 'assets' and 'balance', (+) indicates outflow of capital and (−) indicates inflow of capital. For items in 'liabilities', (+) indicates inflow of capital and (−) indicates outflow of capital.

foreign exchange bank sector. These items are ordinarily included in the short-term capital account, but Japan separates them out (and uses reversed sign in equation 4 above) so that the amount of foreign exchange available is readily apparent. In the 1950s and early 1960s, Japan had a chronic shortage of foreign exchange, so great emphasis was placed on monitoring and maintaining foreign exchange reserves. When presented as in Table 31.1, a line is drawn between Balance of Monetary Movements and all the other items, showing that it has been separated out. Thus Balance of Monetary Movements is called 'below the line' while all the other items are called 'above the line'.

Errors and Omissions

In principle, the sum of all the entries in the balance of payments statement should sum to zero, as in equation 3. In practice, due to various errors and inconsistencies in the estimates as well as omissions (due to time-lags and other reasons) from the statement, the sum inevitably shows a net credit or debit. Thus, a separate item called Errors and Omissions is included to offset (cancel out) the credit or debit.

Available Statistics

Denomination of Currencies

Figures in major categories of BOP statistics are available both in $US and yen terms. Figures for detailed items are available only in $US.

Seasonal Adjustment

Seasonally adjusted figures are obtained by the Census X-11 method. Figures for investment income are not seasonally adjusted. Seasonally adjusted figures other than investment income and original figures for investment income are summed up to obtain seasonally adjusted figures for services balance, current account balance, and overall balance.

Regional Balance of Payments

Regional balance of payments are reported twice a year in the April and November issues of *Balance of Payments Monthly* (see Table 31.4).

External Assets and Liabilities of Japan

External assets and liabilities of Japan are available in the April issue (see Table 31.5). Note that the increase in net foreign assets (before valuation adjustments) is equal to the deficit in the capital account (including BMM), which is equal to the current account surplus (plus errors and omissions). The figures in Table 31.5 include an adjustment for changes in the valuation of outstanding foreign assets and liabilities.

Table 31.4. Balance of Payments by Region
Calendar Year 1992, Billion $US

	Current Account Balance	Trade Balance	Services Balance	Long-term Capital Balance
Total	117.6	132.3	−10.1	−28.5
OECD countries	80.6	88.2	−6.3	−37.5
USA	44.5	50.2	−4.8	−27.2
Canada	2.0	−0.0	2.1	−2.1
EC	37.4	39.4	−1.9	−6.7
France	−0.3	1.6	−1.9	−0.6
Germany	10.0	10.3	−0.3	−3.9
Italy	−0.4	0.0	−0.4	0.5
UK	7.6	13.5	−5.7	−1.8
Australia	−2.7	−4.2	1.6	2.0
South-East Asia	43.6	50.0	−5.6	12.1
NIEs	41.6	48.4	−7.0	13.5
Russia, China, Eastern Europe, etc.	−4.8	−4.4	−0.1	−1.7
China	−4.0	−3.4	−0.4	0.1
USSR	−1.3	−1.1	−0.1	−1.2
Others	−3.7	−1.4	−1.3	−3.8
International organization	1.9	--	3.1	−1.2
Not included elsewhere	--	--	--	3.7

Note: NIEs consist of Korea, Taiwan, Hong Kong, and Singapore. Russia, China, Eastern Europe, etc. includes: Albania; Bulgaria; Cambodia; PR China; Czechoslovakia; Hungary; DPR Korea; former USSR countries; Lao PDR; Mongolia; Poland; Romania; and Vietnam.

Source: Bank of Japan, *Balance of Payments Monthly* (April 1993), 81-2.

Features and Problems

Growth in Services, Especially Investment Income

Trade in services has been growing rapidly, and imports of services now roughly equal merchandise imports. Investment income accounts for 75 and 50 percent of exports and imports of services, respectively, and has grown as the result of the increase in Japan's external assets and liabilities (see Table 31.5).

Change in Item in Capital Transaction

Beginning in January 1995, the Bank of Japan and the Ministry of Finance are going to unify two items (long-term and short-term capital balances) into a single item 'capital balance'. This is the current practice in the United States.

Relation between BOP and SNA Statistics

'Net increase in claims on foreign assets' in the system of national accounts (SNA) corresponds to the current account surplus in terms of yen in BOP statistics (see Tables 2.15 and 2.16).

Table 31.5. External Assets and Liabilities of Japan
End-of-Calendar Years 1987–1992, Billion $US

	1987	1988	1989	1990	1991	1992
Total external assets	1,071.6	1,469.3	1,771.0	1,857.9	2,006.5	2,035.2
Long-term assets	646.2	832.7	1,019.2	1,096.1	1,247.8	1,315.6
Private sector	565.1	728.2	901.7	973.6	1,090.1	1,132.2
Direct investment	77.0	110.8	154.4	201.4	231.8	248.1
Trade credits	37.2	48.8	52.9	47.1	47.3	44.6
Loans	97.5	123.7	137.1	130.1	141.2	143.4
Securities	339.7	427.2	533.8	563.8	632.1	655.5
Others	13.7	17.7	23.6	31.2	37.6	40.7
Government sector	81.1	104.5	117.5	122.5	157.8	183.4
Trade credits	1.7	1.9	1.8	1.4	1.5	1.4
Loans	43.1	55.6	60.5	60.9	77.3	88.3
Others	36.3	47.0	55.3	60.1	79.0	93.7
Short-term assets	425.4	636.7	751.8	761.8	758.7	719.7
Private sector	343.3	538.8	666.7	682.1	685.4	646.9
Monetary movements	320.2	502.3	627.8	644.5	640.8	599.9
Others	23.1	36.5	38.9	37.5	44.6	47.0
Government sector	82.2	97.9	85.1	79.7	73.3	72.8
Monetary movements	82.2	97.9	85.1	79.7	73.3	72.8
Others	0.0	0.0	0.0	0.0	0.0	0.0
Total external liabilities	830.9	1,177.6	1,477.8	1,529.8	1,623.4	1,521.6
Long-term liabilities	236.2	311.6	447.5	464.0	647.4	658.5
Private sector	178.8	268.4	405.5	408.1	565.2	578.8
Direct investment	9.0	10.4	9.2	9.9	12.3	15.5
Trade credits	0.0	0.0	0.0	0.0	0.0	0.0
Loans	1.1	1.1	18.9	58.0	99.7	119.7
Securities	166.2	254.9	374.0	334.5	443.8	431.4
Others	2.5	2.0	3.4	5.7	9.4	12.2
Government sector	57.4	43.2	42.0	55.9	82.2	79.6
Loans	0.0	0.0	0.0	0.0	0.0	0.0
Securities	57.3	43.2	42.0	55.9	82.2	79.6
Others	--	--	--	--	--	--
Short-term liabilities	594.7	866.0	1,030.3	1,065.8	976.0	863.2
Private sector	583.1	851.0	1,004.1	1,028.8	924.7	807.2
Monetary movements	530.1	765.2	894.7	898.9	803.5	684.7
Others	53.0	85.8	109.4	129.9	121.1	122.5
Government sector	11.6	15.0	26.2	37.0	51.4	55.9
Monetary movements	3.9	5.1	17.0	28.8	42.9	46.6
Others	7.7	9.9	9.2	8.2	8.5	9.3
Net external assets	240.7	291.7	293.2	328.1	383.1	513.6
Private sector	146.5	147.6	158.8	218.8	285.5	393.1
Government sector	94.3	144.2	134.4	109.2	97.5	120.6

Source: Bank of Japan.

Differences between BOP and Customs Clearance Statistics

As mentioned above, merchandise exports and imports in customs clearance statistics are adjusted to account for the difference in the valuation of imports (CIF vs. FOB in balance of payments) and for differences in coverage (for example, the value of reimports are excluded from BOP statistics because residents maintain ownership, but are included in customs clearance statistics because the goods pass through customs). Table 31.6 shows the difference between BOP and customs clearance values (as a percentage of the customs clearance values).

While the difference for exports is relatively stable at 1–2 percent of the customs values, that of imports has varied substantially in the past few years. The fluctuation in the difference for imports can be largely explained by 'gold savings accounts'. These accounts were popular because of regulations on short-term interest rates available to small depositors (see Chapter 48). By using arbitrage in the gold futures market, it was possible to earn a higher rate of return than a small depositor could get at banks.

These accounts appeared as imports of gold in the BOP statistics, but did not appear in customs clearance statistics because nothing physically passed through customs. This had the effect of narrowing the gap between BOP and customs clearance imports in 1989–90. The gold accounts lost momentum with the economic slowdown in 1991, and the creation of Money Management Fund (MMF) accounts in 1992 made them obsolete. The resulting decrease in gold savings accounts was recorded as a reduction of gold imports in BOP statistics in 1991 and 1992, which widened the difference with customs clearance statistics.

Treatment of Retained Earnings in Foreign Affiliates

The *Balance of Payments Manual* (fourth edition) suggests that the accumulation

Table 31.6. Difference between BOP and Customs Clearance Statistics
Calendar Years 1983–1992,
Percent of Customs Clearance Values

	Exports	Imports
1983	–1.0	–9.8
1984	–1.1	–9.1
1985	–0.9	–8.9
1986	–1.7	–10.8
1987	–2.0	–14.2
1988	–1.9	–12.1
1989	–2.0	–8.6
1990	–2.3	–7.6
1991	–2.5	–14.0
1992	–2.6	–14.8

Sources: Ministry of Finance, Bank of Japan.

of retained earnings in foreign subsidiaries be included in direct investment (capital account) and investment income (current account), as if retained earnings in a foreign subsidiary were repatriated to the home country and then reinvested in the affiliate. In Japan, these retained earnings are currently not recorded in either the capital or current accounts. When the standards in the fifth edition of the manual are adopted in January 1995, Japan is expected to revise this approach.

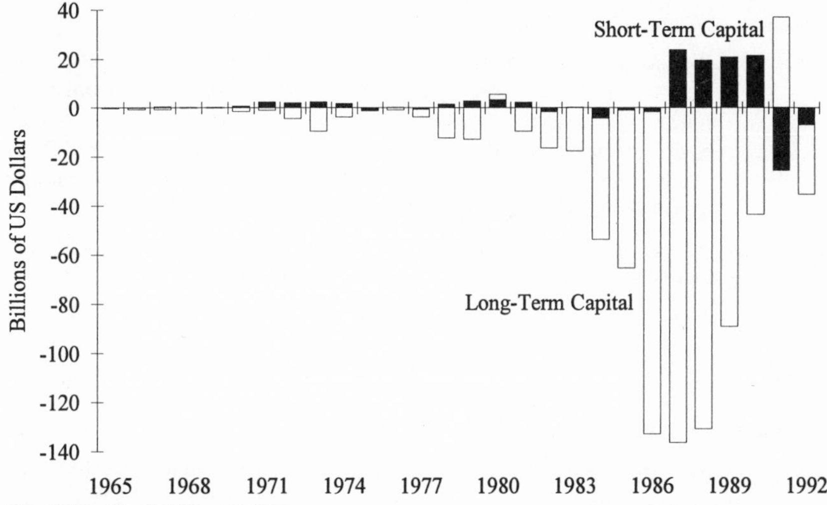

Fig. 31.2. Capital Transactions

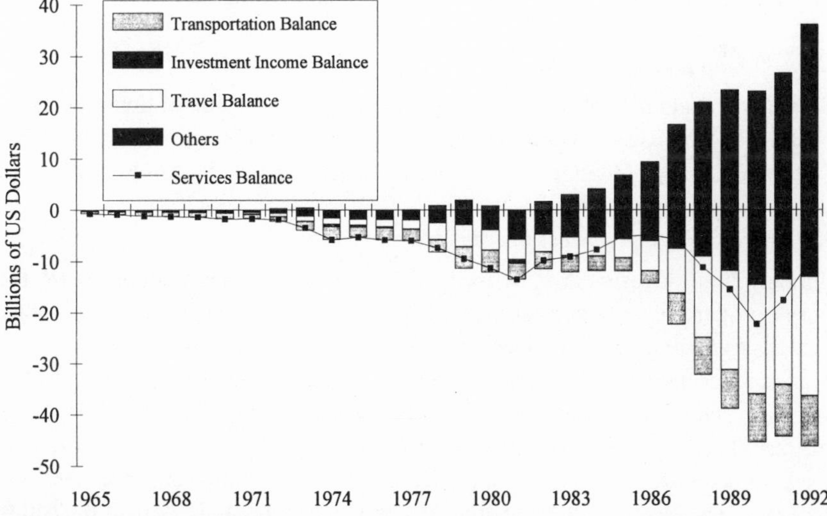

Fig. 31.3. Service Transactions

32 Foreign Direct Investment

Source: International Finance Bureau, Ministry of Finance.

Frequency: Monthly, semi-annual, and annual.

Release: Figures are released at the beginning of each month with a two-month lag. They are available in *Monthly Finance Review* published by the Ministry of Finance. Semi-annual figures are released in June and December. Annual figures for the previous fiscal year are available in *Financial Statistics of Japan* and occasionally in the December issue of *Monthly Report of Fiscal and Monetary Statistics* both published by the Ministry of Finance.

Availability: Annual figures are available for 1951 onward for outward direct investment, and 1950 onward for inward direct investment.

Details

Monthly Release

Monthly figures reveal only the number of investments, the value of total investment, and the value of investment by type. Values are available both in $US and yen (*Monthly Finance Review* gives only $US values). There are no figures by country; they are available only in the semi-annual and annual releases.

Semi-Annual and Annual Release

Semi-annual and annual releases reveal the number and value of investments by country and industry. More detailed figures are available occasionally in the December issue of *Monthly Report of Fiscal and Monetary Statistics*.

Definition of Foreign Direct Investment

Foreign direct investment is defined as investment in foreign countries for the purpose of managerial control or participation in management of foreign companies. *Indirect* investment does not involve managerial control.

In practice, the distinction between direct and indirect investment is unclear. In Japanese statistics, outward direct investment (in foreign countries by Japanese residents) includes: (1) acquisition of securities issued by foreign companies; (2) loans to a foreign company; and (3) investments for establishing branches and factories. Usually, the Japanese company must own more than 10% of the equity of the foreign company in order to be included in foreign direct investment. If the relationship between the two companies is close enough, the investment will be included in direct investment even if the Japanese company owns less than 10% of equity (or even no equity). Having a Japanese board member, long-term contracts between two companies on purchases of goods, provision of technology, and agency operations are all regarded as a basis for outward foreign direct investment.

The definition for inward direct investment (in Japan by foreigners) is somewhat different. Payments for opening and expanding branches are not included, and loans were not included until March 1985. Acquisition of non-listed stocks and foreign ownership worth less than 10% of equity has been excluded since January 1992.

Coverage

Prior to the enactment of the new Foreign Exchange and Foreign Trade Control Law in December 1980, outward and inward foreign direct investment had required approval from the Ministry of Finance. Afterward, the MOF simply had to be notified prior to the investment. This advance notice requirement was, in principle, replaced by ex-post notification in January 1992 for inward direct investment.

The statistics cover only transactions which require notification to the MOF. Investments worth less than 30 million yen are not included in the statistics. Acquisitions of real estate in foreign countries by Japanese residents have not been included in the statistics since December 1980.

Timing of Entry

Entries are recorded not on the date of investment, but on the date of acceptance by the MOF. There is usually a lag between the time of entry and the actual

Table 32.1. Foreign Direct Investment
Fiscal Years 1987–1992, Million $US

	1987	1988	1989	1990	1991	1992
Inward direct investment by foreigners						
Total	2,214	3,243	2,860	2,778	4,339	4,084
Acquisition of stocks and ownership	1,453	2,576	1,941	2,585	3,164	2,792
Loans	761	667	919	193	1,175	1,292
Outward direct investment by Japanese						
Total	33,364	47,023	67,540	56,911	41,584	34,137
Acquisition of stocks, ownership, and corporate bonds	19,941	28,638	43,169	38,507	27,129	21,667
Loans	12,971	17,801	23,632	17,598	13,991	12,110
Payments for opening and expanding branches, etc.	452	584	739	806	464	360

Note: For inward direct investments, acquisitions involving less than 10% of ownership (equity) are excluded from January 1992 onward.

Source: Ministry of Finance.

disbursement. Even for a multiple-year investment, the entire value of the investment is recorded on the acceptance date.

Investment by Country and Industry

Semi-annual and annual releases reveal the value and number of direct investments by country (see Table 32.2 and Fig. 32.2) and by industry (see Table 32.3). The cumulative outstanding value and number of investments from fiscal 1951 onward (1950 for inward investment) is also available. This is simply the sum of the past investment flows; no valuation adjustment is made for depreciation, obsolescence, or exchange rate fluctuation.

Table 32.2. Foreign Direct Investment by Country
Fiscal Year 1992, Million $US, unless otherwise noted

	Outward Investment [Destination]	Percent of Total	Inward Investment [Origination]	Percent of Total
Total	34,138	100.0	4,084	100.0
North America	14,572	42.7	1,424	34.9
US	13,819	40.5	1,337	32.7
Canada	753	2.2	87	2.1
Latin America	2,726	8.0	756	18.5
Panama	938	2.7	28	0.7
Asia	6,425	18.8	99	2.4
Korea	225	0.7	12	0.3
Taiwan	292	0.9	25	0.6
Hong Kong	735	2.2	38	0.9
Singapore	670	2.0	18	0.4
Malaysia	704	2.1	0	0.0
Thailand	657	1.9	0	0.0
Philippines	160	0.5	0	0.0
Indonesia	1,676	4.9	0	0.0
China	1,070	3.1	5	0.1
Europe	7,061	20.7	1,450	35.5
UK	2,948	8.6	254	6.2
Switzerland	144	0.4	513	12.6
Netherlands	1,446	4.2	207	5.1
Germany	769	2.3	125	3.1
France	456	1.3	167	4.1
Spain	332	1.0	0	0.0
Belgium	281	0.8	109	2.7
Italy	216	0.6	3	0.1
Middle East	709	2.1	10	0.2
Africa	238	0.7	13	0.3
Oceania	2,406	7.0	0	0.0
Australia	2,150	6.3	0	0.0
New Zealand	67	0.2	0	0.0
Foreign firms in Japan	--	--	334	8.2

Source: Ministry of Finance.

Table 32.3. Foreign Direct Investment by Industry
Fiscal Year 1992, Million $US, unless otherwise noted

	Outward Investment [Destination]	Percent of Total	Inward Investment [Origination]	Percent of Total
Total	34,138	100.0	4,085	100.0
Manufacturing	10,057	29.5	1,609	39.4
Food	517	1.5	9	0.2
Apparel and textile	428	1.3	5	0.1
Lumber and pulp	431	1.3	n.a.	n.a.
Chemical	2,015	5.9	710	17.4
Steel and nonferrous metal	824	2.4	40	1.0
General machinery	1,104	3.2	653	16.0
Electric machinery	1,817	5.3	n.a.	n.a.
Transportation machinery	1,188	3.5	n.a.	n.a.
Others	1,732	5.1	192	4.7
Non-manufacturing	23,720	69.5	2,476	60.6
Agriculture and forestry	139	0.4	n.a.	n.a.
Fishery and acquatic	91	0.3	n.a.	n.a.
Mining	1,270	3.7	n.a.	n.a.
Construction	534	1.6	0	0.0
Wholesale and retail trade	3,705	10.9	1,194	29.2
Finance and insurance	4,579	13.4	147	3.6
Services	6,530	19.1	823	20.1
Transportation	1,725	5.1	19	0.5
Real estate	5,147	15.1	230	5.6
Others	0	0.0	63	1.5
Branch opening and expansion	360	1.1	--	--

Source: Ministry of Finance.

Features and Problems

Large Share of Non-Manufacturing Sector in Outward Investment

It is worth noting that non-manufacturing sectors account for around 70 percent of the total value of outward direct investment by Japanese. The finance and insurance, wholesale and retail trade, service, and real estate industries are the four major investors, accounting for nearly 60 percent of the total value invested in fiscal 1992.

Balance of Payments Statistics and Foreign Direct Investment

There are two source statistics on foreign direct investment: Balance of Payments Statistics from the Bank of Japan (hereafter, BOP statistics, see Chapter 31) and Foreign Direct Investment Statistics from the Ministry of Finance (hereafter, MOF statistics). Differences between these two statistics are explained below (also see Fig. 32.1).

1. Differences in Coverage

The MOF statistics are based on the notifications submitted to the MOF (notification basis), while the BOP statistics are compiled based on the reports on invisible trade receipts and payments from the authorized foreign exchange banks submitted to the Bank of Japan (disbursement basis). The notification to the MOF should be in advance of the investment and the entire value is recorded in the initial entry. The MOF statistics also include investments that are suspended or reduced after the notification. These factors result in overestimation in the MOF statistics.

2. Minimum Denomination for Reporting

The MOF statistics exclude investments of 30 million yen or less, while the BOP statistics exclude those with value of 5 million yen or less.

3. Acquisition of Real Estate

The MOF does not require notification of acquisition of real estate (and thus it is not included in the statistics), while the BOP statistics include real estate purchased for business purposes in foreign countries by Japanese residents.

4. Payments to Overseas Branches

The MOF statistics only cover payments for opening and expanding branches, while the BOP statistics also cover payments for establishment of businesses, additional operating funds, repayment of loans and redemption of debt securities by the foreign subsidiary, and the closure or trimming of business operations.

5. Loans for Mines Overseas

The MOF statistics include loans, cash payments, and payments in kind to foreign mine operators from which the Japanese counterpart will import minerals, petroleum, or gas by offsetting the loans disbursed in advance. The BOP statistics treat these loans as 'loans' rather than as 'direct investment'.

Limited Coverage of the Statistics

As mentioned above, the distinction between direct and indirect investment is unclear. For example, when a Japanese subsidiary located in a tax haven country makes an investment in a third country, it is usually not included in Japan's foreign direct investment.

A construction project by a Japanese company in a foreign country (without establishing a subsidiary) or by a joint-venture which does not possess a corporate entity would not be counted as foreign direct investment. On the other hand, if a Japanese company establishes a subsidiary or a joint-venture owning a corporate entity, remittances from Japan to the subsidiary or the joint-venture are included in foreign direct investment.

Fund raising (bank borrowings, issue of debt securities and stocks) by foreign subsidiaries of Japanese companies is not included in foreign direct investment.

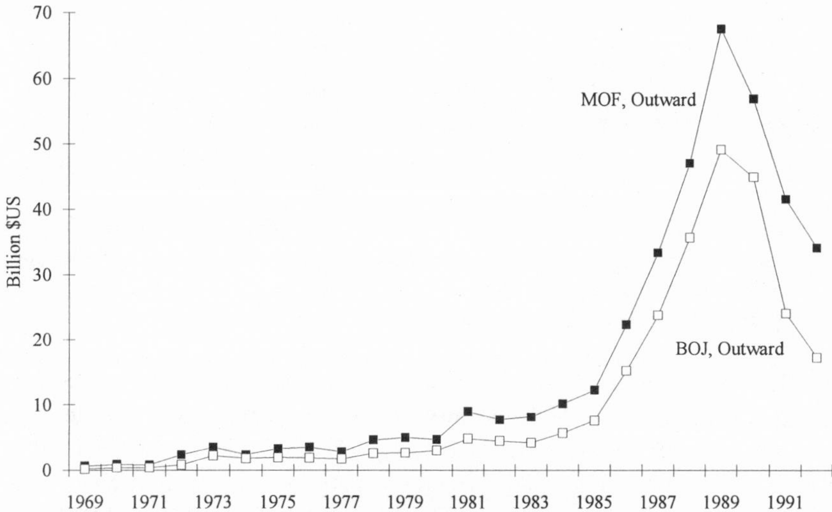

Fig. 32.1. Comparison of Foreign Direct Investment Statistics

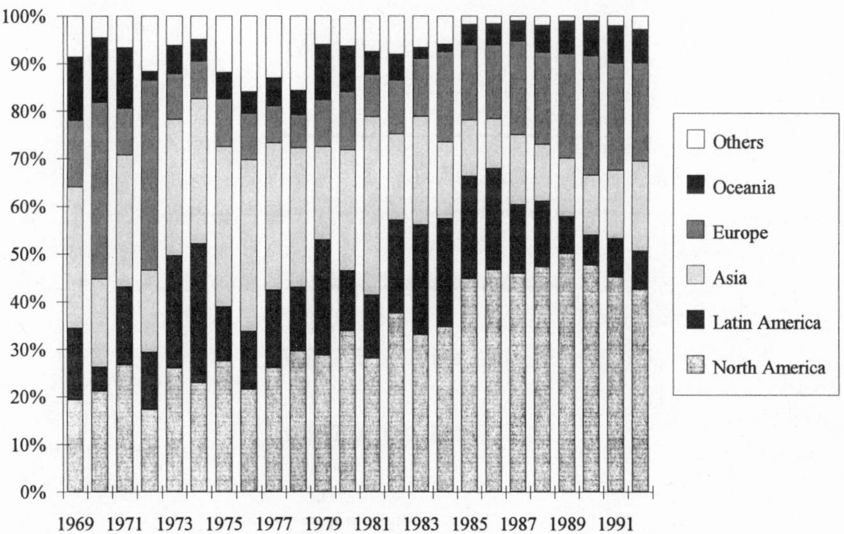

Fig. 32.2. Outward Direct Investment by Destination

33 Survey on Foreign Business Activity of Japanese Firms

Source:	Ministry of International Trade and Industry.
Frequency:	Annual (questionnaire is usually in fiscal year terms).
Release:	The survey is conducted every March, and the results are released in March of the following year.
Availability:	Survey results are available since fiscal 1970. The questionnaires are subject to change, reflecting the prevailing economic environment. New questionnaires on capital investment of foreign affiliates, destination, and sources of affiliates' exports and imports are available only for recent years.

The Survey on Foreign Business Activity of Japanese Firms provides statistics regarding the operation of Japanese firms overseas. It contains basic statistics such as outward investment of parent companies and sales, profits, and capital investment of overseas affiliates; certain detailed information, such as foreign production to consolidated sales ratio, and the ratio of host country- to- total procurement of parts by industry, is also available. Although the data may not be fully reliable due to possible sampling biases, this survey is extremely useful for analyzing the overseas business activities of Japanese companies, especially manufacturing companies.

Details

Coverage and Methodology of the Survey

MITI sends questionnaires to Japanese parent companies regarding the operation of their overseas affiliates as of March every year. Finance, insurance, and real estate companies are excluded from the survey. Sub-classifications in manufacturing industries are available for most survey results.

A company is designated as a foreign affiliate if more than 10% of its stock is held by the Japanese parent company, and a subsidiary if more than 50% is held. All questions are asked in terms of fiscal year. When a company's accounting year is different from the fiscal year, it is asked to use the available accounting year which overlaps the fiscal year the most. Companies not giving answers are omitted when calculating various ratios. The average foreign exchange rate is used for conversion.

In the fiscal 1991 survey (conducted as of the end of March 1992), 1,789 parent companies out of the 3,368 companies surveyed responded. Among the 1,789 respondents, 15 had already retreated from the foreign market and 111 were outside the covered industries. The remaining 1,663 parent companies have 8,505 foreign affiliates as of March 1992 (see Tables 33.1 and 33.2).

Table 33.1. Foreign Business Activities of Japanese Companies By Industry of Parent Companies
Fiscal 1991 (March 1992) Survey

	Number of Companies	Exports to Affiliates (% of Total)	Imports from Affiliates (% of Total)
Total	1,663	48.9	27.4
Agriculture, forestry, and fishery	18	8.8	41.7
Mining	28	11.0	10.2
Construction	63	18.7	12.1
Manufacturing	1,008	53.7	26.5
Food	43	19.6	27.8
Apparel	51	6.3	28.2
Wood, paper, and pulp	24	4.7	23.8
Chemical	127	29.2	7.2
Steel	28	5.2	4.5
Nonferrous metals	29	29.1	8.7
General machinery	108	39.4	23.6
Electrical machinery	206	59.0	36.1
Transportation machinery	119	55.1	21.3
Precision machinery	49	77.1	43.8
Petroleum and coal	14	17.9	29.9
Others	210	53.0	30.7
Commerce	344	27.3	28.5
Services	95	13.1	16.7
Others	107	10.2	55.9

Note: Exports to Affiliates = percent of exports to affiliates in total exports of the parent companies, and likewise for imports.

Source: Ministry of International Trade and Industry.

Other available statistics on affiliates include:

1. Outstanding investment and loans by parent company to affiliates.
2. Percentage of shares held by parent company.
3. Sales and profits (estimates) [Fig. 33.3].
4. Foreign production ratio [Figs. 33.1 and 33.2].
5. Destination countries of exports [Fig. 33.4].
6. Originating countries of imports [Fig. 33.5].
7. Capital investment.
8. Numbers of employees.
9. Community activities.

Table 33.2. Foreign Affiliates of Japanese Parent Companies by Area and Industry
Fiscal 1991 (March 1992) Survey

	NA	LA	AA	ME	EU	OC	AF	Total
Total	2,399	584	3,156	51	1,785	407	123	8,505
Agriculture, forestry, and fishery	18	22	33	0	9	16	2	100
Mining	46	6	10	5	12	39	3	121
Construction	49	16	147	9	24	7	3	255
Manufacturing	845	203	1,828	12	530	87	23	3,528
Food	52	11	67	0	10	15	2	157
Apparel	13	25	132	0	9	4	2	185
Wood, paper, and pulp	27	7	20	0	2	5	0	61
Chemical	107	23	280	2	75	7	1	495
Steel	42	7	62	2	3	1	4	121
Nonferrous metals	32	4	49	0	5	4	1	95
General machinery	80	20	113	1	70	7	0	291
Electrical machinery	192	49	489	4	187	13	6	940
Transportation machinery	124	24	200	1	57	15	4	425
Precision machinery	38	7	77	0	14	3	0	139
Petroleum and coal	4	3	8	0	2	1	0	18
Others	134	23	331	2	96	12	3	601
Commerce	785	147	672	22	811	138	14	2,589
Services	202	42	197	3	116	53	6	619
Others	454	148	269	0	283	67	72	1,293

Note: *NA* North America, *LA* Latin America, *AA* Asia, *ME* Middle East, *EU* Europe, *OC* Oceania, *AF* Africa.

Source: Ministry of International Trade and Industry.

Features and Problems

Sampling Biases and Discontinuity in Series

The response ratio for this survey is low, and it is not known whether the sample accurately represents all Japanese companies having foreign affiliates. Because the sample changes every year, it is not recommended to use the raw level figures for time series comparison.

Foreign Production Ratio on the Rise

The 'foreign production ratio' for manufacturing companies is the ratio of 'sales of foreign affiliates' to 'total domestic sales' of the parent companies. It rose to 6.6% in fiscal 1992 (estimate) from 1.6% in fiscal 1978 (see Fig. 33.1). The ratio suddenly decreased from 1984 to 1985 (the result of the yen's sudden rise in 1985, which had the effect of reducing the yen value of foreign affiliates' sales), but continued to increase afterward. The increase in the foreign production ratio is particularly striking for the machinery industries (see Fig. 33.2).

Destination of Sales and Source of Procurement

Destination of sales and source of procurement of the foreign affiliates are available by area and by sub-classified industry for manufacturing. As shown in the Fig. 33.4, the Japanese foreign affiliates in the US and Europe have about 90% of their sales in their host country, but less than 60% for the affiliates in Asian countries.

One of the politically controversial issues in international trade is procurement by Japanese foreign affiliates. In response to sharp criticism, mainly from the US, the Japanese affiliates have increased their share of materials procured from their host country to 48.1% in fiscal 1991 from 40.1% in fiscal 1986 (see Fig. 33.5).

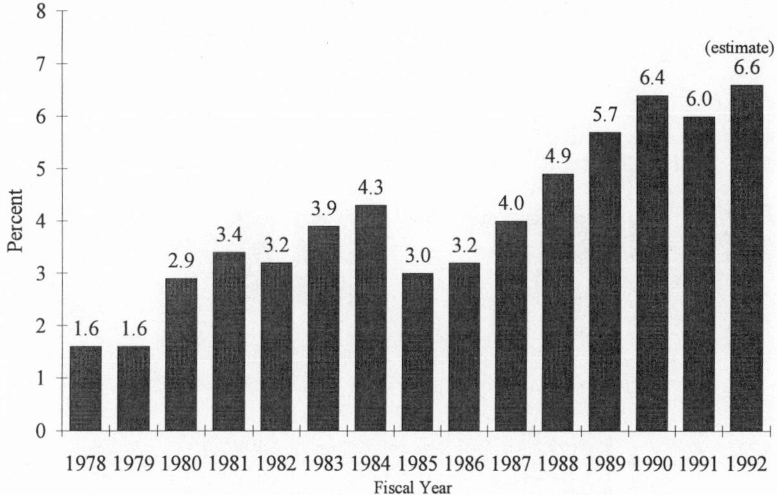

Fig. 33.1. Foreign Production Ratio of Japanese Manufacturing Companies

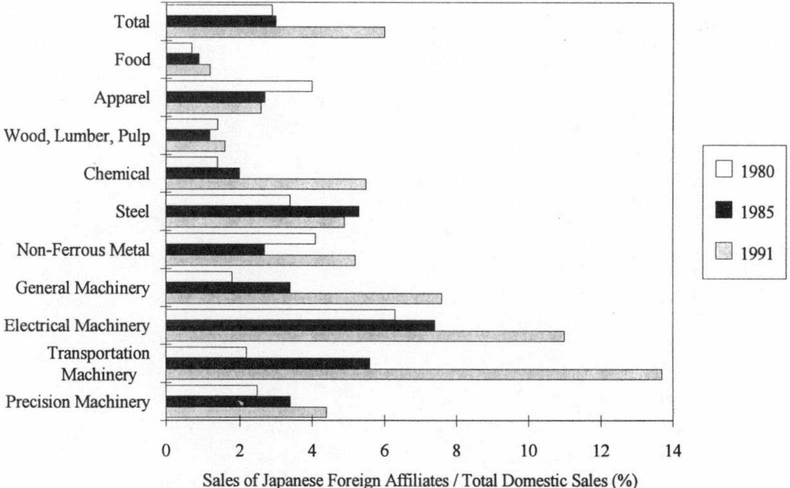

Fig. 33.2. Foreign Production Ratio of Japanese Manufacturing Companies, by Industry

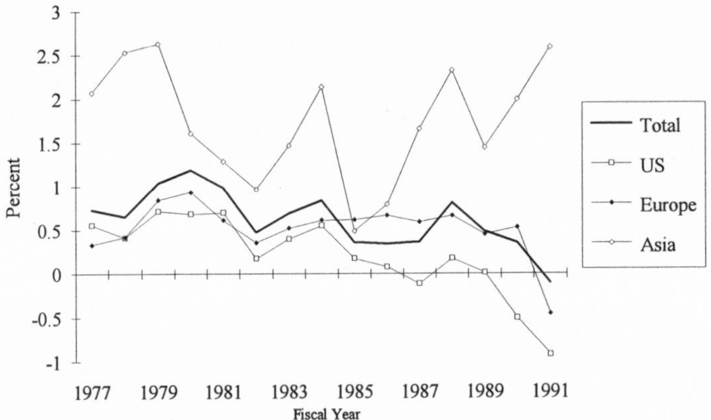

Fig. 33.3. After-tax Profit to Sales Ratio of Japanese Foreign Affiliates

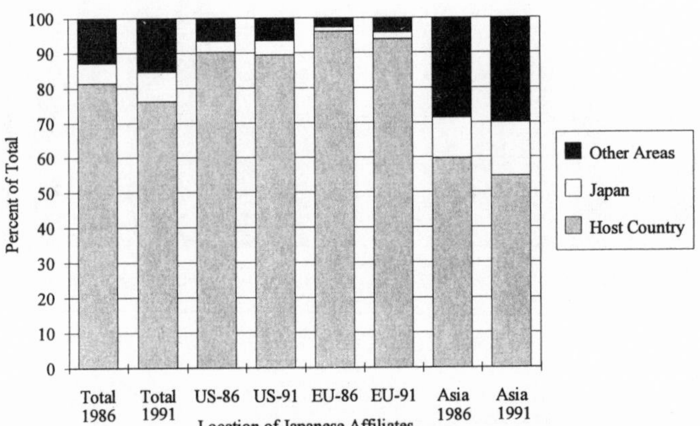

Fig. 33.4. Destination of Sales of Japanese Affiliates

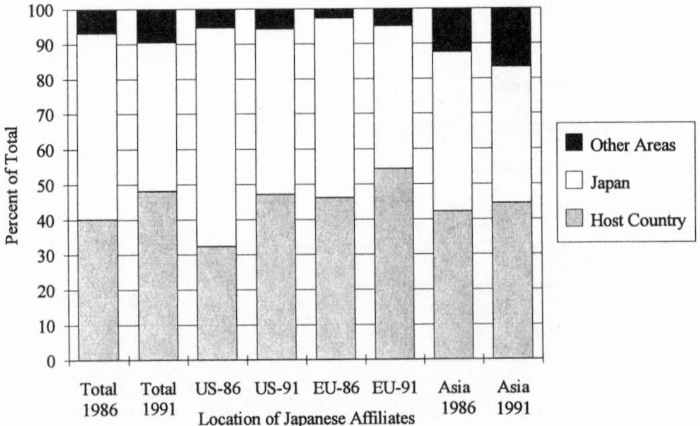

Fig. 33.5. Source of Procurement of Japanese Affiliates

Government Sector

34 Government Budget

Source: Ministry of Finance.

Frequency: Annual. Fiscal year starts on 1 April and ends 31 March.

Release: The central government budget is approved by the Diet, usually in the latter half of March or the beginning of April. A supplementary budget is usually adopted during the fiscal year.

Availability: Historical series are available in *Fiscal Statistics* (available in Japanese only and not listed in Appendix 3) published by the Ministry of Finance.

Details

Types of Budgets

The central (national) government has three types of budgets: (1) general account budget; (2) special accounts budget; and (3) government agency budget. The general accounts budget controls basic revenues and disbursements. The special account budget consists of numerous independent accounts (38 as of fiscal 1993). Some special accounts are for specific projects, such as airport construction, while others fund specific expenditures with specific revenues, such as social security. The government agency budget covers government agencies which are wholly owned by the nation. These three types of budgets all require approval by the Diet. The term 'government budget' usually refers to the general account budget only.

Drafting and Approval of the General Account Budget

The Cabinet, especially the minister of finance, is responsible for organization of the general account budget and its submission to the Diet. Typically, in July the Ministry of Finance (MOF) proposes a ceiling on the budget of each ministry and government agency. Under this constraint, each ministry and agency submits its budget request to the MOF in August. After negotiations, the MOF presents a draft to the cabinet, which approves it in late December. The Cabinet plan is submitted to the House of Representatives (Lower House) around the end of January. The budget is usually approved by the Diet around the end of March (end of the fiscal year). In practice, there is usually little difference between the MOF draft submitted to the Cabinet and the budget finally approved.

Provisional Budget

In case the budget is not approved by the end of March, the Cabinet prepares a provisional budget so that it can avoid interruptions in the day-to-day operations of the government. After the Diet approves the actual budget, it supersedes the provisional budget. Any disbursement in the provisional budget is treated as disbursement in the actual budget.

Supplementary Budget

A supplementary budget is organized when it becomes 'necessary' to change the budget after it is approved. Supplementary budget funds are often used to increase public investment or for restoration following natural disasters, as well as civil servant pay increases. A supplementary budget has been organized every year recently (see Fig. 34.1). The expenditures in the supplementary budget are covered by government securities issuance or other (sometimes unspecified) sources.

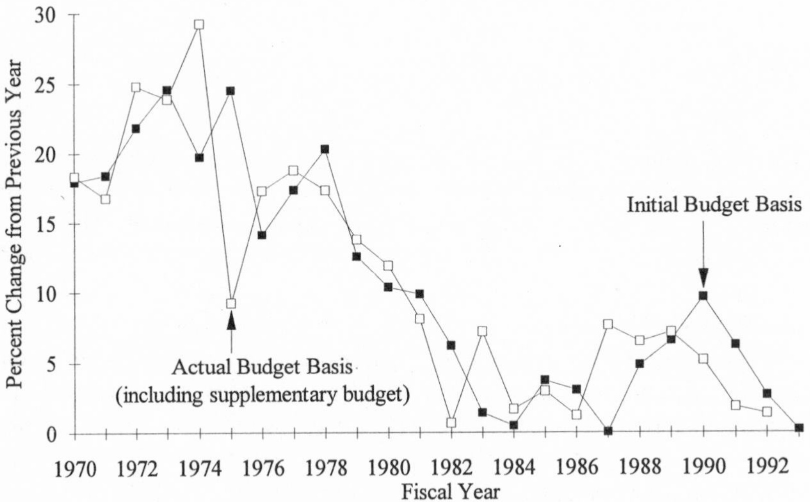

Note: Figure for FY 1992 Actual Budget Basis is an estimate.

Fig. 34.1. General Account Budget Disbursements

General Account Budget Revenues and Disbursements

Tables 34.1 and 34.2 show General Account Budget revenues and disbursements. Distribution of local allocation tax is a disbursement of central government revenue to local governments (prefectures and municipalities). Disbursements in other categories, especially education and public investment, include subsidies given to local governments. In total, about 40 percent of central government revenues are transferred to the local governments.

Table 34.1. General Account Budget Revenues: Initial Budget Basis
Fiscal Years 1988–1993, Billion Yen, unless otherwise noted

	1988	1989	1990	1991	1992	(Est.) 1993	1993 % of Total
Total revenue	64,607	67,248	71,703	70,613	72,218	72,355	100.0
Tax and stamp revenue	50,827	54,922	60,106	58,990	62,504	61,303	84.7
Personal income tax	17,954	21,382	25,996	26,749	25,350	27,046	37.4
Corporate income tax	18,438	18,993	18,384	16,595	14,981	15,952	22.0
Consumption tax	2,043	3,270	4,623	4,976	4,968	5,458	7.5
Inheritance tax	1,831	2,018	1,918	2,583	2,720	2,699	3.7
Liquor tax	2,202	1,786	1,935	1,974	2,025	2,051	2.8
Stamp revenue	1,932	1,960	1,894	1,749	1,663	1,756	2.4
Others	6,426	5,513	5,357	4,363	10,797	6,341	8.8
Government bonds	7,152	6,639	7,312	6,730	7,280	8,130	11.2
Surplus in the preceding fiscal year	3,658	3,136	1,389	1,504	84	4	0.0
Other revenues	2,971	2,551	2,897	3,390	2,350	2,918	4.0

Note: Consumption tax was introduced in April 1989. Prior to FY 1989, consumption tax consisted of commodity taxes.

Sources: Ministry of Finance, *Fiscal Statistics*. Bank of Japan, *Economic Statistics Annual*.

Table 34.2. General Account Budget Disbursements: Initial Budget Basis
Fiscal Years 1988–1993, Billion Yen, unless otherwise noted

	1988	1989	1990	1991	1992	(Est.) 1993	1993 % of Total
Total	61,852	66,312	69,651	70,613	72,218	72,355	100.0
General disbursements	35,490	37,957	37,971	37,977	39,782	41,109	56.8
Social security	11,802	12,475	11,545	12,196	12,737	13,146	18.2
Pension	1,880	1,856	1,837	1,808	1,784	1,777	2.5
Education and science	4,982	5,075	5,359	5,563	5,683	5,820	8.0
National defense	3,728	3,970	4,254	4,440	4,552	4,641	6.4
Public investment	6,683	7,399	7,013	7,343	8,024	8,527	11.8
Overseas economic aid	719	771	802	865	905	957	1.3
Others	5,696	6,412	7,160	5,762	6,097	6,241	8.6
Distribution of local allocation tax	13,031	14,965	15,931	15,800	15,772	15,617	21.6
Disbursements for government debt (interest and principal)	12,031	12,090	14,449	15,537	16,447	15,442	21.3
Transfer to Industrial Investment Special Account	1,300	1,300	1,300	1,300	217	187	0.3

Sources: Ministry of Finance, *Fiscal Statistics*. Bank of Japan, *Economic Statistics Annual*.

Features and Problems

Public Sector Expenditures in National Income Statistics

The government sector in the national income statistics (SNA) consists of three components: (1) central government; (2) local governments; and (3) social security fund. Public corporations and public financial institutions are not included in the government sector. They are classified as non-financial business and financial business, respectively. The sum of the government sector, public corporations, and public financial institutions is sometimes called the public sector.

Government expenditures in the SNA are divided into three types: (1) government final consumption expenditures; (2) government fixed capital formation (investment); and (3) increase in government stock (see Table 34.3). Expenditures for land purchase are not included in the SNA because they do not produce value added.

Local governments account for about 75% of the total government expenditures in the SNA. This is mainly due to the fact that the central government collects revenues and transfers them to the local governments which actually spend them.

Table 34.3. Government Sector in SNA
Fiscal Years 1987–1991, Trillion Yen, unless otherwise noted

	1987	1988	1989	1990	1991	1991 % of Total
Total government sector	57.8	59.1	63.1	68.2	72.6	100.0
Government consumption expenditures	33.2	34.6	36.7	39.5	41.7	57.4
Central government	8.0	8.3	8.9	9.4	9.9	13.6
Local governments	24.6	25.6	57.2	29.3	31.0	42.7
Social security fund	0.7	0.7	0.7	0.8	0.8	1.1
Government fixed capital formation	24.5	24.9	26.4	28.6	31.2	43.0
Central government	6.6	6.1	6.2	6.5	6.9	9.5
Local governments	17.9	18.7	20.2	21.9	24.2	33.3
Social security fund	0.1	0.1	0.1	0.1	0.1	0.1
Increase in government stock	0.0	–0.4	–0.1	0.1	–0.2	–0.3

Source: Economic Planning Agency, *Annual Report on National Accounts* (1993), 240–1.

Large Amount of Fixed Capital Formation

Fixed capital formation (investment) in Japan accounts for a much higher percentage of total government expenditures than in other G-7 countries (see Table 34.4).

Table 34.4. General Government Investment
Calendar Year 1990, Percent

	FCF/GDP	FCF/GGE
Japan	5.1	35.7
Canada	2.6	11.4
United States	1.6	8.4
France	3.3	15.3
Germany	2.3	11.0
Italy	3.5	16.8
United Kingdom	2.3	10.3

Note: General government includes central and local governments and social security funds. *FCF* gross fixed capital formation of general government, *GGE* total general government expenditures (= fixed capital formation + final consumption expenditure).

Source: OECD, *National Accounts 1978–1990*.

Financing of Budget Deficits

The Japanese government has issued two types of bonds to finance budget 'deficits' (revenue minus consumption and investment): construction bonds, which can only be used for public works and are authorized under the Public Finance Law of 1947; and deficit-financing bonds, which must be issued under a special law enacted each year of issue.

Construction bonds were first issued in 1965 to make up for an unexpected shortfall in revenues. Deficit-financing bonds were first issued in 1975 (following the first oil crisis), and large amounts were issued as the government maintained a loose fiscal policy. A tighter fiscal policy was adopted in the 1980s, when the MOF set very low ceilings on the central account budget (see Fig. 34.1); in addition, some burdens were shifted from the central government to local governments. Annual issuance of deficit-financing bonds to finance budget deficits was ended in fiscal 1990. The recession which began around the beginning of 1991 has hurt government revenues (especially corporate income taxes -- see Table 34.1), and has led to increased issuance of construction bonds. Although construction bonds are essentially the same as deficit-financing bonds in the market and from a macroeconomic viewpoint, they are treated differently under the SNA (see Chapter 2). While construction bonds appear (as negative saving) in the capital finance account, deficit-financing bonds appear in the income-outlay account.

The ratio of government bond revenues to total revenues is estimated at 11.2% in fiscal 1993 (see Fig. 34.2). The ratio of interest payments to total disbursements is 16.1%, which is higher than in most other industrialized countries.

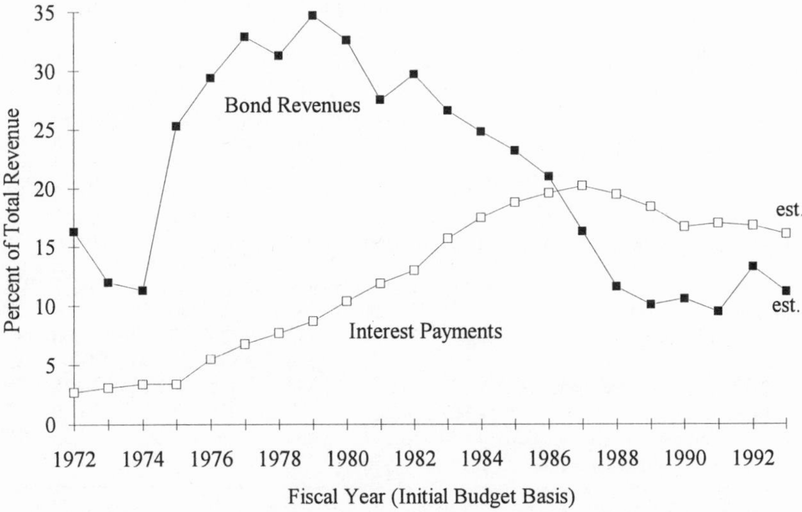

Fig. 34.2. General Account Budget: Bond Revenues and Interest Payments

Fiscal Investment and Loan Program

The FILP is often called the nation's 'second general account budget' and is regarded as the nation's 'capital budget'. The size of the FILP is more than 50 percent of the general account budget. It is planned in parallel with the general account budget and requires approval by the Diet. The major source of funds comes from the Trust Fund Bureau of the MOF, which collects public funds mainly in the form of Postal Saving deposits, social security contributions, and Postal Insurance premiums.

The FILP consists of general FILP and fund operation service. General FILP includes funds that are disbursed to public financial institutions, public corporations, and local governments so that these institutions can invest in public infrastructure or lend the funds at subsidized interest rates to stimulate private investment. The fund operation service consists of funds which are first deposited with the Trust Fund Bureau then later used by the depositing institution (usually Postal Savings or Postal Insurance) for investments in securities or loans.

In the 1950s, the FILP was primarily used for investment in industrial facilities. During the period of double-digit growth in the 1960s, when private investment led the economy, the FILP allocated funds to lower-productivity industries and investment in infrastructure. Recently, the emphasis has shifted away from industrial infrastructure toward housing and related projects.

For further details on the FILP, see Chapter 46.

Table 34.6. Fiscal Investment and Loan Program
Fiscal Years 1988–1993, Billion Yen

	1988	1989	1990	1991	1992	(Est.) 1993	1993 % of Total
Total disbursement	33,114	34,571	36,572	37,406	41,402	46,771	100.0
FILP disbursement	29,614	32,271	34,572	36,806	40,802	45,771	97.9
General FILP	25,344	26,341	27,622	29,106	32,262	36,596	78.2
Public investment institutions	4,122	4,183	4,302	4,713	5,224	5,870	12.6
Government financial inst.	16,477	17,947	19,151	20,027	22,144	25,026	53.5
Local governments	4,745	4,210	4,170	4,365	4,895	5,700	12.2
Fund operation service	4,270	5,930	6,950	7,700	8,540	9,175	19.6
Purchase of government bonds	3,500	2,300	2,000	600	600	1,000	2.1
Total inflow of funds	33,114	34,571	36,572	37,406	41,402	46,771	100.0
Industrial Investment Special Acct.	91	85	64	66	58	58	0.1
Trust Fund Bureau	26,207	26,871	28,453	29,135	33,489	37,660	80.5
Postal Saving	7,900	8,500	7,200	8,800	9,900	10,400	22.2
Welfare insurance/natl. annuities	3,500	4,310	5,540	6,430	7,230	7,190	15.4
Repayment to FILP	14,807	14,061	15,713	13,905	16,359	20,070	42.9
Postal life insurance/postal annuities	4,409	5,614	6,055	6,305	6,055	7,053	15.1
Government guaranteed bonds	2,407	2,000	2,000	1,900	1,800	2,000	4.3

Note: Initial Budget Basis.
Source: Ministry of Finance.

Part II

Monetary Economy

Financial Institutions and Money Markets

35 Major Financial Institutions

Source: Research and Statistics Department, Bank of Japan.

Frequency: Monthly.

Release: Figures are released with a two- or three-month lag in *Economic Statistics Monthly*.

Availability: Figures are available from as early as 1950, depending on the series. There are many discontinuities in the series, especially for those regarding banking accounts.

This chapter gives an outline of the major financial institutions in Japan (other than the Bank of Japan). Financial structure is dealt with in Chapter 36 (Flow of Funds). For a detailed and comprehensive review of financial institutions in Japan, see Suzuki 1990.

Historical Perspective -- Separation and Specialization

After World War II, Japan's financial system was reconstructed so that it could meet the requirements for recovery from the war. Various types of regulations were adopted to ensure low interest rates, an adequate supply of long-term funds to industries, and stability. Although these regulations have been liberalized or relaxed, they still represent the basis of Japan's financial system. Among these, the following separation/specialization by lines of business are frequently cited:

1. Separation of long-term and short-term financing.
2. Separation of trust business from commercial banking.
3. Separation of banking from commerce and securities business.
4. Specialization in foreign exchange business.
5. Specialization in banking for small and medium-sized companies.
6. Specialization in banking for certain industries such as agriculture, fishery, and housing finance.

Distinction among various types of financial institutions has become blurred because of the liberalization of deposit interest rates and separation regulations. In addition, as a result of various types of regulation, the government has been strongly involved in the financial system in the form of Postal Savings and government-owned financial institutions.

Types of Financial Institutions

There are three types of financial institutions: central bank -- the Bank of Japan; private financial institutions; and public financial institutions. Among private financial institutions, there are private financial intermediaries and 'other financial institutions'. The former issues indirect securities such as deposits, bank debentures, or insurance certificates to transfer funds to the ultimate borrowers, while the latter sells primary securities issued by the ultimate borrowers. The private financial intermediaries can be subdivided into two groups: depository institutions and non-depository institutions. Depository institutions include various types of banks which accept demand deposits. Non-depository institutions include insurance companies, securities investment trust management companies, private housing finance companies, consumer credit institutions, etc. Private depository institutions are discussed in detail below.

Private Depository Institutions

Included in this category are the following institutions:

1. Commercial banks.
2. Long-term financial institutions.
3. Financial institutions for small business.
4. Financial institutions for agriculture, forestry, and fishery.

1. Commercial Banks (Ordinary Banks)

Commercial banks consist of city banks, regional banks (Regional Banks I), member banks of the Second Association of Regional Banks (Regional Banks II), and foreign banks. They mainly deal with short-term lending and deposits, although they are permitted to participate in long-term lending. There is no legal distinction among these first three types of institutions. City banks are usually large in size, have large branch networks nationwide, and are headquartered in metropolitan areas. Main borrowers of City banks have been large corporate customers, although lending in other markets such as small and medium-sized companies and individuals has grown rapidly. Regional banks tend to have their headquarters in a city that is the seat of a prefectural government, and a limited branch network in a few prefectures. They have strong ties with local corporations and local governments. Member banks of the Second Association of Regional Banks are banks which were converted to commercial banks from sogo (mutual) banks. They are generally smaller in size than regional banks, have smaller branch networks, and serve smaller companies.

2. Long-Term Financial Institutions

Long-term financial institutions consist of long-term credit banks and trust banks. Long-term credit banks were established to supply long-term lending. They are strictly limited in deposit taking activity. Their main source of funds comes from issuance of five-year interest-bearing notes and one-year discount debentures. Trust banks can conduct both trust and banking business. However, their main business is to gather funds in the form of loan trusts and money in trust, and to lend them to corporations for capital investment.

3. Financial Institutions for Small Business

There are four types of financial institutions serving small business: Shinkin banks; credit cooperatives; labor credit associations; and the Shoko Chukin Bank. A Shinkin bank can only lend to its members, although it is allowed to gather deposits from both members and non-members. Credit cooperatives are generally smaller than shinkin banks. Both lending and deposits are limited to members. Labor credit associations are non-profit organizations which promote the welfare activities of labor unions, consumer cooperatives, and other labor bodies. These three types of financial institutions have their own associations: Zenshinren Bank; National Federation of Credit Cooperatives; and National Federation of Labor Credit Associations. Major activities of these associations are deposit taking from and lending to members, and to a lesser extent non-members, as designated by the Ministry of Finance.

The Shoko Chukin Bank is a special corporation serving cooperative societies of small businesses and organizations of small-business operators. The Government is rather strongly involved in its operation. It lends mainly to small businesses and issues five-year debentures as the main source of its funding.

4. Financial Institutions for Agriculture, Forestry, and Fisheries

There is a pyramid of three levels in financial institutions for agriculture, forestry, and fisheries: cooperatives; cooperative credit federations; and the Norinchukin Bank. Cooperatives are located in individual villages, towns, and cities. Their main business includes deposit-taking from members and redepositing surplus funds to their respective prefectural organizations, i.e. the cooperative credit federations. The Norinchukin Bank is the national level organization which accepts surplus funds from cooperative credit federations and issues debentures.

Public Financial Institutions

Public financial institutions consist of government financial institutions and postal savings. The former includes two government banks and nine public corporations.

They are designed to supplement private-sector finance and are prohibited by law from competing with private-sector institutions. They cannot obtain funds through deposits. Their main source of funds is the Fiscal Investment and Loan Program (FILP). The Postal Savings system is the major source of funds of the FILP (along with repayment of previous loans -- see Table 34.6). The postal savings system has more than 24,000 branches in its nationwide network, and gathers personal deposits up to 10 million yen per person. The original purpose of the postal savings system was to serve small individual depositors. However, recent financial liberalization has allowed the postal savings system to provide a variety of new services. (See Chapter 47 for details.)

Size of Assets and Liabilities by Type of Financial Institution

Table 35.1 shows total assets, outstanding loans, securities, deposits, and debentures by type of financial institution. All Banks (zengin), which does not literally include every bank, consists of city banks, regional banks, member banks of the Second Association of Regional Banks (Regional Banks II), banking accounts of trust banks, and long-term credit banks. Other major institutions in terms of size are shinkin banks, life insurance companies and the postal savings system.

Table 35.1. Major Assets and Liabilities by Type of Financial Institution
End-of-Calendar Year 1992, Trillion Yen

	Assets	Loans	Securities	Deposits	Debentures
Banking accounts of All Banks	728.0	471.8	118.1	428.0	58.1
City banks	338.8	223.6	45.9	196.3	4.6
Regional Banks I	187.3	125.6	32.4	155.8	--
Regional Banks II	70.1	50.9	9.5	59.6	--
Trust banks	53.1	24.5	15.3	9.5	--
Long-term credit banks	78.6	47.2	15.0	6.7	53.4
Trust accounts of All Banks	197.3	35.0	92.2	--	--
Overseas branches of All Banks	149.9	72.3	7.6	111.0	--
Foreign banks	21.3	9.3	2.3	1.7	--
Shinkin banks and Zenshinren Bank	104.4	69.1	17.2	86.9	1.0
Shoko Chukin Bank	15.2	11.5	2.9	2.2	12.2
Credit coops. and its national federation	25.8	19.9	2.3	21.6	--
Labor credit assoc. and its national fed.	11.1	4.4	3.1	10.0	--
Norinchukin Bank, its credit fed. and coops.	82.1	41.9	28.8	67.8	8.6
Life insurance	151.6	60.1	65.1	--	--
Non-life insurance	27.3	7.3	12.3	--	--
Postal Saving	--	--	--	167.1	--

Note: *Regional Banks II* member banks of the Second Association of Regional Banks. Assets for Zenshinren Bank, Shoko Chukin Bank, Credit coops. and its national fed., Norinchukin Bank and its credit fed. and coops. include only principal assets. Redeposits of Shinkin banks, credit coops., labor credit assoc., and agricultural coops. and its federation exclude higher level (prefectural or national) institutions when calculating assets and deposits. Deposits include Certificates of Deposit. Securities in All Bank trust accounts include domestic and foreign securities held for securities investment trust.

Source: Bank of Japan.

36 Flow of Funds Accounts

Source:	Research and Statistics Department, Bank of Japan.
Frequency:	Quarterly and Annual.
Release:	Figures for the previous quarter are released at the end of the first month of each quarter. They are published in *Economic Statistics Monthly*. Historical series are obtained from *Flow of Funds Accounts in Japan*, published every five to seven years.
Availability:	Annual (both calendar and fiscal year basis) figures are available from 1954 onward. Quarterly figures are available from 1965 onward.

Flow of Funds Accounts (FFA) reveal the flows of financial assets between economic sectors, as well as the level of financial assets and liabilities outstanding of each sector. This makes it possible to investigate how each sector allocates funds to competing financial assets in response to changes in financial market conditions (such as interest rates and stock market prices). The Bank of Japan releases a paper titled 'Flow of Funds in Japan' in June every year where detailed analysis based on Flow of Funds Accounts is described. The English version becomes available in July or August.

Details

FFA includes the following four tables, each of which is explained below:

1. Financial Transaction Accounts (Flow).
2. Financial Assets and Liabilities Accounts (Stock).
3. Time Series Presentation (Flow).
4. Time Series Presentation (Stock).

In FFA, the economy is divided into six major economic sectors:

1. Financial institutions (Bank of Japan, private and public financial institutions).
2. Central government.
3. Public corporations and local authorities.
4. Corporate business.
5. Personal.
6. Rest of the world.

Financial Transaction Accounts (Flow)

Financial Transaction Accounts reveal the flow of financial assets between economic sectors. Essentially, they show the *change* in the balance sheet of financial assets for each sector for a certain time period (either one quarter or one year). The accounts are constructed on a double-entry bookkeeping basis, so that an increase in assets of one sector is also recorded as an increase in liabilities of another sector.

Table 36.1 is an abridged example of Financial Transaction Accounts (the figures shown are only for explanatory purposes). Each column shows the *change* in financial assets and liabilities for a sector (the *amount* outstanding is shown in 'Financial Assets and Liabilities Accounts'). Each row shows the flow of funds between sectors for a particular asset. For example, the row labelled 'demand deposits' indicates that the liabilities of financial institutions increased by 6 units, while the assets of the corporate business and personal sectors increased by a total of 6 units. The penultimate row, 'financial surplus or deficit', is simply the increase in the net value of financial assets (increase in assets less increase in liabilities) for each sector, entered under liabilities so that total assets and liabilities will balance. In the last column, 'total' is the sum of assets (or liabilities) in each row, indicating the change in the amount outstanding of the asset.

Table 36.1. Abridged Example of Flow of Funds: Financial Transaction Accounts

	Financial Inst.		Corp. Business		Personal		Total
	Asset	Liab.	Asset	Liab.	Asset	Liab.	
Deposits with BOJ	−10	−10					−10
Cash		5			5		5
Demand deposits		6	4		2		6
Time deposits		15	5		10		15
Trusts		12	4		8		12
Insurance		8			8		8
Securities	5	10	5	10	10		20
BOJ loans	3	3					3
Call money	−4	−4					−4
CP	2		4	6			6
Loans	35			25		10	35
Trade credit			7	7			7
Financial surplus (+) or deficit (-)		−14		−19		33	
Total	31	31	29	29	43	43	103

Financial Assets and Liabilities Accounts (Stock)

Financial Assets and Liabilities Accounts use the same format as Financial Transaction Accounts, except that they show the *amount* of financial assets and liabilities for each sector instead of the *change* for each sector. Financial Assets and Liabilities Accounts are published twice a year (at the end of March and December).

Time Series Presentation (Stock)

Time Series Presentation (Stock) provides more detailed figures than Financial Assets and Liabilities Accounts (for domestic non-financial sectors only), with disaggregated figures by type of asset and sector. It includes data for the past few years, so that trends in the stock of financial assets can be followed. Conceptually, the stock figures are the sum of past flows in Time Series Presentation (Flow).

Time Series Presentation (Flow)

Time Series Presentation (Flow) provides historical series of frequently used items from the Financial Transactions Accounts so that the trends of particular sectors and/or transactions can be followed.

Series in the following classifications are available:

Financial surplus or deficit (and ratio to nominal GNP) by sector (Table 36.2).
Fund raising by domestic non-financial sectors by source and sector (Tables 36.3 and 36.4).
Fund intermediation in broadly-defined financial markets (Table 36.5).
Financial investment by domestic non-financial sectors by item and sector (Table 36.6).
Trade credit.

Table 36.2. Financial Surplus or Deficit by Sector
Calendar Years 1987–1992, % of Nominal GNP

	1987	1988	1989	1990	1991	1992
Corporate business	−2.2	−4.5	−6.7	−9.0	−6.9	−6.0
Personal	7.8	7.4	9.1	9.9	8.4	9.9
Public	−1.4	0.6	0.6	0.8	0.7	−1.6
Financial institutions	−0.7	−0.7	−1.0	−0.4	−0.1	0.9
Rest of the world	−3.6	−2.7	−2.0	−1.2	−2.2	−3.2

Source: Bank of Japan, *Economic Statistics Monthly*.

Table 36.3. Fund Raising by Domestic Non-Financial Sectors by Source
Calendar Years 1987–1992, % of Total, unless otherwise noted

	1987	1988	1989	1990	1991	1992
Borrowing	68.2	68.4	68.9	69.8	78.4	67.4
Private financial institutions	56.7	55.4	58.3	57.6	55.4	31.8
Public financial institutions	11.5	13.0	10.6	12.1	22.9	35.6
Issues of securities	26.4	21.0	24.4	21.0	27.3	33.4
Commercial Paper	1.9	8.9	3.4	2.6	−5.5	−0.4
Foreign credit	3.4	1.8	3.4	6.6	−0.2	−0.5
Total funds raised (trillion yen)	87.3	85.5	112.4	104.6	60.8	52.6
Total as percent of nominal GNP	24.9	22.9	28.2	24.5	13.4	11.2

Source: Bank of Japan, *Economic Statistics Monthly*.

Table 36.4. Fund Raising by Corporate Business Sector by Source
Calendar Years 1987–1992, % of Total, unless otherwise noted

	1987	1988	1989	1990	1991	1992
Borrowing	65.0	62.7	60.7	68.6	79.1	81.8
Industrial bonds	5.5	3.0	2.0	4.7	9.5	15.6
Stocks	9.7	9.6	13.9	6.6	3.3	1.7
Foreign bonds	8.8	7.9	13.0	5.6	17.1	2.6
Foreign credit	7.0	2.8	5.2	10.4	–0.2	–0.9
Total funds raised (trillion yen)	42.7	54.2	73.0	66.7	38.3	27.4
Total as percent of nominal GNP	12.2	14.5	18.3	15.6	8.4	5.8

Note: Items do not sum to 100% due to exclusion of minor items.
Source: Bank of Japan, *Economic Statistics Monthly*.

Table 36.5. Fund Intermediation in Broadly-Defined Financial Markets
Calendar Years 1987–1992, % of Total, unless otherwise noted

	1987	1988	1989	1990	1991	1992
Financial institutions	97.6	97.2	87.7	76.1	82.6	109.2
Banks, etc.	52.2	56.9	48.5	52.2	30.9	36.9
Trust accounts	6.8	4.1	5.2	–2.2	2.1	–0.8
Investment trusts	5.0	2.2	–1.8	1.4	–6.0	7.6
Insurance institutions	6.0	8.8	9.8	11.6	15.0	13.0
Public financial institutions	18.7	19.6	19.1	13.3	47.8	55.6
Securities markets	–0.6	–3.1	0.4	13.3	–8.1	–11.7
Foreign capital markets	3.0	5.9	11.9	10.6	25.5	2.5
Total fund intermediation (tril. yen)	90.6	92.8	117.2	104.7	59.8	54.5
Total as percent of nominal GNP	25.8	24.8	29.4	24.5	13.2	11.6

Note: Each supplier of funds is pooled into hypothetical, broadly-defined markets. Unlike Table 36.4, securities with intermediation by banks are classified under 'financial institutions' not 'securities markets'.
Source: Bank of Japan, *Economic Statistics Monthly*.

Table 36.6. Financial Investment by Domestic Non-Financial Sectors
Calendar Years 1987–1992, % of Total (Flow), unless otherwise noted

	1987	1988	1989	1990	1991	1992
Cash currency	2.2	2.7	3.9	0.3	1.1	0.3
Demand deposits	2.8	6.1	–0.2	3.7	15.9	8.7
Time deposits	35.7	31.1	38.7	32.4	8.1	4.5
Foreign currency deposits	–1.2	0.8	1.3	3.6	2.8	–5.8
Certificates of Deposits (CDs)	–0.6	1.9	1.4	–2.0	–1.4	–0.3
Postal Savings	6.9	7.3	7.0	0.7	25.8	23.0
Trust	12.2	10.6	10.9	8.3	9.2	16.2
Insurance	17.2	22.2	19.7	19.7	26.3	33.2
Securities	10.1	1.2	1.8	12.6	–10.0	0.3
Commercial Paper	0.1	1.6	0.8	2.1	–1.3	–0.4
Government current deposits	0.0	0.0	0.1	–0.1	0.0	–0.0
Deposits with Trust Fund Bureau	6.9	6.8	6.8	8.9	14.5	15.6
Foreign credit	7.7	7.6	8.1	9.8	8.9	4.7
Total financial investment (tril. yen)	105.4	106.0	128.7	113.8	72.5	63.7
Total as percent of nominal GNP	30.1	28.4	32.2	26.6	16.0	13.6

Source: Bank of Japan, *Economic Statistics Monthly*.

Features and Problems

Difference in Classification of Economic Sectors: FFA vs. SNA

The division into six economic sectors adopted in the Flow of Funds Accounts (FFA) is different from the classifications adopted in the System of National Accounts (SNA). Fig. 36.1 is given to reconcile these differences.

No Seasonally Adjusted Figures

There are no seasonally adjusted figures for the Flow of Funds Accounts. Seasonal fluctuation in the Flow of Funds Accounts is so large that readers are recommended to use year-on-year comparisons. In June, the *White Paper on the Monetary Economy* published by the Bank of Japan reveals recent developments of the financial markets in Japan. It uses a seasonally adjusted, three-quarter moving average for financial surplus or deficit by sector with weights of 1:2:1.

Financial Surplus or Deficit in FFA vs. Capital Finance Accounts in SNA

Financial surplus or deficit in Flow of Funds Accounts roughly corresponds to the saving-investment balance in the System of National Accounts. The saving-investment balance in SNA is expressed in two different measures: real (non-financial) transactions and financial transactions. Table 36.7 shows financial surplus or deficit in FFA and the two different measures of saving-investment balance in SNA for each sector. The difference in these three measures reflects different classifications in each sector as well as statistical discrepancies in compiling SNA figures from FFA. Note that the figures for the foreign sector in the SNA and FFA are identical. Financial deficit of the foreign sector in the FFA is conceptually the same as that of 'net increase in claims on foreign assets' in the SNA and current account surplus in Balance of Payments statistics (see Chapter 31).

Limited Availability of Source Statistics

Because the balance sheets of each sector are not always available at the time of compilation, the Bank of Japan uses various supplementary source statistics, including sample surveys which are considered less reliable than actual balance sheets.

Statistical Discrepancy in Flow and Stock Data

In theory, the change in financial assets between years in the Time Series Presentation (Stock) table should equal the flow during the year. However, due to limitations on the timely availability of statistics and differences in valuation methods, the figures from the two tables may be different, especially for stocks (see Tables 36.8 and 36.9). Since the stock data for stocks is on a market value basis, and stock prices declined in value in 1991, the theoretical value calculated using flow data (acquisition value basis) is much too high.

Table 36.7. Financial Surplus or Deficit (FFA) and Saving-Investment Balance (SNA) Calendar Years 1987–1991, Billion Yen

	1987	1988	1989	1990	1991
Households (1)					
FFA	27,386	27,743	36,391	42,142	38,190
SNA (Non-financial)	29,616	31,685	36,709	40,776	44,066
SNA (Financial)	31,989	28,184	34,966	38,514	35,548
Non-financial corporate					
FFA	−7,721	−16,933	−26,863	−38,679	−31,109
SNA (Non-financial)	−12,928	−20,694	−29,597	−40,225	−40,134
SNA (Financial)	−22,426	−23,055	−30,015	−48,799	−41,074
General government (2)					
FFA	−4,804	2,176	2,327	3,310	2,973
SNA (Non-financial)	1,607	5,586	9,964	12,342	13,341
SNA (Financial)	5,241	7,730	6,708	16,955	15,477
Foreign (3)					
FFA	−12,541	−10,192	−7,853	−5,203	−9,767
SNA (Non-financial)	−12,541	−10,192	−7,853	−5,203	−9,767
SNA (Financial)	−12,541	−10,192	−7,853	−5,203	−9,767

Notes: (1) In SNA figures, households and private non-profit institutions serving households are combined. (2) In FFA figures, central government and public corporations and local authorities are combined. (3) In SNA, figures for the foreign sector are obtained as the 'net increase in claims on foreign assets' with reversed sign.

Sources: Bank of Japan, Economic Planning Agency.

Table 36.8. Change in Financial Assets of Corporate Business Sector Trillion Yen

	Stock at end of		Flow during		End of FY 1991 Stock	
	FY 1990		FY 1991		Theoretical	Actual
Demand Deposits	44.34	+	3.38	=	47.72	47.72
Stocks	139.62	+	−1.48	=	138.14	99.12

Source: Bank of Japan, *Economic Statistics Monthly*.

Table 36.9. Stock Valuation Methods in Flow of Funds Accounts

	Prior to 1982		Since 1983	
	Flow Data	Stock Data	Flow Data	Stock Data
Assets				
Financial institutions	B	B	B	B
Domestic non-financial corporate business	(1)	B	A	M
Foreign sector	A	--	A	--
Liabilities				
Financial institutions			(2)	(3)
Domestic non-financial corporate business			(2)	(3)

Notes: *A* Acquisition value, *B* Book value, *M* Market value, (1) Changes in par value + excess of par value − new bonus issue, (2) Stock issuance + converted convertible bonds, (3) Paid-in capital.

Source: Bank of Japan.

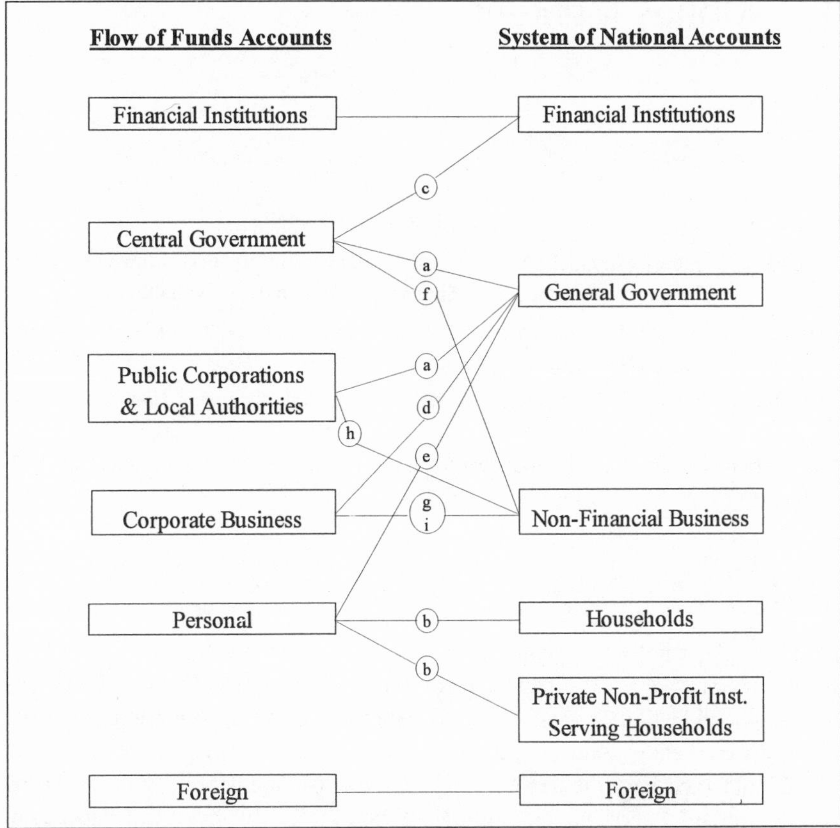

(a) There are two separate sectors 'Central Government' and 'Public Corporations and Local Authorities' in FFA while central government and local authorities (with the exception noted in 'h') are included in 'General Government' in SNA.
(b) There is a single 'Personal' sector in FFA while this is divided into two separate sectors ('Households' and 'Private Non-Profit Institutions Serving Households') in SNA.
(c) Public insurance and two special budget accounts (Industrial Investment and Urban Development Finance) included in 'Central Government' in FFA are classified as 'Financial Institutions' in SNA.
(d) Government corporations included in 'Corporate Business' in FFA are classified as 'General Government' in SNA.
(e) Health Insurance Unions included in 'Personal Sector' in FFA are classified as 'General Government' in SNA.
(f) Six special budget accounts (Coinage, Postal Service, National Forests and Fields, Alcohol, Printing, and Food Control) included in 'Central Government' in FFA are classified as 'Non-Financial Corporate Business' in SNA.
(g) Four Public Corporations included in 'Corporate Business' in FFA are classified as 'Non-Financial Corporate Business' in SNA.
(h) Public corporations and local government business budgets (excluding hospital and sewage) included in 'Public Corporations and Local Authorities' in FFA are classified as 'Non-Financial Corporate Business' in SNA.
(i) Local Public Corporations for land development, housing supply, and local roads included in 'Corporate Business' in FFA are classified as 'Non-Financial Corporate Business' in SNA.

Fig. 36.1. Comparison of Classifications in FFA and SNA

37 Money Markets

Source: Research and Statistics Department, Bank of Japan.

Frequency: Interest rates in these markets are available on a daily basis from newspapers. Figures for amount outstanding are available only on a monthly basis.

Release: Figures for amount outstanding are made available with a one- or two-month lag, depending on the type of market.

Availability: In general, figures are available from the market's opening date.

Money markets are financial markets for lending and borrowing transactions with maturities of one year or less.

Details

Money markets include two types of markets: interbank markets and open markets. In interbank markets only financial institutions participate, while in open markets both financial institutions and non-financial corporate businesses can participate. Interbank markets include: (1) call; and (2) bill. Open markets consist of: (1) CD (negotiable certificate of deposit); (2) Gensaki (or bond repurchase); (3) FB (Financing Bills) and TB (Treasury Bills); and (4) CP (Commercial Paper). In addition to these markets, US dollar call, Euro-Yen, CP and CD issued overseas, and the Japan Offshore Market (JOM) are sometimes included in money markets.

Table 37.1. Money Markets
End-of-Calendar Year Outstanding, Trillion Yen, unless otherwise noted

	1980	1985	1988	1989	1990	1991	1992	1992 % of Total
Total	16.7	34.1	69.4	89.7	90.9	96.6	109.9	100.0
Interbank markets	9.9	19.8	33.7	45.2	41.0	51.8	60.1	54.7
Call	4.1	5.1	15.7	24.5	24.0	35.3	44.5	40.5
Uncollateralized	--	0.8	6.0	10.1	12.3	23.4	31.7	28.8
Bill	5.7	14.7	18.0	20.8	17.1	16.5	15.6	14.2
Open markets	6.9	14.3	35.6	44.5	49.8	44.8	49.8	45.3
CD	2.4	9.7	16.0	21.1	18.9	17.3	16.6	15.1
Gensaki (RPs)	4.5	4.6	7.4	6.3	6.6	6.0	8.8	8.1
FB/TB	--	0.0	3.0	4.0	8.6	9.0	12.2	11.1
CP	--	--	9.3	13.1	15.8	12.4	12.2	11.1

Source: Bank of Japan, *Economic Statistics Annual*.

Interbank Markets

1. Call Market

The call market mainly deals with money transactions with maturities of less than one month. This market functions to adjust the financial position (temporary surplus or deficit of funds) of each financial institution. There are basically four types of transactions, depending on collateral (collateralized or uncollateralized) and maturity (fixed-date or unconditional). Uncollateralized call transactions were introduced in July 1985 and maturities of these transactions were extended to up to one year in April 1989. Currently, they make up 70% of total transactions. Fixed-date call transactions refer to those with a fixed date of maturity. Unconditional call transactions refer to those for which the date of maturity is automatically extended if neither party indicates a desire for repayment of the loan. If one party requests repayment, they are settled on the day after the date of the transaction at the time of clearing of the market. Overnight call transactions are classified as unconditional.

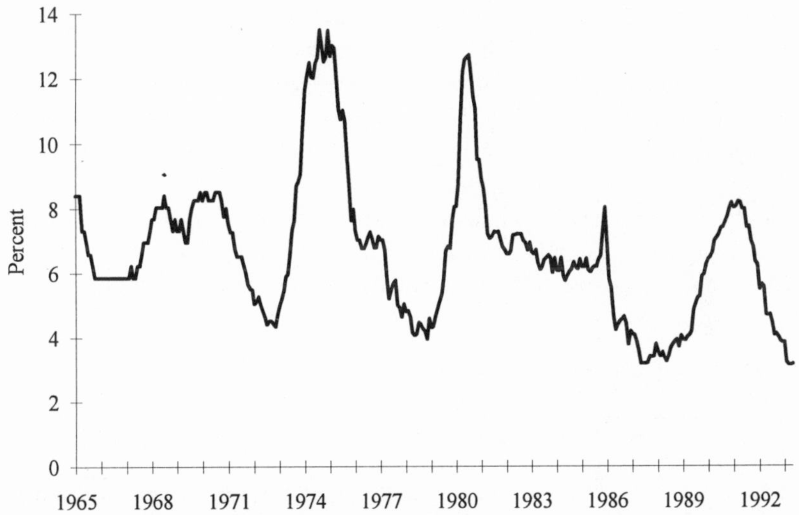

Fig. 37.1. Overnight Call Rate (unconditional)

2. Bill Market

The bill market mainly refers to interbank transactions with maturities of more than one month. Eligible bills include various types, such as high-grade commercial and industrial bills, trade bills, high-grade promissory notes, yen-denominated fixed-term export and import bills, and bank-issued bills of exchange.

Figures for monthly average outstanding and end-of-month outstanding are available for each interbank market. Data on monthly average outstanding by lender and borrower is available. City banks are usually the largest borrowers in these markets. Foreign banks also actively borrow in the markets, while trust banks, the Norinchukin Bank, the Zenshinren Bank, and shinkin banks are usually lenders.

Interbank markets are considered to reflect most precisely the monetary policy of the Bank of Japan. The interest rate on uncollateralized overnight call loans is most frequently used for analysis of the supply-demand conditions of the market.

In addition to general business conditions, the seasonality of interbank markets contributes to the fluctuation of interest rates. An increase in the demand for bank notes and net receipts of Treasury Funds puts upward pressure on interest rates in interbank markets (for details, see Chapter 40). This seasonality is, to a large extent, offset by money market operations of the Bank of Japan.

Open Markets

1. CD Market

Certificates of Deposit are issued by banks, with an interest rate determined by money market conditions. CDs are negotiable, or transferable. The issuing of CDs was authorized in May 1979, and current regulations require a minimum of 50 million yen and maturities of two weeks to two years. City banks are by far the largest issuers of CDs (see Table 37.2). Non-financial corporations are thought to be the largest purchasers of CDs, but there are no official statistics classified by purchaser.

The Bank of Japan has been indirectly participating in CD markets since March 1986, via loans to money market dealers for the purchase of CDs. The interest rate on CDs is considered one of the representative money market rates because of the lack of a sufficiently active Treasury bill market.

Table 37.2. Certificates of Deposit by Issuer
End-of-Calendar Year Outstanding, Billion Yen, unless otherwise noted

	1980	1985	1988	1989	1990	1991	1992	1992 % of Total
Total	2,357	9,657	15,973	21,086	18,860	17,298	16,603	100.0
All Banks (Zengin)	2,041	8,655	15,368	20,393	18,248	16,864	16,364	98.6
City banks	1,061	4,891	9,510	10,960	11,750	10,976	12,297	74.1
Regional Banks I	374	1,763	1,069	1,741	1,805	993	748	4.5
Regional Banks II	110	676	1,528	2,576	2,648	2,232	1,291	7.8
Trust banks	299	748	654	1,972	728	867	660	4.0
Long-term credit banks	196	578	2,607	3,144	1,317	1,796	1,368	8.2
Shinkin banks	24	203	469	462	374	236	133	0.8
Foreign banks	257	754	101	211	189	107	90	0.5
Others	35	45	35	20	49	91	16	0.1

Note: Regional Banks II are member banks of the Second Association of Regional Banks. Others include the Shoko Chukin Bank and the Norinchukin Bank.

Source: Bank of Japan, *Economic Statistics Annual*.

2. Gensaki Market

Gensaki are repurchase/resale agreements with securities used as collateral. Gensaki is, therefore, a kind of short-term financing and investing activity with securities as collateral. Purchasing Gensaki is equivalent to lending, while selling is equivalent to borrowing. Participants in Gensaki markets include securities companies, financial institutions, business corporations, public financial institutions, and non-residents. Business corporations and trust banks are the largest buyers, while securities companies are the largest sellers.

Gensaki transactions are usually for a minimum of 10 million yen and have maturities of one week to three months. The amount outstanding of bond Gensaki has been on the decline due to the heavy burden of the security transaction tax, which has caused participants to shift their lending and borrowing activities to other instruments. On the other hand, T-bill Gensaki, on which there is no such tax, has increased its share. The Bank of Japan has participated in Gensaki markets via buying operations of Gensaki since December 1987.

3. TB, FB Market

There are two types of short-term government securities: Treasury Bills (TB) and Financing Bills (FB). TB (or *tanki kokusai*) were first issued in February 1986 with a minimum of 100 million yen (reduced to 10 million yen in April 1990). TB are intended to smooth the redemption and refunding of the large amounts of government bonds due from 1985 onward. TB have maturities of either three or six months. They are floated through public auction. Contrary to TB, FB (or *seifu tanki shoken*) is a traditional instrument with a maturity of 60 days used to cover temporary shortages of funds of the Treasury. The interest rate on FB is below the official discount rate. Because of its low interest rate, FB are sold almost exclusively to the Bank of Japan.

The Bank of Japan started selling operations of FB in May 1981. Selling with repurchase agreement was implemented in January 1986. Selling operations of TB were implemented in January 1990.

4. CP Market

The Commercial Paper market was established in November 1987. CP is a short-term financing instrument (without collateral) for eligible corporations. Maturity is set between two weeks and nine months. Issuance of CP by non-residents was authorized in January 1988. Guidelines regarding eligible corporations have been relaxed. The Bank of Japan started buying operations of CP in May 1989.

The amount outstanding (but not the interest rate) of CP is available in *Economic Statistics Monthly* published by the Bank of Japan (see Fig. 37.3).

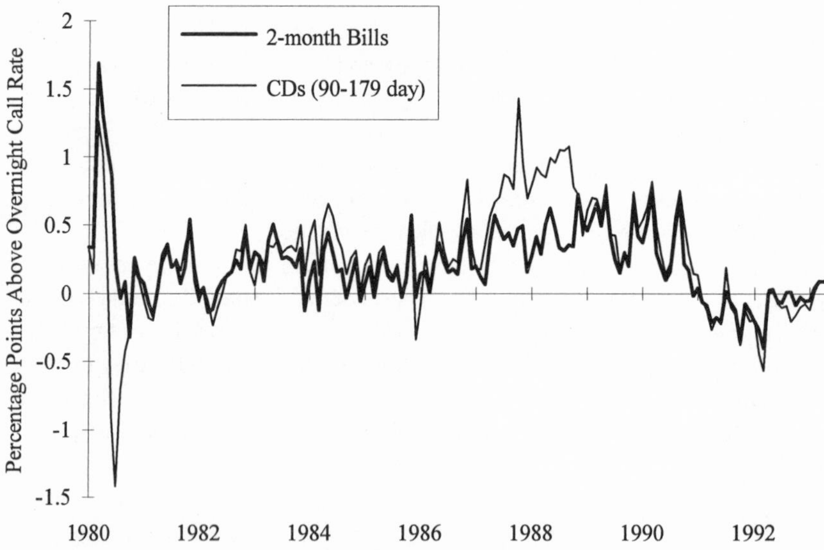

Fig. 37.2. Comparison of Short-Term Interest Rates

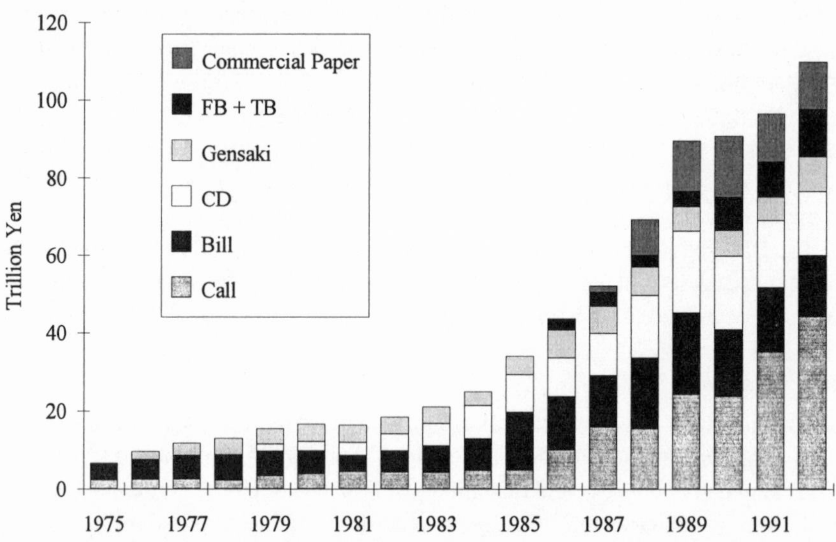

Fig. 37.3. Amount Outstanding of Money Market Instruments (end-of-calendar year values)

Money

38 Money Stock

Source: Research and Statistics Department, Bank of Japan.

Frequency: Monthly.

Release: Preliminary figures for the previous month are released in the middle of each month. Revised figures are released one month later.

Availability: Monthly average outstanding figures for M1 and M2+CDs are available from 1965 and 1967 respectively, while end-of-month outstanding is available from 1955 onward. Monthly average outstanding of 'broadly-defined liquidity' is available from 1981 onward.

Money stock statistics are important in evaluating both business conditions and the monetary policy stance of the Bank of Japan. The broadly defined money supply, M2+CDs (average monthly outstanding), is the most frequently used category of money stock in Japan. The Bank of Japan watches the year-on-year growth rate of M2+CDs closely in formulating its monetary policy, although recently it has started to place more emphasis on broadly-defined liquidity. M2+CDs is included in the leading index of Diffusion Indexes compiled by the EPA. Monetary base is covered in Chapter 39.

Details

Coverage of Financial Institutions

Money stock statistics cover only the following financial institutions:

- All Banks excluding trust accounts
  - City banks (excluding trust accounts)
  - Regional Banks I
  - Regional Banks II
  - Long-term credit banks
  - Trust banks (excluding trust accounts)
- Shinkin banks
- Norinchukin Bank
- Shoko Chukin Bank

These institutions are the same as those included under 'Private Financial Institutions' in 'Monetary Survey' (see Chapter 40).

Components of Money Stock

M2+CDs consists of the components shown in Table 38.1.

Table 38.1. Components of Money Stock
Calendar Years 1987–1992, Trillion Yen, unless otherwise noted

	1987	1988	1989	1990	1991	1992	1992 % of Total
M1	96.1	104.2	108.5	111.3	117.1	122.4	24.3
Cash currency in circulation	23.8	26.2	28.8	31.2	31.9	32.7	6.5
Deposit money	72.4	78.0	79.7	80.1	85.1	89.7	17.8
Quasi-money	248.0	279.2	312.8	361.4	374.3	372.7	74.0
Regulated rates	198.3	185.2	159.8	108.6	86.4	99.3	19.7
Unregulated rates	49.7	94.0	153.0	252.7	287.9	273.3	54.3
Certificates of Deposit (CDs)	9.9	10.2	11.3	10.4	9.3	8.5	1.7
M2+CDs	354.0	393.7	432.7	483.1	500.7	503.6	100.0
Growth rate (%)	10.4	11.2	9.9	11.7	3.6	0.6	--
Broadly-defined liquidity	677.9	744.6	814.9	893.0	940.3	973.6	--
Growth rate (%)	10.1	9.8	9.4	9.6	5.3	3.5	--

Note: Figures are average outstanding. Unregulated rate quasi-money includes large time deposits, money market certificates (MMC), small-MMC, non-resident yen deposits, and foreign deposits.
Source: Bank of Japan, *Economic Statistics Annual*.

Definition of Components

'Cash currency in circulation' represents the amount of bank notes issued and coins in circulation less the amount of cash currency held by the financial institutions surveyed. 'Deposit money' is the total of demand deposits (current deposits, ordinary deposits, deposits at notice, special deposits and deposits for tax payments) among private and public deposits with the financial institutions surveyed minus the checks and bills held by these institutions. 'Quasi-money' represents the total of private and public deposits less demand deposits with the financial institutions surveyed. 'Quasi-money with unregulated rates' consists of time deposits with unregulated rates (large time deposits), Money Market Certificates (MMCs), small denomination MMCs, non-residents' yen deposits, and foreign currency deposits.

Both average monthly outstanding and end-of-month outstanding of these components are available. Seasonally adjusted figures are available for M1 and M2+CDs only. The Census X-11 method is applied for seasonal adjustment.

Broader measures of money stock include M3+CDs and broadly-defined liquidity. For M3+CDs, only end-of-month outstanding figures are available, while for broadly-defined liquidity, only average outstanding figures are available.

M3+CDs consists of: M2+CDs; deposits with Post Offices, Agricultural Cooperatives, Fishery Cooperatives, Credit Cooperatives and Labor Credit Associations (including CDs); and money in trust and loan trusts of All Banks (excluding inter-financial institution deposits, trust accounts and the checks and bills held by the financial institutions surveyed).

Broadly-defined liquidity consists of: M3+CDs; bonds with repurchase agreements; bank debentures; government bonds; investment trusts; money deposited other than money in trust; and foreign bonds.

Fig. 38.1 shows a comparison of money supply measures.

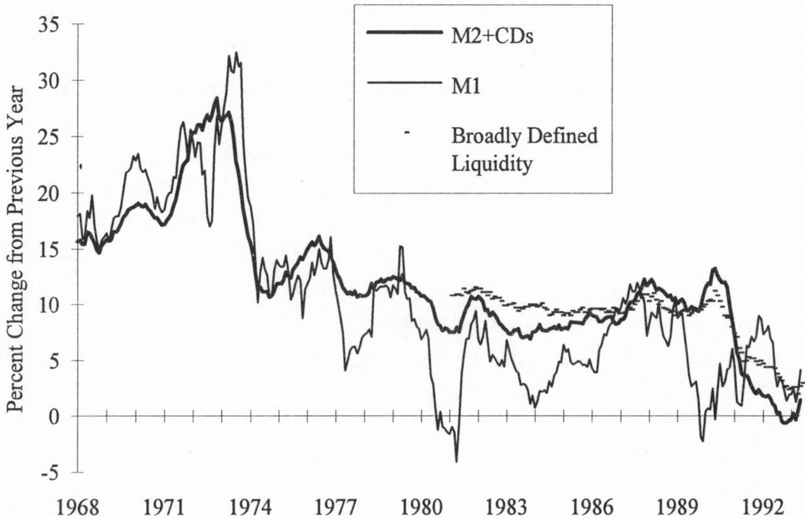

Fig. 38.1. Comparison of Money Supply Measures (Average Outstanding)

Features and Problems

Forecast of M2+CDs by BOJ

The Bank of Japan publishes its forecast of the growth rate of M2+CDs for each quarter in the first month of the quarter, in *Monthly Economic Review*. While the forecast is not considered to be a target, it reflects the Bank of Japan's emphasis on the movement of M2+CDs in formulating monetary policy.

Judgement on Tightness of Monetary Policy: Velocity of M2+CDs

One way to judge the tightness of monetary policy is based on deviation from the trend velocity of M2+CDs. Velocity of money is defined as PQ/M, where P is the price level (GNP deflator), Q is the quantity of output (real GNP), and M is the money supply (M2+CDs). In other words, velocity is nominal GNP (PQ) divided by money supply. In Japan, the velocity of M2+CDs has a downward trend.

Fig. 38.2 shows the actual and trend velocity of M2+CDs. The trend was calculated using data for the period from 1975 to the fourth quarter of 1985 (the time of the Plaza Agreement). Upward deviation of velocity from the trend reflects tight monetary policy while downward deviation from the trend velocity reflects accommodative monetary policy. The gap between velocity and its trend widened from 1987 to 1989, reflecting the accommodative monetary policy of this period. When monetary policy was tightened in 1990, velocity began to rise and is currently above its trend.

Liberalization of Interest Rates on Deposits and M2+CDs

When analyzing the growth of M2+CDs, it is important to consider the ongoing liberalization of deposit rates (see Chapter 48 for details) and movement of money between instruments. In 1988, when the growth of M2+CDs surged, the BOJ stated that the liberalization of interest-bearing deposits, such as large time deposits, was responsible. In 1990, the high interest rates caused by the tight monetary policy of the Bank of Japan may have reduced the stock of M2+CDs via transfers of money from M2+CDs components to instruments outside M2+CDs, such as five-year debentures of long-term credit banks and ten-year time deposits of Postal Savings. Even during the declining interest rate environment in 1991–2, these long-term debentures and deposits have attracted huge amounts of money from instruments inside M2+CDs. This may (at least partially) account for the rise in velocity seen in Figure 38.2. These movements have led the BOJ to put greater emphasis on broadly-defined liquidity.

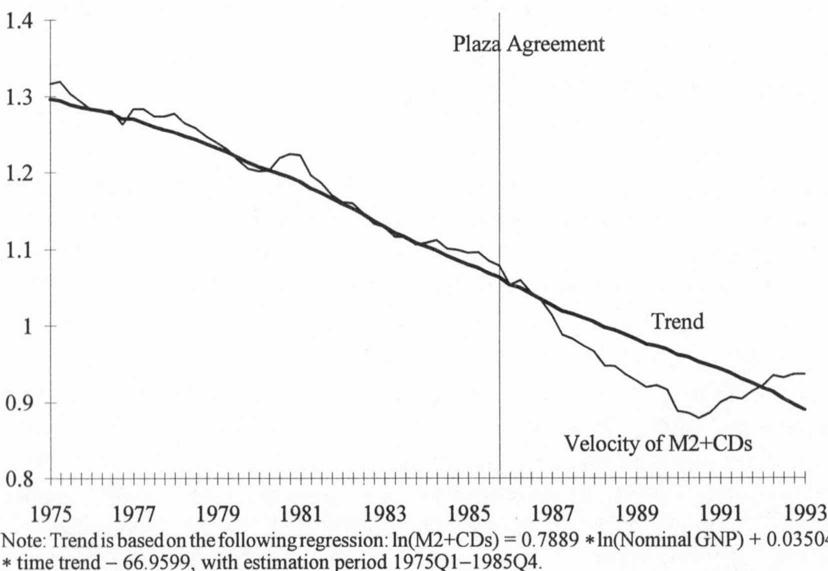

Note: Trend is based on the following regression: ln(M2+CDs) = 0.7889 * ln(Nominal GNP) + 0.03504 * time trend – 66.9599, with estimation period 1975Q1–1985Q4.

Fig. 38.2. Velocity of Money

39 Monetary Base

Source: Research and Statistics Department, Bank of Japan.

Frequency: Monthly.

Release: Figures are released each month with a two-month lag. End-of-month figures only are available.

Availability: End-of-month outstanding for the components of monetary base are available from January 1970 onward. There are no official statistics for monthly average outstanding of monetary base.

Monetary base (also called high-powered money or reserve money) is defined as the sum of cash currency (coins and notes) holdings of the public and reserves (defined here as deposits of financial institutions at the central bank). It is the narrowest definition of money supply. Since it is composed primarily of liabilities of the central bank, it is usually considered to be a variable that the central bank can influence directly. It is also considered to reflect the monetary policy stance of the central bank. End-of-month figures are available, but average outstanding figures must be estimated (see Chapter 40 for method of estimation).

Details

Monetary Survey

End-of-the-month figures for monetary base are available in 'Monetary Survey', which appears in *Economic Statistics Monthly* published by the Bank of Japan. Table 2 in Monetary Survey is *Accounts of Monetary Authorities* (Monetary Authorities includes the BOJ and monetary authority functions undertaken by the central government). The item 'reserve money' is the sum of 'cash currency issued' and 'deposits from Deposit Money Banks'. 'Cash currency issued' is the same as cash currency holdings of the public. Deposits from Deposit Money Banks are deposits of financial institutions with the BOJ, or reserves. (Deposit Money Banks, or DMBs, include every bank subject to reserve requirements with the exception of foreign banks.) Thus, 'reserve money' is (with the exception noted) equivalent to monetary base, i.e. cash currency holdings of the public and reserves.

'Cash currency issued' can be decomposed into currency held by DMBs and currency outside DMBs using table 3, *Accounts of Deposit Money Banks*. The item 'reserves at Bank of Japan' is not 'reserves' as defined above, but the sum of currency held by DMBs and 'deposits from DMBs'. By subtracting 'deposits from DMBs' from 'reserves at Bank of Japan' the figure for currency held by DMBs is obtained. Currency outside DMBs is then 'cash currency issued' less currency held by DMBs. Figures for monetary base and its components are shown in Table 39.1.

The coverage of Monetary Survey includes the Bank of Japan, Foreign Exchange Fund, All Banks excluding trust accounts (city banks, regional banks, member banks of the Second Association of Regional Banks, long-term credit banks, and trust banks), Shinkin banks, the Norinchukin Bank, and the Shoko Chukin Bank.

Table 39.1. Monetary Base
Calendar Years 1987–1992 (End-of-Year Outstanding)
Billion Yen, unless otherwise noted

	1987	1988	1989	1990	1991	1992	1992 % of Total
Monetary base: total	34,919	39,463	44,568	47,865	47,192	45,396	100.0
Cash currency issued	31,927	35,180	40,449	43,017	43,318	42,511	93.6
Cash currency held by DMBs (A)	3,344	3,658	3,768	5,763	5,348	4,408	9.7
Cash currency outside DMBs	28,583	31,521	36,681	37,254	37,970	38,103	83.9
Deposits from DMBs (B)	2,993	4,283	4,119	4,848	3,874	2,885	6.4
Reserves at BOJ (A)+(B)	6,337	7,941	7,887	10,610	9,222	7,293	16.1

Source: Bank of Japan.

Features and Problems

Growth Rate of Monetary Base

The growth rate of monetary base is considered to reflect the monetary policy stance of the central bank more precisely than that of M2+CDs. Dramatic reduction in monetary base growth in 1974–6, 1980–1, and 1990–2 reflects tight monetary policy, while the relatively high growth rate in the latter half of the 1980s reflects accommodative monetary policy (see Fig. 39.1).

One problem in calculating the growth rate of monetary base is that when reserve requirements are changed, the amount of reserves changes, which affects the growth rate of monetary base. Under some circumstances it is better to adjust the amount of reserves to what they would have been if the reserve requirements had been the same as in some base period. A simple method is to use the reserves/M2+CDs ratio as a proxy for the reserve requirement ratio, and calculate adjusted reserves as:

$$\text{Adjusted Reserves} = \text{Actual Reserves} * \frac{\text{(Reserves/M2+CDs) in base period}}{\text{(Reserves/M2+CDs) in current period}}$$

Money Multiplier

The money multiplier is defined as the broadly defined money supply (M2+CDs) divided by the monetary base. The traditional view of monetary policy is based on stability of (or, at least, predictable movement of) the money multiplier. If the central bank can control the monetary base and the money multiplier is constant, then it can indirectly control the broadly defined money supply. Since monetary base consists of central bank liabilities (except for coins in the case of Japan), the central bank should have almost complete control over it. The Bank of Japan, however, has sometimes claimed that monetary base is beyond their control, or that changes in broadly defined money determine changes in monetary base.

Instead of adopting the multiplier approach, the Bank of Japan focuses on changes in interest rates in the call and bill markets and their effect on the growth of broadly defined money.

Note that it may be appropriate to use adjusted reserves (adjusted monetary base figures) when calculating the money multiplier, as in Fig. 39.2.

End-of-month vs. Average Outstanding of Monetary Base

Figures for end-of-month outstanding of monetary base may reflect special factors affecting demand and supply of the components of monetary base that happen to occur at the end of a month (for example, holidays). In such a case, it is desirable to use the monthly or quarterly average outstanding values to smooth out the special factors (see Chapter 40 for method of calculation).

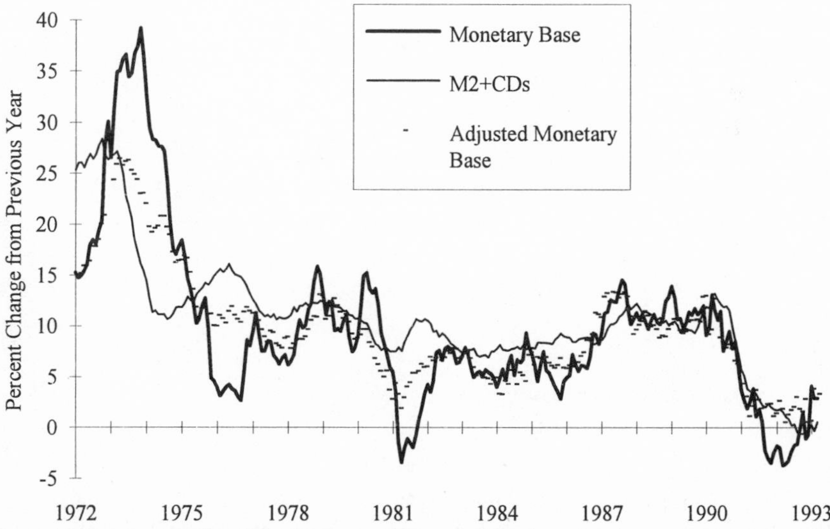

Note: All figures seasonally adjusted. Monetary base and adjusted monetary base are two-period moving average of end-of-month figures.

Fig. 39.1. Comparison of Money Supply Measures

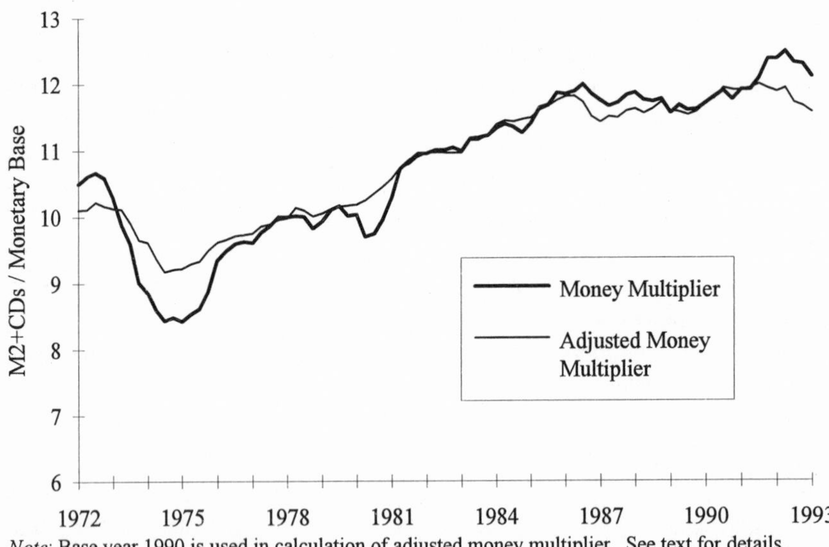

Note: Base year 1990 is used in calculation of adjusted money multiplier. See text for details.

Fig. 39.2. Money Multiplier

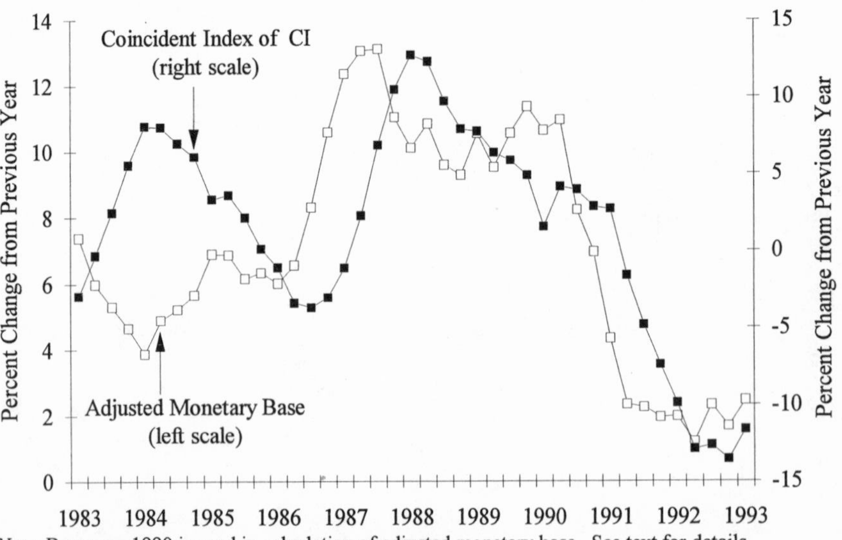

Note: Base year 1990 is used in calculation of adjusted monetary base. See text for details.

Fig. 39.3. Monetary Base and Real Economic Activity

Operations of the Bank of Japan

40 Supply and Demand of Funds

Source: Research and Statistics Department, Bank of Japan.

Frequency: Daily and Monthly.

Release: Figures for the previous day are published in newspapers (including the *Nikkei Financial Daily*). Quick estimates for the previous month are released at the beginning of each month. Revised monthly figures are published in *Economic Statistics Monthly* with a two-month lag.

Availability: Figures are available from 1950 onward.

Supply and Demand of Funds reveals the factors responsible for changes in the level of reserve deposits as well as the supply and demand for monetary base. These statistics are fundamental to the Bank of Japan's day-to-day operations in money markets.

Details

Factors Affecting the Level of Reserve Deposits

The three main factors affecting the level of reserve deposits are (throughout this chapter, reserve deposits, or simply reserves, are the deposits of private financial institutions with the BOJ): (1) flows of banknotes between financial institutions and the public; (2) payments and receipts of the government; and (3) credit provided by the BOJ to other financial institutions. An example of each of these is discussed (in an oversimplified manner) below.

1. Banknotes

Suppose the public desires to increase its holding of banknotes. People will withdraw cash from their deposit accounts, and the financial institutions will replenish their cash holdings by withdrawing from their accounts with the BOJ (i.e. by decreasing reserves). Thus an increase in banknotes (outflow from the BOJ) leads to a reduction in reserves. It should be noted that coins are not included in banknotes, and are a liability of the Ministry of Finance. An increase in coins would also lead to a reduction in reserves, and is included in Treasury funds (as part of the entry 'others' in Table 40.2).

2. Payments and Receipts of the Government

In Japan, corporations make tax payments by requesting their banks to transfer the funds to the government. The banks cover the transfer by withdrawing from their accounts with the BOJ (i.e. by reducing reserves). The government's deposits with the BOJ increase by an equal amount, but this has no effect on reserves. Thus receipts of the government lead to a reduction in reserves.

3. Credit Provided by the BOJ

The BOJ can lend to a financial institution by simply crediting the institution's account with the BOJ. Thus provision of credit by the BOJ leads to an increase in reserves. The BOJ can also provide credit by purchasing financial assets in money markets which, just like lending, amounts to the BOJ providing funds in return for payments in the future.

Fundamental Formula of Monetary Control

The factors affecting reserves can be gathered into a single equation:

Increases (decreases) in reserve deposits
= Inflows (outflows) of banknotes
+ Payments (receipts) of the government
+ Provision (absorption) of credit by the BOJ [1]

This equation is the fundamental formula that the BOJ uses in its monetary control. Each of these components is published in 'Supply and Demand of Funds' (see Table 40.1). All figures in Supply and Demand of Funds are on a flow basis, giving the change in each item during the given time period. From the point of view of the BOJ, positive figures represent increases in the net financial assets of the BOJ. Since banknotes are liabilities of the BOJ, positive (negative) figures for banknotes represent inflows (outflows) of banknotes to (from) the BOJ. Treasury funds are the deposits of the government with the BOJ, and represent a liability of the BOJ. Positive figures for Treasury funds mean that the BOJ's liabilities have been reduced, i.e. the government's deposits have been reduced. This happens when the government makes net payments to the private sector. 'BOJ credit' is the amount of credit provided by the BOJ, i.e. how much financial institutions owe to it plus the amount of financial assets purchased in money markets. Thus BOJ credit is an asset, and positive figures represent provision of credit. By summing the entries for banknotes, Treasury funds, and BOJ credit, the increase in reserve deposits is obtained, as in Equation 1. Below, it is demonstrated that Equation 1 is equivalent to the equilibrium of supply and demand for monetary base.

Table 40.1. Supply and Demand of Funds
Calendar Years 1987–1992, Billion Yen

	1987	1988	1989	1990	1991	1992
Banknotes	–2,302	–3,132	–5,102	–2,378	–85	857
+ Treasury funds	297	609	399	3,637	–19,245	–1,368
(+ other funds)	1,334	1,234	–1,026	1,327	5,343	–76
= excess / shortage (–) of funds	–671	–1,289	–5,728	2,586	–13,988	–512
+ BOJ credit	1,060	2,571	5,586	–1,847	12,939	–408
= reserves	389	1,282	–142	739	–1,049	–919

Note: Prior to August 1992, Treasury funds did not include 'other funds'. 1992 Figure for Treasury funds includes 'other funds' for all of 1992. See Chapter 45 for details.

Source: Bank of Japan, *Economic Statistics Annual.*

Table 40.2. Components of BOJ Credit and Treasury Funds in Supply and Demand of Funds Statistics
Calendar Years 1987–1992, Billion Yen

	1987	1988	1989	1990	1991	1992
Treasury funds - total	297	609	399	3,636	–19,245	–1,368
General funds	–2,633	–401	3,690	10,617	–8,701	3,281
Real general funds	–2,799	–334	3,481	10,421	–8,770	3,112
Special account for food control	183	–87	146	189	170	199
Government bonds	–2,498	206	–359	–5,066	–10,336	–3,885
Foreign exchange funds	5,427	804	–2,933	–1,915	–208	–688
(Other funds)	1,334	1,234	–1,026	1,327	5,343	–76
BOJ credit -- total	1,060	2,671	7,115	–1,847	12,939	5,041
Lending	44	1,907	–1,529	–642	3,964	–3,049
Bills purchased	99	301	4,100	–2,294	3,914	2,180
Commercial Paper purchased	--	--	--	--	--	--
Sales of Treasury Bills	--	--	--	454	69	109
Sales of Financing Bills	–0	–100	995	–991	991	–1,792
Short-term sales of securities	178	42	305	–525	1,689	–609
Sales of securities	738	422	1,715	2,151	2,312	2,752

Note: Figures for sub-categories of real general funds in Treasury funds are published in *Economic Statistics Annual.* Note in Table 40.1 also applies to this table.

Source: Bank of Japan, *Economic Statistics Annual.*

Estimation Average Outstanding of Monetary Base

As mentioned in Chapter 39, there are no official statistics for monthly average outstanding of monetary base. This must be constructed by estimating the outstanding amount of monetary base on a daily basis, then taking the average of the daily figures. Rearranging equation 1 to gather the components of monetary base on the left-hand side yields:

Increase (decrease) in reserves deposits – Inflow (outflow) of banknotes
= Payments (receipts) of the government
+ Provision (absorption) of credit by the BOJ [2]

In this equation, the left-hand side is the demand for monetary base (from the private sector on a flow basis), while the right-hand side is the supply of monetary base (by the BOJ). Thus Equation 1 is analogous to the equilibrium of supply and demand for monetary base on a flow basis. Either side of Equation 2 gives the change in monetary base. Each of the components in Equation 2 (as well as the components of BOJ credit in Table 40.2) is published daily. The daily figures for monetary base are obtained by adding the daily changes in monetary base to the end-of-month outstanding values, e.g. to calculate monetary base as of the end of July 1:

Monetary base as of the end of July 1
= Monetary base as of the end of June
+ (Increase in reserve deposits on July 1)
– (Inflow of banknotes on July 1)

Two problems with this estimation are: changes in coins outstanding (which are a part of monetary base) are not included; reserve deposits include foreign banks in Supply and Demand of Funds but not in monetary base figures (which are taken from Monetary Survey).

Excess and Shortage of Funds

The BOJ refers to the total of the inflows or outflows of banknotes and payments or receipts of the government in equation 1 as 'Excess and Shortage of Funds'. An increase in shortage of funds (outflow of banknotes and receipts of the government) is interpreted as tightening of supply-demand conditions in the money market, since a shortage of funds tends to decrease reserve deposits *as long as the amount of credit provision by the BOJ remains unchanged.* A decrease in reserve deposits forces banks to try to borrow funds in the money market, driving up interest rates.

To control day-to-day fluctuations in the market, the BOJ chiefly uses provision and absorption of credit. By examining excess and shortage of funds, it can determine how much credit will have to be provided (or absorbed) in order to achieve its desired effect on interest rates. The BOJ releases daily a forecast for the following day's excess and shortage of funds, along with its planned provision/absorption of credit.

Seasonal Fluctuation

Seasonal fluctuations of monthly figures for banknotes and Treasury funds are large (see Figs. 40.1, 40.2, and 40.3). Demand for banknotes increases in June and December for bonus payments (which appear as large negative figures in the statistics), and recedes in January and May (positive figures). Treasury funds shows positive figures (net payments) in February to May and November, while it shows negative figures in January, June, July, and December. These seasonal fluctuations are (at least partially) offset by monetary operations of the BOJ.

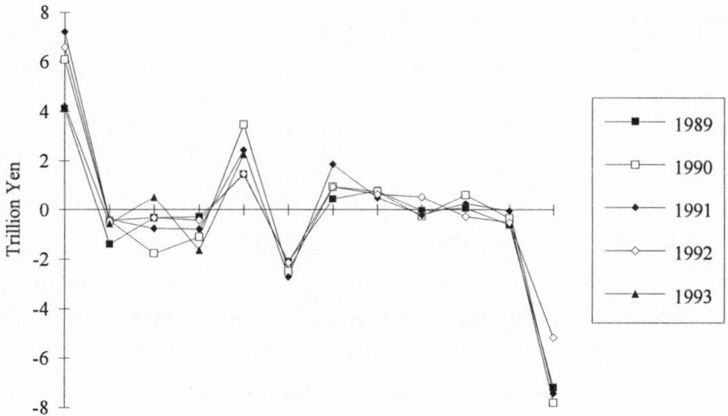

Fig. 40.1. Seasonal Fluctuation in Banknotes

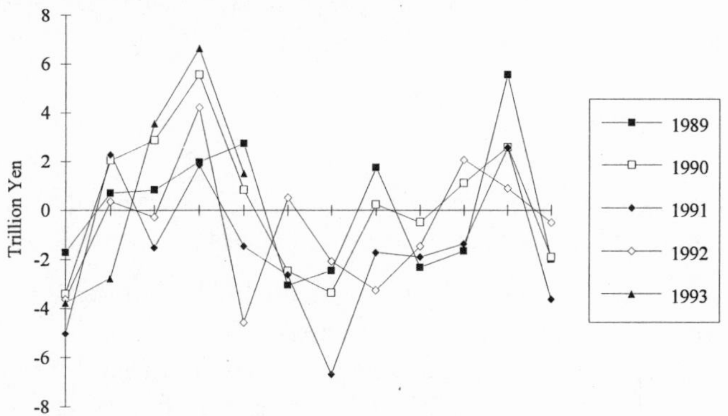

Fig. 40.2. Seasonal Fluctuation in Treasury Funds

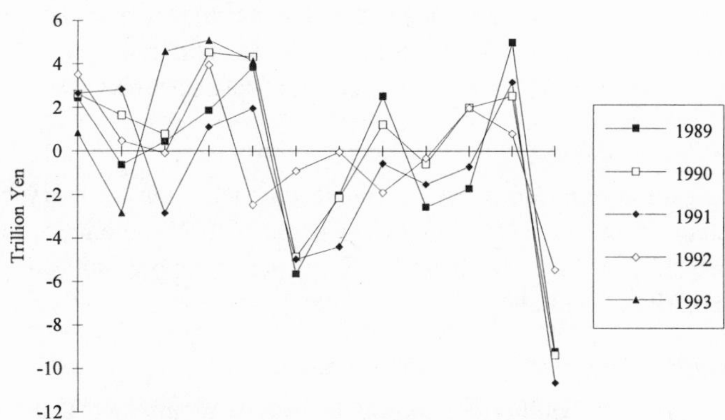

Fig. 40.3. Seasonal Fluctuation in Shortage of Funds

41 Reserve Requirements

Source: Research and Statistics Department, Bank of Japan.

Frequency: Reserve requirements on the liabilities of financial institutions are not changed frequently. Monthly data on legal requirements and actual reserves outstanding are available in *Economic Statistics Monthly* published by the Bank of Japan.

Release: Daily outstanding of reserves is available in the *Nihon Keizai Shimbun* (newspaper). End-of-month outstanding is released two months later and average outstanding four months later in *Economic Statistics Monthly*.

Availability: Reserve requirements were introduced in September 1959. Historical reserve requirement rates are shown in *Economic Statistics Annual*.

Details

Table 41.1 compares reserve requirement systems in five industrialized countries.

The main features of the system of reserve requirements in Japan are:

1. Only deposits with the Bank of Japan can be used to fulfill reserve requirements; vault cash is not counted as reserve assets.
2. Required reserves are based on the average outstanding balance of deposits during one calendar month. The 'maintenance period' (the period in which financial institutions must actually fulfill the reserve requirements) begins on the sixteenth day of that month and ends on the fifteenth day of the next.
3. Any shortage in reserve deposits in a certain maintenance period is subject to a penalty rate, which is 3.75% above the official discount rate.
4. Excess reserves may not be carried over from one maintenance period to the next.

Financial Institutions Subject to Reserve Requirements

The financial institutions subject to reserve requirements are: ordinary banks (including foreign banks in Japan); long-term credit banks; authorized foreign exchange banks; Shinkin banks (with outstanding deposits of more than 160 billion yen); and the Norinchukin Bank.

Types of Liabilities Subject to Reserve Requirements

The following types of liability are subject to reserve requirements: deposits, debentures, principal of money in trust, and 'foreign' (accounts relating to foreign currency and non-residents). Table 41.2 shows the reserve rate (reserve require-

Table 41.1. Comparison of Reserve Requirement Systems

	Japan	USA	UK	Germany	France
Carry Over	No	Yes	No	Yes	Yes[1]
Maintenance Period	1 month	2 weeks.	6 months	1 month	1 month
Lag[2]	Half-month	2 days[3] or 1 month[4]	Half-year	Half-month	Half-month
Inclusion of vault cash	No	Yes	No	Yes	No
Penalty on shortage[5]	Yes	Yes	No	Yes	Yes
Progressive requirement	Yes	Yes	No	Yes	No

Notes: 1. Only for excess reserves. 2. Lag between the period of calculation of required reserves and the maintenance period. 3. For demand deposits. 4. For other deposits. 5. Japan: official discount rate + 3.75%; USA: official discount rate + 2%; Germany: Lombard rate + 3% is maximum; France: overnight call + 3%.

Source: Ministry of Finance.

ment ratio) for each type of liability (the reserve rate for 'foreign' is excluded to avoid complexity).

Reserve Progress Ratio and Monetary Operations

The reserve progress ratio is the sum of the daily balances of actual reserves divided by the total cumulative required reserves for a maintenance period. The reserve progress ratio has a value of 0 –100%. In the last day of the maintenance period, this ratio should be equal to (or more than) 100%. For example, suppose a bank's total cumulative required reserves are 50 billion yen-days during a maintenance period (assume this to be 30 days). If the bank has a total of 1 billion yen in reserve deposits during the first 10 days of the maintenance period, then the reserve progress ratio will increase by 2% (1 billion yen / 50 billion yen) per day, reaching 20% after 10 days. If the bank increases its reserve deposits to 2 billion yen on the eleventh day, and maintains this level for the last 20 days of the maintenance period, the reserve progress ratio increases by 4% per day, reaching 100% on the final day. Total cumulative reserve deposits would then equal required reserves:

1 billion yen * 10 days + 2 billion yen * 20 days = 50 billion yen-days

The Bank of Japan watches the reserve progress ratio closely to monitor the financial positions of banks. The BOJ can facilitate (delay) the reserve progress of banks by supplying funds to (absorbing funds from) money markets. If the BOJ delays the reserve progress of banks by absorbing funds from the market, banks are forced to borrow larger amounts of money from the market, which tends to raise money market interest rates.

Table 41.2. Reserve Rates by Type of Liability
Percent

	Effective date	
	16 Oct. 1991	1 July 1986
Deposits of banks[1]		
Time deposits		
50–500 billion yen	0.05	0.125
500–1,200 billion yen	0.05	0.125
1.2–2.5 trillion yen	0.9	1.375
Over 2.5 trillion yen	1.2	1.75
Other deposits		
50–500 billion yen	0.1	0.25
500–1,200 billion yen	0.8	1.875
1.2–2.5 trillion yen	1.3	2.5
Over 2.5 trillion yen	1.3	2.5
Deposits of the Norinchukin Bank		
Time deposits	0.05	0.125
Other deposits	0.1	0.25
Debentures	0.1	0.125[2]
Principal of money in trust	0.1	0.125[2]

Notes: 1. Ordinary banks, long-term credit banks, authorized foreign exchange banks, and Shinkin banks. No reserve ratio was set for amounts of 50 billion yen or less. 2. Effective as of April 1, 1981.

Source: Bank of Japan, *Economic Statistics Monthly*.

Average Outstanding for Maintenance Period

It should be noted that the average outstanding of legal reserve requirements shown in *Economic Statistics Monthly* is *not* the average outstanding for the *calendar* month but rather for the *maintenance period.* For example, the figure given for January is the average outstanding between 16 January and 15 February.

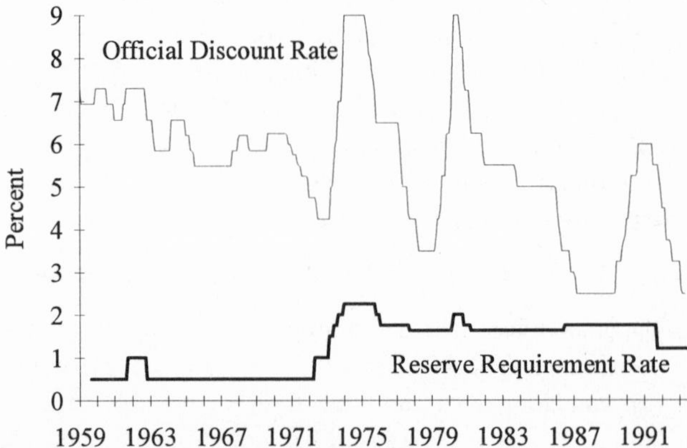

Note: End-of-month figures. Reserve requirement rate is rate for the highest category of time deposits.

Fig. 41.1. Reserve Requirement Rate

42 Official Discount Rate and Lending Policy of the BOJ

Source: Research and Statistics Department, Bank of Japan.

Availability: Historical time series for the official discount rate is available in *Economic Statistics Monthly* published by the Bank of Japan.

Details

The official discount rate is the lending rate of the Bank of Japan to private financial institutions. There are actually two types of official discount rates, depending on the type of collateral:

1. Discount rate of commercial bills and interest rates on loans secured by government bonds, specially designated securities and bills corresponding to commercial bills.
2. Interest rate on loans secured by other collateral.

The interest rate with collateral of type 1 is usually referred to as the official discount rate. Changes in the discount rate are determined by the Policy Committee of the BOJ (of which the chairman is the BOJ governor).

Credit Ceiling

There is a credit ceiling so that banks are not allowed to borrow too heavily from the BOJ. Currently, this ceiling is applied to city banks and is set to a total of 5 trillion yen.

Special Lending Facility

The special lending facility was introduced in March 1981. The BOJ can lend money to banks at a different interest rate from the prevailing discount rate in response to an abrupt change or disturbance in economic conditions, such as wide fluctuations of foreign interest rates or exchange rates. This facility has never been implemented.

Impact of Change in the Discount Rate on Economic Activities

A change in the discount rate might be expected to affect the amount borrowed from the central bank, but this is not the case under the current interest rate structure in Japan. The discount rate is usually set lower than the call and bill market rates, which means that banks would (in general) like to borrow as much as possible at the discount rate. Thus, the BOJ is free to determine how much will be lent to each bank (credit rationing), and a change in the discount rate does not affect the amount borrowed. This does not, however, imply that there will be no effect on interest rates. Changes in the discount rate usually reflect the stance of the central bank. If, for example, the discount rate is raised, banks may believe the central bank will tighten its monetary policy, and are likely to tighten credit standards and to raise their lending rates. This is called the announcement effect; the BOJ usually attempts to time changes in the discount rate to create the greatest possible announcement effect.

Weakening Link with Other Interest Rates

In the past, when most interest rates were regulated, a change in the discount rate triggered changes in other lending and deposit rates. For example, the short-term prime rate and regulated deposit rates had been linked to the discount rate. Recent liberalization of interest rates on deposits, however, have weakened this link. The short-term prime rate and interest rates on money market certificates are determined by the prevailing money market rates (for details, see Chapter 48). Therefore, changes in the discount rate have tended to follow, not lead the changes in money market rates. This is sometimes called 'market-induced change in the discount rate'.

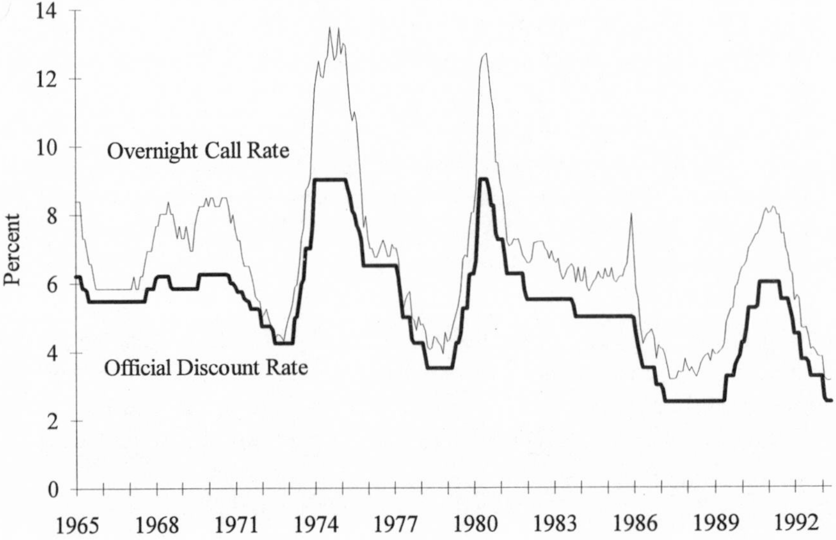

Fig. 42.1. Official Discount Rate

43 Open Market Operations

Source: Research and Statistics Department, Bank of Japan.

Frequency: Daily and Monthly.

Release: Results of open market operations by the BOJ during the previous month are published in *Economic Statistics Monthly*. Daily results are published in newspapers.

Along with changes in reserve requirements (see Chapter 41) and the discount rate (see Chapter 42), open market operations represent one of the three main instruments of monetary policy of the Bank of Japan. The role of open market operations among the policy instruments has become increasingly important.

Details

The Bank of Japan can affect the reserve positions of private banks, and thus money market rates, by open market operations (below we do not distinguish between operations conducted in open markets and those conducted in interbank markets). It is useful to classify open market operations into three categories: (1) defensive operations; (2) dynamic operations; and (3) supply of money for economic growth.

While the first two operations are mainly concerned with short-term adjustment of supply and demand of funds, the third operation is deemed as concerning the long-term supply of money for economic growth. Defensive operations by the BOJ are used to neutralize daily or seasonal excess demand (supply) of funds in money markets via supply (absorption) of funds to (from) the market by buying (selling) operations. Dynamic operations are intended to affect the 'reserve progress ratio' of private banks so that they can understand the BOJ's intention of maintaining or changing demand/supply conditions in the money markets. Because these two operations are short-term adjustments of daily or seasonal fluctuations in supply and demand of funds, the BOJ usually conducts them with resale or repurchase agreements. Supply of money for economic growth, on the other hand, has the long-term objective of supplying money necessary for economic growth. Based on this viewpoint, money for economic growth is supplied by the outright purchase of securities (government bonds).

Types of Securities and Bills for Operations

Open market operations are conducted via purchase or sales of various types of securities and bills. They include:

1. Bills (high-grade commercial and industrial bills, trade bills, high-grade promissory notes, yen-denominated fixed-term export and import bills, and bank-issued bills of exchange).
2. Commercial Paper (CP).
3. Treasury Bills (TB).
4. Financing Bills (FB).
5. Government bonds with repurchase/resale agreement.
6. Government bonds.

Among these instruments, items 1–5 are typically used for daily or seasonal operations while item 6 is used to supply money for economic growth. Interest rates on all open market operations are tendered or based on the prevailing money market rates. Table 43.1 summarizes the types of open market operations and their instruments.

Table 43.1. Monetary Operations and Instruments

	Date Introduced	Daily Adjustment	Seasonal Adjustment	Money for Growth
BOJ Lending	Nov. 1962	x		
Bills[1]	Aug. 1971	x	x	
CP	May 1989	x[2]	x	
TB	Jan. 1990		x	
FB[3]	May 1981		x	
Bonds, Repo[4]	Dec. 1987		x	
Bonds[5]	Nov. 1962			x

Notes: 1. Sales of bills were introduced in August 1971, while purchase of bills were introduced in June 1972. 2. In principle daily adjustment, but in practice usually conducted for seasonal adjustment. 3. Due to lack of a mature secondary market for FB, only sales of FB are currently conducted. 4. Operation via bonds with repurchase/resale agreement. 5. Outright purchase of bonds.

Monetary Operations and Supply and Demand of Funds

Table 43.1 corresponds to the sub-categories of the item 'BOJ credit' in 'Supply and Demand of Funds' statistics (see Table 40.2).

Results of Open Market Operations

The results of open market operations for the most recent month are available in the table 'Bank of Japan Operations in the Money Markets' in *Economic Statistics Monthly* published by the BOJ. Type of instrument, date of resale/repurchase, period, amount and interest rate are available.

44 Accounts of the Bank of Japan

Source:	Research and Statistics Department, Bank of Japan.
Frequency:	Daily and Monthly.
Release:	Daily figures for outstanding banknotes, lending, and government bonds are released on the following day in newspapers. Figures for the previous month are released at the end of each month.
Availability:	Figures are available for 1947 onward.

The accounts of the Bank of Japan reveals the results of its various operations. There are two related statistics for market operations of the BOJ: (1) Monetary Survey; and (2) Supply and Demand of Funds (see Chapter 40 for details). 'Accounts of Monetary Authorities' in the former includes not only the BOJ but also monetary authority functions undertaken by the central government. The latter does not include transactions by the BOJ with the government. Comparison of the BOJ balance sheet with related statistics is useful for understanding the transactions of the BOJ. Only end-of-month figures are available in the 'BOJ Accounts' statistics published in *Economic Statistics Monthly*.

Details

Balance Sheet Items

Table 44.1 presents the balance sheet of the Bank of Japan. On the asset side, 'loans and discounts' are the sum of outstanding bills discounted from private banks and loans extended to private banks. 'Bills purchased' are those purchased from private banks. 'Government bonds' reveal the results of transactions with both private banks and the Government. 'Foreign assets accounts' are foreign assets bought with Foreign Exchange Funds in the BOJ's capacity as agent for the Government. These include deposits of the BOJ with foreign central banks and foreign government securities. 'Agents accounts' is the net outstanding of tax receipts less Treasury expenditures by the BOJ's agents at private banks.

On the liability side, 'banknotes issued' include only outstanding banknotes (coins are not included since they are a liability of the Ministry of Finance). 'Financial institutions' deposits' are the reserves of private banks in the form of deposits with the BOJ. This roughly corresponds to 'deposits from Deposit Money

Table 44.1. Balance Sheet of the Bank of Japan
Calendar Years 1988–1992, Billion Yen, end-of-year figures

	1988	1989	1990	1991	1992	Change [91-90]
Total assets	39,644	45,131	49,157	49,591	47,989	434
Gold bullion	140	140	140	140	140	0
Cash	287	290	431	483	513	52
Loans and discounts	8,474	6,945	6,303	10,267	7,218	3,964
Bills discounted	187	237	144	135	121	–9
Loans	8,287	6,708	6,160	10,132	7,098	3,972
Bills purchased[1]	5,100	9,200	6,906	10,820	13,000	3,914
Government bonds	22,521	25,348	31,542	24,147	23,305	–7,395
Financing Bills (FBs)	15,383	20,845	22,541	17,976	15,039	–4,565
Foreign assets accounts	2,681	2,634	2,996	2,964	2,994	–32
Agents accounts	2	64	71	*	*	–71
Others	438	508	766	770	817	4
Liabilities and net worth	39,644	45,131	49,157	49,591	47,989	434
Banknotes issued	32,318	37,420	39,798	39,883	39,026	85
Financial institutions' deposits	4,284	4,143	4,881	3,832	2,912	–1,049
Government deposits	373	495	521	621	623	100
Other deposits	9	5	424	212	324	–212
Other accounts	492	470	1,071	1,368	1,175	297
Allowances	770	1,178	1,027	2,157	2,182	1,130
Capital	*	*	*	*	*	*
Reserves	1,398	1,420	1,435	1,518	1,747	83

Notes: 1. Bills purchased includes Commercial Paper purchased. (*) indicates less than 0.5 billion yen.
Source: Bank of Japan, *Economic Statistics Annual*.

Banks' in 'Accounts of Monetary Authorities' in *Monetary Survey* (see Chapter 39). 'Financial institutions' deposits' shown in the BOJ's balance sheet is usually slightly larger than that of 'deposits from Deposit Money Banks' in *Monetary Survey* because the latter does not include foreign banks. However, the latter are estimates which are not subject to revision, and occasionally exceed the former. 'Government deposits' include transactions between the government and both the private sector and BOJ. It shows relatively little seasonal fluctuation, since transactions with the BOJ tend to offset transactions with the private sector (see Chapter 45). 'Other deposits' are those by foreign central banks and international organizations with the BOJ. As is shown in Table 44.1, most of the BOJ's liability is banknotes.

Loans and Discounts by the Bank of Japan

Figures for loans and discounts by the BOJ to private banks are available by type of bank, as shown in Table 44.2.

Table 44.2. Loans and Discounts by the Bank of Japan, by Type of Bank
End-of-Calendar Years 1987-1992, Billion Yen

	1987	1988	1989	1990	1991	1992
Total	6,567	8,474	6,945	6,303	10,267	7,218
All Banks (Zengin)	5,944	6,501	6,376	5,872	9,459	6,786
City banks	5,156	5,456	4,568	4,273	5,199	3,973
Regional Banks I	319	486	1,078	648	1,663	900
Regional Banks II[1]	--	--	114	67	268	194
Trust banks	20	25	27	150	1,022	814
Long-term credit banks	449	534	589	734	1,306	905
Shoko Chukin Bank, Norinchukin Bank	6	7	6	5	357	142
Shinkin banks, etc.[2]	617	1,965	563	426	452	290

Notes: 1. Member banks of the Second Association of Regional Banks. 2. Includes money market dealers.

Source: Bank of Japan, *Economic Statistics Annual.*

Features and Problems

Transactions with Government Outside Money Markets

The Bank of Japan makes transactions not only with private banks, but also with the government. Since the 'BOJ Accounts' include government transactions while 'Supply and Demand of Funds' excludes them, a comparison of the statistics can reveal transactions of the government with the BOJ.

Table 44.3 reconciles the BOJ's transactions with banks in 'Supply and Demand of Funds' and 'BOJ Accounts'. In the latter statistics, as shown in Table 44.1, loans and discounts increased by 3,964 (= 10,267 – 6,303) billion yen while bills purchased increased by 3,914 (= 10,820 – 6,906) billion yen during calendar year

Table 44.3. Reconciliation of Accounts and Implied Transactions by the BOJ
Calendar Year 1991, Billion Yen

	Supply and Demand of Funds Table 40.2	BOJ Accounts Table 44.1
Loans and discounts	3,964	[3,964] (=10,267 – 6,303)
Bills purchases	3,914	[3,914] (=10,820 – 6,906)
Government bond purchases		–7,395
from private banks	5,061	
from government	[–12,456] (= –7,395 – 5,061)	

Note: Negative figure in 'government bond purchases' indicates sales. Figures in brackets are indirectly obtained, as explained in the text.

Source: Bank of Japan, *Economic Statistics Annual.*

1991. These two figures are exactly the same as shown in lendings (3,964 billion yen) and bills purchased (3,914 billion yen) in BOJ Credit of 'Supply and Demand of Funds' statistics (see Table 40.2).

However, this reconciliation is not possible for government bonds. In 'BOJ Accounts', government bond holdings declined by 7,395 billion yen in calendar year 1991 while the 'Supply and Demand of Funds' statistics show that the BOJ bought 5,061 billion yen of government bonds in money markets (this figure is the sum of the last four items in Table 40.2). These two figures imply net sales and redemptions of government bonds by the BOJ of 12,456 billion yen to a third party outside of financial markets. This third party must be the government because the BOJ does not make transactions outside of financial markets with the private sector.

This striking contrast reminds us of the fact that, unlike Supply and Demand of Funds statistics, the balance sheet of the BOJ reflects not only its transactions with private banks but also those with the government. The missing link between these two statistics is provided by the 'Statement of Receipts and Payments of Treasury Accounts', covered in Chapter 45.

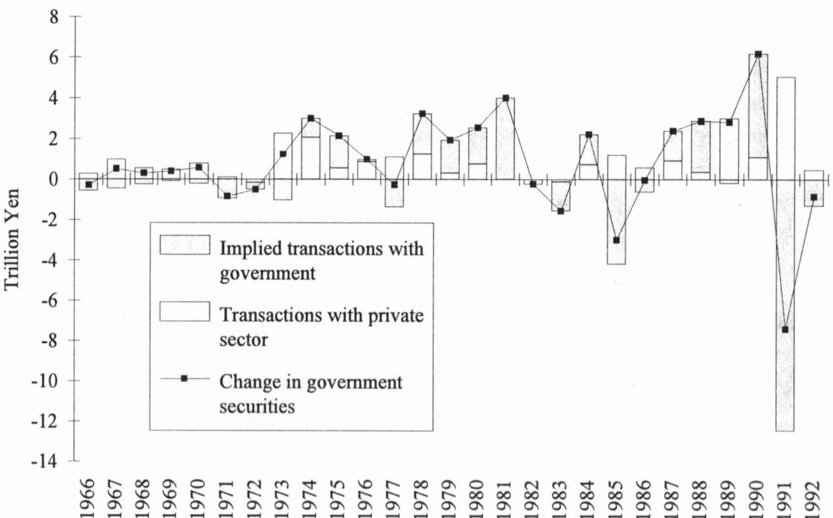

Fig. 44.1. Change in BOJ's Holdings of Government Securities

45 Statement of Receipts and Payments of Treasury Accounts

Source: Research and Statistics Department, Bank of Japan.

Frequency: Daily and Monthly.

Release: Figures for the previous month are released on the 1st of each month. A forecast for the month is made available at the same time. Figures are available in *Economic Statistics Monthly* published by the Bank of Japan, with a two-month lag. Daily figures are published in newspapers.

The Statement of Receipts and Payments of Treasury Accounts reveals the result of transactions of the government with the private sector and the Bank of Japan. This statement has a close relationship with 'Supply and Demand of Funds' (see Chapter 40) published by the Bank of Japan, and is useful for understanding demand/supply conditions in money markets.

Details

Government transactions can be divided into three categories:

1. Transactions with the private sector.
2. Transactions with the Bank of Japan.
3. Transactions with intra-government entities.

Because the balance of transactions with intra-government entities sum to zero by definition (they do not affect the deposits outstanding of the government), the sum of transactions with the private sector and with the Bank of Japan comprise government transactions. They are shown in 'Consolidated Receipts and Payments of the Treasury'. The 'Transactions with the Private Sector' account is frequently used in analyzing the financial activities of the government sector.

1. Transactions with the Private Sector

All transactions of the government with the private sector are conducted through the government account with the BOJ. Thus, government transactions with the private sector are reflected as changes in the current deposits outstanding with the BOJ; these are referred to as 'Transactions with the Private Sector of Government Current

Deposits' in the statistics. By making some adjustments to this item, 'Receipts and Payments of Treasury Accounts with the Private Sector' (hereafter, RPTAPS) is obtained. The latter figure is usually used when examining government transactions with the private sector.

Coverage

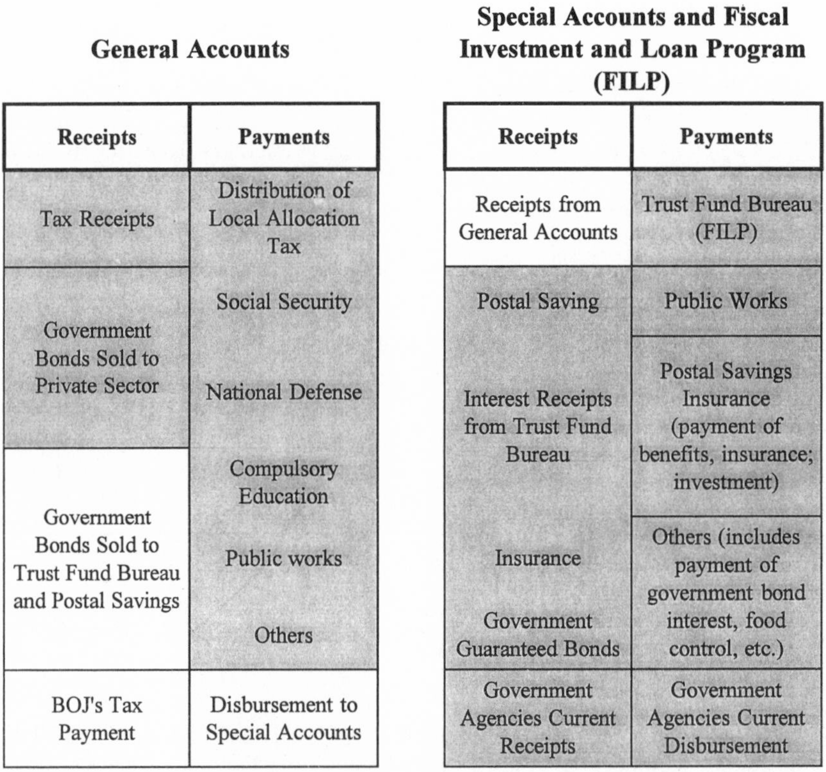

General Accounts

Receipts	Payments
Tax Receipts	Distribution of Local Allocation Tax
Government Bonds Sold to Private Sector	Social Security
	National Defense
Government Bonds Sold to Trust Fund Bureau and Postal Savings	Compulsory Education
	Public works
	Others
BOJ's Tax Payment	Disbursement to Special Accounts

Special Accounts and Fiscal Investment and Loan Program (FILP)

Receipts	Payments
Receipts from General Accounts	Trust Fund Bureau (FILP)
Postal Saving	Public Works
Interest Receipts from Trust Fund Bureau	Postal Savings Insurance (payment of benefits, insurance; investment)
Insurance	Others (includes payment of government bond interest, food control, etc.)
Government Guaranteed Bonds	
Government Agencies Current Receipts	Government Agencies Current Disbursement

Fig. 45.1. Coverage of RPTAPS (Shaded Areas)

RPTAPS covers not only General Accounts and Special Accounts, but also two government-owned banks (Japan Development Bank and Japan Export-Import Bank), and nine government financial corporations that are included in the Fiscal Investment and Loan Program (see Chapter 34 for FILP). Therefore, the coverage of RPTAPS is broader than the budget of the central government. Table 45.1 shows the major categories available.

In General Accounts, government bonds sold to the Trust Fund Bureau of the Ministry of Finance and Postal Savings are not included (they are included in 'intra-

Table 45.1. Statement of Receipts and Payments of Treasury Accounts Transactions with the Private Sector
Fiscal Year 1992, Billion Yen

	Receipts	Payments	Balance[1]
General accounts	58,911	43,400	15,511
Special accounts etc.	164,489	182,638	−18,149
Government bonds	35,213	25,002	10,211
Sub-total[2]	258,614	251,041	7,573
Adjustments etc.	6,109	6,524	−415
Total[3]	264,723	257,564	7,158
Balance of receipts and payments of Treasury funds excluding foreign exchange funds[4]			−4,359
Balance of foreign exchange funds			1,306

Notes: 1. Positive figures show net receipts (or net absorption from the markets). 2. Transactions with the Private Sector of Government Current Deposits. 3. Receipts and Payments of Treasury Accounts with the Private Sector. 4. Sum of General Accounts, Special Accounts, and adjustments less balance of Foreign Exchange Funds.

Source: Bank of Japan, *Economic Statistics Annual*.

government transactions'). The BOJ's contribution of surplus ('profits') to the Treasury are also not included (they are included in 'transactions with the BOJ').

In Special Accounts, receipts from General Accounts are not included. For the Trust Fund Bureau and Postal Insurance, which invest funds into Special Accounts and government financial institutions having deposit accounts with the BOJ, disbursements are not counted as 'payments'; they are recorded as intra-government transactions, then counted as 'payments' of Special Accounts and government financial institutions when the funds are actually disbursed to the private sector.

Reconciliation with 'Supply and Demand of Funds' Statistics

Up until 1992, the components of Total Net Balance in RPTAPS had been roughly equal to the components of Treasury Funds in 'Supply and Demand of Funds' (SDF) statistics (see Table 45.2). The sign of the corresponding figures in the two statistics is opposite, reflecting the difference in viewpoints: RPTAPS is from the viewpoint of the government while SDF is from the viewpoint of the BOJ.

The sum (difference in magnitude) of these two statistics (shown in the last column of Table 45.2) suddenly became significant in fiscal 1992. For example, the sum of 'total net balance' in RPTAPS and 'Treasury funds total' in SDF increased from zero in fiscal 1991 to 3.5 trillion yen in fiscal 1992. Effective August 1992, Treasury Funds in SDF includes 'other funds', and part of 'other funds' were reclassified into 'government bonds'. (This reclassification consists mainly of transactions with foreign central banks.) This has no effect on the change in reserves or 'excess and shortage of funds' in SDF statistics, but 'net balance' and 'Government bond' figures in RPTAPS no longer match the corresponding figures in SDF.

Table 45.2. Reconciliation with Supply and Demand of Funds Statistics
Fiscal Years 1991–1992, Billion Yen

RPTAPS[1]	1991	1992	SDF[2]	1991	1992	RPTAPS + SDF 1991	RPTAPS + SDF 1992
Total net balance[3]	18,512	7,158	Treasury funds total	−18,512	−3,670	0	3,488
Government bonds	10,672	10,211	Government bonds	−10,758	−6,649	−86	3,562
Net balance[4]	7,635	−4,359	General funds	−7,549	4,444	86	85
Foreign exchange	205	1,306	Foreign exchange	−205	−1,306	0	0

Notes: 1. Positive figures represent net receipts of the government. 2. All figures for 1992 are sums of monthly data. Positive figures represent net payments of the government. 3. Balance of Receipts and Payments of Treasury Accounts with the Private Sector. 4. Balance of Receipts and Payments of Treasury Funds excluding Foreign Exchange Funds and Government bonds.

Source: Bank of Japan, *Economic Statistics Monthly*.

2. Transactions with the BOJ

Receipts and Payments of Treasury Accounts with the Bank of Japan (hereafter referred as RPTABOJ) cover receipts of surplus from the BOJ and payments of interest and principle on the government bonds and interest on short-term government securities (FB) held by the BOJ. In addition to these transactions which are included in the government budget, issuance and redemption of short-term government securities to the BOJ, and buying and selling operations of government bonds between the Trust Fund Bureau and the BOJ, are also included.

Table 45.3. Receipts and Payments of Treasury Accounts Transactions with the Bank of Japan
Fiscal Year 1992, Billion Yen

	Receipts	Payments	Balance
Total	317,706	324,558	−6,851
Ordinary receipts and payments	8,742	15,768	−7,026
Raising and repayments of funds	154,458	154,560	−102
Treasury financing bills	61,011	60,176	835
Food financing bills	2,431	2,526	−95
Foreign exchange fund financing bills	91,016	91,858	−842
Investment and withdrawal of surplus funds	154,507	154,230	277
Trust fund bureau	108,757	107,254	1,503
Postal life insurance	40	44	−4
Debt consolidation fund	45,014	46,239	−1,225
Finance corporations	697	694	3

Source: Bank of Japan, *Economic Statistics Monthly*.

Relationship with RPTAPS

The balance in RPTABOJ is usually at least partially offset by the balance in RPTAPS. If the balance in RPTAPS shows net payments, the government's funds are declining, so it tends to borrow funds by issuing short-term government securities to the BOJ. The payment by the BOJ to the government for these securities is recorded as net receipts in the government's account with the BOJ (RPTABOJ). On the other hand, if the balance in RPTAPS shows net receipts, the government can use the receipts to repurchase its short-term obligations from the BOJ, in which case the balance in RPTABOJ shows net payments.

Features and Problems

Seasonal Fluctuation

RPTAPS has large seasonal fluctuations reflecting seasonality of tax receipts, bonus payments, social security expenses, etc. In addition, issuance and redemption of government bonds and movement of Foreign Exchange Funds show large volatility. Monthly fluctuation in RPTAPS is shown in Fig. 45.1 and Table 45.4.

Table 45.4. Seasonal Fluctuations in RPTAPS

Month	Balance	Factors
January	++	Income Tax receipts and Postal Savings (reflecting bonus)
February	–	
March	–	Local Allocation Tax disbursement
April	– –	Local Allocation Tax disbursement Disbursement from Trust Fund Bureau and Insurance
May	–	Disbursement from Trust Fund Bureau and Insurance Interest payments on government bonds Social Security expenses
June	+	Corporate Tax receipts and Postal Savings
July	++	Income Tax receipts and Postal Savings
August	+	Social Security expenses Interest payments on government bonds
September	+	Interest receipts from Trust Fund Bureau
October	+	
November	– –	Disbursement of Local Allocation Tax Social Security expenses Interest payments on government bonds
December	++	Postal Savings Income and Corporate Tax receipts

Note: Positive (negative) figures represent net receipts (payments) of the government.

Annual Fluctuation in RPTAPS

Revenues and disbursements in the budget of the central government and Fiscal Investment and Loan Program (FILP) is designed to be balanced each year. This implies that the balance in RPTAPS should be close to zero each fiscal year. The

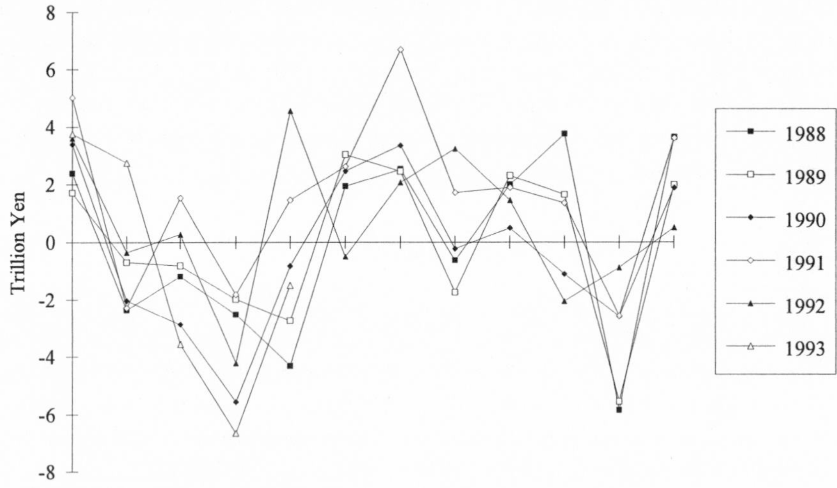

Fig. 45.1. Monthly Fluctuation in RPTAPS

annual balance in RPTAPS, however, shows considerable fluctuation. This is mainly due to the fact that: (1) there is a time lag between actual and planned receipts and disbursements beyond and/or prior to the current fiscal year; and (2) RPTAPS covers only transactions with the private sector while the budget and the FILP also cover transactions with the BOJ.

Relationship between RPTA, SDF, and BOJ Balance Sheet

It is worthwhile to clarify the relationship among: (1) Statement of Receipts and Payments of Treasury Accounts (RPTA, this chapter); (2) Supply and Demand of Funds (SDF, Chapter 40); and (3) Accounts of the Bank of Japan (Chapter 44). Fig. 45.2 shows this relationship. While RPTA covers all government transactions, and BOJ Accounts cover all BOJ transactions, SDF includes government and BOJ transactions with the private sector.

Alternative Interpretation of BOJ's Monetary Policy

This relationship among the three statistics reveals an alternative interpretation of the BOJ's monetary policy stance. As shown in Fig. 45.2, in calendar year 1991, the Bank of Japan extended credit to private banks by 12.9 trillion yen (BOJ credit in 'Supply and Demand of Funds'). This is the largest figure ever, and seems to indicate easy monetary policy. However, the BOJ had net receipts of 19.0 trillion yen from the government (Transactions with the BOJ, 'Receipts and Payments of Treasury

Account'), most of it in the form of a reduction in net lending, resulting in net absorption of funds of around 5 trillion yen from the economy as a whole (subtracting 1.0 trillion yen in reduced reserves).

In 1991, 16 trillion yen flowed into postal savings accounts, much of it transferred from private banks (see Chapter 47). This brought about historically tight money market conditions and record low growth in broadly defined money (M2+CDs). Although the BOJ extended a large amount of credit to banks to compensate for this, it reduced credit to the government by an even greater amount, reducing the funds available for government lending to the private sector (e.g. through the FILP).

RPTABOJ shows unusually large net payments to the BOJ of 9 trillion yen by the Trust Fund Bureau in calendar 1991, which probably accounts for the large amount of net government bond sales and redemptions in that year (see 'Features and Problems' in Chapters 44 and 46). Fig. 45.4 reveals that in the past twenty years, only in fiscal years 1990 through 1992 were there net absorption of funds from the economy by the BOJ.

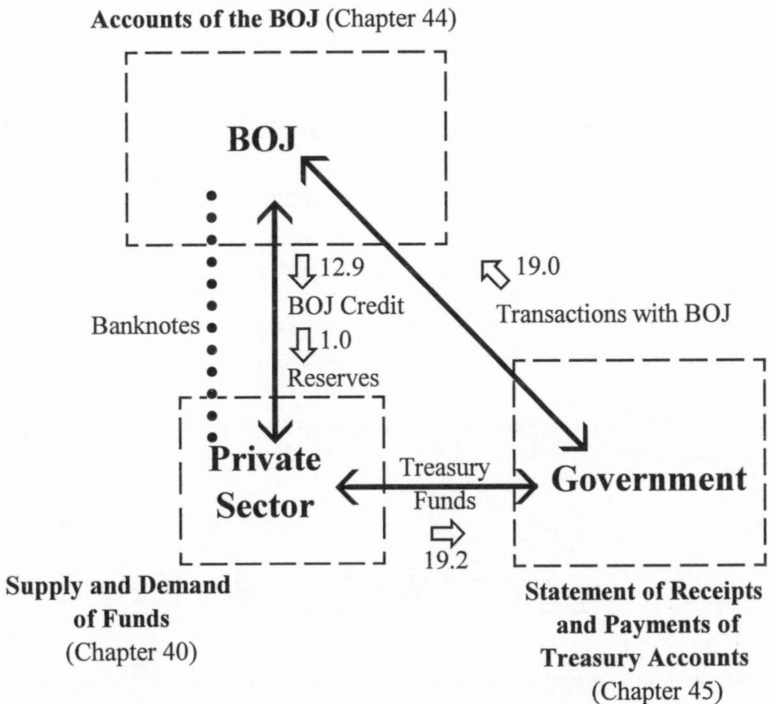

Fig. 45.2. Relationship Between RPTA, SDF, and BOJ Balance Sheet Calendar Year 1991, Trillion Yen

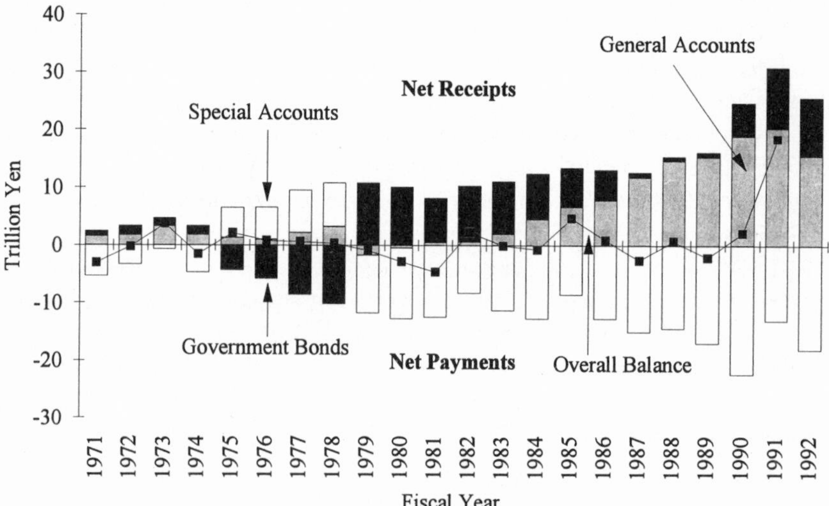

Fig. 45.3. Receipts and Payments of Treasury Accounts -- Transactions with the Private Sector (Balance)

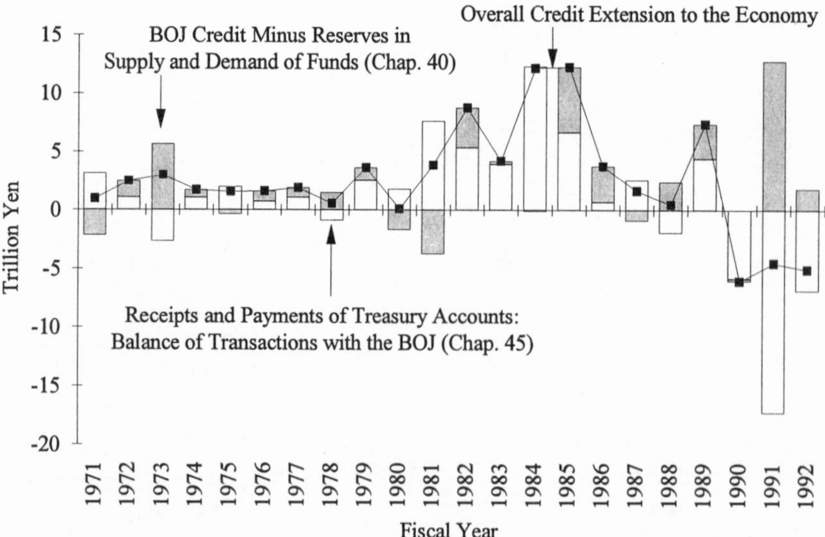

Note: Overall Credit Extension is approximate in that balance of RPTABOJ includes some items not related to credit extension.

Fig. 45.4. BOJ's Transactions with the Private and Public Sectors

Public Financial Institutions

46 Assets and Liabilities of the Trust Fund Bureau

Source: Ministry of Finance; Research and Statistics Department, Bank of Japan.

Frequency: Monthly.

Release: Figures are released at the end of each month with a two-month lag in *Economic Statistics Monthly* published by the Bank of Japan.

Availability: Figures are available from 1950 onward.

The Trust Fund Bureau (TFB) of the Ministry of Finance receives funds from Postal Savings and Insurance, Welfare Insurance, and National Annuities. These funds are invested into government securities and loans to various types of government institutions. The TFB is the major source of funds for the Fiscal Investment and Loan Program (FILP, see Chapter 34) and is considered a kind of national financial institution.

Details

The TFB receives funds from Postal Savings and Insurance, Welfare Insurance, National Annuities, and surplus funds in various Special Accounts. These funds are required to be deposited with the TFB by law. Investment of funds by the TFB is restricted to the following categories (in the form of loans and securities purchases) which seem to be safe and produce a stable flow of interest earnings: (1) the government; (2) government financial institutions; (3) local governments; (4) public corporations; (5) bank debentures; and (6) foreign bonds issued by foreign governments and international organizations. In addition to long-term investments, the TFB can invest short-term idle funds in these instruments. Table 46.1 shows the balance sheet of the TFB.

TFB and Fiscal Investment and Loan Program

The TFB is the major source of funds for the Fiscal Investment and Loan Program. It covers roughly 80 percent of the total FILP budget. Sources of FILP funds also include Postal Insurance Funds, Industrial Investment Special Account, and government guaranteed bonds (see Fig. 46.1). They are consolidated to be allocated to

Table 46.1. Assets and Liabilities of the Trust Fund Bureau
End-of-Calendar Years 1987–1992, Billion Yen

	1987	1988	1989	1990	1991	1992
Total Assets	193,979	209,378	227,625	238,408	266,158	294,106
Cash	1	1	1	1	1	1
Securities	58,660	62,425	68,895	67,004	81,813	89,395
Long-term government bonds	51,359	53,842	57,467	52,546	62,766	64,471
Financing bills (FBs)	61	97	112	191	165	886
Bonds of govt.-related organizations	4,202	5,300	6,813	8,969	10,320	13,178
Bank debentures	3,038	3,186	4,504	5,299	8,563	10,860
Loans	134,273	145,803	157,469	170,909	184,217	204,602
Loans to general and special accounts	24,403	26,506	27,431	29,337	32,551	39,015
Loans to local public organizations	27,036	29,646	31,602	33,372	35,168	36,970
Loans to govt.-related organizations	82,834	89,651	98,435	108,199	116,498	128,617
Others	1,046	1,150	1,261	494	128	108
Total Liabilities	193,979	209,378	227,625	238,408	266,158	294,106
Deposits of Postal Savings	115,521	123,416	132,396	132,590	148,879	165,043
Deposits of postal life insurance and annuities	3,147	3,351	3,806	4,136	4,802	5,886
Deposits of welfare insurance special accts.	57,646	61,784	67,600	72,751	79,754	85,907
Deposits of funds of national annuities	3,335	3,982	4,493	4,817	5,548	6,404
Deposits of others	14,210	16,718	19,194	23,968	26,921	29,935
Others	121	127	136	145	254	932

Source: Bank of Japan, *Economic Statistics Monthly*.

government financial institutions, government agencies, and local governments. These FILP-implementing entities make loans or disbursements to the private sector.

Interest Rates on TFB Funds

The interest rates that the TFB pays and receives are determined by law. These two interest rates are basically set equal so that the TFB's interest margin is zero (although the former varies depending on maturity). The level of interest rates reflects the coupon rate of the most recently issued ten-year government bonds.

The interest rate that TFB pays to Postal Savings, Welfare Insurance, National Annuities, and Postal Insurance is called the lending rate on deposits with the TFB (shown as 'A' in Fig. 46.1). This lending rate is determined by a Cabinet order based on a referral to the Trust Fund Investment Commission. The lending rate should be consistent with the coupon rate of currently issued government bonds and sound operation of Postal Savings and government insurance programs.

The lending rate on deposits with maturities of seven years or longer is frequently cited for analysis because a large portion of postal savings, which is the major source of deposits of the TFB, has a maturity of 10 years.

The interest rate that the TFB receives from FILP-implementing institutions, which is shown as 'B' in Fig. 46.1, is set by the Minister of Finance based on a referral to the Trust Fund Investment Commission. In practice, this TFB-receiving interest

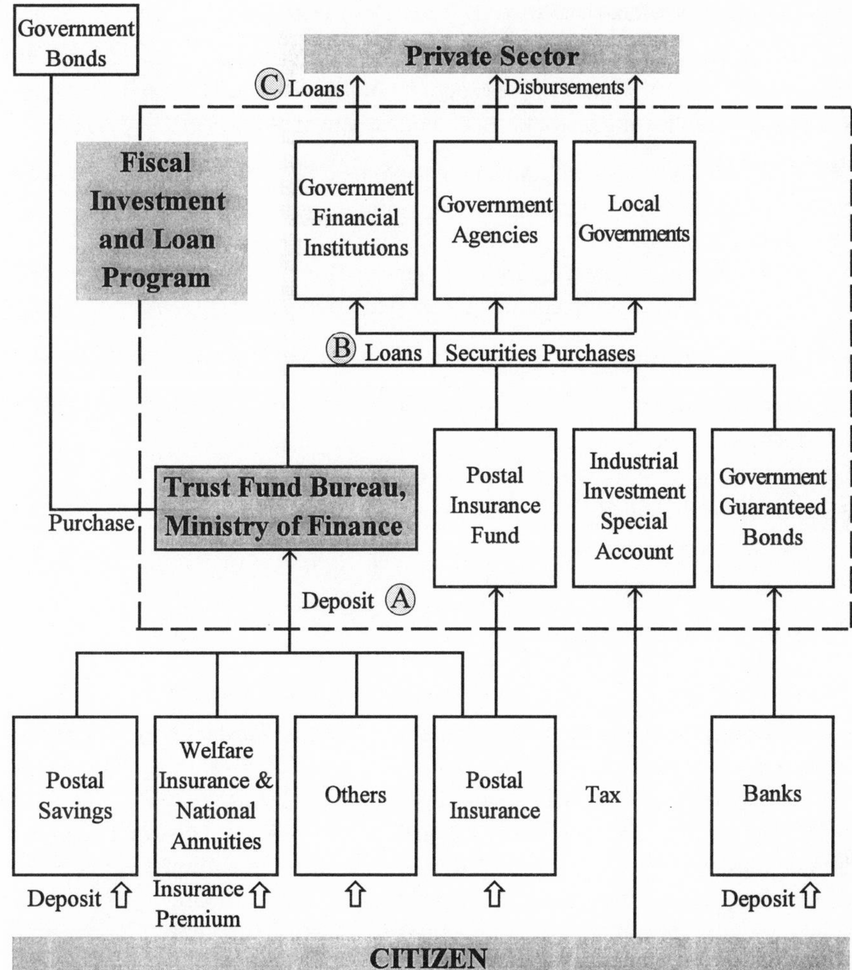

Fig. 46.1 Trust Fund Bureau and the FILP

rate is set equal to the lending rate on deposits with the TFB with maturities of seven years or longer. Thus, the interest margin of the TFB is basically zero.

In addition to these two interest rates, there is another interest rate, 'C', which government financial institutions, or FILP-implementing institutions, charge on lending to the private sector. It is called the 'key rate of government financial institutions'. This lending rate by government financial institutions is determined either by each institution or by a Cabinet order. Typically, it is set equal to the long-term prime rate, which is usually determined by the currently prevailing market yield on five-year bank debentures.

Investment of TFB Funds

Investment of TFB funds is not restricted to FILP purposes. In addition to investment in FILP, which requires approval of the Diet, the TFB can invest their funds into the following instruments without approval of the Diet:

1. Medium- and long-term government bonds and foreign bonds (other than FILP).
2. Short-term loans to Special Accounts.
3. Short-term government securities (Financing Bills), discount bank debentures, and long-term government bonds with resale agreement.

Category 3 is called 'idle funds investment'. Sources of idle funds investment are:

a. New deposits from Postal Savings, government insurance programs, and Postal Insurance.
b. Receipts of interest and principal from past investments.
c. Withdrawal from surplus and sales of government bonds with repurchase agreements.

Features and Problems

TFB Transactions in Receipts and Payments of Treasury Accounts

Results of transactions of the TFB with the private sector and the BOJ are available in 'Statement of Receipts and Payments of Treasury Accounts' (see Chapter 45). Receipt, payment, and net balance are shown in the statistics.

However, readers should pay attention to the coverage of the statistics. Part of the transactions of the TFB are not recorded due to intra-government transactions. Most of the source of funds of the TFB are recorded neither in 'transactions with the private sector (RPTAPS)' nor in 'transactions with the BOJ (RPTABOJ)', since they represent intra-government transactions. Only transactions with some government agencies which do not have accounts with the BOJ and receipts of interest and principal on loans from local governments are recorded in RPTAPS. On the other hand, loans to and securities purchase from FILP-implementing institutions, purchases of bank debentures, and purchases of government bonds from the private sector with resale agreement are recorded as payments in RPTAPS. As a result, for the TFB, RPTAPS usually shows net payment.

47 Postal Savings

Source: Postal Savings Bureau, Ministry of Posts and Telecommunications.

Frequency: Monthly.

Release: Preliminary figures are released in the first week of each month with a one-month lag and are revised five months later. Preliminary figures are available in *Economic Statistics Monthly* published by the Bank of Japan with a two-month lag.

Postal Savings was designed for small savers to accumulate assets in a safe financial instrument. The total outstanding deposits of Postal Savings has grown to more than 167 trillion yen (as of the end of 1992), nearly three times as large as the assets of the largest city bank in Japan. Deposits from Postal Savings are in turn deposited with the Trust Fund Bureau of the Ministry of Finance. They are the major source of new funds for the Fiscal Investment and Loan Program.

Details

Types of Deposits

Postal Savings is available at more than 24,000 post offices nationwide. Postal Savings offers various types of deposits such as ordinary deposits, savings certificates, time deposits, money market certificates, installment deposits, housing deposits, and education deposits (there are no checking accounts offered). Among them, savings certificates has the largest share, around 90 percent of total deposits. Savings certificates have a fixed, semi-annually compounded interest rate with maturity of up to ten years. Certificates with longer maturities offer higher interest rates. In addition, they include an option to cancel the savings certificate (to switch to a new savings certificate with a higher interest rate). This cancellation is available without penalty if the funds are deposited for more than six months. In an increasing interest rate environment, this option is very attractive. Private financial institutions complain about this characteristic because it is too risky for them to offer such an option.

Postal Savings has several competitive advantages over the private financial institutions it competes with:

1. Full faith and credit of the Government of Japan.
2. No tax obligations.
3. No reserve requirements.
4. No payment of deposit insurance premiums.
5. Scale economies resulting from the simultaneous mail, insurance, pension, and deposit operations at each post office.

Interest Rates on Postal Savings

Interest rates on Postal Savings are determined by a Cabinet order after a referral to the Postal Services Council. Most interest rates are regulated by this Cabinet order. Interest rates on money market certificates (MMC) are based on the currently prevailing rates offered by private banks.

Up until May 1993, interest rates on saving certificates had been pegged to the official discount rate, which was sharply criticized by private financial institutions. Postal Savings could attract a huge volume of deposits when short-term interest rates were high because of its longer maturity. In response to the criticism, interest rates on postal savings are now based on the prevailing market rates of either 3-year time deposits of private banks (when short-term rates are lower than long-term ones) or the 10-year government bond yield (when short-term rates are higher than long-term ones).

Postal Savings and the Trust Fund Bureau

Funds collected via Postal Savings are deposited with the Trust Fund Bureau of the Ministry of Finance. Postal Savings is the largest supplier of funds to the TFB. As of the end of March 1993, Postal Savings accounts for 56 percent of total liabilities of the TFB. These funds are used as a source for the Fiscal Investment and Loan Program (FILP).

In fiscal 1987, Postal Savings was allowed to begin investing part of its deposits at its own discretion (as part of a political deal to compensate the Ministry of Posts and Telecommunications for the elimination of tax-free savings). This is called the 'fund operation service' (see Chapter 34). Postal Savings borrows the funds from the FILP at the same interest rate as the lending rate on deposits with the TFB and invests the funds into instruments which produce a stable flow of interest earnings, such as government and municipal bonds. In fiscal 1992, 4.75 trillion yen was allotted to the fund.

Features and Problems

Transfers of Funds Between Private Banks and Postal Savings

The uniqueness of the ten-year saving certificates has caused large shifts of deposits between private banks and Postal Savings. For example, in 1990 there were a large number of maturing Postal Savings deposits which were deposited ten years earlier (1980) when interest rates were at a historically high level. At the same time, the yield on five-year bank debentures (an alternative to the 10-year savings certificates) was also at a historically high level, and there was an outflow from Postal Savings. Because of this outflow, total deposits of Postal Savings increased only slightly in 1990. In 1991, when the yield on five-year bank debentures declined substantially while the discount rate was lowered only gradually, there was a huge inflow into Postal Savings from deposits of private banks due to the higher interest rate on the 10-year saving certificates. In 1991, deposits of Postal Savings increased by 16 trillion yen to 152 trillion yen (see 'Features and Problems' in Chapter 45).

Large transfers of funds between private banks and Postal Savings are likely to continue, since private banks cannot offer an instrument similar to the savings certificate offered by Postal Savings (cancellation option) because of the huge interest rate risk involved; further, the Bank of Japan does not have a mechanism to control Postal Savings. This brings into question the BOJ's ability to control monetary aggregates. Postal Savings is not included in M2+CDs (but is included in broadly defined liquidity -- see Chapter 38) so a shift of funds from private banks into Postal Savings will lower the level of M2+CDs.

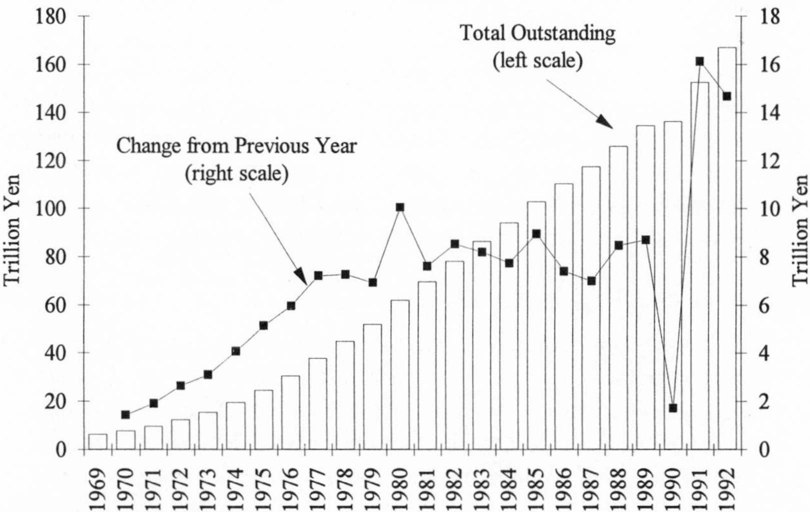

Fig. 47.1. Postal Savings

Interest Rates and Banking Institutions

48 Interest Rate Structure

This chapter describes the relationship between various types of interest rates in Japan. The process of liberalizing (deregulating) interest rates is proceeding quickly, and this has changed the way in which each interest rate is determined. Some rates have been liberalized completely, while others are linked to a reference interest rate or a basket of reference rates. There are two reference rates: the call rate; and the secondary market yield of 10-year government bonds. Many long-term interest rates are linked to the long-term government bond yield or five-year bank debenture yield in the secondary market (see Fig. 48.1). Regulated deposit rates are mostly linked to the official discount rate, while liberalized deposit rates are linked to money market rates such as the three-month CD rate.

1. Official Discount Rate

The Official Discount Rate is determined by the Policy Committee of the Bank of Japan (see Chapter 42). The Policy Committee consists of seven members, including the Chairman of the BOJ and one representative each from: the Ministry of Finance, Economic Planning Agency, city banks, regional banks, manufacturing and commerce industries, and agricultural industry.

2. Short-Term Money Market Rates

Money market rates are determined by the demand and supply conditions of each market. Money markets consist of the following: call; bills; CD; Gensaki; TB; FB; and Commercial Paper (see Chapter 37). Because of arbitrage between markets, the interest rates on instruments with the same maturity move in the same direction. Although when issued FB are sold only to the BOJ at a below-market rate, sales of FB by the BOJ are conducted based on the current money market rates.

3. New Short-Term Prime Rate

Prior to the introduction of the new short-term prime rate in January 1989, the short-term prime rate had been set at 0.5% above the official discount rate. This old rate was first announced by one of the city banks, then followed (after a brief delay in deference to the Anti-Trust Act) by all of the other banks. This formula was altered because of the increasing weight of market rate instruments in banks' source of

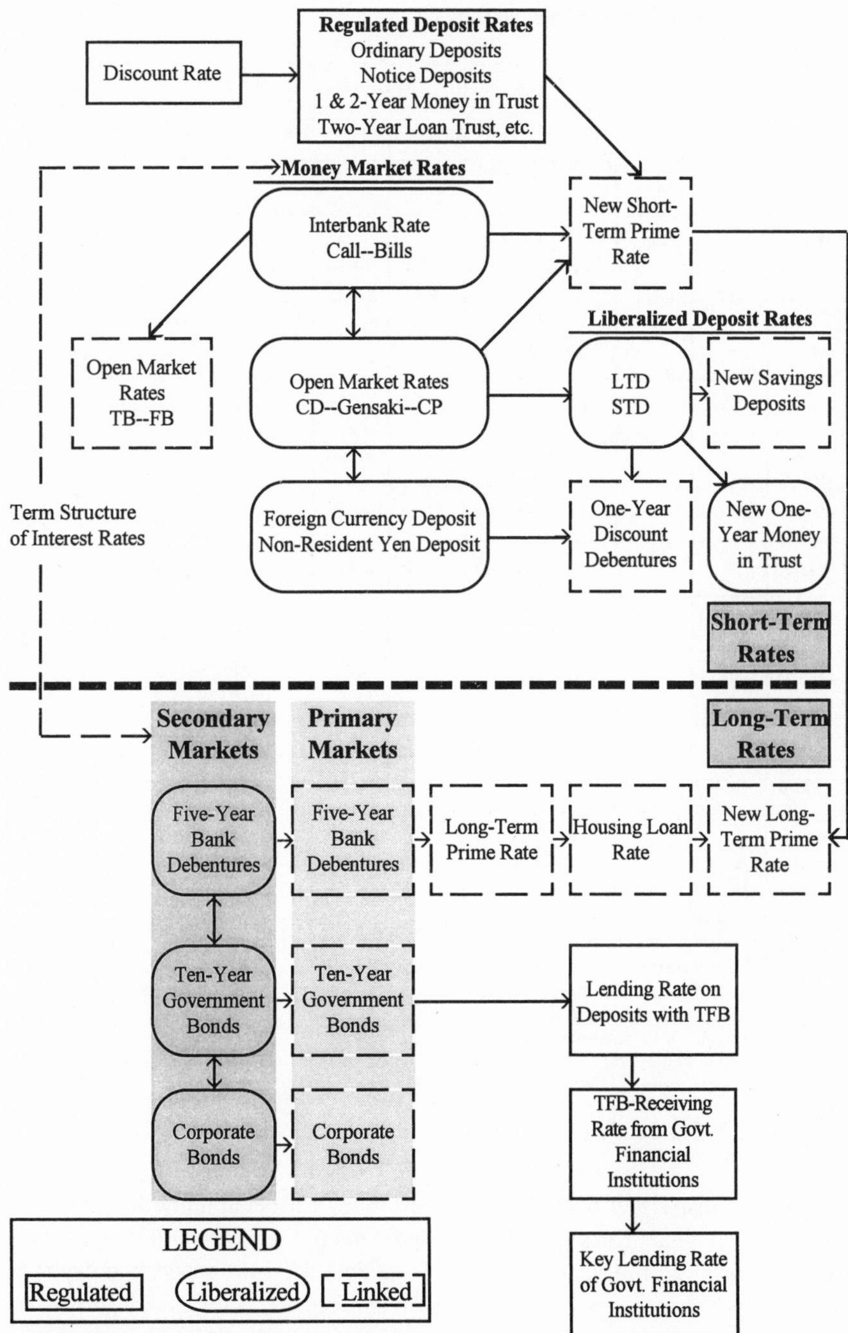

Fig. 48.1. Interest Rate Structure in Japan

Table 48.1. Deregulation of Deposit Rates

	CD		LTD		MMC		Super-MMC		STD	
Yr./m.	Minimum	Term	Minimum	Term	Minimum	Term	Minimum	Term	Minimum	Term
1979/5	500	3-6m.								
1984/1	300	3-6m.								
1985/4	100	1-6m.			50*	1-6m.				
1985/10			1000	3m.-2yr.						
1986/4	100	1m.-1yr.	500	3m.-2yr.	50	1m.-1yr.				
1986/9			300	3m.-2yr.	30	1m.-1yr.				
1987/4			100	3m.-2yr.	20	1m.-2yr.				
1987/10			100	1m.-2yr.	10	1m.-2yr.				
1988/4	50	2 weeks-2yr.	50	1m.-2yr.						
1988/11			30	1m.-2yr.						
1989/4			20	1m.-2yr.						
1989/6							3	6m., 1yr.		
1989/10			10	1m.-2yr.			3	3,6m., 1,2,3yr.		
1990/4							1	3,6m., 1,2,3yr.		
1991/4	All figures are in millions of yen. STD were created in November 1991, with a minimum of 3 million yen, and terms of 3,6,12,24, and 36 months. *: MMC was authorized to small banks in March 1985				Superseded by LTD		0.5	3,6m., 1,2,3yr.		
1991/11									3	3m.-3yr.
1992/6							0	3,6m., 1,2,3yr.		
1993/6							Superseded by STD		0	1m.-3yr.

funds. In January 1989, banks adopted a new formula in determining the short-term prime rate. It is based on a weighted average of interest rates on various types of the banks' sources of funds, such as CDs, large time deposits, super time deposits, saving deposits, etc., and the operating ratio of the banks. Currently, if this basket rate changes by more than 0.25%, the new short-term prime rate is likely to change (in increments of 0.125%). Banks can reflect their own cost of funds by choosing different rates, although in practice most banks still use the same rate. The new short-term prime rate more accurately reflects the movement of money market rates.

4. Liberalized Deposit Rates

Liberalization of deposit rates dates back to the introduction of CDs with a minimum denomination of 500 million yen in May 1979. This was followed by the introduction of Money Market Certificates (MMC) in April 1985 with a minimum of 50 million yen and that of Large Time Deposits (LTD) in October 1985 with a minimum of 1 billion yen. Super-MMC were introduced in June 1989 with a minimum of 3 million yen; the minimum was gradually lowered and finally eliminated in June 1992. Super Time Deposits (STD) were introduced in November 1991, covering deposits of between 3 and 10 million yen. MMC were superseded by LTD in October 1989, when their minimum denominations were made equal. The minimum denomination of STD was eliminated in June 1993. Super-MMC were then replaced by STD.

Currently, there are three types of time deposits with market or quasi-market rates: CD, LTD, and STD. The minimum denomination of CD and LTD are currently 50 million yen and 10 million yen respectively. The minimum denominations on Super-MMC and STD were abolished in June 1992 and June 1993, respectively (see Table 48.1 for details). The interest rate on maturity-designated time deposits was also liberalized in June 1993. Interest rates on CD, LTD, and STD are determined by demand and supply conditions of the markets. The interest rates on CDs changes daily. Interest rates on LTD and STD are changed every week.

The interest rate on one-year discount bank debentures issued by long-term credit banks, the Shoko Chukin Bank, the Norinchukin Bank, and the Bank of Tokyo are based on the one-year STD rate. The minimum denomination of these debentures is 10,000 yen.

Interest rates on foreign currency deposits and non-resident yen deposits are liberalized. In addition, interest rates on ordinary deposits of private banks were partly liberalized in June 1992. There are two types of new savings deposits depending on the minimum denomination: 200,000 and 400,000 yen. Interest rates on both new savings deposits are determined by a formula based on the prevailing rates on 3-month LTD multiplied by a factor of 0.5 or 0.6. The interest rate on ordinary deposits at Postal Savings plus 0.3% is a floor interest rate for new savings deposits. The dividend rate on the newly introduced money in trust called 'hit' (withdrawal is not permitted for at least one month) offered by trust banks was liberalized in June 1992. In the past, the provisional rate was set equal to the one-year time deposit rate plus 0.12%.

5. Regulated Deposit Rates

Interest rates on (traditional) ordinary deposits, installment deposits and notice deposits are regulated. Their rates are linked to the official discount rate. In June 1992, traditional time deposits were abolished and superseded by Super-MMC. Provisional dividend rates (interest rates) on one- and two-year money in trust and two-year loan trust offered by trust banks are also linked to the discount rate.

6. Postal Savings Deposit Rates

Postal Savings offers both regulated and liberalized instruments. Interest rates on regulated deposits such as ordinary deposits, education deposits, installment deposits, and housing deposits are determined by a Cabinet order after a referral to the Postal Services Council. Their change usually coincides with changes in the official discount rate, although in some cases there is a lag. Postal Savings also handles liberalized deposits such as LTD, STD, and saving certificates. These interest rates are determined by Postal Savings based on the average interest rates of the same maturity offered by private banks. Formerly, the interest rate on 10-year saving certificates was fully linked to the official discount rate (see Fig. 48.3), which had been criticized by private banks. Since June 1993, it has been based on the prevailing market rates on either three-year STD of private banks (when short-term rates are lower than long-term ones) or 10-year government bond yield (when short-term rates are higher than long-term ones). There is a ceiling on per-capita deposits at Postal Savings; currently, the ceiling is set at 10 million yen per person.

7. Long-Term Prime Rate

The long-term prime rate is usually determined as the coupon rate of five-year bank debentures of long-term credit banks plus 0.9%. In principle, the rate is determined at the discretion of each bank, but generally the same rate is offered by all banks. Long-term credit banks and trust banks, which mainly engage in long-term financing of corporations, frequently use this prime rate. Recently, the growing participation by commercial banks (city banks, regional banks, etc.) in the field of long-term financing has put less emphasis on the long-term prime rate as a key rate on long-term loans. This rate has been applied to sub-prime borrowers, while below-prime rates have often been given to large borrowers. The provisional dividend rate on five-year money in trust and loan trust offered by trust banks are linked to the long-term prime rate.

8. New Long-Term Prime Rate

The new long-term prime rate was introduced in April 1991 by city banks in response to an inverted yield curve caused by tight monetary policy which, along with deposit rate regulation, seems to have had an adverse effect on their interest margins. The new long-term prime rate is calculated as the new short-term prime rate plus 0.3% for loans with maturity of less than three years, and plus 0.5% for loans with maturity of three years or more. This new long-term prime rate is reviewed when the new short-term prime rate is revised.

9. Coupon Rate on Five-Year Bank Debentures (New Issue)

The coupon rate on five-year bank debentures issued by long-term credit banks is usually based on the secondary market yield of the debentures. If there is a difference of more than 0.2% between the coupon rate and the secondary market yield of debentures issued in the previous month, the coupon rate of debentures for the current month is changed accordingly. All new debentures are issued at par. Movement of the secondary market yield of five-year bank debentures is strongly related to that of long-term government bonds.

10. Coupon Rate on Long-Term Government Bonds (New Issue)

The coupon rate on ten-year government bonds is determined by negotiation of the Ministry of Finance and a syndicate for the subscription, which includes major banks and security companies, based on the currently prevailing secondary market yield of government bonds. The price is determined by public auction. Because over- and under-par issue is possible, the coupon rate (apart from the currently prevailing secondary market yield) can be adjusted by a lower (higher) bid price and hence a higher (lower) subscribers' yield.

11. Lending Rate on Deposits with the Trust Fund Bureau

The lending rate on deposits with the Trust Fund Bureau, or TFB-paying rate, is determined by a Cabinet order after a referral to the Trust Fund Investment Commission. This rate is closely linked to the coupon rate of the most recently issued ten-year government bonds. The lending rate should also be consistent with the sound operation of Postal Savings and other government insurance programs. There are six categories depending on the maturity. The interest rate that the TFB receives from government financial institutions is set equal to the paying rate on deposits in the category with the longest maturity (7 years or longer).

12. Key Lending Rate of Government Financial Institutions

The key lending rate of government financial institutions is set equal to the long-term prime rate. In addition to this basic rate, all government financial institutions have a preferential lending rate below the long-term prime rate.

13. Housing Loan Rate

There are two types of housing loan rates offered by commercial banks: fixed rate and variable rate. Both rates are based on the long-term prime rate. The variable housing loan rate tends to move more sensitively than the fixed loan rate in response to changes in the long-term prime rate.

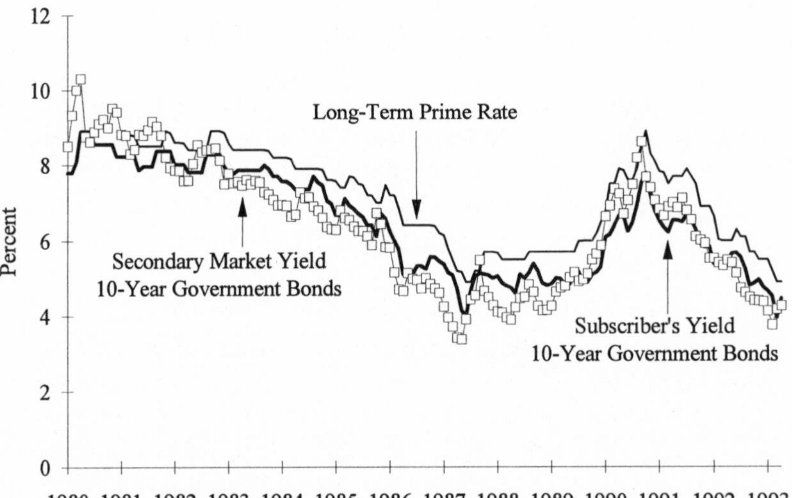

Fig. 48.2. Long-Term Interest Rates

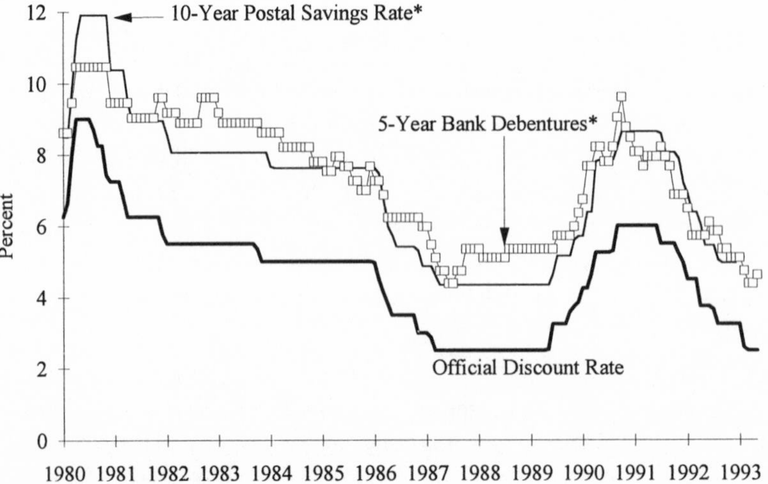

Note: * indicates semi-annual compounded rate.

Fig. 48.3. 10-Year Postal Savings Rate

49 Average Contracted Interest Rates on Loans and Discounts

Source: Research and Statistics Department, Bank of Japan.

Frequency: Monthly.

Release: Figures are released in the first half of each month with a two-month lag. They are available in *Economic Statistics Monthly* published by the Bank of Japan.

Availability: *Average* lending rates are available from 1950 onward. *New* lending rates are available from August 1978 onward.

These statistics cover loans and discounts executed by domestic branches of banks (foreign branches of banks are excluded). The average contracted lending rate of All Banks is included in the lagging index of Diffusion Indexes compiled by the EPA.

Details

The average contracted interest rates on loans and discounts (hereafter, average lending rate) is calculated by summing up the various lending rates of banks weighted by the loan volume at that rate and dividing by total loans outstanding:

$$\text{Average lending rate} = [r_1 * L_1 + r_2 * L_2 + ...] \div L$$

where r_i represents the ith lending rate, L_i the loan volume at the ith lending rate, and L total loans outstanding. In addition to the average lending rate, a new lending rate for the latest month (average contracted interest rates on new loans and discounts) is available. This is defined as the lending rate on new loans and discounts weighted by the loan volume at each rate divided by total new loans and discounts:

$$\text{New lending rate} = [r\text{-}new_1 * L\text{-}new_1 + r\text{-}new_2 * L\text{-}new_2 + ...] \div L\text{-}new$$

where $r\text{-}new_i$ represents the ith lending rate on new loans, $L\text{-}new_i$ the volume of new loans at the ith lending rate, and $L\text{-}new$ the total volume of new loans originated during the month. In general, the average lending rate is used more frequently than the new lending rate (see Figs. 49.1 and 49.2).

In June 1993, the BOJ released average lending rates including overdraft. According to the BOJ survey of private banks, the share of lending via overdraft in total lending has increased substantially, from 1.4% at the end of 1980 to 16.6% at

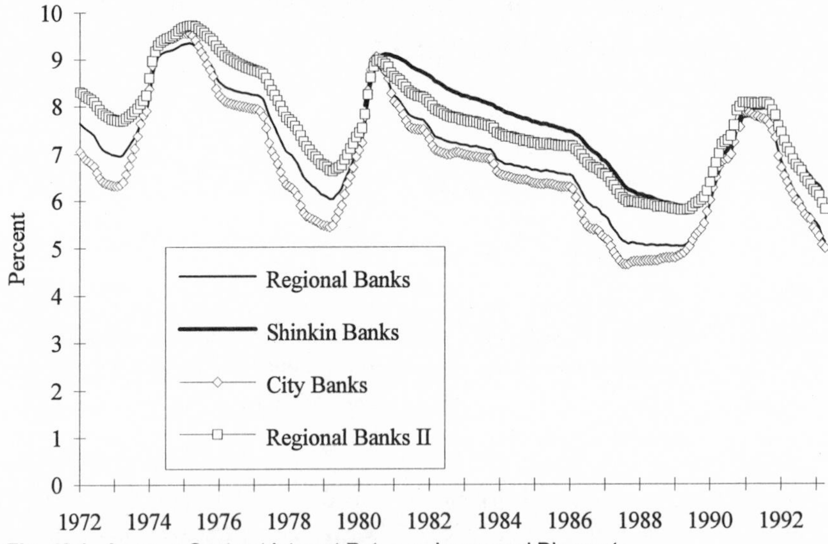

Fig. 49.1. Average Contract Interest Rates on Loans and Discounts

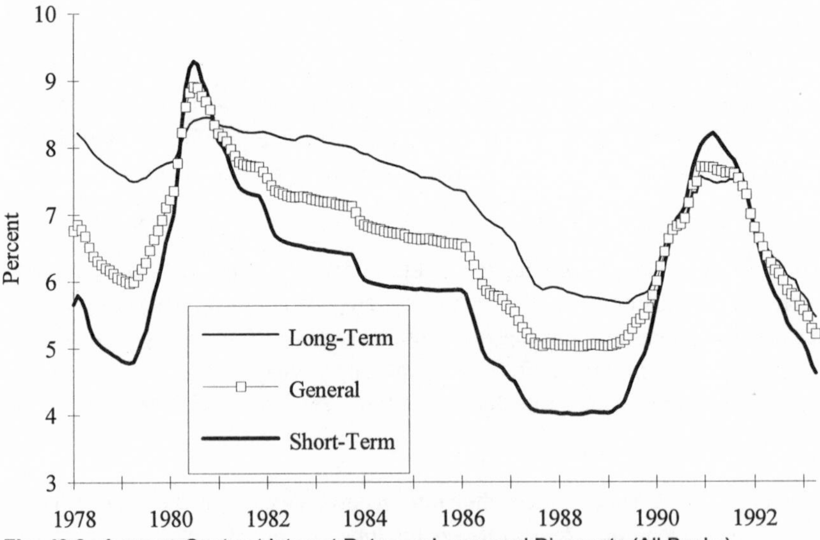

Fig. 49.2. Average Contract Interest Rates on Loans and Discounts (All Banks)

the end of 1992. From July 1993 onward, only average lending rates including overdraft will be released. Average lending rates excluding overdraft are, however, available upon request to the BOJ. There is not a significant difference in the level and movement between these two rates (in April 1993 it was only 0.081%).

Features and Problems

Compensating Balance

The statistics given reveal only the nominal, or contractual lending rate of banks. There is a business tradition, though less frequent in recent years, that corporations maintain a portion of loans in accounts with the lending bank. This is called a compensating balance. If there is a compensating balance, then the effective interest rate of the loan is higher than the contractual lending rate.

Calculation of Long-Term Loans in Loans Outstanding

Although the percentage of long-term (or short-term) loans in total loans outstanding is not published in the statistics, it can be calculated as follows:

$$\text{percentage of short-term loans} = (R - R_L) / (R_S - R_L) * 100$$

$$\text{percentage of long-term loans} = 100 - \text{percentage of short-term loans}$$

where R, R_S, and R_L represent the lending rate for total (general), short-term, and long-term loans, respectively. Note that this formula becomes inaccurate when the gap between the published short-term and long-term rates becomes too small.

Fig. 49.3 shows the ratio of long-term loans to total loans outstanding by type of bank. It shows a dramatic shift to long-term loans (possibly to real-estate related loans) from short-term ones, especially for city banks. This shift continued even though the yield curve became inverted in 1990. It seems banks attempted to offset part of the adverse effect of deposit rate deregulation on their net interest margin by shifting their assets toward long-term loans.

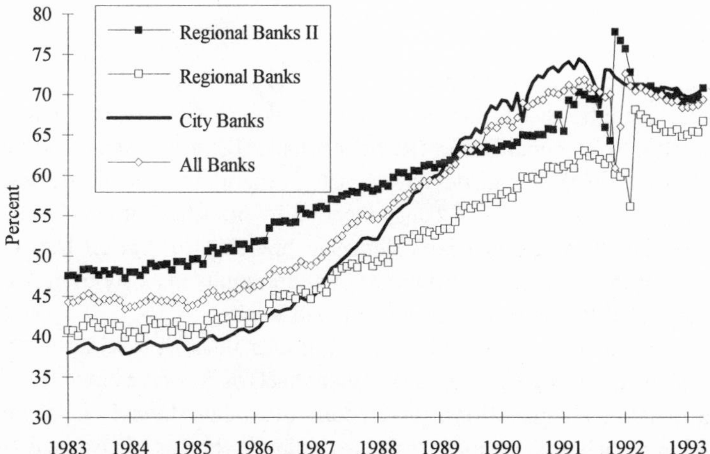

Note: Three points in Regional Banks II curve are average of prior and subsequent months because the gap between short- and long-term lending rates is too small at these points.

Fig. 49.3. Percentage of Long-Term Loans in Loans Outstanding

50 Balance Sheets of All Banks

Source: Research and Statistics Department, Bank of Japan.

Frequency: Monthly.

Release: Figures are released with a one- or two-month lag in *Economic Statistics Monthly*.

Availability: Figures are available from 1950 onward. Only end-of-month figures are available.

Balance sheets of All Banks consist of two accounts: banking accounts and trust accounts. Most major items are classified in the former while items related to trust business are classified in the latter.

These statistics reveal major items in the assets and liabilities of banks, such as loans outstanding by type of borrower and deposits by type. The growth rate of loans outstanding is considered to be a leading indicator of business activities (see Fig. 50.1). The percentage of liberalized time deposits in total deposits has risen, reflecting the ongoing process of deregulation in Japan.

Details

Coverage

All Banks, which does not literally include *every* bank, consists of major private financial institutions: city banks; regional banks; member banks of the Second Association of Regional Banks (Regional Banks II); trust banks; and long-term credit banks. The main statistics cover assets and liabilities of domestic head offices and branches of the banks. Loans extended by branches outside Japan are not included, but those extended by domestic branches to foreign borrowers are included. It should be noted that there is a discontinuity in all series in April 1989, when Regional Banks II were included in All Banks.

In addition to assets and liabilities of All Banks, those of specialized and public financial institutions are available. Balance sheets of domestic branches of foreign banks operating in Japan (Principal Accounts of Foreign Banks in Japan) and those of foreign branches of Japanese banks (Principal Accounts of Overseas Branches of All Banks) are available separately. Hereafter, we focus on All Banks figures.

All figures are as of the end-of-month or end-of-year. There are no monthly average figures or seasonally adjusted figures.

Table 50.1 shows the major assets and liabilities of All Banks (these items are also available for each type of bank separately). Classification of each item is more or less similar across the different types of institutions. Differences arise from the inclusion of various types of banks such as trust banks, which conduct trust business, and long-term credit banks, which mainly issue bank debentures. Detailed figures for loans and deposits are available, as described below.

Table 50.1. Major Assets and Liabilities in Banking Accounts of All Banks
End-of-Calendar Years 1988–1992, Trillion Yen, unless otherwise noted

	1988	1989	1990	1991	1992	1992 % of Total
Assets	526.5	676.4	728.6	730.8	728.0	100.0
Cash and deposits	40.0	47.4	46.8	35.2	21.8	3.0
Call loans	14.2	17.7	17.1	16.1	17.0	2.3
Bills purchased	0.9	1.6	1.2	0.7	0.3	0.0
Trading accounts bonds	2.9	4.7	4.7	4.3	4.8	0.7
Securities	88.0	112.6	124.0	120.6	118.1	16.2
Loans and discounts	332.5	410.6	441.2	460.5	471.8	64.8
Foreign exchange	5.6	6.7	9.5	6.4	6.3	0.9
Others	42.4	75.2	84.0	87.0	87.8	12.1
Liabilities and net worth	526.5	676.4	728.6	730.8	728.0	100.0
Deposits	310.6	405.5	436.2	428.5	411.6	56.5
Certificates of Deposit (CDs)	13.8	20.4	18.2	16.9	16.4	2.2
Bank debentures	41.5	44.6	51.8	55.0	58.1	8.0
Call money	24.3	34.4	33.7	40.4	49.3	6.8
Bills sold	16.9	20.4	15.9	15.5	14.8	2.0
Borrowed money	7.2	7.3	9.6	16.6	18.0	2.5
Due to trust account	15.7	14.8	18.3	21.5	30.1	4.1
Others	73.4	97.5	108.5	99.3	90.6	12.4
Net worth	23.1	31.5	36.3	37.3	39.3	5.4

Note: There is a discontinuity in all figures in April 1989, when Regional Banks II were included in All Banks.

Source: Bank of Japan, *Economic Statistics Annual.*

Loans

Detailed loan figures are available in separate statistics in *Economic Statistics Monthly,* including:

1. Loans and discounts outstanding by industry (see Table 50.2).
2. New loans for equipment funds by industry (same categories of industries as in Table 50.2).
3. Loans and discounts outstanding of banking accounts of All Banks by interest rate .

Table 50.2. Loans and Discounts Outstanding by Industry and by Type of Bank: Banking Accounts of All Banks
End-of-Calendar Years 1988–1992, Trillion Yen, unless otherwise noted

	1988	1989	1990	1991	1992	1992 % of Total
By Industry						
Total	288.2	355.1	376.0	385.7	393.0	100.0
Manufacturing	53.9	59.1	59.2	60.0	59.2	15.1
Foodstuffs and beverages	4.3	5.0	5.1	5.0	5.0	1.3
Textile products	4.8	5.4	5.4	5.4	5.2	1.3
Chemical products	4.7	4.8	4.8	4.8	4.8	1.2
Petroleum refining	1.1	1.2	1.2	1.2	1.2	0.3
Iron and steel	4.7	4.3	4.1	4.3	4.1	1.0
General machinery	4.7	5.2	5.4	5.5	5.2	1.3
Electrical machinery	4.9	5.4	5.5	5.7	5.5	1.4
Transportation machinery	4.0	4.1	4.1	4.2	4.4	1.1
Non-manufacturing	187.7	204.0	244.5	249.4	255.6	65.0
Construction	14.8	19.2	20.0	21.6	23.4	5.9
Electricity, gas, heat, and water supply	5.4	5.1	5.1	5.3	5.4	1.4
Transportation and communications	9.9	11.7	12.8	14.0	14.3	3.6
Wholesale and retail trade, and restaurants	53.3	63.1	65.6	64.3	62.7	16.0
Finance and insurance	30.3	36.7	37.7	36.1	36.3	9.2
Real estate	31.4	41.0	42.4	44.7	47.5	12.1
Services	40.0	51.3	57.8	60.3	62.8	16.0
Local government	2.0	2.0	1.9	2.3	2.9	0.7
Individuals	36.3	54.1	61.2	65.0	66.0	16.8
Overseas	8.4	8.9	9.2	9.0	9.4	2.4
(Small enterprises)	n.a.	247.0	264.5	273.2	279.5	71.1
By Type of bank						
City banks	149.9	163.8	173.2	176.9	179.1	45.6
Regional Banks I	82.8	92.0	97.5	100.7	103.6	26.4
Regional Banks II	35.8	39.5	42.7	44.4	44.9	11.4
Long-term credit banks	36.0	39.9	43.4	45.2	44.9	11.4
Trust banks	19.5	19.9	19.2	18.5	20.5	5.2

Notes: There is a discontinuity in all figures in April 1989, when Regional Banks II were included. Overdraft is not included. Loans for business by individuals are classified in terms of their activities. Small enterprises cover companies with a capital of 100 million yen or less or with 300 regular employees or less. Loans to local governments are classified in terms of their activities.

Source: Bank of Japan, *Economic Statistics Annual*.

Deposits

Detailed deposits figures are also available in *Economic Statistics Monthly*, including the following:

Banking accounts of All Banks.
Deposit rates by type of deposits.
Maturity distribution of LTD and Super-MMC.
Amount of deposits by depositor (semi-annual).

Banking Accounts of All Banks

The classification of deposit liabilities shown in Table 50.3 are available in 'Banking Accounts of All Banks'. Major liabilities of trust business such as money in trust, pension trusts, loans trusts, and securities investment trusts are not included; they are given in 'Trust Accounts of All Banks'.

Time Deposits consist of: (1) maturity-designated time deposits; (2) Large Time Deposits (LTD); (3) Super Time Deposits (STD); and (4) Super-MMC. Interest rates on item 1 are regulated, while those on items 2, 3, and 4 have been liberalized. Interest rates on ordinary deposits, deposits at notice, and deposits for tax payments are regulated. Interest rates on deposits at notice are set at 0.25% above the rate for ordinary deposits. Deposits at notice requires a ban on withdrawals for at least seven days and a two-day notice prior to withdrawal. Special deposits are those for temporary funds kept at banks. No interest rates are offered on special and current (demand) deposits.

The ratio of liberalized time deposits to total deposits has risen for all types of financial institutions as shown in Table 50.4.

Details on the interest rate structure in Japan and the process of interest rate deregulation are presented in Chapter 48.

Table 50.3. Deposits Outstanding: All Banks
End-of-Calendar Years 1988–1992, Trillion Yen, unless otherwise noted

	1988	1989	1990	1991	1992	1992 % of Total
Deposits	310.6	405.5	436.2	428.5	411.6	100.0
Current deposits	17.7	24.6	23.4	23.4	19.8	4.8
Ordinary deposits	45.8	56.6	60.5	62.6	63.4	15.4
Notice deposits	16.0	14.4	12.9	11.8	10.3	2.5
Special deposits	3.3	4.1	5.0	4.6	3.1	0.8
Deposits for tax purposes	0.2	0.2	0.2	0.2	0.2	0.1
Time deposits	202.8	273.5	294.8	290.2	285.8	69.4
with unregulated rates (LTD and STD)	73.7	152.6	192.3	194.5	204.6	49.7
MMC	22.8	11.2	0.2	0.0	--	0.0
Super-MMC	--	19.3	53.9	31.5	--	0.0
Installment savings	2.5	4.3	3.7	3.6	3.7	0.9
Non-resident yen deposits	2.1	2.1	2.2	1.6	1.6	0.4
Foreign currency deposits	20.2	25.6	33.6	30.4	23.1	5.6
Certificates of Deposit (CDs)	13.8	20.4	18.2	16.9	16.4	4.0
Bank debentures	41.5	44.6	51.8	55.0	58.1	14.1

Notes: There is a discontinuity in all figures in April 1989 when Regional Banks II were included. Large Time Deposits (LTD) were introduced in October 1985. Money Market Certificates (MMC) were introduced in March 1985 and superseded by LTD in October 1989. Small-MMC were introduced in June 1989 and superseded by Super Time Deposits (STD) in June 1993. Super Time Deposits (STD) were introduced in November 1991.

Source: Bank of Japan, *Economic Statistics Annual*.

Table 50.4. Liberalized Time Deposits
End-of-Calendar Years 1985–1992,
% of Total Deposits

	City Banks	Regional Banks I	Regional Banks II	Shinkin Banks
1985	8.7	4.5	4.3	1.5
1986	15.7	6.9	7.5	2.5
1987	27.4	13.8	14.9	7.4
1988	39.4	23.1	23.6	13.6
1989	55.0	38.2	36.9	26.4
1990	63.7	52.9	53.6	42.3
1991	59.3	49.6	50.5	43.6
1992	56.9	46.2	47.5	39.6

Note: Liberalized time deposits and total deposits include CDs.
Source: Bank of Japan, *Economic Statistics Annual*.

Amount of Deposits by Depositor (semi-annual)

Amount of Deposits by Depositor is released twice a year with figures as of the end of March and September. Figures for All Banks (and each of its components) are released in May and November issues of *Economic Statistics Monthly*, while figures for shinkin banks are given in June and December issues. Amount of Deposits by Depositor shows classification by type of deposit, type of depositor, and size of deposit. In addition to the classifications for total deposits, time deposits are further broken down by maturity.

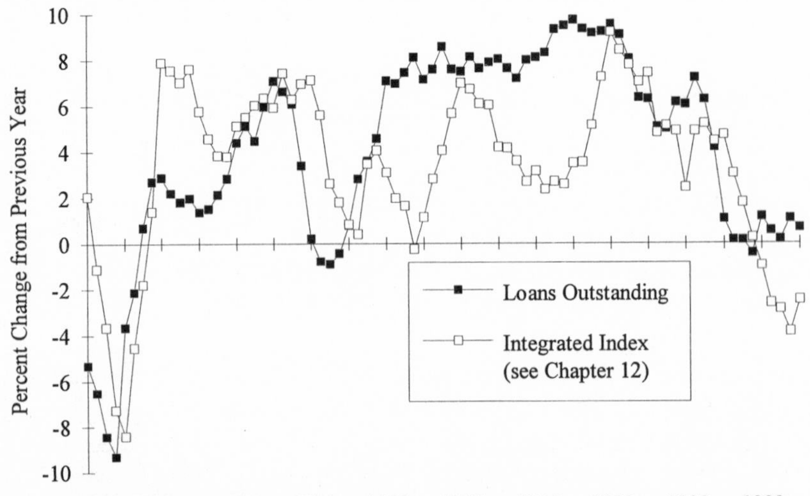

Note: Loans Outstanding is a seasonally adjusted, two-period moving average of end-of-month figures, adjusted for inflation using CPI.

Fig. 50.1. Loans Outstanding of All Banks (Adjusted for Inflation using CPI)

Securities Markets

51 Public and Private Bond Markets

Source:	Research and Statistics Department of the Bank of Japan and The Bond Underwriters Association of Japan.
Frequency:	Daily and Monthly.
Release:	Figures are released with a one- or two-month lag. Daily figures for secondary market yields are published in newspapers.

Details

Types of Bonds

The various types of public and private bonds issued in Japan are classified into five categories by type of issuer: government bonds; local government bonds; government-agency bonds (government guaranteed bonds); industrial bonds; and bank debentures. Amount issued, amount of redemption, and amount outstanding for each of the five categories are available in both *Economic Statistics Monthly* published by the Bank of Japan and *Bond Review* published by the Bond Underwriters Association of Japan.

As Table 51.1 shows, banks as a group and the central government are the two largest issuers of bonds in Japan (Financing Bills are issued to cover seasonal gaps in the cash position of the government, which results in a relatively small amount of outstanding bills compared with the annual issuance). Hereafter, we focus mainly on government bonds.

Primary (Issuing) Markets

Currently, there are three methods of government bond issuance: underwriting by a syndicate; public offering with price bidding; and public offering under non-competitive terms.

In underwriting by a syndicate, a syndicate composed of major securities companies, banks, and insurance companies negotiates terms of issuance with the Ministry of Finance. The terms are determined based on the currently prevailing market yield of government bonds. The syndicate sells bonds to the public on the determined terms (price and coupon) then undertake the unsold portion, if any. This method is used for 40% of the bonds offered at the monthly 10-year government bond auctions.

Table 51.1. Total Issue and Outstanding Bonds by Issuer
Fiscal Years 1988–1992, Billion Yen, unless otherwise noted

	1988	1989	1990	1991	1992	Outstanding March 1993
Domestic flotation	74,939	82,668	101,213	99,393	111,884	354,310
Central government securities	23,303	27,003	39,032	37,296	46,146	178,331
Long-term bonds	15,679	14,255	16,363	15,393	19,002	162,468
Medium-term notes	3,182	1,977	2,218	1,948	1,859	5,209
Treasury Bills	4,441	10,771	20,451	19,955	25,285	10,655
(Financing Bills)	156,163	158,472	167,339	157,578	155,208	22,770
Local government bonds	2,272	2,461	2,061	2,588	2,776	13,260
Government guaranteed bonds	7,039	6,868	7,624	7,640	7,365	41,969
Bank debentures	33,594	35,685	46,908	45,417	48,787	76,634
Corporate (straight) bonds	1,082	1,096	2,925	4,081	4,666	18,704
Convertible bonds	6,995	7,640	911	1,279	575	16,776
Bonds with warrants attached	--	915	395	382	--	1,764
Yen-denominated foreign bonds	655	1,001	1,358	711	1,569	6,873
Overseas flotation						
Local government bonds						
$US (million)	515	665	525	400	340	n.a.
Swiss franc (million)	350	100	100	340	--	n.a.
Government guaranteed bonds						
$US (million)	1,280	1,930	2,460	1,120	1,600	n.a.
Deutschmark (million)	670	150	--	100	300	n.a.
Swiss franc (million)	300	--	370	500	500	n.a.
Bank debentures						
$US (million)	1,180	1,855	--	--	250	n.a.
Deutschmark (million)	400	1,000	--	--	--	n.a.
Swiss franc (million)	3,150	4,090	--	--	--	n.a.
Corporate bonds						
$US (million)	38,915	56,240	18,198	20,797	14,893	n.a.
Deutschmark (million)	1,230	5,247	2,782	8,750	4,650	n.a.
Swiss franc (million)	12,147	18,010	8,943	12,997	7,753	n.a.
Pound sterling (million)	150	--	--	250	150	n.a.
Yen (billion)	--	20	1,464	3,060	2,687	n.a.

Notes: Overseas flotation excludes those issued by overseas affiliates, but includes convertible bonds. Central government securities do not include Financing Bills.

Sources: The Bond Underwriters Association, *Bond Review*. Bank of Japan, *Economic Statistics Monthly/Annual*.

In public offering with price bidding, the Ministry invites a large number of subscribers to bid a price on a pre-determined coupon rate. This method is more market-determined than the first method. It is used in 20-year government bonds, medium-term government notes, and 60 percent of the bonds offered at the monthly 10-year government bond auctions. In public offering under non-competitive terms, coupon and price are predetermined. Subscribers' yield is usually lower than the current market yield of the same maturity instrument. This method is used for Financing Bills and a portion of medium-term notes.

Issue of ordinary industrial bonds, or straight bonds, is limited both in numbers and amounts because of complex procedures and high costs, such as fees paid to trust companies, collateral requirements, standards regarding eligibility for issuance, etc.

Purchases of new issues of public and private bonds by type of bond and by purchaser are also available. *Bond Review* shows more detailed figures by type of bond. Most of the figures of new issues, redemptions, and outstanding by type of securities are identical to those in *Economic Statistics Monthly*. BOJ statistics do not include private offerings of government guaranteed bonds while *Bond Review* does.

Secondary Markets

Secondary markets for bonds consist of the following three markets: transactions at stock exchanges; over-the-counter transactions (OTC); and inter-dealer transactions. Transactions at stock exchanges reflect fair and actual prevailing yields and prices of bonds listed. In addition to these transactions, financial institutions (securities companies, banks, etc.) engage in transactions with each other and with other investors without using a stock exchange. These are called OTC transactions. Financial institutions also make transactions to adjust their inventories of bonds through 'Brokers' Broker' (BB). These transactions are called inter-dealer transactions. Inter-dealer transactions have gained growing importance in determining prevailing market prices.

Most transactions in the secondary markets are conducted in OTC markets, not at stock exchanges. In fiscal 1992, total transactions at eight stock exchanges in Japan was 18.8 trillion yen, while at the OTC markets in Tokyo the total was 3,244 trillion yen.

This concentration in OTC trading reflects the following factors:

1. There are too many issues to be listed at stock exchanges.
2. Transactions at stock exchanges require actual certificates, while most bonds are registered, which does not require issuance of actual certificates to investors.
3. Transactions at stock exchanges require standardized formulas of amount, settlement day, etc., while investors usually have diversified needs in these respects.

Volume of the transactions at exchanges and in OTC markets is available by type of bonds. Purchases and sales of bonds by type of investors and bonds are also available.

Coupon, Subscribers' Yield, Yield to Maturity

In a new issue of interest-bearing bonds, the coupon and issue price are determined, which determines subscribers' yield. Coupon is an interest payment received by bondholders semi-annually (there is no coupon for discount securities). If the coupon is 6%, the holder will receive 6% of principal, or par value, in a year as interest. If the bond is issued at par (100 yen), the coupon and subscribers' yield are equal. In some cases, however, bonds are issued at over- or under-par. This will result in a loss or gain in the investor's initial investment value at the time of redemption. Subscribers' yield takes into account this effect. If a 10-year bond is issued at 98 yen with a coupon of 6%, the subscriber gains an average of 0.2 yen a year [(100–98)/10] in addition to the 6 yen coupon. In Japan, subscribers' yield is calculated as the average annual receipt (6.2) divided by the value invested (98), which result in a subscribers' yield of 6.327%. Thus, subscribers' yield can be expressed as follows:

Subscribers' Yield (%)

$$= [\text{ coupon} + (100 - \text{issue price}) \div \text{years to maturity }] \div \text{issue price}$$

Yield to maturity is the yield on bonds purchased in a secondary market:

Yield to Maturity (%)

$$= [\text{ coupon} + (100 - \text{purchase price}) \div \text{years to maturity }] \div \text{purchase price}$$

Features and Problems

Developments in Secondary Markets

A huge increase in the transaction volume of government bonds reflects accumulation of government debt and deregulation of trading in the secondary markets. From the initial issuance of government bonds in January 1966 up until April 1977, banks were requested by the Ministry of Finance not to sell government bonds in the secondary market. Banks were only able to sell them to the BOJ, as the MOF was afraid that the huge supply of bonds in the secondary market would cause prices in the primary market to collapse. In other words, there had been no secondary market for government bonds. The huge accumulation of government bond-holding at banks since the first oil crisis in 1973–4, however, had a significant impact on liberalizing the secondary market of government bonds, and restrictions have been relaxed several times. Banks were allowed to participate in the dealing of government bonds in June 1985, which has contributed to a growing secondary market for government bonds. In addition, development of the TB market was remarkable following the liberalization of TB issuing procedures. The transaction values of TBs in the Tokyo OTC market exceeded those of government bonds in fiscal 1992.

Benchmark Issue

10-year government bonds are issued every month at terms (price, coupon) depending on the currently prevailing secondary market conditions. On the other hand, financial institutions are heavily engaged in bond dealing in the secondary market (OTC). This requires a standard, or benchmark issue of government bonds so that financial institutions can make transactions efficiently on the same, unified issue. As of end of June 1993, the current benchmark issue is the government bond #145, issued in January–April 1992 at a coupon of 5.5% with total amount issued of about 4.45 trillion yen (see Fig. 51.1).

Because of this concentration on a single issue, the yield of the benchmark issue is usually lower than other issues preceding and following the benchmark issue. Financial institutions demand the benchmark issue for the purpose of dealing, which produces a premium for the benchmark issue.

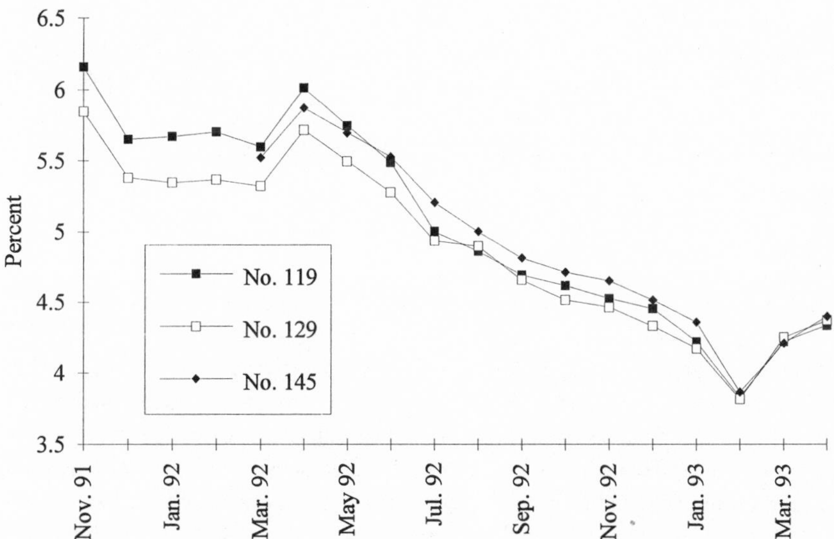

Fig. 51.1. Secondary Market Yield of 10-Year Government Bonds -- Benchmark Issues

52 Stock Markets

Source: Tokyo Stock Exchange, Japan Securities Dealers Association, *Nihon Keizai Shimbun*.

Frequency: Daily, monthly, and annual.

Release: Most daily figures are available in the *Nihon Keizai Shimbun* and other newspapers. Monthly figures are published around the last week of the following month in the *Monthly Statistics Report* by the Tokyo Stock Exchange. *Annual Securities Statistics* is published every April by the TSE.

TOPIX (Tokyo Stock Price Index) and the Nikkei Stock Price Average are the two most popular indicators of stock market prices in Japan. The former is a market value-weighted index which relates all Tokyo Stock Exchange-1st Section stocks to an aggregate market value as of January 4, 1968, adjusted for capitalization changes. The latter, the oldest and most widely quoted of all market indicators, is the price-weighted average of 225 major stocks listed on the Tokyo Stock Exchange-1st Section, and is calculated by the same method as the Dow Jones Industrial Average. Both indexes have performed similarly in trends, though the former is exempt from the possible influence of short-term sudden movements of narrow-market, high-price issues that is sometimes observed in the latter.

Details

Some 1,200 stocks and 425 stocks are listed on the 1st and 2nd sections respectively of the Tokyo Stock Exchange (TSE), which is by far the largest of the eight stock exchanges in Japan. Some 460 stocks are registered on the over-the-counter market. In general, young companies, when they go public, are first registered on the OTC market. As they become more established and are able to meet listing requirements, they are promoted to listing on the stock exchange. An exception was NTT (Nippon Telegraph and Telephone), a mammoth privatized company, which was listed on the Tokyo Stock Exchange-1st Section when it went public. Some 115 foreign issues are listed on the TSE.

Table 52.1. Summary Statistics for Tokyo Stock Exchange-1st Section
Calendar Years 1971–1992, units vary as shown

Calendar Year	Nikkei 225	TOPIX	No. of Listed Cos.	Total Market Value	Daily Trading Volume	Daily Trading Value	Price–Earnings Ratio	New Shares Issued
		1968.1.4 =100	End of Year	Billion Yen	Million Shares	Billion Yen	Times	Billion Yen
1971	2,385.72	163.48	771	21,500	197.4	45.2	14.9	537.0
1972	3,755.12	179.62	806	45,950	327.8	69.4	25.5	1,041.4
1973	4,759.25	282.42	849	36,507	201.7	50.6	13.3	939.3
1974	4,276.05	362.46	881	34,420	174.7	42.4	13.0	544.0
1975	4,243.05	307.21	901	41,468	178.7	53.5	27.0	1,001.1
1976	4,651.42	311.67	914	50,751	235.3	79.3	46.3	688.7
1977	5,029.69	347.40	926	49,350	239.4	72.2	24.2	922.6
1978	5,537.73	376.75	936	62,704	327.1	106.3	34.3	896.7
1979	6,272.33	415.15	950	65,909	332.0	117.0	23.3	953.4
1980	6,870.15	450.02	960	73,221	351.6	124.2	20.4	1,052.1
1981	7,510.73	474.11	974	87,978	371.7	169.5	21.1	1,926.4
1982	7,399.36	551.46	982	93,605	268.0	123.4	25.8	1,349.3
1983	8,806.57	549.02	1,003	119,505	349.9	177.9	34.7	801.8
1984	10,567.42	647.15	1,032	154,842	345.8	221.4	37.9	1,043.1
1985	12,556.63	815.86	1,052	182,697	414.8	264.7	35.2	859.1
1986	16,386.06	996.57	1,075	277,056	693.9	558.8	47.3	872.5
1987	23,176.03	1,323.93	1,101	325,478	946.8	896.3	58.3	3,013.0
1988	27,011.33	1,957.67	1,130	462,896	1,020.5	1,024.7	58.4	4,782.3
1989	34,042.79	2,131.91	1,161	590,909	876.9	1,308.5	70.6	8,848.6
1990	29,474.77	2,568.69	1,191	365,155	483.9	716.7	39.8	3,792.4
1991	24,298.20	2,180.67	1,223	365,939	372.9	435.4	37.8	807.7
1992	18,179.40	1,842.24	1,229	281,006	264.9	238.4	36.7	419.9

Note: Figures are annual averages unless otherwise indicated. Total Market Value is as of year end. New Shares Issued is the sum for all eight stock exchanges over the calendar year.
Source: Tokyo Stock Exchange

Primary Market

New share issuance is made by one of the three methods shown in Fig. 52.1. Public offering at market price is by far the most common method in recent years, in contrast to the situation up until the early 1970s, when most new share issuance was made through share allotment to existing shareholders. Incidentally, the latter method still prevails in many Asian markets.

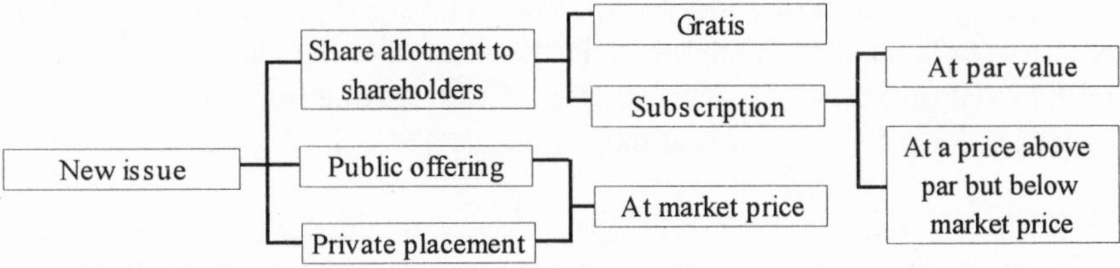

Fig. 52.1. Three Methods of New Share Issuance

In case of initial public offer (IPO) -- when a company goes public and is registered on the OTC market (or listed on the exchange), the initial offering price must be determined; two or three companies similar to the issuing company from the viewpoint of type of business are selected; then, earnings and book value (net assets) of the issuing company are compared with those of the selected companies, and after considering the current market sentiment and any special factors, some adjustments may be made to the theoretical price before deciding on the final initial offering price.

	Issuing company	Similar company
Earnings per share	B	***B***
Book value per share	C	***C***
Share price	A	***A***

Theoretical price A = ***A*** * (B/***B*** + C/***C***)/2

Secondary Markets

Tradings of stocks are made on exchange floors for listed stocks or on the OTC market for OTC-registered stocks. Following a revision of the Commercial Code, the unit share system was introduced in October 1982. With certain exceptions, trading is usually effected in units of 1,000 shares for 50 yen par value issues, and in units of 100 shares for 500 yen par value issues*. In order to avoid violent fluctuations in stock prices, daily stock price gain and loss limits are set by stock exchanges. These limits are approximately 10% on either side of a stock's price. For stocks priced at 1,000 yen or 10,000 yen, for example, the maximum daily gain or loss would be 100 yen and 1,000 yen respectively. However, for higher priced stocks, a smaller percentage limit is set, so that for a 50,000 yen stock, the limit is 3,000 yen. Daily price limits are practiced by neighboring South Korea and Taiwan, but not in the US.

Most companies have par values of 50 yen, and some 500 yen. Par values have been decreasing in importance because stock prices have gone up to three or four digits, and also because public offerings at market price have increased. Nevertheless, par value remains alive, as evidenced by the trading units mentioned above.

The Tokyo stock market, like its New York counterpart, has become institutionalized since around the mid-1980s, in the sense that the share of trading by institutional investors has exceeded 50% of total trading (excluding trading by securities firms for their own accounts) on the TSE. In the US, the mainstay

*With respect to less-than-one-unit shares arising from stock dividends, gratis issues, etc., no share certificates are issued, and only the number of such shares is recorded on the issuing company's shareholders' register. Less-than-one-unit shares are not entitled to voting rights.

institutional investors are pension funds and mutual funds, but in Japan, institutional investors can be broken down into four main groups: banks and insurance companies, corporations, foreigners, and investment trusts (see Table 52.2).

Features and Problems

High Price–Earnings Ratio

As financial assets accumulated and easier money prevailed in Japan's economy of the 1970s and 1980s, the price–earnings ratio of the Tokyo market rose to higher and higher levels, reflecting the increasingly optimistic sentiments of investors. Indeed, stock prices nose-dived entering the 1990s, but earnings also declined dramatically. Thus, as of the end of April 1993, Japanese stocks sold at around 50 times earnings, in contrast to 23 for the USA, 20 for the UK and 12-25 for some other European markets (see Table 52.3).

Factors generally cited for Japan's high price–earnings ratios include: long-term interest rates are lower than in other countries; shares available in the market are very limited, as most shares are cross-held by financial institutions and corporations as permanent shareholders; Japanese investors are fond of asset (especially land) values so much that stock prices reflect the value of assets, not earnings; and corporate accounting is generally very conservative, as exemplified by large depreciation charges.

As for this last point, Japanese companies in general follow the declining-balance method, and their depreciation costs thus charged are indicated on their financial statements as well as for tax purposes. This method, on top of their aggressive investments in plant, equipment, and other depreciable assets in the 1980s, led to very large depreciation charges. Remarkably, while the price–earnings ratio of the Tokyo market is much higher than its New York counterpart, Tokyo's price–cash earnings ratio (cash earnings = earnings + depreciation), at around 10 as of the end of April 1993, is about the same as New York's.

Primary Market Temporarily Suspended

Entering the 1990s, the Tokyo equity market became extremely sluggish, dipping in prices and thinning in turnover. It was feared that should new shares be supplied, the secondary market would be further damaged. Thus the securities industry, issuer companies, and the authorities concerned have cooperated to largely suspend new share issuance since March 1990. Such suspension is expected to be lifted sometime in late 1993, though still with some restrictions. This type of cooperative regulation shows that Japan still does not operate under a US-style free market mechanism.

Large Share Ownership of Financial Institutions and Corporations

Unlike the US, major shareholders of Japanese listed companies are financial institutions (banks and insurance companies) and corporations, and not individual investors. They do not hold shares to sell; instead, they mutually cross-hold each other's stocks, thereby strengthening their mutual business relationship. It is said that this cross-holding largely restricts the availability of shares in the market. Since those shareholders are permissive of each other's management, some criticize that Japanese management is unduly free from the discipline of the market. Some US investors criticize this system as virtually closing the door to takeover chances, while some Asian leaders view it as an acceptable way to consolidate their own countries' industries.

Table 52.2. Stock Ownership
End-of-Fiscal Year, % of Total, unless otherwise noted

	1971	1976	1981	1986	1991	1992	1993
Government	0.7	0.4	0.4	0.3	0.3	0.3	0.3
Business	56.8	63.9	65.9	70.4	74.7	73.4	72.6
Financial institutions	31.6	35.5	38.2	39.8	43.0	42.8	42.9
Banks and trust banks	13.7	16.8	17.9	19.2	21.8	21.9	22.4
Investment trusts	2.1	2.2	1.9	1.7	3.7	3.4	3.2
Life-insurance	10.0	10.2	11.5	12.3	12.0	12.2	12.4
Non-life insurance	3.7	4.4	4.6	4.1	3.9	3.9	3.8
Other financial	2.1	2.0	2.3	2.4	1.6	1.4	1.2
Non-financial business	23.9	27.0	26.2	28.8	30.1	29.0	28.5
Securities companies	1.3	1.4	1.5	1.9	1.7	1.5	1.2
Personal	37.7	32.1	27.9	22.3	20.4	20.3	20.7
Foreigners	4.9	3.6	5.8	7.0	4.7	6.0	6.3
(Total value in trillion yen)	20.0	47.7	86.3	236.1	449.4	326.0	328.0

Source: The National Conference of Stock Exchanges.

Table 52.3. International Comparison of Japan's Stock Markets
As of the end of April 1993

	Japan	US	UK	France	Germany
Price–book value ratio	2.2	2.5	2.1	1.6	1.7
Price–cash earnings ratio	10.4	10.1	10.8	6.5	4.2
Price–earnings ratio	50.7	22.6	20.5	18.9	18.9
Yield (%)	0.8	2.9	4.3	3.4	3.4
Market capitalization ($US billion)	1,839.8	2,379.0	642.0	225.1	227.6

Source: Morgan Stanley, *Capital International Perspective* (May 1993), 2, 5.

Household Savings

53 Personal Savings

Source: Research and Statistics Department, Bank of Japan.

Frequency: Quarterly.

Release: Figures for the previous quarter are released in the latter half of the last month of each quarter. They are available in *Economic Statistics Monthly*.

Availability: Figures are available from 1978 onward.

Details

These statistics reveal the amount of personal savings by type of instrument (see Table 53.1). The Bank of Japan compiles the figures from 'Flow of Funds Accounts' (see Chapter 36) where 'Financial Transactions Accounts (Flow)' and 'Financial Assets and Liabilities Accounts (Stock)' provide data for the personal sector.

Features and Problems

Comparison with Flow of Funds Statistics

In general, figures for each instrument in Personal Savings roughly correspond to the amount of each instrument held by the household sector in 'Financial Assets of Liabilities Accounts (Stock)' of Flow of Funds Accounts. Table 53.2 presents the data on financial assets for the personal sector available in Flow of Funds Accounts.

There are two major differences between the two statistics. First, Personal Savings does not include private non-profit institutions serving households while Flow of Funds Accounts does. Second, Personal Savings does not include cash currency, negotiable certificates of deposit (CD), or stocks, while Flow of Funds Accounts does. In the former, figures for stocks are available as a memo item valued at the market prices of listed stocks.

In addition to the above differences in coverage, there is a large difference in the figures for trusts and insurance between the two statistics. Coverage of Flow of Funds statistics on trusts and insurances is larger than that of Personal Savings. For example, Flow of Funds statistics cover broader types of trusts, such as pension trusts and property accumulation annuity for employees.

Table 53.1. Personal Savings
End-of-Calendar Years 1988–1991, Billion Yen, unless otherwise noted

	1988	1989	1990	1991	1991 % of Total
Total	629,805	700,064	754,202	804,358	100.0
Deposits and savings	389,596	430,654	465,030	503,347	62.6
Banks[1]	154,375	174,994	196,900	208,334	25.9
Shinkin banks	45,684	50,629	56,202	59,393	7.4
Credit cooperatives	11,738	13,686	14,625	14,449	1.8
Agricultural and fishery cooperatives	47,896	51,936	56,630	61,312	7.6
Labor credit associations	5,967	6,483	6,976	7,445	0.9
Post offices	123,938	132,926	133,698	152,415	18.9
Trusts	30,872	34,114	39,988	43,410	5.4
Public and corporate bonds	50,755	52,513	51,738	53,696	6.7
Investment trusts	41,013	44,205	42,885	36,603	4.6
Insurance	117,570	138,578	154,560	167,302	20.8
Life insurance	104,227	122,639	136,685	147,911	18.4
Non-life insurance	13,343	15,939	17,876	19,392	2.4
Stocks (memo)[2]	99,568	125,410	80,684	79,807	--

Notes: 1. Banks includes City banks, Regional Banks I and II, and long-term credit banks. 2. Figures for stocks are not included under total, and are valued at the market prices of listed stocks.

Source: Bank of Japan, *Economic Statistics Monthly*.

Table 53.2. Financial Assets Outstanding for Personal Sector: Flow of Funds Accounts
End-of-Calendar Year 1991, Billion Yen, unless otherwise noted

	1991	1991 % of Total Excluding Stocks and Cash Currency
Total	980,906	
Total excluding stocks and cash currency	868,333	100.0
Cash currency	33,073	--
Deposits and savings	505,204	58.2
Demand deposits	58,337	6.7
Time deposits	446,868	51.5
Trusts	69,171	8.0
Insurance	213,177	24.6
Securities	159,866	--
Government bonds	11,096	1.3
Bank debentures	25,324	2.9
Stocks	79,501	--
Securities investment trusts	34,602	4.0

Note: Sub-categories do not sum to total due to omissions in the published figures.

Source: Bank of Japan, *Economic Statistics Monthly*.

54 Family Savings Survey

Source: Statistical Bureau, Management and Coordination Agency.

Frequency: Annual.

Release: Figures for the previous year are released each March.

Availability: Annual figures are available from 1958 onward.

The Family Savings Survey has been conducted since 1958 to trace (both the stock and flow of) households' savings, debt, and investment in real assets. This survey supplements the Family Income and Expenditure Survey (FIES, see Chapter 4), providing detailed information on savings lacking in the FIES.

Details

Coverage

The Family Savings Survey (FSS) is conducted as of the end of each year. It covers 168 municipalities nationwide, the same as those covered by the Family Income and Expenditure Survey (FIES). Currently, the FSS covers about 6,300 households. Sample households are surveyed for two consecutive years, with roughly half replaced each year. The households are surveyed under both the FIES and FSS for the first year (they are called the 'current-year' sample), but only under FSS during the second year (called the 'previous-year' sample).

Items Surveyed

The following items are surveyed:

1. Year-end outstanding and increase/decrease of savings by type of instrument.
2. Year-end outstanding and increase/decrease of liabilities by type of lender; liabilities and annual repayments for purchases of housing and land.
3. Amount invested in housing and land during the year, and future housing/land investment plans.
4. Characteristics of the household and housing.
5. Annual income of the household.

Explanation of Terms

Yearly Income

Yearly income includes: pre-tax gross wage earnings; operating profits of the self-employed (sales less operating costs and taxes); interest and dividend income; pension income; rental income; and remittance received. Lump-sum retirement allowance, receipts of insurance compensation, inherited deposits, and income from sales of securities, housing, and land are not included.

Savings

Savings include: deposits at banks, post offices, and other financial institutions; insurance premiums; stocks; bonds; investment trusts; loan trusts; money in trust; and 'deposits in one's own companies' (interest-earning deposits with a company the respondent works for). Savings in insurance is calculated as the sum of insurance premium payments since the purchase of the policies. Stocks and investment trusts are valued at market prices while bonds, loan trusts, and money in trust are valued at their face values.

Savings is defined as the sum of savings of all family members, including savings for business purposes by self-employed households. Term insurance without maturity payment and public pension plans are not included in savings. Equity in housing is not included in savings, but debt related to housing is included in liabilities.

Liabilities

Liabilities include those to private and public financial institutions, post offices, life insurance companies, one's own companies, individuals, and installments. Business related liabilities are included.

Investments in Fixed Assets

Investments in fixed assets consist of those for households and those for businesses during the year. They are calculated as the purchase of land and housing (buildings), construction of new housing (buildings), extension and rebuilding of housing (buildings) less proceeds from sales of houses (buildings) and land.

Groups: Quartile, Quintile, Decile, Median, and Mode

Households are divided into four (five, ten) groups from lowest to highest income. The lowest 25 (20, 10) percent of total households are called the Group I quartile (quintile, decile). The next 25 (20, 10) percent of households are called Group II, etc. The household in the very middle of the total distribution (half of all households are above it, half are below) is called the median household. The value of income and savings for the median household are called median income and median savings respectively. In some cases, households are grouped into fixed intervals of income or savings (e.g. less than 1 million yen, between 1 and 2 million yen, etc.). The group which shows the highest number of households is called the mode.

Features and Problems

Biased Nature of Sample

The warnings regarding the biased nature of the sample given for the FIES (see Chapter 4) also apply to the FSS.

Average Savings More Than Median Savings

In 1992, the average savings outstanding per workers' household was 11.87 million yen, 1.55 times annual income (see Fig. 54.1). Median savings was 7.44 million yen, and the mode (using 1 million yen intervals) was the 5–6 million yen category.

Comparison with Family Income and Expenditure Survey

The Family Savings Survey (FSS) reveals the increase/decrease of savings/liabilities of households (more precisely, the increase in savings less the increase in liabilities plus investment in fixed assets). This roughly corresponds to the concept of 'surplus' in the FIES. Disposable income is not given in the FSS, but 'yearly income' in the FSS roughly corresponds to 'income' in the FIES. Fig. 54.2 compares the 'surplus-to-yearly income ratio' obtained from the FSS and the FIES.

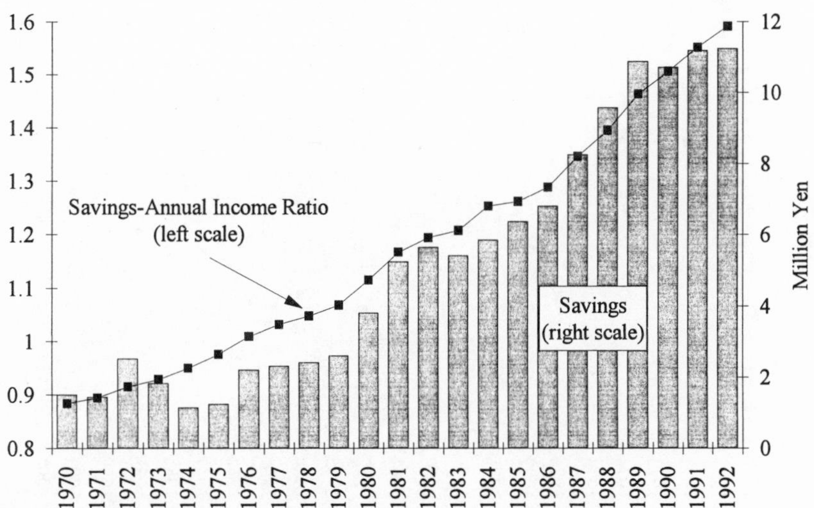

Fig. 54.1. Family Savings, Workers' Households

Table 54.1. Savings and Liabilities Held per Household: All Households
End-of-Calendar Years 1987–1992, Thousand Yen, unless otherwise noted

	1987	1988	1989	1990	1991	1992	1992 % of Total
Savings	10,452	11,198	13,110	13,530	14,654	15,368	100.0
Financial institutions	10,170	10,880	12,760	13,212	14,289	14,914	97.0
Demand deposits	735	788	895	957	937	989	6.4
Time deposits	4,502	4,685	4,999	5,734	6,687	7,343	47.8
Post offices	1,269	1,315	1,367	1,632	1,940	2,181	14.2
Banks	1,823	1,858	2,285	2,832	3,343	3,706	24.1
Others	1,409	1,512	1,347	1,270	1,405	1,456	9.5
Gold accounts	--	--	--	--	64	39	0.3
Life and non-life insurance	2,346	2,665	3,114	3,365	3,573	3,848	25.0
Postal life insurance	811	881	890	997	1,119	1,198	7.8
Life insurance companies	1,535	1,784	2,020	2,117	2,218	2,393	15.6
Non-life insurance companies	--	--	204	251	236	257	1.7
Securities	2,587	2,742	3,752	3,155	3,029	2,695	17.5
Stocks and shares	1,441	1,434	2,335	1,829	1,594	1,331	8.7
Public and corporate bonds	377	366	380	366	346	359	2.3
Unit and open-end trust	244	335	445	257	232	186	1.2
Open-end bond trust	112	154	141	161	158	182	1.2
Loan trust and money in trust	414	454	451	549	699	637	4.1
Non-financial institutions	283	318	350	318	366	454	3.0
Liabilities	3,113	3,096	3,742	3,592	3,753	3,926	--
For purchase of houses/land	2,595	2,657	3,256	3,147	3,169	3,200	--
Yearly income	5,923	6,075	6,413	6,773	7,189	7,505	--

Source: Management and Coordination Agency, *Family Savings Survey*, 1992.

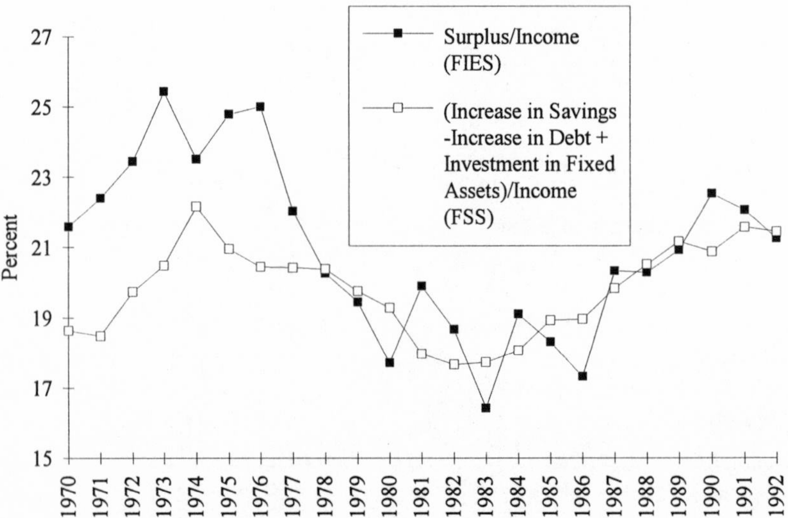

Fig. 54.2. Comparison of Surplus/Income Ratio in FIES and FSS

Appendices

A1 Theory and Practice of Index Numbers

Index numbers are frequently used in statistics as value, price, and quantity indexes. Despite their frequent use in economic analysis, many readers may be unfamiliar with the different types of indexes and the theoretical concepts behind them. This section provides the theory and practical use of index numbers so that readers can more readily understand the calculations used in forming the statistics. We focus mainly on price indexes, as they are the most frequently used.

Types of Index Numbers

In general, there are three types of price index numbers used in economic statistics: Laspeyres [L]; Paasche [P]; and Fisher [F] indexes. Each attempts to measure the level of current prices (or year 't' prices) compared to prices at a specific time in the past, called the base year (benchmark year) or year '0'. In the equations below, $P_{t,x}$ represents the price of good 'x' in year 't', $P_{0,x}$ represents the price of good 'x' in the base year, $Q_{t,x}$ represents the quantity of good 'x' in year 't', and $Q_{0,x}$ represents the quantity of good 'x' in the base year.

$$[L] = \frac{P_{t,1}*Q_{0,1} + P_{t,2}*Q_{0,2} + P_{t,3}*Q_{0,3} + \ldots \text{ (Current year cost of \textit{base} year goods)}}{P_{0,1}*Q_{0,1} + P_{0,2}*Q_{0,2} + P_{0,3}*Q_{0,3} + \ldots \text{ (Base year cost of \textit{base} year goods)}}$$

$$[P] = \frac{P_{t,1}*Q_{t,1} + P_{t,2}*Q_{t,2} + P_{t,3}*Q_{t,3} + \ldots \text{ (Current year cost of \textit{current} year goods)}}{P_{0,1}*Q_{t,1} + P_{0,2}*Q_{t,2} + P_{0,3}*Q_{t,3} + \ldots \text{ (Base year cost of \textit{current} year goods)}}$$

$$[F] = (L * P)^{1/2}$$

The Laspeyres index uses the quantity of each good in the *base* year. It is also called a 'fixed-weight' price index because the relative weight (i.e. the quantity of the good) assigned to each price is fixed in the base year. The Laspeyres index tells us how much it would cost today, relative to the base year, to buy the same goods as were bought in the base year.

The Paasche index uses the quantity of each good in the *current* year. The Paasche index is also called a 'variable-weight' price index because the weights (quantities) are changing every year, and the weights must be calculated every year. The Paasche index tells us how much it costs today, relative to the base year, to buy the goods sold during the current year.

The problem with these price indexes is that, in general, people do not buy the same goods every year. In fact, if the price of a certain good increases substantially, people will probably buy less of it. A simple example reveals the problem with each index. Suppose that the price of lettuce this year is much higher than it was last year (the base year), but the price of everything else is the same. People buy no lettuce at all, and instead buy cabbage or some other vegetable. The Laspeyres index assumes that the amount of lettuce bought this year is the same as last year (the weight on the price of lettuce is unchanged), and indicates that overall, prices have increased greatly. In the Paasche index, the reduction in the quantity of lettuce this year means that the weight on the price of lettuce is zero; the weight on cabbage increases, but since the price of cabbage is unchanged, that does not affect the index. Overall, the Paasche index will show no change in prices.

Reality lies somewhere between these two extremes. The question we would like to answer is: how much worse off are we because the price of lettuce increased? The Laspeyres index overstates how much worse off we are. It tells us how much worse off we would be if we were *forced* to buy the same amount of lettuce as last year despite the price increase. However, since we can choose to buy cabbage instead, the effects of the price increase are somewhat mitigated. On the other hand, the Paasche index understates how much worse off we are. Last year we were able to buy lettuce at a cheaper price, and this year we can not, so our choices are more limited and we are at least somewhat worse off.

The index that would correctly answer the question above is called the *true index* or *economic theoretic index*. Unfortunately, in practice it is impossible to calculate the true index, since it would require information that is not readily available. All we can state is the Laspeyres index is greater than, and the Paasche index is less than, the true index.

A compromise between the Laspeyres index [L] and Paasche index [P] is the Fisher index. The Fisher index is the geometric mean of the Laspeyres and Paasche indexes, i.e. the square root of L*P, and by definition lies between the Laspeyres index and Paasche index. If the quantity of goods were the same in the current and base years, all three indexes would be the same.

Currently, Laspeyres indexes are used in Japan's statistics, with the exception of *trade price indexes* (Fisher) and *implicit deflators* of national income components (Paasche).

Quantity Indexes

Corresponding to each price index is a quantity index. A quantity index tells us how much quantity has increased relative to the base year, taking into consideration the relative price of each good.

$$[L] = \frac{P_{0,1}*Q_{t,1} + P_{0,2}*Q_{t,2} + P_{0,3}*Q_{t,3} + \ldots \text{ (Current year value at } \textit{base} \text{ year prices)}}{P_{0,1}*Q_{0,1} + P_{0,2}*Q_{0,2} + P_{0,3}*Q_{0,3} + \ldots \text{ (Base year value at } \textit{base} \text{ year prices)}}$$

$$[P] = \frac{P_{t,1}*Q_{t,1} + P_{t,2}*Q_{t,2} + P_{t,3}*Q_{t,3} + \ldots \text{ (Current year value at } \textit{current} \text{ year prices)}}{P_{t,1}*Q_{0,1} + P_{t,2}*Q_{0,2} + P_{t,3}*Q_{0,3} + \ldots \text{ (Base year value at } \textit{current} \text{ year prices)}}$$

$$[F] = (L * P)^{1/2}$$

Technological Progress and Price Indexes

Technological progress embedded in a new product raises its benefit to the consumer even if the price of the new product is the same as that of the old one. In theory, the benefits of technological progress should be reflected as a decline in the price index. For example, if a new, more powerful computer is introduced at the same price as the old model, the price index should fall, reflecting the fact that consumers are made better off by the introduction of the new model. In actual practice, the distinction between a change in price attributable to technological progress and one attributable to some other factor (say the cost of a factor of production) is rather ambiguous and subject to the compiler's judgement.

In compiling the Wholesale and Consumer Price Indexes, the Bank of Japan and Management and Coordination Agency try to separate these two effects. For example, they conduct a direct survey on producers to obtain cost estimates of new and old products. Problems still remain because both indexes are fixed-weight indexes and the base year is revised only once every five years. This seems to produce a smaller overlap of products surveyed between the two base years. The interruption is particularly severe for computers and machinery equipment, which display rapid technological progress.

The BOJ now employs a *hedonic price index* (regression method) for certain goods such as information processing equipment. This index uses a linear regression to estimate a formula for the value of a good based on its main characteristics (for a computer, perhaps amount of memory, speed of CPU, etc.). The price of the good can then be adjusted to take account of any improvement in quality. For further details, see Griliches 1971.

A2 Seasonal Adjustment

Economic variables are affected by many seasonal factors. They include weather conditions, number of trading days, and social and business traditions such as payment of bonuses and summer vacations. Sales of beer tend to peak in the hot summer season while a simultaneous slowdown in factory operations due to summer vacations tends to reduce production. Seasonal adjustments attempt to take these seasonal factors out of the not-adjusted, or raw, time series as accurately as possible to provide more useful time series reflecting true economic conditions. The basic concepts of seasonal adjustment are outlined below.

In Japan, *Census X-11* and *MITI-III-R* are employed for seasonal adjustment. MITI-IIIR is employed only for the industrial production, shipments, and inventory statistics published by MITI. Other agencies have adopted the Census X-11 method. Although there are differences in several aspects between these two, their main property is the same. Their method of excluding seasonal factors is called 'ratio-to-moving-average'.

Excluding Seasonal Factors from Time Series

Let us suppose that each time series consists of four components:

1. Trend Component: reflecting long-run growth or decline.
2. Cyclical Component: swing with interval of more than one year.
3. Seasonal Component: regular movement within a year.
4. Irregular Component: movements not explained by 1–3.

An original, or raw, time series Y is taken to be the *product* of T, C, S, and I. If the original series includes zero and/or negative values, it is taken to be the *sum* of T, C, S, and I.

$Y_m = T * C * S * I$ (multiplicative assumption)

or $Y_a = T + C + S + I$ (additive assumption)

In short, seasonal adjustment attempts to somehow exclude S to obtain the adjusted figure (AY) $AY_m = T*C*I$, or $AY_a = T + C + I$. Below, we consider the multiplicative assumption.

In the first step, trend and cyclical components are calculated by the moving average of the original time series. If the time series is a monthly variable, an estimated product of the trend and cyclical components $(T*C)_t^e$ is expressed as:

$(T*C)_t^e = 1/12\ (1/2\ Y_{t-6} + Y_{t-5} + ...\ Y_t + ... + 1/2\ Y_{t+6})$

The estimated product of seasonal and irregular components $(S*I)_t^e$ is obtained by dividing Y_t by $(T*C)_t^e$:

$(S*I)_t^e = Y_t\ /\ (T*C)_t^e$

The next step is to exclude the irregular factor I from the $(S*I)^e$ component. Again, the moving average method is employed. This assumes that the moving average will smooth out the movement of the irregular factor thus isolating the seasonal factor.

$S_t^e = 1/5\ [\ (S*I)_{t-24}^{\ e} + (S*I)_{t-12}^{\ e} + (S*I)_t^e + (S*I)_{t+12}^{\ e} + (S*I)_{t+24}^{\ e}\ ]$

The seasonally adjusted figure, AY^e is obtained by dividing the original Y_t by the estimated seasonal factor, S_t^e.

$AY^e = Y_t\ /\ S_t^e = (T*C*I)_t^e$

In both X-11 and MITI-III-R, this process is repeated to obtain a more accurate seasonal factor. In theory, a seasonal factor should be recalculated for the entire period upon the latest release; in practice, there is a revision of figures only once a year after the figures for the whole year are available.

Differences between X-11 and MITI-III-R

1. The minimum period required for X-11 is 36 months while the period of calculation is fixed at 64 months for MITI-III-R. MITI-III-R incorporates a seasonal adjustment upon the release of February figures.
2. Seasonal factors for the entire period are subject to change in X-11 while they are fixed except for the latest year in MITI-III-R.
3. A trading day adjustment is available as an option in X-11 but not in MITI-III-R.
4. For calculation of seasonal factors of the current year, X-11 uses seasonal factors of the past two years ($S_t + 1/2(S_t - S_{t-1})$) while MITI-III-R uses only those of the past one year.
5. In general, X-11 incorporates various options to be applied in a particular case while MITI-III-R adopts a more concise method of calculation.

Problems of Seasonal Adjustment

1. The sum of seasonally adjusted figures, in general, does not equal the sum of the original figures. While the adjusted and not-adjusted merchandise trade balance figures published by the Bureau of Census, US Department of Commerce are calculated so that their sums are equal, it is not the case for Japan.
2. Because both X-11 and MITI-III-R adopt a moving-average method, figures in the latest periods are calculated using preliminary estimates of seasonal factors. Therefore, they should be regarded as preliminary figures subject to revision.

A3 Source Statistics

This Appendix provides a list of source statistics useful for analysis of Japan's economy, including some statistics not cited in this book. When calling the telephone numbers listed below from outside Japan, use 81 for the country code and drop the leading 0. Most official statistics are available from:

The Government Publication Service Center
1-2-1, Kasumigaseki
Chiyoda-ku, Tokyo 100
(TEL 03-3504-3885)

Some Ministries and Agencies have their own sales agents which are given below. The symbol [J] after the title of the statistics means that the statistics do not contain an English translation. The letters in the parenthesis indicate the frequency of release: (5) Every five years; (A) Annual; (SA) Semi Annual; (Q) Quarterly; (M) Monthly; and (O) Occasional.

A. Management and Coordination Agency

Statistics Bureau
Management and Coordination Agency
19-1, Wakamatsu-cho
Shinjuku-ku, Tokyo 162
(TEL 03-3202-1111)

Sales Agent: Japan Statistics Association (except no.12)
Crest 21
6-21, Yocho-machi
Shinjuku-ku, Tokyo 162
(TEL 03-5269-3051)

1. Monthly Statistics of Japan (M)
2. Japan Statistical Yearbook (A)
3. Historical Statistics of Japan: Volumes 1 to 5 (O)
4. Monthly Report on the Family Income and Expenditure Survey (M)
5. Annual Report on the Family Income and Expenditure Survey (A)
6. Comprehensive Time Series Report on the Family Income and Expenditure Survey: 1947–1986 (O)

7. Family Savings Survey (A)
8. National Survey of Family Income and Expenditure (5)
9. Monthly Report on the Labor Force Survey (M)
10. Annual Report on the Labor Force Survey (A)
11. Employment Status Survey (5)
12. Monthly Report on Current Population Estimates (M)
13. Population Census of Japan (5)
14. Monthly Report of Retail Prices: Consumer Price Index (M)
15. Annual Report on the Consumer Price Index (A)
16. Housing Survey of Japan (5)
17. Establishment Census of Japan (5)

B. Economic Planning Agency

Business Statistics Research Div. (except nos.18, 20–2, and 29)
or Economic Research Institute (nos. 18, 20–2, and 29)
Economic Planning Agency
3-1-1, Kasumigaseki
Chiyoda-ku, Tokyo 100
(TEL 03-3581-0261)

Sales Agent: Economic Planning Association (except nos. 18 and 29)
5-19-1, Shinbashi
Minato-ku, Tokyo 105
(TEL 03-3437-0571)

18. Preliminary Quarterly Estimates of National Accounts {QE} (Q)
19. National Economic Accounts Quarterly (Q) [J]
20. Annual Report on National Accounts (A) [J]
21. Report on National Accounts from 1955 to 1989 (O) [J]
22. Report on Revised National Accounts on the basis of 1985, vols. 1 and 2 (O) [J]
23. Indexes of Business Conditions (M)
24. Main Economic Indicators (Quick Report) (M)
25. Japanese Economic Indicators Quarterly (Q)
26. Annual Report on Business Cycle Indicators (A)
27. Monthly Machinery Orders Statistics (M) [J]
28. Annual Report on Machinery Orders (A) [J]
29. Quarterly Fixed Capital Stock of Private Non-Financial Enterprises (Q) [J]
30. Business Investment Survey of Incorporated Enterprises (Q) [J]
31. Consumer Behavioral Survey (Q) [J]

C. Ministry of Finance

Customs and Tariff Bureau (nos. 32 and 33)
or Institute of Fiscal and Monetary Affairs (nos. 34 and 35)
or International Finance Bureau (no. 36)
Ministry of Finance
3-1-1, Kasumigaseki
Chiyoda-ku, Tokyo 100
(TEL 03-3581-4111)

Sales Agent: Japan Tariff Association (nos. 32 and 33)
4-7-8, Kojimachi
Chiyoda-ku, Tokyo 100
(TEL 03-3263-7221)

Printing Office (nos. 34 and 35)
Ministry of Finance
2-2-4, Toranomon
Minato-ku, Tokyo 105
(TEL 03-3587-4283)

32. The Summary Report on Trade of Japan (M)
33. Japan Exports and Imports: Commodity by Country (M)
34. Monthly Statistics on Government Finance and Banking <Zaisei kinyu tokei geppo> (M) [J]
35. Statistical Survey of Incorporated Enterprises <Quarterly Financial Report of Non-Financial Businesses> (Q) [J]
36. Foreign Direct Investment (M, SA) [J]

D. Ministry of International Trade and Industry

Research and Statistics Department (except no. 44)
or Industrial Policy Bureau (no. 44)
Ministry of International Trade and Industry
1-3-1, Kasumigaseki
Chiyoda-ku, Tokyo 100
(TEL 03-3501-1511)

Sales Agent: Research Institute of International Trade and Industries (except nos. 38–40)
2-8-9, Ginza
Chuo-ku, Tokyo 104
(TEL 03-3535-4881)

37. Industrial Statistics Monthly (M)
38. Year Book of Indices of Industrial Production (A)

39. Activity Index of Tertiary Industry (Q) [J]
40. Input-Output Tables (A) [J]
41. Census of Manufactures (A) [J]
42. Monthly Statistics of Large-Scale Retail Store Sales (M) [J]
43. Monthly Statistics of the Current Survey of Commerce (M) [J]
44. Survey on Foreign Business Activity of Japanese Firms (A) [J]
    (Wagakuni kigyo no kaigai jigyo katsudo doko chosa)

E. Ministry of Labour

Policy Planning and Research Department (except no. 48)
or Employment Security Bureau (no. 48)
Ministry of Labour
1-2-2, Kasumigaseki
Chiyoda-ku, Tokyo 100
(TEL 03-3593-1211)

Sales Agent: Rodo Horei Kyokai Foundation
3-18-6, Hatchobori
Chuo-ku, Tokyo 103
(TEL 03-3552-4851)

45. Monthly Labour Survey (M)
46. Annual Report on Labour Survey (A) [J]
47. Yearbook of Labour Statistics (A)
48. Monthly Report of Employment Security Business (M) [J]

F. Ministry of Construction

Economic Affairs Bureau
Ministry of Construction
2-1-3, Kasumigaseki
Chiyoda-ku, Tokyo 100
(TEL 03-3580-4311)

Sales Agent: Construction Research Institute
13-4, Kodenma-cho, Nihonbashi
Chuo-ku, Tokyo 103
(TEL 03-3663-2411)

49. Monthly of Construction Statistics (M)
50. Yearbook on Construction Statistics (A) [J]

G. National Land Agency

Land Bureau
National Land Agency
1-2-2, Kasumigaseki
Chiyoda-ku, Tokyo 100
(TEL 03-3593-3311)

Sales Agent: Printing Bureau
Ministry of Finance
2-2-4, Toranomon
Minato-ku, Tokyo 105
(TEL 03-3587-4283)

51. Official Land Price Survey (A) [J]
52. Prefectural Land Price Survey (A) [J]

H. The Bank of Japan

Research and Statistics Department (except no. 57)
or International Department (no. 57)
The Bank of Japan
2-1-1, Hongoku-cho, Nihonbashi
Chuo-ku, Tokyo 103
(TEL 03-3663-5681)

Sales Agent: The Credit Information Company of Japan
6-1, Kobuna-cho, Nihonbashi
Chuo-ku, Tokyo 103
(TEL 03-3663-5681)

53. Economic Statistics Monthly (M)
54. Economic Statistics Annual (A)
55. Price Indexes Monthly (M)
56. Price Indexes Annual (A)
57. Balance of Payments Monthly (M)
58. Short-Term Economic Survey of Enterprises (TANKAN) (Q)
59. Comparative Economic and Financial Statistics: Japan and Other Major Countries (A)

I. The Bond Underwriters Association of Japan

1-5-8, Kayaba-cho, Nihonbashi
Chuo-ku, Tokyo 103
(TEL 03-3667-2435)

60. Bond Review (M)

J. Tokyo Stock Exchange

1-2, Kabuto-cho, Nihonbashi
Chuo-ku, Tokyo 103
(TEL 03-3666-0140)

61. Monthly Statistics Report (M)
62. Annual Securities Statistics (A)

K. The Investment Trusts Association

1-5-8, Kayaba-cho, Nihonbashi
Chuo-ku, Tokyo 103
(TEL 03-3667-7471)

63. Monthly Report of Investment Trust (M)

L. Japan Security Dealers Association

1-5-8, Kayaba-cho, Nihonbashi
Chuo-ku, Tokyo 103
(TEL 03-3667-8454)

64. Shoken Gyoho (M)

M. Toyo Keizai Shimpo Sha

1-2-1, Hongoku-cho, Nihonbashi
Chuo-ku, Tokyo 103
(TEL 03-3246-5451)

65. Toyo Keizai Monthly Statistics (M)
66. Toyo Keizai Data Bank (A) [J]

N. Japan Productivity Center

3-1-1, Shibuya
Shibuya-ku, Tokyo
(TEL 03-3409-1111)

67. Quarterly Journal of Productivity Statistics (Q)

O. Japan Department Stores Association

2-1-10, Nihonbashi
Chuo-ku, Tokyo 103
(TEL 03-3272-1666)

68. Monthly Department Store Sales (M) [J]

P. Japan Automotive Dealers Association

5-7-17, Minami-Aoyama
Minato-ku, Tokyo 107
(TEL 03-3400-8404)

69. Monthly New Vehicle Registration (M) [J]

Q. Organization of Economic Cooperation and Development (OECD)

Publications Service
OECD
2 rue André-Pascal
75775 Paris Cedex 16
France

70. Quarterly National Accounts (Q)
71. National Accounts, Volume 1: Main Aggregates (A)
72. National Accounts, Volume 2: Detailed Tables (A)
73. Main Economic Indicators (M)
74. Main Economic Indicators -- Historical Statistics: 1969–1988 (O)
75. Quarterly Labor Force Statistics (Q)
76. Labor Force Statistics (A)
77. Monthly Statistics of Foreign Trade, Series A (M)
78. Foreign Trade by Commodities: Series C (A)
79. Indicators of Industrial Activity (Q)
80. Financial Statistics Monthly -- Part 1, Section 1: International Markets (M)
81. Financial Statistics Monthly -- Part 1, Section 2: Domestic Markets -- Interest Rates (M)

R. International Monetary Fund (IMF)

Publication Services
International Monetary Fund
700 19th St., NW, Suite C-100
Washington, DC 20431
USA

82. International Financial Statistics (M)
83. International Financial Statistics Yearbook (A)
84. Direction of Trade Statistics (M)
85. Direction of Trade Statistics Yearbook (A)

Tables A3.1, A3.2 and A3.3 summarize the sources of the statistics used in each chapter of this book. If the symbol 'J' appears below the statistics' number, the statistics do not contain any English translation. Statistics without the 'J' symbol may contain English translation for only a part of the statistics.

Each row of the table indicates the source of statistics for a particular chapter. 'S' indicates a source which contains a complete set of statistics, while 'x' indicates that only some of the statistics are available. There are four groups of statistics which contain a large portion of the statistics cited throughout the book: statistics no. 1, no. 2, and no. 3 published by the Management and Coordination Agency, no. 24, no. 25, and no. 26 from the Economic Planning Agency, no. 53 and no. 54 from the Bank of Japan, and no. 65 and no. 66 from Toyo Keizai Shinpo Sha, a private publishing company. If you are interested in not only economic but also other social statistics, no. 1 and no. 2 provide the widest coverage. Two sources which offer a quick release are no. 24 and no. 65, although no. 24 contains only basic items. While no. 24 and no. 25 feature the real economy, no. 53 and no. 54 emphasize the monetary economy. If you need historical time series, no. 3, no. 20, no. 21, no. 22, no. 26, and no. 66 are the primary sources, although the English translation of no. 66 is incomplete. Statistics no. 3 consists of 5 volumes containing the most comprehensive historical series available, from as early as 1900 up until 1985 (vol. 1: land and population, vol. 2: industry, vol. 3: foreign trade, money, and public finance, vol. 4: enterprises, labor, price, and household, vol. 5: social and cultural statistics); statistics no. 1 and no. 2 will provide much of the more recent data. The combination of no. 18, no. 26, no. 53, no. 54, and no. 65 would provide the key statistics needed for most purposes.

In addition to publications, there are data-base services from private companies. The largest supplier is Nihon Keizai Shimbun Sha, or NIKKEI. The coverage of their service includes the entire contents of this book and more:

Information Service Department
The Nihon Keizai Shimbun
1-9-5, Otemachi
Chiyoda-ku, Tokyo 100
(TEL 03-3270-0251)

International organizations such as OECD and IMF also provide data-base services. Most publications from OECD are available on magnetic tapes and diskettes. *International Financial Statistics* from the IMF is available on CD-ROM.

Table A3.1. Summary of Source Statistics: 1–30

	1	2	3	4	5	6	7	8	9	10	11	12	13	14	15	16	17	18	19	20	21	22	23	24	25	26	27	28	29	30
	M	A	O	M	A	O	A	5	M	A	5	M	5	M	A	5	5	Q	Q	A	O	O	M	M	Q	A	M	A	Q	Q
																			J	J	J	J					J	J	J	J
1	x	x	x															S	S	S	S	S	x	x	x	x				
2		x	x															S	S	S	S	S								
3	x																						S	x	x	S				
4	x	x	x	S	S	S		S															x	x	x	x				
5	x	x	x																				x	x	x	x				
6																														
7	x		x																					x	x					
8		x	x																					x	x	x				
9	x	x																					x	x	x	x	S	S		
10	x	x	x																				x	x	x	x				
11	x	x	x																				x	x	x	x				
12																														
13		x																	S					x	x	x			S	
14	x	x																								x				
15	x	x	x																				x	x	x	x				
16		x															S													
17		x																												
18	x	x	x																				x	x	x	x				
19	x	x	x																					x		x				
20	x	x	x													S							x	x	x	x				
21	x	x	x																					x	x	x				
22	x	x	x											S	S									x	x	x				
23	x																													
24		x																												
25	x	x	x						S	S	S												x	x	x	x				
26	x	x	x																				x	x	x	x				
27	x	x	x																				x	x	x	x				
28		x	x									x	S																	
29	x	x	x									S													x					
30	x	x	x																					x	x	x				
31	x	x	x																					x	x	x				
32		x																												
33																														
34	x	x	x																						x					
35		x	x																											
36		x	x																											
37	x	x																						x	x	x				
38	x	x	x																				x	x	x	x				
39		x	x																											
40	x	x																						x	x	x				
41																														
42	x	x																							x					
43	x	x																												
44		x	x																						x					
45	x	x																								x				
46		x	x																											
47		x	x																					x						
48	x	x																						x	x	x				
49	x	x																					x	x	x	x				
50	x	x	x																					x	x	x				
51	x	x	x																					x	x	x				
52	x	x	x																					x	x	x				
53																														
54		x	x				S																							

Note: *A* Annual, *Q* Quarterly, *M* Monthly, *O* Occasional, *J* Japanese Only, *S* Source, *x* Incomplete

Table A3.2. Summary of Source Statistics: 31–60

	31	32	33	34	35	36	37	38	39	40	41	42	43	44	45	46	47	48	49	50	51	52	53	54	55	56	57	58	59	60
	Q	M	M	M	Q	M	M	A	Q	A	A	M	M	A	M	A	A	M	M	A	A	A	M	A	M	A	M	Q	A	M
	J			J	J	J			J	J	J	J	J	J		J		J		J	J	J								
1																							x	x					x	
2																														
3																							x	x						
4																							x	x						
5							x					S											x	x						
6																							x	x						
7																							x	x					x	
8	S																													
9																							x	x					x	
10							S	S															x	x					x	
11							S	S															x	x				S	x	
12									S														x	x						
13																													x	
14																							x	x						
15				S	S																			x						
16																														
17											S																			
18																			S	S			x	x						
19																			S	S			x	x						
20																			S	S			x	x					x	
21																							x	x	S	S			x	
22																							x	x					x	
23																							x	x	S	S				
24																							x	x					x	
25																	x						x	x					x	
26															S	S	S						x	x					x	
27																	S	S					x	x					x	
28																													x	
29																													x	
30		S	S																				x	x						
31																							x	x			S		x	
32				x		S																					x		x	
33														S							S									
34				x																			x	x					x	
35																							S	S						
36																							S	S					x	
37																							S	S					x	x
38																							S	S					x	
39																							S	S					x	
40																							S	S						
41																							S	S						
42																							S	S					x	
43																							S	S						
44																							S	S						
45																							S	S						
46																							S	S						
47																							x	x						
48																							S	S					x	x
49																							S	S						
50																							S	S					x	
51																							S	S					x	S
52																							x	x					x	
53																							S	S						
54																														

Note: *A* Annual, *Q* Quarterly, *M* Monthly, *O* Occasional, *J* Japanese Only, *S* Source, *x* Incomplete

Table A3.3. Summary of Source Statistics: 61–85

	61 M	62 A	63 M	64 M	65 M	66 A J	67 Q	68 M J	69 M J	70 Q	71 A	72 A	73 M	74 O	75 Q	76 A	77 M	78 A	79 Q	80 M	81 M	82 M	83 A	84 M	85 A
1					x	x				x	x	x	x	x								x	x		
2						x				x	x	x													
3					x	x							x												
4					x	x																			
5					x	x																			
6					x	x		S																	
7					x	x			S				x	x											
8					x	x																			
9					x	x							x	x											
10					x	x							x	x					x			x	x		
11					x	x							x	x											
12					x	x																			
13						x																			
14					x	x							x	x					x						
15				x	x	x																			
16																						x	x		
17																						x	x		
18					x	x							x	x											
19					x	x																			
20					x	x							x	x											
21					x	x							x	x					x						
22					x	x							x	x											
23						x							x												
24																									
25					x	x							x	x	x	x						x	x		
26					x	x							x	x											
27					x	x							x	x											
28						x																			
29					x	x										x									
30					x	x							x	x			x	x				x	x	x	x
31					x	x							x	x								x	x		
32					x	x																			
33						x																			
34					x	x																			
35						x																x	x		
36						x																			
37				x	x	x																			
38					x	x							x	x								x	x		
39						x																x	x		
40					x	x																			
41						x																			
42				x	x	x							x	x							x				
43					x	x																			
44					x	x																			
45					x	x																			
46					x																				
47					x	x																			
48				x	x	x							x	x							x	x	x		
49					x	x															x				
50				x	x	x																x	x		
51				S	x	x							x	x						x	x	x	x		
52	S	S		S	x	x							x	x							x	x	x		
53																									
54						x																			

Note: *A* Annual, *Q* Quarterly, *M* Monthly, *O* Occasional, *J* Japanese Only, *S* Source, *x* Incomplete

A4 List of Capital Investment Surveys

There are many business surveys on capital investment plans, all of which are written only in Japanese, with the exception of TANKAN and the survey conducted by the Japan Development Bank (JDB), which also have English language versions. The Long-Term Credit Bank of Japan (LTCB) has published English summaries of its surveys. Some surveys are conducted quarterly, while others are on a semi-annual basis. Summary information regarding 10 surveys is presented in Table A4.1.

Most surveys have the same inherent biases discussed in Chapter 14 (TANKAN). Therefore, readers should be careful in interpreting the results. All of the surveys ask companies the planned value of capital investment for *fiscal* years rather than *calendar* years.

As is the case for TANKAN, at the beginning of the year the capital investment plans are generally underestimated, then revised upward as time passes; the actual results are usually somewhat lower than the end-of-year estimates. Thus, the margin of revision is given attention, especially in the TANKAN and JDB studies.

The samples of most surveys are limited to relatively large corporations, although some cover small and medium-sized companies as well, such as nos. 2, 5, and 10. It is also important to distinguish the relative weights of manufacturing and non-manufacturing companies. The Bank of Japan's surveys (nos. 1 and 2) tend to sample manufacturing companies more extensively than non-manufacturers.

Some surveys include the cost of land purchases in capital investment while others do not. There is also a difference in the definition of capital investment. Some adopt an 'installation-in-progress' basis while others adopt a 'payment-of-proceeds' basis. The former is considered to lead the latter by about two quarters. Classification of companies by industry also varies. Some classify the entire company by their 'mainly-engaged business' while others consider each 'business unit' of a company separately. The Industrial Bank of Japan, Nippon Credit Bank, and LTCB studies are limited in that they have the bank's major clients as the base. The figures given for a particular industry are only those reported by the bank's clients in that industry.

In addition to the capital investment survey, some surveys include related information such as judgement of business conditions, estimates of sales and profits, fund-raising plans, and purposes of investment.

Table A4.1. Capital Investment Surveys

Capital investment survey no.	(1)	(2)	(3)	(4)	(5)
Source	BOJ	BOJ	EPA	MITI	MOF
Frequency	Quarterly	Quarterly	Quarterly	Semi-Annual	Quarterly
Surveyed month	2, 5, 8, 11	2, 5, 8, 11	3, 6, 9, 12	3, 10	2, 5, 8, 11
Released month	3, 6, 9, 12	3, 6, 9, 12	5, 8, 11, 2	6, 12	3, 6, 9, 12
As of	May-93	May-93	March-93	March-93	May-93
No. of companies with reply	716	6,753	4,322	1,758	9,900
Criteria	Annual sales 1 bil. yen +		Paid-in-capital 100 mil. yen +	Paid-in-capital 100 mil. yen +	Paid-in-capital 10 mil. yen +
Financial companies	no	no	yes	no	no
Weight of manufacturing	54.9%	54.1%	37.1%	36.0%	37.1%
Industry classification	Main business	Main business	Main business	Main business	Main business
Appropriation	Construction-in-progress	Construction-in-progress	Construction-in-progress	Construction-in-progress	Construction-in-progress
Land purchases	Included	Included	Excluded	Included	Incl./Excluded
Business conditions judgement	Available	Available	Available	N.A.	Available
Sales/profit estimates	Available	Available	N.A.	N.A.	Available
Funds raising plan	N.A.	N.A.	N.A.	Available	N.A.
Purpose of investment	Available	N.A.	N.A.	Available	Available
Overseas direct investment	N.A.	N.A.	Available	Available	N.A.
English translation	Available	N.A.	N.A.	N.A.	N.A.

Capital investment survey no.	(6)	(7)	(8)	(9)	(10)
Source	JDB	IBJ	LTCB	NCB	SBFCJ
Frequency	Semi-Annual	Semi-Annual	Semi-Annual	Semi-Annual	Semi-Annual
Surveyed month	2, 8	2, 8	2, 7	1, 7	4, 9
Released month	3, 9	3, 9	3, 8	2, 8	6, 11
As of	March-93	March-93	February-93	January-93	April-93
No. of companies with reply	2,343	3,477	1,550	1,507	11,479
Criteria	Paid-in-capital 1 bil. yen +	Clients	Clients	Clients	Manufacturing 20-299 emplys.
Financial companies	no	no	no	no	no
Weight of manufacturing	36.0%	29.3%	30.6%	30.4%	100%
Industry classification	Business unit/ main business	Main business	Main business	Main business	Main business
Appropriation	Construction-in-progress	Construction-in-progress/ payment-of-proceeds	Construction-in-progress	Construction-in-progress/ payment-of-proceeds	Payment-of-proceeds
Land purchases	Incl./Excluded	Included	Included	Included	Included
Business conditions judgement	N.A.	N.A.	N.A.	N.A.	Available
Sales/profit estimates	Available	N.A.	Available	N.A.	N.A.
Funds raising plan	N.A.	Available	Available	Available	Available
Purpose of investment	Available	N.A.	Available	Available	Available
Overseas direct investment	N.A.	Available	Available	Available	N.A.
English translation	Available	N.A.	Summary	N.A.	N.A.

Note: *BOJ* Bank of Japan, *EPA* Economic Planning Agency, *MITI* Ministry of International Trade and Industry, *MOF* Ministry of Finance, *JDB* Japan Development Bank, *IBJ* Industrial Bank of Japan, *LTCB* Long-Term Credit Bank of Japan, *NCB* Nippon Credit Bank, *SBFCJ* Small Business Finance Corporation of Japan. Figures for weight of manufacturing (in total industries) is based on planned value of capital investment in fiscal 1992, except for nos. 1, 2, and 5 which are based on the number of companies surveyed.

A5 Data Stream of Monthly and Quarterly Statistics

This appendix shows the release dates of monthly and quarterly statistics (most daily statistics are available in newspapers). Most monthly and quarterly statistics are first made available in the form of a press release, then appear in a publication or a completed book. Tables A5.1 and A5.2 show the approximate date of initial release.

The name of each chapter is given in the first column, followed by the name of the agency releasing the statistics. The number of the source statistics (the same numbers used in Appendix 3) appears in the third column. The remaining six columns indicate the approximate date of release. The figure in brackets indicates the number of months or quarters lagged. In Table A5.2, 'P' indicates the release of preliminary figures while 'R' indicates revised figures; all dates in Table A5.1 are preliminary releases. For example, in Table A5.2, preliminary March figures for *Sales of Large-Scale Retail Stores* (Chapter 5) are released around 26–31 April, while revised figures are released around 21–5 May. The exact date of release is not always announced in advance. Some statistics contain the schedule of release in coming months while others do not.

Table A5.1. Data Stream of Quarterly Data

			Day and Month of Each Quarter					
			1st Month		2nd Month		3rd Month	
Chapter No. and Title	Source	Stat. no.	1–15	16–31	1–15	16–31	1–15	16–31
1 National Income Statistics	EPA	18/19					[1]	
8 Consumer Behavioral Survey	EPA	31		[1]				
9 Outlook of Machinery Orders	EPA	27			[1]			
12 Index of Tertiary Industry Activity	MITI	39					[1]	
13 Gross Fixed Private Capital Stock	EPA	29					[1]	
14 Short-Term Eco. Survey (TANKAN)	BJ	58					[1]	
15 Quarterly Financial Report (QFR)	MF	35					[1]	
25 Corporate Service Price Index	BJ	55		[1]				
36 Flow of Funds Accounts	BJ	53						[1]
53 Personal Savings	BJ	53						[1]

Note: Figures in brackets show the number of quarters lagged. For example, national income statistics are released in the first half of the third month of each quarter (March, June, September, and December) with a one-quarter lag. Thus, first quarter figures are released in the first half of June, second quarter figures are released in the first half of September, etc.. *BJ* Bank of Japan, *EPA* Economic Planning Agency, *MF* Ministry of Finance, *MITI* Ministry of International Trade and Industry.

Table A5.2. Data Stream of Monthly Statistics

Chapter No. and Title	Source	Stat. no.	Day of Month 1–5	6–10	11–15	16–20	21–25	26–31
3 Indexes of Business Conditions	EPA	23					[2]	
4 Family Income and Expenditure Survey	MCA	4					[2]	
5 Sales of Large-Scale Retail Stores	MITI	42					R[2]	P[1]
6 Department Store Sales	JDSA	68					[1]	
7 New Vehicle Registrations	JADA	69	[1]					
9 New Machinery Orders	EPA	27			P[2]			
10 Industrial Production	MITI	37				R[2]		P[1]
11 Operating Rate and Production Capacity	MITI	37				[2]		
18 Orders Received for Construction	MC	49						[1]
19 Public Construction Started	MC	49		[2]				
20 New Housing Construction Started	MC	49						[1]
21 Wholesale Price Index	BJ	55			[1]			
22 Consumer Price Index	MCA	14			R[2]			P[1]
25 Monthly Report on the Labor Force Survey	MCA	9						[1]
26 Monthly Labour Survey	ML	45						P[1] R[2]
27 Job Offers and Applicants	ML	48						[1]
29 Monthly Current Population Estimates	MCA	12		P[1] R[5]				
30 Summary Report on Trade	MF	32			P[1]			R[1]
31 Balance of Payments Statistics	MF/BJ	57	[2]					
32 Foreign Direct Investment	MF	36	[2]					
35 Major Financial Institutions	BJ	53						[2],[3]
37 Money Markets	BJ	53						[1],[2]
38 Money Stock	BJ	53				P[1] R[2]		
39 Monetary Base	BJ	53						[2]
40 Supply and Demand of Funds	BJ	53	[1]					
41 Reserve Rquirements	BJ	53						[2],[4]
42 Official Discount Rate	BJ	53						[1]
43 Open Market Operations	BJ	53						[1]
44 Accounts of the Bank of Japan	BJ	53						[1]
45 Receipts/Payments of Treasury Accounts	MF/BJ	53	[1]					
46 Trust Fund Bureau	MF/BJ	53						[2]
47 Postal Savings	MPT	53		P[1]				R[5]
49 Interest Rates on Loans and Discounts	BJ	53		[2]				
50 Balance Sheets of All Banks	BJ	53						[2]
51 Public and Private Bond Markets	BJ/BUAJ	53/60						[1],[2]
52 Stock Markets	TSE/BJ	53/61						[1],[2]

Note: *P* Preliminary, *R* Revised. Figures in brackets show the number of months lagged. For example, P[1] indicates preliminary figures are released with a one-month lag. *BJ* Bank of Japan, *BUAJ* Bond Underwriters Association of Japan, *EPA* Economic Planning Agency, *JADA* Japan Automotive Dealers Association, *JDSA* Japan Department Stores Association, *MCA* Management and Coordination Agency, *MITI* Ministry of International Trade and Industry, *MC* Ministry of Construction, *ML* Ministry of Labour, *MPT* Ministry of Posts and Telecommunication, *TSE* Tokyo Stock Exchange.

Select Bibliography

References are provided to facilitate further research for those who are interested in a particular sector of the Japanese economy. First, various white papers published by government agencies are cited. Then, other books and papers are listed by sector: households and savings; corporate sector; labor markets; external sector; and monetary sector. Finally, references on index numbers are given. The following lists are far from comprehensive, and are limited mainly to recent writings in English.

White Papers (published annually)

Economic Planning Agency, *Economic Survey of Japan* available from:
Printing Bureau of Ministry of Finance
2-2-4, Toranomon
Minato-ku, Tokyo 105
(TEL 03-3587-4283)

Ministry of Labour, *White Paper on Labour* available from:
The Japan Institute for Labour
1-7-6, Shiba-Koen
Minato-ku, Tokyo 105
(TEL 03-5470-4034)

Ministry of Health and Welfare, *Annual Report on Health and Welfare* available from:
Japan International Corporation of Welfare Services
1-2-9, Shinjuku
Shinjuku-ku, Tokyo 160
(TEL 03-3225-6591)

Ministry of International Trade and Industry, *White Paper on International Trade Japan* available from:
Japan External Trade Organization (JETRO)
2-2-5, Toranomon
Minato-ku, Tokyo 105
(TEL 03-3582-5547)

Ministry of Construction, *White Paper on Construction* available from:
Research Institute of Construction and Economy

39, Mori-Building
2-4-5, Azabu-dai
Minato-ku, Tokyo 106
(TEL 03-3433-5011)

In addition to these white papers, the following book will be helpful to understand the structure of the central government of Japan.

Management and Coordination Agency, *Organization of Government of Japan* available from:
Institute of Administrative Management
P.O. Box 1106
Sun-Shine 60
3-1-1, Higashi-Ikebukuro
Toshima-ku, 170 Tokyo
(TEL 03-3981-0441)

Other Books and Papers

General Topics

A System of National Accounts, Studies in Methods, Series F, no. 2, Rev. 3, United Nations, 1968.

Barro, Robert J., and Sala-i-Martin, Xavier, 'Regional Growth and Migration: A Japan-United States Comparison', *Journal of the Japanese and International Economies*, Dec. 1992.

Balassa, Bela, and Noland, Marcus, *Japan in the World Economy*, Institute for International Economics, Washington, DC, 1988.

Fruin, W. Mark, *The Japanese Enterprise System: Competitive Strategies and Co-operative Structures*, Oxford University Press, 1992.

Hulten, Charles R. (ed.), *Productivity Growth in Japan and the United States*, University of Chicago Press, 1991.

Hutchinson, Michael M., 'Structural Change and the Macroeconomic Effects of Oil Shocks: Empirical Evidence from the United States and Japan', *Pacific Basin Working Paper Series,* no. PB92-06, Federal Reserve Bank of San Francisco, 1992.

Inada, Ken-ichi, Sekiguchi, Sueo, and Shoda, Yasutoyo, *The Mechanism of Economic Development: Growth in the Japanese and East Asian Economies*, Clarendon Press, Oxford, 1993.

Ito, Takatoshi, *The Japanese Economy*, MIT Press, Cambridge, Mass., 1992.

Komiya, Ryutaro, *The Japanese Economy: Trade, Investment, and Government*, University of Tokyo Press, 1990.

Kosai, Yutaka, *The Era of High-Speed Growth*, University of Tokyo Press, 1986.

Krugman, Paul (ed.), *Trade with Japan*, University of Chicago Press, 1992.

Masson, Paul R., and Tryon, Ralph W., 'Macroeconomic Effects of Projected Population Aging in Industrial Countries', *IMF Staff Papers*, Sept. 1990.

Miyazaki, Isamu, *The Japanese Economy*, The Simul Press, Tokyo, 1990.

Moreno, Ramon, 'How Big is the Permanent Component in GNP? The Evidence from Japan and Australia', *Pacific Basin Working Paper Series*, no. PB92-02, Federal Reserve Bank of San Francisco, 1992.

Moreno, Ramon, 'Are the Forces Shaping Business Cycles Alike? The Evidence from Japan', *Pacific Basin Working Paper Series*, no. PB92-10, Federal Reserve Bank of San Francisco, 1992.

Nakamura, Takafusa, *The Postwar Japanese Economy: Its Development and Structure*, University of Tokyo Press, 1981.

Nelson, Charles R., 'Implicit Estimates of the Natural and Cyclical Components of Japan's Real GNP', *The Bank of Japan Monetary and Economic Studies*, August 1989.

Odagiri, Hiroyuki, *Growth Through Competition, Competition through Growth: Strategic Management and the Economy in Japan*, Oxford University Press, 1992.

Okawa, Kazushi, and Shinohara, Miyohei, *Patterns of Japanese Economic Development: A Quantitative Appraisal*, Yale University Press, New Haven, Conn., 1979.

Owen, Robert F., 'The Evolution in Japan's Relative Technological Competitiveness since the 1960s: A Cross-Sectional, Time-Series Analysis', *The Bank of Japan Monetary and Economic Studies*, Nov.1988.

Patrick, Hugh, and Tachi, Ryuichiro (eds.), *Japan and the United States Today*, Columbia University Press, New York, 1987.

Shinohara, Miyohei, *Industrial Growth, Trade, and Dynamic Patterns in the Japanese Economy*, University of Tokyo Press, 1982.

Takenaka, Heizo, *Contemporary Japanese Economy & Economic Policy*, The University of Michigan Press, Ann Arbor, 1991.

Taylor, John B., 'Differences in Economic Fluctuations in Japan and the U.S.: The Role of Nominal Rigidities', *Journal of the Japanese and International Economies*, 1989.

Teranishi, Juro, and Kosai, Yutaka (eds.), *The Japanese Experience of Economic Reforms*, Macmillan, Basingstoke, 1993.

Torres, Raymond, and Martin, John P., 'Measuring Potential Output in the Seven Major OECD Countries', *OECD Economic Studies*, 14, Spring 1990.

West, Kenneth D., 'Sources of Cycles in Japan, 1975-1987', *Journal of the Japanese and International Economies*, Mar. 1992.

Yamamura, K., and Yasuba, Y. (eds.), *The Political Economy of Japan,* vol. 1, *The Domestic Transformation*, Stanford University Press, 1987.

Yamazawa, Ippei, *Economic Development and International Trade: The Japanese Model*, Resource Systems Institute, East-West Center, Hawaii, 1990.

Yoshikawa, Hiroshi, and Takeuchi, Yoshiyuki, 'Real Wages and Japanese Economy', *The Bank of Japan Monetary and Economic Studies*, Apr. 1989.

Yoshikawa, Hiroshi, and Ohtake, Fumio, 'Postwar Business Cycle in Japan: A Quest for the Right Explanation', *Journal of the Japanese and International Economies*, Dec. 1987.

Households and Savings

Aghevli, Bijan B., Boughton, James M., Montiel, Peter J., Villanueva, Delano, and Woglom, Geoffrey, 'The Role of National Saving in the World Economy: Recent Trends and Prospects', *International Monetary Fund, Occasional Paper*, no. 67, Mar. 1990.

Blades, Derek W., and Strum, Peter H., 'The Concept and Measurement of Savings: The United States and Other Industrialized Countries', in Federal Reserve Bank of Boston, *Saving and Government Policy*, Conference Series, no. 25, Oct. 1982.

Bovenberg, A. Lans, and Evans, Owen, 'National and Personal Saving in the United States', *IMF Staff Papers*, 37/3, Sept. 1990.

Bradford, David F., 'What is National Saving? Alternative Measures in Historical and International Context', *NBER Working Paper*, no. 3341., Apr. 1990.

Christiano, Lawrence J., 'Understanding Japan's Saving Rate: The Reconstruction Hypothesis', Federal Reserve Bank of Minneapolis, *Quarterly Review*, Spring 1989.

Dekle, Robert, 'A Simulation Model of Saving, Residential Choice, and Bequests of the Japanese Elderly', *Economics Letters*, 1989.

Dekle, Robert, 'Saving, Bequests, and Living Arrangements of the Japanese Elderly', *Journal of the Japanese and International Economies*, Sept. 1989.

Dekle, Robert, 'Do the Japanese Elderly Reduce Their Total Wealth? A New Look with Different Data', *Journal of the Japanese and International Economies*, 4/3, 1990.

Dekle, Robert, and Summers, Lawrence, 'Japan's High Saving Rate Reaffirmed', *BOJ Monetary and Economic Studies*, 9/ 2, Sept. 1991.

Egebo, Thomas, Richardson, Pete, and Lienert, Ian, 'A Model of Housing Investment for the Major OECD Economies', *OECD Economic Studies*, 14, Spring 1990.

Hayashi, Fumio, 'Why is Japan's Saving Rate So Apparently High?', in Stanley Fischer and Olivier Blanchard (eds.) *NBER Macroeconomics Annual*, MIT Press, Cambridge, Mass., 1986.

Hayashi, Fumio, 'Japan's Saving Rate: New Data and Reflections', *NBER Working Paper*, no. 3205, Dec. 1989.

Hayashi, Fumio, 'Rejoinder to Dekle and Summers', *The Bank of Japan Monetary and Economic Studies*, Sept. 1991.

Hayashi, Fumio, 'Explaining Japan's Saving: A Review of Recent Literature', *The Bank of Japan Monetary and Economic Studies*, Nov. 1992.

Hayashi, Fumio, Ando, Albert, and Ferris, Richard, 'Life Cycle and Bequest Savings -- A Study of Japanese and U.S. Households Based on Data from the 1984 NSFIE and the 1983 Survey of Consumer Finances', *Journal of the Japanese and International Economies*, 24, Dec. 1988.

Hayashi, Fumio, Ito, Takatoshi, and Slemrod, Joel, 'Housing Finance Imperfections, Taxation, and Private Saving: A Comparative Simulation Analysis of the United States and Japan', *Journal of the Japanese and International Economies*, 2/3, 1988.

Horioka, Charles Y., 'Saving for Housing Purchase in Japan', *Journal of the Japanese and International Economies*, 1988.

Horioka, Charles Y., 'Why Is Japan's Saving Rate So High', in Ryuzo Sato and Takashi Negishi (eds.), *Developments in Japanese Economics*, Academic Press, New York, 1989.

Ishikawa, Tsuneo, and Ueda, Kazuo, 'The Bonus Payment System and Japanese Personal Savings', in Masahiko Aoki (ed.), *The Economic Analysis of the Japanese Firm*, North-Holland, Amsterdam, 1984.

Kawasaki, Ken'ichi, 'The Saving Behavior of Japanese Households', *OECD Working Papers*, 73, Jan. 1990.

Shibuya, Hiroshi, 'Japan's Household Saving Rate: An Application of the Life Cycle Hypothesis', *IMF Working Paper* no. 87-15, 1987.

Tachibanaki, Toshiaki, 'Housing and Saving', *Kyoto Institute of Economic Research, Discussion Paper*, no. 324, 1991.

Tachibanaki, Toshiaki, and Shimono, Keiko, 'Saving and Life-Cycle: A Cohort Analysis', *Journal of Public Economies*, 31/1, Oct. 1986.

Tachibanaki, Toshiaki, and Shimono, Keiko, 'Wealth Accumulation Process by Income Class', *Journal of the Japanese and International Economies*, 5/3, Sept. 1991.

Corporate Sector

Ando, Albert, and Auerbach, Alan J., 'The Cost of Capital in the United States and Japan: A Comparison', *Journal of the Japanese and International Economies*, 2, 1988.

Ando, Albert, and Auerbach, Alan J., 'The Cost of Capital in Japan: Recent Evidence and Further Results', *Journal of the Japanese and International Economies*, 4/ 4, 1990.

Aoki, Masahiko, 'Toward an Economic Model of the Japanese Firm', *Journal of Economic Literature*, 28/1, 1990.

De Long, J. Bradford, and Summers, Lawrence H., 'Equipment Investment and Economic Growth', *Quarterly Journal of Economics*, May 1991.

Ford, Robert, and Poret, Pierre, 'Business Investment: Recent Performance and Some Implications for Policy', *OECD Economic Studies*, 16, Spring 1991.

Flath, D., 'Vertical Restraints in Japan', *Japan and the World Economy*, 2, 1989.

Frankel, Jeffrey A., 'The Cost of Capital in Japan: A Survey', *Pacific Basin Working Paper Series,* no. PB91-05, Federal Reserve Bank of San Francisco, 1991.

Hodder, James, 'Is the Cost of Capital Lower in Japan?', *Journal of the Japanese and International Economies*, Mar. 1991.

Hoshi, T., and Kashyap, A., 'Evidence on *q* and Investment for Japanese Firms', *Journal of the Japanese and International Economies*, 4/4, 1990.

Hoshi, T., Kashyap, A., and Scharfstein, D., 'Corporate Structure, Liquidity, and Investment: Evidence from Japanese Industrial Groups', *Quarterly Journal of Economics*, 106, Feb. 1991.

McCauley, Robert N., and Zimmer, Steven A., 'Explaining International Difference in the Cost of Capital', Federal Reserve Bank of New York, *Quarterly Review*, Summer 1989.

McDonald, Jack, 'The *Mochiai* Effect: Japanese Corporate Cross-Holdings', *Journal of Portfolio Management*, Fall 1989.

Nachbar, John H., 'The Cost of Capital in the United States and Japan: A Survey of Some Recent Literature', *A Rand Note*, N-3088-CUSJR, Sept. 1990.

Poterba, James M., 'Comparing the Cost of Capital in the United States and Japan: A Survey of Methods', Federal Reserve Bank of New York, *Quarterly Review*, Winter 1991.

Tachibanaki, Toshiaki, and Taki, Atsuhiro, 'Shareholding and Lending Activity of Financial Institutions in Japan', *The Bank of Japan Monetary and Economic Studies*, Mar. 1991.

Takagi, Keizo, 'The Rise of Land Prices in Japan: the Determination Mechanism and the Effect of the Taxation System', *The Bank of Japan Monetary and Economic Studies*, Aug. 1989.

Labor Markets

Ariga, Kenn, Brunello, Giorgio, Ohkusa, Yasushi and Yoshihiko Nishiyama, 'Corporate Hierarchy, Promotion, and Firm Growth: Japanese Internal Labor Market in Transition', *Journal of the Japanese and International Economies*, Dec. 1992.

Clark, Robert L, and Ogawa, Naohiro, 'Employment Tenure and Earnings Profiles in Japan and the United States: Comment', *American Economic Review*, Mar. 1992.

Clark, Robert L., *Japanese Retirement Systems*, Dow Jones-Irwin, New York, 1990.

Hamada, Koichi, and Kurosaka, Yoshio, 'The Relationship between Production and Unemployment in Japan: Okun's Law in Comparative Perspective', *European Economic Review*, 25/1, June 1984.

Hashimoto, Masanori, 'Employment and Wage Systems in Japan and Their Implications for Productivity', in Alan S. Blinder (ed.), *Paying for Productivity: A Look at the Evidence*, The Brookings Institution, Washington, DC, 1990.

Hashimoto, Masanori, *The Japanese Labor Market in a Comparative Perspective with the United States: A Transaction-Cost Interpretation*, W. E. Upjohn Institute for Employment Research, Kalamazoo, Mich., 1990.

Hashimoto, Masanori, and Raisian, John, 'Employment Tenure and Earnings Profiles in Japan and the United States: Reply', *American Economic Review*, Mar. 1992.

Ishikawa, Tsuneo, 'Saving and Labor Supply Behavior of Aged Households in Japan', *Journal of the Japanese and International Economies*, 2, 1988.

Mincer, Jacob and Higuchi, Yoshio, 'Wage Structure and Labor Turnover in the United States and Japan', *Journal of the Japanese and International Economies*, June 1988.

Rebick, Marcus E., 'The Persistence of Firm-Size Earnings Differentials and Labor Market Segmentation in Japan', *Journal of the Japanese and International Economies*, June 1993.

Seike, Atsushi, 'The Employment Adjustment in Japanese Manufacturing Industries in the 1970s', *Keio Business Review*, 22/3, 1985.

Shimada, Haruo, *The Japanese Employment System*, Japan Institute of Labor, 1980.

Sorrentino, C., 'Japan's Low Unemployment: An In-Depth Analysis', US Dept. of Labor, *Monthly Labor Review*, 107/3, Mar. 1984.

Tachibanaki, Toshiaki, 'Labour Market Flexibility in Japan in Comparison with Europe and the U.S.', *European Economic Review*, 31/3, Apr. 1987.

Taira, Koji, 'Japan's Low Unemployment: Economic Miracle or Statistical Artifact?', US Dept. of Labor, *Monthly Labor Review*, 106/ 7, July 1983.

Takayama, Noriyuki, *The Greying of Japan: An Economic Perspective on Public Pensions*, Oxford University Press, 1992.

Weitzman, Martin L., *The Share Economy*, Harvard University Press, Cambridge, Mass., 1984.

Yagi, Tadashi, and Tachibanaki, Toshiaki, 'Behavior of the Aged under Uncertainty -- Theory and Empirical Evidence', *Kyoto Institute of Economic Research Discussion Paper*, 287, Jan. 1990.

Yamada, Tetsuji, 'The Labor Force Participation of Elderly Males in Japan', *Journal of the Japanese and International Economies*, 4, 1990.

Yamada, Tetsuji, and Yamada, Tadashi, 'The Effects of Japanese Social Security Retirement Benefits on Personal Savings and Elderly Labor Force Behavior', *NBER Working Paper*, no. 2661, 1988.

Yamada, Tetsuji, Yamada, Tadashi, and Liu, G., 'Determinants of Saving and Labor Force Participation of the Elderly in Japan', *NBER Working Paper*, no. 3292, Mar. 1990.

Yoshikawa, Hiroshi, and Ohtake, Fumio, 'An Analysis of Female Labor Supply, Housing Demand, and the Saving Rate in Japan', *European Economic Review*, 33/ 5, 1989.

External Sector

Bergsten, C. Fred (ed.), *International Adjustment and Finance: The Lessons of 1985-1991*, Institute for International Economics, Washington, DC, 1991.

Citrin, Daniel, 'The Recent Behavior of U.S. Trade Prices', *IMF Staff Papers,* 36/4, Dec. 1989.

Dornbusch, Rudiger W., 'Policy Options for Freer Trade: The Case for Bilateralism', in Robert Z. Lawrence and Charles L. Schultze (eds.), *An American Trade Strategy: Options for the 1990s*, The Brookings Institution, Washington, DC, 1990.

Drake, Tracey A., and Caves, Richard E., 'Changing Determinants of Japanese Foreign Direct Investment in the United States', *Journal of the Japanese and International Economies*, Sept. 1992.

Fukao, Mitsuhiro, 'Exchange Rate Fluctuations, Balance of Payments Imbalances and Internationalization of Financial Markets', *BOJ Monetary and Economic Studies*, 7/2, Aug. 1989.

Gagnon, Joseph E., and Rose, Andrew K., 'How Pervasive Is the Product Cycle? The Empirical Dynamics of American and Japanese Trade Flows', Board of Governors of the Federal Reserve System, *International Finance Discussion Paper*, no. 420, Sept. 1991.

Hickok, Susan, 'Japanese Trade Balance Adjustment to Yen Appreciation', Federal Reserve Bank of New York, *Quarterly Review*, Autumn 1989.

Hooper, Peter, and Mann, Catherine L., 'Exchange Rate Pass-Through in the 1980s: The Case of U.S. Imports of Manufactures', *Brookings Papers on Economic Activity*, 1:1989.

Krugman, Paul (ed.), *The US and Japan: Trade and Investment*, University of Chicago Press, 1991.

Lawrence, Robert Z., 'How Open Is Japan?', in Paul R. Krugman (ed.), *The U.S. and Japan: Trade and Investment*, University of Chicago Press, 1991.

Marston, Richard C., 'Pricing to Market in Japanese Manufacturing', *Journal of International Economics*, 29, March 1990.

McKibbin, Warwick J., and Sachs, Jeffrey D., *Global Linkages: Macroeconomic Interdependence and Cooperation in the World Economy*, The Brookings Institution, Washington, DC, 1991.

Nishikawa, Hirochika, 'Influence of Exchange Rate Fluctuation on Japan's Manufacturing Industry -- Empirical Analysis: 1980–88', *The Bank of Japan Monetary and Economic Studies*, Jan. 1990.

Ohno, Kenichi, 'Export Pricing Behavior of Manufacturing: A U.S.–Japan Comparison', *IMF Staff Papers*, 36/3, Sept. 1989.

Orr, James, 'The Trade Balance Effects of Foreign Direct Investment in U.S. Manufacturing', Federal Reserve Bank of New York, *Quarterly Review*, Summer 1991.

Rogoff, Kenneth, 'Oil, Productivity, Government Spending and the Real Yen-Dollar Exchange Rate', *Pacific Basin Working Paper Series*, no. PB91-06, Federal Reserve Bank of San Francisco, 1991.

Shinjo, Koji, 'Exchange Rate Changes and Pricing Behavior of Japanese Firms: A Cross-Section Analysis', *Journal of the Japanese and International Economies*, June 1993.

Stern, Robert M., (ed.), *Trade and Investment Relations among the United States, Canada, and Japan*, University of Chicago Press, 1989.

Taylor, John B., 'Japanese Macroeconomic Policy and the Current Account under Alternative International Monetary Regimes', *The Bank of Japan Monetary and Economic Studies*, May 1988.

Tyson, Laura D'Andrea, 'Managed Trade: Making the Best of the Second Best', in Robert Z. Lawrence and Charles L. Schultze (eds.), *An American Trade Strategy: Options for the 1990s*, The Brookings Institution, Washington, DC, 1990.

Monetary Sector

Bernanke, Ben, and Mishkin, Frederic, 'Central Bank Behavior and the Strategy of Monetary Policy: Observations from Six Industrialized Countries', in Stanley Fischer and Olivier Blanchard (eds.) *NBER Macroeconomics Annual*, MIT Press, Cambridge, Mass., 1992.

Boughton, James M., and Tavlas, George S., 'Modeling Money Demand in Large Industrial Countries: Buffer Stock and Error Correction Approaches', *Journal of Policy Modeling*, 12/2, Summer 1990.

Browne, Frank, and Tease, Warren, 'The Information Content of Interest Rate Spreads Across Financial Systems', *Economic Letters*, 39, Aug. 1992.

Bryant, Ralph C., 'Model Representations of Japanese Monetary Policy', *BOJ Monetary and Economic Studies*, 9/2, Sept. 1991.

Dotsey, Michael, 'Japanese Monetary Policy: A Comparative Analysis', *BOJ Monetary and Economic Studies*, 4/2, Oct. 1986.

Federation of Bankers Associations of Japan (ed.), *The Banking System in Japan*, 1989.

Feldman, Robert, *Japanese Financial Markets: Deficits, Dilemmas, and Deregulation*, MIT Press, Cambridge, Mass., 1986.

Foundation for Advanced Information and Research, Japan (ed.), *Japan's Financial Markets*, Tokyo, 1991.

Frankel, Allen B., and Montgomery, John D., 'Financial Structure: An International Perspective', *Brookings Papers on Economic Activity*, 1, 1991.

Frankel, Allen B., and Morgan, Paul B., 'Deregulation and Competition in Japanese Banking', *Federal Reserve Bulletin*, Aug. 1992.

French, Kenneth R., and James M. Poterba, 'Were Japanese Stock Prices Too High?', *Journal of Financial Economics*, Oct. 1991.

Goodhard, Charles A. E., and Sutija, George, (eds.), *Japanese Financial Growth*, Macmillan, Basingstoke, 1990.

Hoeller, Peter, and Poret, Pierre, 'P Star as an Indicator of Inflationary Pressure', *OECD Working Paper,* no. 101, 1991.

Ito, Takatoshi, 'Is the Bank of Japan a Closet Monetarist? Monetary Targeting in Japan, 1978-1988', *NBER Working Paper,* no. 2879, Mar. 1989.

Ito, Takatoshi, and Ueda, Kazuo, 'Tests of the Equilibrium Hypothesis in Disequilibrium Econometrics: An International Comparison of Credit Rationing', *International Economic Review*, 22, Oct. 1981.

Iwamura, Mitsuru, 'The Determination Mechanism of Monetary Aggregates and Interest Rates', *The Bank of Japan Monetary and Economic Studies*, Feb. 1992.

Japan Securities Research Institute (ed.), *Securities Market in Japan*, Tokyo, 1992.

Kasuya, Munehisa, 'Economies of Scope: Theory and Application to Banking', *The Bank of Japan Monetary and Economic Studies*, Oct. 1986.

Kato, Kengo, 'The Information Content of Financial and Economic Variables: Empirical Test of Information Variables in Japan', *The Bank of Japan Monetary and Economic Studies*, Mar. 1991.

Kole, Linda S., and Leahy, Michael P., 'The Usefulness of P^* Measures for Japan and Germany', Board of Governors of the Federal Reserve System, *International Finance Discussion Paper*, no. 414, Nov. 1991.

Matsuoka, Mikihiro, 'Credit Crunch in Japan: Reality or Myth? - Analysis on Competition in Bank Loan Markets', *DIR Working Paper*, Mar. 1993.

McKenzie, Colin R., 'Money Demand in an Open Economy', *Journal of the Japanese and International Economies*, June 1992.

McNelis, Paul, and Yoshino, Naoyuki, 'Monetary Stabilization with Interest Rate Instruments in Japan: A Linear Quadratic Control Analysis', *The Bank of Japan Monetary and Economic Studies*, Nov. 1992.

Okina, Kunio, 'Reexamination of the Empirical Study Using Granger Causality: "Causality" between Money Supply and Nominal Income', *BOJ Monetary and Economic Studies*, 3/3, Dec. 1985.

Okina, Kunio, 'Relationship between Money Stock and Real Output in the Japanese Economy: Survey on the Empirical Tests of the LSW Proposition', *The Bank of Japan Monetary and Economic Studies*, Apr. 1986.

Rasche, Robert H., 'Equilibrium Income and Interest Elasticities of Demand for M1 in Japan', *The Bank of Japan Monetary and Economic Studies*, Sept. 1990.

Sakakibara, Shigeki, Yamaji, Hidetoshi, Sakurai, Hisakatsu, Shinoshita, Kengo and Fukuda, Shimon, *The Japanese Stock Market: Pricing Systems and Accounting Information*, Praeger, New York, 1988.

Shigehara, Kumiharu, 'Japan's Experience with Use of Monetary Policy and the Process of Liberalization', *BOJ Monetary and Economic Studies*, 9/1, 1991.

Shigehara, Kumiharu, 'Some Reflections on Monetary Policy Issues in Japan', *The Bank of Japan Monetary and Economic Studies*, Sept. 1990.

Shirakawa, Hiromichi, 'Fluctuations in Yields on Bonds: A Reasessment of the Expectations Theory Based on Japanese and U.S. Data', *The Bank of Japan Monetary and Economic Studies*, Sept. 1987.

Singleton, Kenneth J. (ed.), *Japanese Monetary Policy*, University of Chicago Press, 1993.

Suzuki, Yoshio, 'Monetary Policy in Japan: Transmission Mechanism and Effectiveness', *BOJ Monetary and Economic Studies*, 2/2, Sept. 1985.

Suzuki, Yoshio, (ed.), *The Japanese Financial System*, Clarendon Paperback, Oxford University Press, 1990.

Suzuki, Yoshio, Kuroda, Akio, and Shirakawa, Hiromichi, 'Monetary Control Mechanisms in Japan', in Peter Hooper, Karen H. Johnson, Donald L. Kohn, David E. Lindsey, Richard D. Porter, and Ralph Tryon (eds.), *Financial Sectors in Open Economies: Empirical Analysis and Policy Issues*, Board of Governors of the Federal Reserve System, Washington, DC, 1990.

Takagi, Shinji (ed.), *Japanese Capital Markets*, Basil Blackwell, Oxford, 1993.

Tatewaki, Kazuo, *Banking and Finance in Japan: An Introduction to the Tokyo Market*, Routledge, London, 1991.

Ueda, Kazuo, 'Are Japanese Stock Prices Too High?', *Journal of the Japanese and International Economies*, 4, 1990.

Ueda, Kazuo, 'Financial Deregulation and the Demand for Money in Japan', in Peter Hooper, Karen H. Johnson, Donald L. Kohn, David E. Lindsey, Richard D. Porter, and Ralph Tryon (eds.), *Financial Sectors in Open Economies: Empirical Analysis and Policy Issues*, Board of Governors of the Federal Reserve System, Washington, DC, 1990.

Yoshida, Tomoo, 'On the Stability of the Japanese Money Demand Function: Estimation Results Using the Error-Correction Model', *The Bank of Japan Monetary and Economic Studies*, Jan. 1990.

Yoshida, Tomoo, and Rasche, Robert H., 'The M2 Demand in Japan: Shifted and Unstable?', *The Bank of Japan Monetary and Economic Studies*, Sept. 1990.

Index Numbers and Measurement Issues

Berndt, Ernst R., *The Practice of Econometrics: Classics and Contemporary*, Addison Wesley, Reading, Mass., 1991.

Davis, Richard G., 'Inflation: Measurement and Policy Issues', Federal Reserve Bank of New York, *Quarterly Review*, Summer 1991.

Gordon, Robert J., *The Measurement of Durable Goods Prices*, University of Chicago Press, 1989.

Gordon, Robert J., 'The Postwar Evolution of Computer Prices', in Dale W. Jorgenson and Ralph Landau (eds.), *Technology and Capital Formation*, MIT Press, Cambridge, Mass. 1989.

Gordon, Robert J., and Baily, Martin N., 'Measurement Issues and the Productivity Slowdown in Five Major Industrial Countries', *Technology and Productivity: The Challenge for Economic Policy*, OECD, Paris, 1991.

Griliches, Zvi (ed.), Price Indexes and Quality Change, Harvard University Press, Cambridge, Mass., 1971.

Griliches, Zvi, 'Productivity and Technological Change: Some Measurement Issues', *Technology and Productivity: The Challenge for Economic Policy*, OECD, Paris, 1991.

Hill, Peter, 'Recent Developments in Index Number Theory and Practice', OECD, *Economic Studies*, Paris, Spring 1988.

Meade, Ellen E., 'Computers and the Trade Deficit: The Case of the Falling Prices', Board of Governors of the Federal Reserve System, *International Finance Discussion Papers*, no. 389, Apr. 1990.

Trajtenberg, M, 'Quality-Adjusted Price Indices and the Measurement of Economic Growth', *Technology and Productivity: The Challenge for Economic Policy*, OECD, 1991.

Triplett, Jack E., 'Economic Theory and BEA's Alternative Quantity and Price Indexes', US Dept. of Commerce, *Survey of Current Business*, Apr. 1992.

Young, Allan H., 'Alternative Measures of Change in Real Output and Prices', US Dept. of Commerce, *Survey of Current Business*, Apr. 1992.

Index

Eyewitness Accounts of the American Revolution

Memoirs of the Duc de Lauzun

Translated by C. K. Scott Moncrieff

The New York Times & Arno Press

Reprinted from a copy in the
University of Chicago Libraries

*

*

Library of Congress Catalog Card No. 74-77105

*

Manufactured in the United States of America

THE DUC DE LAUZUN

MEMOIRS

ARMAND LOUIS DE GONTAUT BIRON, DUC DE LAUZUN

(*After Delpech*)

[*frontispiece*

MEMOIRS OF THE DUC DE LAUZUN

Translated, with an Appendix, by C. K. Scott Moncrieff
Introduction by Richard Aldington
Notes by G. Rutherford

WITH FIVE PLATES

Published by
GEORGE ROUTLEDGE & SONS, LTD
BROADWAY HOUSE, CARTER LANE, LONDON

First published in 1928

PRINTED IN GREAT BRITAIN BY
BILLING AND SONS, LTD., GUILDFORD AND ESHER

To
B. L. R.

R.A.

C.K.S.M.

INTRODUCTION

I

THE chief authority for the life of Lauzun is the volume of memoirs here translated. Mr. Scott Moncrieff has added a brief account of Lauzun's career from the moment when the memoirs break off, and has given the facts and dates of the Duke's early life and family. Miss G. Rutherford, who has made a special study of Lauzun, has most kindly offered for this edition the notes which are printed at the end of the volume. These notes clear up difficulties which have puzzled the French editors. Very little than can possibly be useful to the reader remains to be said, and the chief merit of this Introduction will be its brevity.

The *Mémoires de Lauzun*, like the *Vie Privée du Maréchal Duc de Richelieu* (also published in this series), have been denounced as false and apocryphal. There is a certain similarity between the two books, *i.e.*, both are intimate confessions written apparently for the amusement of one or more ladies, both contain revelations which were exceedingly disagreeable to the restored French monarchy and aristocracy of the early nineteenth century, which was anxious to show how mighty moral it was and always had been. The great difference between the two books is that Richelieu is shown as a cynical blackguard, while Lauzun is a sort of romantic madcap. The adventures related by Lauzun might have been duplicated by the Prince de Ligne if he had chosen to be indiscreet. Richelieu, Ligne, Lauzun, are typical figures of pre-Revolution Versailles; but, whereas the cynicism and cruelty of the elderly Regency beau make him rather repellent, Ligne has a gaiety and polish, Lauzun a romantic gallantry which make them both sympathetic as well as interesting historical characters. In the present state of the evidence, no one can vouch for the authenticity of Richelieu's *Vie Privée*. It is far otherwise with the memoirs of Lauzun, and I shall put before the reader the remarks of two French critics who have investigated this topic.

In the fourth volume of the *Causeries du Lundi*, under the date of the 15th June, 1851, Sainte-Beuve gives a characteristic essay on the Duc de Lauzun. Hypocritically anxious, as usual, to pose as a pillar of bourgeois morality, Sainte-Beuve judges the Duke with considerable severity, refusing him even that military talent which Washington warmly praised and even Napoleon is said to have acknowledged. But this hostile respectability renders Sainte-Beuve's remarks on the authenticity of the memoirs all the more convincing. Sainte-Beuve says:

"The fate of these Memoirs, moreover, was curious, and will suggest more than one reflection. Written by Lauzun, as it appears, to amuse some of the women among his friends, the Memoirs were copied, and little by little were handed about and widely circulated. During the early years of the Restauration, the upper rank of society was warned of the existence of these Memoirs, and was positively terrified by the news. Indeed, several of the women mentioned for light conduct and adventures in their youth were still alive, and had since posed as solemn defenders of good principles, supporters of the altar as well as of the throne. M. de Talleyrand, who had known Lauzun, came to the aid of these ladies and their distressed families. In a letter signed by him, which was inserted in the *Moniteur* of the 27th of March, 1818, he said:

INTRODUCTION

" 'The Duc de Lauzun, who was a friend of mine, had written his Memoirs; he read them to me. I do not know into what hands copies may have fallen; but what I know with certainty is that they have been horribly falsified.

" 'All who knew the Duc de Lauzun know that he needed only the natural gifts of his mind to give charm to his narrative, that he was above everything a man of taste and fashion, and that no one was ever less capable than he of willingly injuring another. Yet they have dared to attribute to this man the most odious satires against French and foreign women, and the grossest calumnies against an August Personage (Marie Antoinette), who showed in her exalted rank as much goodness as in her days of misfortune she manifested grandeur of spirit. That is the most striking thing in the pretended Memoirs of the Duc de Lauzun, which for some time have been circulating in manuscript, and a copy of which is now in my hands.

" 'I should maintain silence towards this work of darkness, if I had not reason to suppose that this kind of manuscript is about to be given to the press.

" 'Forgeries and falsifications of books are not a new thing. From all time impassioned or mercenary persons have abused the facilities offered them by private Memoirs in order to diffuse under another's name that venom which is in them. But this sort of crime seems to become more common, instead of diminishing; and no doubt it will continue to increase if we continue to complain of it without employing a remedy.'

"After proposing a somewhat vague and unintelligible law against defamation and every kind of imputation of a personal character, M. de Talleyrand continued:

" 'But, as these laws do not yet exist, I think I owe it to the memory of a man who was my friend to declare that *he did not write*, that *he was incapable of writing*, and *would feel a horror at writing* the Memoirs which they have dared to put forth under his name. If I do not wait for them to be published, the reason is that in all probability they will appear while I am in the country and without my knowing of it.

" 'I did not wish my protest to arrive too late through being delayed.

" '(*Signed*) LE PRINCE DE TALLEYRAND.'

"When he wrote this" (Sainte-Beuve goes on), "M. de Talleyrand thought he was performing a good deed; he was at least performing a deed agreeable to persons in high society, but he lied, and lied wittingly, which is always regrettable when one desires to perform a public action in the name of morality.

"I have in my possession a letter of thanks and gratitude written to him on the 28th of March, just after the letter, by a noble lady of that time, Mme. la duchesse d'Es. . . . She says:

" 'I wish it to be felt here, Prince, how important is the service you have rendered. Nobody reads history, and the information of the salons is based on Memoirs. You proved to me the other day that their opinion carried great weight. A letter from you, depriving these Memoirs of their authenticity, crushes them, and foreigners, whom our misfortunes have rendered so important, will think them nothing but a novel. Anything which attacks the morals of the Queen diminishes the respect due to Madame (the Duchess of Angoulême). So that you have rendered a most important service. Yesterday, they were dangerous; to-day, they no longer exist.'

"But here" (says Sainte-Beuve) "we have a right to interrupt the person in society who judges in this way so lightly, and to say to her:

INTRODUCTION

"No, Madam, it is in the power of no man, however eminent his name and influence, to challenge in this way and by a stroke of the pen to annihilate indiscretions, even if scandalous and prejudicial to a whole order of society. In default of M. de Talleyrand, a Cato even could not do it. The society of the old regime chose to live in a certain way, to use and to abuse all the goods which were granted it. The men themselves are not denounced; others, in their place, would have done the same; newly-rich plebeians would have acted like Lauzun, but with less elegance. But, then, as the society of the old regime lived in that manner, it has no right to every privilege, nor can it add to the excess of past prodigalities and pleasures that final esteem which it would only owe to complete discretion and silence. The society of the old regime abused its position; it has been punished and destroyed, and that punishment and ruin are justified this very day by the successive admissions which come from its own bosom. Lauzun's Memoirs existed before M. de Talleyrand's denial; they still exist and count for twice as much after it, for their importance is more apparent. At first they seem only frivolous; they have a serious and far more durable side, and history will note them among the incriminating documents in the great impeachment of the eighteenth century."

How venomous the little bourgeois is! One feels convinced that the ancestors of M. Sainte-Beuve took no part in "the prodigalities and pleasures" of Versailles, for the plain reason that they were not invited. But, in his excuse, it must be mentioned that he wrote during the second French Republic, and even under the Prince-President a certain amount of democratic cant was expected. But the main point is that Sainte-Beuve, unequalled in his knowledge of eighteenth-century history and literature, felt not the slightest doubt about the authenticity of Lauzun's memoirs. It is true that he brings no proof to back his assertion, but that we can find elsewhere. At any rate, the most respectable Monsieur Sainte-Beuve throws his influence on the side of authenticity.

We now move from 1851 to 1893, when M. Gaston Maugras published his *Le Duc de Lauzun et la Cour Intime de Louis XV*. M. Gaston Maugras does not affect the austere and republican virtues of M. Sainte-Beuve, but he has a real sympathy with and understanding for the society of the eighteenth century, and his two volumes on Lauzun are a mine of amusing and witty information. M. Maugras writes well and in a most attractive way, so we cannot therefore claim for him the status of a scholar. However, since M. Maugras is a foreigner and wrote thirty-five years ago, perhaps his union of taste with knowledge may be forgiven. This is what M. Maugras says in his Preface:

In 1811 the police of the First Empire were informed that a MS. by the Duc de Lauzun was about to be printed and that a great scandal would result. The manuscript was seized. Queen Hortense asked to read it, and had it hastily copied. The MS. was then returned to the police and burned in the presence of Napoleon.

The first edition of Lauzun's memoirs appeared in 1821, and was printed from a copy of the copy made by the Queen Hortense. This publication aroused great excitement and the book was suppressed. It was, moreover, declared to be the work of a forger, and Mme. de Genlis (good, virtuous lady!) vowed that she had seen and read the true memoirs of Lauzun (even as M. de Talleyrand), and pledged her word that they were totally unlike the printed memoirs. "*Malheureusement*," says M. Maugras, "*Malheureusement*, the word of Mme. de Genlis does not carry much weight."

M. Maugras then proceeds to refute the ordinary objections made against the memoirs, and ends up with this fairly decisive declaration:

"In my view the authenticity of Lauzun's Memoirs is not disputable, and here is the reason: at every point —and they are very numerous—where my private documents have permitted me to check the Memoirs, I have never found the least error; important incidents, details, dates, are all absolutely exact and true. Who else could have known Lauzun's life in so precise a manner and could have penetrated into its most minute details?"

This accuracy of detail is confirmed by a small point concerning our own country which came up during the discussion in *The Times* Literary Supplement on the meaning of the word "keilets"—an obvious misprint in the French text. Now Lauzun mentions a horse-racing country gentleman named Sir Marmaduke "Hewell," and Miss Rutherford, in her letter, mentioned this personage as a puzzle. Next week the Literary Supplement published a letter from Sir Algernon Law identifying Sir Marmaduke "Hewell" as Sir Marmaduke Wyvill, Bt., of Burton Constable, Yorks. When the accuracy of Lauzun's memoirs is confirmed in so many points, this additional identification of an accidentally misspelled name with a real person is striking. There seems little room for further doubt.

II

There is every probability, then, that the stories Lauzun tells about himself and Mme. de Stainville, Lady Sarah Bunbury, the Princess Czartoryska and many other ladies, are true. Though the admission may cost me the esteem of some persons who are very virtuous (on paper), I confess I am not so scandalised as, I fear, some people will have to pretend to be. Hypocrisy is seldom pretty, even where it is a national institution, and it is particularly misplaced in literary and historical judgments. The elegant and powerful aristocracy to which Lauzun belonged has been "judged and punished," as M. Sainte-Beuve remarked; or, as I prefer to put it, abdicated and was assassinated. The French aristocracy of the eighteenth century is hated, not because some of its members were licentious, but because it was a privileged class, gay, witty, rich, brave, free and superbly insolent. According to figures published in *The Times*, England to-day contains 138 persons who pay income-tax on an annual revenue of £100,000 and upwards; the number of millionaires in the United States is said to baffle description. How many nobles at the Court of Louis XVI could spend 2,000,000 livres a year? Into the delicate question of comparative or competitive morals I shall not enter; the reader presumably has eyes and ears. It is possible, also, that one might be prejudiced in trying to establish a comparison between the respective encouragement given in the two epochs to the major and minor arts, to literature and the amenities of life. But, so far as one may judge, the aristocrats of the eighteenth century were more polished, more witty, more amusing, more curious people, living with more ease and gaiety in high places, more accustomed to ceremony, and less dependent for their eminence on the size of their income. But it is easy to be generous to the dead; so let it be with Lauzun.

RICHARD ALDINGTON.

P.S.—Miss Rutherford's notes are serially numbered from 1 upwards, to facilitate reference.

Memoirs of the Duc de Lauzun

MY life has been interspersed with such remarkable happenings; I have, from my earliest years, been a witness of such important events, that I have felt myself entitled to leave behind me these memoirs for the persons who are dear to me. They are written for such persons only, and it will be hard indeed for me to arrange them in the order necessary to a work intended to face the judgment of the public. I shall pride myself upon my veracity alone; I shall frequently retrace my steps; my narrative will have scarcely more sequence than had my conduct in the past, and the reader will see me in turn as lover, gambler, politician, soldier, sportsman, philosopher, and often more than one of these at a time.

I must say something to those who are to be my readers of the character of my father. M. le Duc de Gontaut,[1] my father, was a man of the most perfect honour, of a compassionate and charitable heart, sincere but controlled in his religious belief. He was not brilliantly clever, nor had he any great learning; but an accurate and sound judgment, a vast experience of the world and of the court, an excellent tone, a noble and charming way of expressing himself, a great natural cheerfulness, a profound aversion to intrigue, and a modest ambition had made him a pleasant and a popular man. A serious wound, which he received at the battle of Dettingen, gave him an honourable pretext for leaving the service. Promoted Lieutenant-General, he took his place at court, became the intimate friend of Madame de Châteauroux,[2] and consequently was admitted to the familiar circle of the King. The assiduous devotion which he paid to her during her fatal illness raised him to even higher favour; and presently he won that of Madame de Pompadour also: he was as well received by her as by her predecessor. The generous use that he made of his influence won him universal popularity, and I have seldom seen a man who had fewer enemies.

It was at court, therefore, and, so to speak, in the lap of the King's mistress, that the earliest years of my childhood were spent. The difficulty of finding me a good tutor led my father to entrust me to the care of a servant of my late mother, who could read and write a passable hand, and was granted the title of *valet de chambre* as an indication of his respectable position. I was given, besides, the masters most in fashion in every branch; but M. Roch (such was my mentor's name) was not capable of directing their lessons or of enabling me to profit by them. He confined himself to imparting to me his talent for writing, in which he took great pride, and with very fair success, as well as to teaching me to read aloud, more fluently and agreeably than is customary in France. This little talent made me almost indispensable to Madame de Pompadour, who continually made me read to her and write for her, and sometimes even for the King. Our visits to Versailles became all the more frequent, and my education the more neglected. I was, moreover, like all the boys of my age and condition: the most becoming clothes for out of doors, rags and starvation at home. At the age of twelve I was placed in the Regiment of Guards,[3] the reversion of which the King promised me, and I realised at that age that I was destined to enjoy an immense fortune and the finest position in the realm, without being obliged to take the pains to deserve them.

M. le Comte de Stainville[4] and my father had

married a pair of sisters—I am the son of the elder, who died in giving me birth. This marriage had brought them into close alliance, and my father's credit with Madame de Pompadour had led to M. de Stainville's appointment as Ambassador to Rome and then to Vienna; had made him a Duke, secured for him the Blue Riband, and finally the Ministry of Foreign Affairs, in which his natural charm and his talents soon won him an influence over her and, in time, over the King.

M. le Duc de Choiseul had a sister,[5] a Canoness of Remiremont, who had no fortune beyond her stall, but who combined with all the charms of her sex the character of a man fitted for great affairs and for great intrigues; he took her into his house. Madame de Choiseul was plain, but with the sort of plainness that generally proves attractive: one might with justice describe her as a desirable woman. It was not long before she decided to secure the control of her brother, and she saw clearly that the most certain way of securing control for herself and preventing that of a mistress was to make him her lover. But to play this part without risk to herself, she required a substance, a position, and these were lacking. She was obliged, therefore, to seek a marriage and a husband that would at once satisfy her self-esteem and ensure her safety. Her eye fell upon M. le Duc de Gramont,[6] a man devoid of character, incapable of anything, who for some years had been forbidden the court, and spent his days in a small house outside Paris, among musicians and women of the town of the humblest kind. Nothing could suit Madame de Choiseul better, since nothing would be easier than to set M. le Duc de Gramont back where she had found him, as soon as he should become a nuisance: my father lent his aid; the ban was removed, and the marriage celebrated.

I was now fourteen years old;[7] and of a pleasing

exterior. Madame la Duchesse de Gramont was as friendly as could be, with the intention, I dare say, of quietly furnishing herself with a young lover, who should be entirely hers and without risk to herself: her influence, I should say her mastery, over M. le Duc de Choiseul increased daily. Madame la Duchesse de Choiseul, who was passionately in love with her husband, was jealous of this undue affection, and, in a few months' time, the sisters-in-law were no longer on speaking terms. My father, with his usual moderation, contrived to take neither side in the quarrel and to remain equally in favour with both. I did well in following his example; but I must confess to my shame that I followed my natural inclination, and gave, in my heart, my entire support to Madame la Duchesse de Gramont, who was exceedingly grateful to me. About this time she carried me to Ménars,[8] to wait upon Madame de Pompadour. Miss Julia, her waiting woman, who was wholly in her confidence and had already become a personage of considerable importance, decided that what her mistress was keeping for herself might very well be to her own taste also, and marked me down for the honour of being initiated into the ways of the world by her; she lavished upon me caresses and provocations, but to no avail, for I was entirely innocent: one day she placed my hand upon her bosom, all my body was still aflame hours afterwards; but I was no farther advanced. And yet I knew no keener pleasure than that of meeting her and of being in her company. My absorption was remarked by M. Roch, who readily guessed its object and, tactfully, forbade me upon any consideration all commerce with Miss Julia; I was greatly distressed by this. An event of greater interest made me forget her, or did at least provide me with a distraction. M. le Duc de Choiseul, become Minister of War upon the death of Marshal

Belleisle, promoted to Lieutenant-General in the French service M. le Comte de Stainville, his younger brother, an officer of repute and at the time Major-General in the Emperor's service. He had no fortune; but his brother's favour and the King's liberality assured him an advantageous marriage; the choice fell upon Mademoiselle de Clermont-Reynel,[9] who combined an ample fortune with a charming person, and was not turned fifteen. All was arranged while M. de Stainville was still with the army. Winter came, an order was dispatched recalling him, and he was married within six hours after his reaching Paris.

I saw Madame de Stainville for the first time upon her wedding day, and she made an impression upon me which has persisted ever since: I at once fell passionately in love with her, and was teased over my love so much that she came to learn of it; she was touched by the news; but she was too strictly guarded by Madame la Duchesse de Choiseul, her sister-in-law, who had taken charge of her, for there to be any danger as yet. Madame de Gramont, who had no love for her younger brother, and was afraid the young Madam might prove too attractive to the Duc de Choiseul, who appeared to be taken up with her, was not sorry to provide her with a cavalier; it was no obstacle to her designs upon myself, whom she believed that she could recall to her side when she chose, and it seemed likely to forestal an attachment, the inevitable result of which must be to destroy her own situation. She therefore gave her protection to our infant love, and often caused us to meet in her own house.

Madame de Stainville told me one day at dinner at Madame de Choiseul's that she would be dining, the next day, with Madame de Gramont, and that we might spend the whole day there together. I was beside myself with joy; but M. Roch, who discovered our plan, and whose strict principles allowed of no exception, insisted the next morning, which was a Sunday, upon making me hear mass; I refused, we came to argument; he threatened me with my father, of whom I lived in terror; I gave way with the bitterest regret; he took me to mass at the Little Fathers',[10] where, choked by misery and anger, I swooned; I lost consciousness altogether; and, when I recovered it, found myself lying upon the steps of the church, surrounded by old women, who, to give me air, had unbuttoned my breeches. I was carried back to the house, where I arrived in a helpless state enough. I said that I was unwell, and they made me retire to bed. The Duchesse de Gramont came to see me, and brought me Madame de Stainville. I told her my story; she laughed to hear it, went to find my father, got M. Roch a scolding, and obtained leave to treat my malady and to carry me off to dine at her own table. This day was one of the happiest in my life. I spent the whole of it with my young mistress, and almost all the time by ourselves. She showed me how deeply she was touched by my affection, and granted me all the innocent favours that I asked of her (and they were all that I knew). I kissed her hands; she swore to me that she would love me all her life; I wished for nothing else in the world. A lingering whooping-cough made her keep her chamber for near six months. The door was barred to me; I saw her but seldom, and never without Madame de Choiseul. The physicians ordered her to take the waters at Cotterets; she was sent there in the spring, and returned in excellent health at the beginning of winter. She went out a great deal with the Duchesse de Choiseul; she danced to perfection. She had the greatest success at all the balls, was the centre of an admiring throng that included all the men of fashion; ashamed to have a boy for a lover, she cast me off, treated me harshly, and took a fancy for M. de Jaucourt;[11] I was jealous, indignant, desperate, but it availed me nothing.

My father, about this time, arranged for me to marry Mademoiselle de Boufflers,[12] granddaughter to Marshal Luxembourg's lady, her intimate companion, the heiress to her fortune, and consequently a very great match indeed. I was vexed at this, because the marriage was not to the liking of Madame la Duchesse de Gramont, who, not without reason, detested the Marshal's lady and told me many things against her. It was decided that I must meet the person whom I was to marry; it was arranged that I should attend a ball in the afternoon that Marshal Mirepoix's lady[13] was giving; that Mademoiselle de Boufflers should take her dinner there; that I should arrive early, and should see her. I was, in short, taken to the house at four o'clock, and found there a charming young person, who pleased me vastly, and whom I took to be herself. I was, alas! mistaken, and the person was Mademoiselle de Roth.[14] I realised my error with all the more regret in that Mademoiselle de Boufflers, who appeared from Madame de Mirepoix's bedchamber, did not gain by the comparison.

Madame la Princesse de Beauvau[15] was at this ball with Mademoiselle de Beauvau. It would be difficult for anyone to combine a greater variety of charms, greater natural parts and greater attraction; I was fully conscious of her rarity. I used to meet Mademoiselle de Beauvau[16] at all the balls; I saw her constantly at Madame la Duchesse de Gramont's, who was her mother's dearest friend. I sought to find favour with her; she received my endeavours without repugnance; she was far more to my liking in every respect than Mademoiselle de Boufflers. I desired to marry her; I spoke of my intention to Madame de Gramont, who gave me her strong approval. I found the courage to mention it to my father, who received me with the worst of graces, told me that he had pledged his word and intended to abide by it. I vowed to myself, however, that I would not let myself be married against my will. The attachment that I displayed to Madame la Princesse de Beauvau found favour with her. Before setting off upon a long tour which she was obliged to make in Lorraine, she was so good as to assure me that she was no less anxious than myself for the success of my projects, and that it would not be her fault should they be defeated. Mademoiselle de Beauvau herself kindly allowed me to hope that she would think of me sometimes during her absence. This tour was prolonged; and, as it was coming to an end, Madame la Princesse de Beauvau took the small-pox and died of it.[17] Mademoiselle de Beauvau returned to Paris a few months later, and was placed in the convent of Port-Royal. I had sincerely regretted Madame de Beauvau: her death had altered nothing of my intentions; I was anxious to learn, what were those of her daughter. I conveyed secretly to her convent a letter expressed in the following terms:

"I have not ventured, Mademoiselle, to disturb your grief with my own: you will do justice to it, when you consider that my loss has been as great as yours. My father seeks to have me married, Mademoiselle; but the more I feel how greatly I am honoured by an alliance with Mademoiselle de Boufflers, and how great are her merits, the more convinced I am that we are not suited. There exists but one happiness for me, Mademoiselle; the hope that I may be able to contribute to yours: I attach a value beyond words to your confirmation of that hope. I dare not request my father to approach M. le Prince de Beauvau, until I know that such a step will not meet with your disapproval. It is a question of contracting a lifelong tie, and it appears to me that you can grant or refuse me the permission that I ask of you, without departing from the strictest propriety. I await your answer, Mademoiselle, with far more anxiety and impatience than if it were merely my life that was in jeopardy.

"I am, with the most profound respect, Mademoiselle, your most humble and most obedient servant,

"Le Comte de Biron."

Mademoiselle de Beauvau's governess received my letter, and read it before handing it to her.

"I ought not, perhaps, to give you this letter," she said to her; "but it contains matters of such importance to yourself, that I feel that I must not only show it to you, but even leave you at liberty to reply to it." Mademoiselle de Beauvau sealed my letter and sent it back to me without a word in reply; I was hurt by a treatment which I did not deserve; it made me decide to promise my father that I would consent to the marriage that he desired; I made the condition that it should be postponed for two years, and that I should be allowed for the present to enjoy my freedom.

I took a fancy for a little actress at the playhouse of Versailles, aged fifteen, named Eugénie Beaubours, and even more innocent than myself, for I had already read several improper books, and required only the opportunity to put in practice what they had taught me. I set to work to instruct my little mistress, who loved me too sincerely not to yield herself to all my desires. One of her fellow-actresses lent us her room, or, to be precise, a little closet in which she slept, and which was entirely filled by a bed and a couple of chairs. An enormous spider appeared to interrupt our dalliance: we were both of us in mortal terror; neither of us could summon up courage to kill it. Instead, we parted, promising each other that we would meet again in a more commodious place, where there would be no such terrifying monsters.

My father heard of our relations, was alarmed at the news, I know not why, and, within a week, sent mother and daughter packing, without my having a chance of seeing them again before their departure. I was not aware that he had any hand in it, and supposed that my only grievance was against Madame Beaubours; a few days sufficed to bring me consolation, and my heart remained unattached.

I attracted, shortly after this, the attention of Madame la Comtesse d'Esparbès,[18] a cousin of Madame de Pompadour, fetching, pretty, and gay; she made many overtures to me in vain, for I did not understand them; I was flattered, at length, by the deference with which she treated me, and fell in love with her. One day when the King was supping in the Royal private apartments at Fontainebleau, with Madame de Pompadour and but a small party else, I took supper in town with Madame d'Esparbès, and Madame d'Amblimont,[19] another of Madame de Pompadour's cousins. Madame d'Amblimont withdrew to her chamber after supper. Madame d'Esparbès, pleading a headache, retired to bed; discretion bade me take my leave, but she told me to stay, and asked me to read to her a little play, entitled *Heureusement*,[20] in which we had taken part together, since when she had called me her young cousin. "My young cousin," she said to me, after I had been reading for a while, "this book bores me; sit down upon my bed and let us talk; that will be more amusing." She complained of the heat, and threw open her garments. My head swam, I was all afire; but I was afraid of offending her; I dared run no risk; I contented myself with kissing her hands and gazing at her bosom with an avidity which did not displease her, but was not followed by the actions that she was entitled to expect. She told me repeatedly to behave myself, as a hint to me that I was behaving myself all too well. I followed her advice to the letter. It teased her, meanwhile, that I should be covering her with caresses and kisses, and she was hoping in vain that I might grow bolder. When she was quite assured of my imbecility, she ordered me, somewhat coldly, to be gone; I obeyed without uttering a word, and was no sooner out of the room than I repented of my timidity, and vowed that I would make a better use of my time should the opportunity present itself again.

I happened some days later to be at the Opera ball. A girl of some beauty, named Mademoiselle Desmarques, excited my interest; I thought her charming; she had instructed the greater part of the young men at court, was pleased to undertake my education, and carried me home with her, where she gave me delicious lessons, of which the reader has seen that I stood in great need: she continued them for a fortnight, after which we parted. I was anxious to give her a present; she declined it, telling me that I had already paid her in a coin so hard to come by, that she had no need of any other.

I encountered Madame d'Esparbès again at Versailles; I offered her my arm one evening, as we were coming from Madame de Pompadour's, after supper. When I was in her chamber, she would have had me go: "One moment," I said to her, "my fair cousin, it is not late. Let us talk a while. I could read to you, if I bore you." My eyes were glowing with a fire which she had never before seen in them. "I should like it," she told me; "but on condition that you behave as properly as you did before: go into the other room; I am going to undress; you shall come in when I am in bed." I did, in fact, return a few minutes later. I sat down upon her bed, unchecked by her. "Aren't you going to read to me?" said she. "No;

it gives me such pleasure to see you, to gaze at you, that I could not see a word of what is printed in the book." My eyes devoured her; I let the book fall from my hands; I disarranged, meeting no great opposition, the kerchief that was covering her bosom. She endeavoured to speak, my lips stopped hers; I was burning; I guided her hand to the most ardent portion of my body; the whole of hers quivered at the contact. When she touched me, she caused me to make an effort which broke all the bonds that were restraining me. I tore aside everything that could conceal from sight one of the most beautiful persons that I have ever in my life beheld; she refused me nothing; but my undue ardour sadly curtailed her enjoyment. I very soon made amends for this and continued until daybreak, when she made me depart with the greatest secrecy. On the morrow, I was awakened by the following note:

"How did you sleep, my charming young cousin? Have you been thinking of me? Are you longing to see me again? I am obliged to go to Paris, upon certain errands for Madame de Pompadour; come and drink chocolate with me before I start, and, what is more important, tell me that you love me."

This attention enchanted me, and appeared to me designed for myself. I blamed myself for not having sent word to Madame d'Esparbès; I allowed myself barely time to put on my clothes, and hastened to her. I found her still abed, and gave such an account of myself as showed that I was wholly recovered from the fatigues of the night: I was overjoyed by this. In her person, Madame d'Esparbès pleased me greatly, and it flattered my self-esteem vastly to possess a woman. I was too much a man of honour to publish the truth; but people gave me an unspeakable pleasure by guessing it; and in this respect she gave me entire satisfaction; for she treated me in such a manner as proclaimed the truth to all the world. A cockade upon which she had embroidered her name, which I wore at the King's review, published my triumph, which was not of long duration, for she took in the course of the summer Monsieur le Prince de Condé.[21] This distressed me, shocked me, I threatened her; all to no effect. She sent me my formal dismissal, couched in these terms:

"It grieves me, Monsieur le Comte, that my conduct should have caused you annoyance. It is impossible for me to alter anything, let alone sacrificing to your whims the persons who do not enjoy your favour. I hope that the public will judge of the attentions that they pay me less severely than yourself. I hope that you will pardon me, considering my frankness, the wrong that you suppose me to have done. Many reasons, which it would take too long to enumerate severally, oblige me to request you to make your visits less frequent. I hold too high an opinion of you to fear any discreditable action from so honourable a man.

I have the honour to be, etc."

I begged a final meeting, which was granted me without hesitation. Madame d'Esparbès displayed a calm that put me to confusion. "You have insisted upon seeing me," she said; "in a like position, any other woman would have declined, but I felt myself obliged to pay some heed to the interests that are always inspired by an old acquaintance. You are, in truth, singularly childish: your principles, your outlook, lack all common sense. Believe me, cousin, a man can no longer succeed by being romantic; it makes him ridiculous, and that is an end of the matter.*

* Madame d'Esparbès had some excuse for this reproach; I had been allowed to read endless novels throughout my boyhood, and this reading had so strong an influence upon my character that I am still

I had a great liking for you, my boy; it is not my fault if you mistook it for a grand passion and persuaded yourself that it must endure for ever. What matter to you, once that liking has passed, whether I grow fond of another or remain without a lover; you have many claims to the favour of women: make the most of them, so as to win it, and be assured that the loss of one may always be remedied with another: that is the way to be fortunate and loved. You are too much a man of honour to seek my harm; it would turn more against yourself than against me. You have no proof of what has passed between us; nobody would believe you; and, if any did, to what extent do you suppose that the public is interested in such matters? If people did know that I had taken you up, they never expected that I would keep you for ever. The date of our rupture is to them a matter of perfect indifference. Moreover, the bad opinion and mistrust that other women would have of you would avenge me upon you, were you capable of dishonourable conduct. The advice that I am giving you should prove to you that interest and friendship outlast the sentiments that I once had for you." I was embarrassed, and cut but a sorry figure: protestations, a few somewhat clumsy compliments. . . . She relieved my embarrassment, by ringing for her women to dress her. I stayed in the room a moment longer, then took my leave.

Time brought me a measure of consolation, and I remained without any serious attachment. Next I found the prettiest little girl, in the house of a woman famed by her talent for procuring such. The modesty

---

conscious of its effects. They have often proved to my disadvantage; but if I have exaggerated my own sentiments and my own sensations, I am at least indebted to my romantic nature for an abhorrence of the treachery and dishonourable conduct towards women, from which many men of honour are not exempt.—L.

of my offers did not disgust her; she was content with a small apartment up three pair of stairs, and meagrely furnished. I had but to hire one for the few months of our connexion. She never appeared dissatisfied with her lot, nor to wish for more money than I was able to give her. Returning after a se'nnight in the country, I arrived at the house in the evening; she was no longer there, and the servant handed me a note which ran as follows:

" I cannot part from you without regret, my kind friend, and I am vexed that you should have cause to complain of my behaviour; I hope, though, that you will forgive me for not refusing an advantageous position which you are not rich enough to secure for me. I confess to you that the certainty of being plunged in poverty and shame, were I to lose you, alarms me. Farewell, my kind friend, I assure you that, notwithstanding what I am doing, I love you, I regret you with all my heart, and that Rosalie will never forget you."

Rosalie was a charming child. I was sorry to lose her; but I bore her no ill-will for having sacrificed me to an assured position, for I did not suspect her of infidelity to myself. I could have wished, though, that she had had sufficient confidence in me not to conceal her plans from me. I continued for some time to frequent the ladies, like any other young man of my age, without fastening my affections upon any. Madame de Pompadour's death was the first remarkable incident in my life;[22] my attachment to her, and her tender regard for myself, made her loss irreparable; I formed, during her illness, a friendship with Monsieur le Prince de Guéménée,[23] which nothing has been able to destroy and which will certainly endure as long as we live. A serious affection of the chest, which continued above a year, kept me from thinking of anything but my health until it was restored.

Monsieur le Prince de Tingry Montmorency[24] took as his second wife, in 1765, Mademoiselle de Laurens,[25] a great girl, stout and rosy, about twenty years old, but seeming thirty; a good creature, merry and fond of pleasure; being on intimate terms with Monsieur le Chevalier de Luxembourg,[26] nephew to Monsieur le Prince de Tingry, I was constantly at their house and had frequent opportunities of meeting Madame de Tingry; I attracted her, and was aware of it; she herself was not unpleasing, and nothing could suit me better than to become the master in a perfectly respectable household. Madame de Tingry's intellect was not unbounded, still less her experience of the world. It was not very difficult to discover what was in her mind, and her fondness for myself was soon remarked by all. I went with her to the country, where we amused ourselves in play-acting; I made a foil to her talent, and was in the highest favour; she was responsible for a practical joke which I should not record here, had it not caused the greatest stir at the time.

Monsieur le Marquis de Gèvres[27] had a house at Fontainebleau, in which he had given a very poor apartment to Madame la Duchesse d'Havré;[28] Madame de Tingry, having failed to prevail upon him to be gallant and to give up his own, told us that he must not be allowed to enter the house: we lay in wait for him that evening as he came out from the house where he was supping; stopped the chaise; carried him off; set him in a cabriolet, and conveyed him to the heart of the forest of Fontainebleau, where we recommended him, in the most friendly spirit, to do things with a good grace and to give up his apartment to Madame d'Havré; he would not agree; we proceeded on our way, assuring him that we should continue the expedition until he had given us the token of friendship that we asked of him; we took fresh horses at a post called Bouron, two leagues from Fontainebleau; he offered resistance, but we had no difficulty in persuading the people of the house that he was one of our family who had gone mad, whom we were taking to Provence, to the mansion of Saint-Cyprien, where he was to be confined. So persuasive were we, that in half an hour the postilions swore that they had seen him running along the manger-rack in the stables. Before we were half a league from the post, he promised to do everything that we asked, and we brought him home. The party was composed of Monsieur le Duc d'Havré, the Marquis de Royan[29] (the Chevalier de Luxembourg's brother), Monsieur le Prince de Guéménée and myself: two of us rode in the cabriolet with Monsieur de Gèvres, and the rest on horseback. We were on good enough terms when we parted from him; but his valet assured him that he ought to take offence, and he charged Monsieur le Duc de Trèmes,[30] his father, to lay a complaint before the King.

Having been scolded for an hour on end by every one who had any control over me, I decided that I could not do better than to retire to Paris, to await the sequel of this incident. A few hours after my arrival I received a letter from my father, who informed me that it had been decided that we should all of us be clapped in the Bastille, and that I would probably be arrested during the night. What made our position more critical was the state of Monsieur le Dauphin, who was dangerously ill and almost breathing his last,[31] a time indeed hardly suited for practical jokes; but the King was not fond enough of his son to take offence at this, nor even to punish us for the sake of propriety. I decided at least to make a happy ending, and invited some pretty girls from the Opera to supper, to while away the time until the constable should appear. Seeing that he did not come, I took the bold course of going to Fontainebleau, to hunt with the King; he never spoke to me throughout the day; a fact which made our disgrace so evident, that people refrained from bowing to us on our return. I was nothing daunted; I attended his orders that evening; the King came up to me: "You have all of you," he said, "bad heads, but merry bodies; come to supper, and bring Monsieur de Guéménée and the Prince de Luxembourg." The case was altered, and we found ourselves, next day, restored to all the consideration that we had enjoyed three days earlier: we kept Madame de Tingry's part in the matter secret, nor was her name ever mentioned; which might have proved embarrassing to her. She treated me a little less kindly; she began to bore me; I discreetly withdrew, and we met upon comparatively cold terms.

Madame la Duchesse de Gramont began again to have designs upon me, in which she became busily engaged. Madame de Stainville was growing prettier every day, and Monsieur le Duc de Choiseul was aware of this: she and I were on cold terms; I had not forgotten the scorn with which she had treated me, and she was remarking that I no longer deserved it, and that I had become quite a personable youth, when Monsieur de Stainville took a house in the Faubourg Saint-Germain, and let her go by herself.

Madame la Duchesse de Gramont's predilection and her efforts did not escape Madame de Stainville; she began to show greater interest in myself. She sent word to me one day that a severe headache prevented her from going to dine with M. le Duc de Choiseul, and would oblige her to stay indoors. I called in the evening to inquire after her, purely from politeness, with no intention of entering the house. They told me that she was at home, and I found her by herself. She gave me the warmest welcome. We talked for some time of trivial matters. She then spoke to me of Madame de Tingry, and her notorious fondness for myself. "You are going," she said, "to play a great part in the world, and nothing can bring you such renown as the conquest of Madame de Gramont." "I don't know what you mean," I replied, slightly embarrassed; "you are aware that Madame de Gramont has long honoured me with her friendship, and you cannot suppose her capable of any warmer sentiment." "I beg pardon for my indiscretion," she replied; "I see now, how foolish I have been. The thought of the sorrow that such an event must have caused me, and of the difference it must have made to my happiness, had I placed that in your hands, and had I been persuaded by your promises, that you would never alter, has recurred to my mind too often for me not to speak of it almost unawares." "It is a fine thing to hear you reproaching my fickleness, forgetting that you once thought you loved me, and that you scornfully forsook me; whereas I was making no mistake as to my own feelings, when I saw how difficult it was to cease to adore you." "I admit that I have treated you amiss; I might urge, however, in my defence, my youth, the strength of the prejudices common at such an age, and my fear of all the obstacles that appeared to be raised in our path; but I prefer to admit quite frankly that I have done amiss; that I did not see you with the same eyes, and that I supposed you less worthy of my affections." Notwithstanding that Madame de Stainville left me entirely unmoved, and had forfeited the rights that at first passion always has over the heart, her speech embarrassed me. "Indeed!" I said to her, "what matters it to you what I become, or whether another woman sets a value upon a heart which you have scorned? Have you not a lover, and have you spared me any of the torments which your fondness for M. de Jaucourt caused me?" "I shall not deny to you my connexion with M. de Jaucourt, M. de Biron; he is no longer anything to me; he has suffered too much by comparison with yourself: I have thought of you more than once with regret. I have often intended to tell you so: your various amours have prevented me. I could not discover any serious attachment on your part: I hoped one day to regain my former sway over you, which I had by my own fault lost; but, I must admit, my sister-in-law alarms me greatly. You can see the opinion that I hold of you, by my frankness: be no less frank with me. Are you in love with Madame de Gramont? Is it thought for your own welfare alone that binds you to her?" I could not answer at once: I was filled with strange emotions. I could not deny to myself that I was flattered by the favour I found in Madame de Gramont's eyes, and by having at my disposal a person already famous, who had the whole court at her feet. On the other hand, never had Madame de Stainville seemed to me so pretty, or so charming. I had to choose what I was to say: I broke the silence at length. "I have loved you too well, not to find pleasure in making you read what is in my heart. Madame de Gramont has many claims upon my gratitude: I should have grudged her no token of it an hour ago; but I feel all too plainly that a certain old wound has not yet closed, and that it has now burst open afresh. I would wish not to appear ungrateful, and yet at the same time to prove to you that nothing is so dear to me as yourself." "I do not wish you," she replied, as she held out the prettiest hand in the world, "to be ungrateful; but I do wish to take upon myself the task of modifying the tokens of your gratitude. Friendship, respect, deference—so much I allow to my sister-in-law: all the rest belongs to me. I shall be discreet and prudent. I insist upon knowing, without reservation, everything that she says to you, and upon reading everything that she writes to you. I should not be so exacting and curious, were I less tender." All that youth can combine of graces and charms, Madame de Stainville's eyes offered me. Madame de Gramont was sacrificed: we were too much in love with one another, my mistress and I, for our secret to be as impenetrable as we supposed. Madame de Gramont did not fail to observe what was going on. She was too sensible a woman to show any sign: she contented herself with treating me coldly, and with forming, for her poor little sister-in-law, an aversion of which to the last moment she gave her terrible proofs.

After our return to Paris, Madame de Stainville said to me one day: "We are quits, my friend; you have a rival who is all-powerful, though not powerful enough to be set above yourself. M. le Duc de Choiseul called this morning to lay his homage and his influence at my feet. Notwithstanding the coldness and severity of my answers, he was most pressing. I did what was required to deprive him of any hope, and I hope now to be rid of him." She was mistaken: so far from abating, his persecution of her increased. He became jealous of myself; he tried to extort from her a promise that she would not see me again. She replied firmly that, whether he supposed me her lover or her friend, nothing would alter her sentiments, or make her renounce me. M. de Stainville too became jealous of me, forbade her strictly to see me, and closed his door to me. A little box which we had secretly engaged at the Comédie Italienne was the only place in which we could meet; nor even there were we free from danger. Her servants adored her. I had always treated them liberally and well: they were devoted to me also. Her porter told her waiting woman that he would let me in by night, if she wished, by a door from the stables, unknown to anybody. The proposal was joyfully accepted, and was put into practice many times without untoward consequences. Once, however, we thought that we were surprised, as here follows: Madame de Stainville had set out one evening for Versailles, leaving word that she would be staying there for two or three days. I had at once been informed of this, and had arrived at the house as soon as I supposed that everybody would be gone to bed. I had wasted no time over my toilet, and in an instant was in the arms and in the bed of my mistress: we were tasting the most exquisite pleasures with complete security, when a loud knock sounded from the street door. Her woman burst into the room in great dismay. "All is lost," she cried; "it is M. le Comte! It is too late to go across the courtyard; run down at once into the garden: we shall get you away as best we can." I sprang out of bed in my shirt, and was going down the stair that led to the closet, when I caught sight of M. de Stainville coming up. Happily, I did not lose my head, but blew out the only light that was burning on the stair. He passed so close to me that his coat brushed against my shirt, and I could feel the braid upon it. I made a dash for freedom; and climbed the garden wall, high as it was; but, as I jumped down into the street, I was arrested by the mounted guard, who took me for a robber. A hundred louis, which I promised him and sent home to fetch, procured my liberty, and bought a promise of secrecy, which was indeed faithfully kept. A few weeks later we were surprised by one of her lackeys, in circumstances that admitted but little doubt. Money, promises, and threats delivered us once again. The fellow gave notice on the morrow, and I took good care to see that he left Paris at once.

The time fixed for my marriage drew round. It was celebrated upon the 4th of February, 1766, and my father was as proud of having given me a wife who neither loved me nor appealed to my taste, as if he had united a pair of lovers who longed ardently for union. I called, after the nuptial mass, at Madame la Duchesse de Choiseul's, where I dined. Madame de Stainville arrived. We sought in vain to conceal our misery. She took her leave early; I gave her my hand to help her into her carriage; this was hardly prudent, but so necessary to us both, that I could not help doing it. "My friend," she said to me as she left, "I could no longer endure the insolent delight of M. de Choiseul. He hopes that you are going to attach yourself to the moping child they have made you marry, and that I shall be only too glad to return to him; but I would sooner die. Tell me that you will not change, for he has frightened me." I had no time to answer; but a glance showed her clearly the state of my heart. I lived most honourably, and indeed most attentively with my wife, who displayed a revulsion that would have pained a man with less self-esteem than myself. I was too honest to demand affection from a woman who inspired none in myself.

Madame de Stainville occupied me entirely, and appeared to be growing fonder of me every day. It was difficult for us to meet, as I dared not approach her house in the daytime. She sent word to me one morning to come at once and speak to her, bidding me enter by the garden gate: I arrived in haste. "M. le Duc de Choiseul has bidden me give him an assignation," she told me. "I wish you to listen to our conversation, so that you can judge for yourself how we stand together; hide yourself in that grated cupboard among my gowns, and do not stir." I was no sooner in my hiding-place than M. de Choiseul entered. "I have been most anxious to see you alone, my dear little sister! I have a number of interesting things to tell you, which are important to you as well as to myself. No one loves you more than I do, my dear child, no one is more anxious to prove his love for you; judge therefore how pained and shocked I must be by the cold and indifferent manner in which you treat me, and what it has obliged me to think." "I do not know, brother," she replied, "of what you complain; I should be very sorry to learn that my behaviour displeased you; but I have no cause to reproach myself with any failure to entertain for you all the sentiments that are proper." "It is not that!" he went on with heat, "for I am very much in love with you, and nothing would be wanting to my happiness and your own, if you chose to . . ." "What would your brother say, if he heard you?" she interrupted him, with a smile. "I know very well that it is not my brother that prevents you: yes, my dear little sister, if you have no lover, you will lie with me." (Here he attempted to embrace her. She drew back.) "I have no lover, Monsieur, nor do I wish for one." "You will repent, my fine lady, of that fine resolution." (He advanced upon her again, and tried to lay his hand upon her bosom.) "I beg you to understand" (she spoke a little crossly) "that if I were to give myself to a man, at least I should first have to be in love with him." "You may lay aside this mask of virtue, Madame la Comtesse, you have had M. de Jaucourt, and at present you have M. de Biron; take heed of this last warning that I shall give you, for my patience is at an end, and I cannot allow you to make a fool of me; your young lover is an insolent fop; you will remember this day, and will repent of it, both of you!" "A moment's reflexion, brother, will bring you to reason; and certainly I have no reason to fear any dishonourable treatment from you." "Do not make an implacable enemy of a man who loves you to distraction; who will, if you wish, do everything in his power to please you, and to whom nothing is easier than to destroy a rival so little worthy of him." (With this he sought to venture farther than he had hitherto gone.) She rose to her feet in anger: "You are all-powerful, Sir; of that I am well aware; but I do not love you, nor am I capable of loving you. M. de Biron is my lover, I admit, since you force the admission; he is dearer to me than anyone; and neither your tyrannical power, nor all the harm that you are able to do us, will make either of us forsake the other." (He rose in a fury.) "Reflect, Madame, that nothing will preserve you from my vengeance, if this conversation is not buried in the most profound silence!" And he left the room. Madame de Stainville released me from my prison, and took me in her arms. "I cannot tell, dear heart," she said to me, "what will be the outcome of all this; but at least we are rid of him, and that is always a blessing. With love and courage, one can always defy the world."

M. de Choiseul learned, how I do not know, that I had heard everything, and flew into a rage which he managed to conceal, but the effects of which were terrible.

As I came away alone, on foot, one night, from Madame de Stainville's, a man who was lurking behind a stone, near the Palais-Bourbon, rose and dealt me a furious blow with a stick, which fortunately was countered in part by the brim of my hat, and fell upon my shoulder. I drew my sword and thrust it well into my assailant's body, so far as I could judge. Two other men sprang up from behind the stones and came to the help of the first. A carriage, behind which were several lackeys with a pair of torches, put them to flight, and effected my rescue. I followed the carriage across the Pont-Royal. I went on the morrow to report my adventure to M. de Sartines,[32] who was then Lieutenant General of Police; he told me that the men were probably drunk, and advised me to say no more about the matter. All these obstacles and dangers made Madame de Stainville waver. We began to see one another more rarely. Her fondness for myself diminished, and in a few months I was no more to her than a friend; but the most affectionate of friends, and almost as affectionate as any lover could be. I felt the loss of her less, having been prepared for it by degrees.

I came across my little mistress of Versailles, Eugénie; I did not choose at first to take her up again, out of respect for Madame de Biron, whose favour I was seeking to win with the utmost good faith, but in vain; her cold and disdainful manner ended by bringing about a complete revulsion. I established Eugénie at Rouen, and, as I was in a bold and active mood, I used to visit her there twice in the week. When winter made these frequent journeys tedious, I set her up in a small and uncomfortable house at Passy. The King created me Duke about this time, and, to avoid confusion with my father and uncles, I was styled Duc de Lauzun.

I supped one evening at Marshal Luxembourg's lady's, with Madame la Vicomtesse de Cambis,[33] the sister of M. le Prince d'Hénin, with whom I was on excellent terms: an elegant figure, wit, talents, grace, abundant art and coquetry made her an attractive woman. I was by this time sufficiently in the fashion for her not to be above courting my favour. I had a marked success with her; and, from the first moment, we adopted a playful tone. When on guard at Versailles, where I was exceedingly bored, I was led by idleness to pay a call upon Madame de Boisgelin,[34] a monster of ugliness, but a pleasant enough woman, and as gay as any beauty; we spoke of Madame de Cambis. "Make her come here," she said, "write her a line; I have every reason to believe that she wants you, and she will come." Nothing but an abounding extravagance and fatuity can excuse my action. I wrote upon a scrap of paper: "M. de Lauzun orders Madame de Cambis to come and keep him company at Versailles, where he is on guard, and bored to death." Greatly to my surprise, she arrived four hours after the dispatch of my note. The reader may imagine that, after such haste in obeying, it was not long before we came to an understanding.

Oh, for the moment my hands were full, and nothing could have been more pleasant than my manner of life. I behaved in the most honourable, and indeed scrupulous, fashion towards Madame de Lauzun; I was notoriously the lover of Madame de Cambis, to whom I paid little heed; I was keeping little Eugénie, to whom I was devoted; I was playing for big stakes; I was paying my court to the King, and went hunting most diligently with him. Abundant gaiety, great activity and little sleep gave me time to attend to everything. Without entering into great detail, I am now so entirely changed that I feel that I have acquired the right to say that I was at the time a most attractive fellow; a character so formed for society was bound to succeed, and had won me the warmest friendship of M. le Prince de Conti,[35] who could not, I might almost say, let me out of his sight, and admitted me into his most intimate circle.

I had not ceased to see Madame de Stainville. A prolonged absence, due to her having gone with her husband to Lorraine, where he was in command, had cured him of jealousy. Being less devoted, I had naturally become less suspect, and besides we were no longer behaving imprudently. I continued, however, to take the keenest interest in her. Finding her one day in floods of tears and in the most deplorable state, I pressed her so hard to tell me the cause of her sufferings, that she confessed to me amid her sobs that she had fallen in love with Clairval,[36] and that she adored him. She had already told herself a thousand times over, but in vain, everything that I could say to her against so misguided an inclination, the consequences of which were bound to prove fatal. I endeavoured to bring her to reason: I preached to her, I persuaded her to give him up; she gave me a promise which she did not keep. I was painfully distressed to witness the downfall of a person who was so dear to me. I waited upon Clairval: I made him aware of all the dangers that he was incurring, and was making Madame de Stainville incur. I was pleased with his answers: they were both noble and sensible. "Sir," he said to me, "if I alone were in danger, a glance from Madame de Stainville would pay for the loss of my life; I feel myself capable of enduring anything for her sake without complaint; but if it is a question of her happiness, of her peace of mind, tell me the line of conduct that I ought to follow, and you may be sure that I shall not depart from it." He was no more true to his promise than herself. People were beginning to suspect their intrigue. M. le Duc de Choiseul and Madame de Gramont did everything in their power to find out something about it from me. I was loyal to her, nor could either endearments or threats draw anything from me. I sought to alarm her with a picture of the fearful storm that was gathering over her head, without making her alter her conduct. She merely entrusted her papers to my care.

Such was the state of affairs, when Lady Sarah Bunbury,[37] with her husband, Sir Charles Bunbury, arrived in Paris. I was then on duty at Versailles, and did not meet them at first. I feel that I owe my reader some information with regard to this charming woman.

Lady Sarah Lennox was sister to the Duke of Richmond;[38] she is tall; her figure is inclined to stoutness, her hair of the most elegant black, and of a perfect growth; her bosom of a dazzling whiteness, and fresh as rose-leaves. Eyes full of fire and character spoke the seductive and artless graces of her mind. The King of England had been passionately in love with her, and had wished to marry her; but he had lacked the courage to surmount all the obstacles that stood in his way, and she had married a mere baronet of the county of Suffolk. Lady Sarah was kind, sensitive, tender, frank, not to say impulsive, but unfortunately coquettish and fickle. I had been on duty at Versailles for some days when she arrived; and I had heard mention a score of times of her successes in Paris, when I set eyes on her at the Temple[39] for the first time, on my return from Versailles. I arrived in the middle of the concert. M. le Prince de Conti came up to me with his customary kindness, and led me to Lady Sarah: " I beg your kindness, Milady," he said to her, " for my Lauzun; he is very wild, very extravagant, very pleasant; he will do you the honours of Paris better than anyone: permit me to do you his. I stand surety for his desire to win your favour." A respectful curtsey, a few words muttered between her teeth were all Lady Sarah's answer. I scarcely listened to the music: I paid my respects to all the women that I knew. Madame de Cambis summoned me a score of times, spoke to me in a whisper, spared no pains to let all the world know that I had the honour to belong to her. The young men pressed round me. They were interested to learn my opinion of the latest comer: the majority were waiting for my opinion before determining their own, or at least expressing it. I was beginning to be greatly in the fashion; and, without flattering myself that I was an excellent original, I am bound to confess that I had plenty of imitators, without there being one of them successful. " She is not bad," I said; " but I do not see that there is anything in her to turn a man's head. If she spoke good French, and came from Limoges, nobody would give her a thought." There was general laughter at my remark. The self-esteem of Madame de Cambis, who had overheard it, was struck by it. " He is quite right," she said; " it is charming!" And behold our poor Milady fallen from the skies. She had already spoken to her of me as a man whose attentions might be flattering to a woman who was sought after, and had made no secret of the rights that she enjoyed over this famous fop. Supper was announced. M. le Prince de Conti made me take my place at table between Lady Sarah and Madame de Cambis, which brought the latter's triumph to an abrupt conclusion. I was barely conscious of her ill humour at my excessive absorption in the fair stranger: I could think of nothing else. I made friends with her husband; I paid him attentions for which he was grateful, and found a way of establishing myself in their household. Shortly afterwards I made a declaration: she appeared not to hear me; I wrote, my letter was returned to me, and I was informed at the first opportunity, quite casually and without anger: " I do not wish to have a lover. Imagine whether I can have a French lover, who is as bad as ten others by the scandal he creates and the trouble he causes; and you especially, M. le Duc, you do me too great an honour. Do not waste your time upon me; do not speak of love, unless you wish me to bar my door to you." I was too genuinely in love to take offence; I decided to keep my own counsel, and to wait for better times.

Madame de Cambis, growing angry at my neglect, wrote to me that I must choose between her and Lady Sarah, and give up one of them. I was not long in making my choice: all that I did was to make a packet of her letters and send them back to her. That same evening she consoled herself for the loss of me by taking the Chevalier de Coigny,[40] whom she knew that I did not like.

I was distracted from my love-affairs by one of the most painful incidents of my life, one the consequences of which threatened to be even more cruel and more horrible than they proved, in fact, to be. I have spoken already of Madame de Stainville's unfortunate passion for Clairval, and of the precaution that she had taken of giving me her papers to keep. They were in a closet which none but myself ever entered, the key of which remained in my pocket. This closet communicated with the Hôtel de Choiseul, next door to which I was living. An old footman of my father's came one day to see me, and asked me whether I had much money in my closet. Speaking at a venture, I said that I had. "Very well," said he, "take care; someone is certainly trying to rob you; for yesterday evening, as I came in, I saw a man picking the lock of the door that opens into the Hôtel de Choiseul; he made off as soon as he saw me, and I could not tell who he was." I thanked him for his warning. I did not speak of the matter. As I went downstairs that night to Madame de Lauzun's chamber, I told one of my servants, in whom I had full confidence, to make a pretence of going up to his own quarters and to conceal himself without a light outside the closet; to come down to Madame de Lauzun's chamber, if he heard any sound, to warn me; adding that I should leave the door of her closet ajar. About an hour after I was in bed, my man came to tell me that there was somebody in my closet; I went up at once, armed with a brace of pistols; I did indeed find the door of my closet standing ajar; but it was very dark and I had no light: I could make out nothing. I shouted twice:

"Who is there?" but got no answer. A sound which I heard close at hand, and the faint light shed by a few stars, made me decide to fire a pistol at what seemed to me to be a man. The rustle of a silken dressing-gown which I heard at that moment stayed my hand; and fortunately for myself! It occurred to me that the man might be my father, utterly improbable as that was. The man, for it was a man, thrust me rudely aside, and fled, shutting each of the doors upon me in turn, as he made his escape through the Hôtel de Choiseul, into which I pursued him, and lost sight of him, as I heard the door of my father's apartment close with a loud noise. It is easy to imagine with what gloomy thoughts my mind was filled. I spent the night in this closet, and on the next day learned that Madame de Stainville had set off with her husband for Nancy, where she was to be enclosed in a convent by the King's command.

My father sent for me. I found M. le Duc de Choiseul with him, who reproached me with having been in Madame de Stainville's confidence. I replied that there was a vast difference between approving a person's misconduct and keeping a secret. He asked me for the letters that had been entrusted to me, I refused bluntly; my father tried to interpose an exercise of authority which was no more successful. They addressed me in sharp terms; to which I retorted, perhaps with more justification, and the outcome of the conversation was a complete rupture with both of them.

Overcome with grief at the misfortunes of Madame de Stainville, whom I loved as my own sister, I remained for some days without leaving the house. At length I resumed my normal existence; but I felt a sorrow which it was hard to dispel. Lady Sarah perceived this, and spoke to me of it with interest: "I am," I told her, "as wretched as it is possible for a man to be;

LADY SARAH BUNBURY

[*face p.* 32

I am losing, in a horrible manner, a woman who is very dear to me, and I shall never be anything to her whom I adore." I told her the painful story of my poor friend, by which she was deeply touched. I read in her eyes the most tender compassion: a visitor interrupted us; she had just time to tell me: "I am supping to-night with Madame du Deffand."[41]

Although I had not been to Madame du Deffand's for five or six years, I succeeded in having myself taken to the house by Madame de Luxembourg, who was supping there also. Lady Sarah's manner to myself had altogether changed. Her eyes, fastened upon mine, told me a hundred things which I dared not interpret, and I supposed that I was indebted to pity alone for her entire absorption in myself. Her vivacity seemed modified by a gentle languor. She showed a distraction which had great charm for me, since I had reason to believe that I was the cause of it.

When everybody was taking leave of Madame du Deffand, she wrote a few words upon a scrap of paper, and said to me as she went downstairs: "Read this when you go to bed." It may be imagined with what eagerness I returned home! I read these three words written in English: "I love you . . ."* I did not know one word of the English language. It seemed to me that the words must mean: "*Je vous aime*"; but I desired this too ardently to venture to flatter myself that they did. My night passed in reflexions of every kind. At six o'clock in the morning I hastened out in person to buy an English dictionary, which confirmed me in the supposition that I was loved. The reader must have been as passionately in love as I was at that moment to form an idea of my joy. I flew to Lady Sarah, as soon as I might suppose her to be awake. "I have risen betimes," she told

* The paper was torn at this point, and I could not make out the last of the English words.—L.

me with a charming grace, " for I had no doubt that you would come to ask me for breakfast. Let us begin with breakfast. Dismiss your cabriolet, or people will see that you are here, for I mean to bar my door to everyone, so that we can talk without being interrupted. Sir Charles is at the tennis-court, and so is my Lord Carlisle,[42] and they will not come home until dinner-time." We took breakfast: she gave out that she was not at home, and the conversation which I am about to report began:

" I love you, M. de Lauzun, and, seeing you very unhappy and very sensitive, I have been persuaded of your love, and have been unable to resist the pleasure of assuaging your sorrows, by making a confession of my own. Ordinarily, a lover is barely an event in the life of a Frenchwoman; it is the greatest event of all for an Englishwoman: from that moment everything is changed for her, and the loss of her existence and of her repose is commonly the end of a sentiment which in France has none but agreeable consequences, that involve little danger. This certainty, however, does not always restrain us. As we choose our husbands, it is less permissible to us not to love them, and the crime of deceiving them is never forgiven us. I might add to this a genuine remorse for showing such ingratitude for the kindness of Sir Charles, who has made my happiness his principal occupation. I take pleasure in saying to you: I love you; but I am none the less convinced that we need expect nothing but unhappiness from our love. Our nations are always divided by the sea, and often by war. We shall pass the greater part of our lives without meeting one another, and our destiny must incessantly hang upon a lost or intercepted letter. We have everything to fear from my Lord Carlisle; he is in love with me; he has long been reasonable, because he thinks it impossible that I should have a lover; but jealousy will very soon open his eyes, and make him capable of anything. I must also speak to you of my own character: I am by nature a coquette; I will sacrifice my coquetry to you with pleasure, if it rests with me; but your jealousy might bring great unhappiness to us both. I have too good an opinion of you to take into account the risk of surrendering my honour and happiness to your honesty and discretion; judge whether I should, whether I can have a lover!"

"I wish," was my answer, "that you should be happy; but there is no power in the world that can prevent me from adoring you." We promised each other that we would not depart from the strictest circumspection and prudence, and our oaths were soon broken. Lady Sarah loved me warmly, and granted me nothing. Our sincerity, our gaiety interested the world, which, this time, was most indulgent. Lord Carlisle said nothing, in the hope that Lady Sarah would forget me as soon as she left France. I continued to be on the best of terms with the Baronet; Madame de Cambis was for the second time forsaken, by M. le Chevalier de Coigny, for Lady Sarah.

The Chevalier gave himself great pains to win her favour, and great airs to make people think that he had won it. He was pleasant and attractive, and he amused her. I tried in vain to conceal the fact that I was dying of jealousy. One day when I had taken breakfast with Lady Sarah, and was very sad, she rang the bell and said, gazing at me with all the graces which she alone possessed: "Understand that I am never at home to M. le Chevalier de Coigny, upon any pretext"; and, throwing her arms round my neck as soon as we were alone: "You have taught me, my dear," she said, "that a woman may find great pleasure in foregoing the homage of other men when she is in love with one and one only." The time for her departure drew near, and at length the fatal evening came.

Sir Charles Bunbury suggested to Lord Carlisle and myself that we should accompany them for part of the way; we agreed, and we stopped for the first night at Pont-Sainte-Maxence, by Chantilly.

The spectacle of that evening will always remain before me: a single candle illuminated a room that was both dark and dirty, as are almost all the inns of France. Sir Charles sat writing; Lord Carlisle, his head buried in his hands, seemed to be plunged in the profoundest meditations. An old English serving-woman, who had been with him in his childhood, devoured me with a look of hatred, and seemed to pierce me to the marrow. Lady Sarah was crying, and a few tears rolled down my own cheeks in spite of myself. I lay in the same chamber with Lord Carlisle; he could contain himself no longer, and proposed that we should fight a duel upon our return to Paris. My love was returned; it was natural to me to be reasonable, and I answered him with moderation, expecting nevertheless that he would seek a quarrel with me as soon as he could do so without compromising Lady Sarah. We parted at Arras. Lord Carlisle could not bring himself to leave a person who was so dear to him; he returned to England instead of coming back to Paris and proceeding to Italy, as had been his intention. I think that I may here give the letter which Lady Sarah entrusted to me for M. le Prince de Conti, and that which she wrote me from Calais:

"You have been so good to me, Monseigneur, that it would be very bad in me, were I to leave your charming country without thanking you. In truth, I did not believe that it was possible that I should be distressed at leaving France, and that I should leave there the better part of myself. Yes, Monseigneur, it breaks my heart to return to my own land and to leave behind the one man whom I am capable of loving. Lauzun loves me more than everything in the world, and, utterly wretched not to accompany me, there is no sacrifice that he would not make. I tremble lest he come to England without leave, and lest such action involve him in serious consequences. Grant him your protection, Monseigneur, and that leave of absence which will make me so happy. I shall be still happier to be thus indebted to you, for no one, Monseigneur, is more respectfully attached to you than your most humble and most obedient servant,

"SARAH BUNBURY.[43]

"*Arras, the 4th of February*, 1767."

"You have utterly changed my heart, my friend: it is sad and broken; and, although you hurt me so, I can have no thought save for my love. I had no idea that such a thing could happen, and I imagined myself too proud, too virtuous for my happiness ever to depend upon a French lover. The wind is against us, and I am not sorry: it is better to be in the same country. I shed copious tears. I told Sir Charles that I had a headache, and he was satisfied with that. Lord Carlisle did not believe it, for he gazed at me very seriously. . . . Heavens! All this that I am doing must be very wicked, since I try to conceal it, and I, the most truthful woman living, am obliged to lie and to deceive two people whom I esteem so highly! They are gone out, and I have chosen to stay indoors to write to him who is dearer to me than the repose which I have lost for his sake. I dare not send my letter to the post by one of our servants; I have appealed to a waiter in this inn. He has an honest, kindly face; he promises that he will be careful and say nothing to anybody: I should be utterly ruined were he to betray me. Everything vexes and tires me, and so it must be until I can see you. Come as soon as you can without imprudence; for I forbid you to do anything that you may have cause to regret. Obtain leave of absence; M. le Prince de Conti is extremely friendly to you and will help you. Come, so as by your presence to fill your mistress with the greatest joy to which she can look forward. I have no fear of your not understanding my ridiculous French; your heart and mine will always understand each other. Adieu; for I am afraid of being taken by surprise. Remember that it is for you alone that there exists your

"SARAH.

"*Calais, the 6th of February*, 1767."

I returned to Paris, on horseback, and in the most wretched state. A malignant fever would not have altered me more. M. le Prince de Conti was flattered by Lady Sarah's confidence, and responded so readily that at the end of a fortnight I obtained leave to proceed to England. I was received there in a manner calculated to increase my love still further, had that been possible.

After the ceremonies of presentation and official visits which the formal habit of M. le Comte de Guerchy,[44] who was at that time the French Ambassador, would have made unending, I set forth at length for the country with Sir Charles Bunbury and Lady Sarah.

On the morning of our departure, I found at their house a man who resembled nothing so much as a great ostler, and to whom I was presented as to one of the family. He was the guest of honour, and took his place in Lady Sarah's post-chaise. At the first post he complained to Sir Charles that his wife bored him, and they put us together. At the second post he complained that the Frenchman bored him even more than the lady; he then rode with Sir Charles, whom he left half an hour later for a meet of foxhounds where he had caught sight of somebody of his acquaintance. This person was Mr. Lee,[45] at present in the service of the Independent Colonies in America.

The time that I spent at Barton[46] was certainly the happiest of my life. After a few days, the Baronet was obliged to absent himself for three weeks, which I spent in the company of his wife. She showed the most tender affection for me, but would allow me no favour. At length one evening she told me that I might come down to her chamber when the household were gone to bed. I awaited this longed-for moment with the utmost impatience. I found her in bed, and supposed that I might take a few liberties; she appeared so offended and distressed by them that I did not persist. She allowed me, however, to lie down beside her; but she required of me a moderation and reserve of which I thought I should die. This charming torment continued for several nights. I had ceased to hope for a consummation when, clasping me on one occasion in her arms with the liveliest ardour, she gratified all my desires. "I did not wish," she told me, "my lover to take anything from me by force, or to owe anything to my frailty or to his want of respect for me. I wished him to receive everything from my love. I give myself to you; yes, your Sarah is all yours." We went out riding together the next day. "Do you love me more than anything in the world?" she asked me, "and do you feel yourself capable of sacrificing all?" "Oh! as for that, yes," I replied without hesitation, and with the certainty that I would never repent of what I was saying. "Very well!" she continued, gazing at me with those peerless eyes, "are you willing to forsake everything, leave everything to fly to Jamaica, with no thought but for the happiness of your mistress? I have a wealthy kinsman there, with no children, of whose friendship and indulgence I am sure; he will give us an asylum with pleasure." As I was beginning to reply: "Wait," she broke in, "I do not wish to hear your answer for a week." What Lady Sarah was proposing was indeed calculated to secure my greatest happiness. I regretted none of the sacrifices which would probably have cost another man dear; but I could not conceal from myself that she was coquettish, fickle. It seemed to me impossible that she would not cease to love me, that she would not one day repent of having taken so violent a course. Lady Sarah, wretched, complaining, with no position, no social life, at the world's end, able to reproach me with her ruin, it would be hell, and the prospect alarmed me.

The week passed. I confided my fears to her: "It is well, my friend," she remarked, somewhat coldly; "you are more prudent, you have greater foresight than I; you are doubtless right; let us say no more about it." Her manner towards me was unaltered. I seemed, however, to detect a certain constraint in her which disturbed me. Her husband joined us again, and we returned to town. The physicians ordered Sir Charles, who was in somewhat delicate health, to take the waters at Bath; he went there, leaving his wife in London. I felt that it would be proper to go and spend two or three days there with him: I mentioned this to Lady Sarah, who approved and seemed to be grateful to me for the thought. I set off on a Monday, meaning to be in London on the Friday following, before noon. She promised that she would expect me then, would close her door, and spend the whole day with me. I returned to London with all the eagerness of a man who is deeply in love: I was dismayed to find Lady Sarah no longer there, and that she had set off with my Lord Carlisle to go to Goodwood on a visit to the Duke of Richmond, her brother.

All the most rending anguish that rage and jealousy

can inspire took possession of my heart. I wrote Lady Sarah a letter dictated by anger and excitement: I sent it to her at Goodwood by one of my servants. I told her that, if she did not return at once to London, I should regard her as the most wicked, false, and perfidious of women. I awaited the return of my messenger with an unspeakable impatience. He came at length, and brought me a reply which was mild and indeed tender: with certain reproaches as to the way in which I poisoned all the charms of love by my violence. She promised me that she would be in London in two days' time. I waited for her at her house until midnight. During the time that she had fixed, every coach that entered Whitehall seemed as though it must be bringing her, and I saw my hopes revive and perish at every moment throughout that day, the longest perhaps in my life. I returned home, and spent the whole night pacing the floor of my chamber, a prey to the most harassing reflexions.

At six o'clock in the morning came a knock at my door: I was the first to open it. Lady Sarah had just arrived and had sent for me. I ran or rather flew to her side. I found her with a serious and composed expression: a table, upon which everything was set for breakfast, before her, and several servants in the room. More than an hour passed before we were left to ourselves. "Now," she began, "while I need fear no interruption, I have to speak to you of matters which concern both of us alike. You know what charming qualities have won you my heart, you know whether any man was ever so dear to a woman. The very extravagance of your jealousy did not displease me: that of your love was so great a compensation! Your anger, when you thought me a coquette, I have always borne with submission, without resentment, and it has never cost me anything to beg your pardon, when you were not always in the right. You have not had sufficient confidence either in your own constancy or in mine. You have not found that I was necessary to your happiness, nor have you cared to bind yourself to me by ties which nothing could ever break. By rending my heart, you have dimmed your own image in it; you have continued to be jealous and violent, after forfeiting the right to be so: I am conscious now of all the dangers. Nothing can ever make me forget them. If my brother had asked me to show him your letter, how could I have refused him? And if the Duke of Richmond had read it, I was undone, and sacrificed for whom? . . . You have yourself destroyed the sentiment that attached me to you: I no longer love you; but that sentiment has been too tender for its impression, henceforth painful, not to persist for a long while still. From now until a time that is perhaps remote, we cannot expect to meet with indifference; I venture, therefore, to ask you as a favour to leave England, and to count now only upon the tender friendship which I have vowed to you for life."

Thunderstruck by so severe, so unexpected a blow, I swooned away. Lady Sarah, touched by my condition, seated on the ground by my side, tried to restore me, bathing my face with her tears. Mrs. Soames,[47] a sister of Sir Charles Bunbury, came into the room; and, astonished by the spectacle, drew back. "Come in, Mrs. Soames," she said to her; "look after this poor wretch: he is my lover, and I leave him to you." With which words she left the room, stepped into her chaise, and set off to join her husband at Bath. I recovered my senses and returned home, with a show of calm. I decided to take horse and follow Lady Sarah. I had so many things to say to her, that it seemed to me that she would not be lost to me if I could speak to her once again. After going a few miles, I swooned again and vomited a quantity of blood.

LADY SARAH BUNBURY, DISGUISED AS A CLERGYMAN GOING TO MEET LORD WILLIAM GORDON

[*face p. 42*

I found myself in so weak a state that it was impossible for me to proceed any farther. I had great difficulty in reaching London, where I was dangerously ill for many days, and where I received the most generous attention from Mrs. Soames.

Lady Sarah wrote to me with an urgent request that I would not leave the country without coming to bid her farewell at Bath.[48] I could not resist the pleasure, or rather the necessity of seeing her, and of having a final explanation with her. She received me with interest, with friendship; but she had so altered towards me that, so far from thinking of prolonging my stay, I considered hastening my departure. I returned to France very different from the man I had been when I left for England: nothing could distract my mind from a sentiment which was making me so wretched. Lady Sarah was scrupulous meanwhile in writing to me. I knew of no rival lover, but I had been loved by her, and she loved me no more. I was in a state of *savagery* which nothing could diminish. I heard that Lady Sarah was lying ill in London; nothing could restrain me. I set off alone, on horseback, without leave, without a passport.[49] She received with pleasure and gratitude this mark of my affection. " Go, my friend," she said to me after twenty-four hours, " remember that Lady Sarah is nothing more now than your friend. Do not for her sake run all the risks that would be incurred by a longer absence." I received her letters more rarely after my return; finally they ceased altogether. I sought every possible way of forgetting her, but without success. I tried to lead the same sort of life as before I had met her. I could no longer attach myself to any woman; any comparison was too greatly to their disadvantage: my whole character was altered. I had lost my gaiety, all the attractions that had made me popular. I was no longer sensible of the pleasures that formerly had had the greatest charm for me.

I did nevertheless seize every occasion that offered to distract myself from so profound a grief, but almost always without success. I made the acquaintance, at the Opera ball, of an extremely pretty girl. She has made too much stir to pass without mention; her name was Mademoiselle Vaubernier: she was known as "the Angel" on account of her heavenly countenance; she was living with M. le Comte du Barry,[50] who maintained her only by his intrigues, and by having recourse to the most desperate expedients. I was bidden to sup at the house, which had an excellent style, and where there were some most presentable persons; but it would be impossible to conceive a greater figure of fun than that of my host. M. du Barry was wearing a superb dressing gown, with his hat on his head, balancing two baked apples which he had been ordered to place upon his eyes. I met there one Madame de Fontanès, come up from Lyons with the plan of becoming King's mistress, and ready in the meantime to be mistress to the first comer: I felt a desire, and M. le Comte du Barry, always obliging, enabled me to achieve my purpose on the very next day; I do not think that I ever saw this Madame de Fontanès again. After this, the Angel aroused desires in me and did not refuse to satisfy them; but I was overawed by the red eyes and feeble health of M. du Barry. M. de Fitz-James[51] was bolder than I, won and kept her; which did not prevent her from treating me with all the little courtesies that meant no danger to either.

About this time, M. le Duc de Choiseul decided upon the conquest of Corsica, and dispatched there M. le Marquis de Chauvelin with sixteen battalions.[52] Such a chance of tasting powder and shot was too precious to be neglected. I was not on such good terms with all my relatives that they were afraid of my being killed. And so I received employment as aide-de-camp to M. de Chauvelin. The day on which my appointment was published, M. le Prince de Conti spoke of it, in his box at the Opera, in the presence of several girls; one of them, who was very pretty, very headstrong, burst into tears, saying amid her sobs: " I am in despair, for I see now that I am madly in love with him. Monsieur," she said to me, " I give myself absolutely to you; you shall do with me whatever you choose until your departure." It would indeed be impossible to find a wilder and more amiable mistress. She was maintained by a rich man, named M. de Romé,[53] who was greatly annoyed to see me often consorting with her. Mademoiselle Têtard declared to him that he positively must consent, or else lose her for ever. He tried one day to find fault with her for having spent the night with me, and to make a scandal: I treated him somewhat cavalierly. He was positively driven from the house; but, as I was to be leaving shortly afterwards, and it might be to his advantage to show some consideration for so respectable a person, he gave me a thousand louis, begged pardon for his crossness, and consented to Mademoiselle Têtard's retaining me, on condition that the secret was shared by no more than a dozen discreet persons. Before I cease to speak of Mademoiselle Têtard, I ought to tell you of a rather amusing thing that she did, when the rumour was going about that I had been killed in Corsica. She went to find the Abbé d'Artis, with whom she had previously lived, and who was a priest; she obliged him to go on pilgrimage to Notre-Dame, to say a mass for my soul, and happily this mass brought me no mishap.

A few days before my departure for Corsica, I was told that the King had seen the Angel, that he had remarked her, and that it was thought that he would take a fancy to her. I went to take leave of her, and to congratulate her upon so brilliant a success. "If you are the King's mistress, fair Angel," I said to her, "bear in mind that I wish to have command of the army." "That is not enough," she replied; "you shall be at least First Minister." The Angel had had dealings with M. de Choiseul, and had been anxious to sleep with him in order to ensure their success. M. le Duc de Choiseul, prejudiced, with good reason, against M. du Barry, refused to hear of such a thing. She is perhaps the only woman whose favours he ever refused, and the whole of Europe has shared in the important consequences of this refusal.

I cannot pass in silence over a distinctly singular event which occurred shortly before my departure for Corsica. On the day of M. le Prince de Lamballe's funeral, I went to see Madame Brissard,[54] who combined with her eight and seventy years a wide acquaintance and a mind as obstinate as it was original. She had a mania for hearing her fortune told, and ran after all the soothsayers in Paris. She told me that she had seen one of these the day before who had told her the most extraordinary things and, she believed, the most secret: she filled me with a curiosity, and gave me the address of M. Dubuisson (such was the soothsayer's name). I called upon him in the rue Saint-André-des-Arts. He lodged, according to the custom, on the fifth floor. He appeared to me to be merely a fool, and told me what follows: "that, upon returning home that same day, I should find a letter which would distress me greatly; that a month later, to the day, I should receive a most comforting letter from the same person; that I should have a quarrel, that I should be on the point of fighting with a person who would offer me an apology; that I should take an illness of which I should think myself in no danger; that I should make war in a country to which I was not expecting to go, and that I should be killed upon an island at nightfall after a battle had been fought and lost." I received the two letters, I had my sword in my hand when an apology was offered me; I fell ill, and I started for Corsica in the month of June 1768. I found at Toulon M. Chardon,[55] the Lieutenant of Corsica, who was taking with him his wife, eighteen years old, and pretty; she seemed to me to be a gift from the gods, and I began, in all sincerity, to pay her attentions which were not well received.

I had orders not to proceed to Corsica without M. de Chauvelin, whom I had left behind in Paris. I heard that there would be fighting, and embarked upon His Majesty's xebec, *Le Singe*, bound for Saint-Florent. M. de Bompart,[56] commander of the naval forces, procured me a landing order. I landed on the island. I took nobody but Madame Chardon into my confidence, and spent the evening in a fisherman's boat. M. de Chauvelin arrived three weeks after me,[57] and placed me under arrest for some days.

I went to war with the ardour and activity of a light-hearted man who is anxious to show his worth. My affair with Madame Chardon made no headway; she was polite, but nothing more than polite. I needed only a mistress to be perfectly happy, and did not at all lose heart. M. de Chauvelin's initial success did not long continue: the infantry of the Royal Legion, the company of Languedoc Grenadiers, etc., had been shut up in Borgo, ill fortified, and attacked for five and thirty days by all the most formidable elements in Corsica, when M. de Chauvelin determined to relieve Borgo, and with such a disposal of his forces that it was impossible to doubt the evil issue of that day; nor have I ever beheld such consternation as prevailed in Bastia. The danger in which we all believed ourselves when we emerged made us forget every other consideration. Madame Chardon gave me a white plume which I wore in my hat, and which certainly brought me good luck, since it did not cause my death; it marked me out in such a way that every shot was aimed by preference at myself. All the world knows how the day went at Borgo, and how disastrous it was to our little army.[58] The battle was lost; M. de Chauvelin, hotly pressed, had been obliged to retire in such confusion that the shots even reached his field ambulance.

We perceived, with despair, that we were abandoning M. de Marbœuf,[59] with a third of our troops, on the other side of Golo, and that all communication with them was severed. There remained a way of escape along the sea which we could indicate to M. le Comte de Marbœuf, supporting him with a few companies of grenadiers; but he must first be reached, and this dangerous commission required a reconnaissance of the country which no one had made but myself, who had already been in Corsica with M. de Marbœuf. I volunteered and set off alone with my hussar. When I had gone about five hundred yards, several shots were fired at me, from the bushes, which did not stop me, and I rode on at full gallop; but I was soon held up by a considerable belt of musketry, which must, I thought, come from one of the principal bodies of the Corsican army. I turned back, preferring to make my way down to the coast and pass along the water's edge.

The Regiment of Soissons, which was escorting M. de Chauvelin, had formed in battle order and had begun to advance as soon as the first shots were heard, replying to them with a brisk and sustained fire from both battalions, under which I must pass. I retired nevertheless upon this fire, and at that moment M. Dubuisson's prediction came into my mind; and, I confess to my shame, I thought myself lost. I rode up to a company which had ceased fire, and was recognised. I proceeded along the shore among the rocks, and joined M. de Marbœuf, who was being hotly pursued by the Corsicans and was wounded, as were MM. d'Arcambale[60] and Campême, while I was speaking to him. I indicated to him the safest way of reaching M. de Chauvelin, whom he joined without mishap. M. de Chauvelin told me that his misfortunes did not prevent him from being conscious of the value of the service that I had rendered; that he would ask for the Cross of Saint-Louis for me, and believed that he could promise me it before the whole army. He never said a word of it to anybody again.

I found at headquarters a little note from Madame Chardon, who, already informed of our defeat, begged me to husband the days of a life in which she took an interest, and promised me that she would make them happy. The army was retiring slowly upon Bastia; I outstripped it by paths which were known to me, and was in the town two hours before the rest. Madame Chardon kept her word and gave herself to me with a sincerity and affection which made me remember her kindly ever since. Her husband, who was beginning to be jealous of me, returned; he supposed that I had remained in the rear, and decided to take advantage of the moment to lay a trap for his wife and discover her feelings: he told her as he came in that all was lost; that the army had been almost destroyed; many of his acquaintance slain, and named myself among the dead. "Then I have restored him to life," she told him with a laugh, "for he is in the next room, dead tired it is true, but I can assure you that he is not dead."

A number of other reverses followed the unhappy day of Borgo. Shots were fired up to the gates of Bastia: this was the kind of life that suited me best; to be under fire all day and to sup at night with my mistress! M. Chardon's jealousy was somewhat disturbing to my happiness: his wife was to be pitied and was often harshly treated; but we all know that a moment of love will pay for an age of suffering.

M. de Chauvelin went. M. le Comte de Marbœuf became friendly and acquired confidence in me. We were in the month of January: all was quiet. I asked his leave to go and spend a couple of days on the Cape of Corsica, and he granted it. He learned during my absence that Clemente Paoli[61] had formed the plan of passing through the redoubts, penetrating to the Cape, and attacking it, at the same moment, from every point. M. de Marbœuf did not hear of this plan until almost the moment of its execution. It was important to occupy Montebello, in front of Bastia; he wished to send me there with some companies of grenadiers; but I was not to be had; and it was necessary that they should march that evening. He asked Madame Chardon repeatedly whether I was going to return that day. She perceived that there was something in the wind, pressed him closely, and discovered his secret. She flung herself, weeping, upon the bosom of M. de Marbœuf, who loved her dearly. "You know M. de Lauzun," she said to him: "he would be less dear to me, were he capable of forgiving me for making him lose, by my negligence, an opportunity of distinguishing himself, however dangerous it might be. I am going to send him a message, without telling him what is in the air, and I give you my word that he will be here before the detachment moves." I arrived at her house without suspecting anything. "Do not lose an instant," she said to me, as she took me in her arms; "go to M. de Marbœuf; he has something to say to you. He will prove to you that I am as devoted to your renown as to your person." I was not sorry to take possession of Montebello before the Corsicans. I should have spent a very cold night there, had it not been warmed by frequent attacks. I discovered

M. de Marbœuf in the plain at daybreak. We passed, with fixed bayonets, through the surrounding Corsicans, and joined forces with him. They retired in considerable numbers upon the village of Barbaggio, which we continued to bombard throughout the day without success.

On the following day people came out from Bastia to watch our siege, as though to a play. The position itself provided shelter for those who chose only to be spectators. Madame Chardon came out on horseback, and kept by the side of M. de Marbœuf. Her husband returned to town to take command of a second ambulance, the number of our wounded being very considerable. A numerous force from the Pieve of Rostino gained a small plain, from which they opened a murderous fire upon our battery, and killed many of our gunners. M. de Marbœuf ordered me to charge them with five dragoons of the Soubise Legion. I obeyed at once. Madame Chardon wished to accompany me. I tried to prevent her, and then to have her arrested so as to send her back to M. de Marbœuf; but she sprang upon a horse, and galloped past me. "Do you suppose," she said to me, "that a woman is never to risk her life save in childbed; and cannot she be permitted once in her life to follow her lover?" She bore a heavy fire with the utmost calm; giving all the money she had in her pockets to the soldiers and dragoons, and did not come back to me until the affair was at an end. The whole army kept the secret of this charming piece of folly, with a loyalty which one would not have dared expect of three or four persons.

All the world knows the outcome of the affair of Barbaggio, and that the modesty of M. de Marbœuf, who would not have the news conveyed by an officer, cost him the command of the army; the post vessel having been detained in Italy, instead of proceeding to

France, the news arrived there only after the appointment of M. le Comte de Vaux.[62]

To soothe M. Chardon's jealousy, I went to spend six weeks at Roscane: I then returned to Corsica, where I heard of the marriage and presentation of Madame la Comtesse du Barry. I served through the campaign with M. le Comte de Vaux, as adjutant-general of his army. Nothing remarkable happened to me, and he sent me home on the 24th of June to convey to the court the news of the complete submission of the island, and of M. Paoli's departure. I did not leave Corsica without regret, and I have often since then thought with regret of the rocks among which I spent what was perhaps the happiest year of my life. It cost me a great deal to abandon Madame Chardon, for whom I felt the most tender love and affection, and whom I was leaving in so wretched a plight. I foresaw all the obstacles that would stand in the way of our reunion, and this parting was truly painful to us both. I set sail, therefore, from Bognomana sorrowful and sick; for I had just had the measles. I posted day and night, and arrived, half dead with exhaustion, at Saint-Hubert,[63] upon the 29th of June 1769, at five o'clock in the evening.

The King was in Council: I asked for M. le Duc de Choiseul, and handed him my dispatches. The King bade me come in, received me with all sorts of kindness, and ordered me to remain at Saint-Hubert, as I was, in a travelling coat and boots. My curiosity to see the Angel in so different a state made me remain with pleasure: I waited in the saloon for the Council to finish; she was not long in appearing, came and embraced me in the most friendly fashion, and said with a laugh: "Who would ever have thought that we should meet again here?" The King, seeing that she appeared to be on the most familiar terms with me, asked her whether she knew me. "He has long," she replied without embarrassment, "been one of my friends." M. le Duc de Choiseul was anxious to make his peace with me, and did so with such good grace, that I was touched by it, and vowed an attachment to him of which I have often given him proof since then, and which would never have altered, had he chosen. I was given the Cross of Saint-Louis as a reward for my tidings: this honour, flattering at my age, did no harm to anyone, and gave me great pleasure.

I accompanied the King to Compiègne,[64] and continued to be kindly treated by him, as well as by Madame du Barry. The King proposed to Marshal Biron[65] to give me the reversion of the Regiment of French Guards. Whether he thought that the King had been advised by M. le Duc de Choiseul, or because he felt the repugnance natural in old men to a successor, he raised the objection of my youth and refused. M. le Duc de Choiseul wished to give me the Corsican Legion which he was then raising, which tempted me greatly, or a regiment of four battalions: I refused, and remained in the Guards regiment out of deference to my father.

In the course of our progress from Compiègne, M. du Barry bade me meet him in the forest, and I joined him there on the following morning. He complained to me of the spite that M. le Duc de Choiseul was showing against Madame du Barry and himself; told me that she did justice to so great a Minister, and ardently desired to live on good terms with him, and that he should not force her to be his enemy; that she had more influence over the King than Madame de Pompadour had ever had, and that it would distress her greatly if he obliged her to employ it to his hurt. He begged me to make a report of this conversation to M. le Duc de Choiseul, and to make him all manner of protestations of attachment. I executed my commision. M. le Duc de Choiseul received it with the arrogance of a Minister persecuted by the ladies, who imagines that he has nothing to fear. And so an implacable war was declared between him and the King's mistress; and Madame la Duchesse de Gramont, in her outrageous remarks, did not spare even the King himself.

I continued to be kindly treated by one and all; I could see that this state of things could not last, and gradually decreased my assiduity at court. M. Chardon obtained leave of absence for his private affairs, and brought to Paris his wife, driven to desperation by his harsh treatment, and desiring nothing better than to be parted from him. Her father, M. de Maupassant, had given 200,000 francs to Madame de Langeac[66] for the promise of the first vacant billet as farmer-general, which she had secured for someone else, without restoring his money to him, which was quite in her style. This unhappy man, who had borrowed the greater part of the sum, was ruined, and saw the prospect of passing the rest of his life in a prison. He was very far from being devoid of talent; he was gifted in many ways. I came to his rescue; went bail for him; lent him all the money that he required; spoke of him to M. de Choiseul, who promised me, for M. de Maupassant, a place as farmer-general of the posts, on condition that Madame Chardon separated from her husband, and that her father gave her a pension of 40,000 francs out of his place. M. Chardon agreed to everything. I was able to see her but rarely, and in a manner that was dangerous for her. M. Chardon had returned to Corsica, and had left his wife in Paris.

I went to Fontainebleau, where the King was; half an hour before the hunt, they came to inform me that there was a lady at the gate who was asking for me; I could not imagine who she might be. I went, and, greatly to my astonishment, found Madame

Chardon on her way to rejoin her husband in Corsica. A priest had turned her head, and had persuaded her that this was an indispensable duty; nothing could stop her. M. le Duc de Choiseul was extremely angry, and refused to give the place in the posts to M. de Maupassant, who died of grief. This cost me more than 100,000 crowns, which I had gone bail for him. I have since then had many opportunities of meeting Madame Chardon; I am bound in justice to her to say that she has never ceased to take the keenest interest in my fortunes.

Towards the end of 1769, a very pretty dancer at the Opera, named Mademoiselle Audinot,[67] reproached me with not having recognised her; I remembered that I had indeed acted in a play with her at l'Île-Adam,[68] when she was a mere child. It would be hard to find a more seductive person. We took a fancy to one another; but it did not, for some time, carry us any farther. She was being sumptuously maintained by Marshal Soubise,[69] closely guarded by her mother and by many other persons. She was living up two pair of stairs, in the Rue de Richelieu, in a fairly ancient house, which shook whenever a coach went past. An idea came to me which proved a complete success; I bribed a maidservant who had a key made for me, and found an English carriage which made a great noise; I made it pass beneath the windows, and, with this aid, entered and left the house so that the mother, who lay in the next room, did not hear me. This state of things continued almost throughout the winter. We were discovered at length, but they were obliged to permit what they could not prevent. The girl loved me dearly; she wished to leave M. de Soubise, but I restrained her; he heard of this and was grateful to me, and told her that she might keep me. He undertook the care of a child to which she gave birth, and which died shortly afterwards.

I was now leading a pleasant and quiet life. I was enjoying all the delights of a brilliant and clamorous society, and all the pleasures that can be afforded by a pretty mistress. The married women, hostile by nature to all girls, found fault with me for not attaching myself to one in good society. The image of Lady Sarah was not effaced from my heart. I had not been able to hear without great emotion that she had ruined herself for Lord William Gordon; I wished to avoid any serious attachment. I met nevertheless at l'Île-Adam Madame la Vicomtesse de Laval.[70] Her manners attracted me as greatly as did her figure. I paid great attention to her, and this did not seem to displease her. I made declarations, but she replied to them always as though they had been pleasantries. Her first lover had sickened her of men, and with some reason: M. le Duc de Luxembourg[71] had exposed her with an impudence and a want of honour which had bidden fair to ruin her. She began nevertheless to show a liking for myself and a pleasure in my company.

One day when, as we were about to leave l'Île-Adam and I was to go on horseback, it was raining in torrents; she said to me: " I should like to save you a drenching, but I dare not take you in my carriage before everyone; if you will leave l'Ile-Adam and enter Paris on horseback, I will take you the rest of the way." I accepted with joy, but unfortunately we had been overheard by Madame de Cambis, who would have been very sorry to let slip this opportunity of thwarting my plans. She waited until the Vicomtesse was ready to step into her carriage, and asked her to take her home, on the pretext that she could not obtain post horses until late in the day. There was no way of refusing her. Madame de Laval appeared quite as impatient as myself, and set off. I accompanied them on horseback; presently, as we climbed a hill, I was on one side of the road and their carriage on the other; Madame de Laval was gazing at me uneasily, and Madame de Cambis was speaking with warmth; it was easy to see that she was speaking evil of me, and I thanked her in an expressive manner for the services that she was rendering me. She was put to confusion: the Vicomtesse began to laugh, and we continued on our way. Madame de Laval, alarmed by her former choice, showed a liking for and an interest in me, but received me coldly as soon as I laid claim to something more.

The rage of M. de Choiseul and his ladies[72] against Madame du Barry was more violent than ever, and the impropriety of their criticisms of a Prince to whom they owed everything infinitely diminished the merit of a noble and courageous conduct. My father lived with Madame du Barry on the same terms as he had lived with all the other mistresses, a little less intimately, however, on account of M. de Choiseul. I visited them rarely, and was in their bad books for having declared that I would never allow Madame de Lauzun to visit them. I was not aware that proposals had been made to Madame de Luxembourg to go on one of the short excursions of the court, and that she had almost made up her mind. My firmness checked her, and she had not the courage to accept. M. le Duc d'Aiguillon and Marshal Richelieu[73] were forming a powerful cabal against M. le Duc de Choiseul. M. le Prince de Condé joined forces with them; in the end they carried the day, and M. le Duc de Choiseul was banished to Chanteloup,[74] on the 24th of December 1770. Never did favour make a Minister so famous as this disgrace. The consternation was general, and in every class of life there was no one who did not seek to show M. de Choiseul some token of attachment and veneration.

I had no hesitation in devoting myself to his cause. I took a large sum of money and letters of credit upon different places in Europe, and prepared to accompany him in his flight. Everyone was convinced that there was a price upon his head, and that he would presently be obliged to leave the country to escape arrest. I received, before starting, two most generous offers from two persons of widely different condition. Mademoiselle Audinot sent me 4,000 louis, which were her whole fortune, and was positively in despair at my refusing them. Madame la Vicomtesse de Laval, who had as yet granted me no favour, wrote to me that she had heard of my decision and that I was going to Madame la Duchesse de Gramont, and begged me to spend the evening before my departure with her. "Your conduct," she told me, "shows me how worthy you are to be loved, and makes me long to be able to have still some part in your happiness." She made me as happy as a man can be, and nothing that has occurred since then could make me forget this charming action.

I stayed for three weeks at Chanteloup, after which I returned to mount guard at Versailles. A few leagues from Paris, I found a letter and horses sent by M. de Guéménée. He informed me that it had been proposed at the Council to clap me in the Bastille, and that Marshal Soubise alone had opposed the plan; that Madame du Barry insisted stoutly that I should be taught not to go to Chanteloup without leave, or to carry letters to M. de Choiseul. I knew very well that they would not dare arrest me in Paris; but I was afraid of the barrier. I made for that of Varennes, quite determined, should I see the slightest movement, to make a dash past the Invalides and swim across the river. I came through without mishap, and arrived at my own little house, in the Rue Saint-Pierre, where I found all the friends of M. le Duc de Choiseul awaiting me.

I appeared that evening at Versailles at Madame la Dauphine's[75] ball, where I caused a stir. Everyone gathered round me to ask the latest news from Chanteloup, and everyone seemed to admire my courage. Never in my life had I a finer part to play. Madame la Dauphine came to me with that grace which was even then inseparable from her actions, and said to me: " How is M. de Choiseul ? When you see him, tell him that I shall never forget what I owe to him, and that I shall always take the most sincere interest in him." I returned to Chanteloup after I had finished my guard, and spent there all the rest of my time when I was not on duty. I was moreover in the most open disgrace. The King no longer spoke to me, and I was never bidden to supper in the Royal private apartments.

Madame de Laval continued to behave in the most perfect manner towards me. Madame de Lauzun was beginning to repent of the sort of disdain with which she had treated me since our marriage. Madame la Princesse de Poix, that same Madame de Poix whom I had wished to marry,[76] inspired her with the desire to master a man whom she had rated too low, and who was now become a general favourite. Sentiment was the one simple way of retracing her steps, and the only one that called for no explanation. And so she played the card of passion, became or pretended to become jealous of Madame de Laval, tried to persuade Madame de Luxembourg to bar her door to her, and was so far successful that, but for M. de Guéménée and my own courageous coolness, the poor little woman must have been ruined for ever or sacrificed to the falsity of Madame de Lauzun's nature. The latter placed herself under the protection of Madame la Duchesse de Gramont, and presently Chanteloup, where I had some title to be left undisturbed, became intolerable to me because of the desperate efforts that were made there to make me fall in love with my wife and to speak evil to me of Madame de Laval.

About this time I came upon an old acquaintance at the moment when I least expected such a thing. One day when I was attending the first performance of a new piece at the Comédie Française, I saw in a box close to my own a woman of very presentable appearance, who was watching me with close attention. I observed that she asked my name, and then began to look at me curiously. As we were leaving the theatre, she came up to me. "May I venture to ask, sir, if your name is not the Comte de Biron?" "Yes, Madame, you never spoke a truer word." "And you do not know me?" "I cannot remember that I have ever had the honour of meeting you." "What! You do not recognise a little girl who treated you very ungratefully; you have forgotten Rosalie?" "Rosalie!" I exclaimed. "Can it be possible?" "If I still arouse in you any interest or any curiosity, come and discuss a bird with me: I am alone, and nothing shall prevent me from telling you all that has happened to me since I left you." I accepted with pleasure. "Dismiss your carriage and servants," she said to me, "and let me take you home." Rosalie had a neat carriage and servants in handsome livery. She took me to a house that was elegantly furnished. "You are now in my house," she told me; "I must begin by begging your pardon, for I have indeed behaved amiss towards you. You will remember doubtless that you were in the country when I deserted, and this is what led me astray. An American of great wealth had seen me several times in town and had desired to have me; he made proposals to me through my maid. I preferred yourself, and refused; finally he offered me an annual income of 10,000 livres if I would go with him to America. This fortune, which I could not expect from you, and my maid's advice made me decide. We sailed soon afterwards. I was distinctly fortunate in having fallen into the hands of an estimable man: I devoted myself to securing his happiness and comfort. He was grateful to me: my care of him helped to save him from two terrible illnesses, when his life was in the greatest danger. Having no family, the sole artisan of his fortune, with no one to whom he need make account, he married me. The climate of San Domingo being bad for his health, which is still delicate, he decided to seek a recovery in Europe, and has brought with him a considerable fortune. We have been here for six months; his health is now perfectly restored, and he is gone to inspect a fine estate in Auvergne, which he intends to purchase and where he means to pass his summers. I have often asked for news of you since I came to Paris; but you had changed your name; and, besides, I see but few people, and those not capable of enlightening me. I was in despair of meeting you, when I happened just now to catch sight of you." An excellent little supper was served, after which I sought to re-establish my former rights. "Stop," she cried; "you must realise that it is impossible for Rosalie to refuse you if you insist: be so generous as not to interrupt my fidelity. I should like to tell my husband that I have found you again, and to tell him all." I did not insist; at midnight she sent me home. She has written to me several times; but I have never seen her again.

I was still in the habit of going to Chanteloup; but all danger to M. le Duc de Choiseul was passed. I no longer thought myself necessary to his safety, and people were teasing me there. I continued to make frequent excursions thither; but was no longer spending my whole time there, as before. I was more intimate than ever with M. le Prince de Guéménée, and we were almost always together. He took me to Madame de Rothes; and I discovered in Madame la Comtesse Dillon[77] that charming person whom I had mistaken for Mademoiselle de Boufflers, some years earlier, at the ball given by Marshal Mirepoix's lady. There can be few women in whom such talent, beauty, and amiable and estimable qualities have been combined: kindly, noble, generous, still a true friend after ten years. I have pleasure in affirming that, granted the desire to attract, the means, and the certainty of doing so, nobody could accuse Madame Dillon of the least shadow of coquetry. A taste for sport and country pleasures made the tie of friendship closer, and I became as constant a visitor to her house as M. de Guéménée. It was not long before I noticed how precious Madame Dillon was to him, and how delicate and discreet was his manner of loving. I did not myself escape from so dangerous a snare. I saw with regret that I was in love with Madame Dillon, but, great God, how little did this love resemble the rest! I hoped for nothing from it; I saw no future prospect; I dared not even desire the possibility of success. I blamed myself, moreover, for such a sentiment, as for an act of betrayal, towards a woman to whom I could not doubt that M. de Guéménée had vowed a lifelong devotion. I furnished the strongest weapons against myself, under the pretext of confidence. I concealed nothing from Madame Dillon that was calculated to repel a woman from me. I displayed my character to her as being far lighter than it really was: I displayed to her my love of independence; I admitted that I was by nature inconstant. I never had girls to supper, I never gratified any fancy that I did not at once report to her; and the life that I was leading could not win the approval of a woman who took any interest in me, after the image that I sought to present.

When I was on guard at Versailles, one evening after supper, at Madame de Guéménée's,[78] the talk ran on sentiment, and I was arguing with Madame de Montesquiou,[79] with all the more eloquence, perhaps, since I dared not avow the sentiment to which I myself was susceptible. Madame la Marquise de Fleury,[80] who had listened to me with an air of astonishment, said to me: "What! M. de Lauzun, you are a man of sentiment? It is inconceivable!" The party broke up. I retired to my quarters in the guard house. At four o'clock in the morning my servant wakened me and gave me a letter which, he said, had been brought by a footman of Madame la Comtesse de Provence.[81] This letter, written in a hand that was strange to me, contained a declaration of the clearest and most passionate kind. I recalled the conversation overnight. I had the bearer sent in, I asked him in whose service he was, and all was made clear, when I learned that he belonged to Madame la Marquise de Fleury. I replied that I would call upon her in the morning; nor did I fail her. I thanked her for the favour that she showed me, and informed her, in so many words, that my heart was pledged to an old attachment, which allowed no room for a new. She would not take this as final, but displayed, with the utmost shamelessness and publicity, her affection for myself, and the scant success with which it had met. She made scenes wherever she met me, and I took as great pains to avoid her as she to pursue me.

There was, about this time, the prospect of a tiresome scene. The Vicomtesse de Laval had her children inoculated at the Gros-Caillou. I went to see her one morning; she invited me to supper that evening; I declined, in fear of meeting Madame la Marquise de Fleury, who was often there, and of incurring a fresh scene. I was to find that I had not been mistaken. She assured me that there would be only herself, perhaps her husband, and two or three persons whom she named to me. I arrived there rather late in the evening, and a moment later the Marquise de Fleury entered, and examined us with the most embarrassing attention. She refused to sit down to table, and wrote me, during supper, a long letter, in which she warned me of a terrible scene after supper, telling me that she could no longer doubt that the Vicomtesse de Laval was the true cause of my coldness towards herself, and that she was going, that very instant, to inform her husband. I had the greatest trouble in calming this fury; she took me home with her, where the whole night passed in tears, explanations, threats. She left a few days later for the country; and, fortunately for myself, a new passion banished the former, which had so greatly alarmed me.

Shortly after this we parted, Madame de Laval and I, without actually parting, and indeed without ceasing to see each other frequently. She did not provide me with a successor that could flatter my self-esteem, for he was the Marquis de Laval,[82] her brother-in-law, whose charms are too well known to require description.

My position began to alarm me: I had no longer a mistress; I had refused one woman, I had parted from the other; and, when I explored my heart, I could not conceal from myself that Madame Dillon was the guiding principle of my conduct. I felt then that it was my duty to warn M. de Guéménée, and to let him read all that was passing in my heart. He received me with that generous confidence to which only honourable hearts are susceptible, did not conceal from me that he adored Madame Dillon, but swore to me that he was still unaware that he had made any impression upon her. She treated us, indeed, with such perfect impartiality, that it was impossible to distinguish the slightest preference. "Let us each work for himself," he said to me, "and if Madame Dillon chooses a lover, let her not lose a friend." I told him that I had made up my mind to travel for a time; he sought in vain to dissuade me, but Madame

Dillon's approaching confinement delayed my departure. I doubt whether anyone has ever seen two rivals show more confidence in one another, or love one another more dearly.

Madame Dillon's confinement was dangerous, long and painful.[83] Our attentions, equally tender, equally untiring, lightened her burden a little; she appeared touched by my situation, and shared it without, however, showing me a preference that could in any way alter my plans. She recovered her health, and I fixed my departure for England for the 15th December 1772. I believed her to feel a strong liking for myself; but I knew that she did not wish to feel it; I did not even desire the greatest happiness that could exist for me on earth. The fifth of December drew round; we were riding through the forest of Compiègne, for the whole party from Hautefontaine[84] were returning that day to Paris. We made little use of the freedom in which the others left us to converse; everyone kept at a distance from us, but I had either nothing or too many things to say. When we reached the carriages, Madame Dillon embraced me, and we parted with tears in our eyes. Madame de Rothes had hitherto appeared neither to take sides nor to advise her daughter; but I fancied that her preference was for myself. My departure for England was an entire renunciation of my rights, or rather a formal admission that I had none, and that I could not honourably expect any.

I arrived in London on the 20th December 1772, and that same evening M. le Comte de Guines,[85] the French Ambassador, took me to the assembly at my Lady Harrington's.[86] I found there various old acquaintances. A woman better dressed both as to her costume and her hair than Englishwomen generally are entertained the room. I asked who she was; I was told that she was a Pole, and that her name was Madame la Princesse Czartoryska.[87] A figure of middling size but perfect, the finest eyes, hair, teeth, a charming foot, very dark, heavily pitted with the smallpox and with no complexion, gentle in her manner, and showing an inimitable grace in every movement, Madame Czartoryska proved that without being beautiful a woman could still be charming. I learned that she had as lover a Russian named Prince Repnin,[88] a man of merit and distinction, formerly Ambassador at Warsaw, who adored her, and had left everything to follow her and to devote himself entirely to her. Madame Czartoryska seemed to me gay, coquettish and amiable; but anyone who told me then that she was to have so great an influence over the rest of my life would have astonished me greatly. Gloomily occupied with all that I regretted leaving behind me in France, I asked for nothing better than a distraction.

M. le Comte de Guines had at that time, with the greatest publicity possible, a very pretty little woman whom her fatuity and the calamities that she thought fit to bring about have made famous in England. Sweet, simple, loving, it was impossible to see Lady Craven[89] without feeling interested in her.

I went often to her house, and always met there one Mrs. Hampden,[90] step-daughter to my Lord Trevor, to whom the Ambassador advised me to pay court. This was a tall woman, straight and stiff, with a good enough figure, a good complexion, fair eyes, and good features; the whole was marred by the absence of a tooth in the front of her mouth, which forced everyone who saw her to exclaim: "What a pity that woman has not good teeth!" My homage was very kindly received; women, in England, love writing letters. I slipped a declaration into Mrs. Hampden's muff, and that evening, at a small dance at the Russian Envoy's, she gave me her answer. It was keen, tender, and promised great things. I had gone into another room to read it: Mrs. Hampden, who had followed me, snatched the letter from my hands as soon as she saw that I had finished reading it, and flung it into the fire; this insulting want of confidence annoyed me, and caused a coolness. Mrs. Hampden made vain attempts afterwards at a reconciliation, but I replied only by sarcasm.

I could not resist the pleasure of seeing Lady Sarah again. I learned that she was occupying a small farm named Halnaker,[91] in the Duke of Richmond's park at Goodwood; that she was living there in the utmost solitude and would see nobody. I set out alone on horseback from London, and arrived after great difficulty at nine o'clock on a winter night at the door of Halnaker. I knocked several times, but no one came; at length a little girl came to inquire what was my errand; I replied that I was a servant of my Lady Holland, and that I had a letter to give to Lady Sarah. "Come in," she said. I went upstairs without any light; I passed through a room of some size which was very dark, and made for the door of a farther room, from which a light seemed to be shining. I opened a door to which Lady Sarah had her back turned; she was engaged in giving supper to a very pretty little girl, who was alarmed at the sight of me. Lady Sarah saw me, took the child in her arms, and came towards me. "Embrace my daughter, Lauzun, do not hate her, forgive her mother; and remember that if she were to lose her, she would have no protector left but yourself."

Lady Sarah, withdrawn from the world, dressed in a plain blue gown, her hair cut quite short and unpowdered, was more beautiful, more seductive than she had ever been. After six years, we were unable to meet without great emotion. I promised to take charge of her daughter whenever she chose. I made her no reproach; she thanked me, and we parted, after conversing for an hour or two together.

I returned to London, where, after renewing my acquaintance with Lady Harland,[92] I met her two daughters; I paid more attention at first to the elder, without however anything in particular occurring between us. One evening, at Lady Craven's, Miss Marianne Harland[93] (the younger) reproached me with being cross and bored. " And so you do not seek to please anyone, and there is nobody in this room who is capable of pleasing you ?" she added with a boundless wealth of expression. I grasped her meaning entirely, but our conversation was interrupted. Miss Marianne Harland was not sixteen; she is small, fetching, has fine hair, beautiful eyes, charming teeth, a voice like the Gabrieli's,[94] of which she makes excellent use; a great fund of coquetry, always subordinated to the ambition of making a brilliant marriage—such is, I think, the exact description of the form and character of Miss Marianne Harland.

I approached her again after supper, and said to her in a whisper: " If I give you a little note to-morrow, will you take it ?" " No; do nothing rash." I went to breakfast the next day at my Lady Harland's. I gave a note to Marianne, which she took very neatly, and a moment later vanished. As I was leaving the house, Miss Harland accosted me on the staircase, and said to me, blushing: " Marianne has given me this message for you: am I not most obliging ?" The note contained the strongest recommendations of discretion and loyalty. I spent all my time at Lady Harland's: I was regarded and treated there as a son of the house. Marianne's self-esteem was highly flattered at the thought of a French lover: she had, moreover, at that time, a great regard for myself; I loved her for my part very tenderly. We wrote to each other incessantly, and handed each other our letters in front of her worthy ladyship, without her suspecting anything. I could not, however, conceal from myself that this intrigue could not last, and that it might have the most tiresome and embarrassing consequences.

M. de Pezai[95] came frequently to the house: he supposed the two Misses Harland to be immensely rich; he spoke of marriage to the elder, and was refused; he fell back upon the younger, and was no better received. In his dismay at not finding adoration, he surmised that Marianne had a fancy for somebody, and, presently, that this was myself. He spoke of the matter to Lady Harland, and left for France. A lackey gave Marianne assurances of discretion and loyalty which beguiled her; she was so rash as to entrust her letters to him.

Lady Harland formed the plan of taking her elder daughter, whose health was greatly impaired, to drink the waters at Bristol. She invited me to spend a fortnight there with her. I accepted with joy, and set forth a few days after her. I went to spend a week at my Lord Pembroke's,[96] and from there made my way to Bath. I there found the Chevalier d'Oraison,[97] who had come from Bristol Hotwells, and informed me that all was discovered, and that Lady Harland was in a terrible rage with myself.

I made up my mind without hesitation: I went to Bristol. I asked my Lady Harland to receive me for a few minutes. After scolding me severely and heaping many reproaches upon me, she forgave me, on condition that I left England without delay. In the end, she could not bring herself to inflict upon me the grief of going without taking leave of Marianne; and, what was amusing, this terrible parent ended by suffering in her presence our assurances of the most tender affection.

Miss Harland recovered her health. The whole family left Bristol, and returned to a fine estate near Ipswich.[98] Marianne presently received the homage of the wealthiest and most disagreeable Baronet in the county of Suffolk. Despite all his grimness, she would have married him, had she not discovered that it was his intention to live in the country, and never to take his wife to London; which made her decide to sacrifice him to me, and to write me the following letter:

"*Sproughton, the 4th of May*, 1773.

"You think yourself forgotten, doubtless, my dear Lauzun, because I have not written to you for a long time. I swear to you that it is not my fault: a girl whom you have honoured with your peculiar attention becomes the object of her parents' attention also and is kept under watch. Pen and ink are refused me: this is not from want of trust in me, according to my mother, but as a precaution. I write to you instead of going to sleep, and this is no sacrifice; for to whom can I give an account of my ridiculous situation, and who is capable of feeling it, but Lauzun? I have an admirer who has not, like yourself, made the mistake of getting married: Sir Marmaduke[99] lays at my feet an immense fortune, and, what is worse, an immense person. He wishes me to adore him; nothing could be fairer; but he wishes it to be in the country: I find that a little beyond my powers. Listen to the description of my new conquest, and see whether he resembles yourself. Sir Marmaduke is the height of one of the old armchairs that stood in our room at Bristol, that room in which you were so welcome a visitor. He is very stout: at present this is merely disagreeable; but he has only to grow a little stouter to become a curiosity. He is excessively fair; a pair of puny, swollen legs convey him with difficulty to my side, where, alas! they leave him all too long: this enormous mass of flesh drinks a quantity of port wine, hunts foxes, and breeds racehorses, like yourself. He assures me that all this will amuse me greatly: in short, he is very suitable, and, if he will live in London, I shall marry him. You will not be annoyed at this, and you have nothing to lose by the comparison. If he must live in the country, I am Sir Marmaduke's humble servant, and remain faithful to you. And I, young, pretty, madly fond of everything pleasant, accustomed to the homage of all the most elegant and sought after men in London, the wife of a *fox-hunter* ! doomed to spend my life between my husband and the old parson of the parish, and to be reduced, if I wish to talk, to conversing with the less tipsy of the two! Think of Marianne, her face, her form, her character, and see whether it is possible. My stout lover is preparing an entertainment for me worthy of himself. The Ipswich races are in a fortnight from now; he has ordered a gold cup, heavier than myself, which is to be won by a horse that cost him two thousand pounds, and which he begs the favour of laying at my feet. Why should not you come to the races? . . . No; when I think it over, do not come: you would be capable of killing the ugly brute; wait at least until I am his wife. Adieu; Fanny sends you a thousand greetings, and I, I love you, in truth, in a manner that would alarm any other girl less sure of her head."

I felt a longing for that big gold cup. I had some quite good horses at Newmarket.[100] I sent one of the best couriers down to Ipswich; his age, his name, ten guineas were sufficient to secure his admission. A little fellow, dressed in black, followed his instructions to the letter, remained modestly, throughout the length of the course, behind Sir Marmaduke's horse, and, within a hundred yards of the winning post, shot past like a flash of lightning. They gave him the cup, he slipped a note inside it and carried it to Marianne " Sir Marmaduke having come in a moment too late, permit me to follow his instructions, and to lay the cup at your feet." Marianne recognised my hand. " He is charming!" she said with a laugh. Lady Harland herself guessed my identity, but without bearing me any malice. They laughed at the unfortunate fox-hunter, who disappeared never to return.

The marriage broken off, Lady Harland returned to London. I managed to make my peace with her, and to gain admission once more to the house. We behaved with more circumspection, and the poor little woman was not a difficult prey. All went wonderfully well for some weeks. A letter which Marianne foolishly mislaid gave us away again; her mother at once left London with her daughters, without saying where she was going. Marianne, whose cleverness always made amends for her folly, wrote upon one of her gloves with a scrap of charcoal: "They are taking me off, Heaven knows where! I shall write upon the windows of the first inn at which we stop: search for it. If we were not, both of us, the most intelligent creatures that exist in the world, we should now be parted for ever." On the outside of the missive was written: "For M. de Lauzun, care of the French Ambassador; he will give the bearer five guineas."

I mounted my horse as soon as I received this pleasant note, which reached me by a lucky chance; and, on the fourth day of my search, I found the window from which I was to learn the fate of my pretty little mistress. She informed me that she was going for three weeks to the country, to a friend of her mother's, and would then return to Ipswich, passing through Winchester; that she awaited a letter from myself, by some means which she could not imagine, but which I would certainly discover. She was not mistaken. I addressed myself to Mr. Sexton, my English master, a poor devil like Don Basilio, ready to undertake anything for a crown. I sent him to Winchester, in a post chaise, with his wife and their three children, to avert suspicion; he performed his errand very skilfully. He waited upon Lady Harland; and, as she entered the room, intercepted Miss Marianne Harland, and said to her: " I have a letter from M. de Lauzun for you: it is in the pocket of that child's pinafore; you can take it when you like." She was not long in going to find it; but she wrote upon a scrap of paper these few words: " I have received the letter; the whole family have done their errand to perfection; I love to distraction the most adroit and most intelligent of men." But, alas! a piece of folly on Marianne's part ruined everything. We were corresponding regularly; she carried her letters herself, and went without subterfuge, when out walking, to collect my letters at the post office. The post office was changed; there was some talk of this at the breakfast table at Sproughton. Marianne foolishly said where the new post office was. Lady Harland asked her how she knew; she replied, slightly embarrassed, that a young lady, their neighbour, with whom she had been out walking that morning, had taken a letter there. Lady Harland left the room and inquired, with more cleverness than she seemed to possess, of the servant who had accompanied her daughter, whether she had forgotten to post a letter which she had entrusted to her. The lackey replied in all innocence that he could testify to her having remembered it. My lady ordered her carriage without another word, drove to the post office, made them give up the letter, and put it in her pocket. You could not imagine anything equal to the anger, the confusion, the rage of Miss Marianne. She was obliged to bow to the storm, and to give me up; she was distressed by this, but even more distressed, however, when she saw that she had brought about her own ruin by a clumsy piece of stupidity. She wrote to me without mentioning any detail, told me that she loved me still, but gave me my dismissal, nevertheless, in the clearest and most absolute form. I was annoyed; but I knew that this intrigue was bound to end badly, and I felt that it was indeed fortunate that its ending was no worse.

And so I was left in London without an occupation; but the notoriety of the affair between the French Ambassador and Lady Craven soon gave me one that was serious. The fatuity of M. le Comte de Guines, and the young woman's imprudence, of necessity brought about a scandal. M. de Guines sought to persuade Lady Craven to procure a separation from her husband, and to yoke herself to his chariot. He urged her with such extravagance that he was involved in legal proceedings with my Lord Craven and sentenced to pay him 10,000 pounds sterling, the most disagreeable and serious trouble that any ambassador could incur: this, combined with the terrible lawsuit that he had with Tort,[101] his secretary, meant his irremediable downfall. I served him with zeal and with success; but everything turned upon the answers made by Lady Craven, who had been carried off and shut up in the country by her husband, with no chance of communicating with anyone.

Princess Czartoryska had the courage to go down and force the door of her retreat and to dictate her course of action, the sole method of saving her as well as her lover. This occurrence enlightened me as to the sensibility and generosity of Madame Czartoryska. She happened by chance to discover all the details of my affair with Lady Sarah, and learned how capable I was of constancy and honourable conduct towards a person whom I had loved. The time fixed for Madame Czartoryska's departure, as it approached, enlightened me as to the sensibility and generosity of her heart; I grew attached to her almost unawares.

A few days before her departure for Spa, the Ambassador gave a dinner for her at Vauxhall, at which were a number of ladies of her acquaintance. She told me that she was sending off her children and servants in advance, and would join them at Calais, but that she was a little afraid to take this journey by herself; I eagerly offered to accompany her. She thanked me, telling me that she was charmed by my offer; and was only afraid that it might not be thought proper. All the ladies assured her that there was no harm in it: the Ambassador appeared slightly annoyed.

I called the next morning upon the Princess, and spoke of our journey. She told me that she was extremely sensible of my honourable intentions, but that she had changed her mind in view of the talk to which it might give rise. I pleaded my cause with so much warmth that I persuaded her; she promised that we should travel together, and appeared conscious of the importance that I attached to escorting her. M. de Guines saw her during the day, and alarmed her once again as to my attentions. I entered the house as he was leaving it, and could easily discern what was passing in her mind. "I no longer insist," I told her; "persecution is proving too much for your courage. I shall regret all my life long an opportunity which I shall never again find of enlightening you as to the truth of many strange events, and proving to you that my conduct is less inconsequent than you perhaps think." I could see in her eyes curiosity, interest, a sort of affection. "You need not be afraid any longer," she told me, "you are too glad to be coming with me, and I should lose too much, were I to prevent you; there will be no further change." She held out her hand to me; I kissed it; and, from that moment, had she chosen, she could not have doubted that she was adored. Our departure was fixed for the following day at noon.

I was punctual in calling upon the Princess. "My trunks," she told me, "will not be ready until five o'clock. Come with me to bid good-bye to Madame Pushkin,[102] who is leaving for Bristol." This lady parted from the Princess with regret, and shed copious tears, as did the Baroness Dierden[103] and Miss Johnson. " I should be far more unhappy than all these women," I murmured to Madame Czartoryska, " were I not going with you." A charming glance was all her answer. I returned to her house at five o'clock; they told me that she was unwell and was sleeping. This sleep seemed to me suspicious. I stopped at a little tavern at the corner of Berkeley Square, and wrote to her begging her to reassure me: she replied that she would not start before the following morning; that she would notify me of the hour.

I cannot describe all the conflicting ideas that entered my head. I saw with pain that M. de Guines, still mourning the loss of Lady Craven, was aspiring to sacrifice to his own vanity the woman to whom he owed everything and the man who had best served him. I then saw clearly that gratitude was less sacred to him than his own self-esteem, and that this man might prove ungrateful. I was too genuinely in love with the Princess not to be made patient and reasonable by the fear of losing her. I returned to the Embassy, where I was to sup with my Lord Sandwich[104] and all the rascals necessary to sing catches. I could not keep my secret any longer. I wrote to the Princess that I had no doubt but that M. de Guines had again upset her plans; that I was bitterly distressed; that I could judge from my own case that he felt how impossible it was to see, let alone know her, without adoring her; that I was far from wishing to speak evil of M. de Guines, but that no happiness could exist for me unless I consecrated the rest of my days to herself, and that I was the most independent creature in the world. I shall here transcribe the Princess's reply; this first note portrays her character as plainly as would a longer letter.

" Nothing in the world could astonish me more than what I have just read; but the thing that does not astonish me and never will, is the frankness and sensibility of your nature. There exist between us certain insurmountable obstacles among which, I swear to you, M. de Guines has no place. I must not, I cannot have a lover; but you inspire me with an interest which will last as long as I live; wherever we may be living, whatever be your fate, I request that you will keep me informed: my tender affection gives me the right to ask this. We cannot go together to Dover, but come and see me before I start."

The Ambassador suggested to me that we should both escort the Princess as far as Dover; I refused in the calmest and most indifferent manner that it was possible for me to assume. I spent the night in convulsions of rage and despair, which I did not myself understand: I was afraid of myself; I should not have answered for myself, had I met M. de Guines at Madame Czartoryska's. I resolved therefore to take precautions against myself. I shut myself up, and told one of my servants to go to her house, and to inform me as soon as she was gone; I intended to overtake her upon the road, to stop her and have that explanation with her which was so important for us both.

I remained in this state until five o'clock, when M. de Guines himself knocked at my door, and inquired whether I would dine with him. I opened the door: he told me that the Princess sent me her compliments: that she had started at midday, greatly astonished not to have seen me: a thunderbolt falling upon my head would have been less stunning. I said to M. de Guines (by whom the servant who was instructed to keep me informed had doubtless been bribed) that I was unable to dine with him. I ran to my stable, with my own hands saddled the first horse I found, and was upon the Dover road without losing an instant. My horse, which was too young and short of wind, foundered at Sittingbourne. I learned that the Princess was but six miles ahead of me and that she had joined her children and servants. I was afraid of compromising her: I wrote her a letter the confusion of which well depicted my love and desperation. I returned to London in haste; I arrived in time to play at a club for such high stakes as to be remarked, and to let it be supposed that I had never left town. On the following day I received a sad and touching reply from Madame Czartoryska; she assured me of her most tender interest, and seemed distressed by the thought of the ties that attached me to her.

After some days I received a letter from the Chevalier d'Oraison; he had seen the Princess on her way to Brussels; she was sick, devoured by some secret sorrow. I remained for more than a month still in England. I went to Portsmouth[105] with the King. I felt at length that I might leave for Spa without comment. We parted somewhat coldly, the Ambassador and I: I had read his secret; henceforth I was only a source of annoyance to him.

At length I arrived at Spa. The Princess received me somewhat coldly, and appeared to me more closely attached than ever to Prince Repnin. M. de Guines had left no stone unturned since her departure from London to persuade me that she was in love with him; that she had given him her portrait, and all the other proofs that a woman can give. I decided accordingly to detach myself from her at all costs, and to treat her with complete indifference. I succeeded famously with Prince Repnin, who never suspected that I was in love. The Princess spoke of the Ambassador with an interest which pained me sufficiently to make me wish her to suppose me attached to someone else; but no object could succeed in detaching me from her.

The routs and assemblies caused me, nevertheless, to make the acquaintance of Mrs. and Miss St. Leger, a pair of Irish ladies. Mrs. St. Leger was between forty and forty-five; she had been a beauty, and, beneath a reserved demeanour, retained a taste for pleasure. Her daughter, aged eighteen, was pretty and attractive. I danced and rode with her: both ladies took a fancy to me. The mother, albeit jealous of her daughter, did justice to her own shortcomings, and felt that she would lose me for ever if she prevented me from seeing her daughter: I therefore became a constant visitor at their house. The Princess teased me about them. "It was your own doing," she told me with a laugh, "and with a word you could put an end to it." My attentions to Miss St. Leger were soon common knowledge. A quarrel which I had with M. Branieski[106] showed the Princess, however, that I had by no means ceased to take an interest in herself.

M. Branieski, who had long been in love with the Princess, and had always been coldly received, spoke of her in a manner which I could not endure; I told him so openly, and we spoke with all the heat of men who are not on good terms. This quarrel would have gone farther but for Lady Spencer.[107] The Princess heard how warmly I had defended her, and was grateful to me. There was a race that was won by one of my horses: I made an offering of the prize to Miss St. Leger. At that very moment, Princess Czartoryska swooned, and was taken home. I was far from suspecting the reason, and barely gave it a thought. A long and dangerous illness followed this swoon. I never left her side, and paid her all the attentions that my heart dictated. I began to withdraw as her health returned, and I felt them to be less necessary.

Everyone was leaving Spa; and I was arranging to go with Mrs. and Miss St. Leger, when Prince Repnin, who had no reason not to trust me, told me that he was obliged to remain for about a fortnight longer, and to escort Madame Chernichef,[108] and that it would certainly please the Princess if I offered to return to Paris with her. I did not wait to be asked twice: the Princess was far dearer to me than he knew. And so we set off, and Prince Repnin accompanied us for several posts. We travelled in short stages, and I was riding my own horses. Madame Czartoryska was still very feeble, and when we reached Brussels was dead tired; she refused supper and went to bed. I remained to keep her company. We talked of England, and the conversation soon turned to the Comte de Guines and Lady Craven. I told her in detail all that I had suffered at her departure: her eyes filled with tears. "Stop," she said, "and let us never return to so dangerous a topic." It was too late, and our destiny must now run its course. The Princess loved me and told me so. This great happiness was poisoned by the alarm that her sentiment caused her, and by the horrible consequences that it could not but entail. She sought to deprive herself of all the means of yielding to it: we parted, and passed the most agitated of nights.

The Prince suggested that we should go the next day to Antwerp, to see a collection of pictures which he wished to buy. It was arranged, without any room for opposition on her part, that she should go with me in a little phaeton, which I had brought from England, with horses which she had often amused herself by driving at Spa. We were no sooner at liberty than the following conversation began:

"It would be futile, M. de Lauzun, to seek to conceal from you how deeply I love you; but I owe it to that very sentiment, which is dearer to me than life, to set before your eyes all the irreparable misfortunes that it will entail for us both, if we do not have the courage to separate promptly. Listen without interrupting me; you shall judge by the avowals that I am about to make what it must cost me to make them.

"Born with certain advantages of station, not to say charms, I began while very young to receive the attentions of men. They flattered my self-esteem; and now that I have come to know myself, I know that I am a coquette. I married my husband without love, and felt no more for him than a very tender affection, of which he becomes more deserving every day. Among all those who have paid court to me, the King of Poland was the most assiduous. The gratification of triumphing over the most beautiful women in Warsaw made me receive his overtures kindly: I did not, however, yield to them.

"Prince Repnin came to Warsaw as Russian Ambassador. He fell in love with me, and was coldly received. The troubles that were rending my unhappy country soon gave him an opportunity of proving to me how dear I was to him. My relatives and my husband greatly annoyed the Empress by always opposing her wishes.[109] Prince Repnin received the most severe orders with regard to them. The Princes Czartoryski continued to offend, and to escape scot-free. The Empress, furious that her orders had not been carried out, commanded Prince Repnin to have the Princes arrested and to confiscate their property. She informed him that his life hung upon his obedience. The Princes were ruined, had not Prince Repnin had the generous courage to disobey her. I felt that I must be the reward of so great an affection: not only that, even when I was giving myself out of gratitude, I believed that I was yielding to love.

"I was soon the only possession that remained to Prince Repnin. He lost his embassy, his pensions, the Empress's favour,[110] and, because he had shown an interest in myself, a bare thousand ducats were left as the sole income of a man who had dazzled all Poland with his splendour. He could not return to Russia; he invited me to travel and to accept his escort:

I had no hesitation in forsaking everything for him. Count Panin,[111] his uncle, made his peace with the Empress, who sent orders to him to take command of a considerable corps in Marshal Rumianzoff's[112] army. He refused, and thereby brought her anger to a head.

"We lived together in perfect happiness until he became jealous of the Comte de Guines; and his jealousy was so violent, so unjustified, that I was offended by it: I felt that I deserved greater confidence from the man for whom I had done everything. I endured his ill humour, nevertheless, in patience; but it made the Ambassador seem to me all the more attractive: I must frankly admit, I was flattered by finding favour with him, and I should certainly have loved him, had he been less exclusively in love with himself. I tore myself from the affection that I felt for him: that which you have formed for me has destroyed it. My heart has only too plainly felt the difference. I am certain, henceforth, that I shall live and die unhappy; but I shall not cause the man to die of grief who has sacrificed everything for me, and to whom I am all that is left now in the world.

"Fly, forget a woman who, were she to follow her inclination, can do nothing for your happiness. Believe me, love which is not based upon confidence is nothing but a torment; and what right have I to yours? Can you have any in a woman who has betrayed Prince Repnin, and who feels affection for M. de Guines? Every token of love that you receive from me will prove to you, will prove to myself, that I am capable of loving twice over: the woman who has changed once may change again; and do you suppose that she who has abandoned without compunction Prince Repnin, to whom she owed everything, will spare you any the more, you whose rights must end with the end of her sentiment for you? You are unaware, moreover, with what excess I am capable of loving you, and of all the misfortunes that may follow such a passion, and all the remorse that will devour me without ceasing: a veil spread between the rest of the universe and my lover will prevent me from seeing everything that is not yourself; the entire oblivion of my own position, of what I owe to my husband, to my children, to my family, to myself, the reasonable jealousy of Prince Repnin; every day will be marked by fears or by untoward events: can such a life endure for long ?"

"You owe too much to Prince Repnin," I told her. "Of the two of us, it is not he who should die of grief! Let me but see you for a few days longer, let me but enjoy a few hours of the last happiness that can exist for me, and I will part from you for ever! Remember now and again that I shall adore you so long as I draw breath, and that I have lost you; that I have loved you sufficiently to fly you: perhaps I should have done more for you than Prince Repnin. O most tender, most honourable of all living creatures! It is to your love that I shall be indebted, if I am not to be a monster of ingratitude; it is to your generosity that I shall owe my honour; this at least is a consolation for us both."

We spoke in good faith; but we did not ourselves know to what an extent we were in love. The two most tender, most ardent hearts, perhaps, in the universe, had met. We did not find at Antwerp the collection for which the Prince had gone there; it was sold: he was told of another that he might have at Amsterdam, which would be more to his taste. This made him decide to take the opportunity for a visit to Holland. I refused courageously to join the party, and held out until the eve of their departure. A look from the Princess made me forget all my intentions; I accepted the Prince's invitation, and the next day we set out together.

The happiness, the danger of being together had filled our heads with an agitation, a confusion that are indescribable. Our travelling companions were all asleep, fortunately for us, and our disturbance passed unobserved: the night came, and we restrained ourselves no longer. The Princess's tears began to flow: I mingled mine with them. Everything to fear, everything to suffer, nothing to hope; our grief overwhelmed us, and did not leave us the strength to think clearly.

We arrived at eleven o'clock in the evening at a wretched hut, where we were obliged to spend the night. The Princess and Bokhdanowicz (her old Polish maid) lay in one chamber, and all the men in the other.

A few hours later, Bokhdanowicz uttered piercing cries which awakened nobody; but I was not asleep; I hastened to see what was the matter: a man, who had been hiding in the room, had nearly made her die of fright. I expelled him with considerable difficulty.

The Princess had been awakened; she called to me. I fell on my knees by her bedside: my eyes were incapable of expressing all the love that was in my heart; but they showed a great deal. "Your sufferings," she said to me, "rend my soul; but they are dear to me; it is so sweet to me to see you sharing mine. If we cannot be happy, let us at least be constant and irreproachable." We promised mutually a courage and a prudence far beyond our power.

We set off again slightly calmer, and with a passable control: we arrived at the Moerdick, which we crossed at once. I remained in the cabin of the yacht with the Princess, while all the rest, afraid of sickness, sat on deck. I read her a charming novel by Dorat, which had just appeared, entitled *The Sacrifices of Love*.[113] Some of the situations bore upon our position: we could not read it without deep interest and emotion. What charms were combined in the person of Madame Czartoryska ! Years of misery and regret have failed to efface their image. We halted at Rotterdam, and arrived on the next day at the Hague, where the Prince and Princess were received with the utmost joy by M. de Lachernéria, the Spanish Ambassador. I had no fault to find with him, and can say nothing that is not to his credit. Madame de Lachernéria, a tall, vigorous, ardent, keen Peruvian, noticed me and, in ten minutes, was like an acquaintance of ten years' standing; she ceased to question the Princess about me only to question myself, and equally embarrassed us both.

We had been but a few hours at the Hague when, at two o'clock in the morning, Bokhdanowicz, who did not speak a word of French, knocked at my door and said to me in bad German: " Come down, the Princess is dying." (The Prince was not at the Hague, having gone to visit the Prince of Orange in the country.) I came downstairs in haste, and found that she was indeed unconscious. It was only after some hours that I succeeded in restoring her to her senses. She held out her hand to me as soon as she saw that I was by her. " I am glad," she said, " I am dying in the arms of the man I love, without having any cause to reproach myself." She had frequent and violent attacks of nerves during the day, and often fainted.

I knew by repute the celebrated Gaubius,[114] Professor of Medicine. I went to consult him at Leyden, starting at daybreak. I explained to Dr. Gaubius, in the fullest detail, the malady that the Princess had had at Spa, and that from which she was now suffering, without mentioning her name; he asked me if she was my wife; I replied that she was not, but that she was my sister. He next asked me if I was a physician or a surgeon; I replied that I was not. " Then," he told me, " you are the most loving and intelligent brother in the world." He reassured me as to the Princess's state, told me that it was not dangerous; adding that he was too old and too gouty for his health to permit him to visit her. He ordered me a treatment for her, the success of which he guaranteed, bade me send him a report of its effect, and told me that he would be very glad to see the patient when she was less weak. I returned to the Hague. The Princess learned with pleasure and gratitude what I had done.

We decided that I should escort her back as far as Brussels, after prolonging the journey from Holland as far as might be possible, and that I should then leave for Italy. Lovers are like children, only at odd moments do they feel a distant grief, and they sacrifice much to the present hour. Ten or twelve days of happiness seemed to us a sufficient ransom for our whole lives. This short respite calmed us. The Princess recovered her health. I did not think of asking her for anything of which she might ever repent. During this time, however, I was jealous without having any object for my jealousy, and it took so extravagant a form, that I cannot refrain from describing it.

I had met in London a young Prince Poniatowski,[115] nephew to the King of Poland, and cousin to the Prince, who had been bred up in England, and to whom I had never paid much attention. Madame Czartoryska told me that he was expected at the Hague. The sole effect upon me of this news was to make me fear the importunity of a third party. One evening when I was at the play with the Prince and Princess, someone came and whispered to him that Prince Poniatowski had arrived, and he rose and left us. I cannot describe the revolution that this created in me. All the attractions of Prince Poniatowski, all the advantages that he possessed for winning the favour of his cousin, in whose society he was destined to live, presented themselves to my mind, and turned my head. I left the theatre, and returned home. I was full of bitter reflexions: the Princess seemed lost to me, and lost from that moment. I was so dismayed, that I decided to flee, and to set off at once for Italy.

I sent out for post horses, and ordered my carriage. It was past ten o'clock. The Princess, astonished that I did not appear at Madame de Lachernéria's, where she was supping, left the house without saying a word, took the first carriage that she saw in the courtyard, and came to our inn. She was greatly surprised to find my post chaise at the door, horsed and loaded. She inquired where I was, and came upstairs to my room. "What does this mean?" she asked me; "where are you going?" "To die remote from yourself," I replied in a tone of despair, "to flee from troubles even greater than that of separation from them." "I do not understand; explain yourself; you are out of your mind; do you suppose that I can live and behold you in the state in which you are?" The Princess's eyes showed me the extent of my error, and how many reasons I had for keeping calm. I was ashamed of my extravagance, and embarrassed how to confess it; I must do so, nevertheless. The Princess neither reproached nor teased me; she took me in her arms. "Never be afraid of losing my heart; I am vexed that you should have suffered so; but how greatly I appreciate the value of so much love. Let us not lose any time; they are expecting us at the Spanish Ambassador's; the slightest pretext will be sufficient to excuse us." She said to my valet as she went downstairs: "He is not leaving, he is never leaving!" with an inexpressible charm. We set off for Amsterdam, and stopped at Leyden to see Dr. Gaubius. He talked at great length with the Princess. "It is," he told her, "one of those maladies which are seldom dangerous to women, and which physicians cannot cure. Your brother," he added with a smile, "knows more about it perhaps than I do "(the Princess blushed); "be constant and prudent, and you will be happy. I have never seen a woman better loved." He spoke to her of our conversation with interest. Nothing was lost upon so tender a spirit. No one could have been more pleasant to love.

We set off late in the day for Amsterdam. The night was dark. I was in the shelter of a large gondola with the Princess; I pressed her hands to my heart, I clasped her in my arms without her offering the least resistance. She retired to bed without supper; and, according to my custom, I remained by her bedside. We embraced tenderly as soon as we were by ourselves; I could not repress desires which she appeared to share; I ventured greatly, and was speedily punished. "I would never have believed," she said to me with pain and indignation, "that the being who is so dear to me would so soon have forgotten his promises and resolutions; or that he would deliberately sacrifice the whole happiness of my life to an instant's pleasure. It was so sweet to me to owe to your love my very honour and tranquillity!" Her maid entered the room; she announced that she wished to sleep, and dismissed me.

There is no more terrible position than to have merited the wrath of one whom we love to excess. I spent the night in grief and penitence. Next morning, M. Onieski called at eight o'clock to fetch me, and, do what I might, took me out to see all that was noteworthy in Amsterdam and its environs, until eight o'clock at night. The Princess treated me with a coldness which dismayed me; she loved me too well not to be moved to pity by my distress. She drew near to me, and murmured: "See how wretched I am, and I am sure that you will not offend again; that I should punish you, that I should distress you,

I cannot bear to think of it." These few words restored me to life. We supped merrily, and fixed our departure for the next day. It was suggested that we should return in little two-seated cabriolets which one drives oneself, and which travel extremely fast. I was appointed to take the Princess, as being the best whip. She began by refusing; but she read so much misery in my eyes that she consented. We set off. I found her serious during the journey, and asked her what was the matter. "I do not wish to scold you," was her reply; "I have forgiven you with my whole heart, but so forcible an impression is not easily obliterated; and it is not with you, it is with myself that I am displeased, and if I have done wrong in reposing a blind confidence in you, I am indeed to blame, I have furious reproaches to make myself." I found it easy to dispel her fears; the tenderest of tears were my reward. We remained for a week longer at the Hague.

At length we were obliged to return to Brussels, where we honestly supposed that we should have to part for ever. We thought that we would die of grief: I drenched several handkerchiefs daily with blood. The Princess was in no better plight than myself; she thought that she would die on the day when we crossed the Moerdick. I spent the night by her side. "We have pledged ourselves," she told me, "to more than we can perform: the excess of your love and of your courage might yet preserve my life. Were you but capable (my only love) of not being jealous of Prince Repnin, of contenting yourself with my love, of laying no claim to anything besides!" A new scheme of life was arranged, in as great good faith as the rest, and, as we shall see in due course, without any greater measure of success. We stopped but a day at Brussels, and returned to Paris.

I left the Princess at Senlis, and went to spend the

night at Hautefontaine, a very different man from when I had left it. I arrived the next evening at nine o'clock in Paris; I stopped at the Hôtel de Chartres where the Princess was staying. I found there Prince Repnin. He received me courteously, but had a cold and constrained air. Madame Czartoryska was in bed; she was feeling unwell, said that she wished to sleep, and dismissed us both. She had only time to give me a little packet in which were a very loving note and a lock of her hair, which I had ardently desired. About eleven o'clock that night, d'Oraison came into my room. "I have just left a madman," he told me, "and have promised to go to him and reassure him to-morrow morning early. This is what brings me to you at such an hour: Prince Repnin has taken it into his head that you are in love with the Princess and that she loves you. I told him that I was sure of the contrary, that I knew you to have an attachment elsewhere, and to make more certain, I have come to speak to you about it." My dismay and confusion showed the Chevalier that he had been mistaken. "You are," he said to me, "the oddest and most fickle of men. And the fair Marianne, are you no longer in love with her?" I told him all that had happened since his departure from London; he blamed me less, pitied me, but gave me no reassurance as to the future.

Distressing thoughts consumed the whole night for me. I went on the next day to inquire after the Princess, and found her no better. Prince Repnin, whom I met, appeared to me fairly tranquil. The Princess received me coldly; I had no wish to complain of this, and suffered in silence. Several days passed in this fashion, without Prince Repnin's allowing me to speak to her alone for one minute. He wore a satisfied and calm air. I could neither sleep nor eat. I spat a quantity of blood; anxious as I was to conceal my state, my handkerchief steeped in blood betrayed me. "What do I see!" she said as she passed by me. "Come at seven o'clock, I shall be alone; I positively must speak to you." I arrived punctually. "My friend," she said to me, as she entered the room, "you are seriously ill; it is doubtless my fault; so, of two people who are dear to me, one must die of grief! What is amiss? Open your heart to me, I wish it, I insist upon it, I beg you upon my knees." "It is nothing" (I clasped her in my arms); "I need only courage, and it rests with yourself alone to supply it. Tell me that you love me, I need to hear it." "Yes, my friend, my dearest friend, I love you, I adore you; there is no power on earth that can prevent me from telling you so. Arm yourself with patience; persist in a line of conduct which makes me add to so much affection the most merited esteem. Your behaviour towards Prince Repnin is more than friendly; he cannot accuse you of rudeness, nor of falsehood. I blame myself most severely for the pain that I am causing you. I spare him, however, as far as it is possible for me; it costs me twice the pain not to be frank, and to treat you in his presence in so different a manner. It is to these precautions, nevertheless, that I owe the security which, I hope, he still enjoys, and the loss of which would involve us all in the most serious consequences. Do not vex yourself, my friend; the mind always pleads, but love commands; and when it speaks, it always prevails. Be sparing with a life which is my sole treasure; be sparing with the blood which I would redeem with all my own." "Oh! my love, you shed a balm on it, a calm which I thought lost for ever. My heart is by no means unworthy of your own; it is capable too of generosity. I do Prince Repnin all the justice that he deserves. Pray God, he may never be made unhappy by my fault! Let every attention, all respect be his! A glance will console me, will remind me that I am dearer to you than any, if I was unjust. My dear friend, I should never suffer so much as if I knew that you had reason to reproach yourself."

Prince Repnin arrived when we least expected him; we were embarrassed, and, notwithstanding our efforts, he perceived it; for, from that moment, it was impossible for him to contain his jealousy; it was such as might be expected in a man at once violent, generous and sensitive. He knew that a scene would be bad for the Princess, he was anxious to spare her one; he left the room when he became afraid that he would be able to control himself no longer. He appeared one evening at Madame l'Huillier's.[116] "I must expire," he said to her, "I can no longer endure the constraint that I have imposed upon myself; I must unbosom myself to you. M. de Lauzun adores the Princess, and is adored by her. He is as proud and as jealous as myself; he cannot but hate me. The honesty and modesty of his conduct is the strongest proof of the power that your friend has over him, a power which she has purchased, doubtless, with the gift of her heart and person. Any base quarrel is beneath the dignity of two men who claim to be worthy of her. One of us must perish, or neither of us can ever be at rest; he is wresting from me the one treasure in which my happiness has dwelt, I shall defend it." It was in vain that Madame l'Huillier sought to calm him. The next morning I received the note which follows:

"My esteem and my hatred are known to you: let us fight for a treasure which we cannot share; one of us must fall by the hand of the other. I leave confidently to yourself the choice of time, place and weapons.

"Nicolas Vassilievitch Repnin."

I made him the following reply:

"Prince Repnin will not suppose me to be capable of fear. I esteem him sufficiently to decline the honour that he offers me. I will on no account agree to a combat which would compromise a person whom I respect and would deprive her of one of her most faithful friends. If the Prince attacks me, I shall defend my life in such a way as will prove to him that I do not wish to shed the blood of a man to whom Princess Czartoryska is so greatly indebted.

"LAUZUN."

After receiving my reply, he sent word begging me to expect him at my house early the next day. He came, sure enough, to the Rue Saint-Pierre, where I was living; the door was shut upon us, and the following conversation began:

PRINCE REPNIN: "Listen, sir, to what I have to say, and you will not refuse me the favour that I have asked of you. It is my rival, it is my enemy that I appoint as judge of what remains for me to do in the dreadful position in which I find myself. I was appointed Russian Ambassador in Poland, at the beginning of the troubles. I saw and adored the Princess; I sacrificed everything to the happiness of proving my adoration. Her family used frequently to offend the Empress. I received the most rigorous orders to punish her relatives: they were not carried out; I was sharply reprimanded for this; my head became the pledge of their good conduct. The Princes Czartoryski never ceased to be culpable, and were never punished. I lost the favour and the confidence of my Sovereign. I saw melt away the most astounding fortune that is recorded in the annals of the Russian Empire.

"I was recalled to justify myself. The influence

of Count Panin, my uncle, saved my life. The Empress appointed another to the Embassy at Warsaw, and I resigned myself to living there as a private citizen. Generous and tender-hearted, Princess Czartoryska felt that she owed me a debt of gratitude; as a reward for such loyal service, I was made happy.

"The Empress ordered me to join Rumianzoff's army: I refused to obey. All her favours were withdrawn from me; there remained only a modest pension, sufficient to maintain life, to the man who had dazzled Poland with his splendour. The Princess was kind enough to leave Warsaw, where I could not remain without danger. She travelled, I accompanied her; everywhere she received attentions, which never deceived her for long. She easily distinguished the vanity, the fatuity, the insincerity of those who paid court to her. She left for London a few weeks later, with myself: I met you at Calais; we crossed the water together. The Chevalier d'Oraison, whom I knew of old, had often spoken to me of you; your attachment to the fair Lady Sarah was known to all England, and made you an object of interest. My first impulse was to fear you. I was speedily reassured when I saw you fix your attention, and begin to pay court to a young and amiable person. The fatuity of your Ambassador caused me no real uneasiness. I set out for Spa, where you came to join us. The Princess was unhappy, out of sorts, all the time there; but I saw you occupied with Miss St. Leger, and never guessed the cause.

"Being pledged, beyond the possibility of withdrawal, to escort Madame de Chernichef to Paris, I carried my feeling of confidence to the pitch of being very glad that you should accompany the Princess. The interest that you had shown in myself, the manner in which we had lived together at Spa, had given me a liking for you: my inclination would have led me on to love you, had not fate compelled me to hate you. I received no news of the Princess throughout her journey from Holland. Terror seized my spirit, the future spread itself before me, I was certain of my calamity before I had any proof of it. Everything has confirmed my suspicion since our arrival in Paris: the Princess loves you. I know her too well not to be aware that she is tormented by remorse; she will not see me without embarrassment, without repugnance. She will suffer inconceivably: but for you, I should still be everything to her. If she loses neither of us, she loses us both. I have no hope of an asylum in my own country, which I have left for her sake. So long as I exist, you will not be the tranquil possessor of a heart whose value you know: so long as you are alive, it will be more yours than mine, and every instant will be marked by fresh uneasiness and fresh rage."

Lauzun: "Your hatred is reasonable, sir, nor is it deliberately criminal, I deserve it all: my heart is, nevertheless, not unworthy of yourself, nor of the homage that it pays to the Princess. I have long fought against a passion the only consequence of which must be the most fearful calamities. I have reckoned as one of the greatest the disturbance of your peace of mind. Carried away in spite of myself by this senseless passion, I have incessantly before my eyes the frightful thought that I may inspire nothing but remorse: ready myself to make any sacrifice, I can never claim any. I know all your advantages over myself, I can but disturb your happiness; but, since I am a foreigner, parted from her of necessity by circumstances, you would speedily destroy the whole of mine, could I hope for any. I will not, however, dishonour, by disputing it, a conquest which, all glorious though it be, must remain secret. I do not wish that the Princess shall be able to reproach me with having cut short the days of one to whom she owes such a debt of gratitude. Were I to perish, my death would easily be avenged; and, after having caused your own, the Princess would not long survive you. I shall go away, sir; I shall seek dangers which will bring me no stain of guilt. I pity you, I esteem you, I hate you; but never of my own free will can I fight with you, and I warn you that I am, and have chosen to be, here unarmed."

PRINCE REPNIN: "That is enough, sir; I must be frank with so generous an enemy. I shall pay regard to Madame Czartoryska's sensibility. I shall in no way compromise her good name, but I am going to employ what influence I have left over her to make her speedily leave a country in which she cannot be happy. I warn you of this, sir, and I ask for your word of honour that you will not follow her."

LAUZUN: "I have no need to promise you anything, sir; I shall never hesitate over doing what I may consider necessary to the Princess's welfare, nor shall I allow anyone but myself to be the judge of my actions."

Prince Repnin left my house and returned to the Princess; I did not see her alone during the rest of the day. She seemed to me to be painfully and profoundly affected. She was unwell, shut herself up at an early hour in her own room, and refused to see either Prince Repnin or myself. There are painful situations that transcend our courage and our strength, that make the most reasonable resolutions vain. It is not in sacrificing everything to the beloved that merit lies, all hearts sincerely touched are capable of that; it is the way in which we endure the sacrifice that gives it its value; by showing too plainly what it is costing us and what we are suffering, we make it impossible. It was at this time that I was carried away by the excess of my passion. I worshipped the Princess, thought absolutely nothing of myself, everything of her, the most frightful calamities seemed to me preferable to that of afflicting her with trouble and remorse; she read what was in my heart; love and despair were depicted in her eyes; she was in love with me and yielded, in spite of herself, to her affection for me; but I wished to be, I felt that I could be generous; I was aware of all the power that I wielded over her; I made use of it to defend her against myself. I inspired her with confidence: sure of me, she no longer sought to avoid me: her tranquillity alarmed me, I became jealous, distrustful, I no longer saw any merit in her conduct, I thought her prudent only because her heart had become more calm; I ventured to show her what I felt; she could withstand anything, except the misery of not seeing me. Fully convinced of her love, she no longer concealed from me the keenness of her affection, nor that of her desires; she no longer sought to put a check to mine; to bring about my own ruin was nothing, I must be certain that I was adored. I was on the point of absenting myself for a week, and the effort was beyond my courage; I was still in the regiment of the French Guards, and nothing could excuse me from mounting guard at Fontainebleau. The Princess felt no other necessity save that of reassuring me by yielding herself to me. Terrible moments recur to me; I shudder as I write, but a solemn vow binds me to this terrible task.

It was the 5th of November. I was to leave two days later for Fontainebleau. Departing from her normal habit, the Princess had barred her door to everyone, even Prince Repnin himself. I was alone with her; I reproached her with being gloomy and serious with me. " I cannot love myself: I am yours," she said to me; "enjoy all your privileges, you must, it is my wish." I flung myself into her arms; I found my happiness, or rather the crime was committed. You may judge of the horror of my lot, even while possessing the woman that I worshipped. She had not an instant's pleasure; the tears flooded her cheeks, she thrust me from her. "That is enough," she said to me, "there is no limit now to my wrongdoing, there will be none to my miseries; leave me!" I sought to remain, she fell at my feet: "Leave me! In God's name, leave me!" Thunderstruck, I did not venture to reply; I returned home. My night was a torment which I alone am capable still of imagining. I returned to her side early the next morning; her curtains were drawn close; I trembled as I parted them. She was unconscious; blood trickled from her lips over her bosom; a little box, lying open upon her bed, told me that she had taken poison. I supposed that she was dead and greedily swallowed what remained in the box. I do not know what happened to me; I vomited a quantity of blood; I suffered throughout that day and the night that followed from violent nervous attacks. I do not know what happened to me during the next twenty-four hours, and can say only that I did not leave my bed, and that I vomited a quantity of blood, which, in all probability, saved my life.

Madame de Lauzun came to fetch me, and to carry me to Fontainebleau, where we were to go together. I was in a feeble and stupefied condition which did not allow me to think of remaining. I begged Madame de Lauzun to wait for me a moment. I rose and dressed myself with great care, and went to inquire for news of the Princess. She was still in a dying state. I set off notwithstanding; I arrived at Fontainebleau like a madman. Except while I was on duty I spoke to nobody. I was really ill. I received there a letter from the Princess, which I feel that I must here transcribe:

"O my friend, my lover! You whom I adore, you in whom all the affections of my heart are united, you are no longer by my side! You have left me, it was my wish. Why did you obey me? Have I then been obliged to pay a penalty for the violation of all my duties? Of the horrors that surround me, those of death are the least fearful; if you knew what a future opens before me! I have lost all hope, every right to happiness. I no longer dare promise anything, I have betrayed my vows. May your love at least, your happiness, take the place of what I have lost. But, alas, I am speaking of the future, and I am dying! I shall not have the barbaric courage to command you to live; I do not know what is happening in me, impulses hitherto unknown. I feel my last breath passing from lips that burn still with your kisses. Come, do not lose a minute; let us die in each other's arms: let happiness and pleasure be our last sensation! No; do not heed my insensate desires. May my remorse, at least, expiate my offence. May the courage to be no longer blameworthy restore to me, at the cost of my life and of my happiness, some spark of self-esteem!"

This letter, written in a tremulous hand, soaked with her tears, drove me altogether out of my senses. I set off by myself for Paris, as soon as night had fallen. I told the Princess of a place where we could meet in safety. Her weakness was extreme, she kept on fainting away. I was but little stronger. I shall not abuse the patience of my readers: if they have never been in love, perhaps even if they are not in love at the moment when they read these pages, they will find me extremely tedious. I shall content myself therefore with saying that this conversation did us great good and great harm. I went back to Fontainebleau; finished my tour of duty, which seemed to me to last for ages, and returned. We were circumspect in our conduct for some weeks. Prince Repnin behaved generously. The fearful change of which I was the cause, the certainty that I was not seeing the Princess in private, the hope that she would soon be leaving, calmed him; he was sorry for me, and recovered his tranquillity.

He was mistaken nevertheless. I saw Madame Czartoryska alone, now and again, out of her own house; the prudence of my conduct, my moderation, seemed to have banished the dangers which she had so prodigiously dreaded. Love and nature have claims which it would be impossible to deny. How can a woman refuse anything to the lover whom she adores, especially when he asks nothing! The Princess was at my disposal, prepared to suffer anything.

As for the future, the rest of our days seemed to us paid for by so much happiness! Incapable of attending to anything else, I would meet the Princess, or would wait for her, and when the hour struck at which I lost all hope of seeing her before the next day, I would go to bed; my body was unable to endure the strain of being absent from her. Prince Repnin became suspicious. The Princess observed that he was having her followed; anything seemed to her preferable to the horror of infidelity. She took the terrible course of confessing everything to him; this confession, made by a generous nature, was received by one no less generous. Prince Repnin allowed himself not one word of complaint or of reproach. "Enjoy your happiness," he bade her; "I do not flatter myself that I possess the courage to witness it. I shall go away in a fortnight; I shall join the Russian army." We felt that we ought not to present before the eyes of this generous man the object and cause of all his sufferings;

I made an effort which I thought to be beyond my strength; I consented to go and stay with M. le Duc de Choiseul, at Chanteloup, until after Prince Repnin's departure.

I went away; I received news of the Princess daily; I suffered, and could not live, apart from her. I returned, and found that Prince Repnin had left. He who has not felt himself in durance vile cannot estimate the full worth of liberty. My happiness was impaired now only by dread of the future, by the horrible certainty of seeing it shortly come to an end. We discussed incessantly how we might avoid any further parting. At times we were hopeful; but the thought of her charming children and their future always checked us. Her interest in them was so touching, they were so necessary to her, they were shaping so well! Accustomed to love everything that belonged to my mistress, I became warmly attached to her children. I felt that ought I to share in their mother's devotion to them: my eyes filled with tears as I caressed them. I preferred to anticipate all the troubles that were gathering to crush me rather than to deprive them of a mother with whom no other could for a moment be compared. She interpreted the sentiments that filled my heart; they strengthened my claim upon her. She knew that I would gladly sacrifice half my life to retain one of her precious children, to whom I felt like a father. We were never apart; we went riding twice daily to escape the tiresome visitors of whom there was no other way of ridding ourselves.

The time for her departure for Poland drew round: her husband was staying behind for a lawsuit.[117] I decided to escort her as secretly and as far as I might: I did not, indeed, take leave of her, until we were within a couple of leagues of Warsaw. The journey had been charming, and the Princess more loving and lovable every day. The moment of our parting was terrible. "My dear," she said to me, "I must at length disclose a secret which I have had great difficulty in concealing from you. You have longed so for one of my children, you shall have one: I am going to leave you the dearest, the best part of myself; I am with child, and I have never lived with my husband since I gave myself to you. I shall have the courage to confess everything to my husband, to arrange that the dearest pledge of our ardent passion shall be sent to you." The reader must know my heart if he would judge of the impression that this speech made upon me. It exhausted my strength in an instant: I fainted, and, when I recovered consciousness, I could find no trace of the Princess. Her father-in-law,[118] who had come to meet her, had obliged her to forsake me; she had left one of her servants to look after me. I was in a state of depression from which nothing could rouse me. I let myself be taken back as far as Breslau, without tasting food or drink, or uttering a single word; there I halted, and waited for tidings of the Princess. These, when they came, restored my balance somewhat, and I continued on my way to Frankfort, where I learned that the King was dangerously ill of the small-pox.

I heard of his death[119] as I passed the Deux-Ponts, and this upset all my plans: I was not in a condition to pay my court to the new King, and I went to join the Royal Legion,[120] of which I was Colonel, at Mouzon in Champagne. I lived there in the strictest retirement, and saw absolutely no one but the officers of my regiment. My time was divided between my military duties and the Princess. I knew that she was sick and unhappy; but she wrote by every post. Then, for several posts, she failed to write: I dispatched a courier who went with the utmost speed. I learned on his return that the Princess had been dangerously ill, and had not had with her the one person who could give me news of her. Her strength had succumbed to the terrible confession which she had made to her husband. He had received it with affection and generosity; but vapours, nervous attacks, a deadly melancholy, combined with the discomforts of her condition, had placed her in the most deplorable situation. She desired anxiously to see me, and did not hope for the possibility. I asked M. de Conflans,[121] under whose command I was, whether he could grant me leave of absence for three weeks, which I should like to spend in the country near Frankfort.

I set off alone, and with all possible secrecy. On the last day of my journey I lost myself and went to ask my way at a house in which I saw a light. I was greatly surprised to find an English family, and learned that I was in the house of the Princess's gardener. I knew that it was not difficult to make a way into the park, but I did not wish to be recognised; I was afraid of being arrested by the Cossack patrols and of not being able to obtain access to her without disclosing who I was. It was eleven o'clock at night; I saw the various pickets come in after going their rounds, and slipped into the garden, where I was at once attacked by two big dogs which were set loose there at night. One of them I had given the Princess in England. I called him by his name; Cæsar recognised me, and came and fawned upon me; the other dog withdrew, and I approached the house: I saw two women strolling together; one went indoors and the other advanced towards me; I recognised Madame Parisot, a maid whom I had placed with the Princess. "Come," she said to me, "neither obstacles nor distance can deceive her heart; she has been expecting you." The Princess clasped me to her bosom. "The necessities of my heart enable me always to divine your actions; it was impossible that you should leave me to the frightful contemplation of all that separates us;

that you should not come to impart fresh charms to my retreat, my sole consolation." Twice I spent twenty-four hours at Powonski:[122] everything there was of interest to me; I was obliged to tear myself away. I had taken steps to be present, without fail, at her confinement, or at least to be close at hand.

I returned slightly more at ease than on the former occasion. After joining my regiment, I procured all the volumes that treated of the affairs of Poland, Prussia and Russia; and upon a great number of works, good and bad, which I had the patience to read, founded a political survey of the interests of those three powers. I drew up a long memorial which I addressed to Prince Adam. He communicated it to M. de Stackelberg,[123] the Russian Minister at Warsaw, who sent it to Moscow without my knowledge. The hope of becoming French Ambassador or Minister at Warsaw gave me an untiring zeal for work. The Princess approved of my plan, and every post brought me fresh encouragement.

She informed me, in the month of September, that she was less pleased with her husband; that the report of my last visit had reached him, and that she feared that the visit which I proposed to make for her confinement might have serious consequences; but that she would die of grief if I did not come. I set off about the end of September, and found at Strasbourg a letter from the Princess, sent by express messenger, begging me urgently to postpone my departure. I found another at Frankfort, even more calculated to alarm me as to the Prince's hostile intentions. Nothing could reconcile me to the thought of being separated from the Princess at the time of her delivery. I sent her a Pole named Miaskowski, whom I had brought with me, and went to wait for him in a little free town situated upon the Vistula and known as Thorn.

Here I received the Princess's reply. She told me that she could not be so near to me without longing to see me, however great the danger; that it was important that I should not let anyone see me; that Madame l'Huillier would conceal me in her house, and that she would come and see me there. I did not lose an instant in getting there; anxiety, agitation, fatigue had so altered me as to make me quite unrecognisable. "You will not see your Princess this evening," said the compassionate Huillier, as she embraced me, "she is in considerable pain and has been ordered to keep her bed; the pain will pass away probably during the night, and she will be here tomorrow morning early."

The next day, on the contrary, her pain increased, and I contrived, with great difficulty, to secure admission to the blue palace,[124] where Madame Parisot shut me up in a large cupboard used as a wardrobe, behind the Princess's bed. She had a painful delivery, which lasted for about thirty-six hours. I could hear her cries, and felt that each of them must be her last. I shall not attempt to describe all that passed in my heart, my misfortunes were the fruit of my crimes; she whom I most loved upon earth was their victim. This torment ended at length, I was released from my prison, and admitted to Madame Czartoryska's chamber. I bathed her face with my tears, but could not utter a single word. "You have saved my life," she told me. "I knew that you were there. I owed my strength only to the courage with which I was inspired by the certainty that you were so near at hand; could my courage fail, when I knew that you would receive my last breath? Kiss this child,[125] which is dearer to me already than all the rest: it would be in such danger, were you discovered! Begone, take up your abode four miles from here, in a farm which is at my disposal. This note will secure you a welcome from the good folk who occupy it; we shall meet again soon; you shall have news of me every day." Once again I was obliged to leave her.

I made a leisurely progress to my new quarters. I found a simple dwelling, but so spotlessly clean that it might be called elegant. I was received by a man of about sixty, of venerable appearance; his wife, slightly younger than himself, looked as though she had once been beautiful. Two young women of agreeable appearance, one of whom was about to become a mother, and a little girl, composed this honest household: I delivered my letter; it was conceived in these terms:

"M. Dembowski, I beg that you will receive into your household the bearer of this note; I am entrusting to you the dearest treasure that I have in the world, and my confidence in your care and discretion is unbounded.

"I. CZARTORYSKA."

"You may make yourself at home here," the good M. Dembowski told me; "you may dispose even of our persons, for we belong to the Princess, far more from our own gratitude than on account of her benefactions to us, vast as they have been."

I retired to my room, finding it impossible to take any supper. Next day I received news of the Princess; she was as well as could be hoped.

I took a stroll in what was quite a large garden with M. Dembowski. He told me his story: he had been born to a fortune that satisfied his ambition. He had married for love a young lady of quality from Kamieniecz, and had had by her several children. There was no situation happier than his, when Prince Radziwill,[126] to whom he had long been attached, obliged him to join the Bar confederacy. Two young Poles, who were passionately in love with his two daughters, thought that they could not prove their devotion better than by accompanying the father. They were wounded, taken, and sent, all three of them, to Siberia; their house burned, their lands laid waste by the Russians, and all their property confiscated by the Empress. Madame Dembowska, who came from Kamieniecz, a territory belonging to the Princess, whom she had known as a child in the house of the Comte de Flemming, her father, went and cast herself at her feet, with her daughters; she had no difficulty in melting so generous and compassionate a heart. The Princess eagerly set to work to repair the wrongs suffered by this unfortunate family; she obtained their pardon, had the men brought back from Siberia, married the two daughters to their suitors, for whom she procured two considerable posts in Lithuania, and gave M. Dembowski and his wife a charming property on which they all lived, and where they never ceased to bless their benefactress. During my life among men, I have never seen any who were more conscious of their good fortune, or for whom gratitude had greater charms.

I received news of Madame Czartoryska daily, and the attentions of my hosts made my stay among them pleasant. I heard incessant prayers for her who was keeping me there. I spent a month without impatience in this tranquil spot. One day when I was uneasy at not having received any letter from the Princess, I saw her arrive in close disguise. A deity descending upon that house would have received less adoration there. We were left to ourselves. " My friend," she said to me, " I owe you a full explanation; I have had the courage to make to my husband the confession which I had planned; he took pity upon the distressing state in which I was when I spoke to him, and offered me no reproach. ' I shall let you have this child,' he told me, ' if you wish;

but you must bind yourself by the most solemn oaths never to see its father.' My tears were my only answer; could I promise to abandon you? You know my husband: stirred up by mischief-makers, he may be for a moment out of temper; but at the core he is kindly and indulgent. He is not at all jealous, and will soon be able to meet you without repugnance. Spend some time in Dresden and Berlin; let it appear that Warsaw is not the only goal of your travels, and I shall soon be able to clasp you once again in my arms." M. Dembowski's elder daughter was brought to bed during this conversation. We stood by the font, and named the child, which was a girl, Isabelle-Armance-Fortunée, after the Princess, myself, and the accident that had given her her godfather and godmother. The Princess returned to Warsaw, and I myself set off, the following morning, for Dresden.

The city and the Elector are as gloomy as the Electress is gay.[127] I was presently in high favour with her; the circumspection with which I received the marks of distinction that she heaped upon me won me great success with the Elector. The Electress decided that she must express herself more clearly. One day at court she took me into the embrasure of a window. "For a Frenchman," she said, "you are neither gallant nor discerning." And, as I made no reply: "Must I then ply you with questions to extract a few words from you? Is it possible that there is not at this court a woman to whom you could pay attention?"—"Nothing could be more true, Ma'am." "And why, may I ask?" "The old women do not tempt me, and all the young ones have lovers." "All? You know nothing about them: I know some who have no lover, and who would perhaps desire your homage, could they believe it to be sincere. Guess!" she added, gazing at me with a wealth of expression. The approach of the Elector interrupted this conversation, which was beginning to be remarked. I did not think that I ought to expose the Electress to a second, and left Dresden for Berlin.

I received news of the Princess regularly; but she would not allow me yet to go to Warsaw. I was giving close study to the military and internal government of Prussia. I sent a number of memorials to Marshal de Muy and to M. de Vergennes,[128] in the absence of M. de Pons, the King's Minister at Berlin. Fräulein von Hatzfeld, maid of honour to the Queen of Prussia, who had previously had a strong passion for the Comte de Guines, knowing that I had married his niece,[129] felt herself obliged to offer me the most cordial treatment. We were soon upon terms of confidence; she confided to me all the details of her attachment to M. de Guines, and ended by taking a fancy to me. The Princess's letters became no more infrequent; but they were colder, and were all aimed at postponing the date of my return to Poland.

I became very intimate with Mr. Harris,[130] the English Minister, whose society formed the chief pleasure of my stay in Berlin. He took me everywhere, and I was soon as well established there as I could have been in Paris. The King[131] returned from Potsdam; I often had the honour of paying court to him; Prince Henry treated me with the greatest friendliness. I was constantly in his company, and heard him speak of war and martial topics with an unwonted admiration. He was so kind as to tell me that the King desired that I should consider becoming the French Minister at his court, and had permitted him to inform me that he would with pleasure take all the steps that might help me to secure the appointment: this accorded in no way with my views; I thanked him and declined, giving as my reason that I was strongly attached to a military career, and I did not feel that I had any talent for politics. Prince Henry was so kind as to repeat his offer several times with insistence; but without making me change my mind.

During this time, Fräulein von Hatzfeld, whom I saw often, acquired a keen liking for myself; to which I was very far from responding. Indeed, I did not conceal from her that I loved another. Such an avowal did not diminish her attachment. I was grateful and touched; I felt that I owed her the warmest friendship. I consoled her, I pitied her, but I did not become her lover, nor did I cease for a minute to adore the Princess. People judged by appearances, and presently there was no doubt in Berlin that I was the lover of Fräulein von Hatzfeld: someone informed Madame Czartoryska; she believed the tale, wrote me a very cold letter, in which she told me that all correspondence between us must be broken off, and begged me insistently not to come to Warsaw.

Abandoned by the Princess, I thought that I would die of grief; I would have given my life to be able to talk to her for a quarter of an hour. A score of projects, each one more extravagant than the last, presented themselves to my mind. The Princess was too precious to me for me not to be swayed by the fear of compromising her. I obeyed therefore, and resolved to set off for France. On the eve of the day fixed for my departure, M. de Rullecour, a French officer who had transferred to the Polish service, came to me with a letter from Prince Adam, who begged me, as the greatest token of friendship that I could give him, to come and spend twenty-four hours at Warsaw, upon affairs of the highest importance, adding that I could easily conceal myself, if I did not wish my presence there to be known. I did not hesitate for an instant, and set off that same evening. I sent all my servants back to Leipsic, and kept with me only a single Polish horseman whom I had engaged at Berlin. I preferred an open carriage to any other, as being the lightest. I was barely conscious of the intense cold, of which many poor wretches died. The hope of seeing the Princess had absorbed all my physical and moral sensations; I arrived, and concealed myself in Marieville,[132] at M. de Rullecour's.

Prince Adam came there immediately to see me. He told me that he had communicated to M. de Stackelberg the memorial relating to the affairs of Poland and Russia which I had previously addressed to him; that this Minister had sent it to his court, where it had made such an impression that he had desired to confer with me about it, and had no doubt that, if France could but lend herself to the task, a rearrangement might be effected of the partition of Poland, restoring to that Power the greater part of the independence which she had lost. I replied to the Prince that I would be pleased to meet M. de Stackelberg; but that I had no authority, and that it was difficult for me to guess the intentions of a Minister whom I scarcely knew. M. de Stackelberg called during the night: we conversed at great length. The result of our conversation was a memorial which I sent to Versailles, and he to Moscow. It was impossible for me to remain in hiding until our couriers returned: I had myself, therefore, presented at court, and went about everywhere.

Madame Czartoryska was in the country, and did not return until a day or two later; she made her appearance at the play. I cannot describe the emotion that I felt in her presence. I went to her box; she received me most coldly. I had difficulty in obtaining permission to see her alone. On the following day she would not listen to a word of my excuses; she insisted that I should give back her letters and her portrait. I did all that she asked, and shut myself up at home, a prey to the blackest despair. She sent for me the next morning: I found her calmer and less severe. She asked me for all the details of what had passed between Fräulein von Hatzfeld and myself. I burned her portrait and her letters in front of the other, and promised not to reply to any that she might afterwards write me, a promise which I have faithfully kept. Fräulein von Hatzfeld is the only woman that I have ever treated in an ungentlemanly fashion, which she certainly did not deserve: and so I have often and severely reproached myself for my treatment of her.

The Princess forgave me with that grace which is inseparable from all her actions. I sought to enter into possession of my former rights; but she refused absolutely. "You would distress me," she said, "you would lose all, if, in your arms, something else occurred to disturb my happiness." M. Branieski, High Constable of the Crown, was more enamoured than ever, and proved his love daily by fresh extravagances. The Princess treated him coldly, and seldom received him in her house; but the whole of the Lady Palatine of Polosk's circle, in which Madame Czartoryska moved, was devoted to him. This was the only house in Warsaw to which no attempt was made to attract me. Princess Poniatowska[133] joined the opposition; and the Princess was so obsessed by all this that the precautions which she found herself obliged to take occupied much of the time that we might otherwise have spent together.

I was annoyed at this, I felt that she was partly to blame, and complained to her Lulli. "She loves you," I was told, "but you are a treasure of which she is over-thrifty. A little jealousy will make her more affectionate than ever, and will give her the courage to thrust aside anything that threatens to stand between her and yourself. Go about more in society; do not appear to be so completely indifferent to all the ladies; you will find it to your advantage." I rashly followed

Lulli's advice. The lover of Madame Czartoryska could not fail to arouse the curiosity of the other ladies; several of them made quite marked overtures to me, among others a young Countess Potoska Tlomocza,[134] who was niece to the High Constable Oginski's lady, whose house I constantly visited, and never failed to find her there. I pretended to be greatly taken up with her; the Princess observed this, and said nothing to me about it. The little lady was a great coquette, especially with myself.

I gave her my arm at a masked ball, where she spoke to me of the conditions upon which she would consent to yield herself to me, and even to accompany me to France. I had not supposed myself so far advanced, and had no wish that matters should go farther. I therefore evaded the question, making no definite reply. A little mask, who was sitting near me, rose quickly and vanished among the crowd. I paid no attention and left the ball-room a moment later. I went the next day, as was my custom, to take the air at Powonski. This was my chief amusement. The Princess arrived there a moment after myself, but as soon as she saw me, turned her carriage. I tried to overtake her; but she told her coachman to drive back to Warsaw as fast as possible. I was unable to conceive the meaning of this behaviour. I called upon her three times during the day without seeing her; I wrote to her that I could not for the life of me understand her behaviour, and that my head was reeling. She replied: "I have seen, I have heard what I could never have believed; you are betraying me for Madame Tlomocza." "You have undone me," I said to Lulli.

I returned home; I was seized by a violent fever, and had the most alarming attack. Lulli went to the Princess. "What have you done!" she said to her; "Lauzun is dying, and it is your work." Madame Czartoryska came to me, spent that day and the whole of the following night beside me, without my recognising her. I saw her at length on her knees by my bedside, in floods of tears. So sudden a transition from desperation to joy nearly cost me my life; I recovered with difficulty; the tender and touching attentions of the Princess made me prefer my extreme weakness to the strength which I had lost, and was beginning to regain. M. Branieski was jealous, complained in public, went so far as to threaten my life. " I am not in love with you," she said to him; " do not force me to hate you." " That is enough, Madame," he replied with fury; " I shall see whether M. de Lauzun is worthy to possess a treasure which I would purchase with all my blood." " Yes, Sir," the Princess answered haughtily; " he knows that my life is attached to his own; he will be capable of defending it; I require nothing more of you." M. Branieski grew calm, and nothing further happened. I was warned, however, that the High Constable would stick at nothing; that I had everything to fear from the mob of cut-throats by whom he was constantly surrounded. I was advised not to go about without an escort; I took no other precaution than that of being well-armed; and nothing happened to me.

I began to go more into society; the manner in which the Princess was treating me enhanced the curiosity that I inspired in all the ladies of Warsaw, who were eager to see me. A review of the hussars was an occasion that brought a great number of them together. They returned afterwards to an assembly given by the High Constable's lady. The Princess appeared to be asking them what they thought of her choice, with a grace that touched me; I let fall the plume from my bonnet as I stooped to pick up something. Madame Tlomocza, whom I had not met since the scene that had cost me so dear, offered me a fine heron's plume which was in her hair. " I beg your pardon," I replied coldly; "I am attached to my own singed plume." Madame Czartoryska, who had heard me, said to me with a charming glance: "Give me your bonnet, and let me put mine in it. I now prefer the singed plume." M. Branieski rose in a temper, and left the room.

That evening, at the masked ball at the Opera, he appeared to be seeking a quarrel with me. "Let us make an end of this, my Lord High Constable," I said to him; "five minutes' conversation at the Wola[135] will suffice. That will be far more worthy of yourself, and of me, than a dispute in a ballroom." He accepted, and we made an appointment for the following morning at eight o'clock. The whole of Warsaw soon knew of this and prepared to act as our seconds. The King was greatly annoyed, and sent, at six o'clock in the morning, for M. Branieski, with whom he held a long conversation, after which the High Constable called upon me with a numerous following, to tell me that he publicly disavowed all the remarks at which I might have taken offence, and that he begged me for my friendship, which he had earned by his esteem and consideration for myself. I had nothing more to say: I was obliged to give in, and Prince Casimir Poniatowski, the King's brother, made us embrace and make friends; Madame Oginska had sent me that morning a superb Turkish horse with a brace of pistols and a sabre, with the message that she hoped that they would bring me good luck.

That evening, our couriers from Versailles and Moscow arrived. The Empress approved my suggestions, wrote me the kindest of letters, and gave me the most ample authority. M. de Vergennes bade me return to court as quickly as possible. I fixed my departure for the evening of the next day but one. I dined at Powonski with the Princess. I clasped her for a long time in my arms; at last I was obliged to leave her. I could not tear myself from Powonski without a pang which the hope of seeing her again presently was powerless to assuage, and which was a genuine presentiment that we should never meet again.

I reached Versailles towards the end of the month of March 1775. M. de Vergennes, with whom I was not acquainted, received me with all the interest that would naturally be aroused by the important errand with which I was charged. He commended my action, and told me to start within a few days for St. Petersburgh, but he soon changed his mind; it did not suit him that the treaty should be made for my sake, and that I should remain there as the King's Minister to the Empress of the Russias, who seemed greatly to desire my appointment. M. de Juigné,[136] his intimate friend, had just been given the post. M. de Vergennes continued to raise absurd difficulties day after day, dragged out the negotiations, and sought to have them broken off, while evading the responsibility for a breach. During this time I lost a lawsuit involving an annual revenue of eighty thousand livres; this affected me little; my fortune was what interested me least of all.

I had on my return found the Queen on the most intimate terms with Madame la Princesse de Guéménée and Madame Dillon; they had spoken to her now and again about myself, and had filled her with curiosity to know me better. She received me kindly; I often had occasion to meet her at Madame de Guéménée's, where she treated me with distinction; I rode out with her regularly, and, in less than two months, became a sort of favourite. My favour was interrupted however by the necessity of joining my regiment. The corn riots in the villages near Paris had led to a concentration of troops. The Queen was anxious that my corps should come there, and that I should not leave the court; I did not feel that I ought to consent, and took my leave of her. She appeared to be genuinely distressed, and came that afternoon to Montreuil,[137] to Madame de Guéménée's, to bid me good-bye, and with an offer to ask the King's leave to summon me back for the Coronation, which I declined.

The Russian matter appeared to have been forgotten. I urged M. de Vergennes in vain to delay no further, but to give me a definite answer: he assured me that he had the treaty more at heart than ever, and that he hoped to conclude his negotiations in the course of the summer; adding that the King would recall me from my regiment, should that prove necessary.

On the very evening of my departure, the Queen sent word to me to wait for a few hours longer, and to meet her the next day at Montreuil. "Do not leave us yet," she said to me most kindly; "the grain riots are obliging us to assemble troops, we shall bring your regiment here." I replied that, if it was not necessary, I did not wish for a movement which would be inconvenient for my legion. "You are a fool," she answered, laughing. Baron de Vioménil,[138] to whom Marshal de Muy had entrusted the movements of troops, entered the room. "Baron," she said to him, "tell the Royal Legion to march, and bring them near enough for this foolish fellow not to leave us, as he proposes." The Baron replied that he would carry out her orders, and appeared surprised. I begged him to make no alteration of his plans. I went hunting again in the Bois de Boulogne with the Queen; she talked to me without ceasing, and from that moment my favour was so widely remarked that it was as well for me, perhaps, that I left that same night.

The Princess's letters became shorter and less frequent; I had word from Warsaw that she was entirely dominated by the Lady Palatine of Polosk and her circle and that M. Branieski never left her side; I wrote to her about this in strong terms; my representations were not well received. Wild with grief, I replied with despair and indignation. I made bold to ask for my child; "I would not have it," I said, "brought up among my enemies;" I was unsuccessful. We broke off relations and ceased to correspond. A profound sadness overwhelmed me. I remained faithful to the Princess and absolutely insensible to all the overtures that were made to me by a pretty little Madame de Monglas, who had been abducted by M. le Prince de Nassau,[139] and was living in retirement near Les Deux-Ponts, where I went frequently. I sought to find some attachment, or rather some distraction; but nothing appealed to me. I was on military duty at Sarreguemines, near Les Deux-Ponts. I was lodging with the mother of an officer of my regiment, and placed him under arrest for foolish conduct; his sister, who was young and pretty, came to me to beg for his release; I refused her. That night, when everyone was gone to bed, Mademoiselle Plunkett came into my room: "Are you really, Sir," she said to me with a smile, "as severe, as strict as you were before everybody this morning?" We conversed; she was merry and impulsive, and made me laugh. I promised to release her brother from his confinement on the following day; she embraced me by way of thanks, and filled me with desires which she shared more fully than she appeared willing to satisfy them. We had another conversation of this sort. She then left for Strasbourg with one of her aunts, and took leave of me in the merriest mood, the pleasure of going to visit a big town overriding any kind of regret.

I was obliged, upon some business relating to my regiment, to go to dinner at a house near Sarreguemines, with M. le Comte de la Leyen.[140] The tone of this household was friendly and polite in the German manner, which was not suited to my tastes. Madame la Baronne Dalberg, Madame de la Leyen's sister-in-law, seemed to me, however, to have a frank and merry nature, very different from the rest of the company. After a few hours, we were on as familiar terms as though we had been acquainted for years. I met her again some days later at Les Deux-Ponts. She confided to me that she had had a lover whom she had loved dearly; that he had behaved ill; that circumstances had separated them; that she no longer loved anybody or anything; that this was a sad plight, but that we must order our lives; that her sole interest lay in the education of her children, and in showing respect for her husband,[141] who was a good enough creature, but incapable of inspiring any respect by his own qualities. I offered myself in all sincerity; I was accepted in a similar spirit, and we agreed that, during the week following, I was to enter upon my new calling, in the huge and ugly castle of Hernsheim, right in the heart of the Palatinate, while the Baron was performing his week of service as Chamberlain to the Elector Palatine. I was given the warmest of welcomes, and, on the first night, made the Baron a cuckold, in the bed in which, for centuries past, the heirs of the house of Dalberg had lain.

The husband returned with his father, and several friends of the same water. I talked politics with some; I drank copiously with the others. I made them expound to me all the genealogical trees of the family: I addressed one and all as Excellency; I assured the old Burgrave that he would live for ever, the Baron that he would one day be a great Palatine Minister, and the Bailiff that the French armies would never again enter the Palatinate. In short, I was brilliantly successful, and had the satisfaction of seeing the Baroness's choice declared good and generally approved.

People have a fancy, in foreign countries, for making the most of their possessions. The Baroness took me to a party given by the Electress Palatine at Ockersheim, where she was by no means loath to display me, as well as a little cream pony which had been sent to her from Mecklenburgh, and which had arrived at the same time as myself. We were both examined with a careful scrutiny.

Four days later I was presented at Schwetzingen, where I was inspected as I had been at Ockersheim.

We returned from there to sup at Mannheim with M. O'Dunn,[142] the French Minister, and I was tempted to behave very badly there. Mademoiselle O'Dunn, a pretty young person, of a coquettish and mocking spirit, sat opposite to me at table and went into fits of laughter whenever she caught my eye. We went for a stroll together after supper: I asked her why she had laughed at me. "I beg your pardon," she said, "seeing that I know you so slightly; but it is because it is too funny and too ridiculous to see you become a lover in Germany. Are you aware that it is an office quite as important as that of Bailiff, and that you will have to appear upon all state occasions?" We teased one another merrily: I offered myself as lover extraordinary, without pretensions, without titles and without rights, but not without desires. Our walk ended, I escorted Mademoiselle home; I went up to her room where we would doubtless have continued moralising for ever, and perhaps have done worse, had not an old servant officiously proposed to light me on my way home. Heaven knows what would have happened, had I gone home in the dark; for Mademoiselle O'Dunn appeared to regard me with the best will in the world.

We set off early the next morning for Hernsheim, and I returned shortly afterwards to my regiment. Madame la Marquise de Chamborant,[143] a fat and foolish woman, whose husband was in command at Sarreguemines, took it into her head to perform a tragedy in society, and to make me take part in it.

As soon as she knew one part, I made her study another, persuading her that she would be infinitely better in it. I discovered every day some fresh difficulty in fixing that of the performance. She gave me to understand that, since she could not appear on the stage, she would gladly play some other part with myself. She was a very worthy woman whom her husband often punished with a hundred blows without any reason, and to whom, had there been the slightest occasion, he would have given a thousand. I felt myself bound to tell her frankly that I was not suited to her, and that what she required was, in every respect, a lover more stalwart than myself. She was not annoyed, thanked me, embraced me, and we continued to live on the best of terms together.

I went back to Paris, and my return to court was quite as brilliant as my departure had been. A race for French horses, which mine, ridden by a boy, won, brought me to the height of fashion.[144] The Queen appeared most anxious to see a race, and a great number were arranged for the following spring. I went to Fontainebleau, where the favour shown me began to have the publicity which has won me so many enemies since.

M. de Vergennes had entirely broken off the treaty with Russia, and, albeit she was offended, the Empress could not abandon it without regret. I became sincerely attached to the Queen, being touched by her kindness and confidence. I was anxious to make her govern a great Empire, to make her play, at twenty, the most brilliant part, which would make her illustrious for all time. I was anxious, in short, that she should become the arbiter of Europe; but the more I longed to cover her with glory, the more it seemed to me that I ought to make straight the road that was to lead her to immortality. I ventured to address myself to the Empress of Russia, and to ask her whether she was willing to let the Empire of the World pass, after herself, into the hands of a woman. I indicated the means of securing this with ease. All that was required was that a treaty advantageous to France, and for which Russia should have no cause to blush, signed by the Empress, and invested with the necessary formalities, should be placed in the hands of the Queen of France, and that, thus armed, she should have the courage to plead before the King and his Council a cause to which there could be no opposition. I had not been mistaken in relying upon the Empress: she received my proposals with avidity, honoured me with unlimited powers, and gave me no other instructions than that I was to ally through the Queen, at all costs, her Empire to ours. The Queen listened to me not without astonishment. The development of so vast a plan impressed her. She asked me to give her time for reflexion, and I saw that all was lost. There was, however, nothing that I would not rather have risked than to have the slightest cause for reproaching myself with negligence or impatience, and so I waited.

I appeared, meanwhile, to have risen to the highest pinnacle of favour. The Queen felt that she could not do too much for a man who wished to do so much for her. Perhaps indeed she was yielding as much to a personal fancy (inspired more by the strangeness of my life than by any other motive) as to what she felt to be her duty towards me. She rarely went out without me, would not allow me to leave the court, which was then at Fontainebleau, always made a place for me by her side at the tables, talked to me incessantly, came every evening to Madame de Guéménée's, and showed resentment if the party there was large enough to interfere with the attention which she almost invariably devoted to myself. It was impossible that such conduct should not be remarked; however, as my manner was not familiar, as I was not an intriguer, as I never asked for anything either for myself or for anyone else, the greedy swarm of courtiers, before declaring themselves for or against me, sought whether they could not derive some advantage from my influence.

Madame la Princesse de Lamballe,[145] Superintendent of the Queen's Household, and her intimate friend at the time, came to Fontainebleau, gave a supper to the people whom the Queen treated with most favour, and did not invite me. The Queen bade me be there. I knew Madame de Lamballe too well to take this command seriously, and did not go. The Queen took me to her the next day, and said, in presenting me to her: " I ask you to love as a brother, the man whom I love best in the world, and to whom I owe most: let your confidence in him be as unbounded as my own." Madame de Lamballe was entitled to regard this presentation as the most important of confidences, and to suppose me to be infinitely dearer to the Queen than I really was. Her behaviour towards me conformed to this idea, and it was not long before our intimacy became noticed.

About this time M. le Chevalier de Luxembourg, to whom the Queen had at one time shown favour, and who was still a sort of favourite of M. le Comte d'Artois,[146] asked her for a private audience in order to lay before her the plan he had devised for setting M. le Comte d'Artois upon the throne of Poland. The Queen listened with embarrassment and dismay, and replied coldly that she did not wish to meddle in any way with affairs of state. She sent for me and repeated to me the conversation that she had had with him: I seized the opportunity to press her strongly to make a statement about the Russian Treaty, and saw with unspeakable grief how far this was beyond either her courage or her power; she showed such alarm and so little strength of character, that for the future I could rely upon her no more.

The Queen felt however that she ought to take an interest in my career, and, a few days later, suggested to me, at Madame de Guéménée's, that she should obtain for me, from the King, the reversion of M. le Duc de Villeroy's command of the bodyguard. I thanked her, and replied that upon no consideration would I accept a post at court; she asked me why. "Because, Madame," I replied, "I wish to be at liberty to retire from the court when I cease to be treated well there, when Your Majesty no longer shows the same kindness for me." "Your pretext is outrageous," she said sharply; "do you say this to me?" "Yes, Madame, I know the unfailing force of intrigue; I must expect to become its victim, to see the Queen withhold from me both her confidence and the protection with which she honours me, and I do not wish that any favour, any benefit, any reward for my services may ever give my enemies an excuse for saying that I have been ungrateful!" This conversation was interrupted but was resumed shortly afterwards before the end of the week.

Madame la Princesse de Bouillon[147] reproached me at Madame de Guéménée's with being gloomy and preoccupied, and told me, with a smile, that I was nursing a great passion in my heart. "If that is so," I jestingly replied, "it is an unhappy one; for you must admit that I rarely set eyes upon its object." "That is not what people are saying," replied Madame de Bouillon, "and I am assured that you are very kindly received." "At least, tell me the name of my passion, it is only fair that I too should know it." "It is too exalted a personage for me to venture to name her; there are, however, so few people in the room that I do not mind admitting to you that it is the Queen." Madame de Guéménée blushed and became embarrassed. "Then," I remarked in the coldest tone possible, "she must be informed of the good news, and

I shall go at once and tell her, without, of course, mentioning any names;" with this I gazed sternly at Madame de Bouillon, who seemed to me to be utterly disconcerted, and left the room.

I went to the Queen's apartments and met her on her way to Benediction: I begged her to grant me half-an-hour's audience after Benediction. She told me to wait, took me into her cabinet as soon as she returned, and said: "What is the news?" "I have felt it my duty to inform Your Majesty that people have ventured to misinterpret my unbounded attachment to her person, and have carried their audacity so far as to condemn the favour with which she honours me. I venture to implore her to modify the most striking proof of that favour, and to permit me to present myself less frequently before her." "You think so?" she replied with heat; "am I to give way to insolent gossip which I have never had any reason to fear? And could I be excused if I sacrificed to it the man upon whom, of all the men in the world, I most rely, and whose attachment is most necessary to me?" "Yes, your Majesty must, and I can expect nothing else; terrible as it is for me to forego the pleasure of consecrating to her my service and my life, I must make up my mind to do so, take advantage, since circumstances so require, of the asylum that is offered me by a great Princess, and flee from the persecutions that are being prepared for me everywhere in my native land." "You think then that I shall not defend you?" "I make bold to implore Your Majesty, I make bold indeed to demand, as the sole reward of my absolute devotion, that she shall not compromise herself in supporting me; I am sufficient for my own defence." "What! You wish me to be so cowardly. . . . No, M. de Lauzun, our cause is indivisible, they shall not destroy you without destroying me!" "Oh, Madame, can the private interests of a subject be compared to the great interests of the Queen?" "Of such a subject as yourself, Lauzun? Do not forsake me, I beg of you. What will become of me, if you forsake me?" Her eyes were filled with tears. Touched myself to the bottom of my heart, I threw myself at her feet: "Oh that I could repay such kindness with my life! So generous a sensibility!" She gave me her hand, I kissed it many times with ardour, without changing my posture. She bent over me with great tenderness; she was in my arms when I rose, I pressed her to my heart, which was throbbing violently; she blushed; but I could see no anger in her eyes.

"Well!" she went on, drawing back a little, "am I to obtain nothing?" "Do you think so?" I retorted hotly, "am I my own master? Are not you everything to me? It is you alone whom I wish to serve, you are my only Sovereign! Yes!" I continued more sadly, "you are my Queen, you are the Queen of France!" Her eyes seemed to be asking me to give her yet another title, I was tempted to enjoy the good fortune which appeared to be offered me. Two reasons restrained me; I have never cared to owe the surrender of a woman to a moment of which she might afterwards repent, and I could not have borne the thought that Madame Czartoryska might suppose herself sacrificed to my ambition; I therefore recovered myself fairly promptly: "I shall not take any step," I said gravely, "without Your Majesty's orders; she shall dispose of my fate." "Go," she said to me; "this conversation has lasted long enough, and has perhaps been too widely remarked already." I made a profound reverence, and withdrew. Closeted in my own room, all the dangers that I had just been incurring presented themselves to my mind, and, although my conduct had been highly imprudent, I thought myself fortunate that it had been no worse. The Queen had been neither courageous nor discreet. The King's Minister's were no longer unaware of the part that I had intended her to play, and were seeking zealously to collect sufficient evidence to have me sent to the Bastille, and to treat me as a state criminal.

I received, during the same week, a reply from the Empress of Russia, who, without entering into great detail as to the negotiations that had been begun, spoke of them as of a matter to which she no longer gave any thought; she made me the most tempting proposals to enter her service. I wrote to the Queen, asking her to hear me at Madame de Guéménée's, and in that lady's presence. She came there that evening. I did not conceal from her that in France I might be arrested at any moment, and that in Russia I was offered the most exalted position to which any subject might aspire: she repeated several times: "The Empress of Russia is very fortunate, and I am very unfortunate;" she then added: " M. de Lauzun, you are lost to us, I have long foreseen it." " Madame," I replied, " as I have already had the honour of saying more than once to Your Majesty, so long as I retain the good opinion and esteem with which Your Majesty honours me, nothing can alarm me; I am afraid of nothing. I shall not leave France like a criminal, I shall not leave the King's service without his permission, and he will not condemn me unheard. If I am attacked, my papers are in a safe place, and my correspondence with his Ministers will justify my conduct. I shall then be free to transfer my services to the Powers that do not disdain them." " They will not attack you, M. de Lauzun; they will not dare; people know that it is the same as attacking myself, and I am very glad that they should know it; but what answer will you send to Russia ?" " I shall accept, Madame, the Empress's offers, on condition that I do not place myself at her disposal until I can leave France in a befitting manner; not for six months, shall I say ?"

"Give me a year; that will be time enough; I hope that I shall find some way of keeping you; there is already one way of attaching you to my person; do not refuse it. M. de Tessé[148] will shortly be resigning his post, and I could make an arrangement that would be agreeable to him; would you not like to be Master of my Horse?" "Overpowered by so much kindness, I am fully conscious of its value without being able to profit by it. Would not this choice seem to justify the insolent remarks that have already been made; and Your Majesty must not be offended if I venture to repeat to her that I never wish to receive any benefactions the inevitable result of which would be first of all to make my disinterestedness suspect and afterwards to make me be accused of ingratitude. I shall wait for one year, since the Queen desires it, but without disguising from myself the impossibility of remaining in the service of France. This period moreover will perhaps be more than sufficient to enable Your Majesty to see me depart without feeling any resentment." Tears streamed from her eyes. "You are treating me very harshly, M. de Lauzun," she said to me, "I do not deserve it;" and, turning to Mme. de Guéménée: "Princess, join with me in making your friend promise that he will not abandon me; and if I should have a son," she continued, blushing, "could I remain happy, seeing him brought up by anyone but yourself!" "To serve him, Madame, as faithfully as yourself, would be all that my zeal could perform: I do not feel that I possess the talents necessary for bringing up, for forming the character of a great King." "There are few men like you, and I should certainly not wish him in better hands: the Princess, I am sure, will be of my opinion." "I should be suspect, Madame: Your Majesty is aware that nobody in the world is dearer to me than M. de Lauzun, and I believe him capable of anything; but

QUEEN MARIE ANTOINETTE
AT THE AGE OF SEVENTEEN

(From the portrait by Drouais (1727-75). Jones Bequest, Victoria and Albert Museum)

[*face p.* **128**

it appears to me as difficult as to himself for him to refuse the glorious position that is offered him, to remain in a country where people are so little conscious of his worth."

The conversation continued for some time longer; afterwards the Queen spoke in a whisper to Madame de Guéménée, who came up to me with a smile and murmured: "Are you greatly attached to my white heron plume which was in your hat when you took leave of me; the Queen is dying to have it, will you refuse it to her?" I replied that I should not dare offer it to her, but that I should be very happy if she would receive it from the hands of Madame de Guéménée. I sent a courier to fetch it from Paris, and Madame de Guéménée took it to her the following evening. She wore it the day after, and, when I appeared at her dinner table, asked me what I thought of her headdress; I replied: "Very fine!" "Never," she replied with infinite charm, "have I worn such an ornament, I feel that I possess inestimable treasures!" She would certainly have done better not to mention it, for the Duc de Coigny[149] remarked the plume and her speech and asked from where the plume came; she said with some embarrassment that I had brought it back from my travels for Madame de Guéménée, who had given it to her. The Duc de Coigny spoke of it during the evening to Madame de Guéménée with considerable temper, told her that nothing could be more ridiculous or more indecent than my behaviour with the Queen, that it was unheard of to play the lover so in public, and incredible that she should appear not to mind. He was none too well received, and began to think of ways of getting rid of me.[150]

My intention, and it was the wisest course, was to spend a great part of the winter in Italy; but the Queen would never agree to such a plan; and so as to absent myself for some days at least from the court, towards the end of the residence at Fontainebleau, I paid a visit to Chanteloup, where I found them all greatly taken up with the favour that I was enjoying. Madame la Duchesse de Gramont in particular was founding the highest hopes upon my influence with the Queen. She was not long in speaking to me on the subject, and saying that the fancy which the Queen had for me made everything easy for me with her. I told her that she treated me with distinction, it was true, but that laying claim to no influence, and being determined never to ask for anything, I could not judge what the extent of my influence was. Madame de Gramont replied that she did not wish to press me to confide my secret to her, if that was not my intention, but that nobody could doubt that the Queen's fancy for me would have the consequences which it must naturally have, or that I was her lover; accordingly, she did not offer me the insult of supposing that I would not make every effort to bring the Duc de Choiseul back at the head of the Ministry. I assured Madame de Gramont that she could not have more misjudged the nature of my connexion with the Queen; that it was by no means within my power to intrigue or to offer her advice; and that, even if I had an influence over her which I had not, I was too deeply attached to her ever to lead her to interfere with the King's Ministry; that everyone knew how devoted I was to M. le Duc de Choiseul; and that, even were it in my power, I felt that I should be doing him a very ill service in placing him at the head of affairs. "And why?" replied Madame de Gramont, with great vivacity. Because, I explained to her, M. le Duc de Choiseul could only suffer by it; that the object of the most ambitious men could be merely to combine a great reputation and general respect with high office and a considerable fortune; that it appeared to me that M. de Choiseul had nothing more to wish for in any of these respects; there was no Minister in Europe who had enjoyed so vast a reputation and such wide respect; that he was perhaps the only person who had seen the Prince who had banished him abandoned by his own courtiers for his sake; that were he to become Minister again, he would perhaps be made responsible for unfortunate events brought about by the mistakes of his predecessors. M. le Duc and Madame la Duchesse de Choiseul were of my opinion; but Madame de Gramont continued to repeat angrily that everyone who cared for M. de Choiseul ought to wish to see him once again governing a great realm, and increasing his fortune in every way. I would not let myself be persuaded; notwithstanding his devotion to the Queen, I could not blind myself to all the inconvenience that must accrue to her from a M. de Choiseul dominated by so imperious a woman as his sister. They continued to treat me very kindly at Chanteloup, where I remained for some days longer; but Madame de Gramont vowed me an undying hatred.

I returned to Paris, and nothing astonished me more than to find at my door a note from my Lady Harland informing me that she was in Paris and would be charmed to see me. Sir Robert Harland, newly arrived from London, was come to spend a few weeks in France in order to see his son,[151] who was at school in Paris. My behaviour towards Marianne was so circumspect that her poor Ladyship recovered all her confidence in myself, and allowed us plentiful opportunities for conversation.

Marianne, as great a coquette and as amusing as ever, admitted that during my absence she had scarcely given me a thought, and had been more occupied in finding a husband to her liking than a lover; but, in truth, she said, she could not find words to express her pleasure at seeing me again, and how I gained in comparison with everyone who had sought to win her favour. Miss Harland, who could not endure life in England and was unhappy at home, obtained leave from her father to spend some years in Paris in a convent, and chose that of the Assumption. As soon as she was installed there, her parents returned home, and on this occasion Marianne parted from me with the most genuine grief.

I had always been tenderly attached to Fanny, who had constantly shown so friendly and active an interest in my affairs; I was much taken up with her. I saw her frequently, and the unhappy Fanny, who had a quick head and a tender heart, and had taken a fancy to me from the first, now took so strong a fancy to me that I was as much embarrassed by it as pained. With any other girl as pretty and charming as Fanny I would have satisfied without attempting to repress the desires that she aroused in me; but, when I had been honourable enough to refuse to ruin Marianne, could I have been forgiven for ruining Fanny, who loved me in far better faith? And so I took the course of making my visits much less frequent, and saw that it was necessary to suppress them altogether. Fanny wrote to me, lamented her plight without offering me any reproach, and contented herself with informing me that in doing an honourable action I was making her extremely wretched, after which she kept the most profound silence.

The Queen had for some time shown a strong liking for the Comtesse Jules de Polignac.[152] A pretty face, a sweet and natural air strengthened this liking daily. It was to her that M. le Duc de Coigny turned to form a party against myself. Madame de Gramont hastened to join the band, and established in this group as her representative the Baron de Besenval,[153] who had formerly been attached to M. le Duc de Choiseul, and had been very kindly treated by the

Queen. The Baron attempted to quiz me; but a bad tone and a want of restraint are a great disadvantage at court. Comtesse Jules made a similar attempt, but with great gallantry, courtesy, and never a trace of ill humour. I very soon tired her of it.

I was still as greatly in favour as before. The Queen confided everything in me, and would scarcely ever allow me to leave Versailles. My behaviour was most circumspect; it was only with an extreme reserve that I allowed myself to give way to a preference which might be remarked. The Queen on the contrary seemed to be making a boast as well of the favour with which she honoured me as of the influence that I had over her. People again began to talk, and it was openly said at court that I was or was about to become the Queen's lover. Madame de Guéménée, who saw us together incessantly, was more convinced of this than anybody, and her extreme indulgence towards myself made her regard the Queen as fortunate in giving herself to a man whose detachment and disinterestedness could lead her only to what was worthy of her.

The Queen indeed showed the most tender affection for Madame de Guéménée and an unbounded confidence in her. She seemed at every moment to be anxious to confide some secret to her and to stop short with embarrassment. She spoke to her incessantly of myself with an interest and enjoyment which she made no attempt to conceal. Many people came to me seeking my protection and support. I received them politely, and assured them that I had no influence, and did not give myself the air of protecting anyone. M. le Comte d'Artois, a certain thermometer of the degree of the Queen's favour, was not content with treating me with the greatest distinction; he positively showed a respect for me, could not get on without me, and was so anxious to have me with him that it became most annoying and often unendurable.

The Queen liked to gamble, and knew that this was displeasing to the King. This obliged her to make some secret of her play, and to select from a very small number of people upon whose discretion she could rely. I represented to her that this was most unwise, and gave rise to gossip that was positively harmful to her. I exhorted her to play in the Royal apartments a game which she could play with anybody, and in front of anybody, adding that, at Madame de Guéménée's, she might do what she chose. This, and the advice that she should pay more attention to the King, are all that I have ever given her. She received them with that grace and that affectionate regard which accompanied all her behaviour towards me.

As I did not wish to appear to be paying court to her alone, I would quite often go hunting with the King; an exercise which bored me to death, as she very well knew. And so she never failed to ride with the hunt on those days, or to drive out in search of the party. The King always sent me to her and told me to stay by her side. He appeared to approve of this attitude towards me, and deserves all the more credit, in that the remarks that were being made in public had come to his ears; he had not been content with replying coldly to such as had ventured to repeat them to him, but from that moment had begun to treat me infinitely better, and to behave as handsomely to me as his nature allowed. He heard one day, during the winter, that M. le Comte d'Artois had ridden out that morning very early; he was greatly disturbed by this, and feared that he might have had some quarrel. They told him that I was with him, and he greatly astonished the people who were in his presence by saying quite calmly: "If M. de Lauzun is with him, I am not alarmed; he will not allow him to do anything foolish, and he would have warned the

Queen had he expected any action which he himself could not prevent."

Such was my position at the beginning of 1776. The reader will see presently the intrigues and vexations of all sorts that followed my rise to favour, and accompanied it for about a year before finishing it altogether.

At the end of 1775 I met at the play my Lady Barrymore,[154] one of my oldest acquaintances in England, although as it happened I had seen very little of her on the different visits that I had paid to that country. She was good-looking, full of wit and charm: I knew that she had a reputation for being impulsive: she appealed to me, and could not be dangerous for me. I went to see her many times. The Vicomte de Pons[155] had established himself in her house, where he gave himself airs of possession which appeared to be not without foundation. I have never cared to take another man's leavings, and I was prepared to withdraw, when M. de Saint-Blancard,[156] my cousin, told me that Lady Barrymore was charming; that I must not allow M. de Pons to boast of a conquest that he had not won, and ought either to make certain of his rights or to make her dismiss him.

This was not at all my habit. However, as she appealed to me, and, so far from any awkwardness, the publicity of our intrigue might have certain advantages, at a moment when the comment upon my attachment to the Queen was becoming too loud; I determined to ask Lady Barrymore what were her relations with the Vicomte de Pons. She swore to me that there was nothing between them. I offered myself: "And the Queen?" she said with a laugh; I told her how absurd and unfounded was anything that she might suppose in that direction.

"Listen," she said to me, "I am prettier than the Queen, and still too young to serve as a cloak for anyone else." I had some difficulty in persuading her that I had never dreamed of making her play any such part; she believed me in the end, as a proof of it applied her lips to mine, and did not postpone my happiness until another occasion; indicated, next day, to M. de Pons that he was free to continue to come to her house as a friend, but that her fondness for myself did not allow her to let him show himself there with any pretensions; and, in less than twenty-four hours, I had a mistress more authentically than it had ever been my lot to have one before.

This made me none too popular at Versailles. Madame de Guéménée was in despair at seeing me tied to a woman's apron-strings, and sought to persuade me that the Queen was greatly distressed. The Queen, indeed, spoke harshly of Lady Barrymore and did not treat her with courtesy when she met her, and, without any great consideration for myself, has always done me the honour of taking an aversion to the women to whom I have been supposed to be attached. I myself, in the meantime, was more in favour than ever, and was going with great regularity to Versailles, since the Queen and M. le Comte d'Artois could not take a step without me. Then the little vexations began: the first of them was as follows.

I had gone to the ball with my Lady Barrymore, who never missed one. I did not know that the Queen was to be there. I met her; she took my arm, talked to me at great length, and this was observed. Some days later, when I was keeping my room, having taken a severe cold, M. d'Esterhazy[157] came to see me, and told me that he had been too good a friend to me, for ten years past, not to warn me that the Queen was displeased with my conduct; that my manner towards her was too sedulous; that I had the appearance of following her about and of being in love with her; that only the other evening, at the ball at the Opera, it had been remarked how greatly I was taken up with her, and that this had embarrassed her. I asked M. d'Esterhazy what made him suppose so. He replied that M. de Lamballe, to whom the Queen herself had spoken about it, had told him. He implored me not to betray him. "I can make no promise," was my answer ; "the Queen owes it to my attachment to herself not to leave me to be informed by a third person, when I have the misfortune to provoke her displeasure." M. d'Esterhazy appeared to me quite disconcerted, and greatly alarmed at seeing me determined to write to the Queen; he dared not protest further, and left me.

I at once wrote to the Queen, and gave her an account of our conversation. She was extremely cold to M. d'Esterhazy, informed me that she had asked him very curtly not to force her to speak, and that I must have seen that what he had told me was plainly nonsense.

A great ball at the Palais-Royal[158] which Madame la Duchesse de Chartres gave for the Queen was, I think, the occasion of Lady Barrymore's first infidelity to me, which was followed by many others. From the Palais-Royal we went to look on at the Opera ball. Lady Barrymore went up to the Duc de Chartres's[159] box with M. le Comte d'Artois, and heaven only knows what happened there. M. le Duc de Chartres, who knew of my relations with Lady Barrymore, told me about it the next day. I mentioned it to her; she replied with an air of veracity that it was true that she had gone upstairs with M. le Comte d'Artois, to have a better view of the ball, that this might have been foolish, might have been scarcely proper, but that there had been no question of anything else, and that she had come down again after a few minutes. I am not suspicious by nature: I was not jealous; I believed her. I discovered in her daily more wit and charm, and she was capable of method, application and serious thought.

I attached myself to her, I was on the point of falling in love with her; but her frivolity, her obstinacy, her absolute want of principles, restrained me: I had, however, no fault to find with her conduct, until one of M. le Comte d'Artois' servants, who had been for a long time one of mine and had been greatly devoted to me, thought to do me a service, and to prevent vexatious consequences, by informing me that M. le Comte d'Artois was enjoying my Lady Barrymore as well as myself, and furnished me with proofs. Shocked at her infidelity, I began to reproach her; she listened to me with a calm which left me speechless. "I do not deny it," she said, "and in truth, I would have told you, had I not feared your hot and sudden temper." I decided to break with her altogether. "Lauzun," she said, "you do wrong to leave me. I like you, you suit me, I am very fond of you, but my freedom is dearer to me than you. I will not sacrifice it to you. I will not allow my lover to be a jealous, interfering, bullying husband, teasing me about my fidelity; I care little for M. le Comte d'Artois; I would give him up without regret, but I do not intend to make sacrifices, let me tell you. I shall keep him without making any ado about him, and I am very far from feeling for him the sentiments that you have inspired in me. Look," she went on, pointing to a portfolio upon the table, "there are all his letters, take them, keep them, do with them what you please; I swear to you, that I shall never make any such use of yours." I was astonished, and made no reply. She continued: "Do not let us quarrel, Lauzun, over so small a matter; the attentions of the King's brother amuse me, flatter my self-esteem, perhaps, and my vanity, what would you have? It is a child's plaything that I do not wish to have snatched from me. But this need not prevent you from finding in me always the most tender devotion, the most genuine interest.

My inclination draws me to you, I have the highest opinion of you, I promise you that you shall never be bothered by my little Prince, that he shall never have a single one of those moments which I have such pleasure in bestowing upon you. I have never taken so true, so keen an interest in anyone as in yourself; I have no wish to be your slave, I should be very sorry were I no longer your mistress."

As she spoke these words, my Lady Barrymore, carelessly reclining upon an ottoman, fairer than the dawn, only partly dressed, aroused desires in me, as she was well aware; passing her arms round my neck she drew me down towards her, and I was soon intoxicated with pleasure. "You find me intelligent," she said, as she showered upon me the most passionate caresses; "you are far more so. I feel that I should be a great deal happier if you converted me, if you won me over to your principles; but I dare not hope for such a thing." The reader can easily imagine that we came to an understanding.

As to M. le Comte d'Artois, she kept her word; I never found him with her. Her conduct was what she had told me that it would be: she was not exacting; and every moment that I could spare from Versailles she desired me to spend on herself, with an infinite grace, and I went to her almost every night. The assignations that she gave M. le Comte d'Artois did not disturb me. In one of the coldest winters that I have ever seen in Paris, she amused herself by making him wait four or five hours in his cabriolet, in the middle of the Place Louis-Quinze, and I did not leave her a moment before my time. As a rule I was not aware of this, and when I appeared to suspect it, she would do everything in her power to make me stay longer: and so the poor Prince began coughing in the most terrible fashion. He knew quite well that he was indebted to me for his treatment; only he never imagined that I was in the secret.

At the beginning of 1776, M. de Saint-Germain[160] decided to reduce all the legions at the moment when it was supposed that he was about to add prodigiously to their strength. The Queen heard of this before it was made public, and came to Madame de Guéménée's greatly embarrassed to know how she should convey the news to me. I could see that something was tormenting her ; but I did not know what it was. The Duc d'Harcourt[161] came in. "I congratulate you," he said to me in the course of conversation; "for it appears certain that M. de Saint-Germain is going to increase the strength of the legions, and raise them to two thousand men." The Queen uttered a cry and left the room. Madame de Guéménée, greatly alarmed, followed her. "I am in despair," she said to her; "you heard what was said about the legions ? Very well, they are being reduced. Your friend will be furious, and nothing can prevent him from leaving us." "He is indeed," said Madame de Guéménée, "greatly attached to his legion ; but if anything could hold him back it would be the interest that your Majesty deigns to take in him, and to learn the news from her lips." She summoned me. "Am I not wretched enough!" the Queen said to me. "The legions are reduced." "This event, Madame," I replied, "will give me back my liberty. I hope that the Queen will not allow the old and gallant officers of the Royal Legion to be harshly treated." She interrupted me. "They are to have excellent pensions; I have already seen to that. And you, what will you do ?" "I, Madame ? If I continue to serve, it will not be in France." "And so," said she, "it has been left to M. de Saint-Germain to rob us of the man upon whom I most relied." I could see the tears in her eyes, and was touched by them. "No," I said to her, "my attachment will never be dependent upon events; you shall dispose once again of my lot: it is no longer the King that I serve, it is the Queen; let her judge whether I am anxious to leave her service!" She gave me her hand without answering me. I kissed it again and again with ardour. She said to Madame de Guéménée, with her eyes upon myself: "I entered your house wretched, and leave it happy;" and away she went.

M. de Saint-Germain attended her orders, and told her that he had never had any intention of depriving me of the means of serving with distinction, by reducing the Royal Legion; that he was anxious, on the contrary, that I should benefit by the change, and that he was proposing to the King to give me a corps of 1,200 mounted chasseurs. He sent Baron Wimpfen,[162] in whom he had full confidence, orders to announce this to me, and to give me his word for it, assuring me that all that would happen was that I should retain the Royal Legion under another name and considerably strengthened. I had no complaint to make, and the Queen was highly pleased.

About a fortnight later, M. de Saint-Germain sent Baron Wimpfen to me again to tell me that, the corps of 1,200 mounted chasseurs which he had intended to raise having come to nothing, he had made an arrangement by which M. de Schomberg was to surrender to me the command of his foreign regiment of dragoons.[163] This arrangement was made, except that nothing had been said about it to M. de Schomberg, who, as was natural, refused to listen to a single word.

M. de Saint-Germain was the first to announce this to the Queen, with evidence of a desire to treat me very well. He said that some way out of the difficulty would be found; he was quite certain that M. de Chamborant would retire with pleasure from his regiment of hussars; whatever conditions he made, they must be granted, and his regiment given to me. M. de Saint-Germain advised me to convey in person to M. de Chamborant, at Sarreguemines, a most advantageous offer, and to try to bring his resignation back with me; which, he said, would be quite easy. This charmed the Queen; she liked the hussars, and nothing could have pleased her more than to see me in command of a Hungarian regiment.

I repaired to Sarreguemines with the greatest promptitude. So far from accepting conditions which were far beyond anything that he could have hoped, M. de Chamborant took offence, and replied to M. de Saint-Germain in a letter full of stupid maxims, in which he declared that he would never retire from his regiment. The failure of my negotiation caused great surprise at Versailles. The Queen, charming as ever, gracious in all her actions, gave me, on my arrival, a superb sabre, and was in despair when she heard that I had not secured Chamborant's regiment. She then decided to ask the King to approve of the Emperor's giving him a Hungarian Noble Guard, the command of which she intended for myself. I pointed out to her that, flattering as this honour might be, I should be obliged to refuse it, since its drawbacks were fully as great as those of an appointment in her household. I said nothing more about my military career, and several months went by without any further activity in the matter.

The affair of Comte de Guines attracted everyone's attention; this is what happened, and the part that I had in the business. Madame de Guéménée was giving a ball for the Queen every Saturday during carnival. Her guests danced in two of the rooms, and played in the rest. This was the time when the most terrible rhymes and songs were being made about the Queen. Fortunately, I had not yet been named;

but the comments upon the favour that was shown me became more disturbing every day, and I could not doubt that my enemies hoped to make use of them to bring about my downfall. I was playing at quinze with M. le Comte d'Artois, M. le Duc de Chartres and two other persons. Madame de Guéménée entered the room with the air of a person who has just received bad news, came up to me, and said: "Finish your game at once, I have something important and urgent to say to you."

I was convinced that the order for my arrest had been issued, and that I was going to be clapped in the Bastille. I rose and followed her. She told me that the Comte de Guines had been recalled from his Embassy in England in the most humiliating fashion; that he was accused of having acted contrary to his instructions, and of having deeply compromised the court of France in regard to the Family Pact.[164] M. de Choiseul, who had taken a strong interest in the Comte de Guines, said that there could be no excuse for him, and that were he his own son, he would ask for no other clemency than an assurance that he would not be brought to trial, and would readily consent to his being sent for a long term to the Bastille.

It seemed impossible to me that the Comte de Guines could have behaved so foolishly, and I decided to serve his interests once again, without expecting any gratitude on his part. The Queen and the Duc de Coigny arrived; and it was decided that she would abandon the Comte de Guines, and would have no hand in the matter whatsoever. I ventured to argue forcibly against such a course, pointing out that the Queen ought not to abandon so light-heartedly a man in whom she had shown so marked an interest. The Duc de Coigny insisted strongly that the Queen should not have any hand in the matter, and I made bold to reply more strongly still. I said that I was certainly not of the opinion that the Queen ought to plead for pardon for the Comte de Guines; but that I did think that the Queen should obtain for him that he should be heard before being sentenced. I added that, without this favour, it would be impossible for the Queen's most loyal servants to count upon her bounty and interest, and that I could judge from my own feelings the effect that this would have upon the rest. "That is enough," said the Queen, "I am convinced, and have made up my mind. I shall follow M. de Lauzun's advice; yes," she repeated in a charming fashion, "I shall gladly do what you consider proper in this affair." She went into the ball-room. Madame de Guéménée had come round to my opinion from the start of the conversation; but the Duc de Coigny left us, mortally offended.

The Comte de Guines returned from London; he obtained a hearing, and was acquitted of the extreme charge. The Queen prevailed upon the King to write to him saying that he was satisfied with his conduct and would raise him to a Dukedom. She sent for him for the first time (for he had never waited upon her until then), about nine o'clock in the morning, to announce this good news to him, and hand him the King's warrant; she said to him: "Be off with this, without losing a moment, to M. de Lauzun, for you owe your good fortune to him more than to anybody. Ask him, at the same time, to come at once to me."

I had been gambling half the night and was still in bed. M. de Guines made them wake me, and showed me the liveliest gratitude. I dressed in haste, and went to the Queen. "Well," she said to me, "are you satisfied, and have I followed your advice?" "How can I not be enchanted," I replied, "to see you just and beneficent!" "Will you employ me," she continued, "always for other people? and shall I never be permitted to do anything for you?" "No,

Madame; you know my profession of faith; I adhere to it more strongly than ever." "Strange pride! It tries my patience, I am more vexed than ever; extraordinary creature!" And she left the room.

Spring came and brought with it the races; I had a number of horses entered, which the Queen always backed, although in society this was not approved. At the beginning of April, I matched a horse against one belonging to M. le Duc de Chartres, for a very considerable sum, far too much no doubt. The Queen was greatly interested, came to the course, and a moment before the start, said to me: "I am so afraid, that if you lose, I think I shall burst into tears." This was overheard and condemned. My horse won with great ease, and the crowd, who preferred me to the Duc de Chartres, cheered me loud and long: the Queen appeared to be transported with joy. I had the greatest difficulty in preventing her from acquiring racehorses, and from riding in the English fashion. This was, I believe, the severest test of my influence over her.

A few days later, when we were out hunting in the Bois de Boulogne, the Queen observed a very neat horse carrying an English groom who was following me, and to whom she often spoke; she asked him whether the horse was quiet, and suited to a lady. The groom replied that he knew no better or nicer horse. The Queen said to me that she would like to have it. I whispered to her teasingly, that I would not give her the horse; she called my groom, bade him change to one of her own horses, and said to me: "Since you will not give it to me, I am taking it." The Duc de Coigny drew near us in time to overhear these last words, which "scandalised him prodigiously" —to borrow his own expression.

My sun appeared now to have reached its zenith, whereas it was presently about to set. The King was beginning also to treat me with great kindness, when M. de Saint-Germain, who had failed to keep one after another of his promises to me, offered me finally the command of the Royal Regiment of Dragoons which at that time was considered the worst and most insubordinate in the service. I refused coldly and without resentment.

The King sent for me to Marly, spoke to me still with a kindness and interest by which it was impossible for me not to be moved; he requested me to take command of the Royal Regiment of Dragoons, promised to make me a gift of the first foreign regiment of horse or foot that should fall vacant or be created, and said, as he left me, to M. de Saint-Germain: "Everything is settled, Lauzun is taking the Royal Regiment." M. de Saint-Germain promised to allow me to choose my station, to do everything that I might think proper, and added that, although the price of this regiment was 40,000 crowns, the King would give it to me without payment.

Towards the end of that week, the Queen heard at Marly that Madame de Lamballe, still her dearest friend, was sick of the measles at Plombières. She was greatly distressed by this, and thought that they were concealing from her her friend's dangerous condition. Nothing could reassure her: I offered to go to Plombières before joining my regiment, and to send her a more exact report. She accepted gratefully, spent the following day writing, and gave me a large packet in which she told me that she had said a great deal about myself. I set off at once, and arrived at Plombières, where I found Madame la Duchesse de Gramont, who, convinced that I must be in higher favour than ever, made me the most marked advances of every sort and did everything in her power to discover whether my visit had not some secret purpose.

Madame de Lamballe, who was doing well, wrote

with her own hand to the Queen, to whom I sent her letter by a courier, and I set off for Sarreguemines, where I was to assist in the disbandment of the Royal Legion, before joining the Royal Regiment. I could not part from those brave fellows, upon whose devotion I could so entirely depend, without the greatest distress. Our parting was truly touching.

I repaired to Sarre-Louis, where my new regiment was quartered, and was greatly astonished, on my arrival, to learn that M. le Comte de Saint-Germain, in addition to all his previous treatment of me, was making me pay 40,000 crowns for the regiment which he had given me for nothing. The Royal Regiment, which had been neglected by its commanding officers for thirty years, and was a stranger to any form of discipline, saw me arrive with an extreme alarm; but we were soon upon the best of terms together; I have never seen in any corps a better spirit, nor so great an anxiety to do good service.

I cannot pass in silence over a rather amusing adventure which befell me while I was stationed at Sarre-Louis. There was, half a league from the town, a chapter of canonesses called Loutre. The Abbess was a lady of quality from Germany, and her chapter was on the whole select. It included a number of pretty young people. Among them was a tall and handsome Mademoiselle de Surin whom the most graceful innocence rendered charming. There was no other society; I went frequently to the chapter, and Mademoiselle de Surin appealed to me more every day. She showed a marked preference for myself, which in any other girl I should have regarded as deliberate provocation; at table her knee often came in contact with mine; she kept treading upon my foot at every moment, and, whenever we were alone for a little, would kiss me in the most affectionate manner. I was greatly tempted to make the most of my opportunity. I was held back by the manner in which the Abbess, Madame de Warstensleben, continually spoke to me of Mademoiselle de Surin's innocence and the purity of her heart. I felt that it would be horrible in me to take advantage of the inexperience of a young lady of quality, and to imperil her honour. I continued therefore to use the same circumspection: I yielded without scruple to the allurements of a little Madame Dupresle, with a husband in Luxembourg, who was plain, but pleasant and gay. I learned in the month of October, as I was leaving Sarre-Louis, that five or six officers of my regiment had enjoyed this innocent Mademoiselle de Surin, and that she had not been afraid to leave the proof of this in their hands in the form of letters that could have but one meaning.

I received at Sarre-Louis a courier from Madame de Guéménée, who wrote to me on behalf of the Queen, and informed me that Madame Jules de Polignac had asked the Queen for the reversion of M. de Tessé's place as Master of the Queen's Horse for her husband; that albeit such an arrangement was possible only upon conditions which must certainly be against my interest, the Queen, who regarded herself as pledged to me, was unwilling to terminate this affair without my consent, and without knowing whether I made any objection: I replied, as I was bound, to the Queen and to Madame de Guéménée, that I had never made the slightest claim to the post in question and that I was enchanted that she should dispose of it to her friend's advantage. I did everything in my power to make my letter convey, in plain and cheerful terms, that the arrangement proposed by the Queen did not offend me in any way.

I returned to Paris at the beginning of October. I went the next day to Choisy, where the King was; the Queen received me most kindly, showed great joy at seeing me again, and talked to me aside for a long time. I left the room, and when I returned to it was in time to hear the Duc de Coigny saying: "You have not kept your word: you promised that you would not say much to him, and would treat him like everybody else." It was not difficult for me to guess that he was referring to myself. A minute later, the Queen came up to me to speak to me, and I said to her: "Take care, or you will get another scolding." She was embarrassed, but ended, however, by admitting the fact and joking with me about it.

The imminent prospect of war turned our attention to the need to put our house in order in India. A report had been called for from M. de Bussy,[165] who had spent many years in that country. This was tempting to me. I had my name mentioned to him by M. de Voyer,[166] who had been the most affectionate friend to me for the last ten years, and M. de Bussy was kind enough to wish to have me as his assistant. I told the Queen, who was strongly opposed to the plan, showed intense grief and annoyance, told me that she would never give her consent, and refused flatly to speak of the matter to the King. I had no other resource, for I had never met M. de Maurepas, whom the Queen disliked and had never allowed me to visit.

During the removal to Fontainebleau, I enjoyed the most absurd degree of favour imaginable; for the Queen was fonder of me than ever, was frightened to death of her own circle, who detested me, appeared to be exclusively taken up with myself, when she was not under observation, and, when people were watching her, often dared not utter a word to me, as she would admit with the greatest good humour. I pressed her to allow me to go to India; this would be the solution of all our troubles; she continued to refuse with the same obstinacy. Her circle supposed my influence to be greatly diminished, at which they rejoiced.

There occurred in the month of November a famous race between two horses owned by M. le Comte d'Artois and M. le Duc de Chartres. The Queen wagered against M. le Duc de Chartres and I against M. le Comte d'Artois. He lost, and, as we came away from the course, the Queen said to me: "Oh! Monster! You were bound to win!" She was overheard. This familiar mode of address alarmed people: they were afraid lest they had been mistaken. Their intrigues became more intense. The Queen's circle and that of the Duc de Choiseul, which clung to it from beneath, foresaw their own ruin if they failed to secure mine.

I had at this time considerable debts, and, whatever people may have said about it, this was in no way surprising. Madame de Lauzun had brought me an income of no more than 150,000 livres. I wished her to live in luxury. Each of us expected to inherit a considerable fortune, and the future could cause us no anxiety. My affairs had been badly administered during my minority. My trustees had made impossible bargains on my behalf by which I had suffered enormous losses. Considerable negligence, a far stronger inclination to extravagance than to method, had, in the ten or twelve years since I had entered society, plunged my estate in confusion. I owed about 1,500,000 livres, against a fortune of more than four millions. My creditors were not pressing, and readily consented to wait until I should be able to pay them without inconvenience. I had seen them all on my return from Fontainebleau, when I was in hopes of going to India.

They had all been satisfied with the arrangements that I had proposed to them; and I was as easy in my mind as if I had had no debts, when some officious persons purchased from my creditors the greater part of their claims. They were so anxious to acquire these titles, that they paid some of my creditors ten per cent. more than was owed them. Writs were served for all of these debts at one time upon the porter at Madame de Luxembourg's house, where I had never lived, and where it was perfectly well known that I was not living. I was then served with a bill for 100,000 livres payable that day se'nnight; it was with this object that the lender had suggested that I should accept liability for that sum, and had fixed the date of payment in the bill.

When all these matters were more or less settled, Madame de Luxembourg sent for me, tried to frighten me, and told me that I had not a farthing left: I replied that this was not true; she was embarrassed by the discovery that I knew more about my affairs than she had supposed. They told me, to frighten me, that my family might have me declared incapable, or even perhaps have me shut up. I assured the Marshal's lady most respectfully that I was afraid of neither of these calamities; she told me that they would come and seize Madame de Lauzun's furniture as security for the 100,000 francs which had to be paid within a week, and that the only recourse left me was to abandon my fortune and person altogether to my family, who would kindly dispose of both. I declined, assuring the Marshal's lady that the 100,000 francs would be paid and that her granddaughter's furniture would not be seized. I bade her good-bye and left her in none too friendly a disposition towards myself.

As for Madame de Lauzun, she was in a plight which nearly made me laugh on more than one occasion, though I was in no laughing mood. She would have liked to appear both responsive and generous, but she did not wish this display to cost her anything or to bind her to any promise. This seriously handicapped all the kind and touching speeches that she meant to make me; and so she decided to seek safety in silence.

I went to see my father, told him what had been happening, and begged him not to take any hand in it, asking him only to inform me, if anyone should suggest to him to have me locked up or declared incapable; this course, which did not compromise him, and would cost him nothing, suited him to perfection.

I went, upon leaving him, to my man of the hundred thousand francs, and reproached him bitterly for his unfriendly action. He agreed, and told me that he had been offered so high a price for the bill payable within a week, that he could not refuse so advantageous a bargain. I did not conceal from him how awkward the consequences of his action had been to myself. He was anxious to repair the damage that he had unintentionally done. He offered very honourably to lend me 100,000 francs for as long a term as I pleased, to enable me to redeem this important bill, an arrangement which was immediately carried out.

I busied myself the next day with assembling all my creditors, whom I found quite prepared to do anything that would be convenient to me, with the exception of those who had recently made themselves my creditors by the purchase of outstanding obligations. They were few in number, and I had, fortunately, enough money to pay them. My plan was to sell my land as soon as possible, to pay my debts, to travel with great economy, and to purchase annuities for myself and Madame de Lauzun, so that she need not in any way diminish her expenditure.

M. de Voyer came to see me, and said with his customary simplicity: " People say that you are ruined beyond remedy: I find it hard to believe; still, it may be so, and this is what I have to suggest. I have an estate which is called La Guerche, four leagues from Les Ormes;[167] the house is quite comfortable, and decently furnished. I offer you the estate and the rental for as long as you may choose to have it: I can do so without inconvenience to myself. If the price of the estate suits you better, I am offered a million for it, I shall give it to you and you shall make use of it: I do not wish to listen to any details. I have no better head, perhaps, for business than yourself." I was deeply grateful for what M. de Voyer was proposing to do for me. I refused his offer, having no need of it, and assured him that I should apply to him rather than to any of my family. The sacrifice was not great; for none of them asked me whether he could be of any use to me. I was afraid that the King might be put on his guard against me and receive an impression which it would be difficult to destroy; I determined to write to him, and to furnish him with an account of my fortune and of my debts.

I went to Versailles to beg the Queen to convey my letter to the King. She received me with an air of constraint and embarrassment, told me that Madame de Lauzun was greatly to be pitied, and that her conduct was very noble and showed great feeling. I replied that, certainly, I never doubted that Madame de Lauzun would show nobility and feeling on every occasion on which that might be necessary, but that I should never put her to the proof on a matter of money. The Queen inquired, blushing, what she could do for me, and offered me her protection, speaking rather more as a Queen that the occasion demanded. This made me decide to cut short the conversation. I begged pardon for having bothered her with the trivialities of my private affairs. I left her in a state of embarrassment for which I could hardly help feeling sorry.

I waited upon M. de Maurepas,[168] to whom I had never yet spoken. I explained my situation to him in a few words, and begged him to convey my letter to the King. He replied, with great kindness: " There is no time to lose; I am going at once to the King;

wait for me." He returned after a quarter of an hour, and told me that the King had been touched by my confidence in him and had bidden him assure me that I might count upon his protection and his interest, of which he intended to furnish me before long with proofs. M. de Maurepas assured me that, since part of my fortune had been employed in the King's service, His Majesty had decided to give me a considerable sum of money and a good pension. I told him that I should decline to accept either; that I had no need of money, what remained of my fortune being more than sufficient to my ambition. I attended the retirement of His Majesty, who treated me with the greatest courtesy.

I returned to Paris. I learned that M. de Guines had accused me, quite undeservedly, of every misdemeanour that could evoke sympathy for Madame de Lauzun. I allowed myself to make fun of him. He called upon me; he wrote to me, but I treated all his overtures with the contempt that they deserved.

I was far more sorry to hear that M. le Duc de Choiseul, to whose interest my constant attachment had given me a certain claim, was speaking of me in the most shocking fashion. As for Madame la Duchesse de Gramont, she said with moderation that I was a liar and a wretch. I felt that my presence was henceforth superfluous to the society of M. le Duc de Choiseul and of Madame, his sister, and ceased entirely to see them. I was sorry because of Madame la Duchesse de Choiseul, of whom I was tenderly fond and for whom I had nothing but praise; but, having ceased to meet M. le Duc de Choiseul, I could no longer call upon Madame de Choiseul. M. le Duc de Choiseul and Madame de Gramont said that I was an ungrateful wretch. M. le Duc de Choiseul had never done anything for me; I had shown the strongest proofs of attachment to him. He had squandered the fortune of Madame de Choiseul, which would eventually have come to me; he persecuted me at a time when I was in distress. It was not difficult to decide between us.

The rumour went about that I had squandered the whole of Madame de Lauzun's fortune and sold her diamonds, that I had given notes of hand and obtained credit on the lives of my father, Marshal Biron, Madame de Choiseul and Madame de Luxembourg. It was important for me to prove the falsehood of all these imputations. This was not difficult. I sold my estates to M. le Prince de Guéménée, charging him to pay certain of my creditors, whom this arrangement suited. I sold a number of drafts upon the King, forfeiting half their value. I settled everything within six weeks. I secured a legal separation from Madame de Lauzun, and proved quite clearly that she had never been asked to sign any document in my favour since the day of our marriage.

After depositing the funds necessary to guarantee all the conditions included in our marriage-contract, I was left with an annuity of 80,000 livres drawn from M. de Guéménée, a floating balance of about 500,000 francs, and a decent enough house in which, to tell the truth, I had but a life interest.

I offered to share what I had left with Madame de Lauzun, but she refused. Madame de Luxembourg insisted upon taking her back, would not allow her to keep even the diamonds that I had given her: they were sent back to me, I refused to take them. They were deposited with a lawyer.

The Queen continued to treat me kindly; it was not difficult, however, to see that I had absolutely fallen from favour. People had already taken care to inform her that I had joined M. de Maurepas in intriguing against her. It was true that this Minister had welcomed me in the most friendly manner, and was beginning to repose confidence in me.

Such was my situation at the beginning of 1777. There was nothing to keep me at home, and I had not lost the desire to visit India, although M. de Maurepas tried to make me abandon the plan. I attached myself to M. de Bussy. I revised his reports, which were useful, but not well written. There could be no question of the advantageous nature of his proposal, but the discussion was endless.

Lady Barrymore, whom I had resigned to a mob of lovers, had returned to England. The report of my ruin brought her back to Paris: she sent for me. "Listen," she said, "and do not interrupt me. People say you are ruined. I am wealthy, young, independent, I have come to propose that I share your fate and you dispose of my fortune; I will travel with you, where you please and for as long as you please. Do not be afraid of the fickleness of my character: nothing promises me so much pleasure and happiness as this plan. I wish you to adopt the authority of the most absolute and severe of husbands; I feel certain that I shall never seek to escape from it." I embraced and thanked Lady Barrymore, who was greatly distressed by my refusal.

It was about this time that Madame de Genlis[169] and Madame Potoczka sought to establish in France, upon the remains of a Polish Order, the Order of Perseverance.

I had furnished too many proofs of my romantic nature, and actually in Poland itself, not to be admitted without scrutiny.[170] The statutes of the Order were charming. It became very numerous, very fashionable, very select. Men of distinction, years and intellect made it a point of honour to secure election. A large wooden shed that stood in my garden became the temple of the Order. The Queen, always athirst for novelty, longed to visit it: they tried to keep her away; and, as was natural, her curiosity increased.

She was on the point of sending us a proposal to have our Order acknowledged by the King, and to make him grant us permission to wear, with our uniform, even when in attendance upon his person, the violet riband of our Order. The whole of her circle trembled at the thought of the Queen in an Order of Knighthood of which I was at the head, which seemed to them the greatest of all perils.

Our Grand Master had not been appointed. Our first rule stated that this must be a prince or sovereign of a reigning house, distinguished above the rest by some famous deed. Monsieur, the King's brother, then took upon himself to offer his candidature. It was rejected. We replied that we were making no appointment to this post, though we had no doubt that Monsieur would at once fulfil the conditions prescribed by our rules. Monsieur took offence. People began to make merry at the expense of our Order, it was turned to ridicule, and the Queen thought no more about it.

A young Madame de Faudouas, sister of the Baronne de Crussol,[171] who as yet was credited with no lover beyond M. de Nassau, whom she had lost, began to show an interest in me at our gatherings. A fine skin, good eyes and hair, simplicity rather than wit made her at this time not unattractive. We soon came to an understanding; but it could not last for long. M. de Faudouas was so jealous, she was so imprudent, that, for fear of a scandal which there was no other way of preventing, I was obliged to break with her.

Fanny Harland, as soon as she heard that I was persecuted, ruined, wrote to me: "Come and see me, I have a lover, give me back a friend." I hastened to her side, and Fanny received me with that tender affection which she retained for me to the end of her life. She told me that M. Edouard Dillon[172] was very much in love with her and that she loved him. I saw Fanny daily; I was sad, worried, surrounded by unpleasantness, and Fanny's attentions charmed away my sorrows and were a great consolation to me. M. Edouard Dillon was very anxious to marry her; he had no fortune. Miss Harland was bound, in any event, to have quite a considerable fortune, and the death of her brother, who was nine or ten years old, might make her one of the greatest matches in England. Marianne had a great influence over Sir Robert Harland, her father, an austere man with whom it was not easy to live. I wrote to Marianne, telling her that she must bring her father and mother to Paris, so that we might decide among us what was to be done to marry Fanny to M. Edouard Dillon. Marianne, who had a heart of gold, and was genuinely fond of her sister, replied that she would do everything that lay in her power, and that she hoped to arrive presently in Paris with the whole family. Lady Harland did come a fortnight later with Marianne; Sir Robert was detained in London upon business.

The good mother made the acquaintance of M. Dillon, who won her favour also; she took him under her wing and wrote to her husband supporting his suit. Marianne wrote to her father, who showed considerably less repugnance to a penniless lover than we had feared. It was impossible to obtain anything from the King to assist M. Dillon's marriage; but M. de Maurepas promised me that he would attend to the matter, and would obtain for him one of the first vacancies that he was qualified to fill. During this time my conduct towards Marianne was the last word in circumspection, and we had nothing to conceal from her lady mother.

Fanny's marriage was well in prospect when I was obliged to join my regiment at Vaucouleurs, the dreariest spot in all Champagne, which is to say in all the world. A month later, I received a letter from Fanny, who informed me that everything was settled, and that she was to be married, in a few days' time, at Haute-Fontaine. I went to Nancy to ask leave of M. de Stainville, under whose command I then was, to spend a few days at Haute-Fontaine. I arrived there two days after the marriage and found that Fanny had already achieved a triumph with Madame de Roth and Madame Dillon. I did not find her in the best of health; but she seemed happy, and showed the greatest delight at seeing me again. She was to spend the autumn in England; she made me promise to go and join her there in the month of October. Marianne was charming to me; since it was supposed that we were no longer interested in one another, we were allowed plenty of liberty.

One day, when I was riding in the Forest of Compiègne, at some distance from the rest of the party, she said to me: "Lauzun, now that my sister is married, we can talk about ourselves. Do you know that I love you more than ever, and that I believe that I shall always love you?" I shall spare her for whose sake I am continuing these Memoirs the rest of the conversation, which was very long and very tender. I shall say merely that we promised to write to one another with the utmost regularity, and that we never failed to keep our promise. Lady Harland returned to England and I to my regiment.

I was leading a life that was easy enough; quiet rather than pleasant, and suited to myself above all men. M. le Comte and Madame la Comtesse de Salles,[173] who lived during the summer on a fine estate a quarter of a league from Vaucouleurs, arrived there. I went, according to the custom, to pay them a formal visit. M. de Gouy, brother to Madame de Salles, was a captain on the unattached list of my regiment. I received the warmest of welcomes.

They gave great dinners, balls and entertainments. Madame de Salles came to return my call on horseback, in a dragoon's uniform, with leather breeches. This was quite enough to disgust me with a woman for ever. It did not however prevent me from enjoying this one, who was neither good-looking nor attractive, and had an appalling manner. I repented at once of my action, and cannot forgive myself even now. Our intimacy became intolerable. I began to seek desperately for some way of breaking it off.

M. de Stainville came to see my regiment, found it already trained according to the new regulations which he had helped to draft, was pleased, urged me to attend the garrison manœuvres at Nancy, an invitation which I accepted. I found at Nancy a number of Englishwomen. One Lady Blower,[174] with whom M. de Liancourt[175] was very much in love, and whose lover he was endeavouring to appear; and a little Mrs. Brown, extremely pretty, like a highly flattering portrait of the Queen, with whom M. de Stainville was greatly taken up; but unfortunately she did not speak a word of French, nor he of English. I was almost the only man in the garrison with whom she was able to converse; this created a close bond between us, and, to provide her with amusement, M. de Stainville would scarcely allow me to stir from Nancy. I fell in love with this charming little lady: but I was prudent and honourable enough to refuse to say anything to her, knowing all the dangers that a French lover might spell for her. She guessed my secret, told me so with a candour the like of which I have scarcely ever seen; she added that she loved me in return. My virtue could hold out no longer; I took advantage of her liking and of her sincerity: we both of us succumbed; but I was so prudent, I kept so close a guard over my conduct, that nobody in the world had the least suspicion of what was afoot. I did not long enjoy this pleasant intercourse. Poor little Mrs. Brown took a malignant fever of which she died, and left me plunged in the keenest and most genuine grief.

I returned to my regiment. As good luck would have it, Madame de Salles was no longer on her country estate. Madame E. Dillon had left for England in very poor health; she wrote to me fairly often; Marianne wrote by every post without fail. She appeared to have no other pleasure left. Before the end of September, her letters became alarming. She informed me, finally, that her sister was in the greatest danger; that the doctors were beginning to despair of her life, and that I had no time to lose if I wished to see her again. M. de Stainville allowed me to leave at once, and I reached London upon the first of October.

I found there a letter from Madame Edouard, written some time back, in which she expressed an ardent desire to see me before she died, and said that she wished to confide in me important secrets, which could be entrusted to no one else but me. I was to receive, after her death, she told me, a box full of papers which would serve at least to justify her whole life. I was about to start for the county of Suffolk, where Madame Dillon was lying ill in her father's house, when I received a latter from Lady Harland, who informed me that her daughter was better, that the doctors had ordered her the Bristol waters, that the whole family would set out at once and would pick me up in London on their way. I decided therefore to wait for them. Towards the end of the week Edouard wrote to me that the improvement was being maintained, and that within a few days they would both be in London. Two days later, I had a letter from Marianne, announcing the death of her sister.[176] I received at the same time an almost illegible letter from poor Madame Edouard, written on the eve of her death. She was distressed that she had not seen me, and spoke again of the box that was to be sent to me after her decease.

Marianne told me that they were plunged in the deepest sorrow, that they could not bring themselves to remain at Sproughton, and were setting off in search of a friend, whose name she did not mention; on their return, which would be in three weeks' time, she would expect me in Suffolk. I had been tenderly attached to Fanny; I was deeply grieved. London became intolerable to me. I went to spend a couple of months at Bath, where there was scarcely anyone; I lived there in great retirement. I took the opportunity to learn English a little more thoroughly; I took a lodging with an intelligent family who did not speak French: I made some progress.

During my stay at Bath, I received some letters from M. de Maurepas, by a special messenger. He told me that there was no longer any thought of M. de Bussy's expedition to India; he asked me to write to him regularly from London. War appeared at that time inevitable between Russia and Turkey. I begged M. de Maurepas to obtain the King's permission for me to go and serve as a volunteer in the Russian army. He replied that he did not think that the Empress would be willing to take French officers in her army; that, if she made an exception in my favour, the King would be charmed; that he would give me the strongest letters of recommendation, and would permit me to accept employment, were it offered me.

I wrote to the Empress: I received from her, by return of post, the most amiable reply. She offered me the command of a corps of light horse, which I accepted. I informed M. de Maurepas of this, and prepared to start for St. Petersburg about the middle of December.

On my return to London, I found that Sir Robert

Harland and his family had arrived two days before me. Edouard came to see me: we went together to dine with his family; they gave me the warmest welcome. I observed that Marianne seemed less at her ease with me than usual. A few days later they left me alone with her, and, with the utmost embarrassment, she asked me to return her letters. I sent them back to her at once; and it was not hard to see that, by his wife's sickbed, Edouard had fallen in love with his sister-in-law, and that he had been led by a touch of jealousy to do everything in his power to keep me away from Sproughton, where he felt that I would have seen too much of Marianne.

I thought only of obtaining the box that Madame E. Dillon had bequeathed to me. Edouard denied all knowledge of it. I plied Madame E. Dillon's maid with questions. She told me that her mistress had given her this box, which was to be delivered to no one but myself; that she had entrusted it to Edouard, who had undertaken to have it conveyed to me. Edouard said that this was not true; that the maid was a senseless creature; and I did not get the box.

I received letters from Madame Dillon in which she referred to poor Madame Edouard as an abominable creature. I was shocked at this, and did not hide my feelings from Madame Dillon, assuring her that I would never allow my friend's memory to be attacked in my hearing.

The news of the defeat of the British Army, under General Burgoyne, at Saratoga,[177] made France decide to support America; and, a few days before my departure for Russia, M. de Maurepas wrote bidding me abandon all thought of going there, since I should presently be employed in the King's service, and bidding me remain in England in the meantime.

One day when I was out riding by myself, in low spirits, on the Richmond road, a woman was carried past me on a runaway horse, in great alarm, and uttering loud cries. I sprang to the saddle, easily overtook her, and stopped her horse before she could meet with any accident. I invited her to mount my horse, which was quieter than her own: she accepted, and two men of a certain age, with the grooms who were riding some way behind her, joined her after a few minutes.

This woman, who might have been about twenty years old, was one of the most charming persons that I have ever seen. I inquired who she was; she told me that she was called Miss Stanton, and that she was niece to one of the Governors of the East India Company. I met her fairly often at the play, at the Pantheon, at Ranelagh, always with the same two men; she always invited me to take tea with her. I found her abounding in wit and charm. The two men appeared pleasant and intelligent, all three of them always had the appearance of being delighted to see me; she never invited me to call at her house, and I did not choose to ask her permission.

One morning when I was taking the air at an early hour, some miles from Chelsea, there came a heavy shower of rain. A passing carriage drew up; and Miss Stanton, who was alone in it, and had recognised me, offered to take me back to Chelsea, where she told me that she had a house. She was alone, I accepted; I took breakfast with her, and we were undisturbed. She plied me with questions which I answered without evasion; she asked me if I was carrying on an intrigue in London, I replied that I was not; she made me swear that I had no mistress, and then told me that it was only fair that I should know also who she was.

She explained that she was not the niece, but the mistress of the elder of the two men with whom I had seen her; that this man, who was honest and respectable in every sense, had an immense fortune, and that she believed that it rested with her to marry him. She never saw anybody but himself and his friend, who also was interested in Indian affairs; otherwise she went out when she chose, went where she chose with one of the two, and generally with both; this life, she said, suited her well enough; but ever since the day when I had stopped her horse, she had taken so strong a fancy to myself, that she would not have concealed it from me but for the fear of distressing a man whom she loved and respected. He had left for Ireland a day or two before this with his friend, his business would detain him there for about six weeks: she ceased speaking. I asked her to let me have those six weeks, of which she might dispose without danger. She consented with pleasure, and I may say that I have never spent six weeks more pleasantly, quietly or happily.

Miss Juliet (for this was her real name) was romantic, frank, sensible, occupied solely with the object of her affection. Her education had not been neglected, she spoke French and Italian well, was a good musician, had a charming voice and played well upon various instruments; she was extremely small, and the best idea that I can give of her appearance is that she closely resembled Madame de Champcenetz,[178] when that lady was at her best.

We took the air together every morning, on horseback or in a phaeton, on the most unfrequented roads. We watched the play from private boxes, and went home together afterwards. Barely once a week did I go into society; every day attached me to her more closely.

Our union had lasted for five weeks when one day I found her in deep mourning and in the greatest distress. "What has happened?" I asked her. "I have lost," she told me, "either my lover, or the man whom I regard as my benefactor and my father. Mr. Stanton returns to-morrow; fulfil your destiny, go to the wars, forget me, be happy. I shall long mourn for you. Do not return here even though I should implore you. I hope to see you again." I could not but feel regret at parting with this amiable creature. I met her two or three times at Ranelagh; she received me in a charming fashion. Mr. Stanton invited me to supper; with a glance she warned me not to accept, and I obeyed. Shortly after this, she went away with Mr. Stanton to an estate which he had purchased in the north of England. I believe that she went back to India with him: she has never written to me.

Living now much more in society than I had since my arrival in England, I began to meet people of all parties who conversed freely before me, and without having to take any trouble I was soon well acquainted with all the public affairs of the time; and I learned many interesting things of which the Marquis de Noailles, our Ambassador, could not have any knowledge. He was intelligent and respected, and, but for the fault of living in too great retirement, I think that he would have been a good Ambassador. I believe that he would have gone far more into society, but for the unimaginable stupidity of his wife, who was a constant source of embarrassment to him, by the incredible things that she used to say and could not be prevented from saying:[179] I cannot refrain from giving an instance.

At a large dinner-party in her own house, all of a sudden she said that she could not conceive why so much was said of the modesty of English women; that there were no women in Europe whose morals were more depraved, and that they spent their time in houses of ill fame. You may imagine the despair and consternation of the Marquis de Noailles. "But, Madame de Noailles, but really . . . just think . . . do you know what you are saying?" She paid no attention, but went on: "Yes, Sir, I am certain of it; and, during the last masked ball, the Duchess of Devonshire and my Lady Granby[180] were seen in a house of ill fame near by." The Ambassador nearly died of confusion, and the rest of us of laughter.

Mention of the Ambassadress has prevented me from saying that when I heard things of which I supposed the Marquis de Noailles not to be informed, I told him them, although I was far from intimate with him, and never thought of reporting them to M. de Maurepas.

Chance having put in my hands Lord North's conciliatory Bill with regard to America, long before he read it in Parliament,[181] I went to the Marquis de Noailles to ask whether he had seen it; he assumed the most important, ministerial air, and told me that he had. I knew that this was impossible: I changed the subject. He tried to question me about the Bill, I made no answer, and took my leave of him. I did not write to M. de Vergennes, with whom I had quarrelled; but I dispatched a courier at once to M. de Maurepas. He showed my letter to the King, and the Marquis de Noailles was unable to furnish a report until a fortnight later. This gave the King and all his Ministers the most exalted idea of the manner in which I learned everything that was going on in England. M. de Vergennes wrote to me, begging me to communicate to him my opinions of everything that I might see or hear. I replied with frigid politeness that I had quite given up any interest in politics and no longer held any political opinions. I continued nevertheless to send M. de Voyer and M. de Maurepas various reports upon matters not generally known, in which the French Ambassadors had taken no interest. My correspondence became very full, and began to occupy much of my time. I went less into society. I became bored with living alone: I adopted a girl who had little intelligence, but was pretty, gentle, neat, and suited me to perfection.

Madame de Lauzun did me the honour, about

this time, to send me a note drawn up by her attorney, concerning the possible effect of our judicial separation in the future, when she inherited the estate of one of her relatives, and dealing especially with the precautions that she would have to take so that I should not interfere with her disposal of her fortune. Madame de Lauzun's attorney had apparently no good opinion of myself, and did not conceal this: his language was absurd and insolent. He repeated incessantly: "Madame de Lauzun's attorney does not know why M. de Lauzun should lay claim. . . . Madame de Lauzun's attorney would be astonished if M. de Lauzun, after the way in which he has behaved, should suppose. . . ." I replied lightly and without resentment to Madame de Lauzun. My reply to her attorney began: "M. de Lauzun informs Madame de Lauzun's attorney, first, that he is an impertinent fellow, secondly that he does not know what he is taking about, and, so as to have done with him, that he whole-heartedly agrees to anything that may be convenient to Madame de Lauzun, whatever it may be."

At the beginning of March 1778, I sent M. de Maurepas a report[182] at great length and in great detail upon the state of the defences of England and of all the English possessions in the four quarters of the globe. He read my report to the Council; it created sufficient effect there for them to consider it necessary to send for me and to consult me about various points in it. M. de Maurepas sent me a courier, informing me that the King desired that I should come to Versailles as promptly and as secretly as possible.

I went to Versailles, I had several private conversations with the King, at the house of M. de Maurepas, who presented me to him with an affection that was positively paternal. M. de Maurepas, distressed that I should have quarrelled with M. de Vergennes, was most anxious to bring about a reconciliation; I had no desire for one. I could not however resist his urgent entreaties. We made friends again without any explanation, and I believe that M. de Vergennes was as sincere as myself, for I have never since had any fault to find with him, and he seems to have sought for opportunities to show his interest in and friendship for myself.

The King's Ministers now showed far greater confidence in me; and, by the measures that I saw adopted, I began to regard war as inevitable. I ventured to propose a great and superb enterprise: I suggested that, before declaring war, we should make the Bank of England bankrupt, and that this would not be difficult. I had managed to ascertain the funds in its possession, which were not considerable, and the resources from which it might derive help in a case of urgency, which were even less. A simple banking operation, the result of which would be to draw, for large sums in gold, from all the important cities of Europe, upon the largest commercial houses in London, in the same week, would force all the bankers immediately to withdraw all their funds from the Bank. The anxiety of the public would increase the loss of credit, and nothing could prevent the Bank from closing its doors.

This proposal was received with the greatest applause by the committee to which I mentioned it. M. de Necker, who was not present, but to whom it was communicated on the following day, was entirely opposed to it. He said that it would ruin all the banking houses in Paris. I did not believe him; I went to Paris to get information; I brought back a statement from all the bankers that they had nothing to lose by the bankruptcy of the Bank of England, except from MM. Germain, a firm which existed as a cover for M. Necker, who had a large interest in the Bank of England. He prevented my proposal from being carried into effect. He did more, he sent to England an immense quantity of gold in specie, to assist the Bank, should there be any attempt to interfere with it.

The King had the intention of beginning the war with an invasion of England at several points. I was too much in the fashion not to be employed in a brilliant capacity, and for the next six months no one could plan any expedition without thinking of making me commander-in-chief or second in command. All of a sudden they changed their minds, and ended with the ridiculous declaration[183] of March 1778, by which England was given a salutary warning to prepare for war.

I did not wish to return to England. M. de Maurepas wished me to do so. He was positive that the King of England would begin by recalling his Ambassador and sending the French Ambassador home, and would shortly afterwards wish to enter into negotiations. He knew that the King of England would rather treat with myself than with anyone else; and so he told me to remain in London as long as I conveniently could; he hoped that a good understanding would be re-established between the two courts; that, once peace was assured, the Baron de Breteuil would return from Vienna, the Marquis de Noailles succeed him there, and I myself be given the Embassy to England. M. de Maurepas urged me above all things to conceal from the Marquis de Noailles the object of my mission, and to find some pretext for remaining in London after his departure. I arranged my arrival two or three days after the declaration. I went at once to call upon the French Ambassador, who was prodigiously astonished to see me. He evidently thought that I had deserted. "Charmed to see you, of course

. . . but by what chance . . . ? Haven't you heard?" "I beg your pardon . . ." "Then you have not seen M. de Maurepas? . . ." "Indeed, here are letters from him and from M. de Vergennes." The latter bade him communicate to me his dispatches and anything of interest that he might learn.

While I was with him, he received a letter from my Lord Weymouth, in reply to the notification of the declaration. He told him that, out of personal consideration for M. le Marquis de Noailles, the King of England permitted him to inform him that he was recalling his Ambassador at the court of France.

M. le Marquis de Noailles told me that he was going at once to send a courier to Versailles, on whose return he was sure to receive orders to leave England immediately. He proposed that we should arrange to cross the Channel together. I told him that this would be impossible for me, and that, so far as I could see, my business would detain me for some weeks after his departure; he replied that he felt it his duty to inform me that this would not be proper, either for France or for England; I assured him that no one in England would take offence at my remaining, and that I hoped that the King of France would see no harm in it. He could not, in reality, fail to agree with me; in case my business were concerned with money, he offered me, with the greatest pleasure in the world, any that I might require.

I suppose that he thought that I was in love; for he suddenly assumed the ministerial air, and told me that it would be his duty to forbid me, in the King's name, to remain in England. I replied coldly that I did not consider that he had the right to do so, that in consequence my plans would remain unaltered; I should merely be sorry that he should do something that would probably incur disapproval. The Ambassador became speechless, while the Ambassadress flew into a passion which made her a hundred times more fatuous and absurd, so that it was all that I could do not to burst out laughing. The Marquis de Noailles's courier returned. He set off for France,[184] leaving me in England.

The Marquis de Noailles's courier brought me letters from M. de Maurepas with instructions at greater length than before, urging me to remain in England as long as I conveniently could. I had an inquiry made of the King by Sir Charles Thompson,[185] one of the men to whom he is most attached, whether my stay in London was offensive to him. He sent word to me with great kindness, that I might remain as long as I chose, and that if I wished to see and speak to him I should find him the following Wednesday, riding along the Richmond road, at eight o'clock in the morning. I was punctually on the spot; he came towards me, and informed me that he was very glad to assure me of his interest and goodwill, before I left England; that it rested with myself to remain there, or to return, whenever it suited me, if I was not afraid of being compromised in my own country; for in England I was too well known ever to be suspected. He personally was offended by France's action; and, accusing her of perfidy, he spoke of her with such warmth, that I was obliged to remind him that I was French. He ended the conversation by saying that no one would be more agreeable to him than myself in treating for peace, or as Ambassador, when circumstances should permit, and that he would then have great pleasure in taking any action that I might deem necessary.

I could not honourably remain any longer in England. I sent a report of this conversation to M. de Maurepas; I asked to be instantly recalled, and warned him that if I did not receive orders from him, I should leave London in a month's time. The month went by without my receiving an answer; I was about to start; the carriage was at my door, when I received by a courier from Spain a letter from M. de Maurepas, who begged me with the most solemn entreaties to remain for six weeks longer. This did not stop me, and off I went. On my arrival at Calais, I explained to M. de Maurepas the reasons that had prevented me from doing as he wished;[186] he was annoyed, but bore me no ill will.

My regiment was lying at Ardres, near Calais; I stopped there instead of going to Paris. I had brought with me a young lady from England. I rented a small mansion a quarter of a league from Ardres. I was greatly taken up with my regiment, and found the time pass pleasantly enough. The pious Duc de Croÿ,[187] under whose command I was, became so friendly towards me that he forgave me for having a mistress and even came to my house to drink tea with her. Miss Paddock had brought from England a young sister far prettier and more agreeable than herself, whom her extreme poverty seemed to destine to the same calling. I felt a scruple about this, respected her innocence, placed her in a convent at Calais, provided her with teachers, and have since been so fortunate as to procure for her an advantageous marriage to a man whom she liked.

Even in my absence, the King's Ministers, whom M. de Voyer never ceased to assure that I was fitted to any task, appointed me to all the expeditions that they were planning in rapid succession, and M. de Voyer proposed that I should undertake the conquest of Jersey and Guernsey; he wrote asking me to try to procure information with regard to these islands and to say how many troops I should want to attack them. Chance had placed in my hands certain reports very well written and in great detail upon Jersey and Guernsey; I sent these to M. de Voyer, and informed him that, given three thousand picked men and entire secrecy, I thought that I could guarantee success. At Versailles the decision was in favour of this expedition, to which they appeared to attach great importance: its success would indeed have made a great difference to our trade; it was necessary however to consult Marshal Broglie,[188] who was in command of His Majesty's troops assembled at the camp of Vaucieux; he was absolutely opposed to the plan, without knowing anything about it; he insisted that it would require at least ten thousand men and several general officers; this upset the Ministers; they preferred to think no more about the matter rather than to dispute it.

M. de Voyer proposed a surprise attack upon the Isle of Wight and Portsmouth, with the complete destruction of the finest establishments of the English Navy; he was to carry out his project himself, and to give me the command of all the grenadiers and chasseurs of his army: they began, as usual, by accepting the plan, then discussed it, and promptly abandoned it. M. de Sartines wished to send me to the Bermudas, to Saint-Helena and various other places, but without any greater success.

In the meantime my regiment received orders to join the camp at Vaucieux, and moved from Ardres about the middle of July; I marched with it; on the second day, I received a courier from M. de Sartines and an order from the King to report at Versailles and to give up my regiment: I arrived at M. de Sartines's; he told me that they were giving M. de Bussy everything he asked in order to stir up a great revolution in India, and that he still desired to have me as his second in command. He proposed to raise a corps of foreign troops of 4,000 men, and to present me with the command of them: he wished me to have two thousand men ready to embark with me in November, and the rest in a condition to follow four months later; I accepted.

I handed over the Regiment of Royal Dragoons, the command of which I obtained for M. de Gontaut.[189] I left the Department of War and passed into that of the Fleet, still retaining however my rank in the land forces. I then did a thing which I believe to be without parallel; for, in less than three months I raised, armed, equipped, and rendered fit for service a superb corps of two thousand men.[190]

I asked the King's permission to tell the Queen what was my destination. I went to her; I asked to be allowed to speak to her in private, an honour which I had not enjoyed for a long time past. I told her that I felt myself bound, in recognition of the kindness with which she had honoured me in the past, to let her know that the King was entrusting to me the post of second in command of his army in the East Indies, under the command of M. de Bussy. I have never seen anybody more prodigiously astonished; she could not without emotion see the man whom, two years earlier, she had treated so kindly, who had been accused at that time of intriguing against her, go to spend several years at the ends of the earth. Tears rolled down her cheeks; for some minutes she could say nothing but: "Oh! M. de Lauzun! Oh! Mon Dieu!" She recovered herself slightly, and went on: "What! Go so far away, separate yourself for so long from everyone that you love and everyone who loves you!" "I have felt, Madame, that in so remote a theatre, my zeal, such small talents as I may possess, would meet with fewer obstacles, would have greater justice done them, would not have to struggle so against intrigue and calumny!" "You are leaving us, M. de Lauzun! You are going to India! Can I do nothing to stop you?" "No, Madame, that is impossible, I am irrevocably bound to this plan, whatever it may cost me in the execution." The King joined us. "Well!" the Queen said to him, "so M. de Lauzun is going to the Indies?" "Yes," replied the King; "it was his own wish: it is a great sacrifice; I have no doubt, he will be most useful there."

The Queen came that evening to Madame de Guéménée's, who had not yet begun to decline in favour; she told her that she was distressed at the decision I had made, and bade her help her to make me change my mind. Madame de Guéménée replied that she was in despair at the thought of my departure, but considered that it would be impossible to keep me at home; her impression was that the Queen had been profoundly moved; she felt that she could answer to me for her good will if I did not go. I resisted every entreaty, albeit I did not conceal from myself the extent of my sacrifice. My vanity was satisfied; I refused the Queen proudly, I showed her that I wished for nothing from her and that I could play an important part without her, and I proved to Madame Czartoryska that Europe no longer held any charm for me.

I went to Haute-Fontaine, which was a severe test of my courage; I could hardly bear to think that perhaps I should never again see persons who were very dear to me. M. de Guéménée was in an indescribable state of grief. Madame Dillon shared it, and twenty times daily the tears started to my eyes: I found Madame de Martainville at Haute-Fontaine; I knew her but slightly; I had given two of her brothers commissions in my regiment, at the request of the Archbishop of Narbonne.[191] She thanked me for this, and appeared to take the greatest interest in my future; this interest grew day by day; she kept on repeating that she could not understand what could have made me decide to exile myself in this way, questioned me in detail as to my position, my troubles, my feelings, paid me, so to speak, unconsciously the most tender attentions. I could see that, by dint of hearing me commiserated, her interest had been aroused, and she had taken a violent fancy to myself. She was good looking and affectionate; I echoed her sentiments; she flew into my arms with unconcealed delight: her intimacy with me was commended at Haute-Fontaine, which is a nest of lovers; I spent all my time there when my business did not oblige me to be in Paris or at Versailles.

One evening, as I was reading the *London Magazine* in my own house, in Paris, I came upon an account of the English possessions on the African coast, and of their garrisons. I saw that they were in very bad order, and that we could easily seize them. I discussed this with M. Francès,[102] who was with me. We spoke of it next day to M. de Sartines. I proposed to him that, while the squadron bound for India was watering at the Cape Verde Islands, I should detach one man-of-war, several frigates and four or five hundred men, to take Senegal, Gambia, and destroy the English settlements upon the coast. This idea pleased him; he asked me whether I would undertake to carry it out.

I felt some reluctance; for nothing could accrue to me but dangers and difficulties, and not the slightest glory from this expedition. I consented at length, and we agreed that I should start at the end of October, that I should go to the Isle of Oléron to inspect my troops, that I should then proceed with great secrecy to Brest, where the garrison was to furnish me with such additional troops as I might require, that the convoy, carrying what I considered indispensable for this enterprise, should join me below Belle-Isle, where I would be anchored; and that after I had taken Senegal, left a garrison there and established order in all the King's conquered territories, a frigate would take me to the Cape Verde Islands, which are quite close, and there I should join M. de Bussy and the army for India.

I set forth on the 28th of October; I left Madame de Martainville broken-hearted, and went to the Isle of Oléron.

The troops that I had raised were superb and were quite ready to embark. I lost no time, and arrived at Landernau near Brest towards the end of November. I had not been there three hours, when I received a courier from M. de Sartines, who asked me to come at once and speak to him at Versailles, and to travel with the utmost speed.

I started a quarter of an hour later; travelled night and day; and arrived at Versailles at four o'clock in the morning. M. de Sartines had left orders that he was to be called. I spoke to him immediately; he told me that certain unforeseen difficulties had indefinitely postponed M. de Bussy's departure, and had indeed made it uncertain whether he would go at all; that the Chevalier de Ternay,[193] Commodore of the Fleet, formerly Governor of Mauritius, was making a similar attempt with a considerably smaller force, and was anxious that I should assume command of the land forces detailed for the landing.

I asked permission to see the general scheme, the Chevalier de Ternay's plan, and his instructions; it was evident to me that he had abused M. de Bussy's confidence, and made use of documents which the latter had communicated to him, in order to supplant him by asking for considerably less. I refused absolutely to serve with M. de Ternay; M. de Sartines did everything in his power to make me change my mind, but in vain.

I saw him again the next day, and he renewed his entreaties, offering me everything that could make my commission more distinguished or pleasant; he went so far as to tell me that if I had a mistress whom I could take with me, he would promise her a considerable fortune in the King's name, and would give me a frigate for my own private use, the command of which I might allot as I chose. I refused all these offers. It was decided that I should go to Senegal; that if, before the 15th of February, I received no orders from the court, I should return to France; that my corps should not serve anywhere without me and should never be separated from me.

No sooner had I left M. de Sartines than M. de Bussy called upon him. M. de Sartines showed him the Chevalier de Ternay's report, without naming its author. M. de Bussy told him that the report was detestable, full of mistakes and false calculations; that if the man who had drafted it was not a fool, he was certainly a knave. M. de Sartines was appalled, and began to think seriously, to repent of having wished to employ M. de Ternay, and to seek out a way of getting rid of him, if that were possible.

I went to spend twenty-four hours in Paris, where I saw nobody but Madame de Martainville, who was overjoyed at so unexpected a visit. I then returned to Brest, where I embarked in a shroud of mystery on board the *Fendant*, a vessel of 74 guns, commanded by M. le Marquis de Vaudreuil.[194] Our little fleet was composed of two ships of the line, two frigates, a few corvettes and a dozen transports.

A succession of contrary winds kept us for a fortnight in harbour, without my venturing to set foot on shore. I received an anonymous letter, quite neatly written, in which I was warned that M. de Sartines, won over by my enemies, and hoping to get rid of me, was seeking to have me killed, and therefore had given me a commission from which I could not return alive.

In proof of this I was assured that none of the things indispensable to the success of my enterprise was on board the vessels on which I expected to find them, and that the inventory which M. de Sartines had given me, and also that which had been sent to me from Lorient, were alike false. The writer expressed his pity for me; paid a tribute to my courage, to my activity; he blamed my imprudence. I had a good opinion of M. de Sartines, I felt confident of his friendship for myself: this letter made no impression upon me; I sent it to him and set sail.[195]

We were obliged to anchor at Capo Blanco, to take on board our transports the things that we required to attack Senegal; I saw with grief and dismay that the anonymous letter had been only too true: whether by the negligence or by the rascality of his subordinates, none of the things that M. de Sartines had promised me, none of the articles named in the list that he had given me was to be found; the river pilots who had been supplied to me by the Navy knew nothing of the channel. M. de Vaudreuil, losing heart, suggested that I should abandon the undertaking. I refused to listen to him. It appeared to me that I should be able to land without exposing the King's vessels; and, if the bar was not defended by batteries, mounted upon unarmed vessels called pontoons, then with only the dangers of the bar to surmount, I might still succeed; but if there was a pontoon, we should have to storm it sword in hand, and probably but few of us would return alive.

The ships anchored inside the bar out of all danger; I stepped into a boat with a naval officer and we set out to sound the bar, which we crossed without difficulty. We pushed up the river and could see no pontoons; we rowed back across the bar and boarded our vessels.

The next day was fairly calm: we embarked our

landing party in sixteen vessels; we crossed the bar* with slightly more difficulty than the day before, but without any accident: we came upon no pontoons, and two days later, on the 30th of January, 1779, we reached the fort,[196] which surrendered after our guns had fired a few rounds.

I spent my time in restoring order, inspiring confidence in the inhabitants, especially the traders, and in seeing that the prisoners were well treated. Everything was far more calm twenty-four hours after my arrival than twenty-four hours before it. On the day after the capture I sent the frigates and corvettes to Gambia and the other settlements along the coast.

I wrote to M. le Marquis de Vaudreuil that, the colony no longer having any need of the protection of the King's ships, he was at liberty to fix the date of his departure for Martinique, where he had orders to join M. d'Estaing. He replied that he would see to that when he had taken on board all the provisions that he needed for himself and for all his sick, who were increasing daily.

As it was possible and indeed quite probable that I should be attacked shortly after M. de Vaudreuil's departure, I wished to put out as a pontoon in the river a corvette which carried quite big guns and was at my disposal; M. de Vaudreuil and all the naval officers decided that she would not be able to cross the bar, that it was impossible. I sounded the channel again, tried to steer my corvette across, and succeeded. M. de Vaudreuil, who had no desire to go and serve under M. d'Estaing,[197] decided to run short of victuals and to use this pretext for returning. He made exorbitant demands upon my commissariat, in the

* This bar is so dangerous that during the three months that I spent at Senegal I saw eighteen vessels of all kinds founder as they were crossing it, although thay had native pilots on board, and were of quite shallow draught.—L.

hope that I should not be able to supply them and that this would be an excuse for not following his instructions: I sent him everything that he applied for, although this was extremely difficult for me; not content with that, he established on shore, on an unhealthy and dangerous spot, a hospital of four hundred patients who behaved in the most disorderly fashion, and nearly involved me in war with the natives of the country; and sent word to me that he could not sail because he was short of seamen.

I disarmed all my vessels, including the one in which I was to return to Europe, and sent him the crews, telling him that I would look after his hospital, as indeed I did, an action which landed us in such straits that for a week or ten days we were reduced, in common with all the able-bodied persons in the colony, to millet bread and stale fish. Seeing that, notwithstanding this, M. de Vaudreuil did not go, I officially requested him to assemble a council of war in order to learn what were his intentions, which made him decide to set sail three days later. He was still able to join M. d'Estaing in time to take part in the fight off Grenada.[198]

I was now undisturbed, and could study with interest and curiosity a country in which nothing resembles Europe. I received visits from several of the neighbouring kings, with whom I made treaties. I received the news of the capture of Gambia and of several other forts. I at once dispatched an officer to France with the news of my easy victories; I decided to remain until I had put the island in a state of defence; I was so far successful that Admiral Hughes,[199] who expected to retake it with a considerable fleet, on his way to India, abandoned his attempt on the second day.

When everything was ready, I armed a merchant vessel as a cartel, in order that I might return on board her with my prisoners. I found myself greatly embarrassed for a moment; I wished to leave behind me money with which to pay the garrison and maintain the colony. It was true that they had supplied me with a paymaster; they had taken the precaution of supplying him with no money, and the little that I had brought for my own purposes had already been spent in the King's service. The English prisoners helped me out of my difficulty by lending to me, personally, all the ready money in their possession. I set forth to the great regret of the entire colony, who showed me every sign of strong attachment. I had been anxious to act for their good; I had been successful in certain respects, and the poor creatures were not accustomed to being governed by men of honour.

After a voyage of six-and-thirty days, I arrived at Lorient in the nick of time; for we had run out of both food and water. I received none too good a welcome at Versailles when I arrived there. M. de Maurepas was not on friendly terms with M. de Sartines; the Senegal expedition had pleased the King: this caused resentment; they were almost angry with me for having taken the place; the King would barely speak to me the first day, though he treated me very well afterwards; I had neither promotion nor pay. M. de Sartines was anxious to give me a gratuity in money, which I refused. Many things had changed during my absence.

The Chevalier de Ternay had been deprived of the command of the Indian fleet. The news of the taking of Pondicherry had suspended any movement of troops in that direction. M. de Sartines had broken his most solemn engagements towards myself; he had scattered my corps over all the globe, so that I could no longer serve in my proper capacity; his conscience pricked him, he did not know what to say to me and took the greatest pains to avoid me. I sent him my resignation, and made no further attempt to see him.

The court was at Marly; I found there Madame de Lauzun, on intimate terms with the friends of Comtesse Jules,[200] and with all the people who were seeking to injure me, succeeding in the attempt, and who were now in favour; you can have no idea of the manner in which I was treated by the Queen, and consequently by everyone else. They scarcely noticed my existence. This provoked much comment, and I was so foolish as to be momentarily embarrassed by it.

One evening they were playing faro: I staked a few louis, to keep myself in countenance, following M. de Fronsac.[201] Madame la Marquise de Coigny,[202] daughter to Madame de Conflans, one of my oldest friends, but herself barely known to me, was sitting beside him. Madame de Coigny spoke to me. I was quite absurdly grateful to her. I found her to be extremely clever and charming: I warned her that she would do herself no good either at court or in her family if she talked so much to myself, and that she must have great courage to do so. She replied that she was well aware of it. Never had anyone struck me as being so charming, so attractive; I became quite indifferent to the rest of the world. She restored my self-confidence, my gaiety; I was less sulky; I spoke to the Queen, I made jokes; she laughed, I became amused; she remembered that it was not for the first time, treated me as she would have treated me three years earlier, and the close of my evening was as brilliant as its opening had been dull.

I came away from Marly, nevertheless, with an impression of gloom: I did not know when I should see that pleasant Madame de Coigny, I had never met anybody like her; she filled my heart, she filled my mind. It was madness to think of her.

M. de Sartines was greatly embarrassed by my resignation; he did not know how he was to explain to the King that I had left the service, that I had been right to leave it, and that it was his own fault. He made an appeal to myself through M. de Maurepas, with whom he was beginning to be on slightly better terms. I told M. de Maurepas that I was leaving the Navy Department, because M. de Sartines had solemnly promised me that he would not separate my corps, and had dispersed it, had promised to complete it as soon as possible, whereas, on the contrary, he had shown his preference in taking under his Department M. de Nassau's corps,[203] which had not been raised for the King's service; I made no complaint (I told him), but I did not choose to serve any longer. The evening after this conversation, the King spoke to me about it very generously and with great kindness. He told me that he would give orders to M. de Sartines, and that he wished me to be well treated and satisfied.

M. le Prince de Nassau made an attempt about this time to take Jersey, but without success: he had been put to enormous expense, and would have been beyond redemption, had not the King taken over his regiment and his debts. M. le Prince de Montbarrey, Minister of War since the death of M. de Saint-Germain, offered to give me the proprietary command of the royal German regiment of which M. de Nassau was proprietary colonel, telling me that the King would pay his debts only upon that condition. I had no need to hesitate; I declared that I would rather never be employed again as long as I lived than take advantage of another's man's misfortune; I refused point-blank.

M. de Sartines was anxious to treat with me with a view to making me return to his Department; I insisted that M. de Vergennes must be a party to our discussion. M. de Sartines made me the following offers, which were confirmed by M. de Montbarrey,[204] which I accepted, and to which neither of them adhered: namely, to make me proprietary colonel inspector of a legion composed of 1,800 infantrymen and 600 cavalrymen, who were never to be broken up, and to give me or rather to renew to me on behalf of the King the promise of the proprietary command of the first regiment of foreign cavalry to fall vacant or to be raised in the Department of War, and in the meantime to attach me to the Hungarian cavalry. When this had been done, and I had given orders for recruiting in Germany, I went to Haute-Fontaine with Madame de Martainville, with whom I continued to be on the friendliest terms.

The bitter and well-founded complaints as to the manner in which prisoners of war were being treated in France, the prodigious mortality that had been the result of this treatment in the prisons, made me decide from motives of humanity to ask M. de Sartines to make me Inspector General of Prisoners of War, without pay, at my own expense. M. de Sartines accepted my offer with joy and gratitude, and gave me all the authority necessary to put a stop to abuses and rascalities.

I was preparing for this new duty when I learned of the formation of an army intended for a landing in England. I asked M. de Montbarrey to give me employment with it; he replied that it was impossible. M. de Sartines told me that he was very sorry, but that it did not rest with him; I was greatly offended: it seemed to me that my services entitled me not to be overlooked. I wrote to the King; he replied that I had done rightly in addressing myself to him, that my request was reasonable, and that I should be employed in the vanguard under M. de Vaux.[205]

My regiment acquitted itself splendidly and with great gusto, although we were worked to death, and M. de Sartines had once again failed to keep his word to us. M. de Vaux was, as usual, tedious, dull and trivial, and beneath his air of austerity, always the vilest flatterer of the men in power.

This army boasted so odd a complement of general officers, that I cannot refrain from describing them. M. de Jaucourt[206] was Quartermaster-General; I heard someone say that he was like the abbé Rognonet, who "could not make his petticoats into a bonnet"; M. de Lambert,[207] his chief of staff, had noticed the likeness and would repeat the rhyme to anyone who cared to listen to him. M. de Jaucourt took his revenge by continually setting him to begin over again the complicated task of embarkation. M. de Puységur,[208] Major-General, kept himself to himself, laughed at his superior officers and colleagues, and would shake his head a hundred times when he spoke of them. M. le Marquis de Créquy,[209] confidential aide-de-camp to the Commander in Chief, helped him to feed us upon poisoned rations and spent the rest of his time playing little tricks upon people, some of which were quite witty. M. le Comte de Coigny,[210] in the disguise of an aide-de-camp to M. de Jaucourt, as Minerva attends Télémaque in the disguise of Mentor, used to smoke in the general's anteroom, to give himself the air of an old campaigner, and when anyone entered his own room would be found writing essays on war. M. le Marquis de Langeron,[211] Lieutenant-General, an honestly boring fellow, an inveterate jester, when he invited anyone to dinner, would say to him: "Will you come and divide a slice of egg off the back of a tin plate with me? If there's not enough to eat, I shall have myself served up." M. de Rochambeau,[212] Brigadier-General commanding the vanguard, spoke of nothing but deeds of martial prowess, manœuvred and took up military positions in the open, indoors, on the table, on your snuffbox, if you took it out of your pocket; entirely absorbed in his profession, he has a marvellous knowledge of it.

M. le Comte de Caraman,[213] a complete dandy, obsequious, fussy, used to stop men in the street whose uniforms were not properly buttoned, and give them earnest little lectures on military discipline; he constantly showed himself to be an excellent officer, full of experience and activity. M. Wall,[214] Brigadier-General, an old Irish officer, reminded one, but for his intelligence, of Arlecchino Balordo, ate heartily, drank punch from morning to night, agreed with everybody and never interfered. M. de Crussol,[215] Brigadier-General, suffered from a violent attack of a disgraceful malady; his shoulders were crooked and his nature none too straight.

While I was at Saint-Malo, M. le Prince de Montbarrey arranged the marriage of his daughter to M. le Prince de Nassau-Saarbruck,[216] and, wishing to treat our M. de Nassau handsomely, employed him with the grenadiers and chasseurs: and, meaning to give him the vanguard of M. de Rochambeau's division, sent orders that his name was to be placed above mine in the Army List. M. de Puységur informed me of this. It was impossible that I should endure it, having been Colonel since 1767, whereas M. de Nassau's seniority dated only from 1770. They could not dispute my claim; for I had commanded detachments in the field in the Corsican campaign in 1768. I wrote to M. le Prince de Montbarrey and to the King; my seniority was restored.

M. de Vaux, to oblige the Minister and leave M. de Nassau in command of the vanguard, proposed to employ me in the third line. I made a vigorous but respectful protest; I asked him whether he was dissatisfied with my regiment or with myself. He replied that he was quite satisfied. Supposing then that it was my person that displeased him, since it was not the manner of my service, I suggested that I should leave his army: he restored my post to me.

M. d'Orvilliers[217] never encountered the English, never came into action; we never embarked, and, at the end of November, we returned to Paris. I found Madame de Coigny on the friendliest terms with Madame Dillon, of which I was glad; I met her quite frequently at Madame de Guéménée's, who gave a theatrical entertainment every Monday; she treated me quite kindly; and when she spoke to me caused me an inexpressible pleasure; I was unable to account to myself for the sentiments that she inspired in me; I did not venture to yield to them; they were no less delicious for that. I! In love with Madame de Coigny, young, lovely, worshipped, surrounded by admirers each of them more seductive than myself; Madame de Coigny in love with me! I, who was barely allowed to do good service at the other end of the world! I was far more certain of being without hope than without love; often I denied myself the pleasure of her company, of gazing at her, of listening to her; I did not wish, moreover, to distress Madame de Martainville, who would easily have read my secret.

I was beginning, however, to be displeased with her. Her behaviour towards Madame Dillon was not what it should have been: she did not listen to my advice, and it was clear that they would presently cease to be friends.

M. de Sartines now found it impossible to fulfil the conditions which he himself had proposed in the presence of M. de Vergennes; I abandoned my claim, and contented myself with what was already in existence, more or less, that is to say with eight hundred infantrymen and four hundred cavalrymen, under the style of Lauzun's Foreign Volunteers, of which I was to be Proprietary Colonel Inspector.

It was decided during the winter to send a corps of French troops to America and to give the command to M. de Rochambeau: I inquired whether I was to be employed in this army. M. de Maurepas told me that it was too far away, and would take too long; that I should have, by arrangement with M. de Bougainville,[218] the command of an interesting expedition to the English or Irish coast. M. de Rochambeau required some light troops; those that they wished to give him did not suit him; he asked for myself, and was at first refused; he insisted, and they agreed; but this was not decided until the day upon which he took leave of the King. I was astounded, when he told me, M. de Sartines having assured me only the day before that there was no possibility of such a thing. Madame de Martainville's feelings were hurt; she wished me to make a sacrifice for her sake. I refused, and we came near to quarrelling.

The day of my departure for Brest drew near; I did not call upon Madame de Coigny, though I was longing to bid her farewell. I met her at Madame de Gontaut's;[219] she proimsed, in fun, to come the next day to the Tuileries to receive my farewells; she did indeed come there with Comtesse Etienne de Durfort and several gentlemen. I saw that day how great my love for her could be. Ten times over I was on the point of telling her; at the moment when I was about to part from her, perhaps for ever, it seemed to me that I risked nothing by opening my heart to her. I felt no attachment to life, she might make life so sweet to me! I did not dare, however; the things that we feel most deeply are often the things that we find it most difficult to express: I set off two days later for Brest.

The troops were embarked at Brest on the 12th of April; contrary winds and a delay in making ready the convoy prevented us from setting sail before the 12th of May;[220] even then, for want of transports, we were obliged to leave behind one brigade of infantry, one-third of the artillery, and one-third of my regiment.[221] M. de Sartines had been scandalously misinformed, with regard to the transport vessels; there were not the half of those that, he was assured, had been assembled; I embarked in the *Provence*, a ship of 64 guns, under an indifferent commander.

We encountered fairly bad weather in the Gascon Gulf; the *Provence* had two of her masts broken. The Captain signalled that he could not face the sea, and asked leave to put into harbour. The Chevalier de Ternay did not share his opinion, sent to inspect our masts, gave us carpenters to repair them, and we continued on our way.

On the 20th of June, we sighted five English men of war and one frigate. This little fleet,[222] greatly inferior to our own, could not have escaped us, had we manœuvred tolerably well; but the Chevalier de Ternay was anxious to avoid fighting; he fought nevertheless for three quarters of an hour at long range; the English vessels escaped, having acquitted themselves far more gloriously than our own.

On the 4th of July, at the entrance to Chesapeake Bay, sails were signalled, and we sighted a convoy escorted by several men of war. After looking through his spy-glass the Chevalier de Ternay, without sending his frigates to reconnoitre, gave chase and lost his course during the night. About midnight, two English frigates steered across his course and fired several shots at him; they were going well, and we failed to overhaul them. We anchored at length in the roadstead of Rhode Island,[223] after a voyage of seventy-two days, with a prodigious number of sick on board, and a shortage of food and water.

Some days later, a squadron of fourteen or fifteen men of war, commanded by Admiral Arbuthnot, came cruising in the Rhode Island channel. We were informed from New York that they had embarked a great part of the army; we expected to be attacked at any moment: if the English had made an attempt in the first month, they were bound to be successful; we had not had time to entrench ourselves; the fleet and the King's army would have been destroyed. Notwithstanding the bad condition of our troops, we toiled without ceasing at building redoubts and fortifying ourselves.

M. de Rochambeau put me in command of the whole of the channel and everywhere within range of possible landing-places, and declared that he would never abandon Rhode Island or the fleet, but that the army would defend itself there to the last man. The English fleet disappeared, our sick men recovered, we began to feel easier in our minds. M. de Rochambeau and General Washington appointed a meeting at a place called Hartford, on the mainland, about one hundred miles from Rhode Island, where they remained in consultation for some days.[224]

During this time, Admiral Rodney arrived from Europe;[225] he began to cruise off Rhode Island with twenty ships of the line. The fleet turned broadside-on at its moorings; once again we expected to be attacked; messenger after messenger was sent to M. de Rochambeau; after cruising for several days, my Lord Rodney sailed away.

We now learned that the convoy to which Chevalier de Ternay had given chase on the 4th of July was carrying three thousand British troops, bound from Charleston to New York, and was escorted by only four or five frigates. With a little less precipitation, the Chevalier de Ternay could quite easily have captured it. His conduct was attacked, in the fleet and in the army, in the most indecent manner. He knew this, and was greatly distressed. It is indisputable that any man who was a little less timid would have arrived in America with three or four English men of war, five or six frigates and three thousand prisoners of war, and that

MARQUIS DE LAFAYETTE

[*face p.* 192

this would have displayed us in a brilliant light to our new allies.

M. de Rochambeau had promised the Americans the second division of his Army, and was awaiting it with extreme impatience. The moment was critical, and our affairs were in a bad way. The American army was short of men, money, rations, and clothing; Arnold's[226] treachery and the defeat of General Gates[227] at Campden added to their distress. M. de Rochambeau thought it necessary to send an officer of his army to France, who would explain the situation, and beg for prompt and powerful support. The general officers of his army, whom he had summoned, strongly approved this decision, and proposed to him that I should be sent, my relations with M. de Maurepas giving me a certain advantage over others who knew him less well. He informed them that he had already appointed his own son.

On the eve of his departure, twelve English vessels appeared off our coast, and caused us some anxiety, but a storm of wind scattered them in the night, and on the following day the Vicomte de Rochambeau set sail in the King's frigate *Amazone*.[228]

General Green,[229] who had taken command of the Southern Army after the defeat of General Gates, called for reinforcements, and above all for cavalry with which to face Colonel Tarleton's corps,[230] which had proved irresistible, saying that otherwise he could not be responsible if the Southern provinces surrendered to the King of England. General Washington was very anxious that M. de Rochambeau should send me. I was equally anxious, hoping to be of use there; I did not hesitate to ask to be employed in the South under the command of M. de La Fayette, although I had served in the field, as Colonel, long before he left school.[231] M. de Rochambeau refused; my action was strongly condemned in the army, especially by

M. le Marquis de Laval,[232] who, with several others, had taken a vow not to serve under M. de La Fayette, and had almost obtained a promise from M. de Rochambeau that he would not employ them under him. General Washington was grateful to me, and frequently showed his gratitude.

M. de Rochambeau moved his army into winter quarters at Newport. The scarcity of forage obliged him to send me to the forests of Connecticut, eight miles away. As I spoke English I was charged with an infinite number of details, boring in the extreme, but necessary. I did not leave Newport without regrets; I had formed a very pleasant circle of acquaintance there.

Mrs. Hunter, a widow of six-and-thirty, had two charming daughters whom she had brought up with great care; they lived in close retirement, and saw scarcely anyone. Chance had led me to make her acquaintance on my arrival in Rhode Island. She had formed a friendship for me; I was soon regarded as one of the family. I spent all my time there; I was taken ill; she took me into her house, where they looked after me with the most touching attentions. I was never in love with the Misses Hunter; but had they been my sisters, I could not have loved them more, especially the elder, who is one of the most agreeable persons I have ever met.[233]

I started for Lebanon on the 10th of November; we had not yet received any letters from France. Siberia alone can furnish any idea of Lebanon, which consists of a few huts scattered among vast forests. I remained there until the 11th of January, 1781, when General Knox, commanding the American artillery, came, on behalf of General Washington, to inform me that the Pennsylvania and New Jersey brigades, grown tired of service, had mutinied, killed their officers, elected leaders from their ranks, and that there seemed to be an equal danger of their marching upon Philadelphia to extort payment by force, or joining the English army, which was not far off.[234]

I mounted my horse at once to ride to Newport and report matters to M. de Rochambeau, who was no less embarrassed than distressed, since he had no means of helping General Washington, being himself short of money, and not having received a letter from Europe since landing in America. A few days later, we heard that Congress had sent them a small sum on account, and that everything was now quiet.

M. de Rochambeau sent me to New Windsor, on the North River, where General Washington had his headquarters, about two hundred miles from the French army. General Washington received me most kindly, and showed a desire to employ me straight away. He told me that he hoped to go at the earliest possible moment to Newport to visit the French army and M. de Rochambeau. He confided to me that, Mr. Arnold having gone down to work great havoc in Virginia, he had formed the plan of seizing him there; that he was going to make M. de La Fayette advance by land with all the light infantry of his army; he was asking that the King's fleet should go and anchor in Chesapeake Bay, and there land a detachment of the French army to cut off Arnold's retreat. He added that he would request M. de Rochambeau to give me the command of this detachment, regarding it as essential that the French and American troops should live together on good terms, as well as the men who commanded them, and that the French officer should be able to speak to the American officers, and to make himself understood by them.

I stayed for two days at General Headquarters,[235] and came near to drowning as I went back over the North River; it was adrift with blocks of ice which the current swept down at such a pace that it was impossible to steer my boat; it swung round and began to fill with water; it was just about to sink when a huge block of ice came alongside; we sprang upon it, and, jumping from block to block, it took us about three hours to get ashore, after we had given ourselves up for lost a score of times.

On reaching Lebanon, I heard of the death of the Chevalier de Ternay,[236] who had died, it was said, of a broken heart, and found orders from M. de Rochambeau which detained me for some days in Connecticut. I then returned to Rhode Island, where they were speaking openly of the movement of the fleet with a detachment of the army. I went to M. de Rochambeau with a request that I might be employed; I was not at all well received; I pointed out to him that I was asking for justice rather than favour, since it was my turn to march. He told me that there were no turns in the vanguard; an hour or two earlier he had said the opposite; he added that he liked zeal, but did not care for ardour. I assured him that he would cure me completely of any ardour to serve under his command; he softened, almost made excuses, informed me privately that he was bound by personal obligations to the Marquis de Laval, and had no other means of showing his gratitude; that he had promised not to employ him under a brigadier; that as this detachment was to operate separately from La Fayette's corps, and to be only indirectly under his orders, the Marquis de Laval had shown a keen desire for it; I made no reply; but he must have seen by my face that this was not fair treatment. I asked to be allowed to go as a volunteer; he said that that would be ridiculous, and refused. In the course of the day, M. de Rochambeau thought the matter over, gave the command of the detachment to the Baron de Vioménil, who had not asked for it, and gave only a subordinate command to the Marquis de Laval, who has never forgiven him.

General Washington arrived at Newport.[237] This arrangement was peculiarly distasteful to him, and he did not conceal his annoyance. M. de Rochambeau had done two things that were bound to displease him: he was not giving him the officer for whom he had asked, and he was giving him one, on the contrary, who would take the command of the expedition from M. de La Fayette, to whom he had intended to give it; he made M. de Rochambeau see that his requests were to be regarded as orders, but he did not choose to alter anything that had been done.

The fleet under the command of M. Destouches,[238] a former Captain in the Navy, set sail with twelve hundred troops, and a few days later General Washington left Rhode Island. I escorted him as far as Stafford, and returned to my regiment, where I received a letter from M. de Rochambeau, who informed me that, as he might easily be attacked during the absence of the fleet, he wished me to return to him. I obeyed.

We had now been ten months away from France; we had not yet received a single letter nor one penny in money; the frigate *Astrée* arrived, and informed us that M. de Montbarrey and M. de Sartines had left the Ministry, and had been succeeded by M. de Ségur and M. de Castries,[239] who had decided against employing the second division; I wrote at once an urgent demand for the four hundred men of my regiment who had been kept at home and who could not be refused me without atrocious injustice.

About eighteen days after the sailing of the fleet, a fleet was signalled in foggy weather, which was entering the channel under full sail; the alarm was sounded, the whole army stood to arms; we supposed that defeat was certain. We never imagined that it was our own fleet, and we were mistaken, for it was; it had manœuvred so adroitly that it arrived at the mouth of Chesapeake Bay twenty-four hours after the English fleet which had sailed three days later. The day[240] had been most glorious for the King's arms; but our enemies had prevented us from entering the Bay, with the consequence that Arnold was out of all danger. M. de La Fayette had failed to secure his object, and was left in some embarrassment. Some of our vessels had suffered severely, especially the *Conquérant*, in which the Marquis de Laval had embarked; she had fought splendidly, with heavy losses.

I returned once again to Lebanon, where M. de Rochambeau ordered me to assemble a great number of horses suited for artillery, and to make all preparations for the advance of the army. At this time the *Concorde*, a frigate hailing from France, brought back M. le Vicomte de Rochambeau,[241] who had not been able even to have himself taken seriously, and M. de Barras,[242] Commodore in the Navy, who was sent out to succeed the Chevalier de Ternay. The latest instructions from the court made M. de Rochambeau anxious for a meeting with General Washington, to settle the plan of campaign for the army and fleet. M. de Barras invested M. de Rochambeau with full powers. The Generals met once again at Hartford.

It was officially decided and signed at this conference[243] that the French army should march to the North River, and there join the American army, and that the two armies combined should approach as near as possible to New York; that the fleet should go to Boston to await the sea forces that were coming from Europe, seeing that it was no longer in safety off Rhode Island, the island being no longer guarded by land forces.

The letters that M. de Rochambeau had received by the *Concorde* had shown him that the men whom he had treated most kindly had by no means spared him in their letters, principally the Marquis de Laval, who, without any evil intention, had written freely to a number of ladies who had shown his letters to others. I had not spoken of him, and my silence became a merit; he displayed greater confidence in me, showed me his plan of campaign, and decided to take me with him to Rhode Island to make certain preliminary arrangements.

We had no sooner arrived at Newport than the Chevalier de Chastellux,[244] who is too hot-headed ever to stick to one idea for any length of time, thought that it would be more to our advantage if the fleet were to wait in Rhode Island roads, since the naval force that was promised us would be able to join it more easily in Chesapeake Bay, where it was probable that it would arrive. The Chevalier de Chastellux discussed this with various naval captains: several were of his opinion. He made M. de Rochambeau agree to speak of the matter to M. de Barras, and to propose to him that the point should be decided by a council of war, composed of officers of the land and sea forces. The council decided that the fleet should remain off Rhode Island. I made what opposition I could: the vote was carried by a majority; all I obtained was that we should leave behind four hundred men of the French troops, and some American militiamen under the command of M. de Choisy.[245]

The council requested me to go and report to General Washington what had been decided. I was inclined to refuse the commission, which was indeed disagreeable: I was quite sure that he would be greatly annoyed to learn that we had referred to the decision of a council of war a matter already decided and signed by himself and M. de Rochambeau. I was the only man, however, whom they could send. I travelled at express speed; I arrived at New Windsor, and handed him a letter from M. de Rochambeau, very awkwardly and badly expressed. It put him in such a rage that he refused to answer it; and it was not until the third day, and then out of regard for myself, that he handed me a very cold answer, in which he said that he abode by the plan to which he had signed his name at the Hartford conference; but that he left M. de Rochambeau free to act as he might choose, and was sending him the necessary orders to assemble such militiamen as he might require. My return embarrassed M. de Rochambeau, from whom I concealed nothing, and who was beginning to repent of what he had done. A second council of war confirmed the decisions of the first: the army began to march.[246]

Throughout the course of this war, the English seemed to be stricken with blindness: they invariably did what ought not to be done, and refused to seize the most obvious and most golden opportunities. After the army had left, they had only to attack the French fleet off Rhode Island, to destroy it. This never even occurred to them. The French army marched through America in perfect order and with perfect discipline, setting an example which neither the English nor the American army had ever furnished. I covered the march of the army at about fifteen miles to the right, and about forty miles from the North River.

M. de Rochambeau received a letter from General Washington,[247] informing him that he had a secret commission for me, and enclosing an order to myself to arrive, by forced marches, with my regiment, within forty-eight hours, at a meeting-place many miles away. M. de Rochambeau sent for me, fifteen miles in the middle of the night, to give me General Washington's orders, which entered into no detail with him. I arrived punctually at the place appointed, although the intense heat and the badness of the roads made this march extremely difficult. General Washington arrived there, a long way in advance of the two armies, and told me that he wished me to capture a body of English troops who were placed in front of New York supporting Fort Kniphausen, which was regarded as the key to the fortifications of New York.

I should have to march all the night, to attack them before daybreak; he added to my regiment one of American dragoons, some companies of light horse, and some battalions of American light infantry. He had dispatched by another road, about six miles to our right, General Lincoln[248] with a corps of three thousand men, to surprise Fort Kniphausen, from which I was to cut off all support. He was not to show himself until my attack was under way, when I should send word to him to launch his own. He amused himself by firing at a little post which had not seen him, and roused the whole of the corps that I was to surprise. It retired into the fort, made a sortie against General Lincoln, who was beaten, and would have been cut off from the rest of the army, had I not come promptly to his rescue.

Although my troops were thoroughly worn out, I advanced upon the English; I charged their cavalry, and my infantry exchanged fire with theirs. General Lincoln took the opportunity to beat a retreat in considerable disorder. He had two or three hundred men killed or taken prisoner, and many wounded. When I saw that he was out of danger, I began my own retreat, which proved most fortunate, for I lost scarcely a man.

I rejoined General Washington, who was marching with a considerable detachment of his army to the support of General Lincoln, about whom he was exceedingly anxious; but his troops were so exhausted that they could not go any farther. He showed the greatest joy on seeing me return, and in his orders paid the most flattering tribute to my troops. He decided to take the opportunity of making a close reconnaissance of New York. I escorted him with a hundred or so of hussars; we came under a considerable fire, both musketry and artillery, but we saw everything that we wished to see. This detachment lasted for three days and three nights[249] and was extremely fatiguing, for we were upon our feet day and night and had nothing to eat save the fruit that we found by the wayside. General Washington wrote M. de Rochambeau a letter in which he commended me warmly; but my general forgot to make any mention of it in his dispatches to France.

I went into camp at White Plains, where the two armies met on the following day.[250] General Washington gave me command of the two vanguards. We spent six weeks in this camp, where I was worked to death, being continually out on long foraging expeditions, within sight of the enemy's outposts. General Washington and M. de Rochambeau decided to make another reconnaissance of New York; I was instructed to cover it with all the cavalry of both armies, all the American light infantry and a battalion of French grenadiers and chasseurs. A considerable detachment from both armies, under the command of Chevalier de Chastellux and General Heath,[251] took up a position at some distance, so that I might retreat upon it in case of accident. The Generals took two days to make their reconnaissance, which was dangerous, for they came under a brisk fire of cannon and musketry.[252]

We marched from White Plains some days later, to cross the North River at Ringsferry. Fortunately the English did not come out from New York in pursuit of us; for our march having started badly, over marshy ground, the whole of our artillery and transport remained stuck for thirty-six hours, with no escort save my regiment and a battalion of grenadiers and chasseurs which formed the whole of the rear-guard under my command. After the crossing of the North River, which was long and difficult, but which the English did not attempt to hinder, the army, for convenience of rationing and foraging, marched in two divisions at one day's distance: the American army marched by another road not far from ours. We were obliged to cross the Jerseys and to cover about seventy miles within fifteen or twenty miles of the enemy, and often nearer. We never doubted that they would attempt to bar our way, in which they would certainly have been successful. M. de Rochambeau had made them suppose that his plan was to attack New York, having dispatched an intelligent commissary with a strong escort to set up field-kitchens and stores at Chatham, near New York.[253]

M. de Rochambeau had gone in advance to Philadelphia with General Washington, to collect everything necessary for the army's march into Virginia. We were encamped in the Jerseys, at Somerset Court House.[254] M. le Baron de Vioménil was in command of the first division of the army, consisting of one brigade of infantry, some artillery, and my regiment. We received warning that a thousand men of the New York garrison had been ordered to hold themselves in readiness to march, and that the light troops were not a mile away from us. M. le Baron de Vioménil, whom a kick from a horse obliged to travel in a carriage, did not know what to make of this. He would, indeed, have been almost helpless, had he been attacked.

I felt that the greatest service that I could render him was to advance as far as possible towards the enemy, so as to give him time to retire into the woods. I sent out strong patrols upon all the roads by which the English might come. I took fifty hussars well mounted and went myself for more than ten miles along the road to Brunswick, by which they would most probably appear. I met two or three strong patrols of light troops, which retired after exchanging a few pistol shots with my hussars. I assured myself that the English army was not on the march, and went back to reassure the Baron de Vioménil.

Notwithstanding the appeals that had been made to Sir Henry Clinton,[255] it had been impossible to make him decide to come out of New York, since he preferred to believe that he was going to be attacked there; he even recalled the light troops that he had outside the town. We arrived at Philadelphia, through which the army marched;[256] it was received with the greatest acclamation and was much admired: we spent one day there, and continued on our way.

At our first halt after Philadelphia, General Washington heard that M. de Grasse[257] had anchored in Chesapeake Bay with more than thirty ships of the line and had there landed M. de Saint-Simon[258] with 3,000 men of the land forces. I have never seen a man more overcome with great and sincere joy than was General Washington. We heard at the same time that Lord Cornwallis[259] had received orders from Sir Henry Clinton not to return to Portsmouth, which was an excellent post, but to fortify himself at Yorktown until relief came to him there.

On arriving at the Head of Elk Creek, an inlet of Chesapeake Bay, fearing lest Lord Cornwallis might greatly hamper M. de La Fayette, whose division consisted of merely two thousand Americans with M. de Saint-Simon's light troops, he made us embark[260] in all manner of craft all the grenadiers and chasseurs of the army and all the infantry of my regiment under the command of M. de Custine.[261] I asked to be allowed to go with my infantry, being convinced that these troops would enter the firing-line before the others. General Lincoln also followed us by water at some distance, with the American light infantry. M. de Custine, eager to arrive first, took a sloop that made good progress, and went on without stopping and without giving me any orders until we reached the James River. On the third day of our voyage we had a very bad time. The boats were vile; two or three of them foundered, and we had seven or eight men drowned. The weather obliged us to anchor off Annapolis; as we were about to set sail again, General Washington sent me a message by an aide-de-camp telling me to land my troops and not to leave until I had received further orders.

The English fleet having appeared outside Chesapeake Bay, M. de Grasse had gone out to give battle, and had not yet returned. Three days later, one of the King's corvettes came to inform us that M. de Grasse had defeated the English force, had captured two frigates, and had returned to anchor in the Bay.[262] I made my troops re-embark immediately. We sailed almost all the time against the wind, and it took us ten days to reach the mouth of the James River.

I there found M. de Custines; and while I was giving him a report of what had occurred in his absence, General Washington and M. de Rochambeau, who were on board a corvette close by, sent word to me to come to them. General Washington told me that, as Lord Cornwallis had sent all his cavalry and a considerable body of troops to Gloucester, opposite York, he was afraid lest he might be seeking to retire in that direction, and therefore was having him watched by a corps of three thousand militiamen under the continental Brigadier-General Weedon,[263] a good enough soldier, but one who hated war, in which he had never wished to engage, and went in deadly fear of coming under fire. Having become Brigadier-General by accident, this worthy officer was my senior in rank; General Washington was more distressed than myself;

for he intended this command for me. He told me that he would write to General Weedon that he would reserve all the honours for him, but forbade him to interfere in any way. I pointed out to him that this form of service was unknown; that, if General Weedon were under my command, I should most certainly make him obey me, but that, being under his, I should obey him most scrupulously; that I felt no repugnance at serving under him, if he saw fit, and that he might count upon our getting on excellently together.

I went with my regiment to join General Weedon's corps. His method of blockading Gloucester was original; he was more than fifteen miles from the enemy's outposts, was frightened to death, and dared not send out a patrol as much as half a mile from his camp. He was the best fellow in the world, and his one desire was not to interfere in anything. I suggested to him that we should move closer to Gloucester, and should go the next day to make a reconnaissance near the English outposts; he agreed, and we set out with fifty hussars. When we were still six or seven miles from the enemy, he said to me that he thought it useless and very dangerous to go any farther, and that we should see no better: I pressed him so hard that he dared not refuse to accompany me. I drove back the enemy's outposts and approached near enough to form an accurate idea of his position. My general was in despair; he told me that he would never go out with me again; that he did not wish to throw away his life.

I made M. de Rochambeau a report of what I had seen; I told him that we could not rely upon the American militia, and that it was essential that he should send me at least two additional battalions of French infantry. I had no artillery, no rations, no powder. I asked him for these: he at once sent artillery and eight hundred men drawn from the garrisons of the ships under M. de Choisy, who, by right of seniority, took command over General Weedon and myself.

M. de Choisy is a good and gallant man, ridiculously violent, constantly in a rage, always making scenes with everyone, and entirely devoid of common sense. He began by finding fault with General Weedon and all the militia, told them that they were cowards, and in five minutes had them almost as frightened of himself as of the English, which is certainly saying a good deal. He decided to move the next day and to occupy the ground that I had reconnoitred. General Weedon preferred to join him a day later, and remained behind with about six hundred men of his division.

Just as we were entering the plain of Gloucester, some dragoons of the State of Virginia came in a great panic to tell us that they had seen some English dragoons in the open, and, for fear of accidents, had ridden away hell for leather, without examining them further. I rode forward to try to find out more about them. I caught sight of a fine-looking woman at the door of a little house, upon the high road; I went to question her; she told me that, at that very moment, Colonel Tarleton had left her house; that she did not know whether many troops had come out of Gloucester; that Colonel Tarleton was most anxious "to shake hands with the French duke." I assured her that I had come there on purpose to give him that satisfaction. She condoled with me, thinking, I suppose, from experience, that it was impossible to resist Tarleton: the American troops were in a similar case.

I had not gone a hundred yards from the house, when I heard my advance guard firing their pistols. I advanced at a gallop to find a terrain upon which I could open battle. I saw as I approached that the English cavalry outnumbered mine by three to one;

I charged them without drawing rein; our lines met. Tarleton caught sight of me, and came towards me with raised pistol. We were about to fight a duel between our lines, when his horse was overthrown by one of his dragoons pursued by one of my lancers. I dashed upon him, to take him prisoner; a troop of English dragoons thrust themselves between us, and covered his retreat: his horse remained in my hands. He charged me a second time without breaking my line; I charged him a third time, routed part of his cavalry, and pursued him as far as the earthworks of Gloucester. He lost one officer and half a hundred men, and I took a good number of prisoners.[264]

M. de Choisy made his camp one mile and a half from Gloucester; our patrols were continually exchanging fire with the English patrols, and we did not sleep for one instant during the siege. As M. le Baron de Vioménil was to attack two of the redoubts of York, M. de Choisy had orders to make a feint attack upon Gloucester; he thought that it was possible to make a genuine attack, and to carry the trenches sword in hand. He therefore had hatchets distributed among the American militia with which to cut down the palisades. At the first shot fired, half of them threw down their hatchets and muskets, to run more quickly. Thus abandoned, he retired upon my lines with some companies of French infantry, and lost a dozen men.

Two days later, my Lord Cornwallis offered to surrender.[265] M. de Rochambeau selected myself to convey these great tidings to France, and sent for me. I had no desire to go to Europe; I advised him to send M. de Charlus;[266] this would put him in the good books of M. de Castries, and might perhaps secure better treatment for the army. I could not bring him to agree; he said to me that I had been the first in action, and ought to carry the news; that

M. le Comte Guillaume des Deux-Ponts[267] had been the second, and should carry the details: the Comte de Charlus never forgave him, nor myself either. I embarked in the King's frigate *Surveillante*, and after a crossing of twenty-two days arrived at Brest and proceeded to Versailles without losing any time.

When I arrived at Versailles, I found M. de Maurepas dying; he was barely conscious: he recognised me, however, and received me in the most touching fashion. He recommended me warmly to the King and his Ministers, who promised him that they would carry out what it had been his intention to do for me. He died two days later,[268] and M. de Castries and M. de Ségur treated me as badly as was in their power.

My news gave the King the greatest joy; I found him with the Queen; he plied me with questions and said many gracious things to me. He asked me whether I expected to return to America; I replied that I did; he added that I might assure his army that it would be treated with great generosity, better than any had ever been treated before. M. de Ségur was present. I replied that I was ready to take the list of awards to America in a fortnight's time. I advised M. de Ségur to set to work at once with the King; he told me that he wished to await the arrival of Comte Guillaume des Deux-Ponts,[269] after which he made no haste, then finished by getting to work with the King and told me that I should leave for Brest in the following week. I asked to see the list of awards that I was to convey; he would not allow it; I learned from the officers that the army was being shockingly treated.

I could, as it happened, judge of this from my own case. What M. de Ségur called a handsome reward was to write to me on the King's behalf that in consideration of my services in America, His Majesty allowed me to retain, in time of peace, my regiment in the Department of War, in the form of a regiment of hussars, and to leave me in command of it for life; this was rather less than the promises made me at the beginning of the war, since I was then to have the proprietary command of the first foreign regiment of horse that should fall vacant or could be raised, and less than I actually had at the moment, since I was inspector of my corps. I refused to convey the awards; M. de Ségur took offence at this, and I paid him no further attention.

M. de Castries had treated me even worse: instead of sending me the four hundred men of my regiment who had been left at Brest, he had used them for the capture of the forts of Demerary and Annamaboo in Africa, and left them there as a garrison until peace was signed, in the unhealthiest spot in the universe; this was a clear indication of his intention to deprive me of all means of doing useful service. M. de Castries, moreover, allotted no award at all to my regiment, not even to the officers who had performed the most brilliant actions.

I found Madame de Coigny more charming than ever; she showed an interest in me, and it was impossible for me not to yield to the irresistible attraction that drew me to her; I saw her almost every day, and every day became more attached to her. I had never seen so much wit and charm, which in no way resembled the wit and charm of other women. I told myself that it was not reasonable to fall in love with her, that it would make me very unhappy; but no other happiness suited me so well. I was told without ceasing that Madame de Coigny was a coquette, that she was light, that she railed without pity at anyone who ventured to fall in love with her. This never alarmed me for an instant; her sensibility had impressed me almost as soon as her wit. I did not hope to win her favour; once she knew the state of my heart, she could not fail to pity me; I kept my secret, but the thought of my departure was beginning to distress me, and it was not difficult for her to guess the reason.

I met in Paris Mrs. Robinson,[270] the first love of the Prince of Wales, of whom the English gossips had said so much under the name of Perdita. She was gay, lively, open, and a good creature; she did not speak French; I was an object to excite her fancy, a man who had brought home great tidings, who came from the war, who was returning there immediately; he had suffered greatly, he would suffer more still. She felt that she could not do too much for him; and so I enjoyed Perdita, and did not conceal my success from Madame de Coigny. "What do my actions matter," I asked myself without ceasing, "if she can read in my heart?"

Perdita succeeded in causing a breach between me and Madame de Martainville; I had found the latter at daggers drawn with Madame Dillon and M. de Guéménée; she had sought to extort a promise from me that I would cease to see them, and I had flatly declined. We were on pretty cold terms; she knew that I had enjoyed Perdita; this increased her resentment; she told me that I must choose, whether I would cease to visit Madame Dillon or herself. My choice was soon made. Madame de Martainville speedily repented, and sought a reconciliation with me, but in vain.

Perdita left for England, and was so insistent that I should accompany her as far as Calais, that I could not refuse. It was a great sacrifice, for that very day I was engaged to dine at Madame de Gontaut's with Madame de Coigny; I wrote to Madame de Coigny to say that I was prevented from dining with her; and seized this singular occasion to assure her that I adored her, and should continue, whatever might befall, to adore her all my life. There was not another woman in the world who could understand me. Madame de Coigny understood me perfectly, believed me, and wrote me a few words in which she made no reply to my declaration. Her conduct towards me was simple and sensible: she showed me no anger because she felt none, no doubt as to my sincerity because she had no doubt; she did not tell me that she would never love me.

I saw many men taken up with her; some of them were redoubtable rivals for me. I was aware of all my own drawbacks; I had no longer either the charm or the gaiety of youth, but I had a heart which she knew, which greatly resembled her own, and I hoped upon both these counts. I found in loving her, quite unexpectedly, a happiness which love had never given me before. I forced myself to be prudent, patient, circumspect. I was ready to sacrifice everything, without hesitation, to the fear of compromising her; nothing was lost upon that heavenly spirit, nothing escaped her, everything was felt and consequently rewarded; I did not call upon Madame de Coigny, I never saw her in private; I could rarely tell her that I loved her, but I could write it to her; I never met her without giving her a note; she would receive it with interest, without appearing annoyed by it; I might have been far more happy; but I knew no one who was even as happy as myself.

At dinner at the Hôtel de Ville,[271] Madame de Coigny, exquisitely attired, was wearing a large black heron's plume, on the front of her dress to the right; seeing that plume and desiring to possess it were the affair of an instant. I looked to it for happiness and courage; never did a knight-errant long for anything with greater ardour and purity.

M. de Coigny wished to go to America.[272] Madame de Coigny was in despair at this. I too was devoured by grief. I did not suppose that M. de Coigny's departure could cost me so much anxiety. Always true, always sensible, Madame de Coigny did not conceal from me either her tears or the pity that I inspired in her. Without saying a word about it she accompanied her husband as far as Rennes; she suspected that this action would meet with disapproval; she wrote to me, before starting, a note that began as follows: "Know how to defend what you know so well how to love." Too superior a woman not to arouse envy, people sought to accuse her of exaggeration, affectation, even of falsehood; I defended her in good faith, I whom her grief had made so wretched. She returned, and was pleased with my conduct.

Chance had made me meet in the course of the winter the Duc de Coigny and Madame de Châlons.[273] I had supped at the Duc de Coigny's; I now visited Madame de Coigny, I saw her almost every day at Madame de Guéménée's, Madame de Gontaut's, or in her own house. This happiness was not to last long. M. de Ségur, with all the rudeness of which he was capable, insisted upon making me go abroad three months earlier than was necessary. I dared not insist too much upon waiting for the second frigate; and yet this would have been quite easy. Everyone was disgusted by the manner in which the Ministers were treating me.

Madame de Polignac, who was no longer afraid of me, and to whom it was sometimes embarrassing to have in her society persons favoured by the Queen, appeared anxious to make friends with me. It was suggested that I should remain in France; a way was to be provided for me to do so; I refused every offer. It was most tempting to remain, for Madame de Coigny's sake; it was for her sake that I left. I was too much afraid that people might guess my true reason for remaining, I dared not even plead the excuse of Madame de Montbazon's[274] confinement, for which M. and

Madame de Guéménée were most anxious that I should remain.

Madame de Coigny was vexed at my departure. I ventured to believe that she was in love with me. She did not, however, tell me so, but continued to be sensible and severe. On the evening of my departure, I cut a lock of her hair; she asked for it back. I gave it to her without hesitation. She gazed at me as she took it; I saw tears in her eyes; I had not lost everything. She alone, I hope, can form an idea of my despair when I was obliged to leave her; she alone could make me feel to what a degree I could be happy or unhappy. I left her; I had never done anything so difficult; my heart was full of love, despair and confidence.

I arrived at Brest on the day on which the English fleet was sighted; this did not prevent the Indian convoy from putting to sea two days later and being captured within twenty-four hours. I wrote by every post to Madame de Coigny. I was afraid that all my letters might bore her. I did what I could to keep them from being long. I was rarely successful; she was sorry for me; she wrote to me often, it is true; I lived upon her letters. I never broke the seal of one without feelings of inexpressible joy and gratitude. We remained for a long while at Brest, confined alternately by the winds and by the English. I pleaded with insistence for that plume to which I had attached so many dreams of happiness. Madame de Coigny replied that it was impossible to send it to me; that one day she would tell me her reasons; I was quite convinced that she was sorry not to give it to me; I could not, however, console myself for not having it.

We sailed at length from Brest, on the 17th of May, in extremely unsettled weather and almost under the eyes of the English; as we came out of Le Goulet we encountered a horrible gale of wind; for four days we were in constant peril of being taken, or dashed upon the coast; I confess that I would have been charmed to be taken. I should have seen Madame de Coigny again; there was no war, no glory worth as much as that. We anchored in the River of Nantes, our frigate greatly damaged. The Captain of the *Gloire* sent a courier to M. de Castries to report this to him, and to say that he would put in for repairs at Lorient, as soon as the wind allowed him. We went to Nantes. I had time to visit Paris; I wrote to Madame de Coigny to ask her if it would not be possible for me to see her for half an hour; I begged her to refuse without hesitation, if she felt that there would be the slightest inconvenience, and to address her reply to the post office at Tours or Orleans, where I would call for it; I implored her to consult no one; she herself was sufficient to dispose of my actions, and I desired that she should take the wiser, even though it were the harder course.

I found no letter either at Tours or at Orleans. I waited; at length one came; it was from M. de Lisle.[275] He informed me that Madame de Coigny would be charmed to see me; but that she thought it would be wiser not to come to Paris; she left me free, however, to decide. Not a word from Madame de Coigny; it would have been so easy for her to refuse and to console me! She had not wished to dispose of my actions; she had not had the kindness to say to me: "I do not wish it." She had employed a third person! She had not written to me! This was more than enough to lacerate my heart. I have experienced great misfortunes, I have never felt any of them so keenly as this; my grief was such, that for ten or twelve days I found it impossible to write to her.

I went to La Rochelle to see M. de Voyer, and returned to Lorient to join my wretched frigate. Madame de Coigny replied to my complaints with an indulgence, a charm that reassured me, and restored my tranquillity; there was nothing left me but to repent of having tormented her with my griefs. Our frigate received orders to go to Rochefort to join the *Aigle* and sail with her. I proceeded there by land. We waited for M. de La Fayette, who was kept by political affairs for three weeks at court; he sent word that he was not coming. M. de la Touche[276] offered me his cabin, which I accepted. We set sail from La Rochelle, upon the 14th of July. On the following day we came into violent collision with the French frigate *Cérès*; she did us considerable damage, and nearly did us far more. Sickness broke out among our crew; not a day passed but one of them died, and the need of nourishment for our sick obliged us to anchor at Terceyre, one of the Azores.[277] I have never seen quainter customs, or so pleasant a mingling of sacred with profane love.

After taking on board cattle, vegetables and water, we set sail again. As I was conversing one day with M. de Bozon,[278] who also was on board the *Aigle*, he spoke to me of Madame de Coigny, and of all her charms. No topic of conversation could have pleased me better: this did not last long; for he told me that M. de Chabot[279] was very much in love with her, and he suspected that she returned his affection. It was dark, fortunately: O my God! . . . I cannot think of it without a shudder; my unshakable confidence in Madame de Coigny sustained me; she had not been false or cruel; I mustered the strength to write to her before we reached the Azores, and my letter went from Terceyre by Portugal. Nothing however could destroy the profound impression that my conversation with Bozon had made upon me: I became more mortally depressed every day; my strength succumbed in the end, and I had a violent fever, with intense paroxysms and delirium. I was conscious of this; I was afraid of betraying myself, and forbade anyone to enter my cabin except two English servants who could barely speak French.

I was right, for I was wholly absorbed in Madame de Coigny; and I was doubly right, for I murmured her name all day long. I wrote to her as often as my fever left me the strength to do so; thinking of her was my only consolation. I had the good fortune to feel the full strength of it: the thought of her, her letters charmed away my ills, although I was suffering keenly. I repeated incessantly: "My thoughts sustain me, I shall not die." In my delirium, I spoke of that plume for which I had so dearly longed.

I had been ill for twelve days when we encountered by night a vessel of 74 guns which we were obliged to fight.[280] My cabin was cleared; I was carried upon the bridge more dead than alive. I had fastened Madame de Coigny's letters over my heart, and had insisted that they should fling me into the sea, fully clothed, if I was killed, or if I died during the battle. I was for three hours the helpless spectator of a very hot engagement. We fought all the time within pistol range, and at length managed to drive off the English vessel, after coming twenty times within an inch of destruction. We had a score of men killed. The English vessel was so severely damaged, that we would easily have captured her, had we not seen upon the horizon other ships bearing down upon her. This vessel was the *Hector*, a French ship of 74 guns, taken from M. de Grasse by Admiral Rodney: she sank some days later on the Banks of Newfoundland,[281] and her crew were saved with great difficulty; we had killed more than one hundred and fifty of her men.

Next day I was worse than ever. A week after our battle, we arrived off the coast of America, at the mouth of the Delaware.[282] We anchored, and sent a boat ashore to procure pilots, the channel of the Delaware being difficult and dangerous. Our boat was submerged by a squall of wind, and almost everyone on board perished; no pilots came to us, but, at daybreak, we sighted an English squadron of seven men of war bearing down upon us under full canvas;[283] we were forced to raise anchor and enter the river without pilots. At length we saw a boat coming towards us from the *Gloire*, which had arrived without mishap and was sending us pilots. We learned from them that we were in the wrong channel, and doomed to destruction. M. de la Touche sailed two leagues farther up the channel; then, seeing that no hope remained, decided to put ashore the packages from the court, the money and the passengers. M. de la Touche ran aground next day, cut his masts, did everything that he could to make the frigate useless to the English, and was taken prisoner; the *Gloire*, which drew less water, arrived safe and sound at Philadelphia. We were put ashore about a league from the nearest habitation, without having brought away so much as a shirt apiece.

I was still in a fever, I could barely stand, and I should never have been able to reach a house had it not been for a powerful negro who gave me his arm. As soon as we had put our money in a safe place, I made my way slowly towards Philadelphia. I was now in a low fever; I kept fainting at every moment: the French and American doctors were agreed in their opinion that I must die before the end of the autumn.

A vessel was sailing for Europe; I had an opportunity of writing to Madame de Coigny, and that did me an infinite deal of good. The doctors had declared that it was impossible that I should think of joining the army, when M. de Rochambeau sent one of his aides-de-camp with letters for the Chevalier de la Luzerne,[284] and wrote bidding me do everything in my power to come to camp, as he had matters of the greatest importance to communicate to me. I made up my mind without consulting anyone; I mounted a horse and rode to camp, death being no worse on the road than in Philadelphia. The ride did me good. I was already much better when I arrived at Headquarters.[285]

M. de Rochambeau was delighted to see me; he told me that the bulk of his army was going to embark at Boston,[286] that he would leave some troops in America, and that he personally would return to France, and would give me the command of his troops. The army struck camp ten or twelve days later.[287] I returned across the North River, and went to take up my winter quarters in the County of Delaware. My health returned, I wished for nothing now but letters, and we received none.

The frigate *Danaë* returned at length;[288] I learned by her of many misfortunes; she did not bring me the consolation for which I hoped, not a word from Madame de Coigny; M. de Voyer was dead, I had lost Madame Dillon, my unfortunate friend[289] had nothing left him in the world; his mistress, his honour, his fortune, that of his children, that of many others, he had lost everything at once; perhaps I had nothing left myself, which was what disturbed me least; I was on the point of throwing up everything to go and join the unfortunate M. de Guéménée wherever he might be; considerations which it would take too long to explain here restrained me.

No letters from M. or Madame de Guéménée, none from my men of business, not the least detail as to the dreadful news, the fear that Madame de Coigny might be ill; she had written to me, or it had been impossible for her to write; I have not to reproach myself with having suspected her for a moment of negligence. When she alone was left to me, sure of her heart as of my own, I kept saying to myself at every moment:

"She cannot love me, but she cannot but wish to console me; alas, two thousand leagues away, does she still exist?" My thoughts and fears varied at every moment, I tormented myself, I reassured myself; everyone was not without pity; no one was in my confidence, but Madame de Montbazon. M. de Lisle knew that Madame de Coigny was very dear to me; they would have sent me news of her to all the ports: a mistake as to a date, the carelessness of a servant, the inexactitude of the posts had often doubtless prevented me from receiving my letters; I had had none from several people who were in the habit of writing to me; I did not suppose that they were ill, I might therefore hope that Madame de Coigny was not.

Such was my cruel situation when M. de Rochambeau left for France.[290] I wrote to Madame de Coigny, I was sure that she would not be hard upon my unhappy friend; I begged her upon my knees to show him a little kindness, he would be so touched by it! I wrote to M. de Guéménée that he had still a friend upon whom he might entirely rely.

The tumult of Philadelphia had become intolerable to me, I decided to escape from it. A visit to Rhode Island combined the advantages of bringing me nearer to the letters that would probably arrive in the North, and of seeing again that charming family who loved me so tenderly. I set off therefore, notwithstanding the rigour of the season.[291] At Newport they were beside themselves with joy at seeing me again. I saw nobody there; I led an easy and quiet life, and they took great care of me.

While I was at Newport, about the middle of the month of March, the American packet *Washington* arrived from France at Philadelphia.[292] The Baron de Foks, my aide-de-camp, brought my letters to Newport: there were two from Madame de Coigny, one from Spa, dated the 26th of July, 1781, and another of the 18th of October in the same year. I mourned sincerely for Madame Dillon and M. de Voyer, but Madame de Coigny was alive and was writing to me: I might have lost her, and I had not lost her. I felt an impulse of joy as keen as had been my grief: what letters! with what touching simplicity they portrayed her soul! She was not at all in love with M. de Chabot, and reproached me for having believed it. All the explanations that could restore my tranquillity she offered me with such a grace! A word was sufficient to reassure me, she had already done what I demanded of her with such persistence! She was sorry for M. de Guéménée, she did not condemn him; she did not tell me that she loved me; but she did tell me that she counted so much upon my sentiments for her, that she made me almost as happy.

The letters that came by the *Washington* spoke of peace as farther off than ever.[293] A week later, I learned from New York that it had been signed. I left Newport: it was not without regret and emotion. I spent some days with General Washington, and returned to Philadelphia. The frigate *Active* brought me orders[294] to take back to France the remains of the French army. I received at the same time a letter from Madame de Coigny of the 22nd September, 1782; it said that all letters that I received from her would be five months old. I lost no time in embarking my troops; and, on the 11th of May,[295] 1783, we set sail from Wilmington for France.

APPENDIX

By C. K. Scott Moncrieff

At this point, the embarkation from Wilmington in May 1783, Lauzun's Memoirs cease, doubtless because they were written for the instruction of Madame de Coigny, and the rest of his adventures would be known to her. He was still in his thirty-sixth year, and might easily have survived until the Restoration; actually, three-fourths of his life were already past. He returned to France, ruined by the bankruptcy of M. de Guéménée, to whom he had sold his landed property in 1776 in exchange for a life-rent of 80,000 livres. He was completely out of favour at court; the King would barely address him, and he dared not approach the Queen's presence. In this situation he naturally gravitated into the orbit of the Duc d'Orléans and joined the Orleanist Party in the Assembly. On the night of the 4th of August, he assisted at the extinction of the feudal system in France. "Gentlemen," exclaimed Biron (he had meanwhile succeeded to the Dukedom of his uncle the Marshal) with a smile, "what have we done? Who knows?" Later, when Orleans fled to England, Biron remained at his post. In October 1790, the officers and men of his regiment of hussars, with those of the Royal Liégeois, attacked the populace of the town in which they were quartered. Biron denounced them in the Assembly, and called for their punishment. On the 27th of April, 1791, we find him writing from Douai: "The King's flight has developed a fresh energy in every heart, and his arrest has caused an outburst of well-nigh universal joy. The people love and bless

the Revolution; their confidence in the National Assembly is unbounded; all hopes are now fused in one: the greatness that you have shown since the King's flight overwhelms your enemies, and you are, more than ever, invincibly strong with all the force of public opinion. We must not leave the National Assembly unaware that their address to the French people has been received with transports of joy by the citizens of the towns which we have visited, and that this refutation of an edict suggested, doubtless, to a Monarch who had been deceived, is regarded as the sole response that need be made to the vain objections of the enemies of the Constitution." Later, he warns the Assembly against the refractory priests, fifty-two of whom he had found in the small town of Cateau-Cambrésis. He is then sent to London with Talleyrand, and is arrested at the instance of one of his former creditors. He returns to France, and is given command of the Army of the North, and serves in the Maritime Alps, where he succeeds in taking Nice from General Devins. Lastly, he is given command of a corps in the Vendée, where he toils in vain to create order and discipline out of a chaotic rabble. The task is too great for any man, and Biron succumbs. He is summoned to Paris and confined in the Abbey. On the 11th of Nivôse in the year II he appears before the Tribunal, receives his sentence with a smile, and on the following day (the first of the year 1794) is led to execution. When the headsman comes for him, he is sitting down to a dish of oysters: "Citizen," he says, "allow me to finish"; and, offering the man a glass: "take this wine, you must have need of courage, in your calling."

His wife did not long survive him. In the summer of 1791 she had retired to Lausanne with the Comtesse de Boufflers. More than a year later, they returned to France and were promptly arrested, on the charge of having left the country. Biron, who had been separated from her for fifteen years, at once wrote to the Convention on her behalf.

STRASBOURG,
The 18*th of November, Year I of the Republic,* 1792.

"Citizen President, I make bold to implore you to lay the following note before the National Convention. A faithful soldier of the Republic makes bold to request the representatives of the people to turn their attention to the fearful position of a woman whom a moment's delirium, of which she can furnish proofs, exposes to the misery of being turned from the bosom of her country. Citizens, this woman is my wife. Judicially separated, parted from her for fifteen years, I feel for the first time with painful remorse, that but for the distance that circumstances have placed between us, more confident, more reassured, proud, it may be, of the patriotism of her husband, this woman, more unfortunate than guilty, would never have deserved to bring upon herself the severity of the laws. It appertains to a free people to be generous rather than severe, to pardon a woman's frailty rather than to punish it. Terrible in its efforts, in its judgments for the maintenance of liberty, it is indulgent whenever it can be so. Citizens, I demand of you for my wife more than justice, I demand generosity. Destined, as I hope, to carry your arms and Liberty into the neighbouring countries, there is no consideration upon earth that can make me quit the honourable post that you have entrusted to me. I have therefore the right to say, without allowing myself to select, Citizens, that one of you shall rise and plead in defence of my wife, since I cannot plead for her myself: this right I claim, and exercise.

"The Citizen General of the Army,
BIRON."

She appears to have been released, for, in October, 1793, Walpole writes to Miss Berry that she is again in prison. Six months after her husband, she went to the scaffold, on a warrant intended, it is said, for her man of business, her name having been written in error in the blank space.

Armand de Gontaut, Duc de Lauzun and afterwards Duc de Biron, was born on the 13th of April, 1747, the son of Charles-Antoine Armand de Gontaut, Marquis de Montferrant and Duc de Gontaut, a General in the Army, and younger brother of the Marshal Duc de Biron. He had married in January, 1744, six months after the battle of Dettingen, Antoinette-Eustachie Crozat du Chatel, elder daughter of Louis-François Crozat, Marquis du Chatel, and of Thérèse-Catherine Gouffier de Heilly; she died in her nineteenth year, after giving birth to our diarist. Her younger sister, Louise-Honorine, was married in December, 1750, to Etienne-François de Choiseul Stainville (1719-1785), Comte de Stainville and afterwards Duc de Choiseul, who figures so frequently in the memoirs. Choiseul was the son of François-Joseph, Marquis de Stainville, and the elder brother of the Duchesse de Gramont and the Comte de Stainville. The former, Béatrix de Choiseul-Stainville (1730-1794), exercised a persistent influence over her brother, both while he was in office and after his disgrace. She took as her husband in August, 1759, Antoine-Antonin de Gramont, Duc de Gramont, Sovereign of Bidache and Governor of Navarre, otherwise a person of no importance. The younger brother, Jacques de Stainville, married in January, 1761, Thomasse-Thérèse de Clermont-Reynel, a fifteen-year-old heiress, in whose sad story Lauzun, who was only a few months her junior, played a considerable part. Lauzun himself was married in his nineteenth year, on the 4th of February, 1766, to Amélie de Boufflers, grand-daughter of a deceased Duc de Boufflers, whose widow (herself the grand-daughter of Marshal Villeroy) had married secondly Marshal Luxembourg.

Of Madame du Barry it is scarcely necessary to say much. She was born at Vaucouleurs (the birthplace also of Joan of Arc, which Lauzun dismisses as "le lieu le plus triste de toute la Champagne, et par conséquent de tout l'univers") in 1741; and christened Marie-Jeanne. Her surname, that of her mother, was Bécu. Her paternity is unknown. At the time of her marriage she had assumed the surname Gomart de Vaubernier. When Lauzun made her acquaintance in 1768, she was living with the Comte Jean du Barry, known variously as the Roué and Mahomet, from the number of his acknowledged mistresses. On the 1st of September in that year she was married to his brother Guillaume, and, as Comtesse du Barry, was presented at court by the Comtesse de Béarn. As is well known, she died on the scaffold in December 1793.

Lady Sarah Lennox was born on the 14th of February, 1745, a day and a year of different but romantic associations, the seventh daughter and eleventh child of Charles Lennox, 2nd Duke of Richmond and Lennox and Duc d'Aubigny (a grandson of Charles II) by Sarah, elder daughter and co-heir of William Earl Cadogan. Her parents had been married when eighteen and thirteen years old, at the Hague, in settlement of a gambling debt between their respective fathers. Her eldest sister, Georgina Carolina Lennox, her senior by nearly twenty-two years, was already the wife of Henry Fox; they, who afterwards were created respectively Baroness and Baron Holland, were the parents of Charles James Fox and his brother, General Henry Edward Fox. The next surviving sister, Emily Mary Lennox, was married in 1747 to James Fitzgerald, 20th Earl of Kildare, afterwards Marquess of Kildare and Duke of Leinster, and became the mother of nineteen children, among whom was the unfortunate Lord Edward Fitzgerald. Lady Sarah is said to have received an offer of marriage from the young King, George III, but to have been at that time in love with Lord Newbottle (William John Ker, 1737-1815), afterwards 5th Marquess of Lothian, K.T.), whose sister was already the wife of her brother, Lord George Lennox (and became the mother of the 4th Duke of Richmond). On the 2nd of June, 1762, Lady Sarah was married to Thomas Charles Bunbury, afterwards 6th baronet of Stanney Hall, in Cheshire, and Barton in Suffolk. By him she had no issue, but in December, 1768, she gave birth to a daughter, styled Louisa Bunbury, apparently the child of Lord William Gordon, for whom she forsook her husband a few months later. Lord William (1744-1823) was second son of Cosmo(named after the Grand Duke of Tuscany), 3rd Duke of Gordon, and elder brother of the notorious Lord George Gordon. In August, 1770, by way of penance for his elopement with Lady Sarah, he cropped his head and set out, with a knapsack and a large dog, to walk to Rome. After his return he became a Member of Parliament, Deputy Ranger of St. James's and Hyde Parks, and Vice-Admiral for Scotland. When Lauzun saw Lady Sarah at Halnaker, she had already parted from Gordon, but their connection was perpetuated by the secret marriage at Gordon Castle in September, 1789 (a fortnight after his duel with the Duke of York upon Wimbledon Common), of Lady Sarah's nephew, Charles Lennox, afterwards 4th Duke of Richmond and Lennox, to Lord William's niece, Lady Charlotte Gordon. The eldest son of this marriage, Charles, 5th Duke of Richmond, succeeded to the Gordon estates, and his eldest son, Charles Henry Gordon-Lennox, K.G., 6th Duke of Richmond and Lennox and Duc d'Aubigny, was created Earl of Kinrara and Duke of Gordon in 1876.

Lady Sarah Bunbury was divorced by Act of Parliament in May, 1776, and five years later became the second wife of Colonel George Napier (reputed the handsomest man in the Army), sixth son of Francis Scott, 5th Lord Napier of Merchiston. Although she was already in her thirty-seventh year, she bore her second husband five sons and three daughters; including Lieut.-General Sir Charles James Napier, G.C.B., Commander-in-Chief in India (1782-1853), General Sir George Thomas Napier, K.C.B., (1784-1855), General Sir William Francis Patrick Napier, K.C.B. (1785-1860), the historian of the Peninsular War, and Captain Henry Edward Napier, R.N., F.R.S. (1789-1853). The last-named had the unusual distinction of being born seventy years after the marriage of his maternal grandparents. Lady Sarah Napier seems to have remained upon the best of terms with her former husband's family; for his nephew and successor, Lieut.-General Sir Henry Edward Bunbury, married first in 1807 the elder daughter of her nephew, General Henry Edward Fox (the younger daughter afterwards becoming the wife of the historian, Sir William Napier), and secondly, after Lady Sarah's death, her own eldest daughter, Emily Louisa Napier. By his first wife, Sir Henry Bunbury had four sons, of whom the third, Colonel Henry Bunbury, who commanded the 23rd Fusiliers at Sebastopol, married his cousin Cecilia, younger daughter of General Sir George Napier, and was by her the father of Sir Henry Charles John Bunbury (1855-   ), 10th baronet of Barton, who is thus descended from Lady Sarah Lennox and from her sister, though not from her husband, Sir Charles Bunbury.

Colonel George Napier died in October, 1804, aged fifty-three. His widow received a pension for herself and his daughters of £1,000 a year in recognition of his services to the State. She, who was senior to him by six years, and to Biron by two, survived both the latter and his more famous English namesake, and died "blind, but still beautiful" in August, 1826.

Princess Czartoryska, an account of whom will be found in Miss Rutherford's notes, was doomed to survive even longer, dying in her ninetieth year in 1835. Three of her children were alive under the second Empire. Her grandson, Prince Alexander Czartoryski, married Princess Marceline Radziwill, well known as a musician in the early part of the last century.

The only other of Lauzun's mistresses that needs be mentioned is Madame de Coigny. This was the daughter of the Marquis de Conflans d'Armentières by his marriage, in 1755, to Marie-Antoinette Portail. She was therefore, unlike her predecessors, Lauzun's junior by about ten years. She was married in 1775 to François de Franquetot, Marquis de Coigny, son of that Duc de Coigny (Marie-François-Henri de Franquetot, 1737-1821) who tactlessly observed the Queen's delight in the acquisition of Lauzun's heron-plume. It was of her that Marie-Antoinette said: "I am only Queen of Versailles; it is Madame de Coigny who is Queen of Paris." She survived until 1832, leaving a son, the Duc de Coigny, who was one of the "Peers of France" under the Restoration and the Bourgeois Monarchy.

NOTES

By G. Rutherford

[1] Charles-Antoine-Armand de Gontaut (1708–*c.* 1796), married 1744 Antoinette-Eustachie Crozat du Châtel (1729–47), daughter of Antoine Crozat, marquis de Thiers.

[2] Marie-Anne de Mailly-Nesle (1717–44), who immediately preceded Mme. de Pompadour as mistress of Louis XV.

[3] He entered the Gardes Françaises as *enseigne à drapeau* on Jan. 18, 1761.

[4] Etienne-François de Choiseul-Stainville (1719–85), afterwards the famous duc de Choiseul. He married in 1750 Louise-Honorine Crozat du Châtel (1736–1801).

[5] Béatrix de Choiseul-Stainville (1730–94).

[6] Antoine-Antonin, duc de Gramont, b. 1722. His first wife was his cousin, Louise-Victoire de Gramont.

[7] Actually between twelve and thirteen. The marriage was celebrated on Aug. 16, 1759.

[8] The chateau of Ménars, near Blois, bought by Mme. de Pompadour in 1760 and later occupied by her brother, the marquis de Marigny.

[9] Thomasse-Thérèse de Clermont d'Amboise, daughter of the marquis de Reynel. She was born in 1746 and married Jacques-Philippe de Choiseul, comte de Stainville, on April 3, 1761.

[10] The church of Notre-Dame-des-Victoires.

[11] Charles-Léopold de Chezelles, b. 1736, chevalier, afterwards marquis de Jaucourt. He was nicknamed *Clair de Lune* because of his round, pale face.

[12] Amélie de Boufflers (1751–94), daughter of Charles-Joseph, duc de Boufflers (who died 1751, son of the maréchale de Luxembourg by her first husband), and of Marie-Anne-Philippine-Thérèse de Montmorency. Besenval said of Mme. de Luxembourg (1707–86) that her one merit was her manner of bringing up her granddaughter, while Mme. du Deffand wrote of the granddaughter: "She is literally exempt from any fault, she is the female Grandison." In her youth her excellent upbringing had the effect of making her almost completely silent.

[13] Anne-Marguérite-Gabrielle de Beauvau-Craon (1707–91), widow of the maréchal de Mirepoix, at one time ambassador to England.

[14] Or Rothe, or Rothes. Lucy de Rothes (1751–82) was the daughter

of General Edward Rothes (d. 1766), whose father had followed James II into exile, and of Lucy Cary, daughter of the 6th Viscount Falkland. Mme. de Rothes was granddaughter through her mother to Arthur Dillon, 1st proprietary colonel of the *Régiment de Dillon*, and was niece to the archbishop of Narbonne, with whom, as will be seen, Lauzun often stayed at Hautefontaine, an estate bought by General Rothes, where his widow and the archbishop had a joint household. Lucy de Rothes married in 1768 her mother's cousin, Arthur Dillon (1750–94), second son of the 11th Viscount Dillon and 6th proprietary colonel of the *Régiment de Dillon*.

[15] Marie-Sophie-Charlotte de la Tour d'Auvergne, sister-in-law of Mme. de Mirepoix.

[16] Anne-Louise-Marie (1750–1834). She married the prince de Poix in 1767.

[17] Sept. 6, 1763.

[18] Born Toinard de Jouy, married 1758 Jean-Jacques, comte d'Esparbès de Lussan. There is a good deal about her in Mme. du Hausset's Memoirs.

[19] See Mme. du Hausset's Memoirs.

[20] By Rochon de Chabannes, after a tale by Marmontel. It was first staged on Nov. 29, 1762.

[21] Louis-Joseph de Bourbon (1736–1818).

[22] April 15, 1764.

[23] Henri-Louis-Marie de Rohan (1745–1807).

[24] Charles-François-Christian de Montmorency-Luxembourg, born 1713. In the preceding year (1764) he had been made Captain of one of the four companies of *Gardes du Corps*, one of the highest posts in the King's Household.

[25] Eléonore-Josèphe-Pulchérie, born 1745. She was his third wife.

[26] Anne-Paul-Emmanuel-Sigismond de Montmorency, born 1742.

[27] Louis-Joachim-Paris Potier, born 1733.

[28] Adelaïde-Louise-Angélique de Croÿ-Solre, born 1741, married 1762 Joseph de Croÿ, duc d'Havré, her cousin three years her junior. The mothers of both the duc d'Havré and the marquis de Gesvres were Montmorencys, sisters of the prince de Tingry, so the escapade which follows was largely a family affair. It caused great annoyance to the staid duc de Croÿ, father of Mme. d'Havré. (See his Memoirs, Vol. II.)

[29] Anne-Charles-Sigismond de Montmorency, born 1737, later duc de Luxembourg.

[30] Louis-Jean Potier de Gesvres (1695–1774).

[31] He died Dec. 20, 1765.

[32] Antoine-Raymond-Jean-Gualbert-Gabriel, comte d'Alby (1729–1801). As will be seen, he was afterwards (1776) Minister for the Navy.

[33] Gabrielle-Charlotte-Françoise de Chimay (1739–1809), married 1755 Jacques-François, vicomte de Cambis. She is often mentioned

in Mme. du Deffand's letters. Her brother, the prince d'Hénin, was a lover of Sophie Arnould, whom he is supposed to have bored to extinction. They were niece and nephew of Mme. de Mirepoix.

34 Louise-Julie de Boufflers (1741–94), sister of the chevalier de Boufflers. She had married in 1760 Louis Bruno, comte de Boisgelin de Cucé, master of the King's Wardrobe.

35 Louis-François de Bourbon, prince de Conti (1717–76). Since 1749 he had been Grand-Prior of France. See Walpole's description of his circle in 1766—the year of which Lauzun is writing.

36 Jean-Baptiste Guignard, known as Clairval (1735–95), principal actor of the *Comédie Italienne*.

37 Lady Sarah Lennox (1745–1826) was the fourth daughter of Charles, 2nd Duke of Richmond, K.G., and of Sarah, daughter of William, Earl Cadogan. The story of how she was nearly married to George III (her cousin after a fashion, for she was descended from Charles II) is well known. In 1761 she was one of the ten trainbearers of his bride, Charlotte of Mecklenburg. On June 2, 1762, she married Thomas Charles Bunbury (1740–1821), who in 1764 succeeded his father as 6th Baronet. His chief claim to distinction was his fine racing stud and the fact that he owned Diomed, winner of the first Derby in 1780, but he also represented Suffolk in Parliament for 43 years. Lady Sarah, "whose least qualification," wrote the first Lord Holland, her brother-in-law, "is her transcendent beauty," left her husband in February 1769 to join Lord William Gordon, taking with her her daughter Louisa, born in the previous December. After a few months with him she returned to her brother, the 3rd Duke of Richmond, and for the next twelve years she lived at Goodwood and at a small house called Halnaker, which the Duke built for her in Goodwood Park. In 1776 Sir Charles Bunbury divorced her. He apparently bore her little malice, and he and his family showed kindness to her child, who was known as Louisa Bunbury. In 1781 Lady Sarah married as his second wife the Hon. George Napier, sixth son of Francis, 6th Baron Napier. They had eight children, among them Generals Sir Charles, Sir George, and Sir William Napier. Louisa Bunbury died of consumption in 1785. Lady Sarah was widowed in 1804, and a few years later became quite blind. The *Life and Letters of Lady Sarah Lennox*, from which the above information has been taken, edited by the Countess of Ilchester and Lord Stavordale, was first published in 1901.

The Bunburys arrived in Paris at the beginning of December, 1766. Lady Sarah had spent a month there with her sisters, Lady Holland and Lady Louisa Conolly, previously, but on that occasion she had not met either Lauzun or Mme. du Deffand, whose letters for 1767 contain many references to her and to her relations with Lauzun. According to Mme. du Deffand, French society was "astonished but not scandalised" by her open encouragement of him.

[38] Charles Lennox, 3rd Duke of Richmond, K.G. (1735–1806), Ambassador to France in 1765. Nine years later Mme. de Cambis was very much in love with him.

[39] The Hôtel du Temple was the residence of the prince de Conti as Grand Prior of the Order of Malta. Built in 1667, it stood within the precincts of the ancient headquarters of the Knights Templar, and here the prince gave sanctuary to Jean-Jacques Rousseau against a *lettre de cachet* in 1765. The *Tour du Temple*, where the Royal Family was confined during the Revolution, was part of the ancient stronghold of the Templars, which was turned into a state prison after the demolition of the Bastille. It was destroyed under Napoleon I and the rest of the buildings under Napoleon III. Their site is now occupied by the Square du Temple. Mme. du Deffand, as is well known, nicknamed the prince de Conti's mistress, Mme. de Boufflers, the *Idole du Temple*.

[40] Jean-Philippe de Franquetot (1743–1806). According to Mme. de Genlis he was nicknamed Mimi.

[41] Marie de Vichy-Chamrond (1697–1780), widow of Jean-Baptiste-Jacques-Charles de la Lande, marquis du Deffand (died 1750). It is as plain from her Letters as from this sole mention of her in Lauzun's Memoirs that there was no love lost between them.

[42] Frederick Howard, 5th Earl of Carlisle, K.G., K.T., P.C. (1748–1825), who in his later years was the much-tried guardian of Lord Byron. His youthful infatuation for Lady Sarah was as little a secret as Lauzun's. Mme. du Deffand thought or pretended to think that Lord Carlisle was the favoured lover and that Lauzun was used as a blind.

[43] According to Mme. du Deffand the Bunburys' departure from Paris was postponed from Monday, Feb. 2, to Saturday, Feb. 7, when Lauzun accompanied them to Arras. If the two letters given by Lauzun are genuine, it looks as if Lady Sarah had written them in Paris before her plans were changed and had forgotten to alter the dates when posting them at Arras and Calais respectively.

[44] Claude-Louis-François de Régnier, born 1715, died Sept. of this same year—1767. Lauzun arrived in England on Feb. 20 or 21 (see Mme. du Deffand), and on Feb. 22 Lady Mary Coke entered in her *Journal* that she had met at the French Ambassadress's "the Duke de Lauzun, who is come from France after Lady Sarah Bunberry. He has no advantage from his person, which is neither agreeable nor in the least conveys the idea of his being of one of the most considerable families in France, & heir to one of the greatest fortunes. L'd Dillon told me he was sure he wou'd not have less than fifty thousand pounds a year English. He married lately the heiress of the Duke de Boufflers, a young lady of sixteen years of age & in all respects amiable; but his attachment to my lady Sarah seems as if he was insensible to her merit. As I was going downstairs I mett him coming up from having attended Lady Sarah to her Chair; he had the polite-

ness to go down again with me, but good breeding is common to all of his Nation."

[45] Major-General Charles Lee (1731–82), son of Major-General John Lee and of Isabella, third daughter of Sir Henry Bunbury, 3rd Baronet. He took service with the Americans in the War of Independence, but his behaviour at the Battle of Monmouth in 1778 was so extraordinary that he was court-martialled and suspended from his command. His manners are reported to have been eccentric and his temper bad.

[46] Sir Charles Bunbury's seat in Suffolk.

[47] The French editions have Soanes. Susanna Bunbury, born 1737, married 1765 the Rev. Henry Soame or Soames, of Thurlow Hall, Suffolk. Both before and after her marriage she lived a great deal with her sister-in-law.

[48] Lady Sarah wrote to Lady Susan O'Brien from Barton on May 7: "Since I came from Paris in Febry, I have been at Bath, at Goodwood, in town, at New[t], & twice here for 10 days."

[49] The Bunburys were to have crossed to France in the middle of June and to have gone via Paris to Spa. Lauzun went to Calais to meet them, but it was finally decided that they should go to Spa direct. On June 24 Mme. du Deffand wrote to Walpole: "I learned yesterday that *le petit Lauzun*, not finding his milady at Calais, had crossed to England, where he did not dare remain; there was some question of putting him in prison for this escapade."

[50] Jean du Barry, who launched *l'Ange*, that is to say, Madame du Barry. She married Guilleaume du Barry, brother of Jean du Barry, in Sept. 1768.

[51] Charles, marquis, afterwards duc, de Fitzjames (1743–*c.* 1803). He was a grandson of the Duke of Berwick, son of James II and Arabella Churchill. For an account of the party given him by the duc de Chartres to celebrate his farewell to his bachelor life see *Journal historique de Collé*, March, 1769. In his latter days he became devout. (See *Jerningham Letters*.)

[52] In 1768 the Genoese, tired of their unsuccessful attempts to control Corsica, ceded it to France under cover of a treaty allowing the King of France to exercise rights of sovereignty over all the places and harbours of Corsica as security for debts owed to France by Genoa. The marquis de Chauvelin (Bernard-Louis, 1716–73) proved unequal to the task of reducing the island, which was finally subdued by the comte de Vaux.

[53] The French editions have Ronné. Probably Albert-Marie, marquis de Romé de Vernouillet (1730–93). According to Dufort de Cheverny, "His extravagant taste for loose women caused his separation from a very rich wife who adored him."

[54] The prince de Lamballe was son of the duc de Penthièvre and husband of the princesse de Lamballe, afterwards the favourite of

Marie-Antoinette. He died May 6, 1768, at the château of Lucienne after he wrote the duc de Croÿ, "a short and not a good life." Mme. Brissard was the wife of a *fermier général.*

[55] Daniel-Marc-Antoine Chardon, born 1730. He was a distinguished lawyer and published several works, including a *Code des Prises* in two quarto volumes, but according to Dufort de Cheverny he was "to the last degree immoral."

[56] This member of a pre-eminently naval family had commanded a squadron during the Seven Years War and had been made *lieutenant-général des armées navales* in 1764.

[57] Lauzun left Toulon on Aug. 9. See Mme. du Deffand's letter to Walpole of Aug. 23, 1768, in which she alludes to the fishing-boat incident. M. de Chauvelin arrived in Corsica on Aug. 29.

[58] Oct 9, 1768.

[59] Louis-Charles-René, comte de Marbeuf (1712–86), who since 1764 had commanded the French troops assisting the Genoese on the island. He continued to command in Corsica after the war, and it was he who obtained for Napoleon a bursary at the military school at Brienne.

[60] Colonel of the regiment of *Rouergue.*

[61] Pascal Paoli's elder brother.

[62] Noël de Jourda, comte de Vaux (1705–88). He was appointed Chauvelin's successor in Feb. 1769, and arrived in Corsica in April.

[63] A château fifteen miles from Versailles between the forests of Saint-Leger and Rambouillet, which Louis XV and XVI used as a hunting-lodge. It was destroyed in the Revolution.

[64] Compiègne, like Fontainebleau, was the abode of the Court for a time each year. These visits were called the *grands voyages,* while those to St Hubert and Marly were *petits voyages* only, of a few days at a time.

[65] Louis-Antoine de Gontaut, duc de Biron (1700–88), maréchal de France in 1751. He was Lauzun's uncle and colonel of the Gardes Françaises. The fact that the regiment was after all given to the duc du Châtelet was one of the causes of Lauzun's later enmity to the court party.

[66] Mistress of the comte de Saint-Florentin (later duc de la Vrillière), who was one of the four Secretaries of State.

[67] Probably a daughter or one of the quasi-wives of Nicolas-Médard Audinot (1732–1801), an actor and theatre-director much in vogue at this time.

[68] The prince de Conti's magnificent château at the village of that name on the Oise. It was destroyed in the Revolution.

[69] Charles de Rohan (1715–87), prince de Soubise, who had been made maréchal de France during the Seven Years War but had not achieved much glory.

[70] Catherine-Jeanne Tavernier de Boullogne, married 1765

Matthieu-Paul-Louis de Montmorency, vicomte de Laval (1748–1809). The vicomtesse de Laval had a reputation for much charm and for changing her lovers often. After the Revolution, when she was over fifty, she became the mistress of the comte de Narbonne, and presided over a Royalist salon at which Talleyrand was a frequent guest as was also her son, the duc Matthieu de Montmorency. She was one of the ladies who was the most scandalised when Lauzun's memoirs were first published in 1822.

71 Formerly marquis de Royan. See note 29.

72 That is, the duchesses de Choiseul and Gramont and the second wife of the prince de Beauvau (Marie-Sylvie de Rohan-Chabot), whom Mme. du Deffand christened the *Dominante*.

73 The duc d'Aiguillon was Armand-Vignerod Duplessis-Richelieu (1720–88). His uncle, the maréchal de Richelieu (Louis François-Armand Duplessis, duc de Richelieu, 1696–1788), used his influence with Mme. du Barry to oust Choiseul, and was helped by the prince de Condé.

74 His château near Amboise. All that remains of it now is the "pagoda," seven stories high, which Choiseul erected at the central point of the converging rides of the forest of Amboise, and furnished with marble tablets bearing the names of those who came to pay him court in his exile.

75 Marie-Antoinette was married to the Dauphin May 16, 1770.

76 As mademoiselle de Beauvau. See note 16.

77 Lucy de Rothes. See note 14.

78 Victoire-Armande-Josephe de Rohan-Soubise, daughter of the maréchal de Soubise. She had married her cousin, the prince de Guéménée (see note 23), in 1761.

79 Jeanne-Marie Hocquart married in 1760 to Anne-Pierre, marquis de Montesquiou (1739–98), since the preceding year First Equerry to the comte de Provence, afterwards Louis XVIII.

80 Claude-Anne-Elisabeth de Montmorency-Laval (1750–84) had married the marquis de Fleury, a collateral descendant of Cardinal Fleury, in 1767. She was possessed of wit and of a mad sort of humour. (See Mme. de Genlis, Bachaumont, etc.) Her son married Aimée de Coigny (*La Jeune Captive*), who, as duchesse de Fleury, played a certain part in Lauzun's later life.

81 Marie-Joséphine-Louise de Savoie had been married to the comte de Provence on May 14, 1771. See note 79.

82 Anne-Alexandre-Marie-Sulpice-Joseph de Montmorency-Laval (1747–1817), afterwards duc de Laval, father of the duc Adrien de Montmorency. He was a supremely good card-player, but famed for the ineptitude of his conversation.

83 This child was a boy who died aged two. Madame Dillon had one surviving child, Henrietta Lucy (1770–1853), who married in 1786 the comte de Gouvernet, later, marquis de la Tour du Pin.

For the Dillon family see this daughter's *Journal d'une femme de cinquante ans*, the comtesse de Boigne's Memoirs, and the *Jerningham Letters*, edited by Egerton Castle.

[84] See note 14. Hautefontaine was between Villers-Cotterets and Soissons.

[85] Adrien-Louis de Bonnières (1735–1806), comte, later duc, de Guines. He was ambassador from 1770 to 1776.

[86] Caroline Fitzroy (d. 1784), eldest daughter of the 2nd Duke of Grafton, married 1746 William Stanhope, 2nd Earl of Harrington. She had been a great beauty and something of a rake. On Dec. 20, 1772, Lady Mary Coke wrote in her *Journal*: "I took the opportunity of being in Town to return the visit Lady Harrington made me six months ago. I mett a Paris acquaintance, the Duke de Lauzon who is come to England for two or three months."

[87] Isabelle (1746–1835), daughter of Count George Flemming—of a Saxon family of Dutch origin which had been brought to Poland by Augustus II—and of Antoinette Czartoryska, daughter of the Grand Chancellor of Lithuania. About 1764 she had married her maternal uncle, Prince Adam Casimir Czartoryski (1734–1823), who was cousin to Stanislas Poniatowski whom he was largely responsible for putting on the Polish throne as King Stanislas II. The Czartoryski family headed a party which was anxious to maintain a constitutional government in Poland by means of Russian aid, but they occasionally defied Russia when patriotism seemed to demand it. Princess Czartoryska and her husband were patrons of art and letters, and the Princess published a book on landscape gardening and another which was intended to give the agricultural classes a taste for Polish history. Lady Craven (see note 89), with whom she was intimate in London and afterwards at Warsaw, wrote of her that "her talents were very superior, and her manners without affectation. She was a perfect musician, and a fine painter; danced inimitably; had knowledge without pedantry, and never displayed her learning with ostentation." The Prince of Nassau-Siegen in a letter written in 1786 described her as having "as many airs and graces as when I saw her fourteen or fifteen years ago, and though they still suit her very well they no longer have quite the same effect on me as they had then." Her son in his memoirs portrays her as a wise and devoted mother, but scandal did not allow all her numerous children the same paternity. In the Polish rising of 1830–31 Princess Czartoryska, though not far from ninety, displayed much energy, turned her country house of Pulawy into a hospital, and was there bombarded by her own grandson, the Prince of Wurtemburg, who was a general in the Russian service. She died at Sienawa in Galicia.

[88] Nicholas-Vassilievitch (1734–1801), general and statesman. During his ambassadorship at Warsaw he had behaved with the utmost arrogance towards the Poles and had violently persecuted their national party.

[89] Elizabeth Berkeley (1750–1828), daughter of Augustus, 4th Earl of Berkeley, married 1767 William Craven, later 6th Lord Craven, from whom she separated in 1780 after the birth of seven children. On 13 October, 1791 (Lord Craven having died on 26 September), she married the Margrave of Anspach whose mistress, or as she declared "sister," she had been for some years. Walpole's description of her agrees with Lauzun's.

[90] Catherine Graeme, daughter of Major-General Graeme, who married 1768 Thomas Hampden, afterwards 2nd Viscount Hampden, elder son of the 4th Baron Trevor (who was created Viscount Hampden in 1776). She died childless in 1804.

[91] Halnaker. See note 37.

[92] Susanna, daughter of Colonel Rowland Reynolds, second wife of Sir Robert Harland (1715?–84), a distinguished admiral and a friend of Keppel. His son Robert (1765–1849) died childless, when the baronetcy became extinct.

[93] Marianne Dorothy (1759–85) married in 1783 Major-General William Dalrymple, brother of the 5th Earl of Stair, and became the mother of the 7th Earl, who died in Paris in 1840 after two disastrous and notorious marriages. Her elder sister Frances married, as will be seen, Count Edward Dillon. They had a younger sister, Susanna Edith, who married in 1785 Sir William Rowley, 2nd Baronet, of Tendering Hall, Suffolk.

[94] Caterina Gabrieli (1730–96), a famous Italian singer. She sang in England in 1775, when Walpole considered her "superannuated."

[95] Alexandre-Frédéric-Jacques de Masson, marquis de Pezai (1741–77). He was son of an official in the French Finance Department, had social and literary pretensions, and though he had also real ability, was laughed at by both courtiers and men of letters. He married a Mlle. Murat in 1776.

[96] Henry Herbert, 10th Earl (1734–94), at Wilton House.

[97] The chevalier d'Oraison was a friend of the Prince of Nassau-Siegen (*q.v.* later in the Memoirs), of the duc de Chartres and of Mme. de Genlis, in short was a member of the Palais Royal circle, to which Lauzun also belonged. He had been round the world with Bougainville and was, says Mme. de Genlis, "prodigiously well-informed . . . without ever having been accused of pedantry."

[98] Sproughton, or Sproughton Hall. The second Sir Robert Harland had it pulled down about 1790, and built himself a house called Wherstead Lodge on his estate at Wherstead.

[99] This personage, who in Lacour's edition of Lauzun's Memoirs is simply called " Sir Marmaduke " and in other editions " Sir Marmaduke Hewel," seems almost certainly to have been Sir Marmaduke Asty Wyvill (1742–74), 7th Baronet, of Constable Burton, Yorkshire. He was the nephew of the sixth baronet and through his mother, the

daughter of Francis Asty, a Hamburgh merchant, succeeded to the estate of Black Notley in Essex. On his death unmarried the baronetcy became dormant (the elder remaining branch of the family having settled in America), and the estates passed to his cousin Christopher Wyvill, the advocate of parliamentary reform, who was also his brother-in-law.

[100] In the course of 1773 Lauzun ran three horses at various meetings—*Patrician*, *Humdrum* and *Taster*—all of which he seems to have bought from Sir Charles Bunbury, who ran them at the early meetings of that year. *Patrician* ran second in a race at Ipswich on June 30, 1773, but that was evidently a later meeting than the one here described.

[101] Tort, who had been using his inside knowledge to gamble with public money, declared when discovered that he had acted on the ambassador's instructions. After a long enquiry Tort's counter-accusations were declared to be false, but the public believed the ambassador guilty.

[102] A lady of this name is mentioned under various spellings by Lady Mary Coke and Mrs. Delaney as being in London in 1767.

[103] Wife of the Danish ambassador.

[104] John Montagu, 4th Earl of Sandwich (1718–92), at this time First Lord of the Admiralty. For a scathing indictment of his public and private life see Trevelyan's *The Early Life of Charles James Fox*.

[105] "On the 22 (June 1773) the King set out for Portsmouth and returned on the 27th. The Ministers attended him and dined with him on board the fleet in their turns, as did several other lords and gentlemen, Monsieur de Guines the French ambassador, and the Duke de Lauzun." Walpole's *Last Journals*.

[106] François-Xavier Branicki (d. 1819), whose real name seems to have been Branetzki, was a foreign adventurer, a favourite of Stanislas II, who became Grand-General of Poland and helped to betray it to the Russians in 1792. He must not be confused with Jean-Clement Branicki, of a noble Polish family, who was also Grand-General and lived 1688–1771.

[107] Margaret Georgiana Poyntz (1737–1814) married in 1755 John Spencer, afterwards created Viscount Althorp and Earl Spencer.

[108] Count Tschernicheff (whom Walpole spells Czernichew) had been Russian ambassador to England in 1768–9. In July, 1773, Lady Mary Coke met him and his wife at Berlin on their way to Aix-la-Chapelle and no doubt to Spa.

[109] Though the Czartoryski had helped Catherine to put her ex-lover Poniatowski on the throne of Poland, they then introduced too many reforms to please the empress.

[110] In 1769.

[111] Nikita-Ivanovich Panin (1718–83), chief minister of Catherine II. He was largely responsible for the first partition of Poland in 1772.

NOTES

[112] Peter, Count Romanzoff (1725–96), a famous Russian general who received from Catherine the additional surname of Zadonaiski because of his deeds against the Turks *beyond the Don*.

[113] Published 1771.

[114] Jerome-David Gaube (1705–80), better known under the name of Gaubius.

[115] Stanislas Poniatowski (1754–1833), afterwards Grand Treasurer of Lithuania. He left Poland in 1793, and spent the latter part of his life in Italy.

[116] Prince Adam Czartoryski, son of the Princess, mentions in his memoirs "a young Genevese called Lhuillier" who was his mathematical tutor.

[117] Prince Czartoryski was arrested on March 30, 1774, at the instance of Count Mostowski, palatine of Moravia, who claimed the sum of 200,000 crowns for which the prince had stood surety for his father-in-law. Owing to Lauzun's exertions he was not put in prison, and in the end he won his case.

[118] Augustus-Alexander Czartoryski (1697–1782), Palatine of Red Russia.

[119] May 10, 1774.

[120] He had bought it from the comte de Coigny in March 1774 for 150,000 francs.

[121] Louis-Gabriel de Conflans d'Armentières, marquis de Conflans, b. 1735.

[122] Near Warsaw where the Czartoryski had a villa.

[123] Otto-Magnus, Count von Stackelberg (1736–1800), a German adventurer who had succeeded Repnin as ambassador and was yet more severe.

[124] The Czartoryski's winter-palace in Warsaw was called by this name.

[125] According to the Memoirs of Prince Adam-George Czartoryski his mother had seven children : Thérèse who was burned to death as a young girl, Marie (1766–1854), who married Prince Louis of Wurtemburg, Adam-George, author of the memoirs (1770–1862), Constantine-Adam (Oct. 28, 1773–1860), Sophie (1776–1836), who married Count Stanislas Zamoyska, Gabrielle, younger than Sophie, and another daughter whose name, fate, date of birth or place in the family are not mentioned. Lacour says in his edition of Lauzun's Memoirs that Prince Constantine-Adam was generally supposed to be Lauzun's son, but owns that there is exactly a year's discrepancy in the date of his birth.

[126] Stanislas-Charles (1734–90), Palatine of Vilna, who opposed the Czartoryski or Russophil faction.

[127] The Elector was Frederick-Augustus (1750–1827), who afterwards became first King of Saxony. In 1769 he had married Maria-Amelia of Zweibrücken or Deux-Ponts.

[128] The maréchal de Muy had been made War Minister in June 1774. He died the following year. Charles Gravier, comte de Vergennes (1717–87), had been appointed Foreign Minister at the same time. These memorials from Lauzun are in the Archives Nationales in Paris.

[129] It was Mme. de Guines who was the duchesse de Lauzun's aunt.

[130] James Harris, afterwards 1st Earl of Malmesbury (1746–1820). He was British Minister at Berlin 1771–76. Later he was to share with Lauzun the favours of the duchesse de Fleury.

[131] Frederick the Great.

[132] A district of Warsaw.

[133] Probably the wife of Casimir Poniatowski, elder brother of the King.

[134] That is to say Madame Potoçka, wife of the *Staroste* of Tlomoçki. Apparently this was Countess Ladislas Potoçka, daughter of Princess Lubomirska, who like Mme. Oginska was a sister of Prince Adam Czartoryski.

[135] The Wola was a plain outside Warsaw where the election of the Polish kings took place and also the duels of their subjects.

[136] The marquis de Juigné, who was appointed in Dec. 1774 and left for Russia in June 1775. A series of letters between Lauzun and Stackelberg on this subject exist (in cipher) in the Archives Nationales. They are quoted by Maugras—*The duc de Lauzun and the court of Marie-Antoinette*.

[137] A district of Versailles where the Guéménée had recently built a house which Louis XVI afterwards bought for Mme. Elisabeth. It still stands in the Avenue de Paris, but it has been enlarged, and the charming garden for which it was famed is no longer laid out as it was.

[138] Antoine-Charles du Houx (1728–92), general, who had served in Russia and was afterwards to serve with Lauzun in America. He was mortally wounded defending the Royal Family at the Tuileries on Aug. 10, 1792.

[139] On Feb. 27, 1774, Mme. du Deffand wrote to Horace Walpole: " It seems that a little Mme. de Monglas who had been ordered to be carried off to a convent at Montpellier and was escorted by three persons of the police, has escaped. I don't know if anyone is chasing after her: the Prince de Nassau and a M. d'Esterhazy had fought about her. . . ." (See also Bachaumont, for an account of the duel in question.) The prince de Nassau was Charles-Henri-Nicolas-Othon de Nassau-Siegen (1745–1808), who will appear again in the Memoirs. Like Lauzun he spent his life in trying to be a hero of romance, and on the whole succeeded.

[140] This family's castle was called Blise-Castel.

[141] Wolfgang-Heribert, Baron Dalberg (1750–1806). He was a Minister of the state of Baden, a writer of plays and a correspondent

of Schiller. One of the children with whose education his wife was so estimably occupied was the duc de Dalberg, who became one of Napoleon's ministers, but welcomed back the Bourbons if he did not actually intrigue for their return.

[142] "Dunn, a Jacobite Irishman" (see Walpole) was French minister to the Elector Palatine from 1764 till 1769. He called himself Count O'Dunn and had married the eldest daughter of Humphrey Parsons, also a Jacobite, who had been Lord Mayor of London. Dufort de Cheverny gives details of his career and marriage.

[143] Marie-Julie Vassal, married 1770 Anne-Claude, marquis de Chamborant, as his second wife.

[144] This race was won on Oct. 4, 1775, on the plain of Sablons "by the address of a little English postillion, who is in such fashion that I don't know whether the Academy will not give him for the subject of a *éloge*" (Walpole to Conway on Oct. 6).

[145] Marie-Louise-Therèse de Savoie-Carignan (1749–92), who perished in the September massacres. She had married the prince de Lamballe in 1767. (See note 54.)

[146] Afterwards Charles X.

[147] Marie-Hedwige-Eleonore-Christine of Hesse-Rheinfels-Rothenburg, born 1747, married the prince de Bouillon in 1766.

[148] René-Mars de Froulay, comte de Tessé, born 1736. He was at this time Marie-Antoinette's First Equerry.

[149] Marie-François-Henri de Franquetot (1737–1821), who died maréchal de France and Governor of the Invalides. At this time and for some years to come he was greatly in Marie-Antoinette's favour. He was one of the four courtiers whom she chose to keep her company at Trianon when she was isolated there with the measles in 1779, the others being the baron de Besenval, Count Esterhazy and the duc de Guines.

[150] Madame Campan gives a counter-version of this incident, composed after reading Lauzun's memoirs.

[151] See note 92.

[152] Gabrielle-Yolande-Claude-Martine de Polastron (1749 ?–1793), married 1767 Armand-Jules-François, comte, afterwards duc, de Polignac.

[153] Pierre-Louis (1722–94). See note 149.

[154] Amelia or Emilia Stanhope (1749–82), third daughter of the 2nd Earl of Harrington (see note 86), and widow of Richard Barry, 6th Earl of Barrymore. Walpole wrote from Paris in Sept. 1775: "Lady Barrymore has taken a house. She will be glutted with conquests: I never saw anyone so much admired. I doubt her poor little head will be quite overset."

[155] Pierre (1723–1805). Not the same as the *marquis* de Pons.

[156] Charles-Michel de Gontaut, who later took the title of vicomte and then of duc de Gontaut-Biron. He and Lauzun were descended

from different sons of the famous maréchal de Biron, friend of Henri IV, so they were not very near cousins. This M. de Gontaut emigrated and returned to France at the Restoration. His wife was made *gouvernante des enfants de France*. Her Memoirs were published in 1891.

[157] Count Valentine-Ladislas Esterhazy (1740-1805), colonel of the Hungarian hussar regiment which bore his name. He was sent to Russia as an emissary by the *Princes* in 1791 and died in Poland. He was a cousin of the Count Esterhazy mentioned in note 139.

[158] On Shrove Thursday. The duchesse de Chartres was Louise-Marie-Adelaide de Bourbon-Penthièvre (1753–1821), who had married the duc de Chartres in 1769.

[159] Louis-Philippe-Joseph (1747–93), later duc d'Orléans (Philippe-Égalité). He was one of Lauzun's earliest friends, and according to Dufort de Cheverny had the worst possible influence over him.

[160] Claude-Louis, comte de St Germaine (1707–78), created War Minister in 1775.

[161] Anne-Pierre (1701–83). He was "Sloth" in the list made by the wits in 1775 likening the seven newly-made Marshals to the seven deadly sins.

[162] George-Felix, baron von Wimpfen (1741–1814).

[163] *Schomberg-Dragons*, formerly the maréchal de Saxe's regiment of Uhlans.

[164] The treaty which united the Bourbon sovereigns (of France, Spain, Naples and Parma) against the rest of Europe in 1761. Having displeased Turgot, Guines was recalled in Feb. 1776. Marie-Antoinette espoused his cause against the King and finally procured his rehabilitation and nomination as Duke—which brought about the fall of the Turgot ministry in May 1776.

[165] Charles-Joseph Patissier, marquis de Bussy-Castelnau (1718–85). He spent most of his life fighting for the French in India, and was at one time a prisoner in England.

[166] Marc-René de Voyer, marquis de Voyer (1722-82), soldier, connoisseur and philosopher. He was son of the comte d'Argenson who had been War Minister under Louis XV.

[167] The domain of the Argenson family, near Tours.

[168] Jean-Frédéric-Phélypeaux, comte de Maurepas (1701–81). Minister at the age of twenty-four, he had been banished in 1749 for an epigram on Mme. de Pompadour. Louis XVI recalled him as soon as he came to the throne, and since then Maurepas had been Prime Minister in fact though not in name, for he was styled only Minister of State and Head of the Finance Council.

[169] Stéphanie-Félicie Ducrest (1746–1830), married to the comte de Genlis, afterwards marquis de Sillery, in 1763. Author of many books and governess to the children of the duc d'Orléans. Madame Potoçka was probably the person of that name mentioned in note 134.

[170] He was the third "knight" to be admitted to the Order which Mme. de Genlis admits in her Memoirs was invented by herself and bore no relation to any Polish one.

[171] They were daughters of Bernard de Boulainvilliers, who was son of Samuel Bernard the great financier. The elder daughter married the baron de Crussol, colonel of the *Régiment de Berry* in 1770, the younger married Marie-Joseph, marquis de Faudoas.

[172] Edward Dillon (1751–1839) was one of the thirteen children of a Mr. Robert Dillon who had settled in business at Bordeaux as a wine merchant. They claimed kinship with the Archbishop of Narbonne, who at any rate did his utmost to further their fortunes. Edward Dillon, who was later colonel of the regiment of *Provence* and gentleman-in-waiting to the comte d'Artois, was one of the many courtiers whose name gossip coupled with that of Marie-Antoinette. He emigrated at the Revolution and held court and diplomatic posts under the Restoration. The comtesse de Boigne, who was his niece, says in her Memoirs that his second wife was a rich Creole and that his daughter Georgina was sought in morganatic marriage by Frederick-William III of Prussia. See also Mme. de la Tour du Pin and the *Jerningham Letters*.

[173] The comte des Salles, Governor of Neufchâteau in Lorraine, married as his second wife in 1769 a demoiselle de Gouy, sister of Louis-Henri-Marthe, marquis de Gouy d'Arsy (1753–94), who was afterwards *colonel en second* of the *Dragons de la Reine*.

[174] Possibly Blount. Sir Walter Blount, 6th Bart., of Sodington married 1766 Mary, eldest daughter of James, 5th Lord Aston of Forfar.

[175] François-Alexandre-Frédéric, duc de la Rochefoucauld-Liancourt (1747–1827), politician and philanthropist. See Arthur Young's *Travels* for a description of his activities.

[176] In October 1777.

[177] Oct. 17, 1777.

[178] The one-time madame Pater or baronne de Niewerkerke, who had been a mistress of Louis XV. She married in March 1777 the marquis de Champcenetz, one of the King's *premiers valets-de-chambre*.

[179] Emmanuel-Marie-Louis, marquis de Noailles (1743–1822), who had replaced M. de Guines as Ambassador, had married in 1762 a demoiselle de Hollencourt de Drosménil, cousin of M. de Genlis. "I met the new French Ambassadress t'other night," wrote Walpole in Aug. 1777. "She is like a little mouse in a cheese, not ugly but with no manner."

[180] The Duchess of Devonshire was Georgiana (d. 1806) ("the beautiful Duchess of Devonshire"), eldest daughter of the Lady Spencer mentioned in note 107. Lady Granby was Lady Mary Somerset, who had married the Marquis of Granby, afterwards 4th Duke of Rutland, in 1775.

181 On Feb. 17, 1778.

182 This memorial is in the Archives of the French Foreign Office.

183 Of France's "Treaty of Commerce and Amity with the Independent States of America." Noailles handed it to Lord Weymouth, English Foreign Minister, on March 13, 1778.

184 On March 20.

185 Sir Charles Hotham-Thompson, 8th Bart., Groom of the Bedchamber to George III (1729–94).

186 From Dover, on April 4, he wrote a letter to Vergennes, given by Maugras—*The duc de Lauzun and the Court of Marie-Antoinette.*

187 Emmanuel, duc de Croÿ (1718–84), who was commandant of the troops in Picardy and Artois. See note 28.

188 Victor-François, duc de Broglie (1718–1804).

189 His cousin Jean-Armand, marquis de Gontaut-Biron (1746–1826), elder brother of the marquis de Saint-Blancard. See note 156.

190 This corps was created by an edict of Sept. 1, 1778, and was called the *Volontaires Etrangers de la Marine.*

191 Mme. de Martainville was a sister of Edward Dillon, and was married to a connexion of Mme. de Pompadour. (See Dufort de Cheverny.) Three of her brothers—Robert, William and Francis—were eventually in Lauzun's regiment. For the Archbishop of Narbonne see note 14.

192 Francès had been First Secretary at the French Embassy in London and had "made himself perfectly master of our language and customs" (Walpole's *Last Journals*). See also Donial: *Participation de la France à l'Etablissement des Etats Unis d'Amérique.*

193 Charles-Henri d'Arsac (d. 1780), who will appear again in the Memoirs.

194 Louis-Philippe de Rigaud (1724–1802), who fought with distinction in the American War.

195 Dec. 25, 1778. The Journal which Lauzun kept of this expedition is in the Archives Nationales, Paris. Quotations from it are given by Maugras.

196 Fort St Louis. The garrison of the fort had mutinied two days before and was in the utmost disorder. It numbered only twenty men. See Lauzun's Journal and Martin, *The British West African Settlements*, 1926. See also Mme. du Deffand for an amusingly spiteful account of the exploit.

197 Charles-Hector, comte d'Estaing (1729–94). The part he took in the American War of Independence is well known.

198 July 6, 1779.

199 Sir Edward Hughes (1720?–94). On his way to India with a strong squadron in the spring of 1779 he dispossessed the French of Goree, but did not retake St Louis.

200 de Polignac. See note 152.

201 First Lord of the Bedchamber. Son of the maréchal de Richelieu.

202 Louise-Marthe de Conflans (1759–1832) had married in 1775 François de Franquetot, marquis de Coigny (1756–1816), son of the duc de Coigny. (See note 149). Her father was the marquis de Conflans (see note 122), her grandfather the marquis d'Armentières, maréchal de France, but her mother, Marie-Antoinette Portail, and her grandmother, belonged to Parliamentary families. Mme. de Coigny, never much in sympathy with the court, eventually, like Lauzun, associated herself entirely with the Orléans party. At the Revolution she fled to England where she associated with the Whigs and the "constitutional" party of the emigrés, while her husband followed the fortunes of Louis XVIII, who rewarded him by making him a general. They divorced during the Emigration, and Mme. de Coigny returned to France in 1801, where she proclaimed herself a fervent admirer of Napoleon. She remained devoted to Lauzun and he to her until his death, though opinions are divided as to the exact nature of their relations. The letters she wrote to him from England in 1791–92 were published by Paul Lacroix in 1884 in an edition of a very few copies. Several are quoted by Maugras. Among Mme. de Coigny's many admirers was the prince de Ligne, whose *Lettres à la marquise de Coigny* were published for the first time as written (and not as doctored by Mme. de Staël) by Henri Lebasteur in 1914.

203 By an edict of June 25, 1779, the *Volontaires Etrangers de la Marine* (see note 190) were amalgamated with the *Volontaires Etrangers de Nassau.*

204 Alexandre-Marie-Léonor de Saint-Mauris (1732–96). He was War Minister from Feb. 1776 till Dec. 1780.

205 Who commanded the army. See note 62.

206 See note 11.

207 Henri-Joseph, marquis de Lambert (1738–1808). He was "Minister of the *Armée des Princes*" with the Prussian army in 1792–93, and in 1794 accepted Catherine II's invitation to take service in Russia.

208 Louis-Pierre de Chastenet, comte de Puységur (1726–1807). He was War Minister for a few months in 1788–9, and on Aug. 10, 1792, commanded the corps of nobles who tried to defend the Tuileries.

209 Charles-Marie, marquis de Créqui (1737–1801).

210 Augustin-Gabriel de Franquetot (1740–1817), brother of the duc de Coigny.

211 Charles-Claude Andrault de Maulévrier, marquis de Langeron, born about 1720.

212 Jean-Baptiste-Donatien de Vimeur, comte de Rochambeau (1725–1807), under whom Lauzun was shortly to serve in America and later in Flanders during the Revolution. He retired from the army in 1792 as the result of a misunderstanding with Dumouriez

(with which Lauzun had something to do), and was later imprisoned, and only saved by 9th Thermidor.

213 Victor-Maurice de Riquet (1727–1807), a friend of Mme. du Deffand, to whom he wrote from this camp at St Malo on July 5, 1779, a letter describing the evil plight of the English, which she forwarded (via Ostend) to Walpole. His wife was a sister of Mme. de Cambis.

214 Patrick, Count Wall, whom the duc de Croÿ had been much annoyed to find as a fellow-commander at Calais in 1764—" a somewhat extraordinary thing seeing he was an Irishman."

215 The baron de Crussol. See note 171.

216 Henri-Charles-Louis, born 1768. Mme. du Deffand wrote on Oct. 8 : " I have just received an invitation to the marriage of the Prince de Montbarey's daughter with the Hereditary Prince of Nassau-Saarbruck; the Princess a girl of twenty-two while the Prince is not yet eleven."

217 Louis-Guillouet (1708–91). The previous year he had commanded the French fleet at the battle of Ouessaint. On the present occasion he, with his Spanish allies, was blown out of the Channel into the presence of a much smaller British fleet under Sir Charles Hardy, which was looking for them beyond the Scilly Isles; but when Hardy retreated towards Spithead they did not follow him. Orvilliers and the Spanish admiral did not work well together, their ships were foul and their crews sickly. After cruising in the Channel for another fortnight they returned to Brest and did not put out again.

218 Louis-Antoine (1729–1814), the famous sailor and explorer.

219 Joséphine de Palerme (1752–1830) married 1771 the marquis de Gontaut-Biron. See note 189.

220 A slip or misprint for May 2 (1780).

221 Three companies of foot were left behind; 600 men embarked, of which 300 were cavalry.

222 It was returning to Jamaica after escorting a convoy of merchantmen as far as the Bermudas, and was commanded by Captain afterwards Admiral Cornwallis.

223 On July 11, 1780.

224 Sept. 20 and 21, 1780, at Hartford, Connecticut.

225 Not from Europe, but from the West Indies. He arrived at New York on Sept. 13 and was in North American waters till the middle of November. His arrival brought the English naval forces up to twenty line-of-battle ships.

226 Benedict Arnold (1741–1801) whose treason in trying to deliver the fortress of West Point to the British was discovered Sept. 25. He escaped and fought as an English general for the rest of the war.

227 General Horatio Gates had been defeated by Lord Cornwallis at Camden in Carolina on Aug. 16. The news reached Newport on Sept. 12.

228 Oct. 28. The vicomte de Rochambeau was Donatien-Marie-

Joseph de Vimeur (1750–1813). Like his father he fought for the Republic. Most of his service was in the West Indies, where he was taken prisoner in 1803 and kept in England till 1811. He was killed at the battle of Leipzig.

229 Nathaniel Greene. His letter asking for Lauzun's Legion is dated Nov. 3, 1780.

230 Banastre Tarleton (1754–1833), commanded the British Legion, a mixed force of cavalry and light infantry. Eventually he rose to the rank of general and died a baronet and Knight of the Bath. He was a magnificent cavalry officer, but less estimable in private life.

231 There was a question at this time of Lafayette and his corps of light infantry joining Greene in Carolina. Lafayette, though he had come to America as a volunteer in 1777, was still only twenty-three.

232 See note 82.

233 Mrs. Hunter was Deborah, daughter of Godfrey Malbone, a well-known Newport merchant and landowner, and widow of Dr. William Hunter, a cousin of the famous doctors William and John Hunter. Her two elder daughters were : Elizabeth (born 1762, died unmarried in France in 1849) and Anne, who married Jean Falconnet, a Swiss banker. There were a younger daughter and a son, William (1774–1849), who became a distinguished American politician and diplomatist. Mrs. Hunter and her daughters went to England in 1785 in hopes of a cure for Elizabeth's eyesight (a vain hope, for she became quite blind), and apparently they never returned to America. For a description of the two Miss Hunters see the Prince de Broglie's *Journal* published by the *Société des Bibliophiles Francais* in 1903, and for a charming account of his own and Lauzun's friendship with the family see Fersen's letters to his sister, published by O. G. de Heidenstam in *Lettres de Marie-Antoinette, Fersen et Barnave* (of which an English translation was published in 1926).

234 Henry Knox (1750–1806), Brigadier-General of Artillery, had been sent by Washington to inform the Governors of the various New England states of the revolt of the Pennsylvania " Line," and to ask for money and clothing to keep other contingents from revolting. His letter to Rochambeau with this news is dated from Lebanon, Jan. 11, 1781.

235 Feb. 13 and 14, 1781.

236 Ternay had died on Dec. 15, 1780.

237 March 6.

238 On March 8. Charles-René-Dominique Sochet, called the chevalier Destouches, commanded the squadron till the arrival of the new naval commander, the comte de Barras. He was born 1728, became an admiral, fought for the Royalists in the Vendée, and is there supposed to have perished.

239 Philippe-Henri, marquis de Ségur (1724–1801) (whose reforms of the French army included the unpopular and dangerous

one of requiring that only nobles should serve as officers), and Charles-Eugène-Gabriel de la Croix, marquis de Castries (1727–1801), who had never been a sailor, and was unpopular on that account.

[240] March 16.

[241] May 9.

[242] Louis, comte de Barras de Laurent. He had already fought in the American war under d'Estaing.

[243] On May 22 at Weathersfield, near Hartford.

[244] François-Jean, chevalier, later marquis de Chastellux, Rochambeau's second-in-command. He had been made an Academician in 1775 on the strength of some not very good comedies and various essays in prose and verse. His *Travels in North America*, of which an English translation was published, gives an amusing account of Lauzun at Lebanon.

[245] Claude-Gabriel, marquis de Choisy (b. 1723). In the Revolution he commanded the Armée du Nord for a few months in 1792–93, and then left the service.

[246] June 10, 1781. The two conferences which Lauzun mentions had taken place on May 31 and June 8—the days of his departure for and return from New Windsor.

[247] On June 30 at Newtown, not far from New York. The operation in question was an attempt at surprising the enemy's outposts in front of New York and at cutting off a corps of Loyalist irregulars which lay about Kingsbridge. As will be seen, it failed.

[248] Major-General Benjamin Lincoln (1733–1810). He was American Secretary of War 1781–84.

[249] July 1-3.

[250] The French and American armies were camped together about the villages of White Plains and Phillipsburg from July 6 till Aug. 19, 1781.

[251] Major-General William Heath (1737–1814).

[252] This reconnaissance took place July 21-23. The French accounts agree that the generals were in some danger, but Washington wrote in his diary for July 23: "Having finished the Reconnoitre without damage, a few harmless shot only being fired at us, we marched back about Six o'clock. . . ."

[253] It had now been decided not to attack New York but to march to join Lafayette in Virginia, where Cornwallis was already entrenching himself at Yorktown, and whither Admiral de Grasse was proceeding with a French fleet and reinforcements from San Domingo.

[254] The French editions have printed this *Summers et Courthouse*. The Legion camped there on Aug. 30.

[255] Sir Henry Clinton (1738 ?–95) had been Commander-in-Chief of the forces in North America since May, 1778. He had distinguished himself in the early part of the war, but his differences with Cornwallis were largely responsible for its humiliating end.

NOTES

[256] Lauzun's division arrived at Philadelphia on Sept. 3 "about eleven o'clock in the morning and in full dress," and left on the fifth for Head of Elk.

[257] François-Joseph-Paul, comte de Grasse (1722–88). In the following year he was vanquished and taken prisoner by Rodney at the Battle of the Saints.

[258] Claude-Anne, marquis (afterwards duc) de Saint-Simon (1740–1819). At the Revolution he entered the Spanish service, and in 1808 defended Madrid against the French.

[259] Charles, 2nd Earl Cornwallis (1738–1805), afterwards Governor-General of India and Marquis Cornwallis. It was by Clinton's orders that he remained in Yorktown where Clinton had promised him reinforcements—which arrived the week after Cornwallis had surrendered.

[260] Sept. 10.

[261] Adam-Philippe, comte de Custine (1740–93). Like Lauzun he became a Revolutionary general and finished on the scaffold. In America he commanded the regiment of *Saintonge*.

[262] The battle, which was undecided, took place on Sept. 5 against Admirals Graves and Hood. Grasse kept them occupied outside the bay till Barras with the French squadron from Newport had slipped within it, and then joined the latter on Sept. 11.

[263] Brigadier-General George Weedon (about 1730–90). He had been an innkeeper in his native town of Fredericksburg, Virginia.

[264] This skirmish took place on Oct. 3. Tarleton's account of it in his *History of the Campaigns of* 1780 *and* 1781 varies a little to his own advantage, as was only to be expected, but Henry Lee's contemporary American account agrees with Lauzun's except that he gives some of the credit to Mercer's Grenadiers, a picked corps of militiamen who supported the hussars.

[265] Oct. 17. The formal surrender took place on Oct. 19, 1781.

[266] Armand-Augustin de la Croix de Castries, comte de Charlus, afterwards duc de Castries (1756–1842), son of the Minister for the Navy. He was second-in-command of the regiment of *Saintonge*.

[267] Second-in-command under his brother Count Christian of Deux-Points of the regiment of that name raised by their family for the French service. He had greatly distinguished himself at an assault on York-town.

[268] Nov. 21, 1781.

[269] Who had followed in another frigate and arrived at Versailles on Nov. 24.

[270] Mary Robinson (1758–1800), who during her stage career, which lasted from 1776 till 1780, had attracted the attention of the Prince of Wales while playing Perdita. She had been abandoned by him before her visit to Paris in 1782. Later she was the mistress for many years of Lauzun's recent antagonist, Colonel Tarleton. She became

paralysed for life through a journey which she took in bitter weather to bring Tarleton a sum of money of which, as frequently, he stood in need.

[271] On Jan. 21, 1782, in celebration of the birth of a Dauphin in the previous October.

[272] He sailed for Martinique on March 16 as second-in-command of *Auxerrois*.

[273] Madame de Châlons, who had been a demoiselle d'Andlau and had married the comte de Châlons in 1768, was a cousin of the duchesse de Polignac and a member of the Queen's most intimate circle.

[274] Aglaë de Conflans, sister of Mme. de Coigny, who had married, on June 1, 1781, Charles de Rohan-Guéménée, duc de Montbazon, son of the prince de Guéménée.

[275] The chevalier Nicolas de Lisle (1735–83), soldier, encyclopedist and correspondent of Voltaire. He died in Mme. de Coigny's house.

[276] Better known as La Touche-Tréville (Louis-René-Madeleine Le Vasseur de, 1745–1804). As an admiral he fought Nelson in 1801.

[277] On Aug. 3, 1782. The "bizarre customs" of Terceiro and Lauzun's participation in them are fully described in the comte de Ségur's Memoirs and also in the prince de Broglie's *Journal*.

[278] Bozon-Jacques, comte de Talleyrand-Perigord (1764–18— ?) brother of "Talleyrand," who, like Ségur and Broglie, was on his way to join the army in America for the first time.

[279] Louis-Antoine-Auguste de Rohan-Chabot, comte de Chabot (1733–1807). He stammered and was ugly, but was considered extremely fascinating.

[280] The *Hector*, a 74, which had been taken by Rodney at the Battle of the Saints and had been separated by storms from the convoy which Admiral Graves was conducting back to England. This fight took place on the night of Sept. 4-5.

[281] This was a misapprehension, for it was not till Oct. 3 that the unfortunate *Hector*, after terrible sufferings, fell in with a Dartmouth merchantman who took on board the survivors of her crew and of the sick and prisoners she carried.

[282] On Sept. 12.

[283] This squadron was commanded by Captain George Keith Elphinstone (1747–1823), later Admiral of the Blue, G.C.B., and Viscount Keith, and ancestor of the late Marquis of Lansdowne. His second wife was Hester Maria Thrale (1762–1857), Dr. Johnson's "Queenie." For details of this affair see Ségur, Broglie and the *London Gazette*.

[284] The French plenipotentiary at Philadelphia.

[285] This was about Oct. 10. Rochambeau's army had been at Crompond in Connecticut since Sept. 23.

[286] For the West Indies.

[287] On Oct. 22. Lauzun left with his legion on Oct. 27 for Wilmington, near Philadelphia.

NOTES

[288] At the end of December, 1782.

[289] The prince de Guéménée, whose gigantic bankruptcy, in which the remnants of Lauzun's own fortune disappeared, had occurred in September. Madame Dillon had died on Sept. 13.

[290] Rochambeau, who had not accompanied the army to the West Indies, sailed for France from Annapolis on Jan. 11, 1783.

[291] In February.

[292] On March 12.

[293] Actually the *Washington* brought news of the signing of the *preliminary articles of peace* (on Nov. 30, 1782), but the baron de Foks had hastened northwards with his general's private letters before Luzerne could communicate the official despatches.

[294] In April.

[295] The French editions have *March* 11, a mistake for May.